Religions of the World
Second Edition

Religions of the World

Second Edition

A COMPREHENSIVE ENCYCLOPEDIA
OF BELIEFS AND PRACTICES

VOLUME ONE: A–B

J. GORDON MELTON
MARTIN BAUMANN
Editors

TODD M. JOHNSON
World Religious Statistics

DONALD WIEBE
Introduction

 ABC-CLIO

Santa Barbara, California • Denver, Colorado • Oxford, England

APR 2011

Library of Congress Cataloging-in-Publication Data

Religions of the world : a comprehensive encyclopedia of beliefs and practices / J. Gordon Melton, Martin Baumann, editors ; Todd M. Johnson, World Religious Statistics ; Donald Wiebe, Introduction. — 2nd ed.
   p. cm.
   Includes bibliographical references and index.
   ISBN 978-1-59884-203-6 — ISBN 978-1-59884-204-3
   1. Religions—Encyclopedias.   I. Melton, J. Gordon.   II. Baumann, Martin.
   BL80.3.R45   2010
   200.3—dc22   2010029403

ISBN: 978-1-59884-203-6
EISBN: 978-1-59884-204-3

14 13 12 11 10   1 2 3 4 5

This book is also available on the World Wide Web as an eBook.
Visit www.abc-clio.com for details.

ABC-CLIO, LLC
130 Cremona Drive, P.O. Box 1911
Santa Barbara, California 93116-1911

This book is printed on acid-free paper ∞
Manufactured in the United States of America

To Robert L. Moore

Contents

A–Z List of Entries

Note: Core essays are indicated with the symbol ◆; country essays are indicated with the symbol ■.

Volume Five

Volume Six

Preface: An Overview of the World's Religions

J. Gordon Melton

This second edition of *Religions of the World: A Comprehensive Encyclopedia of Beliefs and Practices* has been designed to survey the present religious situation around the world as the 21st century begins. To accomplish this task, the text is anchored in a disciplined country-by-country discussion of the emergence of the contemporary religious community in each of the more than 240 nations from the smaller island republics to the larger and more populous countries. This survey is made in the more than 1,700 A-to-Z entries in this work.

In the world of world religions encyclopedias, *Religions of the World* has assumed a unique approach. The great majority of previous world religions encyclopedias have grown out of the disciplines of anthropology and comparative religion. Those volumes have done a monumental job of highlighting the building blocks of the religious life as they have appeared in widely variant cultural contexts. While showing the very different religious structures that have been created by people around the world, they have also tried to discern the common elements that repeatedly appear in all or most religious traditions—prayer and meditational techniques, myth, ritual, devotion, sacred texts, moral perceptions, deities, spirit entities, and so forth.

Rather than attempt to duplicate past endeavors, *Religions of the World* takes a very different approach. It is concerned more with the organization of various religious communities, the history of their origin and growth, their interaction with the larger world, and their present status in the world. Rather than concentrate on the often abstract themes that run throughout the religious world, we have attempted to locate different religious communities in space and time and tried to identify those communities that have secured the greatest support from their ideal constituency and those that have had the greatest impact on the world in which they exist. The attempt to ground each religious community discussed has included the naming of present leadership and giving addresses at which the individual groups may be contacted as well as listing official websites, where applicable.

The production of this encyclopedia has dominated the life of the Institute for the Study of American Religion (ISAR), a religious studies facility in Santa Barbara, California, for more than a decade. Since its founding in 1969, ISAR has concentrated on the production of reference books that have, as its name implies, primarily focused on religion in North America. However, at the end of the 1980s, several factors converged to redirect its research to a larger context. Not the least of these factors was the invitation to the director of the Institute (J. Gordon Melton) to join the international board of the Center for Studies on New Religions (CESNUR) headquartered in Turin, Italy. Board duties required several annual trips overseas and provided the opportunity for comparing the American and European situation and time to consider the possibility of adapting techniques used in producing the reference books in American religion using a global scope. CESNUR provides the context in which this volume's two editors initially met and provided regular opportunities for consultation.

By far the most important element in generating this encyclopedia, however, was the long-term relationship that began in the later 1980s between ISAR and its director and the Institute for World Spirituality (IWS) and its founder, Dr. Robert L. Moore, a professor of Psychoanalysis, Culture, and Spirituality at Chicago Theological Seminary. Moore and Melton had met in the 1970s when ISAR was located in Chicago and together had written a textbook, *The Cult Experience* (1982). Their paths diverged in 1985 when ISAR relocated to California. In the meantime, Moore had founded the Institute for World Spirituality, an organization working toward the creation of interfaith cooperation for the human future. As he began to work in an interfaith context, Moore saw the need for a means of placing religious leaders throughout the world in contact with each other. He initially suggested the idea of creating an "International Directory of the World's Religions," and through the 1990s, IWS and ISAR worked together on the production of such a directory.

The idea of creating *Religions of the World*, as an encyclopedia of the most important of the world's religions, emerged as a logical extension of the directory project in conversations with the wide range of scholars and religious leaders who cooperated with it.

As the 21st century began, ISAR extended its work to China and Southeast Asia and developed a close working relationship with Edward Irons and the Hong Kong Institute for Culture, Commerce and Religion, which he founded and leads.

Scope and Arrangement of Encyclopedia Entries

Religion does not just happen. Religions are created by inspired individuals, spread by faithful devotees, and structured so as to reach specific goals and serve the felt needs of adherents. Religious groups develop an economy to provide for the upkeep of facilities and sustain leadership as they pursue their spiritual visions. Some religions are more successful than others in each of these endeavors, relative success often being dictated by a more or less friendly environment.

In its attempt to describe the present situation to which the religious world has evolved, *Religions of the World* presents four distinct elements. First, the introductory essays by Donald Wiebe and Todd Johnson provide some overall perspective on the basic approach in the body of A-to-Z entries. Wiebe discusses the development and present state of the debate on the question of religion in the academy and how scholars attempting to understand its many manifestations can operate; that is, how an encyclopedia of religions is possible. As a distinct discipline, religious studies is an academic enterprise built around "an organized group of scholars and scientists from a diverse range of disciplines who have gained 'academic identity' by virtue of their common interest in religion. And it is essentially a 'scientific enterprise' because it is chiefly characterized by a cognitive intention, and takes for granted that the natural and social sciences are the only legitimate models for the objective study of religion." Thus, religious studies engages the religious community in terms of its publicly accessible manifestations—its ideas, its behavior, its existence in community, it historical development—rather than the Truth it claims, and compares without making judgment, at least of a religious/theological nature.

Johnson, a religious statistician, provides an overall picture of the world's religious situation in terms of the larger religious groupings and offers some projection of where those different groups will go in the next decades. While religions have dispersed dramatically through the 20th century, the older areas of strength by Christianity, Hinduism, Judaism, Buddhism, and Islam remain and will effect religious life for the foreseeable future.

The main body of the text of *Religions of the World,* the more than 1,700 A-to-Z entries, offer three kinds of material. First, in a series of core essays, the basic data about sixteen major religious traditions are presented. Not only are the five largest communities described, but several smaller groups—Jainism, Shintoism, Zoroastrianism, and Sikism/Sant Mat are highlighted. These core essays include several items often neglected in other volumes on world religions. First, there is an essay on what are termed Ethnoreligions, and a complementary essay on African Traditional Religions. These religions, described under a variety of terms in world religions textbooks, are those religions basically active among one people or ethnic group and in which membership in the ethnic group is basic to membership/participation in the religion. The religions in this highly diverse set are individually quite small but, collectively, remain an important element in the ongoing evolution of the religious community. In the last generation they have, in some places, shown a remarkable resiliency and in others have made a significant comeback.

Second, among the core essays is one on the Western Esoteric tradition. Possibly the most neglected element in religious studies texts, Western Esotericism has been the major alternative to Christianity in the West for the last two thousand years. Often present as a persecuted minority, it has blossomed since the 16th century and has made its presence felt in the last generation as it made a quantum leap forward in a revivalistic movement generally called the New Age. The defining of the Western Esoteric tradition(s) provides a handle for understanding much of the religious/spiritual activity apart from the Christian church in the Western world.

Third, the core essays include a discussion of Unbelief. The modern religious world is in large part defined by the critique on religious claims that began with the Protestant attack on Roman Catholic supernaturalism and then the Unitarian attack upon the basic Christian idea of the Trinity in the 16th century. That critique expanded in the French Enlightenment. Unbelief differs from mere irreligion in that it offers a nonsupernatural perspective from which decisions concerning metaphysics, ethics, and human relations can be constructed. With due deference to the nonreligious nature of the Unbelief community, the fact that it largely concerns itself with traditional religious questions (the existence of God, supernaturalism, normative behavior) and that it offers a replacement (sometimes in an evangelical manner) for traditional "religious" life makes Unbelief and its organizational manifestations an important element in any discussion of the religious world and hence is appropriately included in our text.

Supplementing the core essays are entries that describe the religious situation in each of the countries of the world. The assignment given to each author was to provide some historical perspective on the current religious community with a description that highlights its diversity. Authors come from a variety of scholarly disciplines; they are sociologists, anthropologists, and religious historians, and a few are religious affairs officials serving in government posts. Their entries, while providing the basic sets of facts, reflect their varied approaches to the question. No attempt has been made by the editors to remold these entries into a common format. Their diversity represents the continued diversity of perspectives that informs our knowledge of religious life.

The country essays cover all of the designated countries as recognized by the United Nations, plus several other designated areas now on that list such as Antarctica and the British Indian Ocean Territory. Thus, one will find entries on not only the larger countries (China, Indonesia, Russia) but of smaller ones from Liechtenstein to Niue. Included are those areas of the world still under foreign control from Wake Island to Mayotte. Also covered are the newer countries such as Timor and Bosnia/Herzegovina. Accompanying most country entries are a map and a set of statistics (created by David B. Barrett) that provide helpful additions to the text. It should be noted that the discussion of the Vatican is included in the entry on Italy, and that in addition to the main entry on China, additional entries focus on China: Hong Kong, China: Macau, China: Taiwan, and China: Tibet.

In this second edition, the editors have chosen to focus upon a set of countries that have often been neglected in volumes on the religious world produced in the West, most notably Latin America and Indonesia. In this edition, the country entries for South and Central America and the larger Caribbean islands have been significantly expanded as has the basic entry for Indonesia. We hope that these expanded entries, which include never before compiled information on religion, will also expand the usefulness of this volume. In addition, we have expanded coverage of the world's larger countries not only by expanding the basic essay on the countries of China, India, Russia, Indonesia, and Brazil but also by adding additional essays on specific religious traditions and movements in these countries.

That being said, the bulk of the entries focus upon nearly 1,400 of the most important religious bodies in the world, the great majority being communities within the larger religious groupings that were the subject of the core essays. The list of religious communities was arrived at by a complex but very focused process. First, those larger religious communities notable for having a membership in the millions constituted the original list, to which were added some groups that while relatively small had a significant international presence, with worshipping communities in 50 or more countries.

To ensure broad coverage, each country was surveyed and an entry on the largest religious group in every country added, if it was not already on the list. This list was then circulated to the members of the editorial board (and other colleagues in religious studies), who were asked to suggest additional groups that had some regional significance. A particular effort was made to give expanded coverage to some of the more neglected areas in world religious studies such as Indonesia, central Asia, and the island nations of the Pacific.

In order to give broad coverage to the various religious traditions, it was decided to include an entry on all of the member churches of the World Council of Churches and all of the cooperating organizations of the World Fellowship of Buddhists (whose membership lists have varied during the years of the development of this text). Islam presented a separate problem as divisions within the Muslim community have developed somewhat differently. Thus, entries have been included on the major schools of Muslim jurisprudence (Hanafite, Hanbalite, Ismaili, Malikite, Shafiite, Shi'ite, and Sufi) as well as entries that cover a number of smaller sectarian expressions. In some cases, the Islamic community is covered as the major object of attention in country entries (Oman, Morocco, the Maldives), in some other countries it has received a separate entry (Brunei, Germany, Malaysia, Romania).

The Roman Catholic Church, the largest single religious organization in the world, presented special problems as on the one hand it was merely one community among many, but on the other hand, a single descriptive entry did not seem adequate. The decision was made to expand coverage of the church by including entries on the several Eastern-rite churches that form an important, distinct, but often misunderstood element of its life, and also to include entries on some of the religious orders that have been most important in the spread of Roman Catholicism worldwide (e.g., Dominicans, Franciscans, Holy Ghost Fathers, Jesuits, White Fathers). In like measure, several of the Protestant missionary agencies that were most important in the spread of Protestantism in the 19th century were also given entries (e.g., American Board of Commissioners for Foreign Missions, Basel Mission, Church Missionary Society, London Missionary Society, Paris Mission).

Finally, in keeping with the contemporary emphasis on religious life as the 21st century began, a select number of entries were reserved for groups that though relatively small, in some cases, infinitesimally so, have had an impact due to their interface with the larger religious and secular world. None are more quickly called to mind than the revivalist Islamic movement variously known as Islamic fundamentalism or revivalism. These have been given a set of entries under the general heading of "Islamism," and additional entries cover its development from the Muslim Brotherhood. Similar groups within the Jewish community are also covered. Among the smaller groups that have become of interest because of their involvement in violent incidents are Aum Shinrikyo, the Branch Davidians, the Church of the Lamb of God, the Movement for the Restoration of the Ten Commandments, the Peoples Temple, and the Solar Temple.

The existence of several thousand distinct ethnoreligions presented a particular problem. Space did not allow the inclusion of separate entries of even a representative sample of the varied world of small land-based primal religions, and hence the original decision was made to present a somewhat random selection of groups from different parts of the world (such as the Navaho from North America, the Zulu from Africa, and the Bon of Tibet), and in this edition that selection has expanded. However, in keeping with the contemporary emphasis of this volume, we have moved to include coverage of a small group of 20th-century revivalist ethnoreligions, with examples drawn primarily from North America and Europe, but including a few others such as the Santo Daime movement from Brazil.

The diversity of the world's religious community is in many ways a daunting phenomenon, and it will grow even more complex as we move through the 21st-century, as the population grows, and as an increasing number of individuals exercise their rights to religious self-determination. Meanwhile, running against the trend to greater diversity is the monumental effort of religious leaders to seek out and unite with people in other countries with whom they share both religious affirmations and secular aspirations. The religious community is only partially displayed if we neglect the many interfaith and ecumenical organizations that attempt to bring otherwise differing faith communities together for joint witness and action. While interfaith organizations (from the Council for a Parliament of the World's Religions to the World Conference on Religion and Peace) concentrate on overcoming religious and social conflict, intra-faith ecumenical groups (from the International New Thought Alliance to the World Muslim Congress) attempt to overcome religious differences in order to present a united witness for a particular faith expression. Some 50 encyclopedia entries are devoted to interfaith and ecumenical organizations that operate on an international level.

Cross-Referencing and Indexing

In order to make *Religions of the World* as accessible as possible to readers, an extensive set of cross-references appears throughout the text. These have been grouped at the end of each separate entry. These will be especially helpful in directing users from country entries to entries about particular groups mentioned as existing in a particular country and the exact name under which a group is described. These cross-references will also direct users to other religious bodies closely related to a particular group to which an entry is given, including parent bodies from which a group has originated and ecumenical organizations that it has joined.

A more extensive end-of-book subject index gives access to entries through the names of leaders, concepts which they espouse, and practices they observe.

Contact

While believing that this work makes a valuable contribution to our knowledge, we are quite aware that we are only beginning a process of describing the world's religions, which number in the tens of thousands. It is hoped that this work may in the future be followed by other works that provide coverage of additional religious groups, and the editors are open to suggestions for groups that might be fruitfully included in future editions. We also welcome communications on improving the present text, correcting any errors that might have inadvertently entered into the entries, or expanding coverage of any subjects. Please address correspondence to:

J. Gordon Melton
Institute for the Study of American Religion
P.O. Box 90709
Santa Barbara, CA 93190
jgordon@linkline.com

Martin Baumann
Religionswissenschaftliches Seminar
Kasernenplatz 3
6003 Luzern
Switzerland
martin.baumann@unilu.ch

Acknowledgments

Such a book as *Religions of the World: A Comprehensive Encyclopedia of Beliefs and Practices*, while carrying the names of two coeditors, could not have been produced without the cooperation and assistance of hundreds. And as one arrives at the point of completing such a work, one pauses to call to memory all the many people who have been our teachers throughout a long life. This work would not have been remotely possible without the many teachers and professors who were patient with our growing up process, the students who continue to motivate our growth now that we have assumed some professorial duties, and colleagues who continually supplement our knowledge and enlarge our perspective. To all we offer our first thanks.

This work began with a project on gathering data on world religions funded by the now defunct Institute for World Spirituality (IWS). Through the last decade, the Institute for the Study of American Religion has continued the thrust initiated by Robert L. Moore, Phil Matthews, and the board members of IWS, without whose initial support this project would have remained an unrealized dream.

We also extend our words of appreciation to the editorial board and the more than 250 scholars who contributed articles. The role that these volumes have come to play in filling a gap in library reference bookshelves have made their effort more than worthwhile.

In this second edition, we have also particularly paused to note the passing of six of our valued colleagues who contributed to the first edition:

Thadeus Doktor
Nikandrs Gills
Jeffrey K. Hadden
Phillip E. Hammond
Gail M. Harley
Gary B. McGee.

They will be missed.

Finally, in working on reference books, one becomes aware of the effort contributed by the publisher and staff in bringing a product to completion. It was a genuine pleasure to work with Todd Hallman (acquiring editor) and Martha Whitt (senior production editor) who assumed oversight of the project at various stages of its development and to their assistants who buckled down and dealt with the manuscript of a work of one million and a half-plus words.

Among the ABC-CLIO staff who contributed to this work are: David Tipton (editorial manager); Jennifer Hutchinson (editor); Kim Kennedy White (development editor); Robin Tutt (editorial operations), Caroline Price, Adam Covici, Julie Dunbar, Liz Kincaid, Jason Kniser, and Ellen Rasmussen (media editors); and Vicki Moran (production editor).

J. Gordon Melton
Martin Baumann
January 2010

Basic Bibliography

During the preparation of *Religions of the World*, the editors assembled a set of volumes that served as desk references from which information was drawn and against which entries were checked for accuracy. These volumes served as a reference point for a majority of the encyclopedia entries, but to avoid undue repetition, except in those places where they became the major source, they are not listed as such.

Anderson, Gerald H., ed. *Biographical Dictionary of Christian Missions.* Grand Rapids, MI: William B. Eerdmans, 1998.

Bachmann, E. Theodore, and Mercia Brenne Bachmann. *Lutheran Churches in the World: A Handbook.* Minneapolis, MN: Augsburg Press, 1989.

Barraclough, Geoffrey, ed. *HarperCollins Atlas of World History.* Ann Arbor, MI: Borders Press, 2001.

Barrett, David, George T. Kurian, and Todd M. Johnson. *World Christian Encyclopedia: A Comparative Survey of Churches and Religions in the Modern World.* 2 vols. New York: Oxford University Press, 2001.

Bauswein, Jean-Jacques, and Lukas Vischer, eds. *The Reformed Family Worldwide: A Survey of Reformed Churches, Theological Schools, and International Organizations.* Grand Rapids, MI: William B. Eerdmans, 1999.

Bissio, Roberto Remo, et al. *Third World Guide 93/94.* Montevideo, Uruguay: Instituto del Tercer Mundo, 1992.

The Brethren Encyclopedia. 2 vols. Philadelphia: The Brethren Encyclopedia, Inc., 1983.

Burgess, Stanley M., and Eduard Van der Maas, eds. *The New International Dictionary of Pentecostal and Charismatic Movements.* Grand Rapids, MI: Zondervan, 2002.

Campo, Juan E. *Encyclopedia of Islam.* New York: Facts on File, 2009.

The Church of England Yearbook. London: Church Publishing House, published annually.

Directory–Handbuch. Geneva: Lutheran World Federation, issued annually.

Directory of Sabbath-Observing Groups. Gillette, WY: Bible Sabbath Association, 2001.

Directory–World Council of Churches. Geneva: World Council of Churches, 2005.

Eggenberger, Oswald. *Die Kirchen Sondergruppen und religiösen Vereinigungen.* Zürich: Theologischer Verlag, 1994.

Ehrlich, M. Avrum, ed. *Encyclopedia of the Jewish Diaspora: Origins, Experiences, and Culture.* 3 vols. Santa Barbara, CA: ABC-Clio, 2009.

Flinn, Frank K. *Encyclopedia of Catholicism.* New York: Facts on File, 2007.

Flynn, Tom, ed. *The New Encyclopedia of Unbelief.* Amherst, NY: Prometheus Books, 2007.

Foster, Douglas A., Paul M. Blowers, Anthony L. Dunnavant, and D. Newell Williams, eds. *The Encyclopedia of the Stone-Campbell Movement.* Grand Rapids, MI: Eerdmans, 2004.

Glassé, Cyril. *The New Encyclopedia of Islam.* 3rd ed. Lanham, MD: Rowman & Litlefield, 2008.

Glazier, Stephen. *The Encyclopedia of African and African American Religion.* Boston: Routledge, 2001.

Handbook. Grand Rapids, MI: Reformed Ecumenical Synod, 1997.

Harmon, Nolan B. *Encyclopedia of World Methodism.* 2 vols. Nashville, TN: United Methodist Publishing House, 1974.

Hart, D. G., and Mark A. Noll, eds. *Dictionary of the Presbyterian and Reformed Tradition in America.* Downers Grove, IL: InterVarsity Press, 1999.

Hirschfelder, Arlene, and Paulette Molin. *Encyclopedia of Native American Religions.* 2nd ed. New York: Facts on File, 2000.

Hoke, Donald, ed. *The Church in Asia.* Chicago: Moody Press, 1975.

Irons, Edward A. *Encyclopedia of Buddhism.* New York: Facts on File, 2008.

Jones, Constance A., and James D. Ryan. *Encyclopedia of Hinduism.* New York: Facts on File, 2007.

Kane, J. Herbert. *A Global View of Christian Missions.* Grand Rapids, MI: Baker Book House, 1971.

Keresh, Sara E., and Mitchell M. Hurvitz. *Encyclopedia of Judaism.* New York: Facts on File, 2006.

Ledbetter, Anna, and Roma Wyatt, eds. *World Methodist Council: Handbook of Information, 2002–2006.* Lake Junaluska, NC: World Methodist Council, 2003.

Lorie, Peter, and Julie Foakes. *The Buddhist Directory.* London: Boxtree, 1996.

Melton, J. Gordon. *Encyclopedia of American Religions.* 8th ed. Detroit: Gale/Cengate Learning, 2009.

Melton, J. Gordon. *Encyclopedia of Protestantism.* New York: Facts on File, 2005.

Moreau, A. Scott. *Evangelical Dictionary of World Missions.* Grand Rapids, MI: Baker Books/Carlisle, Cumbria, UK: Paternoster, 2000.

Murphy, Larry G., J. Gordon Melton, and Gary L. Ward. *Encyclopedia of African American Religion.* New York: Garland Publishing, 1993.

Orthodoxia. Regensburg, Germany: Ostkirchliches Institut, issued annually.

Pan, Lynn, ed. *The Encyclopedia of the Chinese Overseas.* 2nd ed. Singapore: Editions Didier Millet, 2006.

Quakers around the World. London: Friends World Committee for Consultation, 1994.

Roberson, Ronald G. *The Eastern Christian Churches—A Brief Survey.* 5th ed. Rome: Edizioni Orientalia Christiana, Pontificio Istituto Orientale, 1995.

Siewert, John A., and Edna G. Valdez, eds. *Mission Handbook: U.S. and Canadian Christian Ministries Overseas.* Monrovia, CA: 1997.

Stein, Gordon, ed. *The Encyclopedia of Unbelief.* 2 vols. Buffalo, NY: Prometheus Books, 1985.

Van Beek, Huiberty, comp. A *Handbook of Churches and Councils: Profiles of Ecumenical Relationships.* Geneva: World Council of Churches, 2006.

Ward, Kevin, and Brian Stanley. *The Church Missionary Society and World Christianity, 1799–1999.* Richmond, Surrey, UK: Curzon Press, 2000.

Wardin, Albert W., ed. *Baptists around the World.* Nashville, TN: Broadman and Holman, 1995.

Weller, Paul, ed. *Religions in the UK: A Multi-Faith Directory.* Derby, UK: University of Derby/Inter Faith Network for the United Kingdom, 1993.

Wingate, Andrew, et al., eds. *Anglicanism: A Global Communion.* London: Mowbray, 1998.

World Methodist Council, Handbook of Information. Lake Junaluska, NC: World Methodist Council, 1997.

Introduction: The Study of Religion

Donald Wiebe

The study of religion is probably as old as religion itself, although there is no single form that defines that notion. The earliest form of the study of religion without doubt is devotional and catechetical. This kind of study of religion is primarily concerned with the edification and spiritual growth of the individual and community and is not capable, therefore, of being clearly differentiated from religion itself. If being religious is in some sense being able to provide a religious account of the world and of human existence in it, then it also necessarily involves a study of religion that will assist the devotee in obtaining the knowledge and skills necessary in providing such an account of life. There can be no doubt that such devotional study involves the intellect and in some sense concerns itself with cognitive issues, but it includes much more than this; training and formation in the practical and ethical requirements of the religious life, that is, are essential to the kind of "understanding" sought by believers of the fundamental religious questions of truth, value, and meaning. This kind of knowing is not primarily about cognition but rather about the construction and organization of meaning. A catechetical and devotional study of religion, therefore, is much less a scholarly or academic undertaking than it is a form of religious formation and education; it provides an "understanding" of religion wholly from the inside and cares little, or not at all, for elaborating a theoretical account of religion. Indeed, it is not a detached study of religious phenomena, nor does it seek objectivity (intersubjective testability) for the claims it makes; it requires of the student, rather, submission to the tradition and the community and therefore exhibits a structure characterized by hierarchy and authority. Religion, however, has also inspired a more scholarly and academic investigation of religious reality and the religious life that—even though directed toward edification of the student/believer—blends both catechetical/devotional and scholarly/cognitive concerns in a quest for a more profound and shareable understanding of religion.

Although both these forms of study—catechetical/devotional and scholarly/cognitive—presume of the student a faith-commitment, in the West the latter eventually produced an elaborate structure of theological disciplines that made possible the development of a more systematic, comprehensive, and therefore "scientific" understanding of the Christian faith. However, "scientific" here does not bear the connotation of the modern notion of science since, in this context, the scholarship involved is still constrained by religious commitment and belief; it is scholarship from the point of view of the religious insider and produces a systematic body of knowledge of (the Christian) religion. Because such a body of knowledge is constructed as an essential element of the "meaning" of the Christian faith it is clearly different from the modern scientific endeavor. Such an academic and scholarly undertaking, therefore, can, at most, be designated a "faith-imbued science." And even though much of the scholarly work in such disciplines as biblical studies and church history, for example, is indistinguishable from that produced by scholars not constrained by a faith-commitment and religious beliefs, it is essentially a theologico-religious exercise.

These religious forms of "the study of religion" do not exhaust that notion—they are simply the earliest forms of that enterprise. And the kind of "scientific" understanding of religion that blends systematic scholarly and catechetical/devotional concerns differs radically from the narrower, more academic and strictly scientific interest in religious phenomena that emerged in the context of the modern Western university in the last quarter of the 19th century. This new academic enterprise is scientific not simply in the sense of producing a systematic body of knowledge of religion, and of religions in their historical manifestation, but in the fuller scientific sense of seeking a natural explanatory and theoretical account of religion. And in embracing the naturalism of the modern sciences this new study of religion transcends the constraints upon research and scholarship imposed by the prior faith-informed framework governing the work of the scholar-devotee. This new study of religion, therefore, cannot be included in the category of "faith-imbued science" but is rather more appropriately given its own designation as the scientific study of religion with "scientific" now being understood to mean a strictly (un-blended) academic undertaking that finds its natural home in the context of the modern research university and affiliated institutes, schools, and associations. Although it is historically connected with the intellectual examination of religion that preceded it, its fundamental objective and methodology represents a radical reorientation of that study. Whereas the devotee-scholar is dedicated to providing a systematic intellectual comprehension of the tradition that is consistent with the faith of the religious community concerned, the modern scientific student of religion aims to *explain* religion (both tradition and faith) as an aspect of the natural world.

This modern approach to the study of religion, it must be noted, has been variously named since its emergence (e.g., *religionswissenschaft,* history of religions, comparative religions, religiology), although the term "religious studies" has become the most frequently used designation for that academic study of religion in colleges and universities since, roughly, the middle of the 20th century. It is also important to recognize, however, that this purely scientific approach to the study of religion has not yet come to full fruition in the modern university. It has rightly been pointed out that even though it is possible to view "religious studies" as a reductionistic scientific project, this does not describe the kind of work in which the majority of those who teach in departments of Religious Studies are engaged. This may be accounted for, in part, by the fact that the formation of departments of Religious Studies has been intertwined in a variety of ways in earlier institutional developments related to religious education and the study of theology in the college and university context. Religious Studies, that is, was often introduced into the university curriculum through pre-existing departments of Theology and simply never fully succeeded in freeing itself from their well-entrenched and well-funded religious agendas. However, the lack of success in fully transforming the study of religion from a faith-based "science" to a "science of religion" may, on the other hand, represent a failure of nerve on the part of later students of religion to follow through on the scientific program for the study of religion set out by its 19th-century founders because of the possible negative affects such a program might have on religion itself. Whatever the cause, the academic study of religion in most colleges and universities today is predominantly a theological or crypto-theological enterprise, and it finds added support for its rejection of the modern scientific ideal in a relatively wide-spread postmodernist backlash against science in general.

Postmodernists are fond of pointing out that science has been under attack since the end of the 19th century as naive in its view of itself as a system or structure that escapes the non-rational determinations of culture affecting other modes of thought. Consequently, postmodern students of religion—whose primary concern, it appears, is with the maintenance and promotion of religion—maintain that the sciences are not simple, rational processes of thought and analysis that can provide a neutral framework for an uncomplicated, objective study of religion. They maintain, therefore, that the academic study of religion can be legitimately undertaken in a "reflective" rather than a reductionistic explanatory manner that not only permits but even requires of the student a conscious engagement with religious truth, value, and meaning offered by religion. "Reflection" on these matters, it is claimed, is not a mere repetition of pious affirmations but rather makes possible a "deeper conversation" with religion that can better reveal religion's essential character than can the reductionistic approach of the theoretical sciences. Such an approach, moreover, is often labelled "postmodern science," even though it bears no resemblance to science as a fundamental set of methods for obtaining knowledge of the world that chiefly characterizes the disciplines of the modern, Western, research university. But there can be no doubt that such a postmodern approach to the study of religion—in its espousal of an (interior) "understanding" of the truth, value, and meaning of religion gained through dialogical engagement rather than an empirically testable theoretical account of religion as its primary goal—more closely resembles the catechetical, devotional, and faith-imbued study of religion dominant in the premodern university. There can be little doubt, that is, that its concerns are more gnostic than epistemic, for it is clear that for the postmodernist rational cognitive inquiry is of little or no importance compared to the issue of determining the meaning of life and the value of religion; making sense of life constitutes its "framework of knowledge" and calls for an immersion of the student in the "wisdom" of the cultural system "studied" rather than description, critical analyses, and explanation of that cultural system.

In light of this overview of historical developments in the "study of religion" it is clear that there is no simple answer to the question of the nature of that study. There are at least two, and possibly three, distinct approaches to the intellectual, scholarly, and academic study of religion: premodern "faith-imbued science" that blends devotional, catechetical, moral, and intellectual concerns; modern scientific study of religion which espouses reason as a non-moral instrument of inquiry that attempts to diminish as much as possible religious, moral, social, cultural, political, and other non-cognitive influences in its quest for knowledge about religion; and "postmodern science" that, in rejecting modern science, appears to be a new form of gnosticism that is only superficially distinguishable from premodern faith-imbued science.

There are many postmodern scholars, but as yet no postmodern universities; postmodernism, that is, has not as yet, so to speak, "convinced" the sciences (which, for this discussion, includes all the academic disciplines and not just the natural sciences) of the modern university that their methods for obtaining objective knowledge of the world are incapable of achieving that end. The primary purpose of the contemporary research university, therefore, still appears to be that of obtaining rationally and empirically sound knowledge (including the skills required in producing it) and of making it available for the management of the affairs of society. Consequently, insofar as the academic student of religion today desires scientific credibility s/he must refuse to expand the Religious Studies portfolio beyond the quest for public knowledge of public facts about religious phenomena, events, and behaviour.

Although it is true that the emergence of "religious studies" as a scientific study of religion in the 19th century was intertwined with earlier institutional developments in religious education and the study of theology, there can be no doubt that the primary impulse that made possible its entry into the university curriculum as a new intellectual enterprise was the rapid development of the natural and social sciences following on from their emancipation from the dominance of theology in the premodern university. The premodern university was essentially a religious institution that concerned itself not simply with the quest for knowledge but also with the moral and religious formation of its students. Nevertheless, as historians have noted, the premodern university, by virtue of legal developments that made them autonomous corporate entities, were also able to provide what has been called intellectual "neutral spaces" in which the natural and social worlds could be subjected to critical analysis and explanation. And the subsequent transformation of the traditional notion of "right reason" to "reason(ing)"—based on the recognition of the possibility of dissociating knowledge from virtue—gave rise to an unrestricted cognitive drive (that is, the quest for knowledge for the sake of knowledge alone) and, in effect, created a non-moral and non-ideological instrument of inquiry that made possible the full exploitation of that neutral intellectual space of the medieval university, and the eventual transformation of the religious university into the modern research university. And these developments also made possible a new conceptual ordering of the world with the mythic ordering of reality giving way to a naturalistic, empirical, and rational framework of understanding within which the critique of religion itself became possible. And it is this new reality that made possible the transformation of "religion" from a supernatural reality to an object of science; "religion," that is, came to function as a taxonomic indicator used to designate a range of human behavior involving belief in the supernatural that was now open to natural explanation.

Understanding these transformations, it should be clear that even though the academic (scientific) study of religion in the West appears to have its beginnings within the framework of Christian theology—because in most cases it found its way into the curriculum of colleges and universities in association with faculties and departments of theology or other institutional arrangements for the "delivery" of religious "services" to undergraduates—it is not so much the "offspring" of theology as it is the result of the critique of religion and theology. And though it is true that many theologians and religious instructors ("faith-imbued scientists") have contributed to the scientific study of religion, they have done so not as theologians or religious educators but as philologists, historians, and social scientists making use of positivist and empiricist methodologies in their broader religio-theological frameworks of thought.

Clearly distinguishing the political from the intellectual aspects of the introduction of the "study of religion" into the modern Western university curriculum, therefore, is helpful in recognizing why "religious studies" is in fact a new enterprise and not simply religion or theology in another guise, nor a mere embellishment of the theological "disciplines" already ensconced in the university setting with which "religious studies" became associated. Indeed, it is in a sense a rival to the theological "disciplines" for—insofar as they are themselves aspects of religion—they will be aspects of the subject matter studied by students of religion. Given these developments it is also clear why talk about the "academic study of religion" ought to be seen as a normative matter rather than merely descriptive of what now passes for academic and scientific work in contemporary departments of Religious Studies for it excludes some traditional scholarly examinations of religion from the field. It is not surprising, therefore, to hear theologians bitterly complain about how quickly the academic study of religion (religious studies) secularized its "host" and converted departments of theology into venues for a non-confessional, naturalistic "discipline" for the study of religion.

If the modern research university is primarily committed to the creation and dissemination of knowledge and to the promotion and development of the skills necessary for acquiring new knowledge, then it is only the modern, strictly scientific, study of religion that is "legitimately" a part of the curriculum of the modern Western university, for it is the only study of religion that transcends the traditional structures of knowledge and authority governing the theological "disciplines" and that, like the other sciences (university "disciplines"), restricts itself to obtaining "public knowledge" of "public facts." The "academic study of religion," therefore, is a new kind of intellectual inquiry into religious phenomena that possesses a normative structure even though it may not be entirely accurate to see it as a discipline with its own peculiar methodology. It is more accurate, rather, to refer to this new inquiry as an academic or scientific "enterprise." To see it as a discipline with a set of methods specific to itself would only be justified, it appears, if religion were a *sui generis* reality explicable solely with reference to its peculiar nature, rather than in relation to other types of human engagements, and the natural world within which human communities exist. However, "religion" now refers merely to a range of human constructions and behavior connected to beliefs in transcendental beings, powers, and states in which scholars from a multiplicity of humanistic, social-scientific, and socio-biological disciplines have an interest and whose work may contribute to achieving an overall understanding (explanation) of religion.

"Religion" no longer designates (refers to) some sacred, mysterious, transcendental or metaphysical reality that sets it wholly apart from mundane reality and therefore beyond the methods of inquiry applicable to the study of everyday, ordinary reality. On the one hand, therefore, the academic study of religion is comparable to economics, political science, sociology, and psychology, among other disciplines, in that, like them, it simply tries to account for a specific range of human behavior in non-religious and non-theological terms. On the other hand, it differs from them in its interdisciplinary and polymethodic character and is better described as an "academic enterprise" because it is essentially an organized group of scholars and scientists from a diverse range of disciplines who have gained "academic identity" by virtue of their common interest in religion's peculiar range of human behavior. And it is essentially a "scientific enterprise" because it is chiefly characterized by a cognitive intention and takes for granted that the natural and social sciences are the only legitimate models for the objective study of all human phenomena—including religion. The multidisciplinary and polymethodic character of this "scientific enterprise" constitutes a centrifugal force that threatens its coherence and identity, but the commitment to finding a theory of religion that will provide a causal explanatory account of the data of religion—which is an essential, even if not yet sufficiently developed element of the "enterprise"—creates a counter-balancing centripetal force. The religious studies enterprise, therefore, even though polymethodic, is more than a miscellaneous agglomeration of humanistic and social-scientific disciplines. The modern student of religion, therefore—whether working at the level of the "naturalist" in the collection, description, and classification of data; or at the level of analysis and interpretation of the meanings that the data have for the devotee; or at the level of comparative analysis of religious systems of thought and practice that might provide useful generalizations about religion; or at the level of theory that might provide a causal explanation for the data—is essentially concerned to find an "account" of religion in terms of scientifically warrantable (testable) claims and therefore contributes to a cumulative body of knowledge about religions and religion.

Whether it is even possible for a postmodern university to take shape and form in the manner of the modern research university is doubtful. And there is no doubt that it does not as yet exist as anything but an idea or ideal. Nevertheless, postmodernists within the precincts of the modern university, in alliance with more general anti-science forces in society at large, exert considerable pressure for radical changes to the structure, curriculum, and operation of the modern university. This is no more evident than in the area of religious studies. What is of particular interest in this case, however, is the affinity between the postmodernists and the premodern students of religion. Both groups of scholars are, in some sense, committed to sound scholarship and science, provided that the scholarship involved does not simply "degenerate" into mere academicism and that the science espoused not simply sink into unrestrained reductionism. Like the premodern theologians, the postmodern "Historians of Religion," (not "historians of religion" who only concern themselves with mundane historical matters) see themselves as spokespersons for an academically grounded study of religion yet use their scholarly careers to reveal the perennial mystery and ultimate truth of religion which they "know" by other than scholarly and scientific means. Like "historians of religion," they engage in philological and historical investigations, but it is by means of some gnostic form of initiation that they seem to possess an esoteric "understanding" of religion—an "understanding" that lies beyond all mundane scholarly and scientific criticism.

Given this stance of the postmodern "Historians of Religion" it is obvious that they are operating with incoherent notions of scholarship and science; rejecting the logical and empirical constraints of normal scholarly and scientific practice in the production of knowledge, yet espousing them as means for the dissemination of a "knowledge" gained by other unspecified (and uncriticizable) means. Furthermore, there is no rationale provided for the implicit claim in such practice that postmodern scholarship and science represents epistemological improvement, development, or progress over that produced by modern scholarship and science in its elaboration of the intellectual "neutral space" provided by the medieval university. Indeed, the so-called postmodern scholarship and science is rather an anti-scholarship and anti-science and is, therefore, subversive of the modern university. It sees scholarship and science as forms of cognitive imperialism that undermine other cultural, religious, and political values and therefore attempts to reconstruct the university so as to provide a framework for their articulation and promotion. Though some see the possibility of a postmodern university as the democratization of scholarship, it is difficult to see how this can be anything other than the balkanization of the university. Given the wide diversity of non-cognitive goals and values seeking attention and place in the public sphere, importation of their agendas into the universities will do little by way of mediating their contending claims for power; indeed, it will simply make the sciences available for the articulation and defence of individual and local social interests. In a postmodern university, therefore, there can be no "growth of knowledge"; such an institution can only encourage an accumulation of contending and contradictory assertions and unsubstantiated claims.

In summary, then, the preceding analysis has shown that "the study of religion" can designate more than simply one kind of intellectual engagement with religion. The study of religion in the premodern university is a form of "faith-imbued" study that is clearly distinguishable from the modern, "strictly scientific" approach to understanding religion; an enterprise that emerged in the late 19th century, spurred on by a period of rapid growth in the natural sciences. And it is the latter approach to the study of religion—one directed to obtaining reliable public knowledge about human religious behavior—that finds legitimation in that peculiar modern institution of the research university. And its success in matters of cognition is incontrovertible, despite the claims of postmodern scholars that science, no more than religion itself, is a culture-transcending mode of thought or source of knowledge. Science may be of little or no help in addressing human problems: in providing people a sense of belonging, in furnishing a basis of obligation and co-operation in society, or in consoling the afflicted, and the like. However, its superiority in the sphere of cognition is wholly conspicuous and distinctive. Postmodern efforts to improve upon the modern university involved transforming the notion of knowledge, incorporating into it the concerns of Truth, Value, and Meaning, and making of it a form of wisdom capable of addressing human problems. Achieving such "wisdom-knowledge," however, involves (an uncritical) immersion in the traditions housing Truths, Values, and Meanings, and is, therefore, a gnostic form of knowing quite incommensurable with scientific knowledge of the modern university; it is, in fact, indistinguishable from the mythopoetic, faith-imbued knowledge of the theologians of the premodern university. "Religious studies," therefore, if it is to be an appropriate *academic* undertaking within the context of the contemporary research university, and a legitimate element of the curriculum in today's colleges and universities, must be a purely cognitive enterprise in the strict sense of "science" set out above. Other styles of the "study of religion" may have their rightful place, but that place is not the modern research university.

Although attention has been focused here on the development of the scientific study of religion in the West, it must be recognized that it is not simply a Western phenomenon. Such an approach to understanding religion also emerged, at least in incipient form, in many non-western cultures and societies. In an important sense, therefore, it is a global phenomenon and not, as some have argued, a "regime of epistemic violence" nurtured by a post-Christian society and foisted upon others. It is neither complicit in a hegemonic political agenda of Western imperialism nor has it suppressed non-Western forms of knowledge and ways of life.

There can be no doubt that the most robust form of the "science of religion" emerged first in Europe and that it did so largely because of the work of a few "religious scholars" who were, so to speak, in the thrall of modern science and who were able to ensconce the enterprise in existing hospitable institutional structures. There is a great deal of evidence, however, to show that the European Enlightenment was not alien to Middle Eastern and Asian intellectual traditions in conceptualizing and analyzing religion. It has been shown, that is, that numerous scholars in non-Western cultures approached religion from a non-confessional and critical point of view and in the process created a religiously independent basis for the historical and comparative study of religion. These parallels between West and East in the scientific study of religion clearly indicate the limitations of a culturally isolationist view of its development and point to the promise of future growth of the field as a inter-culturally shared enterprise.

A Statistical Approach to the World's Religious Adherents, 2000–2050 CE

Todd M. Johnson

About the Statistics Used in this Encyclopedia

Religions of the World: A Comprehensive Encyclopedia of Beliefs and Practices contains a standardized statistical table, with total of followers (adherents) of the 18 largest religions, for each of the world's 239 countries, 20 regions, 7 continents, and the entire globe itself. This listing follows the names and definitions as designated by the United Nations (UN) as of 2009. Tables for the world, the continents, and the continental regions immediately follow this introduction. The tables for the individual countries (as well as Antarctica) appear in the encyclopedia entry for the respective country.

A Standardized Format

The standardized formats and definitions in each of these short religion tables are as follows: Titles follow the format "Status of religions in Afghanistan, 1970–2050," with the largest being "Status of religions in world population, 1970–2050." This latter table lists the world's 18 largest or most significant distinct religious blocs, ranked numerically by number of followers (adherents) in 2010 CE. The largest such religion, Christianity, is then subdivided into the 3 largest of its 6 constituent ecclesiastical megablocs of affiliated church members (Orthodox, Roman Catholics, Anglicans, Protestants, Independents, and Marginal Christians).

Standardized Columns

Scanning across the column heads of each table, readers will note 7 categories of information: (1) name of the religion's followers; (2) total of those followers (including children) in 1970; (3) total of those followers (including children) in 2010; (4) that total expressed as a percentage of total population (which in turn is shown on the bottom line); (5) annual percent rate of growth over the period 2000–2010; (6) projected total followers in 2025 CE; and (7) total projected followers in 2050 CE. The future projections in these last 2 columns are built on the 7 detailed alternate scenarios that are part of the UN's demographic database for every country and every year from 1950 to 2050.

Duplicate Membership

In the interests of brevity, these highly condensed tables abridge an important issue and omit a variety of explanatory categories (which can be studied more completely in the *World Christian Encyclopedia*, 2d ed. [New York: Oxford University Press, 2001], and also in *World Christian Trends* [Pasadena, CA: William Carey Library, 2001]). Among these categories are: (1) Unaffiliated Christians (found in all countries) often called nominal Christians, being professing followers of Christ who are not known to be involved in organized Christianity; (2) Doubly affiliated Christians (found in 173 countries, such as Brazil), being baptized members of a denomination who become baptized or affiliated in a second denomination without renouncing the former; and (3) Disaffiliated Christians (found in 11 countries, such as Italy), being baptized persons who profess to have abandoned Christianity (as in polls) but without renouncing their baptismal membership.

Definitions

The tables use the following categories and subjects:

Continents These follow current UN demographic terminology, which now divides the world into seven major areas including Antarctica. See *World Population Prospects: The 2006 Revision* (New York: United Nations, 2007), which gives populations of all continents, regions, and countries covering the period 1950–2050. Note that "Asia" now includes the former USSR Central Asian states; and "Europe" now includes all of Russia extending eastward to Vladivostok, the Sea of Japan, and the Bering Strait.

Countries This covers sovereign countries (properly termed *nations*) and nonsovereign countries in which each religion or religious grouping has a numerically significant and organized following.

Followers (or Adherents) As defined in the 1948 Universal Declaration of Human Rights, a person's religion is what he or she says it is, and no one has the right to deny such profession. Total are enumerated following the methodology of the *World Christian Encyclopedia* using recent censuses, polls, surveys, reports, Web sites, literature, and other data. All figures are from the *World Christian Database* (Brill, 2009) and the *World Religion Database* (Brill, 2009).

Atheists Persons professing atheism, skepticism, disbelief, or irreligion, including the militantly antireligious (opposed to all religion). Compare with "Nonreligious," below.

Buddhists At the world level, followers of the Buddha are 56 percent Mahayana, 38 percent Theravada (Hinayana), 6 percent Tantrayana (Lamaism).

Chinese folk-religionists An umbrella term for followers of traditional Chinese religion (local deities, ancestor veneration, Confucian ethics, Taoism, traditional universism, divination, some Buddhist elements).

Christians   Followers of Jesus Christ comprising (a) persons affiliated with churches (church members, including children), divided into six standardized ecclesiastical megablocs as enumerated below; plus (b) persons professing in censuses or polls to be Christians though not so affiliated. Each table lists under "Christians" only the three largest such megablocs. Figures for these three megablocs may be larger than the total on the previous line because many Christians are affiliated to more than one denomination. The six megablocs are as follows:

1. *Orthodox.* Churches in communion with the ancient patriarchates of the East, including (a) Eastern Orthodox (Constantinople, Antioch, Jerusalem), (b) Oriental Orthodox (Etchmiadzin, Alexandria, Damascus, Addis Ababa, India), and (c) the Ancient Assyrian Apostolic Church of the East.
2. *Roman Catholics.* Churches and jurisdictions in communion with the Holy See and the Roman papacy.
3. *Anglicans.* Churches in communion with the Archbishop of Canterbury.
4. *Protestants.* Churches tracing their ancestry back to the Protestant Reformation in Europe from 1517 onwards, under Luther, Calvin, Zwingli, et al.
5. *Independents.* Members of churches and networks that regard themselves as postdenominationalist and neo-apostolic and thus are independent of and uninterested in historic, organized, institutionalized, denominationalist Christianity.
6. *Marginal Christians.* Members of denominations regarding themselves as on the margins of organized mainstream Christianity (Mormons, Jehovah's Witnesses, Christian Science, Religious Science, et al.).

Confucians   Non-Chinese followers of Confucius and Confucianism, mostly Koreans in Korea.

Ethnoreligionists   Followers of local, tribal, or shamanistic religions, with members restricted to one ethnic group.

Hindus   At the world level, followers of Hindu deities are 68 percent Vaisnavites, 27 percent Shaivites, and 2 percent neo-Hindus and reform Hindus.

Jews   Adherents of Judaism. For detailed data of "core" Jewish populations, see the annual "World Jewish Populations" article in the American Jewish Committee's *American Jewish Year Book.*

Muslims   At the world level, 84 percent are Sunnites, 14 percent are Shi'ites, and 2 percent are other schools.

New-Religionists   Followers of 20th-century new religions, new religious movements, radical new crisis religions, and non-Christian syncretistic mass religions, all founded since 1800 and most since 1945, mostly Asian in origin and membership but increasingly with worldwide followings.

Nonreligious   Persons professing no religion, nonbelievers, agnostics, freethinkers, indifferent, uninterested, or dereligionized secularists indifferent to all religion but not militantly so. Compare with "Atheists," above.

Other religionists   Includes a handful of smaller religions, quasi-religions, pseudo religions, parareligions, religious or mystic systems, religious and semireligious brotherhoods of numerous varieties.

Total population   UN medium variant figures for 1970, mid-2010, 2025, and 2050, as given in *World Population Prospects: The 2006 Revision*.

Religious Adherents of the World by Continent and Region

The following tables cover the world's countries as recognized by the UN, plus 11 countries not recognized or included by the UN: Bougainville, British Indian Ocean Territory, Christmas Island, Cocos Islands, Mayotte, Norfolk Island, Northern Cyprus, Somaliland, Spanish North Africa, Svalbard and Jan Mayen Islands, and the Republic of China (Taiwan). There is a country entry in the encyclopedia for each country, plus entries for British Indian Ocean Territory, Christmas Island, Cocos Islands, Mayotte, Svalbard and Jan Mayen Islands, and China: Taiwan. There is, in addition, an entry on Antarctica. For statistics and material on the Vatican (Holy See), see Italy; for material on Hong Kong and Macau, see China: Hong Kong and China: Macau. The tables below cover the world, then each continent in alphabetical order. Following each individual continent are the tables for each region of that continent, each with a note detailing the countries that compose that region.

The World

Religion	Followers in 1970	Followers in 2010	% of Population	Annual % growth 2000–2010	Followers in 2025	Followers in 2050
Christians	1,234,969,000	2,292,454,000	33.2	1.44	2,708,029,000	3,220,348,000
Roman Catholics	665,895,000	1,155,627,000	16.7	0.88	1,323,840,000	1,522,294,000
Protestants	210,986,000	419,316,000	6.1	1.85	530,485,000	671,148,000
Independents	86,018,000	369,156,000	5.3	2.69	502,211,000	655,556,000
Muslims	579,875,000	1,549,444,000	22.4	1.86	1,962,881,000	2,494,229,000
Hindus	458,845,000	948,507,000	13.7	1.53	1,098,680,000	1,241,133,000
Agnostics	542,318,000	639,852,000	9.3	−0.58	625,648,000	556,416,000
Chinese folk	231,814,000	458,316,000	6.6	0.87	504,695,000	525,183,000
Buddhists	234,028,000	468,736,000	6.8	1.46	542,372,000	570,283,000
Ethnoreligionists	165,687,000	261,429,000	3.8	1.31	267,440,000	272,450,000
Atheists	165,301,000	138,532,000	2.0	−0.11	133,320,000	132,671,000
New religionists	39,332,000	64,443,000	0.9	0.52	66,677,000	63,657,000
Sikhs	10,677,000	24,591,000	0.4	1.69	29,517,000	34,258,000
Jews	15,100,000	14,641,000	0.2	0.62	15,521,000	16,973,000
Spiritists	4,657,000	13,978,000	0.2	1.10	15,664,000	17,080,000
Daoists	1,734,000	9,017,000	0.1	3.02	13,194,000	15,018,000
Confucianists	4,759,000	6,461,000	0.1	0.22	6,698,000	6,014,000
Baha'is	2,657,000	7,447,000	0.1	1.80	10,491,000	15,113,000
Jains	2,629,000	5,749,000	0.1	1.65	6,845,000	7,943,000
Shintoists	4,175,000	2,782,000	0.0	0.16	2,674,000	2,355,000
Zoroastrians	125,000	181,000	0.0	0.05	166,000	170,000
Total population	**3,698,683,000**	**6,906,560,000**	**100.0**	**1.24**	**8,010,511,000**	**9,191,294,000**

Status of Religions in World Population, 1970–2050

Africa (60 countries)

Religion	Followers in 1970	Followers in 2010	% of Population	Annual % growth 2000–2010	Followers in 2025	Followers in 2050
Christians	144,922,000	384,416,000	47.9	2.58	700,371,000	1,055,401,000
Roman Catholics	45,059,000	128,000,000	16.4	2.52	249,921,000	392,546,000
Protestants	27,322,000	103,437,000	13.3	3.16	194,950,000	292,264,000
Independents	18,218,000	77,946,000	9.6	2.42	136,702,000	197,655,000
Muslims	144,796,000	334,307,000	40.5	2.29	563,140,000	789,149,000
Ethnoreligionists	71,720,000	91,874,000	10.4	1.63	111,005,000	123,124,000
Agnostics	586,000	4,953,000	0.6	2.15	10,058,000	16,335,000
Hindus	994,000	2,484,000	0.3	1.64	3,865,000	5,286,000
Baha'is	698,000	1,718,000	0.2	2.36	3,421,000	5,649,000
Atheists	103,000	514,000	0.1	1.89	948,000	1,508,000
Buddhists	11,600	247,000	0.0	1.62	378,000	506,000
Jews	205,000	125,000	0.0	0.54	138,000	151,000
New religionists	29,400	107,000	0.0	2.13	190,000	294,000
Jains	32,800	73,400	0.0	2.60	143,000	234,000
Chinese folk	7,300	60,500	0.0	1.43	84,200	125,000
Sikhs	25,900	58,200	0.0	2.33	101,000	141,000
Confucianists	0	18,200	0.0	1.09	25,000	30,000
Spiritists	2,300	3,100	0.0	1.03	4,800	6,200
Zoroastrians	480	880	0.0	−0.67	800	700
Total population	**364,135,000**	**820,959,000**	**100.0**	**2.35**	**1,393,872,000**	**1,997,938,000**

Status of Religions in Africa, 1970–2050

Religion	Followers in 1970	Followers in 2010	% of Population	Annual % growth 2000–2010	Followers in 2025	Followers in 2050
Christians	55,091,000	214,842,000	64.7	2.75	313,793,000	483,266,000
Roman Catholics	18,457,000	67,344,000	20.3	2.98	99,411,000	155,269,000
Protestants	7,785,000	60,481,000	18.2	3.09	88,748,000	133,754,000
Orthodox	12,120,000	38,682,000	11.6	2.75	54,033,000	79,449,000
Muslims	21,749,000	72,436,000	21.8	2.80	101,966,000	150,856,000
Ethnoreligionists	31,010,000	40,640,000	12.2	1.60	43,299,000	48,785,000
Hindus	557,000	1,577,000	0.5	1.99	2,110,000	2,995,000
Baha'is	448,000	1,150,000	0.3	2.39	1,797,000	2,871,000
Agnostics	54,100	1,054,000	0.3	2.52	1,810,000	3,225,000
Atheists	6,000	121,000	0.0	2.17	209,000	324,000
Jains	32,800	90,100	0.0	2.64	140,000	230,000
Buddhists	7,800	75,800	0.0	2.44	109,000	159,000
Sikhs	21,900	53,600	0.0	2.53	77,400	110,000
Jews	35,700	34,400	0.0	1.95	40,800	51,800
Chinese folk	5,600	28,200	0.0	1.59	36,100	60,100
New religionists	1,600	3,400	0.0	1.12	5,000	7,900
Zoroastrians	480	850	0.0	−0.67	800	700
Spiritists	300	660	0.0	0.72	800	1,200
Total population	**109,021,000**	**332,107,000**	**100.0**	**2.60**	**465,393,000**	**692,943,000**

Status of religions in Eastern Africa, 1970–2050

Eastern Africa includes 21 countries: British Indian Ocean Territory, Burundi, Comoros, Djibouti, Eritrea, Ethiopia, Kenya, Madagascar, Malawi, Mauritius, Mayotte, Mozambique, Reunion, Rwanda, Seychelles, Somalia, Somaliland, Tanzania, Uganda, Zambia, and Zimbabwe.

Religion	Followers in 1970	Followers in 2010	% of Population	Annual % growth 2000–2010	Followers in 2025	Followers in 2050
Christians	30,667,000	105,830,000	81.7	2.89	159,802,000	266,616,000
Roman Catholics	15,627,000	57,478,000	44.4	1.57	87,747,000	148,234,000
Protestants	6,544,000	26,467,000	20.4	3.48	40,387,000	67,699,000
Independents	4,571,000	19,000,000	14.7	2.58	29,386,000	49,189,000
Muslims	3,546,000	12,403,000	9.6	3.05	18,162,000	28,721,000
Ethnoreligionists	6,861,000	9,840,000	7.6	2.14	10,676,000	11,975,000
Agnostics	34,400	769,000	0.6	4.03	1,448,000	3,051,000
Baha'is	170,000	493,000	0.4	2.99	799,000	1,486,000
Hindus	1,000	105,000	0.1	2.99	201,000	401,000
Atheists	4,500	95,500	0.1	2.66	163,000	289,000
New religionists	2,600	40,900	0.0	2.37	64,000	112,000
Buddhists	400	5,700	0.0	3.19	9,600	20,000
Jews	500	400	0.0	−5.06	500	500
Chinese folk	40	450	0.0	2.66	700	1,200
Total population	**41,289,000**	**129,583,000**	**100.0**	**2.85**	**191,325,000**	**312,672,000**

Status of religions in Middle Africa, 1970–2050
Middle Africa includes 9 countries: Angola, Cameroon, Central African Republic, Chad, Congo (Republic of, Brazzaville), Congo (Democratic Republic, Zaire), Equatorial Guinea, Gabon, and São Tomé and Príncipe

Religion	Followers in 1970	Followers in 2010	% of Population	Annual % growth 2000–2010	Followers in 2025	Followers in 2050
Muslims	74,443,000	182,154,000	88.3	1.68	225,043,000	273,092,000
Christians	7,993,000	17,492,000	8.5	1.61	21,943,000	28,102,000
Orthodox	6,160,000	9,463,000	4.6	1.25	10,202,000	11,242,000
Roman Catholics	1,180,000	4,267,000	2.1	1.61	6,100,000	8,375,000
Anglicans	303,000	2,355,000	1.1	0.98	3,506,000	5,007,000
Ethnoreligionists	3,154,000	4,630,000	2.2	1.95	4,501,000	4,802,000
Agnostics	228,000	1,770,000	0.9	1.53	2,731,000	3,749,000
Atheists	66,200	153,000	0.1	1.89	206,000	296,000
Baha'is	5,300	49,400	0.0	1.31	70,700	104,000
Buddhists	400	22,000	0.0	2.06	32,000	50,000
Jews	49,000	11,900	0.0	0.34	11,800	12,100
Hindus	0	7,600	0.0	2.03	12,200	18,400
Sikhs	0	2,400	0.0	2.06	5,000	8,000
Chinese folk	0	1,800	0.0	2.06	3,000	6,000
Total population	**85,939,000**	**206,295,000**	**100.0**	**1.68**	**254,559,000**	**310,240,000**

Status of religions in Northern Africa, 1970–2050
Northern Africa includes 8 countries: Algeria, Egypt, Libya, Morocco, Sahara, Spanish North Africa, Sudan, and Tunisia

Religion	Followers in 1970	Followers in 2010	% of Population	Annual % growth 2000–2010	Followers in 2025	Followers in 2050
Christians	19,300,000	46,419,000	82.0	1.21	49,798,000	53,010,000
Independents	4,873,000	20,814,000	36.8	2.18	23,033,000	24,380,000
Protestants	7,251,000	12,020,000	21.2	0.80	12,409,000	13,337,000
Roman Catholics	2,171,000	4,841,000	8.6	1.03	5,415,000	6,000,000
Ethnoreligionists	5,127,000	5,358,000	9.5	0.21	4,360,000	3,778,000
Agnostics	150,000	1,591,000	2.8	1.56	2,311,000	3,147,000
Muslims	271,000	1,262,000	2.2	1.10	1,629,000	2,042,000
Hindus	433,000	1,182,000	2.1	1.10	1,511,000	1,808,000
Baha'is	34,700	274,000	0.5	1.11	374,000	532,000
Atheists	5,100	172,000	0.3	1.10	218,000	305,000
Buddhists	2,200	159,000	0.3	1.10	181,000	202,000
Jews	120,000	83,000	0.1	−0.01	83,400	85,300
Chinese folk	1,600	34,000	0.1	1.10	36,200	42,400
New religionists	10,000	22,600	0.0	1.09	30,400	40,000
Confucianists	0	20,000	0.0	1.09	25,000	30,000
Sikhs	4,000	11,300	0.0	1.10	14,400	17,600
Spiritists	2,000	3,000	0.0	1.10	4,000	5,000
Jains	0	2,000	0.0	1.10	3,000	4,000
Total population	**25,462,000**	**56,592,000**	**100.0**	**1.11**	**60,578,000**	**65,050,000**

Status of religions in Southern Africa, 1970–2050
Southern Africa includes 5 countries: Botswana, Lesotho, Namibia, South Africa, and Swaziland

Religion	Followers in 1970	Followers in 2010	% of Population	Annual % growth 2000–2010	Followers in 2025	Followers in 2050
Muslims	44,787,000	149,389,000	48.6	2.78	216,340,000	334,437,000
Christians	31,871,000	110,084,000	35.8	2.80	155,035,000	224,406,000
Protestants	5,532,000	36,265,000	11.8	4.02	50,488,000	72,948,000
Roman Catholics	7,625,000	35,565,000	11.6	3.56	51,248,000	74,668,000
Independents	4,874,000	34,163,000	11.1	2.73	48,223,000	69,593,000
Ethnoreligionists	25,568,000	46,547,000	15.1	1.70	48,169,000	53,784,000
Agnostics	119,000	999,000	0.3	2.64	1,757,000	3,164,000
Baha'is	39,700	210,000	0.1	2.94	381,000	656,000
Atheists	21,000	82,100	0.0	2.53	152,000	295,000
New religionists	15,300	64,700	0.0	2.44	90,600	134,000
Buddhists	800	29,600	0.0	2.06	46,000	74,500
Hindus	3,000	19,900	0.0	2.82	31,400	62,800
Chinese folk	0	5,400	0.0	2.49	8,200	15,500
Sikhs	0	3,300	0.0	3.58	4,000	5,000
Jews	0	1,200	0.0	2.53	1,300	1,400
Total population	**102,424,000**	**307,436,000**	**100.0**	**2.61**	**422,017,000**	**617,034,000**

Status of religions in Western Africa, 1970–2050
Western Africa includes 17 countries: Benin, Burkina Faso, Cape Verde, Gambia, Ghana, Guinea, Guinea-Bissau, Ivory Coast, Liberia, Mali, Mauritania, Niger, Nigeria, Saint Helena, Senegal, Sierra Leone, and Togo

Asia (50 countries)

Religion	Followers in 1970	Followers in 2010	% of Population	Annual % growth 2000–2010	Followers in 2025	Followers in 2050
Muslims	415,784,000	913,408,000	26.0	1.76	1,342,221,000	1,642,640,000
Hindus	456,715,000	814,355,000	22.6	1.53	1,089,550,000	1,229,146,000
Agnostics	437,993,000	513,757,000	11.8	−0.66	442,666,000	336,580,000
Chinese folk	231,539,000	419,866,000	11.0	0.87	502,707,000	522,754,000
Buddhists	232,843,000	407,811,000	11.1	1.45	531,160,000	555,279,000
Christians	96,386,000	278,432,000	8.5	2.72	480,157,000	595,333,000
Independents	16,500,000	101,439,000	3.4	4.22	206,253,000	264,727,000
Roman Catholics	50,983,000	117,456,000	3.3	1.75	175,152,000	210,120,000
Protestants	21,835,000	69,552,000	2.1	2.96	119,678,000	142,706,000
Ethnoreligionists	91,682,000	133,566,000	3.5	1.09	149,905,000	142,768,000
Atheists	109,602,000	116,701,000	2.8	0.13	111,375,000	107,973,000
New religionists	38,268,000	58,079,000	1.4	0.44	60,900,000	56,353,000
Sikhs	10,411,000	19,937,000	0.6	1.63	27,707,000	31,893,000
Daoists	1,734,000	7,065,000	0.2	3.02	13,174,000	14,992,000
Confucianists	4,758,000	6,243,000	0.2	0.20	6,559,000	5,824,000
Jews	2,756,000	4,966,000	0.1	1.93	7,083,000	8,558,000
Jains	2,586,000	4,759,000	0.1	1.63	6,521,000	7,429,000
Baha'is	1,411,000	3,038,000	0.1	1.48	4,579,000	5,988,000
Shintoists	4,173,000	2,700,000	0.1	0.14	2,594,000	2,254,000
Zoroastrians	124,000	156,000	0.0	−0.14	134,000	134,000
Total population	**2,138,766,000**	**3,704,838,000**	**100.0**	**1.23**	**4,778,991,000**	**5,265,897,000**

Status of religions in Asia, 1970–2050

Religion	Followers in 1970	Followers in 2010	% of Population	Annual % growth 2000–2010	Followers in 2025	Followers in 2050
Agnostics	417,318,000	442,219,000	28.3	−0.81	381,167,000	260,727,000
Chinese folk	224,824,000	445,443,000	28.5	0.85	490,386,000	509,538,000
Buddhists	127,980,000	276,177,000	17.7	1.71	325,199,000	335,244,000
Atheists	98,816,000	105,737,000	6.8	0.04	98,530,000	93,820,000
Christians	11,030,000	140,012,000	9.0	3.72	202,035,000	251,337,000
Independents	2,862,000	93,002,000	6.0	5.47	129,543,000	160,508,000
Protestants	3,396,000	35,974,000	2.3	4.81	53,420,000	65,550,000
Roman Catholics	1,919,000	20,991,000	1.3	2.39	31,802,000	41,363,000
Ethnoreligionists	56,360,000	68,515,000	4.4	0.66	66,282,000	54,766,000
New religionists	27,494,000	45,462,000	2.9	0.24	44,170,000	38,276,000
Muslims	12,085,000	21,775,000	1.4	0.85	24,495,000	25,510,000
Daoists	1,734,000	9,000,000	0.6	3.02	13,173,000	14,990,000
Confucianists	4,758,000	5,377,000	0.3	0.09	5,380,000	4,530,000
Shintoists	4,173,000	2,710,000	0.2	0.13	2,590,000	2,250,000
Baha'is	27,300	74,000	0.0	0.48	99,200	138,000
Hindus	17,500	45,700	0.0	0.36	52,500	68,000
Sikhs	8,000	22,700	0.0	0.61	29,800	41,000
Jews	2,000	4,200	0.0	0.47	4,200	4,400
Jains	0	1,600	0.0	0.14	1,800	2,000
Zoroastrians	50	70	0.0	0.63	70	70
Total population	**986,626,000**	**1,562,575,000**	**100.0**	**0.62**	**1,653,595,000**	**1,591,242,000**

Status of religions in Eastern Asia, 1970–2050
Eastern Asia includes 6 countries: China, Peoples Republic of China, Republic of China (Taiwain), Japan, Mongolia, North Korea, and South Korea

Religion	Followers in 1970	Followers in 2010	% of Population	Annual % growth 2000–2010	Followers in 2025	Followers in 2050
Hindus	452,928,000	932,792,000	52.5	1.53	1,079,270,000	1,217,180,000
Muslims	229,477,000	637,021,000	35.8	1.81	808,420,000	1,011,596,000
Christians	27,261,000	69,213,000	3.9	2.80	100,563,000	130,975,000
Roman Catholics	9,895,000	24,905,000	1.4	3.00	31,847,000	38,413,000
Protestants	9,164,000	23,998,000	1.4	2.25	30,756,000	37,972,000
Independents	3,768,000	20,734,000	1.2	3.05	39,159,000	56,039,000
Ethnoreligionists	20,993,000	50,350,000	2.8	1.65	53,492,000	56,199,000
Buddhists	14,154,000	26,764,000	1.5	1.09	30,526,000	33,575,000
Agnostics	11,104,000	25,440,000	1.4	0.60	32,097,000	38,776,000
Sikhs	10,325,000	22,998,000	1.3	1.63	27,323,000	31,370,000
Jains	2,584,000	5,528,000	0.3	1.63	6,510,000	7,415,000
Atheists	7,205,000	4,463,000	0.3	0.45	4,402,000	4,540,000
Baha'is	1,009,000	2,351,000	0.1	1.36	2,850,000	3,646,000
Chinese folk	61,500	195,000	0.0	1.68	296,000	482,000
Zoroastrians	123,000	149,000	0.0	–0.16	132,000	132,000
Jews	195,000	90,300	0.0	–0.18	85,800	81,100
New religionists	13,700	24,000	0.0	0.78	33,400	44,600
Shintoists	0	160	0.0	0.40	400	500
Total population	**777,433,000**	**1,777,378,000**	**100.0**	**1.65**	**2,146,001,000**	**2,536,011,000**

Status of religions in South-Central Asia, 1970–2050

South-Central Asia includes 14 countries: Afghanistan, Bangladesh, Bhutan, India, Iran, Kazakhstan, Kirghizstan, Maldives, Nepal, Pakistan, Sri Lanka, Tajikistan, Turkmenistan, and Uzbekistan

Religion	Followers in 1970	Followers in 2010	% of Population	Annual % growth 2000–2010	Followers in 2025	Followers in 2050
Muslims	101,420,000	217,705,000	36.6	1.38	247,164,000	270,146,000
Buddhists	90,698,000	158,139,000	26.6	1.08	174,915,000	185,755,000
Christians	51,723,000	129,700,000	21.8	1.96	162,782,000	197,185,000
Roman Catholics	37,451,000	88,590,000	14.9	1.28	106,156,000	123,766,000
Independents	9,793,000	28,498,000	4.8	1.62	36,774,000	47,040,000
Protestants	9,154,000	27,184,000	4.6	1.41	35,154,000	38,707,000
Ethnoreligionists	14,314,000	28,697,000	4.8	1.24	30,055,000	31,707,000
Agnostics	5,676,000	17,740,000	3.0	1.38	23,676,000	29,738,000
New religionists	10,665,000	14,614,000	2.5	1.09	16,407,000	17,671,000
Chinese folk	6,645,000	11,063,000	1.9	1.57	11,926,000	12,595,000
Hindus	3,756,000	7,544,000	1.3	1.41	8,609,000	9,494,000
Atheists	1,424,000	6,889,000	1.2	1.46	7,943,000	8,974,000
Confucianists	0	995,000	0.2	0.87	1,179,000	1,294,000
Baha'is	363,000	968,000	0.2	1.61	1,374,000	1,794,000
Sikhs	75,000	152,000	0.0	1.34	204,000	237,000
Jains	1,700	4,600	0.0	1.38	8,000	11,000
Jews	1,300	2,300	0.0	1.75	2,600	2,600
Shintoists	0	1,800	0.0	1.31	3,100	3,900
Zoroastrians	350	950	0.0	1.04	1,000	1,000
Daoists	0	470	0.0	1.58	1,300	2,000
Total population	**286,762,000**	**594,216,000**	**100.0**	**1.41**	**686,251,000**	**766,611,000**

Status of religions in South-Eastern Asia, 1970–2050

South-Eastern Asia includes 11 countries: Brunei, Cambodia, Indonesia, Laos, Malaysia, Myanmar, Philippines, Singapore, Thailand, Timor, and Vietnam

Religion	Followers in 1970	Followers in 2010	% of Population	Annual % growth 2000–2010	Followers in 2025	Followers in 2050
Muslims	72,802,000	206,036,000	88.8	2.11	262,142,000	335,388,000
Christians	6,372,000	13,315,000	5.7	0.35	14,777,000	15,837,000
Orthodox	4,350,000	8,294,000	3.6	−0.56	8,217,000	7,512,000
Roman Catholics	1,719,000	4,216,000	1.8	1.67	5,347,000	6,578,000
Independents	76,900	503,000	0.2	0.98	778,000	1,140,000
Jews	2,557,000	5,873,000	2.5	1.97	6,991,000	8,470,000
Agnostics	3,895,000	4,409,000	1.9	0.94	5,725,000	7,339,000
Hindus	14,600	1,103,000	0.5	2.85	1,619,000	2,404,000
Atheists	2,157,000	411,000	0.2	0.07	500,000	638,000
Buddhists	10,500	384,000	0.2	2.77	519,000	705,000
New religionists	95,600	222,000	0.1	1.75	289,000	361,000
Baha'is	12,900	158,000	0.1	3.02	257,000	409,000
Sikhs	3,100	99,800	0.0	2.41	150,000	245,000
Chinese folk	9,000	65,600	0.0	2.03	98,000	139,000
Ethnoreligionists	15,500	61,400	0.0	2.29	75,800	96,300
Zoroastrians	600	1,000	0.0	1.65	1,000	1,100
Jains	0	250	0.0	3.06	500	800
Total population	**87,945,000**	**232,139,000**	**100.0**	**1.97**	**293,144,000**	**372,033,000**

Status of religions in Western Asia, 1970–2050
Western Asia includes 19 countries: Armenia, Azerbaijan, Bahrain, Cyprus, Georgia, Iraq, Israel, Jordan, Kuwait, Lebanon, Northern Cyprus, Oman, Palestine, Qatar, Saudi Arabia, Syria, Turkey, United Arab Emirates, and Yemen

Europe (48 countries)

Religion	Followers in 1970	Followers in 2010	% of Population	Annual % growth 2000–2010	Followers in 2025	Followers in 2050
Christians	492,531,000	572,479,000	80.2	0.39	563,718,000	508,439,000
Roman Catholics	255,761,000	274,002,000	37.8	0.02	265,866,000	242,868,000
Orthodox	110,684,000	194,205,000	27.5	0.75	190,654,000	161,022,000
Protestants	82,204,000	69,683,000	9.3	−0.50	66,410,000	62,350,000
Agnostics	86,134,000	92,340,000	11.1	−1.88	82,457,000	84,209,000
Muslims	17,922,000	38,635,000	5.6	0.64	46,223,000	46,727,000
Atheists	53,815,000	17,957,000	2.1	−2.20	14,474,000	15,243,000
Jews	4,284,000	1,891,000	0.3	−0.33	1,776,000	1,702,000
Buddhists	552,000	1,719,000	0.3	0.67	2,263,000	2,881,000
Ethnoreligionists	586,000	1,195,000	0.2	−0.32	1,067,000	884,000
Hindus	243,000	871,000	0.1	1.87	1,168,000	1,475,000
Sikhs	202,000	406,000	0.1	3.12	678,000	868,000
New religionists	243,000	353,000	0.1	0.39	479,000	586,000
Chinese folk	60,000	345,000	0.1	2.16	481,000	559,000
Spiritists	36,400	136,000	0.0	0.48	167,000	199,000
Baha'is	56,500	134,000	0.0	0.49	207,000	320,000
Confucianists	1,000	17,500	0.0	0.36	23,000	28,700
Jains	4,000	16,100	0.0	1.89	31,200	51,500
Zoroastrians	410	5,400	0.0	0.60	7,200	9,400
Total population	**656,670,000**	**728,501,000**	**100.0**	**0.07**	**715,221,000**	**664,184,000**

Status of religions in Europe, 1970–2050

Religion	Followers in 1970	Followers in 2010	% of Population	Annual % growth 2000–2010	Followers in 2025	Followers in 2050
Christians	158,219,000	246,495,000	84.8	0.65	233,935,000	196,582,000
Orthodox	92,685,000	177,352,000	61.0	0.85	166,006,000	137,089,000
Roman Catholics	49,631,000	56,517,000	19.4	−0.15	54,458,000	46,658,000
Protestants	7,306,000	7,879,000	2.7	0.81	8,155,000	7,590,000
Agnostics	57,707,000	20,357,000	7.0	−7.79	12,038,000	7,054,000
Muslims	11,545,000	17,417,000	6.0	0.26	17,299,000	14,930,000
Atheists	44,888,000	4,244,000	1.5	−6.89	1,840,000	1,091,000
Ethnoreligionists	535,000	987,000	0.3	−0.46	907,000	707,000
Jews	3,021,000	536,000	0.2	−1.86	469,000	418,000
Buddhists	475,000	604,000	0.2	−0.42	644,000	708,000
Hindus	0	51,000	0.0	1.07	66,000	87,000
Baha'is	2,700	23,500	0.0	−0.38	39,700	67,000
New religionists	23,400	14,800	0.0	−0.23	16,400	20,200
Sikhs	0	11,100	0.0	0.15	11,500	12,000
Spiritists	0	7,600	0.0	−0.12	9,000	10,000
Chinese folk	0	7,300	0.0	−0.31	9,200	11,200
Total population	**276,417,000**	**290,755,000**	**100.0**	**−0.47**	**267,284,000**	**221,697,000**

Status of religions in Eastern Europe, 1970–2050

Eastern Europe includes 10 countries: Belorussia, Bulgaria, Czech Republic, Hungary, Poland, Moldavia, Romania, Russia, Slovakia, and Ukraine

Religion	Followers in 1970	Followers in 2010	% of Population	Annual % growth 2000–2010	Followers in 2025	Followers in 2050
Christians	75,759,000	79,610,000	80.9	0.25	80,334,000	81,004,000
Anglicans	29,265,000	26,099,000	26.5	0.07	25,204,000	25,195,000
Protestants	30,742,000	25,809,000	26.2	−0.42	25,780,000	25,386,000
Roman Catholics	10,727,000	12,541,000	12.8	0.08	12,979,000	13,203,000
Agnostics	7,610,000	11,914,000	12.1	1.22	14,795,000	16,894,000
Atheists	2,224,000	2,392,000	2.4	0.43	2,755,000	3,216,000
Muslims	676,000	2,377,000	2.4	1.59	3,358,000	4,138,000
Hindus	220,000	664,000	0.7	2.15	713,000	894,000
Jews	519,000	322,000	0.3	0.06	316,000	291,000
Sikhs	200,000	422,000	0.4	3.82	578,000	754,000
Buddhists	31,700	282,000	0.3	1.39	369,000	464,000
New religionists	58,400	98,700	0.1	0.44	122,000	141,000
Spiritists	20,600	77,400	0.1	0.48	87,900	103,000
Chinese folk	15,000	80,200	0.1	1.57	71,300	81,500
Baha'is	20,200	52,500	0.1	0.64	62,800	91,500
Ethnoreligionists	100	30,900	0.0	0.50	33,100	36,800
Jains	4,000	18,000	0.0	1.96	30,000	50,000
Confucianists	0	6,000	0.0	0.38	7,000	9,000
Zoroastrians	0	4,800	0.0	0.46	6,000	8,000
Total population	**87,358,000**	**98,352,000**	**100.0**	**0.43**	**103,636,000**	**108,177,000**

Status of religions in Northern Europe, 1970–2050

Northern Europe includes 14 countries: Channel Islands, Denmark, Estonia, Faeroe Islands, Finland, Iceland, Ireland, Isle of Man, Latvia, Lithuania, Norway, Svalbard and Jan Mayen Islands, Sweden, and United Kingdom

Religion	Followers in 1970	Followers in 2010	% of Population	Annual % growth 2000–2010	Followers in 2025	Followers in 2050
Christians	111,625,000	125,796,000	82.3	0.52	123,338,000	115,581,000
Roman Catholics	99,035,000	113,809,000	74.4	0.31	109,895,000	101,388,000
Orthodox	15,462,000	19,562,000	12.8	–0.11	19,918,000	19,092,000
Independents	170,000	1,345,000	0.9	2.46	1,862,000	2,138,000
Agnostics	8,843,000	13,307,000	8.7	1.19	15,193,000	15,856,000
Muslims	3,713,000	10,154,000	6.6	1.13	10,789,000	10,622,000
Atheists	2,979,000	3,280,000	2.1	0.46	3,468,000	3,722,000
Buddhists	2,000	116,000	0.1	1.86	143,000	184,000
Chinese folk	0	67,000	0.0	0.41	75,000	81,000
Jews	58,600	65,600	0.0	0.50	62,900	62,700
Sikhs	0	31,600	0.0	0.36	36,400	39,300
Hindus	310	30,400	0.0	0.38	42,000	56,400
Baha'is	10,500	32,000	0.0	0.76	51,400	72,600
New religionists	12,200	23,200	0.0	0.08	32,500	41,000
Ethnoreligionists	500	5,400	0.0	0.04	6,800	7,700
Spiritists	0	5,000	0.0	0.51	6,500	8,500
Total population	**127,245,000**	**152,913,000**	**100.0**	**0.61**	**153,244,000**	**146,335,000**

Status of religions in Southern Europe, 1970–2050
Southern Europe includes 15 countries: Albania, Andorra, Bosnia-Herzegovina, Croatia, Gibraltar, Greece, Holy See, Italy, Macedonia, Malta, Portugal, San Marino, Slovenia, Spain, and Yugoslavia

Religion	Followers in 1970	Followers in 2010	% of Population	Annual % growth 2000–2010	Followers in 2025	Followers in 2050
Christians	146,927,000	133,838,000	71.0	–0.10	126,111,000	115,272,000
Roman Catholics	96,368,000	92,953,000	49.3	–0.23	88,534,000	81,620,000
Protestants	43,385,000	33,167,000	17.6	–0.88	31,414,000	28,190,000
Independents	1,376,000	2,868,000	1.5	0.86	3,591,000	4,126,000
Agnostics	11,973,000	35,449,000	18.8	1.90	40,431,000	44,405,000
Muslims	1,988,000	11,134,000	5.9	0.59	14,777,000	17,037,000
Atheists	3,725,000	5,250,000	2.8	1.30	6,411,000	7,215,000
Jews	685,000	920,000	0.5	0.45	928,000	930,000
Buddhists	43,000	830,000	0.4	1.07	1,107,000	1,524,000
New religionists	149,000	241,000	0.1	0.45	309,000	384,000
Hindus	23,000	262,000	0.1	1.51	348,000	437,000
Chinese folk	45,000	261,000	0.1	2.99	325,000	386,000
Ethnoreligionists	50,500	121,000	0.1	0.58	120,000	133,000
Spiritists	15,800	55,600	0.0	0.55	64,000	77,400
Sikhs	2,000	45,100	0.0	0.25	52,500	63,000
Baha'is	23,200	35,800	0.0	0.74	53,700	88,800
Confucianists	1,000	12,600	0.0	0.35	16,000	19,700
Zoroastrians	410	970	0.0	1.29	1,200	1,400
Jains	0	900	0.0	0.50	1,200	1,500
Total population	**165,650,000**	**188,457,000**	**100.0**	**0.34**	**191,057,000**	**187,974,000**

Status of religions in Western Europe, 1970–2050
Western Europe includes 9 countries: Austria, Belgium, France, Germany, Liechtenstein, Luxembourg, Monaco, Netherlands, and Switzerland

Latin America and the Caribbean (46 countries)

Religion	Followers in 1970	Followers in 2010	% of Population	Annual % growth 2000–2010	Followers in 2025	Followers in 2050
Christians	271,378,000	483,735,000	92.5	1.31	627,925,000	694,174,000
Roman Catholics	252,160,000	442,632,000	80.5	0.60	527,803,000	559,018,000
Protestants	12,578,000	44,530,000	9.6	3.13	75,801,000	97,973,000
Independents	9,377,000	35,174,000	7.1	2.10	58,521,000	73,201,000
Agnostics	6,048,000	14,926,000	2.9	1.07	27,737,000	38,096,000
Spiritists	4,612,000	12,130,000	2.3	1.11	15,291,000	16,642,000
Ethnoreligionists	1,460,000	3,326,000	0.6	1.38	3,596,000	3,591,000
Atheists	1,265,000	2,517,000	0.5	1.73	3,537,000	4,291,000
Muslims	460,000	1,653,000	0.3	1.07	2,619,000	3,339,000
New religionists	208,000	1,462,000	0.3	2.59	2,888,000	3,539,000
Jews	794,000	907,000	0.2	0.42	910,000	883,000
Baha'is	299,000	786,000	0.2	1.65	1,340,000	1,888,000
Hindus	554,000	747,000	0.1	0.55	815,000	766,000
Buddhists	389,000	672,000	0.1	1.39	1,097,000	1,658,000
Chinese folk	68,900	167,000	0.0	1.31	253,000	335,000
Shintoists	2,000	7,000	0.0	1.42	10,000	16,000
Sikhs	1,500	6,000	0.0	0.91	7,700	9,300
Jains	500	1,200	0.0	0.72	1,500	1,700
Confucianists	0	440	0.0	0.97	600	800
Total population	**287,541,000**	**523,044,000**	**100.0**	**1.30**	**688,027,000**	**769,230,000**

Status of religions in Latin America, 1970–2050

Religion	Followers in 1970	Followers in 2010	% of Population	Annual % growth 2000–2010	Followers in 2025	Followers in 2050
Christians	19,898,000	35,379,000	83.6	1.36	39,718,000	43,071,000
Roman Catholics	15,549,000	26,337,000	62.3	1.37	29,017,000	30,769,000
Protestants	1,761,000	5,307,000	12.5	2.33	6,443,000	7,436,000
Independents	542,000	1,712,000	4.0	2.18	2,247,000	2,876,000
Agnostics	2,794,000	2,740,000	6.5	-2.79	3,071,000	3,109,000
Spiritists	1,860,000	2,787,000	6.6	0.63	2,913,000	2,781,000
Atheists	504,000	729,000	1.7	0.36	682,000	599,000
Hindus	230,000	385,000	0.9	0.64	406,000	399,000
Muslims	70,200	125,000	0.3	0.43	143,000	152,000
Baha'is	30,900	74,000	0.2	1.51	111,000	154,000
Chinese folk	9,700	41,100	0.1	0.56	48,900	57,800
New religionists	6,200	16,800	0.0	1.01	23,000	29,900
Buddhists	9,400	14,700	0.0	0.49	19,500	25,000
Jews	7,900	8,100	0.0	0.79	8,700	9,700
Ethnoreligionists	0	450	0.0	0.23	500	530
Total population	**25,420,000**	**42,300,000**	**100.0**	**0.97**	**47,144,000**	**50,388,000**

Status of religions in the Caribbean, 1970–2050
The Caribbean includes 24 countries: Anguilla, Antigua and Barbuda, Aruba, Bahamas, Barbados, British Virgin Islands, Cayman Islands, Cuba, Dominica, Dominican Republic, Grenada, Guadeloupe, Haiti, Jamaica, Martinique, Montserrat, Netherlands Antilles, Puerto Rico, Saint Kitts and Nevis, Saint Lucia, Saint Vincent and Grenadines, Trinidad and Tobago, Turks and Caicos Islands, and Virgin Islands of the United States

Religion	Followers in 1970	Followers in 2010	% of Population	Annual % growth 2000–2010	Followers in 2025	Followers in 2050
Christians	68,297,000	147,257,000	95.8	1.16	170,480,000	188,759,000
Roman Catholics	62,348,000	134,172,000	87.3	1.12	149,827,000	159,319,000
Protestants	1,442,000	10,646,000	6.9	3.10	15,360,000	20,155,000
Independents	1,430,000	7,506,000	4.9	3.14	11,160,000	15,785,000
Agnostics	890,000	3,504,000	2.3	2.08	6,104,000	8,858,000
Ethnoreligionists	102,000	1,514,000	1.0	1.10	1,492,000	1,517,000
Muslims	81,600	392,000	0.3	1.30	620,000	919,000
Atheists	32,100	239,000	0.2	1.56	390,000	605,000
Baha'is	58,300	208,000	0.1	1.69	333,000	496,000
Spiritists	31,400	206,000	0.1	1.78	262,000	334,000
Jews	41,600	138,000	0.1	0.99	140,000	144,000
Buddhists	22,300	71,400	0.0	1.47	104,000	152,000
Chinese folk	13,800	51,000	0.0	1.70	70,900	103,000
New religionists	6,200	44,400	0.0	1.52	67,500	97,500
Hindus	5,000	27,700	0.0	1.60	39,000	53,500
Sikhs	1,000	5,500	0.0	0.89	6,500	8,000
Total population	**69,581,000**	**153,657,000**	**100.0**	**1.18**	**180,108,000**	**202,045,000**

Status of religions in Central America, 1970–2050
Central America includes 8 countries: Belize, Costa Rica, El Salvador, Guatemala, Honduras, Mexico, Nicaragua, and Panama

Religion	Followers in 1970	Followers in 2010	% of Population	Annual % growth 2000–2010	Followers in 2025	Followers in 2050
Christians	183,183,000	366,322,000	92.1	1.36	417,727,000	462,344,000
Roman Catholics	174,264,000	317,702,000	79.9	0.33	348,959,000	368,931,000
Protestants	9,376,000	41,161,000	10.3	3.25	53,998,000	70,383,000
Independents	7,405,000	32,659,000	8.2	1.88	45,114,000	54,540,000
Spiritists	2,721,000	10,656,000	2.7	1.23	12,116,000	13,528,000
Agnostics	2,365,000	10,878,000	2.7	1.99	18,562,000	26,130,000
Ethnoreligionists	1,358,000	2,202,000	0.6	1.58	2,104,000	2,073,000
Atheists	729,000	1,933,000	0.5	2.33	2,465,000	3,087,000
New religionists	196,000	1,768,000	0.4	2.63	2,797,000	3,411,000
Muslims	308,000	1,342,000	0.3	1.07	1,856,000	2,268,000
Jews	745,000	785,000	0.2	0.31	762,000	730,000
Buddhists	358,000	714,000	0.2	1.41	974,000	1,481,000
Baha'is	210,000	660,000	0.2	1.66	896,000	1,238,000
Hindus	319,000	367,000	0.1	0.39	370,000	314,000
Chinese folk	45,400	99,400	0.0	1.45	133,000	174,000
Shintoists	2,000	8,000	0.0	1.42	10,000	16,000
Jains	500	1,300	0.0	0.72	1,500	1,700
Sikhs	500	1,100	0.0	0.99	1,200	1,300
Confucianists	0	500	0.0	0.97	600	800
Total population	**192,540,000**	**397,739,000**	**100.0**	**1.38**	**460,775,000**	**516,797,000**

Status of religions in South America, 1970–2050
South America includes 14 countries: Argentina, Bolivia, Brazil, Chile, Colombia, Ecuador, Falkland Islands, French Guiana, Guyana, Paraguay, Peru, Suriname, Uruguay, and Venezuela

North America (5 countries)

Religion	Followers in 1970	Followers in 2010	% of Population	Annual % growth 2000–2010	Followers in 2025	Followers in 2050
Christians	211,585,000	283,002,000	81.2	0.83	304,642,000	331,521,000
Roman Catholics	57,384,000	84,485,000	24.2	1.24	95,316,000	106,515,000
Independents	35,190,000	73,759,000	21.2	0.95	85,559,000	102,410,000
Protestants	62,768,000	61,511,000	17.6	–0.13	63,763,000	64,060,000
Agnostics	10,899,000	41,144,000	11.8	2.45	56,659,000	73,412,000
Jews	6,994,000	5,655,000	1.6	–0.22	5,485,000	5,540,000
Muslims	842,000	5,740,000	1.6	1.92	7,850,000	11,020,000
Buddhists	216,000	3,720,000	1.1	2.15	6,550,000	8,751,000
Atheists	300,000	1,900,000	0.5	0.70	2,401,000	2,951,000
Hindus	120,000	1,820,000	0.5	1.73	2,650,000	3,720,000
New religionists	572,000	1,678,000	0.5	1.34	2,085,000	2,695,000
Ethnoreligionists	82,500	1,578,000	0.5	1.27	1,475,000	1,625,000
Chinese folk	120,000	762,000	0.2	1.07	1,000,000	1,200,000
Sikhs	30,000	680,000	0.2	2.59	950,000	1,250,000
Baha'is	162,000	527,000	0.2	2.43	786,000	1,047,000
Spiritists	5,000	173,000	0.0	1.02	192,000	222,000
Jains	4,000	99,000	0.0	1.58	145,000	220,000
Shintoists	0	62,200	0.0	1.03	70,000	85,000
Zoroastrians	0	20,800	0.0	1.03	22,000	23,000
Daoists	0	12,400	0.0	1.03	15,000	20,000
Total population	**231,932,000**	**348,575,000**	**100.0**	**1.03**	**392,978,000**	**445,302,000**

Status of religions in North America, 1970–2050

North America includes 5 countries: Bermuda, Canada, Greenland, Saint Pierre and Miquelon, and United States of America

Oceania (28 countries)

Religion	Followers in 1970	Followers in 2010	% of Population	Annual % growth 2000–2010	Followers in 2025	Followers in 2050
Christians	18,168,000	24,940,000	78.5	1.25	31,217,000	35,479,000
Roman Catholics	4,548,000	8,032,000	25.1	1.04	9,782,000	11,227,000
Protestants	4,279,000	6,860,000	23.7	1.43	9,884,000	11,794,000
Anglicans	4,781,000	4,885,000	14.3	–0.02	5,179,000	5,591,000
Agnostics	659,000	3,750,000	12.9	1.83	6,071,000	7,783,000
Buddhists	16,600	448,000	1.8	3.80	923,000	1,209,000
Hindus	218,000	439,000	1.5	2.79	631,000	741,000
Muslims	71,600	422,000	1.6	3.26	828,000	1,354,000
Atheists	215,000	365,000	1.2	1.39	585,000	706,000
Ethnoreligionists	157,000	293,000	1.0	2.42	392,000	458,000
Jews	66,700	101,000	0.3	1.20	128,000	139,000
Baha'is	29,200	87,400	0.3	2.24	157,000	220,000
Chinese folk	18,500	84,900	0.3	2.38	171,000	210,000
New religionists	11,200	84,600	0.3	2.34	135,000	191,000
Confucianists	150	39,800	0.1	2.44	90,500	131,000
Sikhs	6,500	34,600	0.1	5.85	72,700	97,500
Spiritists	1,000	6,700	0.0	1.26	9,000	11,000
Daoists	0	4,000	0.0	0.92	4,800	5,500
Jains	1,000	2,400	0.0	4.63	4,000	6,500
Zoroastrians	0	1,900	0.0	3.89	2,500	2,500
Total population	**19,639,000**	**31,106,000**	**100.0**	**1.44**	**41,421,000**	**48,743,000**

Status of religions in Oceania, 1970–2050

Religion	Followers in 1970	Followers in 2010	% of Population	Annual % growth 2000–2010	Followers in 2025	Followers in 2050
Christians	14,517,000	18,816,000	73.4	0.86	19,938,000	21,172,000
Roman Catholics	3,464,000	5,982,000	23.3	0.56	6,020,000	6,451,000
Anglicans	4,652,000	4,541,000	17.7	–0.18	4,501,000	4,701,000
Protestants	2,763,000	3,193,000	12.4	0.08	3,440,000	3,651,000
Agnostics	646,000	4,464,000	17.4	1.76	5,901,000	7,530,000
Buddhists	13,400	599,000	2.3	3.87	885,000	1,155,000
Muslims	26,700	518,000	2.0	3.69	761,000	1,281,000
Atheists	215,000	434,000	1.7	1.38	575,000	690,000
Hindus	8,800	271,000	1.1	6.09	370,000	495,000
Jews	66,300	109,000	0.4	1.19	127,000	138,000
Ethnoreligionists	14,000	102,000	0.4	2.93	112,000	130,000
New religionists	11,000	100,000	0.4	2.36	127,000	180,000
Chinese folk	13,600	95,400	0.4	2.43	153,000	187,000
Confucianists	0	50,000	0.2	2.44	90,000	130,000
Sikhs	3,300	45,700	0.2	6.60	65,700	90,500
Baha'is	11,700	27,600	0.1	2.02	35,000	49,000
Spiritists	1,000	7,500	0.0	1.26	9,000	11,000
Daoists	0	4,500	0.0	0.92	4,800	5,500
Zoroastrians	0	2,400	0.0	3.89	2,500	2,500
Jains	0	1,600	0.0	12.42	2,000	4,000
Total population	**15,548,000**	**25,647,000**	**100.0**	**1.20**	**29,157,000**	**33,250,000**

Status of religions in Australia-New Zealand, 1970–2050

Australia-New Zealand includes 5 countries: Australia, Christmas Island, Cocos Islands, New Zealand, and Norfolk Island

Religion	Followers in 1970	Followers in 2010	% of Population	Annual % growth 2000–2010	Followers in 2025	Followers in 2050
Christians	231,000	532,000	92.5	1.56	622,000	723,000
Roman Catholics	132,000	351,000	61.1	1.20	397,000	449,000
Protestants	85,900	197,000	34.2	1.33	229,000	262,000
Marginals	1,500	28,500	5.0	2.34	40,900	56,800
Buddhists	350	12,100	2.1	2.65	16,300	23,400
Baha'is	2,600	8,300	1.5	1.31	12,500	16,500
Chinese folk	1,500	7,600	1.3	2.12	9,300	11,600
Agnostics	1,200	7,200	1.3	4.40	14,200	22,700
Ethnoreligionists	5,100	5,100	0.9	0.29	4,700	4,800
New religionists	0	1,800	0.3	1.81	2,600	3,700
Muslims	0	670	0.1	2.96	1,000	1,400
Confucianists	150	290	0.1	2.14	500	700
Atheists	0	260	0.0	1.49	540	950
Total population	**242,000**	**575,000**	**100.0**	**1.60**	**683,000**	**808,000**

Status of religions in Micronesia, 1970–2050

Micronesia includes 7 countries: Guam, Kiribati, Marshall Islands, Micronesia, Nauru, Northern Mariana Islands, and Palau

Religion	Followers in 1970	Followers in 2010	% of Population	Annual % growth 2000–2010	Followers in 2025	Followers in 2050
Christians	3,005,000	7,847,000	91.4	2.29	9,923,000	12,788,000
Protestants	1,214,000	4,686,000	54.6	2.69	5,862,000	7,508,000
Roman Catholics	855,000	2,388,000	27.8	2.31	3,140,000	4,089,000
Anglicans	127,000	534,000	6.2	1.98	674,000	885,000
Hindus	209,000	253,000	2.9	0.03	261,000	246,000
Ethnoreligionists	138,000	242,000	2.8	2.26	274,000	323,000
Muslims	44,900	63,200	0.7	0.51	65,800	71,000
Agnostics	8,900	81,000	0.9	6.32	132,000	198,000
Baha'is	11,200	66,400	0.8	2.57	99,600	141,000
Buddhists	2,600	15,000	0.2	2.37	20,500	28,400
Chinese folk	2,400	5,500	0.1	2.15	7,100	9,200
Sikhs	3,200	5,000	0.1	0.18	7,000	7,000
Atheists	0	5,300	0.1	2.00	7,600	11,600
New religionists	100	3,100	0.0	2.15	4,600	6,200
Jains	1,000	1,600	0.0	−0.38	2,000	2,500
Jews	400	920	0.0	1.97	930	950
Total population	**3,426,000**	**8,589,000**	**100.0**	**2.23**	**10,806,000**	**13,833,000**

Status of religions in Melanesia, 1970–2050
Melanesia includes 6 countries: Bougainville, Fiji, New Caledonia, Papua New Guinea, Solomon Islands, and Vanuatu

Religion	Followers in 1970	Followers in 2010	% of Population	Annual % growth 2000–2010	Followers in 2025	Followers in 2050
Christians	415,000	653,000	96.0	1.00	735,000	796,000
Protestants	215,000	328,000	48.2	0.64	353,000	373,000
Roman Catholics	96,600	193,000	28.3	1.63	225,000	239,000
Marginals	49,800	181,000	26.6	1.53	202,000	219,000
Agnostics	2,500	15,500	2.3	2.32	23,700	33,600
Baha'is	3,700	6,100	0.9	1.13	9,400	13,200
Atheists	210	1,600	0.2	1.50	2,200	3,100
Chinese folk	1,000	1,400	0.2	1.69	1,800	2,100
Buddhists	300	780	0.1	1.48	1,200	1,800
Ethnoreligionists	100	440	0.1	0.98	510	620
New religionists	100	340	0.1	1.58	500	700
Jews	20	150	0.0	0.13	150	150
Hindus	30	100	0.0	0.20	150	200
Muslims	0	80	0.0	2.83	120	230
Total population	**423,000**	**680,000**	**100.0**	**1.03**	**774,000**	**852,000**

Status of religions in Polynesia, 1970–2050
Polynesia includes 10 countries: American Samoa, Cook Islands, French Polynesia, Niue, Pitcairn Islands, Samoa, Tokelau, Tonga, Tuvalu, and Wallis and Futuna Islands

About the Editors and Contributors

Editors

J. Gordon Melton   J. Gordon Melton is the director of the Institute for the Study of American Religion founded in 1969 in Santa Barbara, California, and a research specialist with the Department of Religious Studies of the University of California at Santa Barbara. In 2009 he was named a Distinguished Scholar with the Institute of Religion at Baylor University. He is the author of more than 40 books on American religion, including the *Encyclopedia of American Religions* (8th ed., Gale/Cengage Learning, 2008), *American Religions: An Illustrated History* (ABC-CLIO, 2001), and *Nelson's Handbook of Denominations* (Thomas Nelson, 2007).

Martin Baumann   Martin Baumann is professor of the Study of Religions at the University of Lucerne in Switzerland. His research interests focus on religious pluralism and public space, migration and religion, diaspora studies, and Hindu and Buddhist traditions in the West. He has published on these topics in both English and German, and his most recent co-edited book is *Eine Schweiz—viele Religionen* (2007).

Buddhism
European Buddhist Union
German Buddhist Union
Germany
Germany, Hinduism in
Germany, Islam in
Hinduism
Maha Bodhi Society
Theravada Buddhism
Trinidad and Tobago
Vipassana International Academy
Western Buddhist Order, Friends of the

Area Editors

Allan H. Anderson Dr. Allan H. Anderson is professor of Global Pentecostal Studies and head of the School of Philosophy, Theology, and Religion at the University of Birmingham. His most recent books are *African Reformation: African Initiated Christianity in the 20th Century* (Africa World Press, 2001), *An Introduction to Pentecostalism* (Cambridge University Press, 2004), and *Spreading Fires* (Orbis & SCM, 2007).

Africa Inland Church
African Apostolic Church of Johane Marange
African Brotherhood Church
African Christian Church and Schools
African Church of the Holy Spirit
African Church, Nigeria
African Independent Pentecostal Church
African Initiated (Independent) Churches
African Israel Church, Ninevah
Aladura Churches
Apostolic Sabbath Church of God
Brotherhood of the Cross and Star
Bwiti
Cherubim and Seraphim/Eternal Sacred Order of the
  Cherubim and Seraphim
Christ Apostolic Church
Church of Pentecost
Church of the Lord
Deeper Life Bible Church
Harrist Church
Kimbanguist Church
Legion of Mary/Maria Legio (Kenya)
Mai Chaza Church/City of Jehovah
Muridîyya
Ngunzist Churches (Congo)
Nomiya Luo Church
Organization of African Instituted Churches
Spiritual Churches (Ghana)
Spiritual Churches (Kenya)
Tocoist Church/ Church of Our Lord Jesus Christ in the
  World
Zimbabwe Assemblies of God Africa
Zion Christian Church (South Africa, Zimbabwe)
Zionist and Apostolic Churches

James A. Beverley James A. Beverley is professor of Christian thought and ethics at Tyndale Seminary in Toronto, Canada, and associate director of the Institute for the Study of American Religion. He is a specialist on new religious movements and the relationship of Christianity to other world religions. He is author and editor of ten books including *Understanding Islam* (Thomas Nelson, 2001), *Islamic Faith in America* (Facts on File, 2002), and *Nelson's Illustrated Guide to Religions* (Thomas Nelson, 2009).

Abu Hanifa
Canada
Chaitanya, Shri Krishna
Eddy, Mary Baker
Ghazali, Abu Hamid al-
God, Existence of
Hubbard, L. Ron
Husayn, ibn Ali ibn Abi Talib Al-
Ibn Hanbal, Ahmad
Islam
Moon, Sun Myung
Smith, Joseph, Jr.
Toronto Airport Christian Fellowship

Gail M. Harley Gail M. Harley was a lecturer with the Department of Religious Studies of the University of South Florida in Tampa. She was the author of *Emma Curtis Hopkins: Forgotten Founder of New Thought* (Syracuse University Press, 2002); and authored a number of articles on American religion, New Thought, and the Middle East. She passed away in 2008.

Church of Christ, Scientist
Turkey
World Brotherhood Union Mevlana Supreme
  Foundation

Clifton L. Holland Clifton L. Holland is director of the Latin American Socio-Religious Studies Program (known as PROLADES in Spanish), which was founded in 1977, and currently has headquarters in San José, Costa Rica. In 1982 he founded and served as the first director of the Missiological Institute of the Americas, which in 1995 became the Evangelical University of the Americas (UNELA). He currently teaches social sciences and religious studies in Costa Rica and in UNELA extension programs in other countries. He has done fieldwork on religious groups in 20 countries throughout the Americas, as well as on Hispanics in the U.S.A. Since 1995 he has edited the monthly news journal *MESOAMERICA,* published by the Institute for Central American Studies (ICAS).

Anguilla
Antigua and Barbuda
Apostolic Assembly of Faith in Jesus Christ, U.S.A.
Apostolic Church of Faith in Jesus Christ of the East
Argentina
Aruba
Bahamas
Belize
Chile
Clavier, Pedro
Colombia
Costa Rica
Cuba
Ecuador
El Salvador
Evangelical Confederation of Latin America
G12 Vision
Garifuna Religion
Guatemala
Honduras
Latin American Council of Churches
Light of the World Church
Mexico
New Acropolis Cultural Association
Nicaragua
Panama
Paraguay
Peru
Peruvian Evangelical Church
Puerto Rico
Spiritual Christian Evangelical Church
Suriname
Uruguay
Venezuela

Massimo Introvigne   Massimo Introvigne received his B.A. in philosophy at the Pontifical Gregorian University and his doctorate in law at Turin University. He is a member of the Italian Association of Sociology and has taught short courses and seminars at several Catholic universities. In 1988 he established CESNUR (Center for Studies on New Religions), Europe's largest research center on new religious movements (see http://www.cesnur.org), and currently serves as its managing director. He is the author, coauthor, or editor of 40 books and of more than 100 chapters and articles published in academic journals in five different languages.

Army of Mary
Church of Satan
Church of the Kingdom of God
Damanhur
Evangelical Baptist Union of Italy
Evangelical Methodist Church of Italy
Fraternity/Society of Saint Pius X
Gnostic Churches
Gnostic Movement
Grail Movement, The
Healing Tao
Iglesia ni Cristo
Italian Assemblies of God
Italy
Lectorium Rosicrucianum
Martinism
Mazdaznan
New Apostolic Church
Ordo Templi Orientis
People of God
Priory of Sion
Sedevacantism and Antipopes
Seventh-day Adventist Reform Movements
Shri Ram Chandra Mission
Spiritual Human Yoga
Universal Church of the Kingdom of God
Universal Life
Universal Soul
Waldensian Church

Edward A. Irons   Edward A. Irons is the director of The Hong Kong Institute for Culture, Religion, and Commerce, a religious studies research facility concentrating on Hong Kong and Chinese cultural studies, Chinese religions, and the interaction of cultural and religious issues with commerce in contemporary society.

Alchemy, Daoist
Ashoka
Bodh-Gaya
Bodhidharma
Bodhisattva
Bukkyo Dendo Kyokai
Chinul
Dalai Lama III, Sonam Gyatso
Falun Gong
Honen
Hua Shan
Hui Neng
Hui Si
Hui Yuan
Ise Shrine, The
Jiu-Hua Shan
Kamakura
Kukai (Kobo Daishi)
Kumarajiva
Kusinagara
Laozi
Lumbini
Meiji Jingu
Mencius
Nagarjuna
Nalanda
Nara
Nichiren
Padmasambhava
Saicho
Shinran
Shwedagon Pagoda
State Shinto
Statues—Buddhist
T'aego Pou
Temples—Buddhist
Tian Dao
Tian Tai/Tendai Buddhism
Tiantan
Tsong Khapa
Uisang
Wang Chongyang
Wesak

Wonhyo
World Buddhist Sangha Council
Zhang Daoling
Zhi Yi
Zhou Dunyi
Zhuangzi

Todd M. Johnson   Todd M. Johnson is research fellow in the Study of Global Christianity and director of the Center for the Study of Global Christianity at Gordon-Conwell Theological Seminary. Johnson is visiting research fellow at Boston University's Institute for Culture, Religion and World Affairs leading a research project on international religious demography. He is co-author of the *Atlas of Global Christianity* (Edinburgh University Press) and co-author of the *World Christian Encyclopedia* (Oxford University Press, 2nd ed.) and *World Christian Trends* (William Carey Library). He is editor of the *World Christian Database* (Brill) and co-editor of the *World Religion Database* (Brill).

Statistical tables

Constance A. Jones   Constance A. Jones is a professor of transformative studies at the California Institute of Integral Studies, San Francisco, California. She received her Ph.D. in sociology from Emory University and was awarded a post-doctoral fellowship at the Center for the Study of New Religious Movements of the Graduate Theological Union in Berkeley, California. Beginning with her doctoral dissertation on the caste system in India, she has pursued a life-long interest in the cultures and religions of the East. As a Fulbright scholar in India, she taught at Banaras Hindu University and Vasanta College and conducted research at the Krishnamurti Study Center, Varanasi. She is a member of the International Advisory Board for "The Complete Teachings of J. Krishnamurti, 1910–1986." Her publications include: the *Encyclopedia of Hinduism* (with James D. Ryan, 2007); *The Legacy of G. I. Gurdjieff* (2005); *G. I. Gurdjieff from South Caucasus to Western World: His Influence on Spirituality, Thought and Culture in Italy, Europe, and the U.S.A.* (2007).

Diwali
Ganesh Chaturthi

Gurdjieff Foundations
Gurdjieff, George Ivanovitch
Guru Purnima
Hanuman Jayanti
Holi
Janmashtami
Krishnamurti Foundations
Mahasivaratri
Meenakshi Temple (Madurai)
Navaratri/Dashain
Patanjali
Patosov
Sharad Purnima
Tirumala/Tirupati

Timothy Miller   Timothy Miller is a professor of religious studies at the University of Kansas. He is the author of *The Quest for Utopia in Twentieth-Century America* (Syracuse University Press, 1998), *The 60s Communes* (Syracuse University Press, 2000), and editor of *America's Alternative Religions* (SUNY Press, 1995), among other works. He is past president of the International Communal Studies Association and a past chair of the New Religious Movements Group of the American Academy of Religion.

Christian Communities International
Communalism
Hutterites

Catherine Wessinger   Catherine Wessinger is the Rev. H. James Yamauchi, S.J. Professor of the History of Religions at Loyola University New Orleans. She is general editor of *Nova Religio: The Journal of Alternative and Emergent Religions*. Her books include *Annie Besant and Progressive Messianism* (Edwin Mellen, 1988) and *How the Millennium Comes Violently: From Jonestown to Heaven's Gate* (Seven Bridges Press, 2000). She edited *Women's Leadership in Marginal Religions: Explorations Outside the Mainstream* (University of Illinois Press, 1993) and *Millennialism, Persecution, and Violence: Historical Cases* (Syracuse University Press, 2000).

Self-Realization Fellowship
Vedanta Societies

Contributors

Andreas Ackermann   Andreas Ackermann is professor of cultural anthropology at the Institute for Studies in Culture (Kulturwissenschaft), University of Koblenz-Landau. His research focuses on identity and migration, particularly diaspora and multiculturalism, as well as visual anthropology. His main regions of research are Singapore, the Kurdish areas of the Middle East and Germany. Currently he researches processes of diasporization among Kurdish Yezidi in Germany. His publications include *Ethnic Identity by Design or by Default? A Comparative Study of Multiculturalism in Singapore and Frankfurt am Main* (1997); *Patchwork: Dimensions of Multicultural Societies* (2002, in German; ed. with Klaus E. Müller); *In the Congo's Shadow: Leo Frobenius, Stereographic Photographs from 1904–1906* (2005, in German; with Ute Röschenthaler and Peter Steigerwald).

Yezidis

Joseph A. Adler   Joseph A. Adler is professor of Asian studies at Kenyon College in Gambier, Ohio, where he teaches courses on East Asian religions. He received his Ph.D. in Religious Studies from the University of California at Santa Barbara. His published work focuses on the "Neo-Confucian" tradition in Song dynasty China. His latest book, *Reconstructing the Confucian Dao: Zhu Xi's Appropriation of Zhou Dunyi*, is nearing completion.

Confucianism
Confucius

Afe Adogame   Afe Adogame holds a Ph.D. in history of religions from the University of Bayreuth in Germany. He is presently an assistant professor of religious studies and World Christianity at the University of Edinburgh. His teaching and research focus includes new African religious movements, Indigenous Religions; and Religion and the new African Diaspora.

Celestial Church of Christ
Council of Christian Churches of an African Approach in Europe
Nigeria

Phyllis D. Airhart   Phyllis D. Airhart is associate professor of the history of Christianity at Emmanuel College in the University of Toronto. Her publications include *Serving the Present Age: Revivalism, Progressivism, and the Methodist Tradition in Canada* (McGill-Queen's University Press, 1992), *Faith Traditions and the Family* (co-editor with Margaret Bendroth, WJKP, 1996), and *Doing Ethics in a Pluralistic World* (coeditor with Marilyn Legge and Gary Redcliffe, Wilfrid Laurier University Press, 2001), and a number of articles on religion in Canada.

United Church of Canada

Mikael Aktor   Mikael Aktor is assistant professor at the Department of the Study of Religions at the University of Southern Denmark. His Ph.D., which he earned from the University of Copenhagen and the School of Oriental and African Studies at the University of London, is an investigation of rules of untouchability in classical Indian law literature (*dharmasastra*). He has published various articles on this and related subjects in Danish and British journals and books.

Ambedkar Buddhism

Milda Ališauskiene   Milda Ališauskiene holds a Ph.D. in sociology from Vytautas Magnus University, Kaunas, Lithuania. She teaches courses on Sociology of Religion and New Religious Movements in Vytautas Magnus University. Her field of research and interest includes religion in contemporary society, religious pluralism and fundamentalism, and New Age. She published a number of scientific publications about contemporary religious phenomena in Lithuania. She is a cofounder of New Religions Research and Information Centre.

Lithuania

Nancy T. Ammerman   Nancy T. Ammerman is professor of sociology of religion at Boston University. She is the author of *Baptist Battles: Social Change and Religious Conflict in the Southern Baptist Convention* (Rutgers, 1990) and *Pillars of Faith: American Congregations and Their Partners* (University of California, 2005).

Cooperative Baptist Fellowship

Galen Amstutz   Galen Amstutz grew up in an Asian-American neighborhood in Sacramento, California, became interested in Buddhism after teaching English in Japan in the 1970s, studied at the Institute of Buddhist Studies in Berkeley, California, and qualified as a minister of the Nishi Honganji True Pure Land organization. Later, having continued his academic study with a Ph.D. in Asian religions from Princeton, he worked for Florida State University, the Reischauer Institute of Japanese Studies at Harvard University, and Ryukoku University in Japan 2004–2009. He is particularly interested in the communication problem related to Shin Buddhism and has published a book on the issue, *Interpreting Amida: History and Orientalism in the Study of Pure Land Buddhism* (SUNY Press, 1997) among other writings.

Pure Land Buddhism

Angela An   Angela An is an undergraduate student at the University of Virginia with a double major in anthropology and sociology. Following graduation in 2003, she plans to work as a Peace Corps volunteer and then pursue graduate education.

Ananda Marga Yoga Society

W. Michael Ashcraft   W. Michael Ashcraft is professor of religion at Truman State University in Kirksville, Missouri. He received his Ph.D. in religious studies from the University of Virginia and specializes in the study of American religions. He published The Dawn of the New Cycle: Point Loma Theosophists and American Culture with the University of Tennessee Press in 2002.

Church Universal and Triumphant
Theosophical Society (America)

Will Bagley   Will Bagley is an independent historian, *Salt Lake Tribune* independent columnist, and writer on the American West. He is editor of the Arthur H. Clark Company's series Forgotten Kingdom: The Mormons and the American Frontier.

Church of Jesus Christ of Latter-day Saints

Eileen Barker   Eileen Barker is the Distinguished Professor of Sociology with special reference to the study of religion at the London School of Economics. She is the author of books such as *The Making of a Moonie: Brainwashing or Choice?* (Blackwell, 1984) and *New Religious Movements: A Practical Introduction* (HMSO, 1989). She is the founder and chairperson of INFORM (Information Network Focus on Religious Movements), a research center on new religious movements.

Armenia
Brahma Kumaris
Subud
United Kingdom

Michelle Barker   Michelle Barker holds a Ph.D. in the sociology of religion from the University of Queenslands in Australia. She has been an assistant professor in Australia, New Zealand and the United States and currently lives in Australia. Her area of research focuses on Buddhism in the West and she has published a book on the growth of Zen Buddhism in Australia. She is currently compiling an edited volume on Buddhism in Australia that combines academic analysis with writings from the Buddhist community.

Diamond Sangha
New Zealand
Sanbo Kyodan
Zen Buddhism

David V. Barrett   Dr. David V. Barrett, a former teacher of religious studies and English, and intelligence analyst for the British and American governments, has since 1991 been a full-time freelance writer concentrating on religious and esoteric subjects. He received his Ph.D. in the sociology of religion from the London School of Economics in 2009. He is the author of *Sects, "Cults" & Alternative Religions* (Blandford, 1996), *Secret Societies* (Blandford, 1997, Constable & Robinson, 2007), and *The New Believers* (Cassell, 2001).

Catholic Apostolic Church
Church of God, International

Emmissaries, The
Living Church of God
Philadelphia Church of God
United Church of God, an International Association
Worldwide Church of God

Gina Ann Bellofatto   Gina A. Bellofatto graduated from Gordon-Conwell Theological Seminary with a master of arts in religion, where her studies focused on Christian mission and its intersections with the world's religions, in particular evangelicals and interfaith dialogue. She has worked at the Center for the Study of Global Christianity under the direction of Todd M. Johnson where she specialized in Jewish demography, contributing to the *World Christian Database* and the *World Religion Database*. Gina also served as senior editorial assistant on the forthcoming *Atlas of Global Christianity* (Edinburgh University Press, 2009).

Occupied Territories

Peter J. Bräeunlein   Peter J. Bräeunlein is currently teaching theory and history of religions at the University of Bremen (Germany). He obtained his master and Ph.D. in cultural anthropology from the University of Freiburg and his habilitation in the study of religion from the University of Bremen. Between 1986–1988, he conducted extensive fieldwork among the Alangan-Mangyans on the island of Mindoro (Philippines). In the years 1996–1998, he conducted fieldwork on "Philippine passion rituals" in the province of Bulacan (Philippines). Research interests include method and theory in the study of religion; religious history of Europe and Southeast Asia; anthropology of Christianity; visible religion; museology; ghosts and modernity.

Flagellation

Behar Bejko   Behar Bejko is the former Chief of the Committee on the Cults of the State of Albania. He has worked with Muslim and Christian humanitarian organizations in Albania, he organized an international seminar that focused on international laws on religious issues and is expected to be the Albanian Ambassador to Egypt.

Albania

Sandra Bell Sandra Bell is a lecturer in anthropology at the University of Durham. She wrote her doctoral thesis on the development and adaptation on Buddhism in Britain and has published a number of articles on Buddhism in the West. She is coeditor, with Elisa Sobo, of *Celibacy, Society and Culture: The Anthropology of Sexual Abstinence* (Wisconsin University Press, 2001).

British Forest Sangha
Shambhala International
Thai Forest Monks

David K. Bernard David K. Bernard is the founder and pastor of the New Life United Pentecostal Church of Austin, Texas, and the president of the Urshan Graduate School of Theology. He holds a doctorate of jurisprudence with honors from the University of Texas and is currently enrolled in the masters of theology program at the University of South Africa. He is the author of 24 books, including *The Trinitarian Controversy in the Fourth Century* (Word Aflame Press, 1993).

United Pentecostal Church International

Roger Bischoff Roger Bischoff heads the International Meditation Centre in the United Kingdom. He has translated a variety of texts of Burmese Buddhism into English and is the author of *Buddhism in Myanmar: A Short History* (Buddhist Publication Society, 1995). In 1998, with William Pruitt, he produced the catalogue of Burmese and Pali manuscripts for the Wellcome Library in London, England.

International Meditation Centres

Sergei Blagov Dr. Sergei Blagov is a part-time lecturer on Vietnamese history and religions at the Institute of Asian and African Studies at the Moscow State University. He has spent a total of seven years in Vietnam as a researcher and a journalist.

Hoa Hao Buddhism

Richard Boeke Dr. Richard Boeke was the secretary of the International Council of Unitarian Universalists and is a vice president of the World Congress of Faiths (WCF). Following his graduation from Yale Divinity School, he served as a U.S. Air Force chaplain from 1955 to 1958. Since 1959 he has been an active Unitarian Universalist minister, most recently in Berkeley, California, and Horsham, England. He is the author of *God is No-Thing*.

International Council of Unitarians and Universalists

Leslaw Borowski Dr. Leslaw Borowski works at the Cathedra of Religious Studies and the Philosophy of the East at Maria Curie-Sklodowska University in Lublin, Poland. He works on neo-Hinduism and general problems of new religious movements and teaches Indian and Chinese philosophy.

Clan of Ausrans
Evangelical Church of the Augsburg Confession in Poland
Old Catholic Church of Mariavites/Catholic Church of
    Mariavites
Orthodox Church of Poland
Polish National Catholic Church/Polish Catholic Church

Martha Sonntag Bradley Martha Sonntag Bradley is a historian of Utah and associate professor in the Graduate School of Architecture of the University of Utah. She is the author of eight books, including *Kidnapped from that Land: The Government Raids on the Short Creek Polygamists* (University of Utah Press, 1993), a social history on polygamists in southern Utah and modern-day Mormon fundamentalism, and *The Four Zinas: A Story of Mothers and Daughters on the Mormon Frontier* (Signature, 2000), a book about nineteenth-century Mormon polygamy. She is currently working on a history of the national fight against the Equal Rights Amendment during 1972 and 1983.

Polygamy-Practicing Mormons

Jan Brzezinski Jan Brzezinski earned his Ph.D. in Sanskrit literature from London's School of Oriental and African Studies. He has taught at the University of Manitoba and McGill University and has translated and published several Sanskrit texts from the Gaudiya Vaisnava tradition.

Gaudiya Math

Christopher Buck Christopher Buck is a Pennsylvania attorney and independent scholar. He holds a Ph.D. from the University of Toronto (1996) and J.D. from Cooley Law School (2006). He previously taught at Michigan State University (2000–2004), Quincy University (1999–2000), Millikin University (1997–1999), and Carleton University (1994–1996). His publications include: *Religious Myths and Visions of America: How Minority Faiths Redefined America's World Role* (2009); *Alain Locke: Faith and Philosophy* (2005); *Paradise and Paradigm: Key Symbols in Persian Christianity and the Bahá'í Faith* (1999); *Symbol and Secret: Qur'an Commentary in Bahá'u'lláh's Kitáb-i Íqán* (1995/2004), various book chapters, encyclopedia articles, and journal articles.

Birth of the Bab
Birth/Ascension of Bahá'u'lláh
Ridvan, Festival of
Temples—Baha'i Faith
World Religion Day

Gary Burlington Gary Burlington is a professor of world missions at Lincoln Christian College in Nebraska, and a former missionary in Zambia. He completed his Ph.D. at Biola University with a dissertation on the Sweet Heart Church of the Clouds (Umutima Uwalowa wa Makumbi) of Zambia and its founder, Emilio Mulolani Chishimba.

Muslim World League

Andrea Cassinasco Andrea Cassinasco is a priest-monk in the Russian Orthodox Church (Moscow Patriarchate) with the monastic name of Fr. Ambrose, and rector of the Russian Orthodox parish of Torino, Italy. He has authored several essays and a book on the Eastern Christian presence in Italy.

Liberal Catholic Church
Serbian Orthodox Church

Kim-Kwong Chan Kim-Kwong Chan, Ph.D. and D.Th., is the Executive Secretary of the Hong Kong Christian Council and the author and coauthor of eight books on Christianity in China. He holds current honorary teaching and research appointments at the Chinese University of Hong Kong, Brigham Young University in the United States, and Zhejiang University in China.

China
China: Hong Kong
China: Macao
Chinese Protestant Three-Self Patriotic Movement/China Christian Council
Hong Kong Council of the Church of Christ in China

James Chancellor James Chancellor, the W. O. Carver Professor of World Religion and World Missions at the Southern Baptist Theological Seminary, is the author of *Life in the Family: An Oral History of the Children of God* (Syracuse University Press, 2000).

Family International, The

Stuart Chandler Stuart Chandler received his Ph.D. from Harvard University. He is a professor at Indiana University of Pennsylvania. His research focuses on modern Chinese and Japanese Buddhism and on the growing religious pluralism of the United States.

Foguangshan

Dorthe Refslund Christensen Dorthe Refslund Christensen, Ph.D., is a lecturer at the Center for the Study of Religion at the Southern Danish University of Odense, Denmark, and the secretary of RENNER (Research Network on New Religion), the Danish-based scholar association. She is the author of *Scientology: Fra Terapi til Religion* (Scientology: From Therapy to Religion; Gyldendal, Nye Religioner, København, 1997), the first Danish introduction to the ideas and practices of the Church of Scientology.

Church of Scientology

Mathew Clark Mathew Clark is head of the Department of the New Testament at the Auckland Park

Theological Seminary in Johannesburg, South Africa. He is also principal of the Durban campus of that seminary. He was the first chair of the Pentecostal Theological Association of Southern Africa, founded in 1998.

Apostolic Faith Mission of South Africa

Peter B. Clarke   Peter Clarke is a professorial member of the Faculty of Theology of the University of Oxford where he teaches the Sociology of Religion. He is also professor emeritus of the history and sociology of Religion in the University of London at King's College. His recent publications include *Encyclopedia of New Religious Movements* (Routledge, London, 2006), *New Religions in Global Perspective* (Routledge, London, 2006), the *Oxford Handbook of the Sociology of Religion* (Oxford University Press, 2009), and with Peter Beyer (eds.) *The World's Religions: Continuities and Transformations* (Routledge, London, 2009). He is the founding and present co-editor of the *Journal of Contemporary Religion*.

Agonshu
Honmichi
Kofuku no Kagaku
Konkokyo
Omoto
Sekai Kyusei Kyo
Shinnyoen
Tenrikyo
Tensho Kotai Jingukyo

Chas S. Clifton   Chas S. Clifton teaches writing at the University of Southern Colorado. He serves as associate editor of *The Pomegranate: A Journal of Pagan Studies* and secretary of the Nature Religions Scholars Network.

Cherry Hill Seminary
Covenant of the Goddess
Gardnerian Wicca

Catherine Cornille   Catherine Cornille is associate professor of Comparative Theology at Boston College. She has published numerous articles on New Japanese Religions in the West. She is author of *The Guru in*

Indian Catholicism: Ambiguity or Opportunity of Inculturation (Peeters, 1991); and *The Im-Possibility of Interreligious Dialogue* (2008) and editor of *Many Mansions? Multiple Religious Belonging and Christian Identity* (Orbis, 2002); *Song Divine: Christian Commentaries on the Bhagavadgita* (Peeters, 2006) and *Criteria of Discernment in Interreligious Dialogue* (Wipf and Stock, 2009).

Mother Meera, Disciples of
Sukyo Mahikari

Diana Cousens   Diana Cousens completed a Ph.D. in Himalayan Studies at Monash University in 2008. She is a regular speaker at international conferences and has published widely. She is also well known in the Buddhist community in Australia for her work in palliative care and in interfaith dialogue. She has an M.A. and a B.A. (Hons) in Tibetan History from La Trobe University. Her Ph.D. was a study of the temple of Triloknath in Lahul, India, near to the Tibetan border.

Aro gTér
Khyentse Foundation, The
Tibetan Nyingma Institute

Douglas E. Cowan   Douglas E. Cowan is professor of religious studies at Renison University College at the University of Waterloo, in Ontario, Canada. He is the author or editor of 10 books and more than 40 articles and scholarly chapters. He is currently working on the final volume of a trilogy examining the relationship between religion and various genres of cinema and television.

Internet and Religion

Frank Cranmer   Frank Cranmer is a graduate of the Cardiff master's course in canon law. A fellow of St Chad's College, Durham and an honorary research fellow in the Centre for Law and Religion at Cardiff Law School, he has recently become secretary of the Churches' Legislation Advisory Service. Recent publications include articles for *Public Law* and the *Ecclesiastical Law Journal*, on Quaker trusteeship, (with Scot Peterson) on clergy employment, (with Tom Heffer) on the interpretation of scripture and Anglican canon law and (with Anna Harlow and Norman Doe) on Bishops in the House of Lords. He is also the parliamentary and synod editor of the *Ecclesiastical Law Journal* and case-notes editor for *Law and Justice*.

Religion-Government Relations

Jamie Cresswell   Jamie Cresswell is the director of the Institute of Oriental Philosophy European Centre in the United Kingdom and is working on a Ph.D. thesis on the development and organization of Buddhism in the West. He has co-edited *New Religious Movements: Challenge and Response* with Dr. Bryan Wilson (Routledge, 1999).

Buddhist Society, The
Foundation for the Preservation of the Mahayana Tradition
Rigpa Fellowship

Vivianne Crowley   Vivianne Crowley, Ph.D., is a practitioner psychologist and was formerly lecturer in Psychology of Religion at King's College, University of London. She is the author of many books and papers on Wicca, Paganism, and the psychology of religion, including *The Natural Magician* (Penguin, 2002) and *Your Dark Side* (Thorsons, 2001).

Fellowship of Isis
Goddess Spirituality
Pagan Federation

Constantin Cuciuc   Dr. Constantin Cuciuc is a professor at the University of Bucharest Scientific Research for the Institute of Sociology at the Romanian Academy in Bucharest, Romania. He is the author of *Tlasul Religiilor si al Monumentelor Istorice Religioase din Romania* (*Atlas of Religions and Religious Historical Monuments in Romania*; Editura Gnosis, 1997) and *Religii noi in Romania* (*New Religions in Romania*; Editura Gnosis, 1996).

Reformed Church in Romania
Romania, Islam in
Romanian Greek Catholic Church
Romanian Orthodox Church

David Daniels   David Daniels is professor of church history at McCormick Theological Seminary in Chicago, Illinois, and an ordained minister in the Church of God in Christ. He is a contributing author to 14 books, including *The Courage to Hope: From Black Suffering to Human Redemption*, edited by Quinton Dixie and Cornel West; *The Globalization of Pentecostalism*, edited by Murray Dempster, et al; *The Century of the Holy Spirit: 100 Years of Pentecostal and Charismatic Renewal*, edited by Vinson Synan; *Portraits of a Generation of Early Pentecostal Leaders*, edited by James Goff and Grant Wacker; and *African Immigrant Religions in America*, edited by Jacob Olupona and Regina Gemignani.

Church of God in Christ

Matthias Dech   Dr. Matthias Dech studied comparative science of religion and Indology in Marburg, Germany, where, in 1999, he completed his Ph.D. thesis on Hindus and Hinduism in Germany. Since 1999, he has been a computer consultant at the Deutsche Börse (German exchange) in Frankfurt, Germany.

Vishwa Hindu Parishad

Dell deChant   Dell deChant is an instructor and associate chair for the Department of Religious Studies at the University of South Florida. He is the author of *The Sacred Santa: The Religious Dimensions of Consumer Culture* (Pilgrim, 2002), and *Religion and Culture in the West: A Primer* (Kendall/Hunt, 2008). He is the coauthor with Darrell Fasching of *Comparative Religious Ethics* (Blackwell, 2000).

International New Thought Alliance
Religious Science
Unity School of Christianity/Association of Unity
   Churches

Max Deeg   Max Deeg is professor of religious studies and Buddhist studies at Cardiff University, Wales, UK.

Mahayana Buddhism

Mahinda Deegalle Dr. Mahinda Deegalle is senior lecturer in the School of Humanities and Cultural Industries at Bath Spa University, UK. He serves in the steering committee of the Buddhism section of the American Academy of Religion and of the managing committee of Spalding Symposium on Indian Religions. He is the editor of the journal of *Buddhist-Christian Studies*, co-editor of the *Journal of South Asian Religions* and book review editor for *Buddhist Studies Review* and *H-Buddhism*. His publications include *Popularizing Buddhism* (SUNY, 2006), *Dharma to the UK* (World Buddhist Foundation, 2008), *Buddhism, Conflict and Violence in Modern Sri Lanka* (Routledge, 2006), and *Pali Buddhism* (Curzon, 1996). His current research focuses on the ethics of war.

All Ceylon Buddhist Congress
Hossoshu
Ontakekyo
Sarvodaya
Young Men's Buddhist Association

Raffaella Di Marzio A graduate in both psychology and religious sciences, Raffaella Di Marzio set up an information and counseling centre in Rome, Italy, about New Religious Movements: the Counseling Center SRS (Sectes, Religions, Spirituality). She is member of managing board of SIPR (Italian Society of Psychology of Religion) and ICAA (International Crime Analysis Association). She has published more than 80 articles on different fringe Catholic movements and New Religious Movements and is a contributor to the "Encyclopedia of Religions in Italy" (2006) assembled by the Center for Studies on New Religion (CESNUR), Turino, Italy.

Missione—Luigia Paparelli, La

Norman Doe Norman Doe is a professor and the director of the Centre for Law and Religion, Cardiff Law School. He studied law at Cardiff, received a master's degree in theology at Oxford, and, for his doctorate, at Cambridge. He is an associate professor at the University of Paris, a member of the European Consortium for Church and State Research, and is author of *Fundamental Authority in Late Medieval English Law* (Cambridge, Cambridge University Press, 1990), *The Legal Framework of the Church of England* (Oxford, Clarendon Press, 1996), *Canon Law in the Anglican Communion* (Oxford, Clarendon Press, 1998), *The Law of the Church in Wales* (Cardiff, University of Wales Press, 2002) and *An Anglican Covenant: Theological and Legal Considerations for a Global Debate* (London, Canterbury Press, 2008). He is a member of the general committee of the Ecclesiastical Law Society and was a member of the Lambeth Commission (2004).

Religion-Government Relations

Thadeus Doktor The late Thadeus Doktor received his doctorate in 1988 from Warsaw University. He was currently an adjunct professor at the Institute of Applied Social Sciences at the Warsaw University. His books include *Spotkania z astrologią* (Meetings with astrology; Iskry, 1987); *Ruchy kultowe: Psychologiczna charakterystyka uczestnikow* (Cult movements: Psychological characteristics of members; Nomos, 1991); *Nowe ruchy religijne i parareligijne w Polsce* (New religious and parareligious movements in Poland; Verbinum, 1999); and (with Irena Borowik) *Pluralizm religijny i mralny w Polsce* (Religions and moral pluralism in Poland; Nomos, 2001).

Poland
Rodzima Wiara (Poland)

Markus Dressler Markus Dressler was, from April 1998 to March 2001, a fellow and doctoral student at the Max Weber Center for Cultural and Social Studies at the Erfurt University in Germany. In March 2001, he finished his doctorate with a thesis on Alevism (published under the title *Die Alevitische Religion: Traditionslinien und Neubestimmungen,* Würzburg: Ergon 2002). In April 2001, provided with a scholarship from the German Academic Exchange Service, he embarked on a post-doctoral project as a visiting researcher at the Orient-Institute of the German Oriental Society in Istanbul, then at the Near Eastern Studies Department of New York University.

Bektashis Order (Bektashiye)

Jan Willem Drijvers Jan Willem Drijvers is lecturer of ancient history at the University of Groningen, Netherlands. His research focuses mainly on Late Antiquity, on which he has published widely, for example, on the christianization of the later Roman Empire, late Roman historiography, and the relations between the Roman and Sasanid Empires. He is the author of *Helena Augusta: The Mother of Constantine the Great and the Legend of Her Finding of the True Cross* (1992) and *Cyril of Jerusalem: Bishop and City* (2004). He is the co-author of the series *Philological and Historical Commentaries on Ammianus Marcellinus* (1995–).

Helena, Flavia Iulia

Neville Drury Dr. Nevill Drury has studied Western magic since the 1970s. He received his Ph.D. from the University of Newcastle, Australia, in 2008 and is the author of several internationally published titles on shamanism and the Western esoteric tradition. His publications include *Magic and Witchcraft: From Shamanism to the Technopagans* (2003); *The New Age: the History of a Movement* (winner of a Silver Award in *ForeWord Magazine's* Book of the Year Awards, New York, 2004); *Homage to Pan: The Life, Art and Magic of Rosaleen Norton* (2009) and *Stealing Fire from Heaven: The Rise of Modern Western Magic* (forthcoming, 2010).

Crowley, Aleister
Hermetic Order of the Golden Dawn
Mathers, Samuel Liddell MacGregor
Thelema

Eugene M. Elliott III Eugene M. Elliott III graduated from the University of Virginia in 2002 with a B.A. in foreign affairs. After graduation he has pursued his interests in environmental policy and environmental education.

Elan Vital/Divine Light Mission

Douglas Ezzy Douglas Ezzy is head of school in sociology and social work at the University of Tasmania, Australia. His books include *Teenage Witchcraft*

(with Helen Berger, Rutgers, 2007) and *Qualitative Analysis* (Routledge, 2002).

Witchcraft

Miguel H. Farias Miguel Farias's research on the psychology of religion covers social psychological and personality aspects of New Age spirituality, and neuroimaging correlates of religious belief and its effect on pain. He currently teaches in the MSc in Psychological Research at Oxford University and at Goldsmiths College, University of London. He is also associated with the Ian Ramsey Centre at Oxford University, where he has been the principal investigator of a project on pilgrimage across Europe, including the Christian sites of Fátima, Lourdes, Santiago de Compostela, and Pagan pilgrimages at Glastonbury and Stonehenge.

Lusitanian Church/Lusitanian Catholic Apostolic
    Evangelical Church
Portugal

Willy Fautré Willy Fautré is the director of *Human Rights Without Frontiers International* based in Brussels, Belgium. He is expert on the religious and linguistic minorities in Europe and has been their advocate at the United Nations, the OSCE, the European Union Fundamental Rights Agency, and the European Parliament. He regularly organizes conferences on religious freedom issues at the European Parliament, and lectures on religious freedom, discrimination, and intolerance. His publications include *Models of State-Church Relationships in the Modern World* (2009) and a report on *Hate Crime, Hate Speech and Discrimination Based on Religion or Belief in Belgium* (2009).

Belgium

Marianne Qvortrup Fibiger Marianne Q. Fibiger received her Ph.D. from Aarhus University in 1999. Her dissertation was entitled "The Sri Lankan Tamil Hindus in Denmark: A Religious Study of the Importance of Religion in an Intercultural Encounter."

Sri Lanka, Hinduism in

Adele Fletcher Adele Fletcher is a researcher currently based in Mito City, Japan. She holds a Ph.D. in Maori and an M.A. in religious studies from the University of Canterbury in New Zealand. Forthcoming publications include two articles on nineteenth-century Maori religion, "Atua, Ancestors and Ghosts" and "Sacred Hierarchies: Maori Ritual and Social Stratification."

Maori Religion

Peter Flügel Dr. Peter Flügel teaches in the Department of the Study of Religions of the School of Oriental and African Studies (SOAS) at the University of London. He is the author of *Asceticism and Devotion: The Ritual System of the Terapanth Svetambara Jains* (Peter Lang, forthcoming) and with G. Houtman is co-editor of *Asceticism and Power in the Asian Context* (Curzon Press, forthcoming).

Sthanakavasi Jain Tradition
Terapanth Svetambar Jain Tradition

Clyde R. Forsberg Jr. Clyde R. Forsberg Jr. is an assistant professor in the English and American Studies Department at Aletheia University, formerly Oxford College (Tamsui, Taiwan). A social and cultural historian and author of *Equal Rites: The Book of Mormon, Masonry, Gender, and American Culture* (Columbia University Press, 2004), his work has been characterized as not simply a new view of Mormonism, but a new view of America of the period, too. Class, race, gender, and sexuality figure prominently in his analysis of new religions. Presently, he is working on a new monograph on the Presbyterian mission to Taiwan, entitled "George Leslie Mackay: Man of Science, Faith, and the Myth of Celtic-Anglo-Saxon Superiority."

Mackay, George Leslie

Judith M. Fox Dr. Judith M. Fox is an independent academic researcher specializing in South Asian new religions. In addition to journal articles and contributions to edited volumes, she has produced *The Way of the Heart: A Study of Rajneeshism* (Aquarian Press, 1986), *Sahaja Yoga* (Curzon Press, 1999), and *Osho Rajneesh: e il suo movimento* (Elledici, 1999).

Sahaja Yoga

Selena Fox Reverend Selena Fox is founder and high priestess of Circle Sanctuary. She also is a writer, photographer, clinical psychotherapist, Pagan religious freedom activist, and guest speaker at colleges and universities. She is a member of the Assembly of Religious and Spiritual Leaders associated with the Parliament of the World's Religion.

Wiccan Religion

Liselotte Frisk Liselotte Frisk received her Ph.D. in 1993 from Åbo Academy in Finland. She was an assistant professor in history of religion at Umeå University in Sweden from 1995 to 1999, and from 1999 to 2001 was an assistant professor in religious studies at Dalarna University in Sweden. Since December 2001, she has been an associate professor of religious studies at Åbo Academy, and since 2006 professor of religious studies, Dalarna University, Sweden.

Satsang Network

David N. Gellner David N. Gellner is a lecturer in social anthropology at the University of Oxford. His books include *Monk, Householder, and Tantric Priest: Newar Buddhism and its Hierarchy of Ritual* (Cambridge University Press, 1992), *Nationalism and Ethnicity in a Hindu Kingdom* (Harwood, 1997), and *The Anthropology of Buddhism and Hinduism: Weberian Themes* (Oxford University Press, 2001).

Nepal

Nikandrs Gills Nikandrs Gills was a researcher at the Academic Center for Study of Religions at the Institute of Philosophy and Sociology, University of Latvia. He studied philosophy, and his research focuses on phenomenology of religion, history of religions, and churches of Latvia, including new religious movements. He was the compiler and editor of *Religious Philosophical Articles*. He passed away in 2009.

Latvia
Latvia, Paganism in
Latvian Evangelical Lutheran Church

Stephen D. Glazier   Stephen D. Glazier is professor of anthropology at the University of Nebraska at Lincoln. He is the editor of *The Encyclopedia of African and African American Religions* (Routledge, 2001), *Anthropology of Religion: A Handbook* (Praeger, 1999), and (with Andrew S. Buckser) *The Anthropology of Religious Conversion* (Rowman and Littlefield, 2003). Glazier currently serves as president of the Society for the Anthropology of Consciousness.

Rada Religion
Rastafarians
Spiritual Baptists

Donatas Glodenis   Donatas Glodenis received his B.A. in Christian studies at Lithuania Christian College in Klaipëda, Lithuania, in 1999, M.A. in religious studies from Vilnius University, Lithuania, and is currently a doctoral candidate in sociology at the Faculty of Philosophy at Vilnius University. He also works for the Ministry of Justice of the Republic of Lithuania. He writes extensively on religious minorities and state-church relations in Lithuania and has coauthored a few books.

Lithuania
Romuva

Joscelyn Godwin   Joscelyn Godwin is professor of music at Colgate University, where he has taught since 1971. He was educated at Magdalene College, Cambridge, and Cornell University, and has written, translated, and edited numerous books in the fields of musicology and esotericism, notably *Harmonies of Heaven and Earth* (Thames & Hudson, 1987), *The Theosophical Enlightenment* (SUNY Press, 1994), and a translation of the *Hypnerotomachia Poliphili of 1499*.

Evola, Julius
Flood, Robert
Western Esoteric Tradition

Marion S. Goldman   Marion S. Goldman is professor of sociology and religious studies at the University of Oregon. She focuses on issues of gender, sexualities, and religious movements. Her 1999 book *Passionate Journeys* (University of Michigan Press) considers the high-achieving women and men who followed Bhagwan Shree Rajneesh (now Osho) to central Oregon in the 1980s. Her recent work is about the Esalen Institute and its profound influence on contemporary culture.

Osho and the International Osho Movement

Arthur L. Greil   Arthur L. Greil is professor of sociology at Alfred University, specializing in the sociology of religion and medical sociology. His work on religion has focused on conversion, quasi-religion, and religion and politics. He is coeditor, with Thomas Robbins, of a volume on quasi-religion and, with David Bromley, a volume on defining religion.

British Israelism
Jehovah's Witnesses

Brian J. Grim   Brian J. Grim, Ph.D., is senior researcher in religion and world affairs at the Pew Research Center's Forum on Religion & Public Life in Washington, DC. Brian also is a research affiliate with Boston University's Institute on Culture, Religion and World Affairs. He previously was a visiting researcher at Georgetown University's Center for Muslim-Christian Understanding and a faculty researcher at Penn State's Survey Research Institute and the Association of Religion Data Archives (ARDA). Brian worked for 20 years as an educator, researcher and development coordinator in China, the former USSR, Kazakhstan, Europe, Malta, and the Middle East. Brian is the co-editor with Todd M. Johnson of the online *World Religion Database* (Brill, 2008). He is currently working on a world Muslim demography project.

Religious Freedom: Contemporary

Céline Grünhagen   Céline Grünhagen is lecturer at the Institute of Oriental & Asian Studies, Department of Comparative Religion at the University of Bonn in Germany. Her research focuses on current problems and developments concerning religions and their social settings as well as religio-ethical questions regarding women and gender issues. She is currently working on her Ph.D. thesis about gender and sexuality in Theravada-Buddhism with special focus on the estimation of sexual aberrance.

Homosexuality

Peter Gyallay-Pap Peter Gyallay-Pap holds a Ph.D. in political science and international relations from the London School of Economics. He is a senior research fellow at the Center of Advanced Study in Phnom Penh, Cambodia, and adjunct faculty at Adams State College in Colorado. He has spent more than fifteen years working with and writing about Buddhism in Cambodia.

Buddhist Institute
Cambodia

Jeffrey K. Hadden Jeffrey K. Hadden earned a Ph.D. in sociology at the University of Wisconsin in 1963. He was professor of sociology at the University of Virginia from 1972 until his death in 2003. His writings in the area of religion have focused on religious movements. His last book, *Religion and the Internet* (JAI, 2001) was co-edited with Douglas E. Cowan.

Ananda Marga Yoga Society
Elan Vital/Divine Light Mission
Integral Yoga International
Serpent Handlers/Signs Following Movement

Olav Hammer Olav Hammer is professor of history of religions at the University of Southern Denmark. He has published extensively, in particular on Western esotericism and on new religious movements. Recent publications include *Alternative Christs* (edited volume, Cambridge University Press, 2009). He is at present executive editor of the journal *Numen*.

Astrology
Egypt in Western Religious Imagination
India in Western Religious Imagination
Tibet in Western Religious Imagination

Phillip E. Hammond Phillip E. Hammond was D. Mackenzie Brown Professor of Religious Studies at the University of California at Santa Barbara. He received a Ph.D. in sociology from Columbia University and taught in the sociology departments of Yale University, the University of Wisconsin, and the University of Arizona before moving to UCSB in 1978. The most recent of his many books was *The Dynamics of Religious Organizations* (Oxford University Press, 2000).

Soka Gakkai International

Jürgen Hanneder Jürgen Hanneder holds a Ph.D. in Indology from the University of Marburg, Germany, and is presently a research scholar in a project located at the University of Halle, Germany, which deals with the Kashmirian version of the Yogavasistha. His teaching and research focus includes Kashmirian Shaivism, classical Sanskrit poetry, and modern Sanskrit literature.

Kashmir Saivism
Pashupata Saivism

Charlotte Hardman Charlotte Hardman is a social anthropologist and head of the Religious Studies Department at the University of Newcastle upon Tyne, England. She has worked in Nepal for many years and has published books and articles on Nepal. She has also carried out research on new religious movements and has written on religion in contemporary society and on children.

Druidism
Nepal, Indigenous Religions in

Carol Harris-Shapiro Carol Harris-Shapiro, the author of *Messianic Judaism: A Rabbi's Journey through Religious Change in America* (Beacon Press, 1999), is an assistant professor of religion at Temple University and a Reconstructionist rabbi. Her research interests include American religion, contemporary American Judaism, and religious/ethnic identity construction.

Messianic Judaism

Christopher H. Hartney Christopher Hartney is lecturer in the Department of Studies in Religion at the University of Sydney.

Caodaism
China: Taiwan
Vietnam

Jan-Peter Hartung Jan-Peter Hartung is a doctoral candidate and researcher in religious studies and Islamic studies at the Max Weber Center for Cultural and Social Studies at Erfurt University in Germany. His fields of research and interest include Islamic scholarship in South Asia in the eighteenth to twenty-first centuries, Sufism, Islamic philosophy, and Muslim revivalist movements in South Asia.

Chistiñiyya Sufi Order
Naqshbandiya Sufi Order

Sarah Harvey Following completion of a masters degree in social research methods at the London School of Economics and Political Science in 2001, Sarah Harvey became a Research Officer at INFORM (Information Network Focus on Religious Movements), a research center on new religious movements, based in London. In September 2009, she began studying for her Ph.D. in the Psychosocial Studies Department at Birkbeck, University of London. Her thesis is on the subject of spirituality and childbirth. At INFORM, her primary responsibility is maintenance of the database of religious movements, but she also responds to many of the enquiries that Inform receives.

Birth

Ariel Hessayon Dr Ariel Hessayon is lecturer in the Department of History at Goldsmiths, University of London. He is the author of *'Gold Tried in the Fire': The Prophet Theaurau John Tany and the English Revolution* (Ashgate, 2007) and has edited collections on *Scripture and Scholarship in Early Modern England* (Aldershot: Ashgate, 2006) and *Radicalism in Seventeenth- and Early Eighteenth-Century Britain, Ireland and Continental Europe* (Ashgate, 2010). He has also written extensively on a variety of early modern topics: book burning, Communism, environmentalism, esotericism, extra-canonical texts, heresy, crypto-Jews, Judaizing, millenarianism, prophecy, and social networks.

Agrippa von Nettesheim, Heinrich Cornelius

Alan Hayes Alan Hayes earned his Ph.D. from McGill University and is currently Bishops Frederick and Heber Wilkinson Professor of Church History of Wycliffe College at the University of Toronto. His teaching and research interests include early Christianity, Anglican history, early modern history, Canadian Christianity, historiography, and worship.

Anglican Church of Canada

Gordon L. Heath Gordon L. Heath, is associate professor of Christian history at McMaster Divinity College in Hamilton, Canada. His most recent books include *A War with a Silver Lining: Canadian Protestant Churches and the South African War, 1899–1902* (MQUP, 2009) and *Doing Church History: A User-friendly Introduction to Researching the History of Christianity* (Clements, 2008).

Christian Church (Disciples of Christ) in Canada
Doukhobors
Evangelical Lutheran Church in Canada
Evangelical Mennonite Conference
Lutheran Church in Canada
Presbyterian Church in Canada

Kathleen Hertzberg Kathleen Hertzberg, a lifelong member of the Society of Friends, is the cofounder of the Canadian Friends Historical Association, founded in 1972. She attended Woodbrooke, the Quaker College in England. Prior to the Second World War, she assisted Jews and others in leaving Germany. She moved to Canada in 1952 and has served as the chair of the Canadian Friends Service Committee and a representative of the Canadian Yearly Meeting on the (international) Friends World Committee for Consultation.

Canadian Yearly Meeting of the Religious Society of
   Friends

Albert W. Hickman Albert W. Hickman is a research associate in global Christianity at the Center for the Study of Global Christianity at Gordon-Conwell Theological Seminary in South Hamilton, Massachusetts. He is an associate editor of the *Atlas of Global Christianity* (Edinburgh University Press, 2009).

AD2000 and Beyond
Lausanne Movement
Mountains

Mark Hill Mark Hill QC is a practicing barrister and honorary professor of law at Cardiff University at its Centre for Law and Religion. His publications include *Ecclesiastical Law* (3rd ed., Oxford, Oxford University Press, 2007) and he is editor of *Religious Liberty and Human Rights* (Cardiff, University of Wales Press, 2002) and the *Ecclesiastical Law Journal* (published by Cambridge University Press). He is a recorder of the Crown Court, and Chancellor of the Dioceses of Chichester and Europe. He regularly lectures in the United Kingdom and abroad on matters concerning the law of Church and State.

Religion-Government Relations

Julie Hirst Julie Hirst is an associate lecturer for the Open University and her doctorate was awarded by the University of York. Her publications include *Jane Leade: A Biography of a Seventeenth-Century Mystic* (2005). She is interested in gender and theology in seventeenth-century women's writing, and her present research focuses on women as religious radicals and visionaries.

Leade, Jane

Norman A. Hjelm Norman A. Hjelm, now retired in Wynnewood, Pennsylvania, served as Lutheran World Federation Director of Communication and Acting Deputy General Secretary for Planning. For a long time he was director and senior editor of *Fortress Press* in Philadelphia. He also served as director of the Commission on Faith and Order of the National Council of the Churches of Christ in the U.S.A.

Lutheran World Federation

Natalie Hobbs Natalie Hobbs is a graduate student in the Department of Religious Studies at the University of South Florida with a research focus in New Religious Movements.

International New Thought Alliance
Religious Science
Unity School of Christianity/Association of Unity
    Churches

E. G. Hoekstra E. G. Hoekstra, M.A., is a retired preuniversity education teacher who wrote many publications on religion in the Netherlands, especially on the diverse churches and religious movements. He is cowriter and editor of *Wegwijs in religieus en levensbeschouwelijk Nederland* (3rd ed., Kampen, 2002) writer of *Handboek christelijk Nederland* (Kampen 2007) and is coeditor of the series "Wegwijs, Kok, Kampen."

Netherlands, The
Netherlands Reformed Churches
Old Catholic Church of the Netherlands
Protestant Church in the Netherlands
Reformed Denomination
Remonstrant Brotherhood
Restored Reformed Church

Michael W. Homer Michael W. Homer is a trial lawyer in private practice in Salt Lake City, Utah. He has written books and articles concerning Mormonism, Freemasonry, Arthur Conan Doyle, and Spiritualism. He is the author of *Lo spiritismo* (Elledici, 1999).

Church of Jesus Christ of Latter-day Saints

Leah Shaw Houghton Leah Shaw Houghton is a graduate of Truman State University in Kirksville, Missouri. She is currently attending graduate school at the University of Missouri at Kansas City where she is working toward a M.S.W. in social work.

Church Universal and Triumphant

Qamar-ul Huda Qamar-ul Huda is assistant professor of Islamic Studies and Comparative Theology in the Department of Theology at Boston College. His area of interests are on Sufism, Qur'anic hermeneutics, Islamic ethics, and history of religious thought.

Mevlevi Sufi Order
Qadiriyya Rifa'i Sufi Order
Qadiriyya Sufi Order
Shadhiliyya Sufi Order
Suhrawardiyya Sufi Order

Neil Hudson Neil Hudson lectures at Regents Theological College in Nantwich, England. He was awarded a doctorate from King's College, London in 1999 for work related to the Elim Pentecostal Church. His research interests include the challenge that contemporary society places before the church and Pentecostal history. He serves on the editorial board of the *Journal of the European Pentecostal Theological Association* and the management board of the Donald Gee Centre for Pentecostal Research.

Elim Pentecostal Church

Lynne Hume Lynne Hume is an anthropologist and senior lecturer in the Department of Studies in Religion at the University of Queensland in Australia. She lectures on Aboriginal religions, women and religion, and new religious movements. Her current research is on altered states of consciousness and religious experience.

Aboriginal Religions

Alan Hunter Dr. Alan Hunter is senior lecturer at the Centre for the Study of Forgiveness and Reconciliation at Coventry University in the United Kingdom. Dr. Hunter has authored several works on religion and society in China, including (with Kim-kwong Chan) *Protestantism in Contemporary China* (Cambridge University Press, 1993) and (with John Sexton) *Contemporary China* (MacMillan, 1999).

China

Harold D. Hunter Harold D. Hunter is the director of the Archives and Research Center of the International Pentecostal Holiness Church in Oklahoma City, Oklahoma, the author of *Spirit Baptism: A*

Pentecostal Alternative (University Press of America, 1983), and a past president of the Society for Pentecostal Studies.

Church of God of Prophecy
International Pentecostal Holiness Church
Pentecostal Church of God
Pentecostal World Fellowship

Dawn L. Hutchinson Dawn Hutchinson is an assistant professor of philosophy and religious studies at Christopher Newport University. She specializes in American religious history, particularly in new religious movements. She is currently writing *Religion in America: A Cultural Analysis* for Rowman & Littlefield and *Antiquity and Social Reform: Religious Experience in the Unification Church, Feminist Wicca and the Nation of Yahweh* for Cambridge Scholars Publishing.

Course in Miracles, A

Manfred Hutter Manfred Hutter is professor for comparative religion at the University of Bonn in Germany. His teachings and current research include Indian religious traditions and spirituality in Europe, the Bahá'í Faith, and traditional and contemporary Zoroastrianism.

Austria
Austrian Buddhist Association
Evangelical Church of the Augsburg and Helvetic
    Confessions in Austria
Old Catholic Church of Austria

Keishin Inaba Keishin Inaba has been associate professor of the Graduate School of Human Development and Environment, Kobe University, since 2003. He studied at the Department of Religious Studies of the University of Tokyo, and obtained his Ph.D. in sociology of religion at King's College, University of London. He has published on the themes of altruism and religion both in English and Japanese. His works include *Altruism in New Religious Movements: The Jesus Army and the Friends of the Western Buddhist Order in Britain* (University Education Press, 19 May 2005), and Ruben Habito and Inaba Keishin, eds., *The*

Practice of Altruism: Caring and Religion in Global Perspective (Cambridge Scholars Press, 2006).

Byakko Shinko Kai
Ennôkyô
Gedatsu Kai
Izumo Ôyashirokyô
Kôdô Kyôdan
Kurozumikyô
Myôchikai Kyôdan
Myanmar Baptist Convention
Nichirin Shoshu
Nichirinshu
Reiha-no-Hikari

Paul O. Ingram   Paul O. Ingram is professor emeritus of religion at Pacific Lutheran University, Tacoma, Washington. He served as president of the Society for Buddhist-Christian Studies and his most recent books include *Wrestling With the Ox: A Theology of Religious Experience; Wrestling with God, Buddhist-Christian Dialogue in an Age of Science;* and *The Process of Buddhist-Christian Dialogue.*

Science and Religion, The Contemporary Scene
Science and Religion, History of the Relationship

Ginette Ishimatsu   Ginette Ishimatsu is associate professor of Asian religions at the University of Denver. She is the author of *Between Text and Tradition: Hindu Ritual and Politics in South India* (Westview, forthcoming) and contributor (with S. S. Janaki, N. R. Bhatt, and Richard Davis) to a critical edition and translation of Aghorashivacharya's *Kriyakramadyotika.*

Tamil Saivism

Forrest Jackson   Forrest Jackson, a graduate of Tulane University, was first entranced by flying saucers at the age of six when his mother, a UFO contactee, took him to see *Close Encounters of the Third Kind.* Along with Rodney Perkins, he cowrote *Cosmic Suicide: The Tragedy and Transcendence of Heaven's Gate* (Pentaradial Press, 1997).

Chen Tao

Kumar Jairamdas   Kumar Jairamdas is a student at the University of South Florida with interests in Vajrayana; Jainism; developmental Hinduism and Buddhism in India; Hindu, Buddhist, and Jain mythology; and the Hindu/Buddhist influence on Tibetan religion. He has traveled to Indonesia to study the ways in which Hindu mythology has been transmitted in non-Indian Hindu culture. He has also visited Singapore to observe secularized Hindu/Buddhist traditions.

Shakta Movement
Smarta Tradition
Yogi Tradition

Abhi P. Janamanchi   Reverend Abhi P. Janamanchi is a Unitarian Universalist minister who currently serves in the Unitarian Universalist Society in Clearwater, Florida. He hails from India and is also a third-generation member of the Brahmo Samaj.

Brahmo Samaj

Andy Brubacher Kaether   Andy Brubacher Kaether completed his M.A. in theology at the Toronto School of Theology, University of Toronto. His thesis is entitled "Christology in African Independent Churches: Theological Reflections in Mennonite Missions Perspective."

Church of Moshoeshoe
Spiritual Healing Church (Botswana)

William K. Kay   William K. Kay is professor of theology at Glyndwr University, which is part of the federal structure of the University of Wales. Among many other publications, he is author of *Pentecostalism* (SCM, 2009), *Apostolic Networks in Britain* (Paternoster, 2007), and coeditor of *Pentecostal and Charismatic Studies: A Reader* (SCM, 2004). He is coeditor of the Brill series in Global Pentecostal and Charismatic Studies and is writing on Pentecostalism in the Very Short Introduction series for Oxford University Press.

Assemblies of God Incorporated

Alexandra Kent Alexandra Kent is an associate professor of social anthropology at the Nordic Institute of Asian Studies in Copenhagen. She completed a doctoral dissertation in 2000 entitled "Ambiguity and the Modern Order: The Sathya Sai Baba Movement in Malaysia" and subsequently carried out post-doctoral research on Chinese participation in the Tamil festival of Thaipusam in Penang, Malaysia. Since 2002, she has been conducting research on the revival of Buddhism in post-conflict Cambodia.

Sathya Sai Baba Movement

Benny Liow Woon Khin Benny Liow Woon Khin earned a B.A. Hons. Ed. in history in 1980 from Universiti Sains Malaysia and in 1985 earned a Master of Public Administration from University of Malaya. He works as a general manager of human resources at a leading Malaysian-based multi-national corporation in Kuala Lumpur. He is editor of *Eastern Horizon*, a journal of the Young Buddhist Association of Malaysia. His most recent publications are *K.Sri Dhammananda Felicitation: Essays in Honor of His 80th Birthday* (BGF, 1999) and *K.Sri Dhamamnanda: A Pictorial Retrospect* (BGF, 1997).

Buddhist Missionary Society Malaysia
Young Buddhist Association

Sallie B. King Sallie B. King is professor of philosophy and religion at James Madison University. She is the author of *Buddha Nature* (SUNY Press, 1991), *Journey in Search of the Way: The Spiritual Autobiography of Satomi Myodo* (SUNY Press, 1993), *Being Benevolence: The Social Ethics of Engaged Buddhism* (Hawaii, 2005), and *Socially Engaged Buddhism* (Hawaii, 2009). She is coeditor of *Engaged Buddhism: Buddhist Liberation Movements in Asia* (SUNY Press, 1996) and *The Sound of Liberating Truth: Buddhist-Christian Dialogues in Honor of Frederick J. Streng* (Curzon Press, 1999).

Unified Buddhist Church

Christoph Kleine Christoph Kleine holds a Ph.D. in religious studies from the University of Marburg, Germany. He is presently professor for the history of religions at the University of Leipzig, Germany. His special field of interest is East Asian religious history—particularly Buddhism, hagiography, religion and politics issues, and methodological questions of the study of religions. His publications include *Hônens Buddhismus des Reinen Landes: A Multilingual Dictionary of Chinese Buddhism* (Peter Lang, 1996) and a number of articles in various journals, books, and reference works.

Jodo-shinshu
Jodo-shu

Alioune Koné Alioune Koné is an independent researcher currently living in Berlin. His dissertation is a sociological analysis of the legacy of Taisen Deshimaru Roshi (1914–1982). His current interests are on recent American New Religions.

International Zen Association

Milan Kováč Milan Kováč, Ph.D., is a Chair of the Department of the History of Religions at the Comenius University in Bratislava, Slovakia. He has concentrated his studies on philosophy, history, and history of religions.

Slovakia

Louise Kretzschmar Louise Kretzschmar is professor of Christian ethics at the University of South Africa in Pretoria, and chairperson of the governing board of the Baptist Convention College in Soweto. She is the author of *The Voice of Black Theology in South Africa* (Ohio University Press, 1986); *Privatization of the Christian Faith: Mission, Social Ethics and the South African Baptists* (Asempa Press, 1998); coeditor (with L. D. Hulley and Luke Lungile Pato) of *Archbishop Tutu: Prophetic Witness in South Africa* (BHB International, 1997); and coeditor (with C. Kourie) of *Christian Spirituality in South Africa* (Cluster, 2000).

Baptist Union of South Africa/Baptist Convention of South Africa
Baptists

Alexei D. Krindatch. Alexei D. Krindatch is sociologist of religion and director for research at the Patriarch Athenagoras Orthodox Institute in Berkeley, CA (www.orthodoxinstitute.org). He graduated from the Moscow State University in 1988, specializing in human geography and geography of religions. Mr. Krindatch's areas of expertise include: Orthodox Christian churches in the USA and religion in the former USSR. He is the author of a monograph, *Geography of Religions in Russia* (Glenmary Research Center, 1996), one of his 50 publications in various languages.

Georgia
Georgian Orthodox Church
Russian Orthodox Church (Moscow Patriarchate)

Solveiga Krumina-Konkova Solveiga Krumina-Konkova is a doctor of philosophy and leading researcher of the Institute of Philosophy and Sociology at the University of Latvia. She is an author of *Evil and Man's Free Will* (Zinatne, 1992, in Latvian), *Religious Diversity in Latvia* (co-authored with Valdis Teraudkalns, Klints, 2007) and of numerous articles on religions in Latvia.

Latvia
Latvia, Paganism in
Latvian Evangelical Lutheran Church

Khun Eng Kuah Khun Eng Kuah holds a Ph.D. in anthropology from Monash University in Australia. She is currently associate professor at the Department of Sociology at the University of Hong Kong. Her teaching and research focus includes Buddhism-society and state, the emigrant villages in China, and ancestor worship in south China. Her recent publications include a book titled *Rebuilding the Ancestral Village: Singaporeans in China* (Ashgate, 2000).

Singapore, Buddhism in

André Laliberté André Laliberté is an associate professor at the School of Political Studies at the University of Ottawa, where he teaches courses and graduate seminars on comparative politics and Chinese politics. He holds a Ph.D. in political science from the University of British Columbia in Canada. He has published on Buddhist associations in Taiwan and China and on relations between state and religions in East Asia. His current research interests include charity and welfare policy in China and Taiwan.

Buddhist Association of the Republic of China
Buddhist Compassion Relief Tzu Chi Association, The
Dharma Drum Mountain Association (Fakushan), The
Master Ching Hai Meditation Association

David Christopher Lane David Christopher Lane is currently a professor of philosophy and sociology at Mount San Antonio College in Walnut, California. He is also a lecturer in religious studies at California State University, Long Beach. Lane is the author of several books, including *The Radhasoami Tradition: A Critical History of Guru Successorship* (Garland, 1992), *Exposing Cults: When the Skeptical Mind Confronts the Mystical* (Garland, 1994), and *The Making of a Spiritual Movement: The Untold Story of Paul Twitchell and Eckankar* (Del Mar Press, 1983). Lane received his Ph.D. from the University of California at San Diego where he was also a recipient of a Regents Fellowship.

Manavta Mandir
Master Ching Hai Meditation Association
Radhasoami
Ruhani Satsang

Laura Maria Latikka Reverend Master of Theology Laura Maria Latikka earned her master of theology at Åbo Akademi University in Turku, Finland in 1996. From 1990 to 1991, she studied at Aarhus University in Denmark. In 1997 she was named the Secretary for Church and People of Other Faiths in the Evangelical Lutheran Church of Finland until 2000.

Evangelical Lutheran Church of Finland
Finland

Paul Alan Laughlin Paul Alan Laughlin is a professor in the Department of Religion and Philosophy at Otterbein College in Ohio, and the author of numerous publications, most in the field of American metaphysical religion. His latest book is *Getting Oriented: What*

Every Christian Should Know about Eastern Religions, But Probably Doesn't (Polebridge Press, 2005).

Seicho-No-Ie

Oliver Leaman   Oliver Leaman is currently teaching at the University of Kentucky, USA. He previously taught in England and the Middle East. He writes mainly in the area of Islamic and Jewish philosophy, and his most recent publications are *Islamic Aesthetics: An Introduction* (Edinburgh University Press, 2004), *Islam: the Key Facts*, co-written with Kecia Ali, and *Jewish Thought: an Introduction* (2006), both published by Routledge. He organized the second edition of Ninian Smart's *World Philosophies*, which appeared in 2008, and the second edition of his *Brief Introduction to Islamic Philosophy* has been published in 2009 as *Islamic Philosophy*.

Gerizim, Mount
Istanbul
Jerusalem
Mecca
Medinah
Meron, Mount
Moses
Muhammad
Temples—Jewish
Zionism

Martha Lee   Martha Lee earned her Ph.D. from Syracuse University and is now associate professor and Stephen Jarislowsky Chair in Religion and Conflict at the University of Windsor in Ontario, Canada. She is the author of *The Nation of Islam, An American Millenarian Movement* (Syracuse University Press, 1996), *Earth First! Environmental Apocalypse* (Syracuse University Press, 1995), and the editor of *Millennial Visions: Essays on Twentieth Century Millenarianism* (Praeger, 2000).

Warith Deen Mohammad, Ministry of

James R. Lewis   James R. Lewis is associate professor of religious studies at the University of Tromsø in Tromsø, Norway. His publications include *Cults in*

America: A Reference Handbook (ABC-CLIO, 1998), *Witchcraft Today: An Encyclopedia of Wiccan and Neopagan Traditions* (ABC-CLIO, 1999), *UFOs and Popular Culture: An Encyclopedia of Contemporary Myth* (ABC-CLIO, 2000), and *Satanism Today: An Encyclopedia of Religion, Folklore, and Popular Culture* (ABC-CLIO, 2001).

Abd al-Aziz ibn Sa'ud
Adidam
Aumist Religion
Branham Tabernacle and Related Assemblies
International Evangelical Church
Movement of Spiritual Inner Awareness
Sikh Dharma
Sikhism/Sant Mat
Way International, The

John LoBreglio   John LoBreglio is a Ph.D. candidate in religious studies at the University of California at Santa Barbara. He has also completed a doctoral course at Kyoto University in Japanese cultural studies.

Japan Buddhist Federation
Nipponzan Myohoji

Carlos Lopez   Carlos Lopez is assistant professor of religious studies at the University of South Florida-Tampa. His research focuses on Vedic religion and culture. His current research focuses on construction of sex, gender and sexuality in South Asian religious traditions. He teaches introductory courses on the Hindu tradition (Religions of Asia, Gods and Goddesses of India), advance topical courses dealing with specific dimensions of the Hindu tradition (Hindu Texts and Contexts, Rebirth and Karma in Ancient Indian Literature, and Hindu Dharma), and Religious themes in Tolkien's Middle Earth.

India, Contemporary Religion in: Asian Religions
India, Contemporary Religions in: Middle Eastern
    Religions
India, Hinduism in: Ancient Vedic Expressions
India, Hinduism in: Classical Period
India, Hinduism in: Medieval Period
India, Hinduism in: Modern Period

Shaivism
Shaktiism
Tantrisam
Vaishnavism

Phillip Charles Lucas Phillip Charles Lucas is professor of religious studies at Stetson University in DeLand, Florida, and a founding editor of *Nova Religio: The Journal of Alternative and Emergent Religions*. He is the author of *The Odyssey of a New Religion: The Holy Order of MANS from New Age to Orthodoxy* (Indiana University Press, 1995), and coeditor of *Cassadaga: The South's Oldest Spiritual Community* (University Press of Florida, 2000), *New Religious Movements in the Twenty-First Century: Legal, Political, and Social Challenges in Global Perspective* (Routledge, 2004), and *Prime Time Religion: An Encyclopedic Guide to Religious Broadcasting* (Oryx Press, 1997). He is the author of numerous articles on new and minority religions.

Ancient and Mystical Order Rosae Crucis
I AM Religious Activity
Sufi Order in North America, The

Dusan Lužný Dušan Lužný is associate professor at the Institute for the Study of Religions at the Faculty of Arts of the Masaryk University in Brno and at the Department of Sociology at the Faculty of Philosophy and Arts of the University of West Bohemia in Plzen in the Czech Republic. He focuses on the issues connected with the existence and activities of new religious movements and on the transformations of religion in the globalization process. He is the author of monographs *Nová náboženská hnutí* (New religious movements; 1997), *Náboženství a moderní společnost: sociologické teorie modernizace a sekularizace* (Religion and modern society: sociological theories of modernization and secularization; 1999), *Zelení bódhisattvové: sociálně a ekologicky angažovaný buddhismus* (The green boddhisattvas: socially and ecologically engaged buddhism; 2000), and *Hledání ztracené jednoty* (Quest for lost unity; 2004).

Evangelical Church of the Czech Brethren
Silesian Evangelical Church of the Augsburg Confession

Richard D. McBride II Richard McBride holds a Ph.D. in East Asian languages and cultures from the University of California at Los Angeles. He is presently an assistant professor of history at Brigham Young University–Hawaii. His research focus includes the development of Buddhist thought and culture in early and medieval Korea and China.

Chogye Order
Korean Buddhism
Pomun Order of Korean Buddhism
Won Buddhism

Gary B. McGee The late Gary B. McGee received his Ph.D. from Saint Louis University. He was the professor of church history and Pentecostal studies at Assemblies of God Theological Seminary in Springfield, Missouri.

Assemblies of God

Marjory A. MacLean Reverend Marjory A. MacLean is deputy clerk (and has served as acting principal clerk) of the General Assembly of the Church of Scotland, and is a former lawyer and parish minister.

Church of Scotland

David Wayne Machacek David Wayne Machacek is a research coordinator at the Center for the Study of Religion and lecturer in religious studies and writing at the University of California at Santa Barbara. His books include *Soka Gakkai in America: Accommodation and Conversion* (with Phillip E. Hammond; Oxford University Press, 1999) and *Global Citizens: The Soka Gakkai Buddhist Movement in the World* (with Bryan Wilson; Oxford University Press, 2000).

Soka Gakkai International

Gilles Marcouiller Gilles Marcouiller is pastor of a French Protestant Evangelical Church in Quebec, Canada. Interested in Faith and Culture, he is producing ressources to help believers (Catholic and Protestant) to understand and engage the Quebec Post-Christian society. He is the author of *Observation des* *rapports entre la foi et la culture dans le Québec du XXe siècle: problèmes d'interprétations.*

Canada (Quebec)

Peter Jan Margry Peter Jan Margry studied history at the University of Amsterdam, the Netherlands. He was awarded his Ph.D. by the University of Tilburg (2000). He became Director of the Department of Ethnology at the Meertens Institute, a research center of the Royal Netherlands Academy of Arts and Sciences in Amsterdam. As a senior researcher at the institute, his current ethnological focus is on cultural memory and contemporary religious cultures in the Netherlands and Europe. His last book was a 2008 edited volume: *Shrines and Pilgrimage in the Modern World: New Itineraries into the Sacred* (Amsterdam University Press).

Fatima (Portugal)
Marian Devotion, World Network of
Medjugorje
Our Lady of All Nations (Netherlands)

Javier Martínez-Torrón Javier Martínez-Torrón is a professor of law at Complutense University (Madrid, Spain). He is a doctor *utroque iure* (Law and Canon Law) and vice-president of the Section of Canon Law and Church-State Relations of the Spanish Royal Academy of Jurisprudence and Legislation. He is also a member of the OSCE/ODIHR Advisory Council for Freedom of Religion or Belief, the Spanish Advisory Commission for Religious Freedom, and the International Academy of Comparative Law. His writings have been published in nineteen countries and in nine languages. His research on law and religion issues is characterized by a predominant interest in international and comparative law.

Spain

Wendy Mason Wendy Mason, ARNP, is a psychiatric nurse practitioner with a background in women's studies, culture, religion and spirituality. She has practiced psychiatry for 12 years while teaching nursing, religion, psychology, culture and women's studies

courses in various colleges and universities. She has published a number of articles on these various topics and is currently working on her doctorate at the California Institute of Integral Studies.

Perrenialism
Women, Status and role of

Giulio Maspero Giulio Maspero was born in Como, Italy, and became a Roman Catholic priest with Ph.D.s in both physics and theology. Presently he is an associate professor of Systematic Theology at the Theological Faculty of the Pontifical University of the Holy Cross in Rome and a Member of the /Association Internationale des Études Patristiques /(AIEP). He has published numerous articles on Gregory of Nyssa and on the relationship between reason and religion.

Theology

Bruce Matthews Bruce Matthews is professor emeritus of comparative religion at Acadia University in Nova Scotia. His research interests and publications have focused largely on Buddhism in the modern world, more particularly the Theravada tradition of Sri Lanka and Myanmar.

Mutima Walowa Wa Mukumbi

Jean-François Mayer Jean-François Mayer is the director of Religioscope Institute (Fribourg, Switzerland). He is the author of a number of books and articles including *I nuovi movimenti religiosi: Sette cristiane e nuovi culti* (with Massimo Introvigne and Ernesto Zucchini; Elledici, 1990); *Las sectas: Inconformismos cristianos y nuevas religiones* (Desclée De Brouwer, 1990); *Les nouvelles voies spirituelles: Enquête sur la religiosité parallèle en Suisse* (Ed. L'Age d'Homme, 1993); *Der Sonnentempel* (Paulusverlag, 1998); *Les fondamentalismes* (Georg Editeur, 2001) and *Internet et religion* (Infolio, 2008).

Arès Pilgrims
Old Catholic Church in Switzerland
Russian Orthodox Church Outside of Russia
Solar Temple, Order of the

Spiritual Human Yoga
Switzerland

Sarah Meadows As a student at the University of Virginia, Sarah Meadows worked closely with Jeffrey K. Hadden and the New Religions project he created.

Integral Yoga International

Andrea Menegotto Andrea Menegotto is a researcher in the field of social and humanistic sciences. He collaborates with different training institutes and organizations. He is Milan Branch Manager of Center for Studies on New Religions (CESNUR) and member of Italian Society of Psychology of Religion (SIPR).

Art of Living Foundation

Michael L. Mickler Michael L. Mickler is professor of church history at the Unification Theological Seminary. He is the author of *Forty Years in America: An Intimate History of the Unification Movement, 1959–1999* (HSA Publications, 2000), *A History of the Unification Church in America, 1959–74* (Garland, 1993), and *The Unification Church in America: A Bibliography and Research Guide* (Garland, 1987), as well as articles and reviews on the Unification Church and other movements.

Unification Movement

Rebecca Moore Rebecca Moore teaches in the Department of Religious Studies at San Diego State University. She has studied the Peoples Temple and the events at Jonestown for the past two decades, and has published a number of books and articles on the subject. She is currently co-general editor of *Nova Religio: The Journal of Alternative and Emergent Religions.*

Peoples Temple
Sri Chinmoy Centers International

A. Scott Moreau A. Scott Moreau served fourteen years on staff with Campus Crusade for Christ, ten in Africa. He taught science at Ntonjeni Swazi National

High School (1978–1980) and missions at the Nairobi International School of Theology (NIST; 1984–1991). In 1991, Scott accepted a position in the Intercultural Studies department at Wheaton College, where he is now professor. In 2000 he became managing editor of the Network for Strategic Missions Knowledge Base, a Web-based database on missions (www.strategic missions.org) and in 2001 the editor of *Evangelical Missions Quarterly.* He has written or edited eleven books and numerous journal and dictionary articles.

Ancestors
Exorcism
Possession

Heinz Muermel Heinz Muermel studied Protestant theology at Karl Marx University in Leipzig. He wrote his Ph.D. dissertation on "Das Magieverstaendnis von Marcel Mauss" (The Concept of Magic with Mauss). His areas of study have included the thought of the French school of sociology on religion, the Theravada Buddhism of Sri Lanka, and Buddhism in Germany and its relation to other religious groups.

Sri Lanka

Ranjana Mukhopadhyaya Ranjana Mukhopadhyaya is a research scholar in sociology of religion at the University of Tokyo, Japan and University of Delhi, India. Her research is on Japanese religions, particularly on modern Japanese Buddhism, new religious movements, and on the public role of religion. Her publications, in English as well as Japanese, are on engaged Buddhism and on state-religion relations and social activism of religious groups in Japan.

Kokuchu-Kai
Reiyukai
Rissho Kosei-kai

Larry G. Murphy. Larry G. Murphy is a professor of the history of Christianity at Garrett Evangelical Theological Seminary in Evanston, Illinois. He is the editor of *Down by the Riverside: A Reader in African American Religion* (New York University Press, 2000) and *African American Faith in America* (Facts on File,

2002). He was coeditor (with Gary Ward and J. Gordon Melton) of the *Encyclopedia of African American Religion* (Garland, 1993).

African Methodist Episcopal Church
African Methodist Episcopal Zion Church
Christian Methodist Episcopal Church

Pamela S. Nadell   Pamela S. Nadell is the Inaugural Patrick Clendenen Professor of History and Director of the Jewish Studies Program at American University. Her books include *Women Who Would Be Rabbis: A History of Women's Ordination, 1889–1985* (1998), which was a finalist for the National Jewish Book Award. She is past chair of the Academic Council of the American Jewish Historical Society, book review editor of the journal *American Jewish History*, and one of four members of the historians' team of the new National Museum of American Jewish History, scheduled to open in Philadelphia in November 2010.

Conservative Judaism
Judaism
Orthodox Judaism
Reconstructionist Judaism
Reform Judaism

Peter Nelson   Dr. Peter Nelson started his scientific career with the study of nerve impulses in the giant axons of squid. From there he moved to psychophysiological studies of human consciousness, arousal, and perception. Later, he became a social scientist and focused his research on how people experience and understand reality—whether seen through the visions of mystics or the daily perceptions of ordinary people. He has worked as a university professor as well as a research consultant to corporations, universities, and government departments.

Dr. Nelson also has specialized in the psychological profiling of individuals for criminal courts in Australia.

Altered States of Consciousness

Frank Neubert   Frank Neubert is currently an Oberassistent at the Department of Religious Studies at the University of Lucerne, Switzerland. His research focuses on theoretical and methodological questions in the study of religions on the one hand, and the history of Hinduism since the early 19th century. His recent research is on Neo-Hindu Movements in the West, especially on the International Society for Krishna Consciousness.

Devotion/Devotional Traditions

Suzanne Newcombe   Suzanne Newcombe is a research officer at INFORM (Information Network Focus on Religious Movements), a research organization based at the London School of Economics, that provides information on new and alternative religions and spiritualities. She also lectures in the field of new and alternative religions with the Open University and Kingston University. Her Ph.D. research at Cambridge University explored the popularization and development of yoga and Ayurvedic medicine in Britain. She has a M.Sc. in Religion in Contemporary Society from the LSE and a B.A. in Religion from Amherst College, USA. She has published a number of articles in places such as the *Journal of Contemporary Religion, Religion Compass*, and *Asian Medicine*.

Energy

Wilson Niwagila   Wilson Niwagila was born in Bukoba, Tanzania, and later studied theology in Tanzania, the United States, and Germany. He became a Lutheran parish pastor in several congregations in Tanzania and Germany. In Tanzania, he was the Lutheran secretary for Christian Education, the director of the Evangelical Academy, and provost of Makumira University College. He resided in Germany for a period as the Executive Secretary for Evangelism of the United Evangelical Mission for Germany, Asia, and Africa. Upon his return to Tanzania, he served as a member of the Task-Force for the establishment of the Bishop Josiah Kibira University College of the Tumaini University in the Kagera Region–Tanzania.

Evangelical Lutheran Church in Tanzania

Lionel Obadia Lionel Obadia is a professor in anthropology at the Université Lyon 2 Lumière, France. A specialist in religions and Asian traditions, he has written more than fifty articles on the diffusion of Buddhism, religion in general, and religion and globalization. He is the author of several books including Bouddhisme en Occident (1999), La religion (2004 – Korean translation in 2007), La sorcellerie (2005), Bouddhisme et Occident (2007 – Italian translation 2009) and L'Anthropologie des religions (2007 – Greek translation in 2008).

Diamond Way Buddhism
France
Kagyupa Tibetan Buddhism
Karma-Kagyupa Tibetan Buddhism

Paul O'Callaghan Paul O'Callaghan holds a Masters in Engineering Science (Electronics) from University College Dublin (1979), was ordained a Roman Catholic priest (1982), and received a Doctor in theology from the University of Navarre (1987). He taught theology at the University of Navarre (1985–90) and since 1990 at the Pontifical University of the Holy Cross, Rome. He occupied the posts of Vice-Rector at "Sedes Sapientiae" International Ecclesiastical College (1991–95), Academic Vice-Rector of the Pontifical University of the Holy Cross (1997–2000), and Dean of the School of Theology of the same University (2000–2008). He is a member of the Governing Council of the Pontifical Academy of Theology. He is Professor of Theological Anthropology at the University of the Holy Cross since 1998. He has authored seven books and more than sixty articles in specialized journals in the areas of anthropology, creation theology, eschatology, theological epistemology and Lutheran theology.

Angels
Death

Javier Farcia Oliva Javier García Oliva studied law at the University of Cadiz, where he obtained his first degree, LL.M and Ph.D. After finishing his first degree, he became a lecturer at the University of Cadiz (1996–2000) and a research fellow at the Centre for Law and Religion at Cardiff University (2001–2004). Javier was appointed lecturer at the University of Wales Bangor in 2004 where he is currently Head of Public Law as well as the Course Leader of Law with Modern Languages. He is also a Research Associate at the Centre for Law and Religion at Cardiff University and he is teaching on a part-time basis at University College London (UCL). Furthermore, he is the convenor of the SLS Public Law Section and book review editor of *Law and Justice*.

Religion-Government Relations

Roger E. Olson Roger E. Olson holds a Ph.D. from Rice University in Houston, Texas. He is author of several books on theology including *The Story of Christian Theology: Twenty Centuries of Tradition & Reform* (InterVarsity Press, 1999). Olson is currently professor of theology at Baylor University in Waco, Texas, and has written articles and essays on new and alternative religious movements.

ECKANKAR

Frands Ole Overgaard Frands Ole Overgaard teaches church history in the Theological Faculty of Aarhus University in Denmark.

Evangelical Lutheran Church in Denmark

David A. Palmer David A. Palmer is assistant professor in the Department of Sociology at Hong Kong University. Trained in anthropology, psychology, and religious studies, he received his Ph.D. from the Ecole Pratique des Hautes Etudes (Sorbonne, Paris) in 2002. He was the Eileen Barker Fellow in Religion and Contemporary Society at the London School of Economics and Political Science and a research fellow at the Ecole Française d'Extrême-Orient (French School of Asian Studies), where he was director of its Hong Kong center from 2004 to 2008. He is the author of *Qigong Fever: Body, Science and Utopia in China* (Columbia University Press, 2007), which was awarded the Francis Hsu Prize for the best book in the Anthropology of East Asia. His forthcoming book projects include the textbook *Chinese Religious Life: Culture,*

Society and Politics; *The Religious Question in Modern China;* and *Dream Trippers: Global Daoism and the Predicament of Modern Spirituality.*

Energy
Qigong

Susan Palmer   Susan Palmer is a lecturer in the religious studies department of Dawson College in Montreal, Quebec, and is a lecturer and research associate at Concordia University in Montreal. She has authored, edited, or coedited nine books, notably *Moon Sisters, Krishna Mothers, Rajneesh Lovers* (Syracuse University Press, 1996), *Children in New Religions* (coedited with Charlotte Hardman; Rutgers University Press, 1999), *Millennium, Messiahs and Mayhem* (coedited with Thomas Robbins, 1998) and *The New Heretics of France*, forthcoming with Oxford University Press. She is currently researching government raids on new religions for a book with Stuart Wright.

Raelian Movement International
Twelve Tribes

Rafael Palomino   Rafael Palomino earned his Ph.D. from the Universidad Complutense de Madrid in 1993, where he is currently professor of law and researcher of the Institute of Human Rights, and a member of the advisory council, ODIHR Panel of Experts on Freedom of Religion or Belief (OSCE). He is author of *Las Objeciones de Conciencia* (*Conflicts between Religious Conscience and Law in the United States of America*; Montecorvo, 1994) and coauthor of *Estado y Religión: Textos para una Reflexión Crítica* (*History of Church-State Relations*; Ariel, 2003).

Spanish Evangelical Church
Spanish Reformed Episcopal Church

Michael Papazian   Michael Papazian is associate professor of philosophy at Berry College at Mt. Berry, Georgia. He is the author of the book *Light from Light: An Introduction to the History and Theology of the Armenian Church* (SIS Publications, 2006) as well as numerous articles on ancient philosophy and Armenian Christianity.

Armenian Apostolic Church (Holy See of Etchmiadzin)
Armenian Apostolic Church (See of the Great House of Cilicia)

Ronan Alves Pereira   Ronan Alves Pereira is professor of Japanese studies at the University of Brasilia, where he was also the chair of its Center for Asian Studies. He has taught and done research on Japanese religions in Japan, USA, Brazil, and New Zealand. His publications include *Spirit Possession and Cultural Innovation: The Religious Experience of Miki Nakayama and Nao Deguchi* (in Portuguese, 1992) and *Japanese Religions in and beyond the Japanese Diaspora* (with Hideaki Matsuoka; University of California-Berkeley, 2007).

Brazil, Japanese religions in

Thomas V. Peterson   Thomas V. Peterson teaches religious studies at Alfred University. Author of *Ham and Japheth: The Mythic World of Whites in the Antebellum South* (Scarecrow Press, 1978) and *Linked Arms: A Rural Community Resists Nuclear Waste* (SUNY Press, 2001), he has written articles on ritual studies, religion and art, religion and homosexuality, and Native American studies.

Lakota, The
Navajo, The

Lopen Karma Phuntsho   Lopen Karma Phuntsho was trained as a monk and holds a Lopen degree from the Nyingma Institute in Mysore and a M.St. in classical Indian religions from Oxford. He is currently writing his Ph.D. thesis and is an associate in Indian and Sanskrit studies at Harvard University and the Centre National de la Recherche Scientifique (CNRS) in Paris. His expertise is in Tibetan Buddhism and his publications include *Steps to Valid Reasoning: A Treatise in Logic and Epistemology* (Ngagyur Nyingma Institute, 1997).

Bhutan

William L. Pitts Jr.   Bill Pitts directs the graduate program in religion and teaches church history at

Baylor University. His professional work focuses on American religious history. He has published in the areas of historiography, spirituality, Baptist history, and new religious movements, including numerous articles on the Davidians and Branch Davidians.

Branch Davidians

John Powers John Powers holds a Ph.D. from the University of Virginia in Buddhist Studies. He is currently professor and head of the Centre for Asian Societies and Histories at Australian National University.

China: Tibet
Gelukpa
Sakyapa
Tibetan Buddhism

Charles S. Prebish Charles S. Prebish holds a Ph.D. in Buddhist studies from the University of Wisconsin. He currently holds the Charles Redd Endowed Chair in Religious Studies at Utah State University. He is a past officer in the International Association of Buddhist Studies and has published more than twenty books. He is best known for his books *Buddhist Monastic Discipline* (Penn State University Press, 1975) and *Luminous Passage: The Practice and Study of Buddhism in America* (University of California Press, 1999).

Insight Meditation Society
Kwan Um School of Zen

Carolyn V. Prorok Carolyn V. Prorok is a professional geographer specializing in the study of sacred places, pilgrimage, and the Hindu diaspora. She has authored book chapters and scholarly articles on these subjects such as, "Transplanting Pilgrimage Traditions in the Americas," in the *Geographical Review*, 93:3:283–307.

Arya Samaj
Divine Life Society
Espiritismo
Iran
Ireland

Presbyterian Church in Trinidad
Trinidad and Tobago, Hinduism in

Kaisa Puhakka Kaisa Puhakka is professor of psychology at the California Institute of Integral Studies in San Francisco where she teaches psychotherapy, Buddhist thought and meditation, and transformation of consciousness. She received her Ph.D. in experimental psychology from the University of Toledo and a postdoctoral diploma in clinical psychology from Adelphi University. She has authored a number of articles and is the coeditor (with Tobin Hart and Peter Nelson) of *Transpersonal Knowing: Exploring the Horizon of Consciousness* (2000). She previously served a term as the editor of *The Journal of Transpersonal Psychology*.

Meditation

Paulson Pulikottil Paulson Pulikottil is a professor at Union Biblical Seminary, Pune, India. He earned his Ph.D. from Sheffield University in 1995 and is currently a member of the World Council of Churches Joint Consultative Group with Pentecostals.

Indian Pentecostal Church of God
Pentecostal Mission, The

Kęstutis Pulokas Kęstutis Pulokas is the chair of the Lithuanian Bible Reading Society (a member of the Scripture Union) and a board member of the Cultural and Historical Society of the Reformation in Lithuania. In 1993 he attended summer courses in Lutheran Theology at Concordia Seminary in St. Louis, Missouri, and from 1993 to 1994 served as editor of *Liuteronu balsas*, the bimonthly publication of the Vilnius Evangelical Lutheran Church. He later graduated from the Philological Faculty of Vilnius University in 1994.

Evangelical Lutheran Church of Lithuania/Lithuanian
    Evangelical Lutheran Church in Diaspora

Kevin Quast For the past twenty-five years, Dr. Kevin Quast has taught in the area of religious studies at colleges, universities, and seminaries across Canada.

Presently, he teaches part-time for Tyndale Seminary (Toronto) and lives in Edmonton, Alberta, Canada. Dr. Quast has published 3 books and more than 100 articles and chapters in academic and popular journals. In addition to his teaching and writing, he has served as a pastor, chaplain and academic dean.

Advent
Ascension Day
Christmas
Easter
Epiphany
Holy Week
Lent
Liturgical Year
Pentecost

Martin Ramstedt Martin Ramstedt holds a Ph.D. in anthropology from Munich University. From 1997 to 2001 he worked as a research fellow at the International Institute for Asian Studies in Leiden, the Netherlands, pursuing research on Hinduism and ethnic religions in modern Indonesia. Since late 2001, he has worked as a research fellow at the Meertens Instituut in Amsterdam, focusing on new forms of religiosity and transcultural religious movements in the Netherlands. He also teaches at the Theological Department at Nijmegen University.

Indonesia, Buddhism in
Indonesia, Confucianism in
Indonesia, Hinduism in

Kari Rantila Kari Rantila is a chief editor, translator, and university teacher with the Finnish Orthodox Church.

Finnish Orthodox Church

Jeremy Rapport Jeremy Rapport is the visiting assistant professor of religious studies at the College of Wooster where he teaches classes on American Religious History and New Religious Movements.

Seventh-day Adventist Church
Universal Faithists of Kosmon
URANTIA Foundation

Ian Reader Ian Reader is professor of Japanese studies at the University of Manchester. Formerly he was professor in religious studies at Lancaster University in England, and he has also worked at universities and research institutes in Japan, Scotland, Hawaii, and Denmark. He has written extensively about religion in Japan and specializes in the study of pilgrimages and of religion in the modern day.

Aum Shinrikyô/Aleph
Japan
Pilgrimage

David A. Reed David A. Reed is professor emeritus of pastoral theology and research professor at Wycliffe College, University of Toronto, Canada. Reared in the Oneness Pentecostal Tradition and now an Anglican minister and theologian, he began his study of the Oneness movement with a doctoral thesis completed in 1978. He is currently writing a book on the Chinese-founded True Jesus Church, whose doctrines of God and salvation are similar to Oneness Pentecostalism.

Church of the Lord Jesus Christ of the Apostolic Faith

Terry Rey Formerly professeur de sociologie des religions at l'Université d'Etat d'Haïti, Terry Rey is associate professor and chair of religion at Temple University. He is author of *Our Lady of Class Struggle* and *Bourdieu on Religion* and co-editor of *Òrìsà Devotion as World Religion and Churches and Charity in the Immigrant City*. Currently he researches the intersections of violence and religion in Haiti and the Congo.

Haiti
Vodou

Keith Richmond Keith Richmond is an historian with a special interest in the Tibetan Bon religion. He has contributed papers on the subject to a number of conferences and journals and is currently completing his Ph.D. at Monash University in Melbourne, Australia.

Bon Religion
Nyingma Tibetan Buddhism

Bernadette Rigal-Cellard Bernadette Rigal-Cellard is professor of North American studies at the University of Bordeaux (France) where she also chairs an interdisciplinary master program in religious studies. She is a specialist of North American religions: in particular NRMs and native Christianity. She has published widely in the field and has edited: *Sectes, Églises, Mystiques: échanges, conquêtes, métamorphoses* (Pleine Page, 2004), *Missions extrêmes en Amérique du Nord: des Jésuites à* Bordeaux (Pleine Page, 2005), *Religions et mondialisation: exil, expansion, résistances (*PUB, 2009), and with Christian Lerat *Les mutations transatlantiques des religions* (PUB, 2000).

Apostles of Infinite Love
Creationism
Native American Religion: Roman Catholicsim

Ringo Ringvee Ringo Ringvee earned his M.A. in theology from the University of Helsinki in 1998. He has been giving courses in several institutions of higher education in Estonia, focusing on religion in contemporary society and on the religious situation in post-Soviet Estonia. He is currently working in the Department of Religious Affairs of the Ministry of Internal Affairs of the Estonian Republic.

Estonia
Estonian Apostolic Orthodox Church
Estonian Evangelical Lutheran Church
Estonian Evangelical Lutheran Church Abroad
Estonian Orthodox Church of Moscow Patriarchate

Ronald Roberson Ronald Roberson holds a doctorate from the Pontifical Oriental Institute in Rome. He is currently an associate director of the Secretariat for Ecumenical and Interreligious Affairs at the United States Conference of Catholic Bishops in Washington, D.C., where he specializes in relations with the Orthodox Churches. He is the author of *The Eastern Christian Churches: A Brief Survey* (7th ed., Pontifical Oriental Institute, 2008).

Ecumenical Patriarchate/Patriarchate of Constantinople
Greek Orthodox Patriarchate of Alexandria and All Africa

Greek Orthodox Patriarchate of Antioch and All the East
Greek Orthodox Patriarchate of Jerusalem
Orthodox Church of Greece

James Burnell Robinson James Burnell Robinson is associate professor of religion at the University of Northern Iowa in Cedar Falls, Iowa. He received his doctorate from the University of Wisconsin at Madison in the area of Buddhist studies with a specialty in Tibetan Buddhism but has since broadened his research to include esoteric religious movements in the West as well. He is presently researching the history of the idea of spiritual hierarchy from a cross-cultural perspective.

Anthroposophical Society
Christian Community

Cristina Rocha Dr. Cristina Rocha teaches at the School of Humanities and Languages, University of Western Sydney, Australia. She is the editor of the *Journal of Global Buddhism*. Her writings include *Zen in Brazil: the Quest for Cosmopolitan Modernity* (University of Hawaii Press, 2006) and *Buddhism in Australia: Traditions in Change* (co-edited with Michelle Barker) (Routledge, 2010) and numerous scholarly articles.

Globalization, Religion and
John of God Movement

Darrin J. Rodgers Darrin J. Rodgers is editor of *Assemblies of God Heritage* magazine and is director of the Flower Pentecostal Heritage Center in Springfield, Missouri.

Assemblies of God

David G. Roebuck David G. Roebuck, Ph.D., is the director of the Dixon Pentecostal Research Center in Cleveland, Tennessee, which serves as the archives for the Church of God. He is an assistant professor of religion at Lee University and also teaches at the Church of God Theological Seminary.

Church of God (Cleveland, Tennessee)

Verónica Roldán Verónica Roldán, has a Ph.D. in sociology and methodology of social science, is professor of sociology at Link Campus University of Malta, Rome; professor of methodology at the Università di Roma Tre and professor of sociology of religious experience at the Pontifical University of Seraphicum, Rome. She is co-author with M. Introvigne, P.L., Zoccatelli and N. Ippolito Macrina of *Enciclopedia delle religioni in Italia* (Elledici, 2001), and she is the author of different articles and books on new religious movements, including *La Chiesa Anima Universale* (Elledici, 2000), *Il rinnovamento carismatico cattolico. Uno studio comparativo Argentina-Italia* (FrancoAngeli, 2009).

Iglesia ni Cristo

Eric Rommeluère Eric Rommeluère is a lecturer and the vice president of the European Buddhist University, an institute for the studies on Buddhism, founded in Paris in 1995. Eric Rommeluère's various publications are about Chan/Zen Buddhism and the acculturation of Buddhism in the West.

Rinzai (Japan), Lin-Chi (China), Imje (Korea), Lam-Te (Vietnam)

Mikael Rothstein Mikael Rothstein is an associate professor in the Department of Cross Cultural and Regional Studies, section for the History of Religions at the University of Copenhagen, Denmark, where he specializes in the study of new religions of the West and the religions of indigenous peoples in Borneo and Hawai'i. Among his several books are *Belief Transformations* (RENNER Studies on New Religions, 1996), *I culti die dischi volanti* (Flying saucer religions; Elledici, 1999), and edited *New Age Religion and Globalization* (RENNER Studies on New Religions, 2001).

Denmark
UFO Religions

Richard C. Salter Richard C. Salter is an assistant professor of religious studies at Hobart and William Smith Colleges in Geneva, New York. From 1986 to 1988 he was a Peace Corps volunteer in Dominica,

and in 1994 he returned there for dissertation research. His dissertation was on religious group formation in Dominica.

Dominica

Russell Sandberg Russell Sandberg is a lecturer at Cardiff Law School and an associate of both the Centre for Law and Religion and the Centre for the Study of Islam in the UK, Cardiff University. After graduating from Cardiff Law School with First Class Honours in July 2005, he commenced doctoral study at Cardiff University examining the relationship between religion, law, and society. He has written widely on religion and human rights, discrimination law, religious dress, and Church-State relations for a wide range of journals including *Public Law*, *Law Quarterly Review*, *Cambridge Law Journal*, the *Modern Law Review* and the *Ecclesiastical Law Journal*. He is co-editor, with Norman Doe, of *Law and Religion: New Horizons* (Leuven, Peeters, 2009).

Religion-Government Relations

Tiago Santos Tiago Santos graduated in sociology from the Universidade Nova de Lisboa in 1997. He was already a research assistant at the time and has since always worked in the craft. In 2001 he became a founding associate of Numena, an independent research center. He currently holds a scholarship from the Fundação para a Ciência e Tecnologia for his work on elective affinities.

Lusitanian Church (Lusitanian Catholic Apostolic Evangelical Church)
Portugal

James A. Santucci James A. Santucci received his Ph.D. in Asian civilization from the Department of Asian Civilizations at the Australian National University in Canberra. He is currently a professor in the Department of Religious Studies at California State University at Fullerton. He is the author of *La società teosofica* (Elledici, 1999) and *Hindu Art in South and Southeast Asia, An Outline of Vedic Literature* (Scholars Press, 1976), and coauthor of *America's Religions*

(Libraries Unlimited, 1997) and most recently of *An Educator's Classroom Guide to America's Religious Beliefs and Practices* (2007). He has written numerous articles for journals and encyclopedias and is currently editor of *Theosophical History*, a quarterly journal.

Reincarnation
Theosophical Society (Adyar)

Peter A. Schalk   Peter Schalk is a professor of the history of religions at Uppsala University. Since receiving his Ph.D. from Lund University in 1972, he has specialized in research on Hinduism and Buddhism, and is at present leading a project on the concept of martyrdom in South Asian religions and political resistance movements.

Martyrdom

Jeffrey M. Schwartz   Jeffrey M. Schwartz, M.D., is a research psychiatrist at the University of California at Los Angeles School of Medicine. He is the author of three books and approximately 100 scientific publications in the fields of neuroscience, psychiatry, and most recently, philosophy of mind and Buddhist meditation. He has maintained a regular practice of Vipassana meditation since 1975.

Buddhasasananuggaha Association

Ruediger Seesemann   Ruediger Seesemann specializes in Islamic studies and works as a research fellow at the University of Bayreuth in Germany. His current research topics include the development of the Tijâniyya Sufi Order in West Africa and Islamic education in East Africa.

Murîdiyya
Tijaniyya Sufi Order

Gaynor Sekimori   Gaynor Sekimori was a research fellow at the Centre for the Study of Japanese Religions at the School of Oriental and African Studies of the University of London from 2000 to 2001 and since November 2001, an associate professor at the University of Tokyo. His research interests include Shugendō,

Japanese combinatory religion, religious art, and gender and religion.

Shugendo

Michael Shermer   Michael Shermer is the founding publisher of *Skeptic* magazine, a monthly columnist for *Scientific American*, and an adjunct professor at Claremont Graduate University. Dr. Shermer's latest book is *The Mind of the Market*, on evolutionary economics. His last book was *Why Darwin Matters: Evolution and the Case Against Intelligent Design*, and he is the author of *The Science of Good and Evil* and of *Why People Believe Weird Things*. Dr. Shermer received his B.A. in psychology from Pepperdine University, M.A. in experimental psychology from California State University, Fullerton, and his Ph.D. in the history of science from Claremont Graduate University (1991). He was a college professor for 20 years, and since his creation of *Skeptic* magazine he has appeared on such shows as *The Colbert Report*, *20/20*, *Dateline*, *Charlie Rose*, and *Larry King Live* (but, proudly, never *Jerry Springer*!). Dr. Shermer was the co-host and co-producer of the 13-hour Family Channel television series, *Exploring the Unknown*.

Agnosticism

Steven L. Shields   Steven L. Shields is the founder of Restoration Research and the Center for the Study of the Latter Day Saint Movement, organizations focusing research and publication on the many splinters of the Latter Day Saints community. He is the author of *Divergent Paths of the Restoration* (4th ed., Herald Publishing House, 2001).

Independence, Missouri
Community of Christ

Larry Dwight Shinn   Larry Dwight Shinn is currently president of Berea College, a liberal arts college in Berea, Kentucky, that is dedicated to serving the Appalachian region. He received his Ph.D. in history of religions from Princeton University, taught at Oberlin College for 14 years, and served as dean and vice president at Bucknell University for 10 years. He has authored 2 books: *Two Sacred Worlds: Experience and Structure in the World Religions* (Abingdon, 1977) and *The Dark Lord: Cult Images and the Hare Krishnas in America* (Westminster John Knox Press, 1987), has coauthored and edited 4 other books, and has written more than 30 published articles.

International Society for Krishna Consciousness

Marat S. Shterin   Marat Shterin holds a Ph.D. in sociology from the London School of Economics and Political Science (LSE) and is currently lecturer in the sociology of religion at King's College London, UK. His research is concerned with various aspects of religion and society in Russia and Britain, in particular religions of ethnic minorities, new religious movements, church–state relations, and religion and conflict. He was the co-editor of *Dying for Faith: Religiously Motivated Violence in the Contemporary World* (Tauris, 2009), and recently completed a monograph on religion in post-Soviet Russia.

Great White Brotherhood
Moscow
Mother of God Centre
Old Believers (Russia)
Russia
Russia, Islam in
Russia, Protestantism in

Elijah Siegler   Elijah Siegler received his B.A. from Harvard University and his M.A. from the University of California at Santa Barbara, both in religious studies. He is currently completing his doctorate at UCSB, writing on the history and practice of Daoism in America. His published works include articles on religion on television police dramas and on New Age channeling groups, and a book, *New Religious Movements* (2006).

Chinese Daoist Association
Chinese Religions
Daoism
Healing Tao
Quanzhen Daoism
Taoist Tai Chi Society
Zhengyi Daoism

Karl Sigurbjörnsson   The Most Reverent Karl Sigurbjörnsson became the Lutheran bishop of Iceland in 1998. Prior to that time he was pastor of Hallgrimskirkja, Reykjavík. Born in 1947, he served in the parish ministry in Iceland from 1973 to 1997. He is the author and translator of several books on the subject of prayer and pastoral care. In 2000, he was awarded an honorary decree in theology by the faculty of theology at the University of Iceland.

Evangelical Lutheran Church in Iceland

Pataraporn Sirikanchana   Pataraporn Sirikanchana holds a Ph.D. in religious studies from the University of Pennsylvania and presently works as chairperson of the Department of Philosophy at Thammasat University, as an advisor for the World Fellowship of Buddhists, and as board member of the Thai Royal Academy. Her publications include *Fundamental Knowledge of Religion* and articles on religion and philosophy both in Thai and in English.

Buddhist Association of Thailand
Dhammakaya Foundation
Santi Asoka
Thailand
World Fellowship of Buddhists

Jaroslav Z. Skira   Jaroslav Z. Skira is an associate professor of historical theology and director of the Eastern Christian Studies Program at Regis College, University of Toronto, Canada.

Roman Catholic Church
Saints

Margareta Skog   Margareta Skog, M.A., is a researcher on the sociology of religion at the Church of Sweden in Uppsala, Sweden. Her studies comprise religious communities beside the Church of Sweden, as the Free Churches, immigrant religions, new religions, and new religiosity.

Sweden

Pedro Soares   Pedro Soares is a social psychologist whose research has focused on minority and messianic religious movements in Portugal. He is the coeditor of *The Experience of the Sacred* (Hugin, 1998) and *Science and the Primacy of Consciousness* (Noetic Press, 2000).

Lusitanian Church/Lusitanian Catholic Apostolic
   Evangelical Church
Portugal

Marika Speckmann   Marika Speckmann received her M.A. degree in study of religions, ethnology, and archaeology at the Philipps Universität Marburg in 1998. Most recently, she has worked in completing her doctoral dissertation concerned with Native American mythology and its meaning for non-American Indian (industrial) cultures.

National Spiritualist Association of Churches
Native American Church

Paul Stange   Paul Stange completed his Ph.D. in history at the University of Wisconsin-Madison. He retired in 2004 after 30 years of teaching Asian studies at Murdoch and Curtin universities in Perth, Australia and at Satyawacana, Malang, and Gadjah Mada universities in Indonesia. He contributed a chapter to the *Cambridge History of Southeast Asia* (Cambridge University Press, 1992), over a dozen essays in scholarly journals, and books (in Indonesian) titled: *The Politics of Attention: Intuition in Javanese Culture* (LKiS, Yogyakarta, 1998), *Modern Javanism: Truth in Sumarah Practice* (LKiS, Yogyakarta, 2009), and *Ancestral Voices in Island Asia* (LKiS, Yogyakarta, forthcoming).

Javanism
Sumarah

Stephen J. Stein   Stephen J. Stein is Chancellors' Professor of Religious Studies and adjunct professor of history at Indiana University in Bloomington. His research interests center on eighteenth-century American intellectual history and on dissenting religious communities throughout American history. He is author of the definitive study *The Shaker Experience in America: A History of the United Society of Believers* (Yale University Press, 1992).

United Society of Believers in Christ's Second Appearing

C. Mark Steinacher   C. Mark Steinacher is a faculty member at Tyndale Seminary, Toronto, Canada. His doctoral dissertation examined the 'Christian Connexion,' a North American Restorationist group, while his Master of Theology thesis analyzed the process of Methodist disunion and reunion in nineteenth-century central Canada. Chaos-Complexity Theory, ecclesiology, eschatology, the Fundamentalist-Modernist conflict, pacifism and religious freedom are his principal research interests.

Evangelicalism
Fundamentalism
Monasticism

H. Christina Steyn   Dr. H. Christina Steyn is senior lecturer in the Department of Religious Studies at the University of South Africa where she specializes in new and alternative religious movements.

South Africa

Robert Stockman   Robert Stockman has a doctorate in history of religion in the United States from Harvard University. He is the author of *The Bahá'í Faith in America, I* (Bahá'í Publishing Trust, 1985) and *The Bahá'í Faith in America, II* (George Ronald, 1994), *Thornton Chase: The First American Bahá'í* (Bahá'í Publishing Trust, 2002), as well as various articles about Bahá'í history and theology. Currently he is director of the Wilmette Institute, an online Bahá'í educational institution, as well as an instructor in religious studies at DePaul University.

Baha'i Faith

Martin Stuart-Fox   Martin Stuart-Fox is emeritus professor in the School of History, Philosophy, Religion and Classics at the University of Queensland, Australia. His publications include *A History of Laos* (Cambridge University Press, 1997), *The Murderous Revolution: Life & Death in Pol Pot's Kampuchea*

(3rd ed., Orchid Press, 1998), and (with R. S. Bucknell) *The Twilight Language: Explorations in Buddhist Meditation and Symbolism* (St. Martin's Press, 1986).

Lao Buddhist Sangha
Laos

William H. Swatos Jr. William H. Swatos Jr. is executive officer of the Association for the Sociology of Religion and of the Religious Research Association. He received his Ph.D. in sociology from the University of Kentucky and was named a distinguished alumnus of that department in 1989. With Loftur Reimar Gissurarson, he is the author of *Icelandic Spiritualism: Mediumship and Modernity* (Transaction, 1996).

Iceland

Vinson Synan Vinson Synan, Ph.D., is dean emeritus of the School of Divinity at Regent University in Virginia Beach, Virginia. He is author of 17 books on Pentecostalism and the Charismatic renewal. His major works include his dissertation, *Holiness Pentecostal Movement*, which he wrote in 1967 while attending the University of Georgia. He also wrote *The Century of the Holy Spirit* (Thomas Nelson, 2001).

Yoido Full Gospel Church

Gyorgy Endre Szönyi Gyorgy E. Szönyi is professor of English (Szeged) and intellectual history (CEU, Budapest). His interests include the Renaissance, the Western Esoteric traditions, and cultural theory and symbolization. Recent monographs include: *Pictura & Scriptura: 20th-Century Theories of Cultural Representations* (in Hungarian, Szeged, 2004); *John Dee's Occultism* (Albany: SUNY Press, 2004). Edited works include: *European Iconography East & West* (Leiden, 1996); *The Iconography of Power* (with Rowland Wymer, Szeged, 2000); "The Voices of the English Renaissance," *Hungarian Journal of English and American Studies* 11.1 (2005); and *The Iconology of Gender* (with Attila Kiss, Szeged, 2008).

Dee, John

Martin Tamcke Martin Tamcke holds a Ph.D. in theology and did post-graduate studies on the history of Eastern Christianity. He is professor for ecumenical theology at the University of Göttingen in Germany and director of the Institute for the History of Oriental Churches and Missions. His studies focus on the past and present of Asian churches. He was recently awarded a Dr.H.C. in Intercultural Theology.

Syrian Orthodox Church of Malabar

Francesca Tarocco Francesca Tarocco lectures on Chinese religions at the Department of the Study of Religions at the School of Oriental and African Studies (SOAS) at the University of London, and on Buddhism at Manchester University. Her research interests include Buddhist apocrypha, Buddhist religious practice in East Asia, and the intellectual history of modern Chinese Buddhism.

Chinese Buddhist Association

Gordon Taylor Gordon Taylor graduated from the University of London in 1972. He served on the staff of the Greater London Council from 1965 to 1986 prior to moving to the international headquarters of The Salvation Army as a researcher in the Literary Department, a position he held from 1986 to 1988. He became a senior researcher at the Army's International Heritage Centre from 1988 to 1997 and since 1997 has been the archivist. He is the author of the *Companion to the Song Book of The Salvation Army* (The Salvation Army International Headquarters, 1989).

Salvation Army

Gene R. Thursby Gene R. Thursby is an emeritus professor of religion with the Department of Religion at the University of Florida. He is the author of *Hindu-Muslim Relations in British India* (Brill, 1975) and *The Sikhs* (Brill, 1992) and the co-editor of *The Hindu World* (Routledge, 2004), *Religions of South Asia* (Routledge, 2006), and *Studying Hinduism* (Routledge, 2008).

Astrology, Hindu
Siddha Yoga
Temples—Hindu

Donald Tinder   Donald Tinnder earned his Ph.D. at Yale and served in various ministries in America while a preacher among the Brethren. He and his wife moved to Europe in 1988 as Brethren missionaries. He served as a professor at Tyndale Seminary, Amsterdam, and Evangelical Theological Faculty, Louvain, Belgium. In 2010 they moved back to America where he is a professor at Olivet Theological Seminary, San Francisco.

Christian Brethren

Francis V. Tiso   Father V. Tiso, a Roman Catholic priest of the Diocese of Isernia-Venafro, Italy, serves (since September 6, 2009) as pastor of the parish of St. Michael in Fornelli. He earned a master of divinity degree (cum laude) at Harvard University and holds a doctorate from Columbia University and Union Theological Seminary where he specialized in Buddhist studies. He served as the Diocesan Delegate for Ecumenical and Inter-religious Affairs (1990–1998) and rector of the Istituto Diocesano delle Scienze Religiose. He was subsequently assigned to the Archdiocese of San Francisco as Parochial Vicar of St. Thomas More Church and chaplain at San Francisco State University and the University of California Medical School. In 2004 he became associate director of the Secretariat for Ecumenical and Interreligious Affairs of the US Conference of Catholic Bishops (2004–2009) and worked as liaison to Islam, Hinduism, Buddhism, the Sikhs, and traditional religions as well as the Reformed confessions.

Asceticism
Spirit Possession

Péter Török   Péter Török received his Ph.D. from the University of Toronto. His research interests include church-state relationships, mental health in social context, and new religious movements. He is currently the director of the Institute of Mental Health at the Semmelweis University, Budapest (Hungary).

Hungary

Will Tuladhar-Douglas   Will Tuladhar-Douglas lectures in the anthropology of environment and religions at the University of Aberdeen and is the director of the Scottish Centre for Himalayan Research.

Newar Buddhism

Frank Usarski   Frank Usarski, Ph.D., lectured on religionswissenschaft (comparative religion) at the universities of Hannover, Oldenburg, Bremen, Erfurt, Chemnitz, and Leizig, between 1988 and 1997. Since 1998, he has been professor at the Pontifical Catholic University of São Paulo, Brazil.

Brazil
Candomblé
Spiritism
Umbanda

Gerard van't Spijker   Dr. Gerard van't Spijker earned his Ph.D. in 1990 from the Free University of Amsterdam, the Netherlands. He was the theological advisor of the Presbyterian Church in Rwanda from 1973 to 1982 and from 1995 to 1999 the coordinator of the Ecumenical Center for Theological Education and Research in Butare, Rwanda. He was research fellow of the Interuniversity Institute for Missiological and Ecumenical Research, at the University of Utrecht, the Netherlands (1999–2004). Now retired, he is visiting professor at theological faculties in Yaounde (Cameroun) and Butare (Rwanda).

Rwanda

Carmen Voigt-Graf   Having completed an M.A. in geography at the Free University in Berlin, Carmen Voigt-Graf is currently working on her Ph.D. in geography at the University of Sydney. Her research interests concern diasporas and transnational communities, in particular the Indian diaspora in Australia, Fiji, and East Africa.

Fiji Islands, Hindu Community of the

Melitta Waligora   Melitta Waligora is a member of the staff of the Seminar for History and Society of South Asia at the Humboldt University of Berlin, Germany. Her teaching and research focus includes Indian modern philosophy, Bengal Renaissance, and gender studies.

Sri Aurobindo Ashram

Graham B. Walker Jr.   Graham B. Walker Jr. holds a Ph.D. degree in theology from the Southern Baptist Theological Seminary and serves as the associate dean of the McAfee School of Theology at Mercer University. For more than 18 years he lived and taught in Southeast Asia. He has authored numerous articles and edited journals related to Filipino religious experience. He is contributor and editor of *Human Fault and Cosmic Fault Lines: Southeast Asian Portraits of Evil* (Mercer University Press, forthcoming). Walker's current research focuses on the South Asian ritual of Thaipusam.

Philippines

Morten Warmind   Morten Warmind is an assistant professor and sociologist of religion with the Department of the History of Religions of the University of Copenhagen, Denmark. He specializes in the study of Celtic and old Norse religion.

Denmark

Helen Waterhouse   Helen Waterhouse is a senior lecturer in religious studies at the Open University in the United Kingdom. She has published on western Buddhism and on reincarnation belief in Britain. Her current chief research interests are British Buddhism and practice in religion and music.

New Kadampa Tradition

James Wellman   James Wellman is associate professor and Chair of the Comparative Religion at the University of Washington. He teaches American religious culture, history, and politics. He has published an award-winning book, *The Gold Church and the Ghetto: Christ and Culture in Mainline Protestantism* (Illinois, 1999). He has published two edited volumes, *The Power of Religious Publics: Staking Claims in*

American Society (Praegers, 1999); *Belief and Bloodshed: Religion and Violence Across Time and Tradition* (Rowman and Littlefield, 2007). His recent book, *Evangelical vs. Liberal: The Clash of Christian Cultures in the Pacific Northwest* (Oxford University Press, 2008) received Honorable Mention for the 2009 SSSR Distinguished Book Award.

Modernity
Secularization
Violence, Religious

Irving A. Whitt   Irving A. Whitt served as a missionary in Kenya from 1970 to 1980. He later chaired the Missions Department at Eastern Pentecostal Bible College in Canada from 1984 to 1991 and chaired the Missions Department at Tyndale Seminary in Toronto from 1991 to 2000. In 2000 he assumed the position of Missions Education Coordinator with the Pentecostal Assemblies of Canada. His masters and doctoral studies were completed in missions at Fuller Theological Seminary.

Pentecostal Assemblies of Canada

Donald Wiebe   Donald Wiebe is a professor of religious studies at Trinity College, University of Toronto. He has taken a primary interest in the problems of the academic and scientific study of religion, and method and theory in the study of religion. He is the author of *Religion and Truth: Towards and Alternative Paradigm for the Study of Religion* (Mouton De Gruyter, 1981), *The Irony of Theology and the Nature of Religious Thought* (McGill-Queens University Press, 1991), *Beyond Legitimation: Essays on the Problem of Religious Knowledge* (Palgrave, 1994), and *The Politics of Religious Studies: The Continuing Conflict with Theology in the Academy* (Palgrave, 1999). In 1985, with Luther H. Martin and E. Thomas Lawson, he cofounded the North American Association for the Study of Religion and has twice served as president of that association—from 1986 to 1987 and from 1991 to 1992.

Introductory Essay

Duncan Williams Duncan Williams is the Shinjo Ito Distinguished Chair of Japanese Buddhism and Director of the Center for Japanese Studies at UC Berkeley. He is the editor of *Buddhism and Ecology* (Harvard, 1997), *American Buddhism* (Curzon, 1999), and author of *The Other Side of Zen* (Princeton, 2005).

Soto Zen Buddhism

Raymond B. Williams Raymond B. Williams is Lafollette Distinguished Professor in the Humanities *Emeritus* at Wabash College and director emeritus of the Wabash Center for Teaching and Learning in Theology and Religion. He is founding editor of the journal *Teaching Theology and Religion.* His most recent book are *An Introduction to Swaminarayan Hinduism* (Cambridge University Press, 2000) and *Williams on South Asian Religions and Immigration* (Ashgate, 2004).

Swaminarayan Hinduism

Jane Williams-Hogan Jane Williams-Hogan earned her Ph.D. from the University of Pennsylvania. She is a professor of sociology, associate dean of graduate studies, and holds the Carpenter Chair in the history of religion at Bryn Athyn College in Bryn Athyn, Pennsylvania. She is the author of numerous articles on Emanuel Swedenborg, Swedenborgianism, and Swedenborg's impact on Western culture. Her book *Swedenborg e le Chiese swedenborgiane* in a series entitled "Religioni e Movimenti" was published by Elledici in 2003. She is currently writing a biography of Swedenborg titled *The Making of a Modern Visionary: Emanuel Swedenborg, Eyewitness to the Apocalypse.*

General Church of the New Jerusalem, The
Swedenborg, Emanuel
Swedenborgian Church of North America
Swedenborgian Movement

Robert S. Wilson Robert S. Wilson received his Ph.D. in British history from the University of Guelph in 1973. He served as the academic dean and professor of history at Atlantic Baptist University in Moncton, New Brunswick from 1971 to 1991, and as professor of church history at Acadia Divinity College since 1991. He is the chair of the Atlantic Baptist Heritage Series Editorial Committee.

Baptist Convention of Ontario and Quebec
Baptist Convention of Western Cuba
Canadian Baptist Ministries
Canadian Baptists of Western Canada
Union d'Églises Baptistes Françaises au Canada

Robert Winterhalter Robert Winterhalter served as president of the Society for the Study of Metaphysical Religion for 12 years (1993–2005). An ordained minister of Divine Science and Unity, he is on the faculty of the Divine Science School in Washington, DC. He has published four books, *The Odes of Solomon* (1986), *The Fifth Gospel* (1988), *Jesus' Parables: Finding Our God Within* (1993), and *The Healing Christ* (2010).

Divine Science Federation/United Divine Science
  Ministries, International

Ali Yaman Ali Yaman received his M.A. and Ph.D. in political history/international relations from Istanbul University. He is the author of six books and numerous articles on Alevism-Bektashism and religious and cultural life in Central Asia. He worked as an assistant professor in political history at Ahmed Yesevi International Turkish-Kazakh University in Turkestan, Kazakhstan, between 2002 and 2005, where he was also the head of the Cultural Studies Department at Yesevi Research Centre in Turkestan. Following his return to Turkey, he taught anthropology of religion at Yeditepe University in Istanbul and political and cultural history at Abant Izzet Baysal University in Bolu as assistant professor. His current teaching and research interests include Alevism-Bektashism, relations between religion, culture and politics of Central Asia and Anatolian studies.

Alevism

Serenity Young Serenity Young is a research associate with the anthropology department of the American Museum of Natural History in New York City. She is the author of *Dreaming in the Lotus: Buddhist Dream*

Narrative, Imagery and Practice (2001) and editor of the *Encyclopedia of Women and World Religion* (1998).

Enlightenment

Ahmad F. Yousif   Professor Ahmad F. Yousif, is currently teaching at the postgraduate International Institute of Islamic Thought and Civilization, Kuala Lumpur, Malaysia. He has previously taught at the University of Ottawa, University of Toronto at Mississauga, International Islamic University Malaysia, and University of Brunei Darussalam. Yousif is the author of three books, and numerous articles published in scholarly journals.

Brunei
Brunei, Islam in

Andrij Yurash   Andrij Yurash received his Ph.D in political science from the Ivan Franko L'viv National University and L'viv Theological Academy in the Ukraine. He is a member of the International Study of Religion in Eastern and Central Europe Association and the American Academy of Religion.

Ukraine
Ukraine, Eastern Orthodoxy in

PierLuigi Zoccatelli   PierLuigi Zoccatelli was born in Verona, Italy, in 1965, and currently works in Turin as deputy director of CESNUR, the Center for Studies on New Religions. He is also a member of the ESSWE (European Society for the Study of Western Esotericism) and of the AIS (Italian Society for the Sociology). He is the author of several articles and books on New Religious Movements and Western Esotericism, subjects on which he has lectured extensively in Italian and international academic and non-academic settings. He has been an associate editor of the monumental encyclopedia *Le religioni in Italia* ("Religions in Italy"; Elledici, 2006).

Army of Mary
Church of the Kingdom of God
Damanhur
Evangelical Baptist Union of Italy
Evangelical Methodist Church of Italy
Fraternity/Society of Saint Pius X
Gnostic Churches
Gnostic Movement
Grail Movement, The
Iglesia ni Cristo
Italian Assemblies of God
Lectorium Rosicrucianum
Martinism
Mazdaznan
New Apostolic Church
Ordo Templi Orientis
People of God
Sedevacantism and Antipopes
Seventh-day Adventist Reform Movement
Shri Ram Chandra Mission
Spiritual Human Yoga
Universal Church of the Kingdom of God
Universal Life
Universal Soul
Waldensian Church

Robert J. Zydenbos   Robert J. Zydenbos is professor of Indology at the University of Munich, Germany, and has previously held Indological teaching positions at universities in Heidelberg, Madras, and Toronto. His main research interests are Kannada language and literature, and the religious traditions of Karnataka, particularly Jainism, Madhva Vaisnavism, and Virasaivism.

Virasaivism

Editorial Board

Religions of the World

Second Edition

A COMPREHENSIVE ENCYCLOPEDIA
OF BELIEFS AND PRACTICES

Volume One: A–B

A

Abd al-Aziz ibn Sa'ud

ca. 1880–1953

Abd al-Aziz ibn Sa'ud was the founder of the modern state of Saudi Arabia. Emerging out of a family that had been identified with the conservative sectarian Wahhabi Islam, he was subsequently able to make an alliance with the highly committed Ikhwan Brotherhood. The Wahhabi and Ikhwan formed his power base for uniting the Arabian peninsula into one political entity that would include the most holy sites of the Islamic world, Mecca and Medina.

Abd al-Aziz was born in Riyadh around 1880 (the exact date, even the year, is a matter of continuing debate). At the time, his family had formed the Emirate of Najd in central Arabia with Riyadh as its capital. To the north and west, Najd touched the Ottoman Empire, which included the western part of the peninsula bordering the Red Sea and territory to the northeast that reached to the Persian Gulf. Between the lands of the Sa'ud clan and the Ottoman to the north lay the land of the Rachidi clan. In 1890, the Rachidi clan, with Ottoman backing, took over the Emirate of Najd and forced the Sa'ud family, including the youthful Abd al-Aziz, into exile in Kuwait.

Still in his early twenties, Abd al-Aziz began the effort to reestablish his family's power in 1901. His first measurable success was the recapture of Riyadh the following year. He subsequently recruited Bedouin tribesmen to form a new fighting force, the Ikhwan Brotherhood. The Ikhwan dedicated itself to both the purification and importantly the unification of Islam based on a belief that the fragmented tribal existence that still typified much of Arabian life was incompatible with practicing Islam correctly. The conquest of

Abd al-Aziz Ibn Sa'ud united the regions of Nedj and Hejaz on September 23, 1932, to create the independent kingdom of Saudi Arabia. (Library of Congress)

the peninsula would keep the Saudi forces in a state of war for more than two decades. Only after World War II, the fall of the Ottoman Empire, and an alliance with the British did Abd al-Aziz feel confident to march against his real enemy, the Rachidi clan. In 1926, Mecca and Medina fell, and subsequently the main religious authorities recognized Abd al-Aziz as the ruler over Hijaz and Najd, the western and central regions of Arabia, respectively. He now essentially ruled the land today known as Saudi Arabia. He had only one remaining task, the putting down of a rebellion among his own Ikhwan troops, an effort that took several years (1927–1930) before he was able to proclaim the founding of the new Kingdom of Saudi Arabia in 1932.

Abd al-Aziz proved as skillful a ruler as he was a military leader. As he attained power over different segments of the peninsula, he moved to create a unified state. He drew a variety of leaders into his circle of advisors and pushed a policy favoring intermarriage across clan and tribal lines. He built the religious component of his kingdom by favoring the leadership of the very conservative Hanbalite School (over against the more "liberal" Hanafite School of Islam) and maintaining close Sa'ud family ties to the equally conservative and even more radical Wahhabi leadership. At the same time he moved to modernize the kingdom, an effort that involved oil.

Saudi Arabia's rise to a powerful oil-producing nation began with Abd al-Aziz granting Standard Oil of California oil exploration rights in 1933. Oil was first discovered in 1938, and began flowing in 1939 just as World War II began. Though oil production was slowed by the war, Standard Oil moved to create a coalition of companies from its own factions along with the Texas Oil Company (Texaco) that emerged as ARAMCO, the Arab American Oil Company, then the largest oil company in the world. At the same time, Abd al-Aziz secured the bulk of the revenues for his large extended family. Islam allowed him to marry multiple wives, with whom he had a number of children.

At the close of World War II, he solidified a working relationship with the United States, a relationship symbolized by his personal meeting with President Franklin Roosevelt in 1945 on the deck of the *USS Quincy*. ARAMCO then became the instrument for building the country's modern infrastructure needed to extract and export the oil.

Since his death on November 9, 1953, Saudi Arabia has been ruled by Abd al-Aziz's descendants. His son and immediate successor King Sa'ud became intoxicated with the wealth and almost bankrupted the kingdom with his palatial lifestyle. He was removed from office in 1964 by a family coup that brought his brother Faisal to the throne. He proved an able ruler who invested the oil revenues in the country and a dedicated believer in Islamic faith and moral practice.

James R. Lewis

See also: Hanbalite School of Islam; Islam; Mecca; Wahhabi Islam.

References

Al-enazy, Askar H. *The Creation of Saudi Arabia: British Foreign Policy and Saudi Expansion, 1914–1927*. New York: Routledge, 2009.

McLoughlin, Leslie J. *Ibn Sa'ud: Founder of a Kingdom*. New York: St. Martin's Press, 1993.

Rashid, Medawi. *A History of Saudi Arabia*. Cambridge: Cambridge University Press, 2002.

Weston, Mark. *Prophets and Princes: Saudi Arabia from Muhammad to the Present*. New York: Wiley, 2008.

Abduh, Muhammad

1849–1905

Muhammad Abduh was an Egyptian scholar and jurist who emerged as the leader of a social reform movement in the Muslim world presenting a modernist interpretation of Islam. Abduh was born in 1849 to a modest family in lower Egypt. He was initially educated by a private tutor but at the age of 13 was enrolled at the Ahmadi mosque in Tanta. He left school without completing his course and later married. In 1866, he picked up his studies again by enrolling at Cairo's famous al-Azhar University. Concluding his studies in 1877, he began teaching at al-Azhar as a religious scholar. About the same time he became politically involved, fueled in part by the nationalist movement that wanted the British out of the country. Eventually he joined the 1882 Urabi Revolt, and when it failed he was exiled by the Egyptian authorities.

Abduh settled in Paris, where he renewed his acquaintance with Jamal al-din al-Afghani (1838–1897), whom he had met in Cairo in the 1870s. In 1884 the two, joined by Saad Zaghloul (1859–1927), later Egypt's prime minister, organized a secret society and launched a newspaper, *al-Urwa al-Wuthqa* (*The Strongest Link*), to stop European expansion in the Muslim world. They argued for the need of revitalization and reform within Islam and called for Muslims' solidarity. They advocated the use of rational interpretation (Arabic: *ijtihad*) as a means of incorporating modern ideas into Islam, which they believed had become stagnant and weak from the unthinking following of old traditions. Abduh came to appreciate the European Enlightenment and saw many parallels between the ideas it advocated and those he found in Islam. He was cautious in his appropriation, however, as he abhorred secularism. He began to call for an enlightened Islam that privileged intellectual pursuits and modern science, but ever affirmed the primacy of Allah as the source of human morality and behavior. He offered a more systematic presentation of his evolving theology in a series of lectures given in Beirut, where he moved in 1885. His lectures were later published as *Risalat al-tawhid* (*The Theology of Unity*).

In 1888 Abduh was able to return to Egypt. Settling in Cairo, he worked for educational and institutional reform. He was appointed to a judgeship in 1890, and eventually (1899) became the mufti in charge of the country's court system, then based on the system of Islamic law, or Sharia. He used his influence to modernize and liberalize the interpretation of Sharia law. Crucial in his effort were changes in the status and role of women. He introduced changes in family law, opposed polygamy, and sought equal opportunities for women in education. He also worked to modernize the curriculum and educational processes at his alma mater, al-Azhar.

For the remainder of his life, Abduh argued for change based on a more comprehensive appropriation of the tradition. He believed that Islam had become bogged down in a narrow following of tradition that ignored the breadth of Islamic knowledge. Change was slowed by an entrenched traditionally oriented leadership that was ignorant of the rich heritage they had inherited.

The reformist effort of Addul and al Afghani begun in Paris was continued by al-Afghani until his death in 1897. One of his young associates, Muhammad Rashid Rida (1865–1935), then moved to Cairo to be near Abduh, and together they launched a new journal, *Al-Manar* (*The Beacon*), which Rashid Rida continued to publish until his death in 1935.

Abduh died in Alexandria on July 11, 1905. The legacy of Abduh is mixed. On the one hand, he is remembered as the founder of a progressive modern approach to Islam that has gained widespread support around the world. He was effective, in particular, in moving Egypt into dialogue with the modern West, a dialogue that has made the country one of the more progressive in the contemporary world. At the same time, his attempt to introduce modernist interpretations of Sharia would lead some of his countrymen toward a total secularist stance, which reached its epitome during the regime of Socialist leader Gamel Abdel Nasser (r. 1954–1970). His Paris colleague Saad Zaghloul would later lead the nationalist movement in Egypt, and when the nationalists finally won an election in 1924 he would briefly serve as Egypt's prime minister.

J. Gordon Melton

See also: Muhammad; Polygamy-Practicing Mormons; Women, Status and Role of.

References

Abduh, Muhammad. *The Theology of Unity*. London: Allen & Unwin, 1966.

Enayat, Hamid. *Modern Islamic Political Thought.* Austin: University of Texas Press, 1982.

Houranui, Albert. *Arabic Thought in the Liberal Age, 1798–1939.* London: Oxford University Press, 1970.

Kerr, Malcolm H. *Islamic Reform: The Political and Legal Theories of Muhammad Abduh and Rashid Rida.* Berkeley: University of California Press, 1966.

Sedgwick, Mark. *Muhammad Abduh.* Oxford: Oneworld Publications, 2009.

Watt, W. Montgomery. *Islamic Philosophy and Theology.* Edinburgh: Edinburgh University Press, 1985.

Abeel, David

1804–1846

David Abeel, a minister of the Reformed Church and a pioneer missionary to China, was the second missionary sent to the Orient by the American Board of Commissioners for Foreign Missions. Already present in Asia when the Nanjing Treaty (1942) opened several Chinese cities to missionary efforts, he moved to Amoy and, in the few years prior to his retirement in 1845, founded what became the first Reformed church in the country.

Abeel was born in New Brunswick, New Jersey, on June 12, 1804. As a youth, he had decided on a career as a doctor, but a profound religious experience sent him into the ministry. He attended Rutgers College (now University) and completed his theological studies at the Theological Seminary of the Reformed Church in New Brunswick, New Jersey. Ordained in 1826, he received his first call to the pastorate from Athens, New York. He remained in Athens for two years, but his health failed and he moved to the West Indies.

Abeel had felt a growing call to foreign missions, and once he had recovered his health, he applied to the Seaman's Friend Society for a position. They appointed him a chaplain and sent him to China in 1829. He sailed on the same ship that took Elijah Coleman Bridgman (1801–1861), the first American missionary. They arrived in Canton early in 1830. He worked with the Society for a year and traveled widely in Southeast Asia, picking up some knowledge of several local languages—Malay, Tahi, and Fukienese. In 1832 he received an appointment, like Bridgman, from the American Board of Commissioners for Foreign Missions, a Congregational agency that also facilitated the work of missionaries from several Reformed and Presbyterian denominations.

Abeel spent his first year with the American Board visiting sites in Southeast Asia and evaluating missionary activity. After several months, and before he could launch his own work in China, his health again failed, and in 1833 he returned to the West. Stopping in England, he became a co-founder of the Society for Promoting Female Education in the East. As his health returned, he spent the next four years promoting the cause of foreign missions, especially in his own Reformed Church in America, in no small part through his books: *The Claims of the World to the Gospel, Journal of a Residence in China*, and *The Missionary Convention at Jerusalem*.

He returned to Asia in 1839, first visiting Malacca and Borneo. He arrived in Canton as the Opium Wars heated up. He retreated from China for two years, but, in 1842, he moved to Amoy, one of five ports just opened to Westerners at the time, where he did his most substantial work. Amoy became the center of Reformed Church activity in China. After only three years his health again forced him back home. He died in Albany, New York, on September 4, 1846. The first Protestant church erected in China would be dedicated two years later by the Reformed Church in Amoy.

J. Gordon Melton

See also: American Board of Commissioners for Foreign Missions; Congregationalism; Reformed Church in America; Reformed/Presbyterian Tradition.

References

Abeel, David. *Journal of a Residence in China*. New York: Leavitt, Lord & Co., 1834.

Abeel, David. *The Missionary Convention at Jerusalem*. New York: John S. Taylor, 1838.

Williamson, G. R. *Memoirs of the Reverend. David Abeel, D.D.: Late Missionary to China*. New York, 1849; rpt.: Wilmington, DE: Scholarly Resources, 1972.

Aboriginal Cult of Maria Lionza

The movement built around the veneration of Maria Lionza originated out of the dissemination of the Spiritism of Allan Kardec in Venezuela at the beginning of the 20th century. As Spiritism became a popular movement, mediums in the countryside began to make contact with what were considered nature spirits. One such spirit was Maria de la Onza, or Maria Lionza, believed to be the guardian spirit of flora and fauna in the area around the holy mountain of Sorte in the state of Yaracuy. Believers could gather at the foot of the mountain, where they would consult her about their personal problems through the instrumentality of a group of mediums.

Over time, additional spirits were also consulted, and as the movement spread around the country, a great variety of new kinds of spirits became available for consultation. As the number of spirits multiplied, leaders began to speak of "courts" of spirits, groups by the 1950s centers could be found across the country. In 1968, an attempt was made to bring some organization to the movement with the founding of the Aboriginal Cult of Maria Lionza, with its headquarters in Caracas. The movement has spread to neighboring countries, some of the larger Caribbean islands, and the United States.

Although consulting the spirits through the mediums was the most important practice in the early days of the movement, over the century a variety of additional rites and ceremonies have emerged. Exorcism rituals are conducted for people, the spirit frequently telling people that troubles are due to evil spirits that have possessed them. The leaders of the group may also practice various alternative healing arts and conduct magical rituals aimed at producing specific sought-for results. Certain ceremonies borrow freely from other religious traditions.

There are no statistics on the exact number of followers of Maria Lionza, but observers have suggested that some 5 percent of the Venezuelan public may be regularly active and that many times that number occasionally participate in various ceremonies. Others have suggested lower numbers, possibly as few as several hundred thousand adherents (not an insignificant figure in a country where only the Catholic Church, the Jehovah's Witnesses, and the Seventh-day Adventists can claim more than 100,000 members). Adherents will attempt to make a pilgrimage to Sorte at least once annually.

J. Gordon Melton

See also: Jehovah's Witnesses; Santeria; Seventh-day Adventist Church; Spiritism; Venezuela.

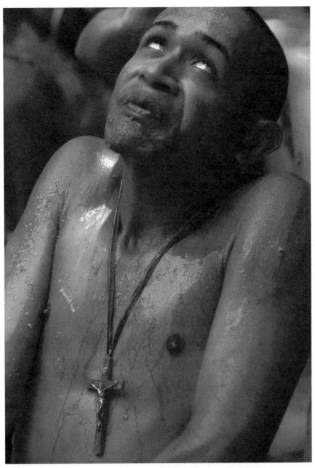

A follower of Maria Lionza's cult looks up while in a trance during an annual gathering at Sorte Mountain, in Venezuela's Yaracuy state, October 12, 2009. The sect follows the goddess Maria Lionza, an indigenous woman who according to tradition was born on Sorte Mountain and whose cult has spread to Colombia, Puerto Rico, the Dominican Republic, and Central America. (AP/Wide World Photos)

References

Garcia, Gavidia, Nelly. *Posesion y ambivalencia en el Culto de Maria Lionza*. Maracaibo, Venezuela: Universidad de Zulia, 1987.

Manata, Bruno. *Maria Lionza, su entitad, su culto y la cosmovision anexa*. Caracas, Venezuela: Universidad Central de Venezuela, 1995.

Pollak-Eltz, Angelina. "The Venezuela Cult of Maria Lionza." In *Encyclopedia of African and African American Religions,* edited by Stephen D. Glazier. New York: Routledge, 2001.

to which the different spirits belonged. Maria Lionza headed the Celestial Court. There is also a court of Patriots, which includes Simon Bolívar and the generals who fought with him, a court of medical doctors, and a court of African figures (which includes the *orishas* of Santeria). The exact spirits available for consultation in any given center vary widely, though the common spirit of Maria Lionza holds the diverse world together. Many people of Roman Catholic background identify Maria Lionza with the Virgin Mary.

The movement found favor in high circles in the Venezuelan government in the 1930s and 1940s, and

Aboriginal Religions

Australian Aboriginal cosmology centers on a concept that has been translated as the Dreaming, or Dreamtime, which refers both to a founding drama of how the Ancestors rose up from beneath the earth to shape and mold an already existing, yet amorphous world, and to an eternal, atemporal metaphysical reality. The term "Dreaming" was the first attempt at understanding the Aranda words *altjiranga ngambakala*. Although Dreaming does not adequately convey the full significance of the complex aspect Aboriginal cosmology, it does suggest the mystery of the connection of Aboriginal people to land, spirituality, and all that exists. Aboriginal people sometimes use the term "Law," or "Eternal Law," to articulate the idea of timelessness that is at the heart of Aboriginal cosmology.

When the Ancestors rose up from beneath the earth, they journeyed from place to place, imbuing all things with their own essence, power, or energy and establishing a set of laws for all to follow. As the Ancestors traveled, they left tangible expressions of themselves in the landscape: here a rocky outcrop, there a tree or waterhole, metamorphosing a part of their own essence into some feature of the environment, or imprinting themselves onto cave walls or ritual objects. When they had completed their journeys, they went back under the earth from whence they had come. The whole continent of Australia is crisscrossed with such landmarks, and these form the basis of Aboriginal lore and law. There is no such thing as original sin; rather, life is a mixture of good and bad, and there is an absence of accountability for one's actions to Ancestral beings. Aboriginal people are linked to the Ancestral Beings through territories (land link), totems (other-species link), and kinship connections (human relationships). When a person is born, by being a member of a particular kin group, its Ancestral associations, and its land connections, he or she automatically fits into a religious framework that is based on this triad.

The trails made by the Ancestors are associated with ritual performance, with song lines (a series or sequence of songs marking a particular event associated with a place along the Ancestral route), and individual and group affiliations that provide Aborigines with identity and kinship connections that extend to everything in their environment. All things—land, humans, and that which is both living and inanimate—are interconnected through these Dreaming (Ancestor) beings. The land is a vast web of sacredness. Land, spirit, and humans are inextricably interwoven. Aborigines say they are caretakers of the land rather than owners.

The Dreaming is not one story but many (for example, Kangaroo Dreaming, Emu Dreaming), and one entire myth complex (stories, songs, ceremonies) associated with each Dreaming story might traverse several linguistic groups. Red Kangaroo, for example, may have emerged from beneath the ground in one place, traversed country that is "owned" by two or three different Aboriginal groups, and went back into the ground at the end of the journey in country belonging to a fourth group. Each group has rights and responsibilities, as guardians and caretakers, for the tract of land associated with their part of the Ancestral route. The responsibilities include taking care of country by periodically following song lines pertaining to the creation stories and keeping up ceremonial performances. These performances may incorporate body painting, objects, artwork, songs, and dances, all of which pertain to the Ancestral story and place connected with the performance. Separate "men's business" (men-only ceremonies) and "women's business" (women-only ceremonies) emphasize distinct gender boundaries for some ceremonies. For other ceremonies, however, men and women perform roles that are complementary and necessary for the proper enactment of a Dreaming performance. Knowledge and beliefs about Ancestral power, myth, and responsibilities are shared, and both women and men have rights and responsibilities in caring for country. Some places belong to women's Dreaming (women's business), some to men's Dreaming (men's business), others to both genders. Both residence and myth link Aborigines to country in a deeply significant spiritual sense. The links are emotional, metaphysical, and situational.

Traditional education on matters pertaining to the Law emphasizes acquisition of knowledge of the Law through ceremonial participation and instruction from the elders who have passed through various stages of initiation. Much knowledge is sacred; some knowledge is both sacred and secret, and only passed on to those

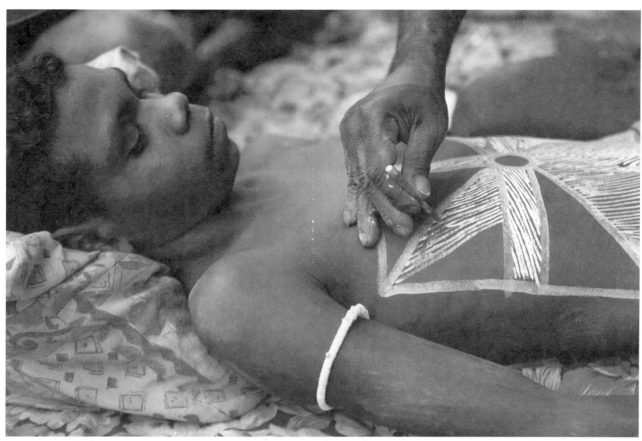

Aboriginal boy being painted for his important initiation and circumcision ceremony at Yathalamarra, Arnhem Land. This is the most important ceremony in a man's life and introduces him to his clan's dreaming stories. (Penny Tweedie/Corbis)

who have accumulated the necessary knowledge to be ready to learn the next level of esoteric information. This is a long, slow process that is tied up with the structure of Aboriginal society. Many Aborigines who have been denied access to such enculturation and instruction, for one reason or another (such as early government policies of assimilation and missionization), and have been raised in urban areas have become Christians, and their links to the land are more tenuous than those created by traditional education. Urban Aborigines tend to have a more generic link to the land; they talk about Mother Earth, as a pan-Australian Aboriginal concept, rather than making associations with creation stories that link people from a particular region to their own local geographic areas.

The responses to Christianity have varied, from outright rejection to syncretism in varying degrees to acceptance. Some Aborigines have become priests and ministers themselves and are attempting a biblical hermeneutic that is culturally relevant to Aborigines. A majority of Aboriginal Australians now profess to be Christians. Although census figures are understated due to incomplete census returns from remote areas of Australia, in the 1991 census, among the 45,208 people who said they spoke an Aboriginal language, 3,802 (9 percent) stated that they followed Aboriginal traditional religious beliefs. Some researchers have estimated that about 10,000 people could be considered adherents of traditional religious beliefs.

The artwork of Aborigines demonstrates the mystique and complexity of their cosmology and epistemology. Aboriginal art, like Aboriginal knowledge, consists of layers of meaning; unless it is executed for commercial purposes, a particular work of art conveys encoded meaning that can be interpreted according to the viewer's access to restricted knowledge. Much contemporary art and literature communicates Aboriginal history since contact, their strong sense of kinship, their feelings about land and spirituality, as well as traditional themes from the Dreaming.

Lynne Hume

See also: Ethnoreligions.

References

Berndt, R. M., and C. H. Berndt. *The World of the First Australians: Aboriginal Traditional Life, Past and Present.* Canberra: Aboriginal Studies Press, 1988.

Charlesworth, Max, ed. *Religious Business: Essays on Australian Aboriginal Spirituality.* Cambridge: Cambridge University Press, 1998.

Hume, Lynne. *Ancestral Power: The Dreaming, Consciousness and Aboriginal Australians.* Melbourne: Melbourne University Press, 2002.

Morphy, Howard. *Ancestral Connections: Art and an Aboriginal System of Knowledge.* Chicago: University of Chicago Press, 1991.

Swain, Tony, and Deborah Bird Rose, eds. *Aboriginal Australians and Christian Missions: Ethnographic and Historical Studies.* Bedford Park, South Australia: Australian Association for the Study of Religions, 1988.

Abraham/Abram

Abraham, one of the ancient Hebrew patriarchs, appears as a character in the book of Genesis in the Jewish Bible. There he receives the promise that God will make of him a great nation through which all peoples will be blessed. He is thus looked upon by contemporary Jewish leaders as both the founder of Judaism and the progenitor of the Jewish people. Both Christianity and Islam hold him in the utmost respect and are, together with Judaism, considered the three Abrahamic religions.

Jews have commonly dated Abraham's birth to around 1800 BCE, a date derived from a literal reading of Genesis and a calculation of the dates from creation and the years of life given for Abraham's reported ancestors. These observations derive from a time in which there was a general consensus that the Torah (the books of Genesis, Exodus, Leviticus, Numbers, and Deuteronomy) were written during or shortly after the time of Moses.

Biblical scholars, even quite conservative ones, now give a range of possible dates for Abraham's birth from 2000 to 1500 BCE. Other scholars who have serious doubts about the historical accuracy of much of Genesis, but who nevertheless agree that Abraham was a real person, tend to accept the broader timeframe in which he could have lived.

Some scholars have also offered a very different interpretation of Abraham, suggesting that it is not the name of an individual so much as a tribal name. In this interpretation, Abraham is the personification of the tribal leadership, and the movement of his family an account of the movement of the tribe. Abraham thus becomes the name of multiple leaders over time.

Even more skeptical scholars have followed what is termed the documentary hypothesis for the origin of the books of the Torah. According to this perspective, the Torah is composed of four documents that were written at different times and places and often giving different accounts of the same events. These documents were written relatively late (beginning in the 10th century BCE, the last around 500 BCE). These documents were later edited together to produce the single text we have today. Such an understanding offers significant room for doubts about the literal accuracy of the text since it described events occurring hundreds of years prior to the written text. Some scholars also point to the lack of independent sources verifying the history recorded in the book of Genesis. The story of Abraham takes up most of chapters 12–25.

Abraham in the Book of Genesis According to the Genesis story, Abram was born in ancient Sumer (later Babylon and today Iraq) in the city of Ur. He lived with his father Terah and brothers Nahor and Haran. He married his half-sister Sarai. His brother Haran died prematurely and his death became the occasion for the family's move first to a place also called Haran, in northern Mesopotamia, where Terah died at the age of 205. Afterward, accompanied by his nephew Lot, Abram and his family moved to Canaan (Palestine) and eventually settled at the Plain of Mamre. Here God appeared to Abram with a promise, "I will give this land to your offspring" (Genesis 12:7).

Once in Canaan, Abram did not stay long in one place and was eventually driven to Egypt by famine conditions. Here, in a famous incident, he passed his wife off as his sister. He returned to Canaan and at Bethel he and Lot separated. Abram settled at Hebron. While at Hebron, he had his encounter with a most interesting character called Melchizedek, described as the king of Salem (possibly Jerusalem) and priest of the Most High God. Melchizedek blessed Abram for his tracking down and killing the marauder Chedorlaomer, who had taken Lot prisoner.

As Abram ages, Sarai's barrenness leads him to take a servant woman, Hagar, to his bed. She produces a son, Ishmael. He was not, however, the heir of God's earlier promise.

When Abram was 90, God came to him and made the covenant that would be so important in establishing what would become Judaism. He changed Abram's name to Abraham (and Sarai's name to Sarah) and promised that he would be the father of many nations. He would give to Abraham's descendants the land of Canaan. As a sign of the covenant, every male was to be circumcised. God also promised a child to be born of Sarah. Shortly thereafter, Abraham and Ishmael (now 13) were circumcised. It would be another 10 years before Sarah's child Isaac was born (Genesis 21); Ishmael was then turned out. Abraham was told not to worry about Ishmael as God would also make a nation of him.

The most important event during Isaac's youth occurred when God tested Abraham's faith by ordering him to sacrifice Isaac. Abraham did as ordered, only to find that God would provide a last-minute substitute in the form of a ram (Genesis 22:1–19). After Sarah died, Abraham remarried. He lived to see Isaac grow to manhood, but died in his 175th year, some 15 years before Isaac married.

Abraham appears to have begun with very little and to have become the leader of a large extended family wealthy enough to have hundreds of servants in his employ. He controlled an unknown quantity of land west of the southern half of the Dead Sea. He bequeathed his land to Isaac and Isaac passed it on to Jacob (also known as Israel).

Abraham in Islam Muslims consider Abraham (or Ibrahim) a Prophet along with both his sons, Isaac (Ishak) and Ishmael (or Ismail). Abraham has a special status as he is considered to have become a monotheist without being taught it by any other human. He is believed to have visited Mecca, where he is credited along with his son Ismail with fixing the Kaaba in its place (Koran 2:125).

Ibrahim is prominently remembered in the annual Hajj, the pilgrimage to Mecca required of every Muslim at least once in his or her lifetime.

The Hajj recalls Allah's testing Ibrahim when he was asked to sacrifice his first-born son Ismail. (Muslims believe that it was Ismail, not Ishak, involved in the request of Ibrahim to sacrifice his son.) Pilgrims pass a site where Iblis (or Satan) attempted to dissuade Ibrahim three times. Each attempt is marked with a symbolic pillar, at which pilgrims throw stones as they pass. This incident is also celebrated during the Muslim holiday, Eid al-Adha.

Another part of the Hajj commemorates the sacrificial efforts of Hajre (Hagar), Ismail's mother, to locate water in the desert for him when he was dying of thirst. To save her son, she is said to have run seven times between the two hills of Safa and Marwa, and during the Hajj the pilgrims reenact her selfless effort. Following the final run, as she approached Mount Marwa, Hajre observed the angel Jibreel (or Gabriel) sheltering Ismail and that a spring of water had emerged beneath his feet. That spring, known as Zam Zam, continues to produce water today.

Abraham/Ibrahim continues to play an important role in contemporary history. It is ultimately the promises of God to Abraham in the book of Genesis upon which the modern state of Israel's claim to Palestine is ultimately based (though it is by no means the only foundation for Israel's claims). That Islam picks up from the biblical account and adds to it, especially in expanding the story of Ismail, has created a situation that makes it possible for Jews and Muslims to ultimately live as neighbors, while at the same time offering the possibility for continued rivalry.

Abraham in Christianity Christians also have a special view of Abraham quite apart from any claim to be the people who should inherit control of Palestine.

The Kaaba is a shrine that houses the Black Stone of Mecca, the focal point for Muslim prayer and final destination for pilgrims to Mecca. According to Islamic tradition, the first building at the site was built by the prophet Abraham and his son Ishmael. (Ayazad/Shutterstock)

He is primarily a hero of faith. In the essay on faith in the eleventh chapter of Hebrews, the author commends Abraham, "By faith Abraham, when called to go to a place he would later receive as his inheritance, obeyed and went, even though he did not know where he was going. By faith he made his home in the promised land like a stranger in a foreign country; he lived in tents, as did Isaac and Jacob, who were heirs with him of the same promise. For he was looking forward to the city with foundations, whose architect and builder is God. By faith Abraham, even though he was past age—and Sarah herself was barren—was enabled to become a father because he considered him faithful who had made the promise. And so from this one man, and he as good as dead, came descendants as numerous as the stars in the sky and as countless as the sand on the seashore" (Hebrews 11:8–12). Paul picks up this theme in Romans 4 and Galatians 3.

Jews, and to some extent Christians, speak of entering into paradise as resting on Abraham's bosom. According to the apocryphal 4 Maccabees 13:17, righteous martyrs will be received by Abraham, Isaac, and Jacob into paradise. In the Christian New Testament, Jesus tells the story of Lazarus and the rich man. When Lazarus, a beggar, died, he was carried to Abraham's bosom by angels (Luke 16:19–31).

J. Gordon Melton

See also: Eid al-Adha; Islam; Jerusalem; Mecca.

References

Alter, Robert, ed. *Genesis: Translation and Commentary*. New York: W. W. Norton & Co., 1997.

Fieler, Bruce. *Abraham: A Journey to the Heart of Three Faiths*. New York: HarperPerennial, 2005.

Fischer, Richard James. *Historical Genesis: From Adam to Abraham.* Lanham, MD: University Press of America, 2008.

Klinghoffer, David. *The Discovery of God: Abraham and the Birth of Monotheism.* Garden City, NY: Doubleday & Company, 2003.

Waskow, Rabbi Arthur, Sister Joan Chittister, and Murshid Saadi Shakur Chishti. *The Tent of Abraham: Stories of Hope and Peace for Jews, Christians, and Muslims.* Boston: Beacon Press, 2007.

Abu Hanifa

ca. 700–767 CE

Abu Hanifa is recognized as the founder of the Hanifi School of Islam, one of the four main schools of Sunni law. As such, he emerged as one of the most influential Muslim jurists in the formative years of Islam.

Abu Hanifa was born around 700 CE in Kufah, in what is now Iraq, of a merchant family. After working in the silk trade, he pursued legal studies under the well-known Iraqi scholar Hammad (d. 732). He was also impacted by the influential Shia jurist Jafar al-Sadiq (d. 765), a fact that shows that the Sunni-Shia divide can be overstated.

Recent historical scholarship suggests that Abu Hanifa's singularity as founder of a school was overstated by his later disciples. It is no insult to his role as founder to recognize the impact of Islamic jurists who came before him. However, there is no doubt that he helped solidify Islamic law into a more coherent body than he inherited as a student. He was faced with laws that contradicted one another and that were often crafted largely as a result of addressing specific problems in very select contexts.

Later critics of Abu Hanifa argued that his jurisprudence was marred by his ignorance and neglect of the hadith (traditions) of the Prophet Muhammad. His detractors had nothing good to say about him and even argued that he was part of a conspiracy against Islam. One critic made the point that it was preferable for towns to have wine stores in abundance than to have one of Abu Hanifa's students around. His apologists wrote biographies to rehabilitate him and establish his knowledge of the hadith material. After two centuries of dispute the Hanifite School became a dominant legal force in the Islamic world.

Abu Hanifa did not seek political office during his life. He was often at odds with the ruling elite and was even imprisoned for a time. Though there are no extant copies of his writings, Abu Hanifa's view of law lived on in his disciples (al-Hasan b. Ziyad, for example) and in the Islamic governments that adopted his jurisprudence. He was held in high esteem by his disciples. A deathbed prayer to God by Abu Yusuf reads: "I put Abu Hanifah between myself and you. I thought him, by God, one who knows your command and would not depart from the truth when he knew it."

Of the four schools, Hanifite law has been most influential in the Middle East and India. The other schools are the Shafiite (East Africa, Malaysia, and Indonesia), Malikite (North, Central, and West Africa), and Hanbalite (Saudi Arabia). Abu Hanifa was a contemporary of Malik ibn-Anas (ca. 710–795), the founder of the Malikite School. The study of Islamic legal history remains a divided field in light of Sunni-Shia divisions and the differences between the four Sunni schools.

As well, more skeptical scholars have contributed to widespread doubts in Western scholarship about whether or not Islamic jurists played a far too creative hand in the formation and selection of so-called authentic hadith. While that charge does not apply as much to Abu Hanifa, it is only in recent years that there is more respect for the view that jurists had access to source material that can be traced back to Muhammad himself.

James A. Beverley

See also: Hanbalite School of Islam; Malikite School of Islam; Shafiite School of Islam; Shia Islam.

References

Hallaq, Wael B. *Authority, Continuity and Change in Islamic Law.* Cambridge: Cambridge University Press, 2001.

Toll, Christopher, and Jakob Skovgaard-Petersen. *Law and the Islamic World.* Copenhagen: Royal Danish Academy of Sciences and Letters, 1995.

AD2000 and Beyond Movement

Originally called the AD2000 movement, the AD2000 and Beyond movement (AD2000) was a global, informal network of Christian missionary agencies, denominations, churches, and individuals committed to world evangelism. It began in the late 1980s, and its international office was closed in early 2001 according to a plan in place from its inception. During its relatively brief lifetime, however, AD2000 and Beyond had a significant impact, including originating the concept of the 10/40 Window and doing much to focus Christian missions on ethnolinguistic peoples rather than geopolitical countries. Among the movement's continuing legacies is the Joshua Project, a research initiative highlighting the people groups with the fewest Christians.

The AD2000 movement had its origins in the Lausanne movement. Thomas Wang, the founder and chairman of AD2000, was also the international director of the Lausanne Committee for World Evangelization and the director of Lausanne's Second International Congress on World Evangelization (held in Manila in 1989). In 1987 Wang noted that numerous mission agencies in a variety of countries were, independently of one another, formulating and propagating plans to evangelize the entire world by the year 2000. During planning for the Manila conference, Wang shared with Lausanne's executive committee the need for cooperation among these various initiatives, both to avoid duplication of effort and to promote their common vision. The committee's conclusion that the Lausanne movement should continue with its broader agenda led to the formation of a separate movement focused on global evangelism and AD 2000.

Wang convened the first Global Consultation on World Evangelization (GCOWE) in Singapore in early 1989. More than 300 delegates from 50 countries met to address the need for cooperation among the 2,000 or so different plans for global evangelization then being pursued. The AD2000 and Beyond movement emerged from the GCOWE to continue its work, adopting as its slogan "A church for every people [the motto of Lausanne's 1980 World Consultation on Frontier Missions] and the Gospel for every person by AD 2000." The GCOWE also helped to cement the shift that had begun among mission agencies toward seeing "mission fields" as peoples rather than countries. Promotion of the AD2000 agenda at Lausanne's Manila congress later that year proved to be ironic, as Lausanne lost much of its earlier momentum to the AD2000 and Beyond movement during the 1990s.

Two additional GCOWE meetings followed, attended by more than 4,000 delegates—the first in South Korea in 1995 (originally intended for 1994) and the second in South Africa in 1997. Celebrate Messiah 2000, a third large gathering with attendees coming primarily from the Global South, was planned as the final public event of the movement. Set to convene in Jerusalem in late December 2000, the celebration had to be canceled at the last minute when Israeli visa workers went on strike. The AD2000 offices were nonetheless closed in early 2001, while the website of the movement has been preserved in archival form.

Perhaps the most influential concept to emerge from the AD2000 and Beyond movement, however, has been that of the 10/40 Window. Lying between 10 degrees and 40 degrees north latitude, the 10/40 Window stretches from northern Africa and the Iberian Peninsula in the west to Japan and the Philippines in the east. As originally conceived in the early 1990s, it included 55 countries, each with at least 50 percent of its land area lying within the window. The countries of the 10/40 Window are the traditional homes of Islam, Hinduism, and Buddhism. Both the world's least-evangelized people and the world's poorest people are concentrated there as well, with considerable overlap between the two groups, making the region a focus of Christian mission.

An ongoing product of the movement is the Joshua Project. Launched in 1995, the Joshua Project initially focused on formulating, for the purpose of cooperation among mission agencies, a listing of the largest ethnolinguistic people groups that were unreached by the Christian gospel (based on the numbers of total Christians and evangelical Christians among them) and of mission work among them. Since its founding, that focus has expanded to include all unreached people groups, regardless of size, and has shifted from ethnolinguistic peoples to purely ethnic peoples. After the AD2000 movement ceased formal operations in 2001, the Joshua Project was connected informally to a number of Christian organizations. In 2006 it became part of the U.S. Center for World Mission and continues to research and offer updated information on the least-evangelized peoples.

Criticisms of the movement have come from a variety of sources. Some focus on the influence of Pentecostal and Charismatic theology and practice within the movement, particularly in the areas of "spiritual warfare" prayer and spiritual mapping. Others have acknowledged the positive aspects of focusing on unreached people groups and the usefulness of the 10/40 Window (as originally described) but point out detrimental consequences. For example, AD2000 movement leaders emphasized that mission to the 10/40 Window should be in addition to, rather than instead of, work currently in place in other areas. Some churches enamored of the 10/40 Window concept, however, declined to fund fruitful, or potentially fruitful, ministries (both existing and new) because they were not directed toward unreached peoples or did not literally take place between 10 and 40 degrees north latitude. (The concept of the 10/40 Window also has evolved over time, with some countries being added and others removed. The meaning of the term as currently used, both in its technical sense and popularly, therefore often differs from its original definition.)

In addition, despite assertions to the contrary by its leaders, the AD2000 and Beyond movement was perceived by many in the Global South as too Western in its leadership, financing, and methodologies. Its emphasis on evangelism (to the exclusion of the "social" aspect of the Christian gospel) and its focus on research and data collection (not always accompanied by action) were also criticized. Whatever one's view of the movement, though, its influence on and importance to the Christian missionary enterprise is undeniable.

Albert W. Hickman

See also: Ethnoreligions.

References

Bush, Luis. "The AD2000 Movement as a Great Commission Catalyst." In *Between Past and Future: Evangelical Mission Entering the Twenty-First Century (Evangelical Missiological Society Series, Number 10),* edited by John Bonk, 17–36. Pasadena, CA: William Carey Library, 2003.

Bush, Luis, ed. *AD 2000 & Beyond Handbook: A Church for Every People and the Gospel for Every Person by AD 2000.* Colorado Springs, CO: AD2000 & Beyond Movement, 1992.

Guthrie, Stan. *Missions in the Third Millennium: 21 Key Trends for the 21st Century.* Waynesboro, GA: Paternoster, 2000.

Joshua Projects website: http://www.ad2000.org; http://www.joshuaproject.net.

Radcliff, Lawrence. "A Field Worker Speaks Out About the Rush to Reach All Peoples." *Mission Frontiers Bulletin* (January–February 1998): 39–46.

Adidam

1939–2008

Adidam (or, more fully, Adidam Ruchiradam) was founded by Avatar Adi Da Samraj, born Franklin Jones, in Long Island, New York. In his autobiography he asserts that he was born into a state of perfect awareness of ultimate reality—a condition he called the "Bright"—but at the age of two he allowed his awareness of that condition to gradually recede in order to completely identify with human limitations. Jones spent his college and subsequent years on a spiritual quest, which eventually led him to Swami Muktananda (1908–1982) and other gurus in that lineage. Jones says that he reawakened to his true state in 1970.

One of the central teachings of Adidam is that no form of seeking for happiness is ever permanently successful, because the means of becoming happy are always transitory. In fact, Adi Da points out that activity actually prevents the conscious realization of perfect happiness in the present. He further asserts that he has realized this Most Perfect Happiness—God, Truth, or Reality—and is able to transmit that Divine Self-Realization to others. Adidam, then, consists of a devotional relationship with Adi Da, who, his devotees assert, is the source of Divine Self-Realization. All the traditional means of religious life—meditation; study; ceremonial worship; community living; moral and ethical observances; disciplines related to diet, health, sexuality, money, and so on—are employed as the conduit to "radical" understanding and devotional communion with Adi Da.

Adi Da began to teach this "radical" understanding —a combination of discriminative self-observation and guru-devotion—in 1972, opening a small ashram in Los Angeles. His method of working with his students was initially quite traditional. It soon became clear, however, that a different approach was necessary, and he switched to a "Crazy-Wise" teaching style. In 1979, he took the name Da Free John. In 1986, he changed his name to Swami Da Love-Ananda. During the late 1980s he was known as Da Avabhasa (The "Bright"). Finally, in 1995, he became Adi Da. This last change, says Adi Da, signaled the completion of his Revelation Work. Adi Da passed from the body on November 27, 2008, on Naitauba Island, Fiji. His devotees continue the Way of Adidam, serving Adi Da's legacy, both spiritually and practically.

The institution of Adidam has an educational organization, the Adidam Academy, which is responsible for conducting courses all over the world to familiarize people with the teaching and the person of Adi Da. Additionally, the institution has a publications mission, the Dawn Horse Press, which publishes books by and about Adi Da; since 1972, more than 80 volumes have been published. The institution also publishes a number of magazines.

Adidam reports a membership of more than 2,000 members, the majority of whom reside in the United States. There are also members in Canada, Fiji, and various European countries. Centers have been opened in northern California, Chicago, Seattle, Boston, New York, Australia, New Zealand, the Netherlands, and Great Britain. Adidam maintains five sanctuaries, located in Fiji, Hawaii, and northern California. For many years Adi Da lived in Fiji, but he spent the last year of his life primarily at the Mount of Attention, the retreat center in California.

Adidam
12040 North Seigler Road
Middletown, CA 95461
www.adidam.org

James R. Lewis

See also: Enlightenment; Hinduism; Meditation.

References

Avatar Adi Da Samraj and the First 25 Years of His Divine Revelation Work. Middletown, CA: Dawn Horse Press, 1997.

The Boundless Self-Confession. Middletown, CA: Dawn Horse Press, 2008.

Feuerstein, Georg. *Holy Madness: Spirituality, Crazy-Wise Teachers, and Enlightenment.* 2nd ed. Prescott, AZ: Hohm Press, 2006.

Lowe, Scott. "Adidam." In *Introduction to New and Alternative Religions in America*, vol. 4, *Asian Traditions*, edited by Eugene V. Gallagher and W. Michael Ashcraft, 85–109. Westport, CT: Greenwood Press, 2006.

Advent

The beginning of the Christian Liturgical Year in Western churches, Advent marks the four Sundays before Christmas. The word "advent" comes from the Latin *adventus,* which means "coming." This season just before Christmas is associated with the coming of Jesus as Messiah and marks a time of penitence, preparation, and anticipation.

Advent always contains four Sundays, beginning on the Sunday nearest to November 30 (the feast of Saint Andrew the Apostle). Consequently, Advent may begin as early as November 27 but always ends on December 24. If Christmas Eve is a Sunday, the last Sunday of Advent falls on that day, as Christmas Eve begins at sundown.

We do not know when the celebration of Advent was first introduced into the church but the first clear reference to its celebration comes in the sixth century. Prior to this time, we find references in the church fathers about homilies, celebrations, and fasts resembling our current Advent season.

Increasingly, in addition to the element of suffering recognized in Advent observances, the season is marked by a spirit of expectation and anticipation. The faithful express a yearning for deliverance by God from the evils of the world following the pattern of Israelite slaves in Egypt. Part of the expectation anticipates a judgment on sin and a calling of the world to accountability before God.

Four burning candles on the Advent wreath. (Ginasanders/Dreamstime.com)

The Roman Catholic and Orthodox churches have set liturgies for Advent emphasizing these themes. Although less scripted, most other denominations have Advent practices that incorporate similar motifs. The traditional color of Advent is purple, the color of penitence. Purple also symbolizes royalty and is associated with the Advent of the King. As well, the purple of Advent is also the color of suffering used during Lent and Holy Week, connecting Jesus' birth and death.

A wreath of evergreens serving as a stand for five candles is used in most Advent celebrations. Evergreens remind us of eternal life, embodied in Jesus, the Light of the world coming into the darkness. The circle signifies God's eternity and endless mercy. Candles mark the light of God coming into the world. The circle usually contains three purple candles and a fourth pink candle, which is lit on the third Sunday of Advent to signify the joy of anticipation for Christ's imminent birth.

While themes vary from church to church and year to year, the first candle is traditionally the candle of Expectation or Hope. The remaining three candles may be organized around characters or themes as a way to unfold the story and direct attention to the celebrations and worship in the season. So, for example, the sequence for the remaining three Sundays might be Bethlehem, Shepherds, and Angels; or Love, Joy, and Peace; or John the Baptist, Mary, and the Magi. The center white candle is the Christ Candle, signifying his incarnation as the heart of the season. It is traditionally lit on Christmas Eve.

Spreading through North America (from Germany) in the late 20th century was the custom of the Advent calendar. Given to children, the card contains

25 flaps, one of which is opened daily from December 1 to Christmas Day. In the more elaborate versions, the opening of the flap reveals a small gift or piece of candy.

Kevin Quast

See also: Christmas; Eastern Orthodoxy; Lent; Liturgical Year; Mary, Blessed Virgin; Roman Catholic Church.

References

Adam, Adolf. *The Liturgical Year: Its History and Meaning After the Reform of the Liturgy.* Collegeville, MN: Pueblo Books, 1978.

Hickman, Hoyt L., et al., *The New Handbook of the Christian Year.* Nashville: Abingdon, 1992.

Mershman, Francis. "Advent." In *The Catholic Encyclopedia.* Vol. 1. New York: Robert Appleton Company, 1907.

Stookey, Laurence Hull. *Calendar: Christ's Time for the Church.* Nashville: Abingdon, 1996.

White, James F. *Introduction to Christian Worship.* Nashville: Abingdon, 2001.

Adventism

Adventism refers generally to those Christian religious groups that place a strong emphasis upon the imminent Second Coming, or Advent, of Jesus Christ to bring history to a culmination, but particularly to those groups that trace their history to the ministry of William Miller (1782–1849), a Baptist lay minister in the 1830s in the eastern United States. From his home in New York in the 1820s, Miller began a study of the Bible that led him to conclude that Christ would return in 1843. In 1831, he began to share the results of his speculations with others, and a movement began to gather around his notions.

Miller built his system on projections from easily dated events in biblical history. When Christ did not return in 1843, and especially after 1844 (termed the Great Disappointment in Adventist history), Miller recanted his ideas, but many of those who had been attracted to his basic perspective continued to believe and developed a spectrum of revised timetables for Christ's return and other end times events. The largest

William Miller was a Protestant leader who attracted a large and enthusiastic following by prophesying the Second Coming of Christ between 1843 and 1844. Miller's followers founded the Adventist Church, which later split into such groups as the Seventh-day Adventists and the Advent Christian Church. (Hayward Cirker and Blanche Cirker, eds. *Dictionary of American Portraits*, 1967)

group gathered around Ellen G. White (1827–1915), who with her husband James White founded the Seventh-day Adventist Church. Later in the century, Pastor Charles Taze Russell (1852–1916) organized a community of Bible students that in the 1930s evolved into the Jehovah's Witnesses. One of the smaller groups to come out of the Millerite enthusiasms was the Seventh-day Church of God, which in the 1930s gave birth to its most successful representative body, the Worldwide Church of God.

During the 20th century, both the Seventh-day Adventists and the Jehovah's Witnesses became large worldwide bodies with members in more than 200 countries. The Worldwide Church of God seemed destined to follow their success until trouble erupted under founder Herbert W. Armstrong's successors and the organization splintered to produce the United Church of God, the Global Church of God, and a host of other lesser groups.

J. Gordon Melton

See also: Jehovah's Witnesses; Russell, Charles Taze; Seventh-day Adventist Church; United Church of God, an International Association; White, Ellen G.; Worldwide Church of God.

References

Bull, Malcolm, and Keith Lockart. *Seeking a Sanctuary: Seventh-day Adventism and the American Dream*. San Francisco: Harper and Row, 1989.

Land, Gary, ed. *Adventism in America: A History*. Berrien Springs, MI: Andrews University Press, 1998.

Morgan, Douglas, and Martin Marty. *Adventism and the American Republic: The Public Involvement of a Major Apocalyptic Movement*. Knoxville: University of Tennessee Press, 2001.

Tkach, Joseph. *Transformed by Truth*. Sisters, OR: Multnomah Books, 1997.

Afghani, Jamal al-Din al-

1838–1897

Jamal al-Din al-Afghani, a 19th-century voice for reform in the Muslim world, helped launch a movement that continues to influence the contemporary Muslim world from quite different perspectives, from the modernist to the ultraconservative. Al-Afghani emerged from obscure beginnings. While his name indicates origins in Afghanistan, most scholars currently place his childhood in Persia (modern-day Iran). It is known that his family adhered to Shia Islam and were designated *sayyids* (that is, descendants of Muhammad). Al-Afghani's origins were further obscured by his early travel.

In Iran al-Afghani had been educated in Islamic theology and philosophy. He seemed to have developed a particular liking for Ibn Sima (known in the West as Avicenna, d. 1037). Moving to India during his youthful years, he studied mathematics and the sciences. It appears that he developed his strong dislike

for British colonial rule at this time. He concluded that Muslims needed to come together, develop a revitalized Islam that integrated the knowledge of modern science, and present a solid front to the intrusion of the British and other Western governments.

In 1871, he moved to Egypt and spent the rest of the decade advocating political reform. His anti-British views finally led to his being banished in 1879 and he settled in Paris. There, in 1881, he published his first major book, *Al-Radd 'ala al-Dahriyyi* (*Refutation of the Materialists*). A few years later he became reacquainted with Muhammad Abduh (1849–1905), banished from Egypt for participation in the unsuccessful Urabi Revolt (1882). The two, joined by Saad Zaghloul (1859–1927), later Egypt's prime minister, launched a newspaper (*al-Urwa al-Wuthqa* [*The Strongest Link*]) in 1884. Saad Zaghloul would return to Egypt and early in the new century emerge as the leader of Egypt's nationalist independence movement. Many consider al-Afghani the father of Muslim nationalism. At the same time, *al-Urwa al-Wuthqa* became a platform for al-Afghani's view that utilized a rational interpretation in understanding Islam. He would advocate that position in discussion with European intellectuals, including the likes of biblical scholar Ernest Renan (1823–1892), as well as his Muslim colleagues.

Al-Afghani continued to travel in his later life. He gave his services to and received patronage from several governments, including the Ottoman Empire and its Sultan, Abd al-Hamid (r. 1806–1909) and Persia and its ruler, Shah Nasir al-Din (r. 1848–1896). He also at times criticized his patrons as facilitators of the growing European influence in the Middle East, including the Tanzimat reforms designed to modernize the failing Ottoman regime. When the British were granted exclusive rights to control the production and export of Persian tobacco, al-Afghani's initial rejection of the agreement led to the Tobacco Protests of 1891–1892 that included a boycott on tobacco use until the agreement was rescinded. The shah was forced to abandon it.

In 1896 one of al-Afghani's followers assassinated Shah Nasir al-Din. Al-Afghani was arrested by the sultan and forced to live the rest of his life in Istanbul under what amounted to house arrest. He died there on

March 9, 1897. He was initially buried in Istanbul, but in 1944, the Afghan government requested his remains. They were transported to Kabul and placed in a mausoleum inside Kabul University.

In the meantime, his reformist impulse was carried into and through the 20th century by the likes of Muhammad Abduh, Muhammad Rashid Rida, and Abu al-Ala Mawdudi (1903–1979).

J. Gordon Melton

See also: Abduh, Muhammad; Islamism; Istanbul; Shia Islam.

References

Hourani, Albert. *Arabic Thought in the Liberal Age, 1798–1939.* London: Oxford University Press, 1970.

Keddie, Nikki R. *An Islamic Response to Imperialism: Political and Religious Writings of Sayyid Jamal al-Din "al-Afghani."* Berkeley: University of California Press, 1983.

Keddie, Nikki R. *Sayyid Jamal ad-Din "al-Afghani": A Political Biography.* Berkeley: University of California Press, 1972.

Watt, William Montgomery. *Islamic Philosophy and Theology.* Edinburgh: Edinburgh University Press, 1985.

■ Afghanistan

The area constituting the present nation of Afghanistan has been inhabited since prehistoric times, many people using the famed Khyber Pass to make their way in and out of India. Crucial to the delineation of present-day Afghanistan was the imposition of the Duran Line defining the border between Afghanistan and British India. The present border between Afghanistan and Pakistan still follows that line. Afghanistan is completely landlocked, sharing its longest borders with Pakistan and Iran. It is a land mostly of deserts and mountains, covering an area of some 402 square miles (comparable to the state of Texas) with a population slightly above 30 million (2006).

The region was conquered by the ancient Persians in the sixth century BCE and then by Alexander the Great. In the first century BCE the nation of Kusana emerged and became an important stop on the trading route that connected Rome with China and India. Persia returned around 240 CE and was still in charge when the Arab Muslims' Umayyad Empire exploded out of the Arabian Peninsula and quickly moved east to the Indus River. Along the way Kandahar and Kabul fell. In the 13th century, Mongols from the east moved into the region. As Mongol power disintegrated, the region became the target of Persians from the southwest, Uzbeks from the north, and Indians from the southeast. An independent state began to take shape in the middle of the 18th century but was immediately faced with Russian pressure to the north and British designs on the Indus Valley. As a result of the British-Afghan War (1878–1880), Afghanistan lost the Khyber Pass, and a British puppet was placed in the ruler's chair. The British, however, granted to Afghanistan a narrow strip of land that extended eastward to the Chinese border. The country overthrew the British protectorate in 1919, but the former Afghan land incorporated into India (now Pakistan) has remained a source of tension.

Since independence in 1919, forces of tradition and modernization have vied for control, and each has succeeded in different ways. Different leaders have attempted to build modern transportation and communications systems, create industry, and reorganize the decentralized government. Attacks on different customs (women's veils, the dowry system) have tended to alienate secularists from traditional religious leaders. The land has never been able to overcome the tensions between the various religious (Shia, Ismaili, and Sunni Islam), language (Pashto, Dari, and Turkic), and ethnic (Pashtun, Tajik, Uzbek, and Hazzara) factions that control different parts of the country. In the modern context, these different factions have looked to various outside forces for support.

Dominating the last half of the 20th century was the country's relationship with the Soviet Union. In 1979, the Soviet Union occupied the country with claims of a friendship agreement. They did not withdraw until 1988, as the Soviet Union was being dismantled. While the Soviets were present, different factions united in opposition, but each had a different vision of Afghanistan's post-Soviet future. Civil war broke out in the 1990s, and as the various factions vied with close ties to Iran. To the north are two other Hanafite Sunni groups, the Tajik (Dari-speaking) and Uzbeks (Turkic-speaking), divided from the Pashtuns by ethnicity and language. The Ismailis draw support from several of the smaller ethnic groups. Like the Tajik and Hazzara, most of the Ismailis speak Dari.

While the various factions were fighting over Kabul, the Taliban emerged out of seclusion. The Taliban movement had grown among students in religious schools that had been established in Pakistan during the days of the Russian occupation. The movement, under the leadership of Mullah Muhammed Rabbani, quickly gained the support of the Pashtun areas of the country and in 1994 moved on Kabul. The Taliban represents an extremely conservative form of Islam and has found an ally in the Wahhabi leadership of Saudi Arabia.

Shia, Ismaili, and Tajik and Uzbek Sunnis, uniting into the Northern Alliance, have opposed the Taliban. At of the end of the 1990s, the Taliban controlled some two-thirds of Afghanistan, while the Alliance held the rest. Neither appeared capable of defeating the other, and a standstill resulted.

The Taliban instituted a traditional Muslim regime in that part of Afghanistan it controlled. It moved to reimpose a spectrum of traditional rules on women.

The area held by the Taliban was also home to a variety of non-Muslim minorities, including Hindus, Punjabi Sikhs, Jews, and a few Christians. All had to conform to Taliban rules, which had become the law of the land.

Prior to the Taliban coming to power there were tens of thousands of Indians (practicing Sikhs and Hindu) residing in Afghanistan. Many left for India or other countries, and that number dwindled to a few thousand, of which approximately 1,700 were Hindus. In 2001, the Taliban announced a program to have the Hindus wear an identifying yellow badge on their clothing. This action brought much criticism, as it appeared to resemble the Nazi imposition of such identifying marks on Jews in prewar Germany. The remaining Indians, Sikhs from the Punjab, took steps to keep their traditional monotheistic worship alive, including the removal of pictures of their gurus from the walls of the *gurdwaras* (temples), so that they would not be considered idolaters.

Muslims pray at the Rauza-Sharif Mosque in the northern Afghanistan city of Mazar-e-Sharif, February 22, 2002, on the Islamic holiday of Eid al-Adha. This mosque complex is the heart of Mazar-e-Sharif. (AP/Wide World Photos)

for dominance, a new force emerged called the Taliban (a Persian word for "students"). Growing in the south, it captured Kabul in 1994. The major opposition came from what was termed the Northern Alliance, a coalition of ethnic groups (including Sunni, Shia, and Ismaili Muslims). The Taliban had a major victory in 1998 but was unable to gain control of the entire country, leaving it divided between two factions at the beginning of the 21st century.

The Hanafite School of Islam came to dominate the Pashtuns, who in turn were the dominant political force in the country through most of the 20th century. Their traditional territory includes the southern half of the nation. In the center of Afghanistan is the homeland of the Hazzara people, who are Shia Muslims

AFGHANISTAN

Jews have resided in Afghanistan, and in the other countries of central Asia, since ancient times. Toward the end of the 19th century, there were some 40,000. Following the establishment of the state of Israel, a mass exodus began and at the beginning of the 21st century there was only a small community (less than 50 people) left in Kabul. A single rabbi remained to oversee the single Jewish synagogue.

Christianity had a presence in Afghanistan from at least the fourth century. In 425, the bishop of Herat was a noted attendee of the Council of Seleucia (Persia). Christian influence in the area was largely eliminated during the years of Mongol rule (14th century). Missionaries were not allowed into the country, and Islamic law calls for death to anyone who leaves Islam

for Christianity. A new Christian presence developed in the 20th century among expatriates working in the country as diplomats or technicians. In 1973, the first Protestant church was erected in Kabul, but it was ordered destroyed two years later. There has been a Roman Catholic chapel and priest at the Italian embassy since 1932.

Buddhism was introduced into Afghanistan in the third century BCE and flourished for many centuries in the eastern part of the country. Buddhist hegemony ended with the coming of the Arabs, and, as in India, over the next centuries it disappeared. There are no Buddhists in Afghanistan today. The Buddhists did leave behind a significant amount of art, including some massive statues of the Buddha. In March 2001, the

Afghanistan

Religion	Followers in 1970	Followers in 2010	% of Population	Annual % growth 2000–2010	Followers in 2025	Followers in 2050
Muslims	11,712,000	30,309,000	99.7	3.86	46,815,000	79,248,000
Hindus	100,000	10,000	0.0	–8.19	10,000	10,000
Baha'is	400	15,000	0.0	3.87	25,000	40,000
Christians	8,000	32,600	0.1	35.26	47,400	85,200
Independents	300	14,000	0.0	24.57	25,000	50,000
Protestants	1,600	12,800	0.0	59.67	15,000	30,000
Roman Catholics	2,000	1,100	0.0	1.13	1,200	1,500
Zoroastrians	3,000	3,500	0.0	–0.67	4,000	4,000
Ethnoreligionists	10,000	4,000	0.0	3.87	4,000	4,000
Sikhs	2,000	2,600	0.0	1.42	3,000	3,000
Agnostics	0	6,800	0.0	24.03	10,000	15,000
Atheists	1,600	500	0.0	28.37	1,000	2,000
Jews	200	10	0.0	–12.94	10	10
Total population	**11,840,000**	**30,389,000**	**100.0**	**3.87**	**46,927,000**	**79,423,000**

Taliban leader ordered all religious statues in Afghanistan destroyed. The world's attention was focused on the Bamiyan Buddha, two large stone statues that the Taliban found religiously offensive. In spite of negative world reaction, including significant negative reaction from other Islamic countries, the statues were destroyed.

The situation in Afghanistan was in flux during the late 1990s, but changed significantly on September 11, 2001, when agents of al-Qaeda, an extreme Islamist group, hijacked four commercial jets and crashed them into the Pentagon in suburban Washington, D.C., the two World Trade Center towers in New York City, and a field near Shanksville in rural Pennsylvania. Al-Qaeda had moved its center to Afghanistan in the mid-1990s and had found protection from the Taliban in return for its financial backing of the Taliban in the continuing civil war and in the attempt to impose a strict form of Islam upon the populace. In reaction to the bombings, the U.S. government launched military operations in Afghanistan, directed against not only al-Qaeda and its leader, Osama bin Laden, but also against the Taliban government, which was charged with being an accessory to al-Qaeda's violence.

The military action quickly led to dramatic changes in the balance of power. A new government was installed in Kabul, but pacification of the country proved far more difficult. As this encyclopedia goes to press, U.S. forces remain in the country (2010) and military operations continue. The volatile situation assures that the religious situation in the country will remain in an unsettled state for the foreseeable future.

J. Gordon Melton

See also: Hanafite School of Islam; Taliban; Wahhabi Islam.

References

Bodansky, Yossef. *Bin Laden: The Man Who Declared War on America.* New York: Forum, 2001.

Crews, Robert D., and Amin Tarz, eds. *The Taliban and the Crisis of Afghanistan.* Cambridge: Harvard University Press, 2006.

Ghani, A. "Afghanistan: Islam and Counter-Revolutionary Movements." In *Islam in Asia: Religion, Politics, and Society,* edited by John L. Esposito. New York: Oxford University Press, 1987.

Juergenmeyer, Mark. *Terror in the Mind of God: The Global Rise of Religious Violence.* Berkeley: University of California Press, 2001.

Maley, William, ed. *Fundamentalism Reborn? Afghanistan and the Taliban.* New York: New York University Press, 1998.

Matinuddin, Kamal. *The Taliban Phenomenon: Afghanistan, 1994–1997.* Karachi, Pakistan: Oxford University Press, 1999.

Olesen, Asta. *Islam and Politics in Afghanistan.* Richmond, Surrey, UK: Curzon Press, 1995.

Africa Inland Church

Africa Inland Church is the name of an autonomous church created as the result of the successful missionary effort launched in the 1890s by the Africa Inland Mission (AIM). AIM was begun by Peter Cameron Scott, a white man living on the coast of Kenya. He developed a vision of a line of Christian missionary stations from Mombasa to Lake Chad, their goal being to resist the further spread of Islam in the region. To that end he founded the Africa Inland Mission as an interdenominational Protestant missionary organization in 1895, and shortly thereafter the first station was opened at Nzaui n (or Nzawe), Kenya, about 200 miles from the coast, among the Akamba people. Before he died the following year, he had obtained the support of a number of conservative church leaders in the United States. He was succeeded by Charles E. Hurlburt, who served as general director of AIM until 1927. After a pause to gather new missionary recruits, the work spread across Kenya (including the Masai and the Tugen peoples) and entered Tanganyika (now Tanzania) in 1909. It pushed on to the eastern Congo among the Zande people in 1912, with the assistance of American president Theodore Roosevelt, who gained the permission of the Belgian government. After World War I, the work expanded to Uganda (1918), the Central African Republic (1924), and the southern part of the Sudan. At the same time, financial support for the work spread through conservative churches throughout the English-speaking world.

Coincidental with its work, schools were founded, most notably the Rift Valley Academy at Kijabe, Kenya (the cornerstone of which was laid by Roosevelt in 1906). These schools (now including secondary schools, Bible schools, and a theological college) began to produce an indigenous leadership, which in turn began to generate indigenous support of the growing mission. The church in Tanzania at one point managed more than 300 primary and secondary schools, but these have now passed into the control of the government.

In 1930, AIM was able to drop support of nationals from its budget. In 1943 the mission in Kenya established the self-governing Africa Inland Church, and in 1971 the church assumed control of the mission's other work and facilities. The church established its own missionary board and commissioned its first missionary in 1960. The church in Tanzania became autonomous in 1964. AIM continues to offer substantial support and remains active across Africa.

The church adheres to a conservative evangelical perspective, but where necessary it has joined with more liberal Protestant churches and even the Roman Catholic Church in common cause. This is especially manifest in the Sudan, where it is a member of the Sudan Council of Churches. It has a congregational organization.

The Africa Inland Church, with more than a million members, is the second largest church body in Kenya (the Roman Catholic Church being larger). It is one of the larger churches in Tanzania, with more than 300,000 members, primarily among the Sukuma people. It has smaller memberships in the Democratic Republic of the Congo, the Sudan, and the Central African Republic, though it has a large constituency among the Sudanese. AIM International (AIM International office: 37 Alexander Park Place, Redland, Bristol, UK BS6 6QB) supports more than 300 missionaries in Kenya and approximately 100 workers in adjacent countries. AIM International has an Internet site at http://www.aimint.org/.

The Africa Inland Church in the Sudan became an autonomous body in 1972. At the time it had about 1,000 members. By the middle of the first decade of the new century, it reported some 123,000 members in 180 congregations. It has also joined the World Council of Churches (2001), being among its most theologically conservative bodies.

Africa Inland Church-Sudan
PO Box 11574
Khartoum
Sudan

J. Gordon Melton

See also: Roman Catholic Church; World Council of Churches.

References

Anderson, Dick. *We Felt like Grasshoppers: The Story of the Africa Inland Mission.* Nottingham: Crossway Books, 1994.

Collins, Robert O. *A History of Modern Sudan.* Cambridge: Cambridge University Press, 2008.

Richardson, Kenneth. *Garden of Miracles: A History of the Africa Inland Mission.* London: Victory Press, 1968.

Van Beek, Huibert. *A Handbook of the Churches and Councils: Profiles of Ecumenical Relationships.* Geneva: World Council of Churches, 2006.

African Apostolic Church of Johane Marange

One of the largest denominations in Zimbabwe is the African Apostolic Church of Johane Marange (AACJM), known as *Vapostori* (Apostles), estimated to have about a million affiliates in Zimbabwe in 2009, with thousands more in countries farther north. The Vapostori have more affinity with Pentecostalism than most other African Initiated Churches (AICs) in Zimbabwe.

Some early Pentecostal preachers of the South African Apostolic Faith Mission in Zimbabwe wore white robes, carried staffs, shaved their heads and grew beards, and taught Old Testament laws—characteristics of both South African Zionists and of African Apostles in Zimbabwe. Johane (John) Marange (also spelled Maranke) (1912–1963), grandson of a chief, received frequent dreams and visions from the time he was six years old. In 1932 an audible voice told him he was "John the Baptist, an Apostle" called to preach internationally and convert people, to baptize them, and to tell them to keep the Old Testament laws and the seventh-day Sabbath. He spoke in tongues and was

Members of the Zimbabwe Apostolic Faith Church sing praises to President Robert Mugabe at a rally at the Chibuku Stadium in Chitungwiza, 30 kilometers (19 miles) south of Harare, Zimbabwe, June 23, 2000. (AP/Wide World Photos)

given other ecstatic manifestations of the Spirit, and he founded the AACJM on the basis of these revelations. In July 1932 the first mass baptism, of 150 people in the Marange chiefdom, took place. Johane Marange in 30 years preached as far afield as Mozambique, Zambia, Malawi, and central Congo, exorcising evil spirits and baptizing thousands of people, commanding them to renounce traditional ritual practices and witchcraft. Abero (Abel) Marange, Johane's son and successor, held a *Pendi* (a Pentecost festival) in the southern Congo in 1964 attended by 10,000 people, but this was only one part of a deeply divided AACJM region. The AACJM has few rivals among AICs for missionary zeal, spreading to many parts of central and southern Africa, as far as Uganda and even Ghana. Although members may make annual pilgrimages to the Marange chiefdom for the main festival of the AACJM in July, the centripetal nature of an African Zion is not emphasized as it is in Zionist churches.

A unique feature of this church is the widespread setting up of hundreds of Pendi centers, where annual festivals are held in which the church leaders minister and give the sacraments to several congregations gathered together from that district. The AACJM also has a canonical addition to the Bible, containing the visions and personal experiences of Marange, called *The New Revelation of the Apostles*. Apart from the characteristic open-air mass services, shaved heads, beards, staffs, and white robes of Marange apostles, the AACJM also practices night vigils known as *mapungwe*, a practice that has become a feature of many types of grassroots Christianity in Zimbabwe. In a *pungwe*, the AACJM practices rituals that involve walking on fire and picking up burning embers with bare hands, symbolizing the power of the Spirit at the end of the world. Sometimes Marange is praised and sung to as "the king of heaven," but he is not regarded as superseding Christ. When Marange died in 1963, a schism occurred between his sons and his cousin, his eldest son Abero succeeding him as priest, the name given to the paramount leader of this church. Johane's cousin, Prophet Simon Mushati, one of the first Vapostori who had assisted Johane on Pendi rounds, began a new church called the African Apostolic Church, St. Simon and St. Johane. There are now several different churches in Zimbabwe using the name African Apostolic Church

and often failing to acknowledge the seminal role of Johane Marange in their genesis.

Allan H. Anderson

See also: African Initiated (Independent) Churches; Pentecostalism; Zionist and Apostolic Churches.

References

Daneel, M. L. *Old and New in Southern Shona Independent Churches*. 2 vols. The Hague: Mouton, 1971, 1974.

Jules-Rosette, Benetta. "Prophecy and Leadership in the Maranke Church." In *African Christianity: Patterns of Religious Continuity*, edited by George Bond et al. New York: Academic Press, 1979.

The New Revelation of the Apostles. N.p.: African Apostolic Church of Johane Marange, n.d.

African Brotherhood Church

The African Brotherhood Church (ABC), predominantly a Kamba church, was founded in 1945 in Nairobi, Kenya, by Simeon Mulandi (1914–1975), a former Salvation Army officer who had received visions about founding a new church. The ABC was a reaction to the missionary attitudes of the time, and most of its first members were dissatisfied members of the Africa Inland Mission, an evangelical missionary organization. Mulandi said that that kind of missionary Christianity meant that "you always had to be apologizing for being an African." Like so many Kenyan independent churches, this church was presumed to be nationalistic and anticolonial from the beginning and was accused of being a front for the Mau Mau resistance movement. It developed independent schools and a "Divinity School" in 1950, and was one of only four African Initiated Churches (AICs) admitted to the All Africa Conference of Churches in 1966. Mulandi himself was dismissed from the church in 1951 for personal misconduct, and his capable administrative assistant Nathan K. Ngala became head of the church, later to be called bishop. He continues to preside over a well-organized episcopal hierarchy.

The church began to expand into non-Kamba areas, but its activities in western Kenya were limited after a Luyia schism in 1952 resulted in the Christian

Brotherhood Church led by Wellington B. Sakwa, who became its bishop. The ABC may be regarded as evangelical: it practices adult baptism by immersion and emphasizes the ministry of all its members, including administration of Communion by lay leaders. This church was one of a few AICs that have officially requested the assistance of foreign Western missionaries. Each church district, with at least 20 congregations, is called a pastorate. Bishop Ngala, like the African Christian Church and Schools, invited the Canadian Baptist Overseas Mission Board to send mission partners in 1979 for an initial period of 10 years, to work mainly in theological and secondary school education under the direction of the African church, and this partnership continues. By 2009 the ABC had some 700 congregations under Bishop Timothy Ndambuki with more than a million members, and had expanded into Tanzania, Uganda, Rwanda, and the Democratic Republic of Congo.

African Brotherhood Church
PO Box 32
Machakos
Kenya

Allan H. Anderson

See also: Africa Inland Church; African Christian Church and Schools; African Initiated (Independent) Churches; All Africa Conference of Churches; Salvation Army.

References

Sandgren, David. "Kamba Christianity: From Africa Inland Mission to African Brotherhood Church." In *East African Expressions of Christianity*, edited by Thomas Spear and Isaria N. Kimambo. Oxford: James Currey, 1999.

World Council of Churches. "The African Brotherhood Church." *Faith and Order Paper 61: Ecumenical Exercise III*. Geneva: World Council of Churches, 1972.

African Christian Church and Schools

The African Christian Church and Schools (ACCS) is an evangelical African Initiated Church founded in the Central Province of Kenya among the Agikuyu people in 1948 as the result of a schism in the Africa Inland Mission. African members and North American missionaries differed over the questions of the ownership of church property and the standards of mission school education. Unlike most of the African churches in Kenya, the ACCS did not begin with a dominant charismatic founder, although Elijah Mbutia was president (later called dignitary) of its first General Council until 1966, and it had only two pastors, Joshua Mudai and Paul Gitau. The ACCS was cooperative with the colonial government and was the first African Initiated Church to be admitted to the ecumenical Christian Council of Kenya in 1954. In 1970 this church, like the African Brotherhood Church later, received the first 8 Canadian Baptist missionaries it had invited to Kenya for an initial 10-year assignment; the relationship continues today. Like the Baptists, the ACCS practices only two sacraments, adult baptism by immersion and the Eucharist.

The church has maintained the traditions of its parent mission in matters of faith, church order, and rules of conduct, and has a Bible college that trains ministers to the diploma level. For higher learning, the ACCS sends its candidates to the local theological colleges and to Canadian and U.S. universities. Four health centers for preventive and curative care are run by the church. It is also actively involved in the fight against HIV/AIDS, which is a major challenge for the Kenyan people.

The church now has a moderator at its helm, and operates more than 60 schools, 3 medical centers, a home for destitute children in Gituru, and a theological college in Kigumo. The estimated membership in 2009, now extended to 7 of the 8 provinces in Kenya, was about 140,000. The church is a member of the World Council of Churches.

African Christian Church
PO Box 1365
Thika
Kenya

Allan H. Anderson

See also: Africa Inland Church; African Brotherhood Church; African Initiated (Independent) Churches; World Council of Churches.

References

Amsler, Karrie M., and Paul Robinson. "The African Christian Church and Schools: Faith and Action." Unpublished paper, 1997. Copy located in the Harold Turner Collection, University of Birmingham, UK.

"The History of A.C.C. & S." Unpublished paper, African Christian Church and Schools, 1973. Copy located in the Harold Turner Collection, University of Birmingham, UK.

Sandgren, David. "Kamba Christianity: From Africa Inland Mission to African Brotherhood Church." In *East African Expressions of Christianity*, edited by Thomas Spear and Isaria N. Kimambo. Oxford: James Currey, 1999.

African Church, Nigeria

One of the oldest of the African Instituted Churches, the African Church was founded in 1901 by a group of dissenting members over the continuing all-European control of the Church of England's mission in Nigeria (one of the most successful efforts of the Church Missionary Society). Instrumental in the church's formation were Jacob Kehinde Coker (1866–1945), a lay warden of a congregation in Lagos, and the Reverend J. S. Williams, a priest who would later become the church's primate. As the issues leading to the founding of the church were organizational and administrative, the new church continued the Anglican doctrine and worship. It merely invited Africans into the priesthood and bishopric. After its formation, it developed a more open attitude toward polygamous families than had its parent body.

As presently organized, the church is led by its primate, seen as the leader of the clergy, and a president, viewed as the head of the lay believers. Legislative authority rests with the general conference. The church founded the African Church School of Theology in 1983, which is presently attached to the University of Ibadan, through which its clergy are trained. The church also sponsors two hospitals and other social services.

By 2006, the church had grown to include 108,000 members organized into 720 parishes and 29 dioceses. The present primate is Most Reverend Abraham Onanuga. It is a member of the All Africa Conference of Churches and since 2005 the World Council of Churches.

J. Gordon Melton

See also: African Initiated (Independent) Churches; All Africa Conference of Churches; Polygamy-Practicing Mormons; World Council of Churches.

References

Adebiyi, Peter. "Jacob Kehinde Coker (1866–1945)." In *Makers of the Church in Nigeria,* edited by J. A. Omoyajowo, 98–115. Lagos, Nigeria: CSS Bookshops Ltd., 1995.

Akinwumi, Elijah Omu. "Coker, Jacob Kehinde, 1866 to 1945, African Church of Nigeria, Nigeria." In *Dictionary of African Christian Biography.* http://www.dacb.org/stories/nigeria/coker_jacobk.html. Accessed January 9, 2009.

Van Beek, Huibert. *A Handbook of the Churches and Councils: Profiles of Ecumenical Relationships.* Geneva: World Council of Churches, 2006.

African Church of the Holy Spirit

After a Pentecostal revival in a Friends Africa Mission in 1927, a "Holy Spirit" movement among the Abaluyia people in western Kenya emerged, encouraged by North American missionary Arthur Chilson. The Abaluyia were undoubtedly influenced by similar movements among the neighboring Luo, and like them, they called their movement Dini ya Roho. The local church leaders and American Friends mission authorities discouraged the revival and banned public confession of sins and spiritual gifts like prophecy and speaking in tongues.

Chilson did not return to Kenya after his furlough in 1928, and the revivalists, expelled from the Friends mission in 1929, eventually organized themselves under their leader Jakobo Buluku in 1933. Buluku died in 1938 as a result of a violent confrontation between his followers and non-Charismatic Friends. As the movement began to organize, a split on the issue of Sabbath observance in 1940 resulted in the Holy Spirit Church of East Africa (HSCEA), eventually led by

Bishop Lucas Nuhu. The main church to emerge was called the African Church of the Holy Spirit (ACHS), led since 1952 by Kefa Ayub Mavuru as high priest; it was officially registered in 1957, and joined the National Christian Council of Kenya in 1960. This church claimed some 700,000 members by 2009. Several schisms from the ACHS resulted in the Church of Quakers in Africa in 1962 (called the African Church of the Red Cross from 1965), the Gospel Holy Spirit Church of East Africa in 1964, and the Lyahuka Church of East Africa in 1971.

These Roho churches, like the Friends, do not have sacraments of water baptism and Communion, but teach the "baptism in the Holy Spirit of adult persons upon repentance." Rituals for purification from evil precede all church services and must occur before meals and before entering and leaving houses. In common with other spiritual and prophetic churches, these Roho churches reject the use of medicines; wear white robes with a red cross, turbans, and beards; and remove shoes in services. The churches emphasize the freedom and power of the Spirit in their church meetings, with ecstatic phenomena, especially prophecy, speaking in tongues, the interpretation of dreams, and healing. The churches have also spread, mainly through migration, to Tanzania and Uganda.

In 1975, the ACHS and the African Israel Nineveh Church were the first two African Initiated Churches in Kenya and the second and third in Africa to become members of the World Council of Churches.

African Church of the Holy Spirit
PO Box 183
Shinyalu, Kakamega
Kenya

Allan H. Anderson

See also: African Initiated (Independent) Churches; African Israel Church, Nineveh; Friends/Quakers; Pentecostalism; World Council of Churches.

References

"Consultation with African Instituted Churches, Ogere, Nigeria, 9–14 January 1996." Geneva: World Council of Churches, 1996.

Hoehler-Fatton, Cynthia. *Women of Fire and Spirit: History, Faith and Gender in Roho Religion in Western Kenya.* Oxford: Oxford University Press, 1996.

Rasmussen, Ane Marie Bak. *Modern African Spirituality: The Independent Spirit Churches in East Africa, 1902–1976.* London and New York: British Academic Press, 1996.

African Independent Pentecostal Church

Churches sticking fairly closely to the churches founded by European missions that they came from, seceding mainly for political reasons and claiming their initial membership from mission churches, began among the Agikuyu in central Kenya as popular movements of protest against the colonial seizure of land and, in particular, against missionary attacks on female circumcision, a central political issue. The African Independent Pentecostal Church of Africa (AIPC) and the African Orthodox Church (AOC) began in a climate of increasing demands by the Agikuyu for political independence, expressed by the Kikuyu Central Association, and in a corresponding struggle for schools independent of European missions. By 1929, the Kikuyu Independent Schools Association (KISA) under Johana Kunyiha and the Kikuyu Karing'a Educational Association (KKEA), which had the support of future president Jomo Kenyatta, had been formed to provide such independent education. And yet, after the model of mission education, the independent schools also sought to provide a Christian foundation, and for this they needed ordained clergy.

The request of KISA to the Anglicans in 1933 to allow two young men to receive theological training was met with such stringent conditions that KISA and KKEA were forced to look elsewhere. KISA invited the AOC archbishop in South Africa, Daniel Alexander, to come and supervise the training of their clergy, at KISA's expense. Alexander had told KISA that the AOC was "perpetually autonomous and controlled by Negroes entirely" and that it was "a church of Africans governed by the Africans and for the Africans." Alexander arrived in Kenya in November 1935 and remained there until July 1937, during which time he opened a theological seminary with eight students, seven of whom were sponsored by KISA and one by KKEA. Before his return to South Africa, he ordained three deacons and two subdeacons.

The newly ordained clergy did not agree among themselves about the organization of their new church. Some, supported by KKEA and including the deacon Arthur Gatung'u Gathuna, wanted to remain in the AOC. Others, supported by KISA, formed a separate church altogether, the AIPC, which adopted the name Pentecostal, not because it emphasized the experience of the Spirit, but because it had clergy appointed by the Spirit and was controlled by the Spirit and not by foreigners. And so, in September 1937, the AIPC emerged from KISA and the AOC out of KKEA. As most African Initiated Churches (AICs) were regarded with suspicion by the British colonial administration, both churches were banned in 1952–1953 during the Mau Mau uprising, and the independent schools were closed. But after independence in 1963, thousands of nominal Presbyterians openly joined the AIPC, which soon had 100,000 members and was led by Archbishop Benjamin Kahihia, one of the original four ordained in 1937. The church is now led by Archbishop Samson Mwangi Gaitho.

By 2009 this church was the largest AIC in Kenya and one of the four largest on the continent, with more than three million adherents.

African Independent Pentecostal Church of Africa
c/o OAIC
PO Box 21736
Nairobi
Kenya

Allan H. Anderson

See also: African Initiated Churches; African Orthodox Church; Pentecostalism.

References

Barrett, David B., and T. John Padwick. *Rise Up and Walk! Conciliarism and the African Indigenous Churches, 1815–1987*. Nairobi: Oxford University Press, 1989.

Githieya, Francis K. *The Freedom of the Spirit: African Indigenous Churches in Kenya*. Atlanta: American Academy of Religion, 1997.

African Initiated (Independent) Churches

In most countries of the sub-Sahara, African Initiated (Independent/Indigenous/Instituted) Churches (AICs) make up a significant section of the Christian population. Although in Africa there are inevitable difficulties with statistics, David Barrett and John Padwick (1989) estimated that from a total of about 42,000 AIC members in 1900, there were some 29 million (or 12 percent of the total Christian population of Africa) in 1985, and by 2000 that figure had at least doubled. Most AIC members are found in southern Africa, Kenya, and the Democratic Republic of Congo and along the West African coast, where the proportion of AICs to the total Christian population is much higher than elsewhere. Whatever the accuracy of the statistics, AICs are undoubtedly a major force in African Christianity today, one manifestation of the shifting of the center of gravity of Christianity in the 20th century from the north to the south. To the consternation of some, this astonishing growth has sometimes been at the expense of older European-founded churches. Living, radical experiments of an indigenized Christianity that has consciously rejected Western ecclesiastical models and forms of being Christian are provided in the AICs.

There are many kinds of AICs, from the earliest "Ethiopian" and "African" churches, which emerged at the end of the 19th century, to the later, more prolific "prophet-healing" and "Spirit" churches, and the most recent Pentecostal and Charismatic churches that emerged after 1970. The birth of the modern AIC movement can be traced to the story of Kimpa Vita (Dona Beatrice) and the Antonian movement in the Kongo Kingdom of the early 18th century, but more immediately in the early "African" churches in West Africa and the "Ethiopian" churches in South Africa at the end of the 19th century. The Liberian prophet William Wade Harris and the Harrist movement that emerged from his remarkable ministry, as well as the ministry of the Nigerian healer-prophet Garrick Braide, influenced the development of a new kind of AIC throughout West Africa, including "spiritual churches" in Ghana and Aladura (praying) churches in Nigeria. Parallel developments took place in AICs south of the

Members of the Zion Christian Church dance during the Easter service in April 1994 at Moria in the Northern Province of South Africa, where up to a million believers gather each year. (Getty Images)

Zambezi, where the greatest proliferation of AICs in the continent is to be found. Zionist and Apostolic churches are found there, the largest of which is the Zion Christian Church, founded by Engenas Lekganyane, and the more unusual but equally significant Zulu movement of Isaiah Shembe, the Nazareth Baptist Church, better known by its Zulu name *amaNazaretha*.

The moving story of Simon Kimbangu and Kimbanguism in the Congo resulted in what is now the largest AIC in the continent, the Kimbanguist Church, Église de Jésus Christ sur la terre par le prophète Simon Kimbangu, and in the rise of Ngunzi ("prophet") churches. Many of these AICs found themselves in violent conflict with both colonial administrations and European missions. Later, the tragic episode of Alice Lenshina and the Lumpa movement in Zambia was an example of an AIC that clashed with the nationalist ideology of a newly independent African nation. In East Africa, and particularly in Kenya, AICs have also proliferated and have become a prominent aspect of Christianity in that region, including the large African Independent Pentecostal Church and several "Spirit" or "Roho" churches. Since the 1960s, AICs have been transplanted and developed in Britain and other parts of Europe, especially those from West Africa. More recent new Pentecostal and Charismatic churches rose up in different parts of Africa in the last three decades of the 20th century, resulting in revivalist and rapidly growing independent Pentecostal or Charismatic churches, some of which propagate a "success" and "prosperity" theology, although forming an increasingly significant part of African Christianity.

Types and Terms The many thousands of AICs today, including the most recent varieties, have become a dominant, as well as the fastest growing, expression of Christianity on the continent. After the European colonization of Africa, a process of religious acculturation took place as older African religious and social traditions were threatened and partially replaced by new ones. The creative independent African Christian churches that began to emerge at the turn of the 20th century were initially snubbed and persecuted. Western mission church leaders and other observers labeled them "sects" and "nativistic," "messianic," "separatist," and "syncretistic" movements. The term "African Independent Churches" was probably the first acceptable, neutral phrase used for these new movements. Harold Turner (1979) defined "African Independent Church" as "a church which has been founded in Africa, by Africans, and primarily for Africans." Later, many African churches founded by European missionaries became independent of European control, and the term "African Indigenous Churches" was proposed to distinguish between the newly independent churches in Africa and those that had formed autonomous churches decades before. After the African states began to emerge one by one from colonial domination in the 1950s and 1960s, there was new impetus toward the Africanization of Christianity. Many European mission-founded churches began to move toward inculturation and sought to be seen as indigenous. The term "African Indigenous Churches" therefore has also become inadequate, particularly because most AICs are not completely free from foreign influence and cannot be regarded as indigenous in any normative sense. "African Initiated Churches" and "African Instituted Churches" are terms more recently deployed, which avoid these difficulties by simply indicating that these churches were initiated by Africans, and not by Western missionaries. The other terms are still used in the literature.

AICs have often flourished in areas where Protestant missions have had the longest histories. There also seems to be a connection between the number of different Protestant missions in a particular region and the emergence of AICs. In any typology of these movements, hasty generalizations or overlooking obvious differences must be avoided, and the distinctive liturgies and healing practices, as well as the different approaches to African religion taken by different AICs, must be appreciated. The many terms used to describe AICs were coined by European researchers and outsiders, and they are not terms familiar to, or always acknowledged by, the vast majority of AICs themselves —although some may have accepted them for their own purposes. A typology can be no more than a hypothesis that depends on further research for its confirmation or correction, as it may overlook the complexities of the subject or may even distort our understanding of it. Harold Turner's (1979) sage advice was that it is better to think of a typology of *tendencies* and *emphases* rather than of individual religious bodies and movements.

Although there has been extensive literature on AICs over the years, the first systematic and comprehensive regional study appeared in 1948, when Swedish Lutheran missionary Bengt Sundkler published *Bantu Prophets in South Africa*. This landmark publication set the standard for the flood of literature that followed, and few were to attain it. Sundkler's own research was conducted in rural Zululand (now KwaZulu Natal) during the mid-1940s, and he identified two main types of AICs in South Africa—Ethiopian and Zionist churches. Most scholars of the movement during the next 40 years followed Sundkler's basic dual typology from southern Africa and placed the many different kinds of AICs from all over the continent into the two broad categories of Ethiopian or African churches, and Zionist or spiritual churches. In West Africa, Turner followed this twofold distinction between Ethiopian type and prophet-healing type; Zimbabwean-born M. L. (Inus) Daneel made the same distinction between Spirit-type and Ethiopian-type churches. Zionist or Spirit-type is the southern African equivalent of the more appropriate continental terms "prophet-healing" and "spiritual," and it distinguishes prophetic churches, emphasizing the revelation of the Spirit from non-prophetic churches.

It is probably true to say that the dual typology no longer applies to southern African churches, let alone those in the rest of Africa. Nevertheless, in the use of any terms at all, it is important to remember that there are many more "types" of churches than those proposed by researchers, and that the churches themselves often do not recognize the categories given them by outsiders. Furthermore, within every type there are exceptions to the general characteristics—so we have to qualify definitions with terms such as "generally" or "usually." Dividing AICs into types is not particularly helpful, and what is offered here is a very brief outline of an extremely complicated subject. (Types are described to facilitate understanding of the broad differences between the movements, but such categorization does not do justice to their diversity. Placing AICs into categories results in generalizations that do not accurately reflect the true nature of each church, and that is not an African concern in any case. Today there are so many recognized exceptions to the "types," and so many new churches being created, that any typology can only outline some of the common characteristics of different "types" in an attempt to make this vast multifarious movement more understandable to the outsider. Turner [1979] suggested that such a framework and language was necessary both for comparative purposes and in order to distinguish the essential features of African religious movements.)

The types are not intended to be definitive, however, especially as the movements they describe are dynamic churches under a constant process of change. Three broad categories of AICs, however, have certain common family likenesses that distinguish them from others, and are described briefly in what follows, while the problems with this categorization are also noted.

African/Ethiopian Churches   AICs that do not claim to be prophetic or to have special manifestations of the Holy Spirit, and which have modeled themselves to a large extent on the European mission churches from which they seceded, have been called "Ethiopian" or "Ethiopian-type" churches in southern Africa, and "African" churches in Nigeria. These were usually the first AICs to emerge. The term "Ethiopian" or "African" is not used or recognized by all churches in this category, however. In Kenya, for example, the terms are not used at all for many AICs there, which would be very similar in character to this type. The largest of these AICs there is the African Independent Pentecostal Church, which further complicates the typology, as it is not a Pentecostal church. Nevertheless, the terms "Ethiopian" and "African" are used for want of better ones to describe AICs generally of earlier origin than the other two types described below, and to describe those that arose primarily as political and administrative reactions to European mission-founded churches. For this reason "African" churches are very similar to

A deacon of the Ethiopian Orthodox Christian church. (Carolyne Pehora/Dreamstime.com)

the churches from which they emerged. They usually practice infant baptism, read liturgies, sing translated European hymns, wear European-type clerical vestments (often black), and are less enthusiastic or emotional in their services than are the "Spirit" churches. They tend to be less prescriptive than other AICs regarding food taboos such as eating pork, the use of medicine, and the consumption of alcohol. Most often not named "Ethiopian" or "African," they originated in secessions from mission-founded churches on racial and political grounds. They were a reaction to the white mission's conquest of African peoples, even though their church organization and Bible interpretation were largely copied from the patterns of those mission churches; sometimes they even include the church's generic name in the church title: "Methodist," "Presbyterian," "Congregational," "Lutheran," and so on.

In southern Africa, the word "Ethiopian" in the church name is more common and had special significance in these countries more heavily colonized than the rest of Africa. Ethiopia, the only African nation that had successfully resisted European colonialism by defeating Italy in war, is mentioned in the Bible as a nation that "stretches out her hands to God" (Psalm 68:32). This verse and the conversion of the Ethiopian court official (Acts 8) formed the basis of the "Ethiopian" ideology that spread in South Africa in the 1890s and may have affected the establishment of these AICs elsewhere. Africans received Christianity before Europeans had, and therefore they had a special place in God's plan of salvation. The "African" and "Ethiopian" churches have declined in the past 50 years and have been somewhat eclipsed by the other, more enthusiastic and more Pentecostal-like churches.

Spirit/Prophet-Healing Churches The "Spirit" or "prophet-healing" churches emphasize spiritual power. They are independent African churches with historical and theological roots in the Pentecostal movement, although they have moved in their own direction away from Western forms of Pentecostalism in several respects over the years, and may not be regarded as "Pentecostal" without further qualification. Like Pentecostals, however, they are churches that emphasize —usually in contrast to "Ethiopian" and "African" churches—the working of the power of the Spirit in the church. Although these AICs differ fundamentally from Western Pentecostal churches, they too emphasize the centrality of the Spirit in faith and (especially) in practice, and therefore have also been termed "African Pentecostal." This is the largest and most significant grouping of AICs and a particularly difficult type to describe, for it includes a vast variety of some of the biggest of all churches in Africa: the Kimbanguist Church and the African Apostolic Church in Central Africa, the Christ Apostolic Church, other Aladura churches and Harrist churches in West Africa, and the Zion Christian Church, other Zionist and Apostolic churches, and the amaNazaretha in southern Africa. These are all churches with hundreds of thousands of members, and, in at least two cases (Kimbanguists and Zionists), millions. Some of these churches are now members of ecumenical bodies such as the different national councils of churches, the continental All Africa Conference of Churches, and the World Council of Churches. In the eyes of those who consider these councils as offering some measure of respectability, these moves are welcomed and give the AICs legitimacy denied them by European churches and colonial powers for so long. But most AICs are not members of ecumenical bodies and are not clamoring to be so. Their legitimacy hails from a belief in divinely appointed leaders who do not feel a need to seek human recognition, and from their time-tested strengths as major denominations in their own right.

Because written theology is not a priority and is generally less precisely formulated in these churches than in European-instituted churches, the differences in belief systems, liturgy, and prophetic healing practices are considerable. Foundational to these churches are definite theological presuppositions, found more in the practice of their Christianity than in formal dogma. Like the new Pentecostal and Charismatic churches described below, there is an emphasis on healing, although the methods of obtaining healing differ. Whereas other Pentecostals generally will practice the laying on of hands or prayer for the sick, that will often be accompanied in prophet-healing churches by the use of various symbolic objects such as blessed water, ropes, staffs, papers, ash, and so on. This constitutes one of the more obvious differences between other Pentecostals and these churches. There are often strong taboos for members prohibiting alcohol, tobacco, and pork. The attitude to traditional religious practices is generally more ambivalent than in the new Pentecostal churches, particularly when it comes to ancestor rituals, and some of these churches also allow polygyny. But for the majority of these churches across Africa, a clear stand is taken against certain traditional practices such as witchcraft and spirit possession.

For the outside observer, the biggest distinguishing feature of these churches in most parts of Africa is the almost universal use of robes and uniforms for members, often white robes with sashes, and in some cases military-like khaki. These obviously non-African accretions notwithstanding, these churches have possibly adapted themselves to and addressed the popular African worldview more substantially than have other churches, and that is their unique contribution toward understanding Christianity in Africa. It is in fact this adaptation to and confrontation with African tradition that constitutes at the same time both the challenge and the problem of these AICs to a contextual African theology, particularly when African theologians have taken on board the entire spectrum of African traditional religion without question.

Pentecostal/Charismatic Churches The newer Pentecostal or Charismatic churches are of more recent origin, and may be regarded as "Pentecostal" movements because they too emphasize the power and the gifts of the Holy Spirit. They vary in nature from hundreds of small independent house churches to rapidly growing and large church organizations, such as the Redeemed Christian Church of God in Nigeria led by Enock Adeboye, the Zimbabwe Assemblies of God Africa of Ezekiel Guti, and the Grace Bible Church of Mosa Sono in South Africa, to name a few. Despite their recent origins, some of these churches are already among the largest and most influential denominations in their respective countries, especially in West Africa.

The rapid growth of these churches over the last two decades of the 20th century indicates that a significant number of their members come from both the older European mission-founded churches and from the Spirit churches. There is a strong Western, especially North American, Pentecostal influence in some of these churches, both in liturgy and in leadership patterns, and North American neo-Pentecostal "prosperity" preachers are sometimes promoted. The difference between these churches and new Pentecostal and Charismatic churches in the West is difficult to discern on the surface, except that the leadership is entirely African and more of a local, autonomous nature. Their founders are generally charismatic and younger men and women who are respected for their preaching and leadership abilities and who are relatively well educated, though not necessarily in theology. These churches tend to be more sharply opposed to traditional practices than are the prophet-healing churches, and they often ban alcohol and tobacco, the use of symbolic healing objects, and the wearing of church uniforms. The membership tends to consist of younger, less economically deprived, and more formally edu-

Parishioners at an all-night Pentecostal mass held by the Redeemed Church of Christ on the Lagos-Ibadan Expressway on October 3, 2003, in Nigeria. Hundreds of thousands of Nigerians, the majority of whom are women parishioners, pray at all night services beginning after work on Friday and lasting until Saturday dawn. (Getty Images)

cated people. They are often seen, particularly by the older AICs, as mounting a sustained attack on traditional African values.

These are three of the ways in which AICs can be described, but these "types" are by no means exhaustive, nor are they the only way a typology could be suggested. There are hundreds of AICs that do not fit neatly into any of these three "types." Deciding on types is so often determined by the criteria used, and by who does the deciding. What is important is how the churches see themselves. The tremendously rich diversity and creativity of the AIC movement will be illustrated in the various entries throughout these volumes, and this discussion of typology is intended merely as an admittedly superficial introduction to the subject. The reader, it is hoped, will be able to make evaluations about the complexity of the AIC movement on the basis of internal evidence from the churches themselves.

The contribution that the AICs make to Christianity in Africa is considerable. It includes innovative adaptations these churches make to older African religious beliefs, such as their approach to the phenomena of ancestors, divination, and traditional medicine and healing. The AICs make a contribution to the understanding of issues such as contextualization, inculturation, syncretism, and how Christianity relates to African culture. This contribution is so far-reaching that we may really consider this to be a reformation of at least the magnitude of the Protestant Reformation in Europe, and perhaps a more profound reformation than the European one ever was.

Allan H. Anderson

See also: African Independent Pentecostal Church; Aladura Churches; All Africa Conference of Churches; Christ Apostolic Church; Kimbanguist Church; Harrist Church; Nazareth (Nazarite) Baptist Church; World Council of Churches; Zimbabwe Assemblies of God Africa; Zion Christian Church (South Africa, Zimbabwe); Zionist and Apostolic Churches.

References

Anderson, Allan H. *African Reformation: African Initiated Christianity in the Twentieth Century.* Trenton, NJ: Africa World Press, 2001.

Barrett, David B. *Schism and Renewal in Africa: An Analysis of Six Thousand Contemporary Religious Movements.* Nairobi: Oxford University Press, 1968.

Barrett, David B., and T. John Padwick. *Rise Up and Walk! Conciliarism and the African Indigenous Churches, 1815–1987.* Nairobi: Oxford University Press, 1989.

Daneel, Inus. *Quest for Belonging.* Gweru, Zimbabwe: Mambo Press, 1987.

Sundkler, Bengt G. M. *Bantu Prophets in South Africa.* London: Oxford University Press, 1948, 1961.

Turner, Harold W. *Religious Innovation in Africa.* Boston: G. K. Hall, 1979.

African Israel Church, Nineveh

One of the most prominent African Initiated Churches (AICs) in Kenya is the African Israel Church, Nineveh, now usually known as the African Israel Nineveh Church (AINC), founded in western Kenya in 1942 by the Pentecostal Luyia evangelist Daudi Zakayo Kivuli (1896–1974). Kivuli associated with the Pentecostal Assemblies of Canada from 1925 and was made a supervisor of schools for this mission. After an ecstatic Spirit baptism experience in 1932, he embarked on an evangelistic and healing ministry officially authorized by the Canadian missionary Otto Keller in 1939, and he was well known among both the Luyia and the Luo. When he was elected liaison leader for the church in 1940, other African leaders did not support him.

Apparently with the blessing of Keller, Kivuli founded his own church organization, called at first Huru Salvation Nineveh and, soon after, African Israel Church, Nineveh. Kivuli took the title high priest, and his home, Nineveh, became the headquarters of the church and the place to which people flocked. The church was registered with the government in 1957.

The AINC has many practices similar to those of other Pentecostal churches in other parts of the continent. Members wear long, flowing white robes and turbans, practice constant singing and dancing, emphasize Spirit possession, observe Old Testament dietary and purification taboos, and have a holy place (Nineveh) where the present archbishop, a grandson of Kivuli, resides. The AINC, like other Roho churches —those with a Quaker background, such as the African Church of the Holy Spirit—is known for its joyful and colorful processions and open air meetings, in which flags, drums, staffs, bells, and trumpets are used in singing to traditional African tunes. Friday, the day of Christ's crucifixion, is declared to be a day of worship together with Sunday, the day of resurrection, and the church places great emphasis on the open confession of sins and daily dawn prayers. Polygamists are accepted as church members, but monogamy is enjoined on all leaders and unmarried members. Alcohol, tobacco, pork, fish without scales, and sexual intercourse on Fridays are all proscribed. This church did not isolate itself as some other Pentecostal churches had done, but after its first application was rejected in 1957, it joined the National Council of Churches of Kenya and was admitted to the World Council of Churches in 1975.

When Kivuli died in 1974, his wife Rabecca Jumba Kivuli (1902–1988) succeeded him as leader and remained high priestess of the AINC until her retirement in 1983. During her leadership a secession occurred, resulting in a new church called the African Israel Church. Kivuli's grandson, John Mweresa Kivuli II (b. 1960), became high priest in 1983, but from 1991 he has been known as archbishop and has embarked on a process of "modernization." Kivuli II, who completed two theological degrees, explained that his change in title was because the AINC had grown in theological understanding, and now it saw all believers as priests and Christ as the only high priest. The church had some 500,000 members in Kenya in 2009, and although Luyia and Luo people dominate the membership, the AINC has become an interethnic national movement.

African Israel Church, Nineveh
PO Box 701
Kisumu
Kenya

Allan H. Anderson

See also: African Church of the Holy Spirit; African Initiated (Independent) Churches; Pentecostal Assemblies of Canada; Pentecostalism; Polygamy-Practicing Mormons; World Council of Churches.

References

Kivuli, John M., II. "The Modernization of an African Independent Church." In *Freedom and Independence*, edited by Stan Nussbaum. Nairobi: Organization of African Instituted Churches, 1994.

Kudoyi, Peter Wilson. "African Israel Nineveh Church: A Theological and Socio-Historical Analysis." M.A. thesis, Kenyatta University, 1991.

Welborn, F. B., and B. A. Ogot. *A Place to Feel at Home*. London: Oxford University Press, 1966.

African Methodist Episcopal Church

The African Methodist Episcopal Church (AMEC) emerged in the social, religious, and political ferment of the late 18th-century United States. Its founder, Richard Allen (1760–1831), converted by a traveling Methodist preacher while yet enslaved, was one of at least two persons of African descent present at the 1784 founding conference of the Methodist Episcopal Church (MEC) (now a constituent part of the United Methodist Church). Just three years later he co-led the movement that came eventually to take form in the founding of the African Methodist Episcopal Church. That body was the first of what are known as the "historically black denominations" to achieve institutional independence. Over the years, it became a major source of advocacy for the social and political elevation of persons of African descent.

The oppressive, discriminatory conditions of life for Africans imported into the United States had the result that this people, who had been of disparate ethnic and regional origins on the African continent, were pulled into a common frame of existential needs and material challenges. The MEC early on distinguished itself among Africans in the Americas by its active evangelistic outreach to them, by the congeniality of its simple style of piety, and by its willingness to admit blacks to certain levels of religious leadership. Nonetheless, the church was not free from discriminatory practices. For instance, the two Methodist congregations in Baltimore, Maryland, had instituted the practice of serving Communion to their black members *after* all whites had been served.

And so, while finding satisfaction in their worship with whites, blacks felt the urge to have devotional time apart, also. Here, in an empathetic atmosphere of mutuality and shared experience, they might find space freely to express their particular concerns and needs and be led in connecting these to the resources of their faith. The first of such separate gatherings among Methodists occurred in 1786 in Baltimore. Then, in November 1787, Richard Allen and other blacks arriving to worship at Philadelphia's St. George Methodist Church were directed to a new gallery seating area. But they took seats in what turned out to be the whites-only

Richard Allen (1760–1831), founder and first bishop of the African Methodist Episcopal Church. (Daniel Alexander Payne. *History of the African Methodist Episcopal Church,* 1891)

section of the gallery. As they knelt for prayer, a church officer approached, insisted that they move, and began physically to remove them, though prayer was still in progress. When the prayer ended, Allen, Absolom Jones, Dorus Ginnings, William White, and several other women and men decided that rather than remain in the face of such indignity, they would leave the church altogether and seek a more fitting and hospitable situation for divine worship.

For several years, this group and those whom they recruited met and conducted religious exercises as part of the Free African Society, which had been formed earlier in 1787 as a mutual aid society, a form of insurance/support organization to address material crises and social and spiritual development.

By 1794, Allen and Jones had raised monies for the erection of a church building. Disagreement among the members of the Free African Society over which denomination they should affiliate with resulted in the formation of two congregations. The structure that had been built and the majority of members became the African Episcopal Church of St. Thomas, which Absolom Jones consented to lead. Allen purchased and remodeled as a worship space an old blacksmith shop, to be the Bethel African Methodist Episcopal Church.

For some 22 years, Bethel functioned as a MEC congregation, with white pastors assigned by the Methodist conference (jurisdictional body). But the assigned pastors treated the congregation rudely. The inability over the years to obtain relief from the conference from this abuse in their own separate facility, combined with a dispute with the conference over the ownership of the church property, led to discussions with other similarly separated black Methodist congregations about the possibility of formal independence. Sixteen clergy and lay representatives of five congregations met in Philadelphia in April 1816 and voted to sue in the Pennsylvania State Supreme Court for legal independence. The suit was granted, and the new denomination was incorporated as the African Methodist Episcopal Church. Daniel Coker, of the Baltimore congregation, was elected the first bishop but declined the next day in favor of Richard Allen.

Home missions began from the first days of the denomination. There was an active effort in the North, but restrictions on the travel of free blacks in the slave South inhibited the work in that area until after the American Civil War. In the trans-Mississippi West, AMEC congregations emerged in each of the territories, most heavily on the Pacific Coast. There were even missions to Native Americans and Mexicans in the Southwest and Mexico.

In 1821, Daniel Coker became the first to undertake overseas mission work, establishing congregations in Liberia and Sierra Leone. Coker's work, however, was not under AMEC sponsorship. Official overseas missions to Africa began in 1824, when the church sent John Boggs to Liberia. In subsequent decades the church sent additional personnel to the work in Liberia and Sierra Leone. In 1864 a Board of Missions was established, and a denominational-level secretary of missions was elected. Though many of the mission initiatives taken by the church from its early days had not been continued due to inadequate support, by 1878

AMEC work on the African continent was permanently established.

In the 1890s, Bishop Henry McNeal Turner (1834–1915) visited West Africa, in part exploring his dream of African American emigration to Africa as the alternative to endemic abuse and discrimination in the United States. While there, he organized annual conferences in Liberia and Sierra Leone. In 1896, in response to appeals from South African Reverend Mangena Maake Mokone for affiliation of his Ethiopian Church of South Africa with the AMEC, Bishop Turner implemented the organization of the work as the Eighteenth Episcopal District of the AMEC. Two years later, the Women's Home and Foreign Missionary Society was established to lend support to missions in Southern Africa. As the 20th century progressed, so, also, did the denomination's work on the continent. There are now six episcopal districts across the African continent.

Whereas the AMEC, practically from the outset, saw a mandate to be in ministry to the people of their homeland, Africa, they also recognized a field of service in the Caribbean. In 1827, the Reverend Scipio Beane was commissioned to initiate work in Haiti. In 1874, the church organized the Women's Parent Mite Missionary Society. Its portfolio included support for the work in the Caribbean Islands and Central and South America, as well as other fields. Under a succession of secretaries of missions, such as the noted L. L. Berry, the work proceeded, ultimately resulting in the permanent planting of the AMEC in Suriname–Guyana, the Windward Islands, the Virgin Islands, the Dominican Republic, Haiti, Jamaica, and Cuba. The annual conferences of those places, along with London, England, constitute the church's Sixteenth Episcopal District.

As with the other large, historically black branches of Methodism, the AMEC through the years has had a particular concern for education. It began one of the first and oldest continuously existing black-run institutions of learning, Wilberforce University, and has maintained numerous other schools, colleges, seminaries, and institutes. The church counts more than 2 million members in 6,200 congregations. It is a member of the World Council of Churches.

African Methodist Episcopal Church
500 Eighth Ave. S.
Nashville, TN 37203
www.amecnet.org

Larry G. Murphy

See also: African Methodist Episcopal Zion Church; Christian Methodist Episcopal Church; United Methodist Church; World Council of Churches.

References

Allen, Richard. *The Life Experience and Gospel Labors of the Rt. Rev. Richard Allen.* Nashville: Abingdon Press, 1983.

Melton, J. Gordon. *A Will to Choose: The Origins of African American Methodism.* Lanham, MD: Rowman & Littlefield, 2007.

Murphy, Larry, et al., eds. *The Encyclopedia of African American Religions.* New York: Garland Publishing, 1993.

Richardson, Harry V. *Dark Salvation: The Story of Methodism as It Developed among Blacks in America.* Garden City, NY: Anchor Press/Doubleday, 1976.

Singleton, George A. *The Romance of African Methodism.* Nashville: AMEC Press, 1985.

African Methodist Episcopal Zion Church

The independent African Methodist Episcopal Zion Church (AMEZ Church) grew from the same sociocultural matrix that produced the African Methodist Episcopal Church under the leadership of Richard Allen (1760–1831) in Philadelphia. While contented with their affiliation to the Methodist Episcopal Church (MEC) (now a constituent part of the United Methodist Church), they desired accommodation within that body to their needs and concern, with equal access to membership privileges and to the liturgical and sacramental life of the church, including full ordination. Their proscribed status in the larger society gave particular impetus to their felt need to hold separate devotional services, in addition to worship shared with whites, services that could connect the resources of the faith to their circumstances as marginalized, often abused Americans.

An African American woman, known to history only as Betty, was among the band of five people who constituted the first recorded Methodist meeting in North America (1766). African Americans contributed toward the construction of the first Methodist meeting-house, to be named the John Street Church, in New York City. It was from this congregation that arose what was ultimately the second major autonomous body of black Methodists. Meeting first informally, under white clergy supervision, the black members of John Street in 1796 requested that they be allowed an official separate meeting, in their own facility. The request was granted by MEC Bishop Francis Asbury (1745–1816). A building belonging to one of the black members was fitted up as a worship space for the new African Chapel. By 1800, another larger, more permanent structure was erected, and in 1801 a congregation was chartered that called itself Zion Church, the name in public records being the African Methodist Episcopal Church of the City of New York.

Still a separate congregation in full communion with the MEC, with white clergy appointed by that body, it might have remained so had not Zion Church been caught up in a controversy of its sister white churches concerning church governance and the ownership of congregational property. Many members in the Methodist congregations desired greater lay participation in denominational legislation and administration. Further, they took issue with the policy of centralized conference ownership and control of all congregational properties. By 1820, the matter came to open legal dispute in the Methodist Conference. Zion Church, which had been granted ownership of its property as one of the terms of its separate status, found itself on the side of the dissidents, who, coincidentally, were led by Zion's white pastor, Reverend William Stillwell (d. 1851). Already disturbed by the continued resistance of the conference to ordaining black clergy, Zion Church was at a point of decision. The resolution reached was to form its own rules of governance, or Discipline, and to move toward full autonomy.

There had been deep dissatisfaction with earlier initiatives by representatives of Richard Allen, sent to New York to recruit members for his Philadelphia-based group, hence a choice was made not to join with the Allenites. Instead, in 1821, Zion joined with another separate New York City body of black Methodists, the Asbury Church, and four other similarly organized groups in New York, Connecticut, and Pennsylvania, to form an independent African Methodist Episcopal Church. One of the early and sustaining Zion leaders, James Varick, was selected in 1822 as the first bishop (bishops then being called superintendents). To establish clearly its identity as distinct from the Philadelphia group of the same name, and in honor of the popular name of the mother church, the General Conference (the national governing body) of 1848 added "Zion" to the denomination's official name.

Though it emerged to independence in New York, many of the AMEZ Church's key judicatory offices and its most enduring educational institutions, Livingstone College and Hood Seminary, came to be located in North Carolina, ultimately the seat of its numerical strength.

Like the AME Church, the AMEZ Church experienced slow early growth, partly as a result of the restrictions imposed by the South on their evangelization among the enslaved, which encompassed the great majority of the black population. Thus it was that with Emancipation, the church experienced a major swelling of its ranks. The work of recruitment among the emancipated was led by Bishop J. J. Clinton (1823–1881), but the impetus for it came from Mrs. Melvina Fletcher, who challenged Bishop Clinton to proceed with this task, which had been assigned to him, and who raised the funds to underwrite the work.

Meanwhile, by the mid-19th century, energetic, highly capable pioneers such as the Reverend John J. Moore began extension of the church's presence to the U.S. Far West. By century's end, Calvin C. Petty (1849–1900), Thomas H. Lomax (1832–1908), and Alexander Walters (1858–1917) (all, like Rev. Moore, later to become bishops) were among those who had continued the westward expansion, including the organization of AMEZ annual conferences in the Southwest and Far West.

The AMEZ Church holds the distinction of being among the first of the independent black denominations to fully ordain women, conferring deacon's orders upon Julia A. J. Foote in 1884 and upon Mary J. Small in 1895. Reverend Foote was ordained elder in 1900.

The AMEZ Church had been active in its participation in the Underground Railroad's conveying of escapees among the enslaved to freedom in Canada. Following through on that ministry, the church extended its full ministry services to this black Canadian population. Work in Canada proceeded, and by 1856 a British North America Conference was established. But the black population of Canada dwindled, and the church found itself with insufficient resources to sustain the work properly. So in 1864 the recently established conference was merged with the New England Conference.

Meanwhile, in the United States, the church pursued a commitment to the civil and social advancement of African Americans. Counting among its membership such noted historical 19th-century personages as Frederick Douglass, Harriet Tubman, and Sojourner Truth, the church forthrightly owned its role in social advocacy and on into the 20th century dubbed itself "the freedom church."

Casting broadly its mission attention, AMEZ work was initiated on the African continent in 1878, when the Reverend Andrew Cartwright formed a congregation in Brewerville, Liberia. In 1880, the General Conference organized the General Home and Foreign Board and the Ladies Mission Society to support the work of foreign missions. In 1896, the church appointed the Reverend John Small (1845–1905) as bishop to Africa. Bishop Small focused on training local leadership for the African work, rather than recruiting black Americans. Small was successful in establishing the AMEZ Church firmly in the Gold Coast (present-day Ghana). Bishops and missionary workers who followed in the path opened by Cartwright and Small extended the work along the West African coast from Liberia to Nigeria, and into South Africa.

Back in the Western Hemisphere, there had been intermittent initiatives to the West Indies and South America. As early as 1856, a church had been established in Demerara, followed a few years later by work in Haiti. By 1899 there were also congregations in Santo Domingo. The 20th century saw further development in the West Indies, with Annual Conferences formed in Guyana, the Bahamas, the Virgin Islands,

and Jamaica. Congregations were also established in England.

At the beginning of the 21st century, the AMEZ Church counted some 1 million in its membership, with 3,000 congregations located on every continent, with the exception of Australia. It is a member of the World Council of Churches.

African Methodist Episcopal Zion Church
PO Box 23843
Charlotte, NC 28232

Larry G. Murphy

See also: African Methodist Episcopal Church; Christian Methodist Episcopal Church; United Methodist Church; World Council of Churches.

References
Bradley, David Henry. *A History of the A.M.E. Zion Church.* Vol. 2. Nashville: The Parthenon Press, 1970.
Melton, J. Gordon. *A Will to Choose: The Origins of African American Methodism.* Lanham, MD: Rowman & Littlefield, 2007.
Murphy, Larry G., J. Gordon Melton, and Gary L. Ward, eds. *The Encyclopedia of African American Religions.* New York: Garland Publishing, 1993.
Richardson, Harry V. *Dark Salvation: The Story of Methodism as It Developed among Blacks in America.* Garden City, NY: Anchor-Press/Doubleday, 1976.
Walls, William J. *The African Methodist Episcopal Zion Church: Reality of the Black Church.* Charlotte, NC: A.M.E. Zion Publishing House, 1974.
www.amez.org/news/amezion/aboutourchurch.html.

African Orthodox Church

The African Orthodox Church is one of several churches that have originated in America but experienced its greatest success outside the country of its origin. The church was founded by George Alexander McGuire (1866–1934), formerly a priest in the Episcopal Church. He had risen as far as an African American could in that church at the time, and in 1919 he left the church and founded the Good Shepherd Independent Episcopal Church. He subsequently sought consecration as a bishop in order to found a church with apostolic succession that would be led and controlled by people of African descent.

McGuire was consecrated in 1921 by Joseph Rene Vilatte (1854–1929), then head of the small American Catholic Church, who had received his orders from the Syro-Jacobite Church of Malabar. McGuire was then installed as the first bishop of the new African Orthodox Church, a church that was orthodox in faith and practice but not in communion with the Ecumenical Patriarchate or other canonical orthodox bishops.

The church found an immediate response, primarily with the community of expatriate West Indians then residing in many American cities. Within two years congregations had been established in Brooklyn, New York; Pittsburgh, Pennsylvania; New Haven, Connecticut; as well as Nova Scotia, Cuba, and Santa Domingo. Additional congregations, including one in the Bahamas, soon emerged.

Following McGuire's death, the church has experienced a bumpy course in the United States. There were several schisms, finally healed in the 1960s. In the 1980s, there were 17 parishes, but the number declined through the 1990s.

The African branch of the church began in 1924 when several members of the African Church left to found an independent body. The leader of the group, Daniel William Alexander (1883–1970), the son of a West Indian immigrant to South Africa, learned of the existence of the African Orthodox Church and in 1927 traveled to the United States, where he was consecrated as bishop (and later elevated to archbishop). Upon his return to South Africa, he established his headquarters in Kimberly. He traveled the countryside establishing churches both across South Africa and in Kenya, Uganda, and Rhodesia (now Zambia).

The amiable relationship between the African and American branches continued through the years, and in 1960 the international leader of the church, Patriarch James I (William E. J. Robertson), traveled to Africa to consecrate the successors of the aging archbishop. While there, the patriarch ordered Alexander to resign in favor of one of the newly consecrated bishops.

The break caused by the incident was healed soon after Patriarch James's death in 1962, and Wafter Mbina succeeded Alexander. However, in 1963, Alexander suddenly reasserted his leadership, broke with both the American church and Mbina, assumed the title of patriarch, and reorganized his following as the African Orthodox Church in the Republic of South Africa. It is that church that has survived to the present. He was succeeded by his godson, Daniel Kanyiles (Patriarch James II). In the 1970s, the church reported 20 parishes in South Africa.

The work in Uganda had begun in 1929 when Ruben Spartas, an Anglican, heard of the African Orthodox Church. In 1932 he obtained ordination from Bishop Alexander, but the following year came to the conclusion that the African Orthodox Church was not fully Orthodox and brought his work under the Greek Orthodox Patriarchate of Alexandria and All Africa, which already had work in the region. The group (some 7,000 strong), however, broke away from the patriarch of Alexander in 1966 and formed the African Greek Orthodox Church.

Early in the 1930s, Alexander spent more than a year working in Kenya, raising a constituency and ordaining two priests. This church ran into trouble in 1952 when it was associated with the Mau Mau terrorism. Its schools were closed, and it was not allowed to conduct public worship. When the ban was lifted in the 1970s, the remaining Orthodox believers transferred their allegiance to the patriarch in Alexandria.

The American branch of the African Orthodox Church has its headquarters in New York. Its current metropolitan primate is Archbishop George Walter Sands. There are some 5,000 members in a dozen congregations scattered across the country from Miami to San Francisco.

African Orthodox Church
International Chancery, Holy Cross Cathedral
122 West 129th St.
New York, NY 10027

J. Gordon Melton

See also: Ecumenical Patriarchate/Patriarchate of Constantinople; Greek Orthodox Patriarchate of Alexandria and All Africa; Syro-Jacobite Malabar Catholic Church.

References

Githieya, Francis Kimani. *The Freedom of the Spirit: African Indigenous Churches in Kenya*. Atlanta, GA: Scholar's Press, 1997.

Newman, Richard. "The Origins of the African Orthodox Church." In *The Negro Churchman*. Millwood, NY: Krause Reprint Co., 1977.

Terry-Thompson, A. C. *The History of the African Orthodox Church*. N.p., 1956.

African Protestant Church

The African Protestant Church originated within the American Presbyterian mission in Cameroon in the 1930s. In 1921 the mission (now the Presbyterian Church of Cameroon) had founded a Bible school (now Dager Theological School) at Bibia. Students were trained in German and then, if deemed worthy, sent to Europe for further training. In 1934, some pastors led by Martin Bambba Minkio and working among the Ngumba people demanded the use of their native language. They left the mission and established an independent church. The church quickly received some 2,000 members from the mission.

Originally the church was named Église Protestante autochtone, but the name was subsequently changed to Église Protestante Ngumba and more recently assumed its present name, in French, Église protestanteafricaine. The church has remained small (some 10,000 members in 32 congregations in 2005), but has become a member of the All Africa Conference of Churches and in 1968 the World Council of Churches. It is headed by the church synod.

African Protestant Church
BP 6754
Yaoundé, Cameroon

J. Gordon Melton

See also: World Council of Churches.

References

Bauswein, Jean-Jacques, and Lukas Vischner, eds. *The Reformed Family Worldwide: A Survey of Reformed Churches, Theological Schools, and International Organizations*. Grand Rapids, MI: Eerdmans, 1999.

Van Beek, Huibert. *A Handbook of the Churches and Councils: Profiles of Ecumenical Relationships*. Geneva: World Council of Churches, 2006.

◆ African Traditional Religions

The term *indigenous* is inadequate, but refers to African societies with a "traditional" religious and cultural orientation with many common characteristics. African peoples do not have the same traditional religious ideas or philosophy, and the existence of common characteristics must be proved through systematic comparative analysis. Any suggestion that there is a "unity" of African indigenous religions must be limited to considering common themes in systems that are often quite different. There are wide divergences between religions, which sometimes develop in isolation from each other. Each "common" phenomenon belongs to a complete whole, which is itself from a unique cultural, historical, and religious context. In this essay we must make generalizations with their accompanying dangers of misrepresentation, although in the indigenous religions of sub-Saharan Africa there is a great degree of affinity. These religions have weathered the ravages of time and the influences of external religions and cultures, and certain expressions of beliefs that have endured for many centuries still persist, even in urbanized and "secularized" societies. When these beliefs come into contact with an imported religion, such as Christianity or Islam, they often remain unaltered or may fundamentally change the character of that religion.

The term *animism*, from the Latin *anima* ("breath" or "soul") was popular in nineteenth-century Europe and is the belief that natural objects or phenomena possess a soul. At best, this idea of a pervasive soul describes only one aspect of African religions and this term, together with "primitive" and even "primal" (basic or primary), should be abandoned. A more satisfactory way of describing African indigenous religions might be to use three interdependent and overlapping terms: (1) *theism*: the belief in a Supreme Being and (sometimes) lesser gods; (2) *spirituality*: the belief in a spiritual world, including ancestors; and (3) *dynamism*: the belief in power working through objects and available to people.

Theism: God and Lesser Divinities   Almost all African religions posit the idea of a single God, a supreme creator. The term *polytheism* (many gods) is a difficult one to sustain in Africa, and writers like Idowu have suggested that an "implicit" or "diffused" *monotheism* is true of African religions. This theism is ambivalent: the Supreme Being is at the same time very near (immanent) and distant (transcendent). But writers like Mbiti have pointed out that the two attributes of God's transcendence and immanence are complementary, and that transcendence cannot be emphasized to the exclusion of immanence. African observers acknowledge that God in traditional religions is predominantly transcendent, which usually means that for most of the time the Supreme Being is remote from everyday affairs. Because of this, he/she (usually male) does not interfere with or harass people, and therefore is regarded as "good." But because of his/her simultaneous nearness, sometimes people live in dread of an unpredictable God who may cause calamity and distress, including affliction, misfortune, diseases, death, and national calamities.

There are no atheists in African religions. Most peoples had a unique name (sometimes several) for a Supreme Being before the introduction of Christianity or Islam. Often one name, or a derivative of it, reappears among different peoples. Although there is widespread belief in a Supreme Being, usually a creator God, most divine functions have been delegated to other beings, lesser gods, spirits, or ancestors. In places where Christianity or Islam predominate there is a stronger belief in monotheism at a popular level, and vaguer traditional ideas of a Supreme Being have been replaced by a definite belief in a monotheistic God. The Supreme Being is a being with personal attributes (although not human) and isolated from other spirit beings. Often the Supreme Being is also the first ancestor and essentially the same name or root word is used for *God* as for *ancestors*. Sometimes the name for God is associated with both the ancestors and with a place where he is believed to live. In these cases the

distinction between *God* and *ancestor* is maintained by the use of different noun classes. In some cases the name for God is a locative related to the place where the spirits live. Usually the Supreme Being is believed to live in the "sky" or "heaven" (in most African languages there is no differentiation between these two words), but some peoples situate him under the earth, where the spirits live. In Yoruba (Nigeria), *Olorun* is "owner of heaven," and in many religions the word for *God* is synonymous with *sun*, and sometimes with *rain*. These ideas indicate that the sun, the rain, the sky (heaven), and other natural phenomena are manifestations of God and among some, God is sometimes identified with nature. In west Africa, the male deity in the sky sends rain to fall upon the female deity, Mother Earth. The Ashanti venerate the Earth Goddess Asase Yaa, as the earth is closely related to the fertility of the Ashanti people as well as being the resting place of their ancestors.

The activity most commonly attributed to the Supreme Being is that of creation, and many of the names for God describe God as creator, molder, and maker. Every new institution and birth is attributed to God's power. However, it is often felt that God has withdrawn from creation usually as the result of some human (or animal) blunder or by God's arbitrary decision, and usually God does not do anything any more. Thus we have the view that the African "high god" is a *dues otiosus*, a passive, inactive God. It is true that many African peoples no longer are able to say who or what God is. Seldom is God worshipped directly, and shrines, altars, temples, or priests do not exist. There is no feeling of guilt in the sight of God and therefore there is no need to try to appease God with gifts or sacrifices. There are exceptions to this general rule, and among some peoples sacrifices and prayers are addressed to and shrines and priests devoted to God. As long as God provides rain, harvests, health, possessions, and children, everyone is satisfied. Nevertheless, God sustains all life, and if he/she chooses to withdraw provisions, then people may have to entreat God. But God is normally too far above humanity to be concerned with their daily affairs. There is no spontaneous longing for God and no desire to enter into relationship with God—religion is practical and material rather than mystical or spiritual.

Nevertheless, belief in the Supreme Being is a central feature of these religions, and it would be wrong to emphasize the remoteness and inactivity to the exclusion of the simultaneous nearness and unceasing activity. God stands behind everything, is mentioned in many proverbs and myths, and is called on in times of crisis. Terrifying and unexplainable natural phenomena (such as storms, earthquakes, lightning, fire, and epidemics) are often attributed to God, who is invoked to account for these otherwise unexplainable things. The basic conception is that God is "good," but this seems to mean that he/she is neutral and does not hamper, irritate, or interfere with humans, and therefore humans should not interfere with God and may ignore him/her. If they do "interfere," this might irritate God and lead to punishment. When God does intervene, a person may never know what God is going to do, and thus there is a strong undertone of fatalism. God becomes arbitrary and unpredictable, merciful or merciless, as God chooses. The comforting thought for those faced with inexplicable events is "God has done it," "it's God's will," or "God knows" (but we do not understand).

Some African peoples, especially in west Africa, have a belief in a pantheon or hierarchy of divinities. They are often associated with some aspect of nature or life, and thus are sometimes called "nature spirits." They have many human characteristics: they can become hungry, jealous, angry, and so on, and people must always endeavor to remain on good terms with them. Some of these divinities used to be human beings, others were created by God or appear as God's wives or children, and some are regarded as more powerful than others. Among west African peoples (unlike most other Africans), there are a great number of divinities and spirits that appear to be personifications of the Supreme Being. But these "gods" are more limited than the Supreme Being and bear a generic name that is not applied to God. Thus, about 1,700 Yoruba divinities are called *orisha*, a term never used to refer to God, which is *Olurun* or *Olodumare*. These divinities, like ancestors, often function as servants and intermediaries of the Supreme Being and are often represented by wooden or metal images. The Yoruba *orisha* are headed by *Orisha-nla* or *Obatala*, the one who gives riches or poverty, strength or deformity.

Ogun is the god of war, *Shango* the god of storms and the anger of *Olurun*, *Shopona* the power of smallpox and fever (*Sapata* among the Ewe in Benin), *Eshu* the power of mischief, *Olokun* the sea god, and so on. The Yoruba pantheon has reappeared in the Caribbean and in Brazil. The divinities derive from the creator and have no existence or authority in their own right. In west Africa, sea deities and many river deities are important. Sky gods distinct from the Supreme Being also exist. The Ewe have twin gods *Mawu* (male) and *Lisa* (female) with fourteen children who become gods of natural phenomena associated with the sky: thunder, lightning, rain, etc.

African societies have myths about the beginning of time, which often reveal beliefs about creation and a supreme creator. These myths are passed on orally from generation to generation, providing fundamental explanations for the order in the universe and society established by a creator, and sometimes explaining why God has "gone away" from creation. Some myths associate human origins with a tree, others tell of the first person's formation out of clay or out of a hole in the ground or a marsh. Others attribute human origins to the knee or leg of a divine being, or to being brought from heaven to earth. The Akan myth (Ghana) has God creating an orderly universe: first the sky, then the earth, rivers, waters, plants, and trees. After that, humans were formed and animals made for them, and nature spirits were formed to protect them. According to many myths, humans originally lived in a state of indescribable bliss, immortality, and unimpeded fellowship with God. Although God lived in heaven, heaven was closely connected to earth at the beginning. God provided all the necessities of food and clothing for people in a paradise and taught them how to till the ground, make beer, hunt, and cook. But this paradise did not last, and after some time God withdrew from people. This withdrawal is not usually attributed to human sin or offence, but to some mistake —although there are some exceptions where myths relate the presence of sin and disobedience. In most of these myths humans are innocent victims of tragic circumstances. Myths go on to explain how people lost their immortality, again through an unfortunate accident. The most common myth in Africa concerns the animal messenger (often the chameleon) who was sent to people with news of immortality or resurrection. But the messenger dawdled on the way, forgot his message or garbled it, stuttered in delivering it, or had his parcel of new skins stolen by the snake (which explains why snakes can have new skins every year). But the most common version of the myth is that the first messenger was overtaken by a second one (often the lizard) whose message was that people would die. The result is irreconcilable separation between humanity and the creator.

Dynamism: Power and Power Specialists Practices associated with the so-called "manipulation of power" ("dynamism") are intimately related to religious practices. The dependence on the Supreme Being, the gods, spirits, or ancestors is revealed in resorting to the "dynamism" specialists for solutions to problems. Africans believe in power, which may reside in charms, amulets, beads, medicines, words, names, and various other inanimate objects. Possessing this power enables people to do supernatural things or to prevent evil from occurring, and so people long for more of it. The greatest disaster possible follows the losing of power. Illnesses, suffering, disappointments, exhaustion, injustice, oppression, and failure are all regarded as a lessening of power, and so everything possible is done to avoid its loss and to promote its increase. The Supreme Being is seen as the source of all power, but this power has no dualism—God can use his power for good or withhold it, resulting in evil. There is a personal quality about the power residing in people, intimately linked to the ancestors and the ongoing life of the community. The interrelatedness between magic, power, and the ancestors is shown in the diviner's capacity to make "magic," ascribed to the power of the ancestors residing within. Life and existence or being itself is inextricably tied up with power. To live is to have power, to be sick or to die is to have less of it. These concepts are not always held by all people in these societies, they sometimes depend upon the level of cultural and technological development, and whether people are in a rural or an urban environment. In these different contexts, although power is sought earnestly, it acquires different meanings.

The principle behind the use of magic and divination in Africa is the ability to strengthen or weaken another person's power through the manipulation of the power of non-human things. In order to obtain power, people make use of charms and medicines, and consult diviners or "witchdoctors," healers, prophets, and mediums. These specialists, who have undergone a long period of training by their elders, use their power for the good of the local community, particularly in providing protection against the illegitimate use of power, the work of evil sorcerers or witches. And so, whenever the lessening of power results in problems, it is usually necessary for people to consult such specialists in order to receive more power. These specialists have power to discern the wishes of the ancestors and to act as protectors of society. They must be heeded, for one who does not follow their instructions courts disaster. The diviner is able to diagnose the cause of the affliction and will usually prescribe some ancestor ritual and sometimes give protective medicines and strong charms to overcome this unseen evil force. The specialist often seeks to discover the source of the trouble and *who* sends it. The answer to the question of who sent the problem takes different forms, but usually involves one of five possibilities that the adversity comes from: (1) an evil wizard; (2) an offended ancestor; (3) the breaking of a taboo; (4) God; or (5) the personal guilt of the sufferer or someone close to her or him. The specialist will be concerned mainly with the first three causes.

These specialists are believed to use their power for the good of the community, and function as doctors, counselors, and pastors at the same time (often the most influential people in the whole community with an all-encompassing mandate). They explain the mysteries of life and death, convey messages from the spirit world, heal sicknesses, give guidance in daily affairs, protect from dangers seen and unseen, resolve quarrels, promote fertility, act as "agony aunts" in affairs of the heart, and ensure success and prosperity in all areas of life. They are in opposition to the evil wizards, who are to be feared and avoided. Sorcery and witchcraft are to be overcome by the strengthening of people through the use of more powerful medicine or magic. In many African languages, different words are used to distinguish between the "good" diviner on the one hand and the enemy of society, the sorcerer or witch, on the other.

Divination is still widely practiced all over Africa, not least of all in urban areas. It is often intimately associated with the ancestor cult, since diviners are traditionally believed to be possessed by ancestors. There are diviners in urban areas throughout Africa whose techniques may differ from rural diviners and who may even consider themselves Christian, although usually they are not. Their healing power is specifically not Christian, coming directly from guiding ancestors, although today the influence of Christianity has contributed to the syncretistic views of many diviners and prophets regarding their source of power. The manipulation of power (magic) may be homeopathic or contagious. The former is based on the principle that power can be harnessed by analogous or imitative actions such as causing smoke to symbolize clouds and produce rain, or piercing a so-called "voodoo doll" in the likeness of a particular person to produce the same effect in that person. Contagious magic likewise is based on the idea that everything closely associated with a person, such as hair, nail clippings, urine, saliva, dirty clothes, and so on, may be used by someone else to do that person harm. The power resident in material substances collectively known as "medicines" is interrelated with the power resident in people and can be used to support that power. Medicines are therefore not exclusively curative in a western sense, but are powerful substances that can be legitimately used for a wide variety of beneficial purposes such as fertility, success, courtship, protection, and even the changing of personality, and also to combat sorcery and witchcraft. These medicines contain (or are) power, which should be used for the benefit of the community, but they are also used illegitimately to harm people or to reduce their power.

Very often there is also the unseen evil and antisocial force of the sorcerer, who has too much power that can be selfishly used to harm others and must be counteracted with a more powerful force. In some African societies a distinction is made between two kinds of wizard. Sorcerers deliberately use medicine against their victims and are the personification of evil in the community. If such a person is discovered or smelled out, there is only one remedy, total extermination by the whole community. The second kind is witches, who are usually female and use medicines and/or some psychic act, usually inadvertently and unconsciously. Witches are believed to leave the bodies of women while they sleep to meet other witches at certain places. They fly around on the backs of birds, fireflies, sticks, and other objects, or they change themselves into owls, bats, or hyenas. They seek to enter other people's bodies and suck out their power. The wizard can sometimes only succeed with an evil intent if some kind of access to the victim is gained through the latter's protective ancestors.

Some make a distinction between Asian shamans who "travel" to cosmic worlds in a state of trance (ecstasy) and African healers who are possessed by guiding ancestors, also resulting in a trance. These are probably different explanations of the same phenomenon, consistent with their own religious contexts. Whether we refer to a shaman or a diviner, both exhibit similar characteristics as spirit mediums. They can be male or female persons who, as a result of a disorientating illness, believe themselves to be called to be healers. After initial resistance to this calling, they accept it and undergo a prolonged period of training often in isolation, usually with an experienced diviner or shaman, and the training ends with a symbolically rich initiation ceremony. Thereafter they enter into periods of purposeful ecstatic communication with the spirits by means of trances or seances, with ancestors or other spiritual entities accepted in their religious contexts, in order to bring health to others and harmony between the community and those spiritual entities they represent. African healers exhibit many similar characteristics to Asian shamans. There are many kinds of healers who divine through wooden divining slabs, shells, or through ancestors or alien spirits, and are distributors of appropriate medicines. This is true whether they are herbalists or diviners/spirit mediums. As long as there is belief in the power of spirits and evil sorcery, the healer's enhanced position as pivotal to the well-being of the community is guaranteed. The healer is called to this position by recurring healing dreams followed by illness, which is sometimes a mental disturbance. Periods of withdrawal and resistance then follow, after which the novice healers accept the calling and enter into training, which involves observing a number of taboos. They must receive their guidance from a spirit or ancestor if they are going to succeed as professional specialists in the spirit world. Various healing techniques and methods used include using herbs, throwing bones, stones, or nuts to divine, and relying on dreams or other forms of communication with guiding ancestors. To increase the power of their patients, specialists use a wide variety of objects: amulets, necklaces, powders, tattoo markings and face painting, incantations, forked sticks, horns, calabashes, and so on. These are all symbols of power intended either to protect or to promote health, happiness, and success. Many healers are also herbalists, with detailed and intimate knowledge of the use of herbs, roots, and other plants as medicines to protect or restore life. In Africa it is not always possible to distinguish between a therapeutic "herbalist" and a diagnostic "diviner," because most specialists use both methods in treating patients. In many of the independent African Initiated Churches, the prophet-healer has taken the place of the traditional healer, and the use of healing symbols with parallels to traditional healing methods is one of the central and most important features.

Spirituality: Ancesters and the Spirit World   Rituals concerning ancestors are the center of many African religions, and this practice is still important for many Africans converted to Christianity. The operating principle is the ancestors' presence and moral influence in the community of which they are part. Ancestors usually manifest themselves through dreams, sicknesses, and other misfortunes. All African peoples take dreams seriously, although not all dreams are sent by ancestors, as these can always be recognized. Africans usually recognize a message from the ancestors by means of a visible manifestation of the dead person in their dreams. It is only when the meaning of a recurring dream is unclear that the diviners are consulted for interpretation. But when an ancestor appears in a dream, the meaning is usually clear enough. Ancestors are limited in that their influence is mainly restricted to their kin of the same lineage. Usually in African societies these will be their patrilineal descendants (male and female), although sometimes an ancestor can even be a younger relative who has predeceased one (hence the inadequacy of the term "ancestor"). The ancestors visit their living kin from time to time by

means of various signs that are interpreted by the family—the most common (besides dreams) being an onslaught of different sicknesses and delay in conception. Various unfortunate and fortunate occurrences will be ascribed respectively to the ancestors' displeasure or their favor. Their main benevolent function is that of protection. If they are neglected (for their main need is to be remembered), then they are capable of unleashing destructive powers on the family concerned. In this respect, ancestors are causative agents of both good and evil. Having protective powers, their exercise of these powers results in good, the withholding of them in evil. Furthermore, the direct actions of their surviving kin, particularly in ritual acts of remembrance or the neglect of such acts, has direct bearing on the conduct of the ancestors.

Ancestors are conceived of as elevated people. Although they are approached with the respect due them as the older and wiser ones of society, it is doubtful whether this approach is the same as that given to God. In other words, such terms as ancestor *worship* or even *veneration* are inaccurate. Of course, the ancestors are known to be dead and therefore they are not the same as living people. They are generally believed to be less fortunate than the living; and because of their limitations, having more power than the living compensates them. African peoples, however, who pray to ancestors also pray to living people. In African societies, elders are believed to have more power and therefore require allegiance from the younger ones. Ancestors are conceived of as quite distinct from the Supreme Being, although they are thought of as nearer to God than are living people. Contact with ancestors on the part of the living is usually made through offerings and ritual killings, which occur when the ancestors are believed to be hungry; essentially, a ritual killing is to participate in a communal meal with the ancestors. People must continually see to it that the ancestors are fed. Thus, apart from ritual killings, beer is poured out for them and food left in the pot. The ancestors are sometimes thought of as unpredictable, capricious, and prone to anger and jealousy, and if they are thought to behave like this they may be scolded. Although ancestors are primarily for the preservation of the family, they are also a threat and are therefore to be feared. No one can ever be sure what they are going to do or not do next. In practice there is an intimate personal relationship between the living and the departed. Supplicants may make suggestions to the ancestors of acceptable alternatives to the course being followed by them, and respectfully request a change in attitude. The language is usually that of polite everyday speech, the address of people to their seniors.

Ancestors are believed to enter into individuals and to use them as mediums of communication. Some African diviners are specialist spirit mediums and are mostly women. Such spirit mediums are "possessed" by ancestors in order to communicate with the living. Various things happen that show that a medium is possessed. Usually she goes into a trance, accompanied by various ritual activities of the people around her, such as singing and dancing. The onset of this trance is accompanied by trembling, rolling of the eyes, falling down in a fit, or supernatural feats, after which the medium begins to speak with the "voice" of the ancestor. After the trance is over, the medium returns to normal. The people inquiring of her are thereafter to carry out the instructions of the ancestor as interpreted by the medium. Spirit possession usually means that a spirit temporarily enters into people and displaces their ability to control themselves while being possessed. Among the Shona and many other African peoples, the desire of an ancestor to possess someone is usually signaled by a lengthy illness. Shaking and grunting noises during dancing and the beating of drums herald the onset of possession. The family may then discuss their problems with the possessed medium, for they are actually talking with the ancestors. A Zulu person possessed by ancestors is expected to become a diviner, for spirit possession is linked to divination. At first, the person will demonstrate strange behavior, will tend to be antisocial, and will be subject to constant dreaming and prolonged illness. The eventual possession is evidenced by frequent yawning and sneezing, by shaking, quivering and convulsions, by belching and hiccuping, and by singing the songs of the ancestors. Ancestors are also believed to reappear in newborn children.

Ancestors who have been forgotten and no longer fulfil their protective function, children who die, and adults who did not have children of their own or did not receive a proper burial are believed to become spirits in the graveyard of time. Their abode is in the earth or in the air, and they seldom fulfill any practical function, but may become angry and vengeful. In many parts of Africa, nature spirits are abundant, such as spirits that dwell in water, sacred stones, caves, hills, springs, trees, groves, forests, and many others. These spirits may have been ancestors buried in or near that particular natural phenomenon, who with the passing of time were identified with that phenomenon. There are also anthropomorphous spirits, often visible to people, which are often ogre-like little creatures, sometimes with strong sexual connotations and associated with natural phenomena. A famous one in southern Africa is the Zulu *thokoloshe*, a creature that is known throughout the region and the subject of many conversations. There are also many spirits identified with particular animals. The origin of all these spirits is not speculated on; they are simply believed to have always existed, and they are omnipresent, very much a part of the world. The main difference between spirits and ancestors in practical terms seems to be that spirits do not appear as often to people. When they do, they may bring adversity or even possess people. In west Africa, nature spirits have become significant deities that must be placated by means of daily sacrifices, offerings, and other ritual acts.

One of the functions of a diviner is to determine the identity of and exorcise evil spirits. These spirits could include nature spirits, spirits under the control of malicious sorcerers, and spirits that come from outside a person's particular ethnic group or lineage, sometimes perceived as avenging spirits. Ancestors are never referred to, nor considered, evil spirits, as their existence depends on the continued respect of their relatives. But once they are forgotten and no rites are performed for them, they may reappear and cause trouble. Many nature spirits are feared, and people go to diviners to seek protection from them. There seems to be a connection in perception between ancestors and all types of spirit; they are all personal spirits with individual identity and characteristics. They often possess people, which in African thought is not always a bad thing. Spirits possess mediums in order to convey significant messages to people and this possession is a treasured feature and not a threat. But at other times, spirits possess people in such a way that they desire to be free from the troublesome consequences through exorcism.

Allan H. Anderson

References

Idowu, E. Bolaji. *African Traditional Religion.* London: SCM, 1973.

Magesa, Laurenti. *African Religion: The Moral Traditions of Abundant Life.* New York: Orbis, 1997.

Mbiti, John. *African Religions and Philosophy.* London: Heinemann, 1969.

Mbiti, John. *Concepts of God in Africa.* London: SPCK, 1971.

Agnosticism

Agnosticism is an intellectual position based on the belief that proving or disproving God's existence is beyond human competence. In 1869, when he coined the term, Thomas Huxley said of the "agnostic," "When I reached intellectual maturity and began to ask myself whether I was an atheist, a theist, or a pantheist . . . I found that the more I learned and reflected, the less ready was the answer. They [believers] were quite sure they had attained a certain 'gnosis,'—had, more or less successfully, solved the problem of existence; while I was quite sure I had not, and had a pretty strong conviction that the problem was insoluble."

There are many positions one can take with regard to the God question. One may be a theist and hold to a "belief in a deity, or deities" and "belief in one God as creator and supreme ruler of the universe." One may be a pantheist and believe that the Deity is to be identified with the whole of the cosmos. Or one may hold to atheism, the disbelief in, or denial of, the existence of a God. Agnosticism, in contrast, defines God as "unknowing, unknown, unknowable." At a party held one evening in 1869, Huxley further clarified the term agnostic, referencing Saint Paul's mention of an altar in Athens to "the Unknown God" in Acts 17:23, as one who holds that the existence of anything beyond and behind material phenomena is unknown and so can be judged unknowable, and especially that a First Cause and an unseen world are subjects of which we know nothing.

Natural scientist and essayist Thomas Henry Huxley (1825–1895) coined the term "agnosticism." (Thomson, J. Arthur. *The Outline of Science,* vol. 1, 1922)

Agnostics make a point of distinguishing between a statement about the universe and a statement about one's personal beliefs. One may personally believe in God and still argue, as the agnostic does, that by the criteria of science and reason God is an unknowable concept. We cannot prove or disprove God's existence through empirical evidence or deductive proof. Therefore, the agnostic suggests that theism and atheism are both indefensible positions as statements about the universe. Thomas Huxley once again clarified this distinction: "Agnosticism is not a creed but a method, the essence of which lies in the vigorous application of a single principle. Positively the principle may be expressed as, in matters of the intellect, follow your reason as far as it can carry you without other considerations. And negatively, in matters of the intellect, do not pretend the conclusions are certain that are not demonstrated or demonstrable. It is wrong for a man to say he is certain of the objective truth of a proposition unless he can produce evidence which logically justifies that certainty" ("Agnosticism," 1889, see *Collected Essays*).

Martin Gardner, one of the founders of the modern skeptical movement, is a believer, but one who believes that the existence of God cannot be proved. He now refers to himself as a fideist, or someone who believes in God for personal or pragmatic reasons, but his position could also be described as agnostic. In defending his position, he noted, "As a fideist I don't think there are any arguments that prove the existence of God or the immortality of the soul. Even more than that, I agree with Unamuno that the atheists have the better arguments. So it is a case of quixotic emotional belief that is really against the evidence and against the odds."

Atheists often accuse agnostics of being wishy-washy. Many atheists would argue that there are really only two positions on the God question: you either believe in God or you do not believe in God—theism or atheism. Agnostics respond that atheism typically means denial of the existence of a God and agnostics argue that denial of a God is an untenable position. It is no more possible to prove God's nonexistence than it is to prove his existence. "There is no God" is no more defensible a statement than "There is a God."

Michael Shermer

See also: Atheism; God, Existence of; Unbelief.

References

Gardner, Martin. *The Whys of a Philosophical Scrivener.* Santa Ana, CA: Griffin, 1999.

Huxley, Thomas H. *Collected Essays.* Vol. 5. New York: D. Appleton, 1894.

Shermer, Michael. *How We Believe: The Search for God in an Age of Science.* New York: W. H. Freeman, 2000.

Agonshu

Agonshu, a Japanese "new, new religion" (in Japanese, *shin shin shukyo*), was established in its present form in 1978 by Kiriyama Seiyu (b. 1921), its founder and *kancho* (leader). Kiriyama started an earlier movement in 1954 known as Kannon Jikeikai, Association for the Worship of the Bodhisattva Kannon, who is regarded as the most potent symbol of compassion and mercy and a widely worshipped Buddhist figure, not only in Japan but also among Japanese and their descendants in other countries, including the United States and Brazil.

In the late 1970s, Kiriyama claimed to have discovered the essentials of original, authentic Buddhism by reading the Agama (in Japanese, Agon, whence the name of the sect) sutras, early Buddhist texts that, he claimed, predate all other Buddhist sutras, including the Lotus Sutra, which is widely revered in Japan. This discovery provided Kiriyama with an unrivalled understanding of the deeper meaning of Buddhism. In practice it meant the development of a system of beliefs and practices, the principal aim of which is to ensure that the sufferings of the spirits of the dead are terminated as they attain *jobutsu,* or Buddhahood.

In its teachings Agonshu stresses that all misfortunes and problems in life can be explained by reference to one's own or one's ancestors' karmic actions. Large-scale *goma* rituals, in which requests or petitions are inscribed on sticks or wood that are then burned on a pyre while invocations are chanted, are performed every Friday in the Sohonzan Main Temple in Kyoto to eliminate negative ancestral karma and transform the sufferings of the spirits of the dead into Buddhahood. The main annual festivals are the Star Festival (Hoshi Matsuri) on February 11, which consists of an outdoor goma ritual on a grand scale; the Flower Festival of April 8 to mark the Buddha's birthday; the Great Buddha Festival (Dai-Butsu Sai) of May 5; and the Tens of Thousands of Lanterns service, held in Kyoto on July 13–15 and in Tokyo on August 13–15, for the liberation and peace of ancestors' souls. Many of those who attend the Tens of Thousands of Lanterns festival at Kyoto also visit the Agonshu cemetery on the Kashihara hills northwest of the ancient capital city of Nara. The unique feature of this cemetery is that every tomb has what is called a *Ho Kyo Into,* in which a small replica of the Busshari and its casket is placed.

Agonshu's principal object of veneration is the Shinsei-busshari (true Buddha relic), a casket said to contain an actual fragment of a bone of the Buddha, and hence his spirit. Three esoteric methods (*shugyo*) form the core of the training undertaken by recruits: *jobutsu-ho,* which provides the necessary sensitivity

A Japanese member of the Agonshu Association practices with a ceremonial sword before a ceremony in Jerusalem, September 10, 2008. (AP/Wide World Photos)

and aptitude for spiritual enlightenment; *noyi hoju-ho*, a practice performed with the shinsei-busshari that enables one to achieve the happiness, good fortune, and insight to cut loose from karma (a rare accomplishment); and *gumonji somei-ho*, a technique for developing profound wisdom and extraordinary mental awareness.

The estimated size of the membership in Japan is 1 million, and Agonshu now has a modest following of between 100 and 1,000 members in most countries of the Far East, Asia, and Africa. It is also present in small numbers in Mongolia, Russia, the United States, Canada, Brazil, and several European countries. The movement is actively engaged in projects for the establishment of world peace and the reform of Buddhism through the teaching of the Agama sutras.

Agonshu is organized into main offices, branch offices, *dojos* (centers or places of worship where teaching and training take place), and local offices. There are seven main offices in different regions of Japan, and a main religious center in Kyoto, while it has administrative headquarters in both Tokyo and Kyoto.

Agonshu
607 Kitakazan Omine-cho
Yamashima, Kyoto
Japan

Peter B. Clarke

See also: Relics.

References

The founder and present leader, Kiriyama Seiyu, has published many treatises in Japanese on the teachings of the movement, including *Henshin no genri* (The Principles of Transformation). Tokyo: Kadokawa Bunsho, 1971.

Agon-shu and Its Activities. Tokyo: Agon-shu Public Information Division, 1990.

The Agon-shu: The Original Teachings of the Lord Buddha. Tokyo: Agonshu, 1989.

Reader, Ian. "Agon Shu: The Rise of a Japanese 'New, New Religion': Themes in the Development of Agon shu." *Japanese Journal of Religious Studies* 15, no. 4 (1988): 231–261.

Agrippa von Nettesheim, Heinrich Cornelius

ca. 1486–ca. 1535

A Renaissance humanist, traveler, and author, Agrippa is best known for several treatises including an exaltation of the virtues of women, an exposition of the vanity of arts and sciences, and an infamous compendium known as *De occulta philosophia sive magia libri tres* (Cologne, 1533). These three books of occult philosophy show great erudition and a familiarity with Latin texts. They incorporate material from a number of sources, notably neo-Pythagorean teaching; Plato's *Timaeus*; Aristotle's, Ovid's, Virgil's, and Pliny's *Historia Naturalis*; the Orphic Hymns and the *Corpus Hermeticum*; neo-Platonic thought; Pseudo-Dionysius; Patristic exegetes such as Clement and Augustine; writings by Marsilio Ficino, Giovanni Pico della Mirandola, Lodovicus Lazarellus, Johannes Reuchlin, Desiderius Erasmus, and Martin Luther; Paulo Ricci's *Portae Lucis* (Augsburg, 1516); and the Venetian Francesco Giorgio's *De Harmonia Mundi* (Venice, 1525). Moreover, *De occulta philosophia* was instrumental in shaping Agrippa's largely tarnished reputation, for it was as a near legendary Doctor Faustus type figure accompanied by a devilish black dog that early moderns knew him.

Heinrich Cornelius Agrippa von Nettesheim was born in Cologne very probably in 1486 (16th-century biographers commonly stated on September 14), enrolling at the Arts Faculty at Cologne University in July 1499. After graduating in 1502 he studied at the University of Paris before apparently undertaking a journey to Spain about 1508, perhaps to engage in military activities. In 1509 he lectured on Johann Reuchlin's *De verbo mirifico* at the University of Dôle in Burgundy. But despite the support of the university's chancellor, Agrippa was denounced in a sermon as

Portrait of Heinrich Cornelius Agrippa von Nettesheim (1486–1535). (National Library of Medicine)

a "judaizing heretic." The following year Agrippa was briefly in London, where he seems to have become acquainted with the humanist John Colet, an expert on Pauline theology, and Thomas Cranmer, a future Protestant Reformer and archbishop of Canterbury. That same year Agrippa dedicated the manuscript of his treatise *De occulta philosophia* to the Benedictine Abbot Johannes Trithemius, who received it at the monastery of St. Jakob, Würzburg, before April 8, 1510. Trithemius, however, counseled Agrippa to read more deeply on these topics and take care in how he chose to reveal them.

From about 1511 until early 1518, Agrippa was in Italy, where he lectured at the University of Pavia on Plato's *Convivium* and the *Pimander,* attributed to Hermes Trismegistus. During and immediately after this period he wrote the unfinished *Dialogus de homine* (1515–1516), *De triplici ratione cognoscendi Deum,* and *De originali peccato* (1519), a prolific output when one also considers that he had written a treatise on the superiority of women, *De nobilitate et praecellentia foeminei sexus* (1509), for Margaret of Austria. From

1518 to 1520 Agrippa was in Metz, then in Geneva from 1521 to 1523, and finally in Freiburg until 1524 as the city's physician. By the spring of 1524 he was in Lyon, where he quickly fell out of favor at the court of the Queen Mother, Louise de Savoy. Shortly after he wrote his *De Incertitudine et Vanitate Scientiarum*, a work described by one modern scholar as "a biting critique of human science," "a ferocious and radical attack on the moral and social assumptions of his day." Eventually, Agrippa made his way to Antwerp, where he secured the imperial privilege for his longer works, notably *De Vanitate Scientiarum* (press of Johannes Graphaeus, 1530) and the first book of an expanded version of *De Occulta Philosophia* (Johannes Graphaeus, 1531) dedicated to the archbishop of Cologne, Hermann von Wied. The theologians of Louvain condemned *De Vanitate* as scandalous, impious, and heretical, while *De Occulta Philosophia* was denounced by a Dominican inquisitor as heretical doctrine. Even so, a complete three-volume version of this text appeared in July 1533 issued in Cologne by Johannes Soter (prudently without a printer's name and the place of publication). The last two years of Agrippa's life are obscure; he returned to France, was arrested on the orders of Francis I, but was soon released. He died apparently in extreme poverty most likely at Grenoble in 1535.

Published versions and manuscript copies of Agrippa's writings circulated widely in several languages throughout Europe among Christians and even some Jews between the 16th and 19th centuries—particularly in England, France, German-speaking areas, the Italian peninsula, and the Netherlands. They influenced views about the Radical Reformation, skepticism, melancholy, physiognomy, angels, Hermeticism, magic, numerology, and Kabbalah. A *Fourth Book of Occult Philosophy*, posthumously attributed to Agrippa and included in the two-volume edition of his collected works (possibly published at Strasbourg ca. 1600 rather than Lyons as the imprint suggests), is a spurious compilation.

Ariel Hessayon

See also: Angels; Luther, Martin; Reuchlin, Johannes; Women, Status and Role of.

References

Agrippa von Nettesheim, Heinrich Cornelius. *De occulta philosophia libri tres*, Ed. by Vittoria Perrone Compagni. Leiden and New York: E. J. Brill, 1992.

Lehrich, Christopher. *The Language of Demons and Angels: Cornelius Agrippa's occult philosophy.* Leiden: Brill, 2003.

Nauert, Charles. *Agrippa and the Crisis of Renaissance Thought.* Urbana: University of Illinois Press, 1965.

van der Poel, Marc. *Cornelius Agrippa, the Humanist Theologian and His Declamations.* Leiden: Brill, 1997.

Zambelli, Paola. *White Magic, Black Magic in the European Renaissance. From Ficino, Pico, Della Porta to Trithemius, Agrippa, Bruno.* Leiden: Brill, 2007.

Ahmad, Mirza Ghulam Hazrat

1835–1908

Mirza Ghulam Hazrat Ahmad, an Indian Muslim, founded the Ahmadiyya movement in Islam. Feeling a call to revive Islam in his day, he came to view himself as the Madhi, the one who would come to reverse the decline of Islam in a time of need. By the time of his death in 1908, his followers had additionally come to view Ahmad as a prophet, equal in stature to Muhammad, a position that had increasingly put the movement at odds with the larger Muslim community.

Ahmad was born February 13, 1835, in what today is Qadian, Pakistan, the son of an old Punjabi family. He was educated at home and married in 1852. In 1865 he entered government service as a minor employee but resigned three years later as he was needed to take charge of the family's lands. This task left him time to study the Koran, the Muslim sacred text, to which he gave an increasing amount of time as the years passed.

Through the 1870s, he concluded that Islam was in a state of decline, due in part to an increasing attack from other religions, especially Christianity. This belief led him in 1879 to begin writing a book,

Portrait of Mirza Ghulam Ahmad, 19th-century Indian prophet and social leader who founded the Ahmadiyya Movement. (Hulton-Deutsch Collection/Corbis)

Barahin-i-Ahmadiyah, an apology for Islam that included an attack upon Christian belief and practice. The book was published in 1880, at which time Ahmad informed the public of his belief that Allah had called him to demonstrate the truth of Islam and he had accomplished his task in his production of the book.

Other books followed, and as they appeared through the 1880s Ahmad assumed the appellation of *mujaddid* (renewer of the faith) for the present age. His work led to an increased appraisal of his own role in history and in 1891 he declared himself to be the Promised Messiah expected by the Christians and the Madhi expected by the Muslims. To increase his identification with Jesus, Ahmad picked up and amplified an Indian legend that Jesus had not died on the cross in Palestine but had survived his crucifixion, after which he traveled to Kashmir in northern India. Here he lived out his remaining days, died a natural death, and was buried. Given that understanding of Jesus' career, Ahmad asserted that the Second Coming would not consist of Jesus' descent from heaven but the appearance of one, such as himself, who manifested the spirit and power of Jesus. As the promised Messiah, he also projected a mission to spread Islam amid the Christian communities in the West.

Through the 1880s, Ahmad gathered a following among people impressed with his writings. In 1889 he formally organized the Ahmadiyya movement in Islam. Two years later he took his boldest step and declared himself a prophet, an assertion of his equality with Muhammad. This assertion, along with his declaring the excommunication of those who did not accept it, placed a barrier between Ahmad and his people and the larger world of Islam.

Problems mounted for Ahmad through the rest of his life. His claims of increased status were accompanied by a growth in the movement's membership but eventually led to defections. Among the early withdrawals were some of his cousins. They in turn convinced his wife to leave, and they were divorced. He later married and raised a new family with his second wife.

At the time of his death on May 26, 1908, at Lahore, India (now Pakistan), Ahmad had become the leader of a large movement. However, it would not be until six years after his death that the mission to the West would begin, in England. Work in America would wait until after World War II. In 1914, the Ahmadiyya movement in Islam split with the dissenting faction, now known as the Ahmadiyya Anjuman Ishaat Islam, Lahore, rejecting the leadership of the larger movement by Ahmad's son and later declining to affirm Ahmad's status as a prophet equal to Muhammad.

Over the century since Ahmad's death, the Ahmadiyya movement in Islam has been established in some 190 countries and has been how most countries were introduced to Islam. In the meantime, several Muslim countries have moved against the Ahmadiyya movement for what are considered heretical beliefs.

J. Gordon Melton

See also: Ahmadiyya Anjuman Ishaat Islam, Lahore; Ahmadiyya Movement in Islam; Muhammad.

References

Ahmad, Bashiruddin Mahmud. *The Ahmadiyya Movement in Islam*. Chicago: The Movement, [1950?].

Ahmad, Mirza Ghulam Hazrat. *Our Teachings*. Rabwah, Pakistan: Ahmadiyya Movement of Islam, 1962.

Ali, Muhammad. *The Founder of the Ahmadiyya Movement: A Short Study*. Newark, CA: Ahmadiyya Anjuman Isha'at Islam, Lahore, 1984.

Dard, A. R. *Life of Ahmad*. Tilford, Surrey, UK: Islam International Publications, 1948, 2008.

Ahmadiyya Anjuman Islaat Islam, Lahore

Following the death of its founder, Hazrat Mirza Ghulam Ahmad (1835–1908), the Ahmadiyya Muslim movement in Islam faced a division concerning his status. During his lifetime, Ahmad had successively declared his calling to help revive Islam; his role as al-Mahdi, the expected Hidden Imam of the Shia Muslims who was expected to return at the end of the age to reform Islam; and then his prophethood, an affirmation that would make him equal in status to Muhammad. Most of the followers, including Ahmad's family, continued to affirm his elevated status, including his prophethood. However, others, under the guidance of Maulawi Muhammad Ali (d. 1951), while considering Ahmad the promised Messiah (expected by both Christians and Muslims), stopped short of affirming his prophethood. Ali argued that Ahmad's references to his prophetic status should be understood allegorically, not literally. Ahmad is the greatest *mujaddid*, a renewer of Islam, but is not equal to Muhammad. Ali especially argued that the acknowledgment of Ahmad's status was not a precondition to being considered a Muslim.

The Lahore Ahmadiyyas assumed control of the Woking Muslim Mission in England, which had been founded at the Woking Mosque in 1913 by Khwaja Kamal-ud-Din (1870–1932). The mission influenced a number of British converts to Islam with its nonsectarian approach to Islam. For the next 50 years the mission was a major center for the dissemination of Islam in the United Kingdom (until its expulsion from the mosque in the 1960s). A mosque and mission were opened in Berlin in 1926. Surviving World War II, it continues as the center of the propagation of Lahore Islam in the German language.

The Ahmadiyya movement spread initially into those countries where Pakistanis and Indians had migrated in numbers. Hence it opened work in Fiji, Suriname, Trinidad, Guyana, South Africa, and Indonesia, where it answered attacks by both Christians and Hindus.

In 1974, the Pakistani government amended its Constitution so as to categorize members of both the Ahmadiyya movement in Islam and the Ahmadiyya Anjuman Islaat Islam, Lahore as being non-Muslims. This opinion was seconded by the World Muslim League, based in Saudi Arabia. Then in 1984, the Pakistanis issued an ordinance prohibiting Ahmadiyyas from referring to themselves as Muslims or representing themselves as Muslims in any manner. They also prohibited members of the movement (with criminal penalties for disobeying) from engaging in some distinctive Muslim practices and using several Muslim terms.

The Lahore Ahmadiyyas denied the validity of these actions, feeling that they are based on new nontraditional criteria for membership in the Muslim community. Muslims have responded that while the Lahore Believers have dropped the offensive reference to Ahmad as a prophet, they have not dropped some of Ahmad's other unique beliefs, especially the end to jihad (holy war), a major belief of Orthodox Islam. The Lahore community has made much of a case in South Africa in which one of their members filed a civil suit against the Muslim Judicial Council. He claimed that the council was defaming him by branding the Ahmadis as unbelievers and apostates. The case was decided in 1985 in his favor.

The Ahmadiyya Anjuman Islaat Islam, Lahore is present is some 16 countries around the world, with a particularly strong following in the Netherlands.

Ahmadiyya Anjuman Islaat Islam, Lahore
5-Usman Block
New Garden Town

PO Box Ferozepur Road
Lahore, PC 54600
Pakistan
www.aaiil.org

J. Gordon Melton

See also: Ahmad, Mirza Ghulam Hazrat; Ahmadiyya Movement in Islam; Muhammad; World Muslim Congress.

References

Ali, Muhammad. *The Founder of the Ahmadiyya Movement.* Newark, CA: Ahmadiyya Anjuman Islaat Islam, Lahore, 1984.

Aziz, Zahid, comp. *The Ahmadiyya Case.* Newark, CA: Ahmadiyya Anjuman Islaat Islam, Lahore, 1987.

Aziz, Zahid, comp. *A Survey of the Lahore Ahmadiyya Movement: History, Beliefs, Aims and Work.* UK: Ahmadiyya Anjuman Lahore Publications, 2008. http://www.ahmadiyya.org/intro/survey.pdf. Accessed March 21, 2009.

Faruqui, N. A. *Ahmadiyyat in the Service of Islam.* Newark, CA: Ahmadiyya Anjuman Islaat Islam, Lahore, 1983.

Ahmadiyya Movement in Islam

The Ahmadiyya movement in Islam began as one aspect of the larger revival of Islam that swept through the Muslim world in the 19th century; in the years after the death of its founder, however, it took a direction that pushed it to the fringe of Islam. The movement was launched by Mirza Ghulam Hazrat Ahmad (1835–1908), a Pakistani government worker, who as a devout Muslim brooded over what he perceived was the decline of the Muslim community. In 1880 he published a book, *Barahin-i-Ahmadiyah*, in which he revealed the calling he felt to help revive Islam in the face of a militant Christian mission in India.

In 1891 he proclaimed that he was al-Mahdi, the expected Hidden Imam of the Shia Muslims who was expected to return at the end of the age to reform Islam. His proclamation came as part of an attack upon Christianity, in which he also declared his belief that Jesus was a prophet (in other words, a person of the same high status as Muhammad) but was not divine. He went on to articulate his unique belief that Jesus had not died on the cross but had survived his ordeal and later moved to Kashmir, where he lived out his normal life. The Second Coming would not involve the reappearance of the resurrected Jesus, but the appearance of someone with the spirit and power of Jesus, a person like Ahmad.

Ahmad began a massive missionary effort directed to the West arguing for Islam, but including as an integral part of his message the claim about his role as the fulfiller of the prophecy of the Second Coming of Jesus. In 1901, he took the additional step of declaring himself a prophet, and hence equal to Muhammad. After his death, those Muslims attracted to his movement argued about his prophethood. The majority continued to align themselves with Ahmad's family and proclaimed his prophethood, even going so far as to suggest that only those who acknowledged the new Prophet Ahmad were true Muslims. But a significant minority rejected the claim (while asserting Ahmad's role as a renewer, or *mujaddid,* of Islam) and organized as the Ahmadiyya Anjuman Islaat Islam, Lahore.

Upon Ahmad's death, a caliphate (without any political powers) was instituted to lead the movement. The first caliph and successor to Ahmad was Hazrat Haji Hakeem Maulvi Nurud-Din Sahib (1841–1914). He was succeeded in turn by Sahibzada Bashirud-Din Mahmud Ahmad Sahib (1889–1965), only 25 years old at the time. He was called to lead the movement through the early 1950s, when popular feeling against it reached a new peak and led to rioting. In 1954 he was almost killed when a man stabbed him in the neck. In 1955, he established an electoral college consisting of some 150 of the movement's leaders, who were to determine his successor.

Following the caliph's death in 1965, his son, Sahibzada Mirza Nasir Ahmad Sahib (1909–1982), was elected to succeed him. He led the movement as it spread internationally, while at the same time fighting for its status in the Muslim world. He was succeeded by Hazrat Mirza Tahir Ahmad (1928–2003) and he in 2003 by the current caliph, His Holiness Mirza Masroor Ahmad Khalifatul Masih V (b. 1950), who is also the son of Sahibzada Mirza Nasir Ahmad Sahib.

Protesters display posters during a demonstration against the possible ban on Ahmadiyya, an Islamic sect founded in Pakistan at the end of the 19th century, in Jakarta, Indonesia, May 6, 2008. The sect has come under attack from hardliners as heretical for its belief that there was a prophet after Muhammad, Mirza Ghulam Hazrat Ahmad, who died in 1908. (AP/Wide World Photos)

The Ahmadiyya movement in Islam holds most beliefs common to Orthodox Sunni Islam, although Ahmad did challenge one of the principal beliefs of Islam by declaring the end to jihad (holy war). The primary belief that separates the movement from the larger world of Islam, however, remains the role it assigns to its founder. That additional affirmation has led to the movement being seen as a sectarian Islamic movement by the great majority of Muslims. In 1974, the Pakistani government declared the movement to be non-Muslim, a move followed by the World Muslim League, which also declared it to be outside of Islam. In 1984, Pakistan also passed an ordinance forbidding Ahmadiyyas to refer to or represent themselves as Muslims. These actions have not stopped the movement's spread, and it now exists in more than 193 countries (2008), its legal status secure in the great majority

where Islam is also a minority faith. It has spread across North America, where it has experienced a significant response from African Americans.

The international headquarters of the movement is in Rabwah, Pakistan. The American branch has developed an expansive Internet site at www.alislam .org. As the new century begins, it claims more than 130 million adherents worldwide. As this encyclopedia goes to press, the Ahmadiyya movement is experiencing significant problems in Indonesia, where Orthodox Sunnis have challenged its legitimacy and called upon the government to suppress it. The Sunni effort challenges the country's commitments to religious freedom.

Masjid Aqsa Goal Bazar Rabwah
Rabwah

Pakistan
www.alislam.org

J. Gordon Melton

See also: Ahmad, Mirza Ghulam Hazrat; Ahmadiyya Anjuman Islaat Islam, Lahore; Muhammad; World Muslim Congress.

References

Dard, A. R. *Life of Ahmad*. Lahore, Pakistan: Tashir Publications, 1948.

Ahmad, Hazrat Mirza Bashiruddin Mahmud. *Ahmadiyyat, or the True Islam*. Washington, DC: American Fazl Mosque, 1951.

Khan, Muhammad Zafrulla. *Ahmadiyya, the Renaissance of Islam*. London: Tabshir Publications, 1978.

Nadwi, S. Abul Hasan Ali. *Qadianism, A Critical Study*. Lucknow, India: Islamic Research and Publications, 1974.

Aivanhov, Omraam Mikhael

1900–1986

Omraam Mikhael Aivanhov, one of the prominent teachers of Western Esotericism in 20th-century Europe, was the founder of the Universal White Brotherhood and Prosveta Publishing, both based in Switzerland and then France.

Aivanhov was born Mikhael Ivanov on January 31, 1900, in Serbtzi, Macedonia. In 1907, his hometown was largely burned to the ground in the general conflict between the people of the area (Greek, Macedonians, and Bulgarians) to throw off control by the Ottoman Empire and establish their own ethnic identity. The Ivanovs moved to Varna, a Bulgarian town on the Black Sea.

In 1914, Ivanov had an intense spiritual experience that began his spiritual awakening. He described it as being plunged into a state of ecstasy during which everything seemed bathed in and suffused with light. Three years later he met the Master Peter Deunov (1864–1944), who had founded a group called the White Brotherhood and had composed the songs and the basic methods and exercises designed to reach enlightenment. Basic to Deunov's system was Paneury-

thmy (rhythm of the cosmos), dance moves that he believed reflected the movements of the solar system and the Creator's natural law. Doing the movements connected the dancers with Earth and heaven.

During his time with Deunov, Ivanhov also attended the university in Sofia (1923–1931) and subsequently made his living as a school teacher and then the director of a high school (1932–1935).

By the mid-1930s, Deunov, fearing the spread of Communism, sent Ivanov to France and told him to work from there to spread the teachings of what would become known as the Universal White Brotherhood. To spread the teachings, Ivanov began to organize conferences, the first being held in Paris and Lyon in 1938. His teaching activity was then abruptly halted by the outbreak of World War II (1939–1945) and the occupation of France by German forces. After the war, however, he picked up his work immediately and before the year was out held the first of a new series of conferences in Lausanne, Switzerland. From that point on his work grew steadily. His talks were recorded by stenographers and later transcribed and published.

In 1959 he traveled to India, while there he met the famous Indian teacher Neem Karoli Baba (d. 1973), whom Baba Ram Dass/Richard Alpert made famous in North America. Neem Karoli Baba gave him the name Omraam Mikhael Aivanhov. After this time, he began to think of himself and allow himself to be addressed as "master." Previously he had considered himself merely another of Deunov's students.

With the founding of Prosveta Publishing in 1971, in Switzerland, the movement began a period of growth. It published the talks from the numerous conferences and launched an effort to translate the subsequent books and booklets into a number of languages. As Aivanhov aged, work began on the publication of a set of his complete works, comprising some 77 volumes.

Having spent his mature life teaching, he passed away on December 25, 1986, in France.

J. Gordon Melton

See also: Enlightenment; Western Esoteric Tradition.

References

Aivanhov, Omraam Mikhael. *Education Begins Before Birth*. Los Angeles: Editions Prosveta, 1982.

Aivanhov, Omraam Mikhael. *Life Force.* Fréjus, France: Editions Prosveta, 1987.

Feuerstein, Georg. *The Mystery of Light: The Life and Teachings of Omraam Michael Aivanhov.* Salt Lake City, UT: Passage Press, 1992.

Frenette, Louise Marie. *Omraam Mikhael Aivanhov: A Biography.* Salt Lake City, UT: Suryoma, 1999.

Lejbowicz, Agnes. *Omraam Michael Aivanhov, Master of the Great White Brotherhood.* Fréjus, France: Editions Prosveta, 1982.

Mukerjee, Dada. *The Near and the Dear: Stories of Neem Karoli Baba and His Devotees.* Taos, NM: Hanuman Foundation, 2001.

Renard, Opierre. *The Solar Revolution and the Prophet.* Fréjus, France: Editions Prosveta, 1980.

Who Is Omraam Michael Aivanhov? Fréjus, France: Editions Prosveta. 1982.

Aladura Churches

The independent West African churches that emerged as reactions to the paternalism of European missions were patterned on the churches from which they had seceded. These African churches began declining in the 1920s and were completely overshadowed by new, rapidly growing prophet-healing, or "spiritual" churches. First, churches associated with the prophets William Wade Harris and Garrick Sokari Braide emerged, followed by churches known by the Yoruba term *Aladura* (prayer people). Like Zionist and Apostolic churches in southern Africa and Holy Spirit churches in East Africa, Aladura churches presented a much more penetrating challenge to older churches than earlier African churches had because they questioned the very heart of Christianity in Africa. In this, they were sometimes aided and abetted by new churches from the North, especially the Pentecostals, whose ideas they borrowed freely yet selectively. Nevertheless, this was a specifically African Christian response, despite the outward trappings of rituals and customs that were innovations rather than continuations of African traditional symbols. In this regard, these new West African churches represent a reformation of African Christianity that reverberates to the present day.

In 1990, African Initiated Churches constituted about 19 percent of the total population of Nigeria, or 38 percent of the Christian population there, in more than 1,000 different churches. These are the "churches of the Spirit," which arose almost simultaneously in many parts of the continent, contemporaneous with Pentecostal movements emerging in other parts of the globe but independent of them. The largest group of these churches is in Yorubaland, where by 1950, Aladura churches were at the very center of society. This movement emphasized prayer, so they were known as Aladura, a term that distinguished them from other Christian churches at the time. The largest Aladura churches are the Christ Apostolic Church, the Church of the Lord (Aladura), the Eternal Sacred Order of the Cherubim and Seraphim, and the Celestial Church of Christ, a church of later origin and different historical roots. Aladura churches in Nigeria have sought cooperation, and when some were refused admission into the Christian Council of Nigeria, they formed the Nigerian Association of Aladura Churches, with 95 denominations and 1.2 million members in 1964, rising to as many as 1,200 member churches by 1996.

During the 1950s, Aladura churches spread to Ghana, Liberia, and Sierra Leone, through the efforts of traveling Nigerian preachers, especially Apostles Oduwole and Adejobi of the Church of the Lord (Aladura), and new Ghanaian churches in the traditions of Aladura seceded. From Africa the Aladura churches spread to Europe and North America. The Aladura churches arrived in Britain in 1964 and in other parts of the North more recently. Like the African Caribbean Pentecostal churches before them, the creation of these West African churches throughout the North was often encouraged by a feeling of estrangement and loneliness, and sometimes, by indifferent and racist attitudes in established churches. But perhaps more important, the intense and holistic spirituality of these churches, their particular contextualization of the Christian message, and their revivalist tendencies were often absent from these churches and left African believers with a sense of emptiness. The African churches in the North are increasing remarkably and some of them are among the largest congregations in Europe.

Allan H. Anderson

Services in the Cherubim and Seraphim Mount Zion Finima Church, 2006. The African-Christian church was founded in Nigeria in the early 20th century and has branches throughout the delta. (Corbis)

See also: African Initiated (Independent) Churches; Celestial Church of Christ; Christ Apostolic Church; Church of the Lord; Cherubim and Seraphim/Eternal Sacred Order of the Cherubim and Seraphim; Zionist and Apostolic Churches.

References

Anderson, Allan H. *African Reformation: African Initiated Christianity in the Twentieth Century.* Trenton, NJ: Africa World Press, 2001.

Peel, J. D. Y. *Aladura: A Religious Movement among the Yoruba.* Oxford: Oxford University Press, 1968.

Turner, Harold W. *History of an African Independent Church.* Vol. 1, *The Church of the Lord (Aladura).* Oxford: Clarendon, 1967.

■ Albania

Albania, a country of some 3.6 million people (2008), is located on the Adriatic Sea and shares borders with Greece, Macedonia, and Kosovo. The 11,100 square miles of territory is overwhelmingly inhabited by people who are ethnically Albanian and speak the Albanian language. Albanians also form a majority of the population in neighboring Kosovo and a significant minority in Macedonia.

During the years of the Roman Empire, Albania constituted the province of Illyria, which became part of the eastern division of the empire as it evolved into the Byzantine Empire. As the Byzantine power crumbled, Albania briefly came under Serbian and Bulgarian rule. In the 14th century, an Albanian state was established, but the Turks overran the Balkans in the 15th century. Albania, under their national hero Scanderberg (1405–1468), a Turkish janissary, led a revolt that kept the Turks busy for a quarter of a century, though ultimately the Turks reestablished their rule.

Albania remained under Turkish rule until it gained its independence in 1912. The country existed as an independent nation for a generation, until annexed by

The Orthodox Church of Saint George in Korca, Albania. Eastern Orthodox Christianity is one of the major religions in Albania. (Itinerantlens/Dreamstime.com)

Italy in 1939. Following the defeat of the occupying forces, a People's Republic was declared by the leaders of the Resistance, who happened to be dedicated Marxists. In 1944, under Enver Hoxha (1908–1985), Albania became a Communist state that pursued an independent course within the wider Communist world until its fall in 1989–1990. Its consciously antireligious stance culminated in constitutional changes, and in 1967 freedom of belief and conscience was prohibited by the Albanian Constitution. Subsequently, the churches and mosques were ordered to close, and later many of them were demolished, and the priests and imams arrested. Albania became the first and only country in the world officially declared atheist.

Since the fall of the Marxist government, Albania has struggled to align itself with the culture of Western Europe, but has been hindered by poverty and an obsolete infrastructure.

To return to the early religious history of Albania, the ancient Pagan faith of the Albanian people was incorporated into the eclectic Paganism of the Roman world, through which a variety of religions spread. The first Christian community was established at Durres in 58 CE. In the year 395, the Roman Empire was divided into the Eastern and Western Empires, and Albania fell into that area controlled by the Eastern, or Byzantine, Empire. In the Byzantine Empire, the Eastern Orthodox Church came into dominance. However, Albania was close enough to the boundary of the two empires that Orthodox and Roman Catholics vied for the allegiance of the Albanian people. That rivalry was somewhat subdued by the incorporation of Albania into the Ottoman Empire in the middle of the 15th century.

The Turks were Sunni Muslims of the Hanafite School, and subsequent to their gaining power, a number of Albanians converted to Islam. A variety of reasons have been offered for the conversion of such a high percentage of Albanians, when compared to neighboring countries so occupied, including proselytization efforts, reaction to anti-Albanian activities of the Orthodox in neighboring countries, and the possibility that high taxes could be avoided by becoming Muslims. In any case, Albania became the first European nation in the Middle Ages to embrace Islam.

Most Muslims in Albania were Hanafis. They were organized into four regions (Tirane, Shkoder, Korce, and Gjirokaster), each under the leadership of a grand mufti. Some 20 percent of Muslim Albanians identified with a Turkish Sufi movement, the Bektashis. This group developed a strong presence within the Turkish army, through which it spread to the Balkans. It suffered when the units in which it was strongest were disbanded in 1826, but it was revived at the end of the 19th century in Albania and Turkey. Then in 1925, all Sufi orders were officially disbanded in Turkey and the Bektashis' center shifted to Albania.

The generation-long battle to prevent the conquest of the nation by the Ottomans was led by Scanderberg (born Gjergj Kastrioti). He died a Christian martyr and was buried in a Christian church but is today considered a national hero by Christians and Muslims alike as a freedom fighter seeking to preserve an independent nation. Albanian religion has always been identified with the desire to establish and preserve the Albanian national identity. This uniting factor has meant that, in spite of the important religious differences between the Christian and Muslim communities, they have been able to live together in relative peace. The tolerant spirit has been demonstrated in numerous mixed marriages and frequent exchange of visits during religious celebrations.

Through the centuries under Muslim rule, the Eastern Orthodox Church survived, but it drew its leadership from neighboring countries. A drive for an autonomous church emerged among Albanians in the 19th century, but this was opposed by the Ecumenical Patriarchate in Istanbul. Thus, an autonomous Albanian church was actually founded in a diaspora community in the United States, under the leadership of Fan S. Noli (1882–1965). He was ordained in 1908 by an America bishop of the Russian Orthodox Church, who directed him to found an Albanian jurisdiction. The work was organized as an independent diocese in 1919. Returning to a now independent Albania in 1920, Noli led in the founding of an autocephalous church in 1922 and became its first bishop in 1923. The Ecumenical Patriarchate eventually recognized it as the Orthodox Autocephalous Church of Albania in 1937.

The newly formed church was an early target of the Marxist government, which ordered the closing of its seminary and stopped the ordination of any new priests. Its churches were closed in 1957 and many priests arrested. Only 22 priests remained when freedom came in 1990. In 1991 the ecumenical patriarch took the lead in rebuilding the church with the appointment of Archbishop Anastasios as the new exarch of Albania. He reestablished the Monastery of St. Viash, Durres, and the Resurrection of Christ Theological Academy. He also opened additional schools and medical facilities. The church now serves approximately 20 percent of the population. It is the only Albanian-based church that is a member of the World Council of Churches.

The Roman Catholic Church has traditionally been strongest in the northern part of the country. As the split developed between the Orthodox and Roman churches, the archdioceses at Durres and Shkoder aligned with Rome. In the 11th century, an Eastern-rite diocese emerged. These were all directly affiliated to the Vatican. Proportionately, the Roman Catholic community suffered the most from the Hoxha regime, in part due to the dislike of Italians that had developed from Italy's attempt to occupy the country. Hoxha moved immediately to expel the apostolic delegate from the Vatican (1944) and then the Italian priests and nuns (1945). But these actions were only the beginning. In 1948, 3 bishops were executed. By the mid-1970s no less than 120 Catholic leaders had been killed. In 1977 the 3 remaining bishops disappeared and were never seen again. By the end of the 1970s, all of the remaining priests were either in prison or in hiding.

With the fall of the Marxist government, a decade of rebirth and revitalization of religion and spiritual life began. Through the 1990s, the older religious communities revived, and a variety of new religions— Protestant/evangelical churches, Church of Jesus Christ

ALBANIA

of Latter-day Saints, Seventh-day Adventist Churches, and various new groups from the spectrum of the world's religions—arrived. Prior to World War II, several Protestant groups, the Seventh-day Adventist Church, the American Board of Commissioners for Foreign Missions, the Baptists, and the Methodist Episcopal Church (now a constituent part of the United Methodist Church), had work in Albania. Most of this work was lost and had to be restarted after 1990. The Adventists were among the first to reestablish work in 1990, at which time they found a few believers from

their earlier efforts. Conservative Baptists arrived in 1991, and shortly thereafter the Baptist World Alliance opened a center for humanitarian aid in Tirana. In 1993, evangelical missionaries formed the Evangelical Brotherhood, which evolved into the Albanian Evangelical Alliance, now a member of the European Evangelical Alliance, through which it relates to the World Evangelical Alliance.

The Church of Jesus Christ of Latter-day Saints entered the country in 1991, and the first permanent missionaries arrived the following year. The work was

Albania

Religion	Followers in 1970	Followers in 2010	% of Population	Annual % growth 2000–2010	Followers in 2025	Followers in 2050
Muslims	600,000	2,083,000	64.2	0.79	2,197,000	2,070,000
Christians	173,000	1,001,000	30.8	1.64	1,170,000	1,310,000
Roman Catholics	70,000	490,000	15.1	−0.30	530,000	530,000
Orthodox	101,000	475,000	14.6	3.54	600,000	720,000
Independents	400	30,000	0.9	11.43	40,000	60,000
Agnostics	1,015,000	135,000	4.2	−7.04	100,000	50,000
Atheists	348,000	18,000	0.6	−3.90	10,000	5,000
Baha'is	0	8,000	0.2	0.47	10,000	15,000
Jews	200	370	0.0	0.47	500	700
Total population	**2,136,000**	**3,245,000**	**100.0**	**0.47**	**3,488,000**	**3,451,000**

originally conducted by the Austria Vienna Mission, but in 1996 the Albania Tirana Mission was officially opened. The church has built a strong humanitarian work assisting the country as a whole to rebuild.

Through the 1990s, the Republic of Albania assumed a very tolerant and even supportive stance toward the traditional religious communities and a non-interfering policy toward the newly arrived groups previously unknown to Albanians. In spite of the appearance of a variety of competing religious groups, the state has refrained from any move to restrict religious freedom. There is no state religion, and the principle of separation of church and state has been written into the law. The parliament has appointed a State Committee for Religious Affairs, which maintains a relationship with the various religious communities in Albania, while refraining from interfering in their internal affairs. Each of the religious groups is, of course, expected to operate under the common law and the Albanian Constitution. An appraisal of the situation as the new century unfolds, especially of the needs of both the Christian and Muslim communities, suggests that, as the country as a whole stabilizes its position economically, the government will assume a more active role in assisting the older larger religious groups in their rebuilding process.

Behar Bejko and J. Gordon Melton

See also: Albania, Orthodox Autocephalous Church of; American Board of Commissioners for Foreign Missions; Atheism; Baptist World Alliance; Baptists; Bektashi Order (Bektashiye); Church of Jesus Christ of Latter-day Saints; Ecumenical Patriarchate/Patriarchate of Constantinople; Hanafite School of Islam; Roman Catholic Church; Seventh-day Adventist Church; United Methodist Church; World Council of Churches; World Evangelical Alliance.

References

Costa, Nicolas J. *Albania: A European Enigma.* Boulder, CO, and New York: East European Monographs and Columbia University Press, 1995.

Hutchings, Raymond. *Historical Dictionary of Albania.* Lanham, MD: Scarecrow Press, 1996.

Schwandner-Sievers, Stephanie, and Bernd Jurgen Fischer. *Albanian Identities: Myth and History.* Bloomington: Indiana University Press, 2002.

Albania, Orthodox Autocephalous Church of

Albanian patriots such as Sami Frashëri (1850–1904) began to agitate for an independent Albanian church in the 1880s. Prior to that time, Eastern Orthodox believers worshipped in churches that drew their leadership from the autonomous churches in neighboring countries (Greece, Bulgaria, Serbia). Orthodoxy had been established in Albania in the days of the Byzantine Empire, but its progress had been stopped and even reversed under the centuries of Turkish rule that began in the 15th century. The drive for autonomy was opposed by the ecumenical patriarch (the patriarch of Constantinople), who included the Albanian parishes in his jurisdiction, and the Turkish government, which ruled the land until the First Balkan War (1912).

Stifled in their homeland, as early as 1900 Albanian expatriates in Romania attempted to create an Orthodox church outside the jurisdiction of the Ecumenical Patriarchate that would use the Albanian language. However, it was in the United States that the first Albanian Orthodox Church was founded. Its founding was occasioned by the refusal of a Greek priest to hold the funeral services for a young Albanian nationalist. The Albanian-American community of Boston designated Fan S. Noli to seek ordination for the purpose of founding an Albanian Orthodox Church. Noli was able to gain the favor of Archbishop Platon of the Russian Orthodox Church (now the Orthodox Church in America), which competed with the Greeks for hegemony in the United States. Noli was ordained on March 8, 1908, and Platon commissioned him to found a missionary church under the jurisdiction of the Russian Orthodox Church. It was organized as an independent diocese in 1919. Noli translated the service from Greek and later translated several liturgical books.

In 1920 Noli returned to Albania, where he enjoyed a promising political career. He served a short term as Albania's prime minister. In 1922 a congress was called to consider religious independence. It declared the existence of an autocephalous church, but the lack of episcopal leadership presented a major problem. That problem was solved the following year when Noli was consecrated as a bishop. Then in 1926 President (later King) Zog became interested in the issue and gave his support to establishing the new church. An initial synod was held in 1929 at the king's villa; autonomous status was finally attained on April 13, 1937, when the Patriarchate released the church from its jurisdiction.

Frustrated at the refusal of the Ecumenical Patriarchate to cooperate with the independence effort, in 1930 Noli returned to the United States, where he reorganized the Albanian parishes as the Albanian Orthodox Archdiocese of America. After the Patriarchate released the Albanian church, the American archdiocese aligned itself with the new autonomous jurisdiction.

The church immediately fell on hard times with the outbreak of World War II and the rise of a Marxist government under the leadership of dictator Enver Hoxha (1908–1985). Hoxha steadily led the country toward atheism, eventually declaring the country officially an atheist state. He initially closed the church's seminary and limited new ordinations. In 1967 he closed all churches and attempted to stop all religious activity. Many churches were destroyed and some priests arrested. Only 22 priests were still alive in 1990.

After Hoxha came to power, the American archdiocese withdrew its connection from the church in Albania, feeling that the leadership had been compromised. Shortly thereafter, in 1950, the ecumenical patriarch designated Mark I. Lipa as his episcopal representative for America, and Lipa began to gather Albanian parishes into the Albanian Orthodox Diocese of America. Lipa's effort split the American Albanian community.

With the fall of the Communist government, religious freedom was restored in May 1990. The ecumenical patriarch took the lead in rebuilding the church and in January 1991 sent His Beatitude Archbishop Anastasios (b. 1929) as the new exarch of Albania. He was enthroned on August 2, 1992, as the archbishop of Tirana, Durres, and all Albania. He moved quickly to reopen the Monastery of St. Vlash, Durres, which became the location of the Resurrection of Christ Theological Academy. He also opened an ecclesiastical high school for boys, nine kindergartens, and five medical clinics.

Finally, in July 1998 the Holy Synod was reestablished. It now includes His Beatitude Archbishop Anastasios; His Eminence Ignati, metropolitan of Berat; His Eminence John, metropolitan of Korca; and His Grace Kosma, bishop of Apollonia. This synod fully restored the autocephalous status of the Church of Albania. The church joined the World Council of Churches in 1994. It now claims the allegiance of some 400,000 believers in Albania, about 12 percent of the population.

Orthodox Autocephalous Church of Albania
Rugae Kavajes 151
AL-Tirana
Albania
http://www.orthodoxalbania.org/

J. Gordon Melton

See also: Eastern Orthodoxy; Ecumenical Patriarchate/Patriarchate of Constantinople; Orthodox Church in America; Russian Orthodox Church Outside of Russia; World Council of Churches

References

De Wall, Clarissa. *Albania Today: A Portrait of Post-Communist Turbulence.* London: I. B. Tauris, 2005.

Forrest, Jim. *The Resurrection of the Church in Albania.* Geneva: World Council of Churches, 2002.

Skendi, Stavro. *The Albanian National Awakening, 1878–1912.* Princeton, NJ: Princeton University Press, 1967.

Van Beek, Huibert. *A Handbook of the Churches and Councils: Profiles of Ecumenical Relationships.* Geneva: World Council of Churches, 2006.

Alchemy, Daoist

Alchemy was an intrinsic part of Daoism in China. In fact, it was the primary orientation, since many Daoist masters were preoccupied with the question of immortality and physical techniques of attaining it. The emphasis during the early and medieval periods of Daoism was on external manipulations of the forces of nature, rather than purification of the self through internal techniques. Internal techniques such as meditation came later, from the 11th century CE, under the influence of a Buddhist faith with a radically different perspective. This early Daoist thought was so obsessed with external manipulation and experiments to further immortality that it was, like its European cousin alchemy, a proto-science.

The Daoist search for immortality was not, however, simply the urge to avoid death. Daoist immortality can be conceived of as attaining a physical presence beyond the degeneration and abandonment of the physical body. This awareness could then easily merge fully with the Dao itself. Hence Daoist immortality included losing the individual sense of identity but did not transcend the forces of the physical universe.

How was the universe conceived in those days? The cosmos was a field of struggle and quiescence, with mirroring, intertwining force-principles, yin and yang, creating the manifest order. The human body was a mini-cosmos of such forces. In particular, the body as well as the cosmos contained three forces or principles, commonly known as *qi* (matter-energy), *jing* (essence), and *shen* (spirit or consciousness). The body was a holding vessel subject to decay through the presence of worms. These worms eventually brought about death. Counter-forces could theoretically be applied. Decay-promoting substances such as grains could be eliminated, and often were proscribed in Daoist diets. Sexual techniques could be practiced to retain energy. And external compounds, especially minerals, could be ingested.

The earliest Daoists, such as the *shanren* (mountain men) mentioned in early texts, were shamans capable of spirit journeys and communing with spirits. These spirits may have been basic forces of nature. At the very least the Daoist masters were keenly aware of nature and the interaction between humans and nature. Part experimenter, part ethno-botanist, he or she categorized herbs and medicinal plants, conducted alchemic experiments at home, and continued to connect to the primal energies of hidden spirits. Early texts also note efforts to create containers of gold that would transform ritual food into pure food for immortals. The concept was later transferred to the view of the human body as a container that if purified would transform its contents into immortal material.

One exemplar of the early alchemist is Li Shaoju (d. 133 BCE), a *fanshi* (technical master) or what we would call a sorcerer. He reportedly persuaded Emperor Wudi (r. 140–187 BCE) to participate in alchemical experiments involving the transformation of cinnabar.

But the best-known Daoist in this pre-Buddhist period is Ge Hong (283–345 CE), a literati bureaucrat forced into an early retirement on a mountain in the far south (Luofu Shan in Guangdong), along with his wife and assistants. In his greatest surviving work, *Baopuzi* (*One Who Embraces Simplicity*), Ge details the transformation of cinnabar into mercury and, finally, gold, through the process of the Nine Transformations and the Nine Returns. Immortality is attained on completion of the eight transmutations, and the ability to fly on the ninth. While such descriptions can be read metaphorically as well as literally, there is little doubt

Iron gate of the White Cloud Daoist Temple, Beijing, China. (iStockPhoto.com)

Daoist alchemists performed actual experiments with real minerals and, in many cases, imbibed the results of such experiments. Due to the high toxicity of such elements as mercury, sulphur, mica, aluminum, and arsenic, some Daoists died from these efforts.

In the early-modern period, with the Song dynasty (960–1260) and thereafter, Daoist preoccupation turned to issues of mind cultivation, and a distinction was created between inner (*neidan*) and outer (*waidan*) forms of alchemy. Inner alchemy is an individual practice still taught today. Its approach and terminology, however, is firmly in the Daoist tradition extending back to the imagery and liturgy of the Book of the Yellow Court and efforts to attain union with the One Primal Essence.

Although neidan techniques vary widely, they share a common picture of the body divided into three cinnabar fields (*dantian*): the abdomen, chest, and head. The aim of meditation was to energize these fields and eventually create a spirit body that would remain upon physical death. The best-known practitioner of waidan was Zhang Boduan (987–1082), who received revelations directly from the immoral Lu Dongbin.

Today most of these currents in Daoist practice are found in the many qigong groups and systems of thought. They generally share a common terminology and intent—health, balance, and the development of supernatural powers.

Edward A. Irons

See also: Daoism; Death; Energy; Meditation; Qigong.

References

Khon, Livia. *Daoism and Chinese Culture.* Cambridge: Three Pines Press, 2001.

Khon, Livia., ed. *Daoism Handbook.* 2 vols. Leiden: Brill, 2004.

Masumi, Chikashige. *Oriental Alchemy.* New York: Samuel Weiser, 1936, 1974.

Robinet, Isabelle. *Taoism: Growth of a Religion.* Trans. by Phyllis Brooks. Stanford, CA: Stanford University Press, 1997.

Schipper, Kristofer. *The Taoist Body.* Trans. by Karen C. Duval. Foreword by Norman Girardot. Berkeley, Los Angeles, and London: University of California Press, 1993.

Willhelm, Richard, and Carl G. Jung. *The Secret of the Golden Flower: A Chinese Book of Life.* London: K. Paul, Trench, Trubner, 1931.

Wong, Eva. *The Shambhala Guide to Taoism.* Boston: Shambhala, 1997.

Alevism

Alevism is a different form of Islam and the major difference between Turkish Alevis and Shia and Sunni Muslims can be found in the worship rituals. Alevis' approach to Islamic rules and religious exercises is strongly criticized by Sunni Muslims. Due to its historical and geographical background from Central Asia to the Balkans, Alevism can be seen as religious syncretism that has incorporated elements of ancient Turkish beliefs and the other religious faiths encountered during the long migration process. Despite some internal political-, ethnic-, and religious-based divisions, Alevis all see themselves as belonging to a distinct, united socio-religious community.

The Arabic term *Alevi* is best defined as "of Ali" or "pertaining to Ali." It also appears in English as *Alouite* or *Alawite*. *Alevism* can be generally defined as the love of Ali and his family line, or as following the Way of the Family of the Prophet. It is generally accepted by believers that this path was founded by Ali ibn Abi Talib (ca. 602–661), who married Fatima, the daughter of Muhammad, the Prophet of Islam. The path continued through Ali's offspring. Ali was the fourth caliph after the death of the Prophet, and Shia Muslims, including the Alevis, consider him the first imam. Over time, the concept of Alevism has been defined in many different ways, from the perspectives of etymology, politics, and Sufism, and it has been supported or attacked with various motives. Alevism is not a faith exclusive to any given ethnic group. Carried by migrations stretching from Central Asia to the Middle East and as far as the Balkans, Alevism found adherents in many countries through adaptation to local faiths and cultures.

The term *Alevi* is used to describe the descendents of Ali in countries like Saudi Arabia, Egypt, Yemen, Iran, Pakistan, India, Iraq, Anatolia (modern Turkey), and the Balkans, as well as in the countries of Central Asia. Groups coming under the category of Alevi are known by different names in various countries: Ismailis in Pakistan, Jaferis in Iran, Zeydi in Egypt and Yemen, Nusayris in Syria, and Druze in Lebanon. The term *Ali Ilahi* was used for Alevi groups in studies done in Moscow under the former Soviet Union.

In today's Turkey, the term *Alevi* is used narrowly to refer to the physical descendents of Ali, but it is also used in a much broader sense. It refers to a type of heterodox Islam, sometimes called folk Islam, practiced by various groups in Anatolia, including the Kizilbash, Tahtaji, Abdal, Yoruk, Zaza, Barak, Avshar, Nalji, Chepni, Sirach, Amujali, Bedreddini, Terekeme, Nusayri, and Bektashi. The different groups are distinguished by their independent interpretations of folk Islam. Alevism, in this sense of folk Islam, was born of historical and social factors that rely more on oral than written traditions. Forms of Alevism continue to survive, with their ancient beliefs and mythology now appearing in Islamic forms.

Turkish tribes, which had been spread across a wide geographical area, had come into contact with and been influenced over the centuries by shamanism, Manicheanism, Christianity, Judaism, and even Buddhism prior to the emergence of Islam. Large-scale Turkish conversion to Islam can be dated to the eighth century, as Arab armies began to conquer Central Asia. As Turks received Islam, they also tended to preserve their ancient beliefs and practices. Most of these Turks did not respect the Muslim sheikhs (elders) and clergy, who spread various restrictive religious laws. Rather, they attached themselves to and came under the influence of "fathers," who filled a role similar to pre-Islamic religious leaders such as shamans. These religious leaders taught more basic religious principles and emphasized the similarities between the Turks' ancient beliefs and the new religion. The result was a variety of syncretistic forms of folk Islam that kept

Alevi men and women perform the *semah* dance during a *cem* ceremony at the Karacaahmet *cem* house in Istanbul, Turkey, December 3, 2006. (AP/Wide World Photos)

ancient beliefs and practices in the forefront and placed religious obligations in the background.

This nominal Islam, which the Turks who moved into Anatolia beginning in the 11th century brought with them, made it quite easy for them to mix in with the local inhabitants. These Turkish immigrants added a combination of Islamic religious law, Arab and Persian religious culture, and traces of native Anatolian culture to their own customs. Anatolian Turkish culture was born from this synthesis.

This synthesis appeared in two distinct forms. Residents of urban areas accepted a more orthodox understanding of Islam, while nomadic and semi-nomadic groups on the fringes of the towns and cities accepted a heterodox Islamic understanding, or Alevism. This division continued through the Seljuk and Ottoman periods. In the Babai Rebellion of 1240, the heterodox groups revolted against the official Sunni Islam of the central administration. This rebellion left deep scars in

Anatolia, and even after the rebellion was crushed, the ideas behind it remained in the minds of the rebels. This heterodox opposition stance was accepted by the groups known as the Vefais, Kalenderis, Haydaris, and Yesevis, and became known by the general name Rum Abdals from the beginning of the 14th century.

From the foundation of the Ottoman state in the 14th century, heterodox dervishes known for the spinning movements in their meditation practices, and called by the names of *abdal, baba, dede,* or *ahi,* were greatly respected by Ottoman sultans and were prominent in former Byzantine lands and in the Balkan areas conquered by the Ottomans. From the 13th century, heterodox babas and abdals started to found small dervish lodges in Anatolia and the Balkans, and their activities were multiplied through their disciples. In the 16th century, sheikhs who had earlier been part of the Kalenderi, Yesevi, and similar movements somehow joined up with the Bektashis, so that by the time of the 17th century, each one of the Rum Abdal lodges had become a Bektashi lodge. In the outlying areas, centers of faith called *ojaks* appeared. The Alevis in the rural areas mostly came under the influence of dedes who were associated with these ojaks.

In the 16th century, the Safawi ruler, Shah Ismail, strengthened his presence in Anatolia and held great influence, especially over the Alevi ojaks. From the 16th century these strong Turkish clans increased their support of the Safawi line, so much so that they became a threat to the Ottoman state, which resorted to strong measures in its opposition to them. The Ottoman administration always saw these heterodox Turkish clans as potential threats and considered them to be irreligious and immoral. Over time, these clans cut every kind of tie with the Ottoman administration and succeeded in pursuing their faith and practices for hundreds of years, closed to the outside world. Unquestionably, this success was due in great part to a vibrant oral and musical tradition. The social and religious organization of what is known today as Alevism, including the institution of *dedelik* (the Alevi equivalent of clergy), is the product of the leadership of the Safawi Shah Ismail. After the death of Shah Ismail, the Alevis of Anatolia lived in continual conflict with the Ottoman administration. In spite of the fact that they were an essential element of the founding of the Ottoman state, Alevis were spurned by the government, so the Alevis did not recognize the authority of the Ottoman administration. They handled all of their social needs and problems among themselves, including holding their own people's courts.

Since they had lived for centuries under the persecution of the Ottoman administration, Alevis received the new Turkish republic's government with joy. They were pleased by most, if not all, of the reforms made in the first years of the republic. Alevis in general supported Mustafa Kemal Ataturk, the founder of the republic, and his Republican People's Party (CHP). Especially after the 1960s, Alevis were active in most leftist movements. Because of this, the dominant mindset in Turkish society equated being Alevi with being leftist, and the marginalization of Alevis was increased. The killings of Alevis in Çorum, Maraş, Sivas, and Istanbul's Gazi neighborhood can be attributed to this marginalization. Even though Alevis are considered

equal by the Constitution, from religious and cultural perspectives they continue to be treated like an unequal Muslim minority.

In today's Turkey, and even more so in Europe, Alevis have organized themselves into associations, foundations, and religious centers (*cem evi*). Unbiased researchers estimate the population of Alevis in Turkey to be at least 15 million. Alevis are found in every part of Turkey, with the exception of the Black Sea and southeastern Anatolia regions, where they are very few. Alevi population is most concentrated in Erzincan, Sivas, Tunceli, Tokat, Kahramanmaraş, and Malatya provinces.

Due to various factors, Alevis historically kept their worship and beliefs secret and perpetuated their culture through oral tradition, but this has changed. This oral tradition expresses itself through the poets and folk literature and music, which is how Alevi faith and culture has come down to us today. Throughout the centuries, Alevi dedes and poets used Turkish, the language of the people, as opposed to the heavily Persian- and Arabic-influenced language of the Ottomans. Alevis consider books like the Koran, the Buyruk, and the Velayetname, obscure texts virtually unknown in the West, to be holy.

Alevi religious leaders are called dede, which is a hereditary office from the various ojaks, or clans, in Anatolia. Alevism's system of morality can be briefly summarized in the two precepts, Love the Family of the Prophet, and Take Moral Responsibility for your Hands, your Tongue, and your Loins, and in the Four Doors, Forty Steps. Those who do not obey these rules are considered fallen and are expelled from the group.

The regular worship service of Alevis is called the *cem*, or assembly. In addition to the cem, important days of celebration are Sultan Nevruz, the Fast of Muharrem, the Fast of Hızır, Hıdırellez, the Sacrifice Feast, and the Feast of Abdal Musa. There are regional variations of the forms of these practices and celebrations. Every year, international festivals are held in honor of Anatolian saints such as Haji Bektash Veli, Abdal Musa, and Pir Sultan Abdal.

There is no central headquarters for the Alevi community in Turkey, divided as it is into various organizations such as CEM Vakfı, Şahkulu Sultan Cemevi, Karaca Ahmet Cemevi, Hacı Bektaş Veli

Dernekleri, and Pir Sultan Abdal Kültür Dernekleri. In Europe, Alevi communities may be contacted through the European Federation of Alevi Unions (Avrupa Alevi Birlikleri Federasyonu), which hosts an Internet site at www.alevi.com/. Other contacts can be found on the Alevi-Bektasi Resources Site at www.alevibektasi.org.

Ali Yaman

See also: Ali ibn Abi Talib; Bektashi Order (Bektashiye); Druze; Ismaili Islam; Sufism.

References

Kehl-Bodrogi, Krisztina. *Die Kizilbas/Aleviten. Untersuchungen über eine esoterische Glaubensgemeinschaft in Anatolien.* Islamkundliche Untersuchungen, Bd. 126. Berlin, 1988.

Kehl-Bodrogi, Krisztina, Barbara Kellner-Heinkele, and Anke Otter-Beaujean, eds. *Collected Papers of the International Symposium «Alevism in Turkey and Comparable Syncretistic Religious Communities in the Near East in the Past and Present,» Berlin, 14–17 April 1995.* In *Syncretistic Religious Communities in the Near East.* Studies in the History of Religions, Numen Book Series, edited by H. G. Kippenberg and E. T. Lawson, vol. 76. Leiden: Brill, 1997.

Mélikoff, Irène. *Hadji Bektach: un mythe et ses avatars. Genèse et évolution du soufisme populaire en Turquie.* Islamic History and Civilization, Studies and Texts 20. Leiden: Brill, 1998.

Olsson, Tord, Elisabeth Ozdalga, and Catharina Raudvere, eds. "Alevi Identity: Cultural Religious and Social Perspectives." *Transactions: Swedish Research Institute in Istanbul* 8 (1998).

Yaman, Ali, Aykan Erdemir. *Alevism-Bektashism: A Brief Introduction.* London: England Alevi Cultural Centre & Cemevi, 2006.

■ Algeria

The area that composes the modern state of Algeria has been inhabited by the Berber people since ancient times, and as early as 1200 BCE, Phoenicians arrived. More than four-fifths of the country's 919,595 square miles of land is desert, and almost all of its 33.5 million residents (2008) reside on the lowlands abutting the Mediterranean Sea. It shares borders with Morocco to the west, Tunisia and Lybia to the east, and Mali, Niger, and Mauritania to the south.

The territory composing the modern state of Algeria was incorporated into the Carthaginian Empire based in neighboring Tunisia, later gradually became part of the Roman Empire, and fell to the Arabs early in the eighth century CE. Since that time Islam has been the dominant religion of the country. In the 12th century, Algeria was incorporated into the Almohad Empire, centered in Morocco. With the fall of the Almohad Empire, an actual Algerian state appeared under Yaglimorossen ibn Zianr and his successors. It had to fight off Spanish incursions at the end of the 15th century.

In the 16th century Algeria was incorporated into the Ottoman Empire (which also drove the Spanish away). Reacting to a supposed insult, the French invaded Algiers during the Napoleonic era. Defeated, the French returned in 1830 and set about conquering the northern coast and then moving south into the Sahara. They were never able to completely pacify the country. In 1873, however, they had enough under their control to begin inviting French settlers to take control of appropriated land. Over a million moved to Algeria by 1950.

The last phase of the colonial era began with renewed resistance to the French in the 1920s. Rebellious activities often met with brutal reaction. In 1962, President Charles De Gaulle signed an agreement that led to independence. Within a short time more than 600,000 French left, and some 500,000 Algerians then living abroad returned. The country passed through several decades of economic and political instability, aggravated by the appearance of radical groups that identified an ultraconservative form of Islam with the cause of helping the poorest and most disenfranchised elements of the society. That instability, often breaking out in terrorist activity, civil war, and suppression of dissent, continued through the 1990s.

To return to the early history of Islam, the Sunni Melekite School of Islam swept across Algeria in the eighth century. However, Algerians tended to dissent from their Sunni conquerors over the issue of the caliphate. They adopted the Ibadite position (popularized in Oman) that the caliphate did not have to remain

Mosque in Algiers. There are a number of historic mosques and churches in Algiers. (iStockPhoto.com)

control of the government, adopting a Socialist and nominally Islamic stance, a variety of dissenting groups based in the mosques in the poorer neighborhoods emerged. In 1989, the government opened the country to a multiparty system, and both Marxist and fundamentalist Muslim organizations emerged. Of the latter, the Islamic Salvation Front (FIS) and the Da'wa Islamic League were the most important. The FIS, demanding that an Islamic state be proclaimed and Islamic law be adopted, won a major victory in the 1992 elections.

In reaction to a possible FIS takeover in a future election, the government arrested all of the FIS's major leaders. The FIS was officially disbanded, and sympathetic imams were replaced in a number of mosques. The actions did not stop the FIS, and it has continued as a strong force in the land. In 1996, parties based on either religion or language were banned, and further violence ensued. The situation has yet to be resolved.

Jewish life in Algeria can be traced to the fourth century BCE. It suffered under the Turkish regime but revived after the French takeover. In 1870, most Jews were given French citizenship. Fearful of the independent Muslim government, soon after the changes of 1962 the great majority of the 120,000 Jews took the opportunity to migrate to France. Today less than 150 Jews are known to live in the country. There is one communal center and synagogue, located in Algiers.

Christianity has an ancient history in Algeria. It spread among the Latin-speaking people living in the area, which was part of the Roman Empire in the first century of the Common Era. Some of the most noteworthy of the church's Latin fathers were Algerians, including Tertullian, Cyprian, and Augustine of Hippo. The Berber tribes were strongly identified with the Donatist movement, which spread from Carthage in the fourth century and incited Augustine to some of his most extreme writing. Both the orthodox and Donatist perspectives survived only to be wiped out in the eighth century by Islam. The Kabyle (a Berber group) are a Christian people who accepted Islam only after lengthy resistance.

Christianity returned to Algeria in the 15th century when a resurgent Spain captured the coastal city of Oran in the 1490s, but the Spaniards were soon driven out by the Ottomans. Then, following the French

in the hands of the family of Muhammad, but belonged to the most qualified. Kharjite Ibada Islam remains strongest in the southern part of the country and operates the Institute al-Haya in Guerara in the Oasis Province. There is now also a small community of followers of the Hanafite School of Islam, most descendents of Turks and Moors. There is a considerable presence by the Sufi brotherhoods, most prominently the Tijaniyya and the Qadiriyya.

The modern history of Islam has been most influenced by the rise of fundamentalist Islam and the tying of Islam, first to the fight for independence from France and then to the struggle to relieve the plight of the poor. Resistance was first formed by the National Liberation Front (FLN), made famous by the writings of Franz Fanon (1925–1961), whose thought helped shape it through the 1950s. However, after the FLN took

ALGERIA

invasion, the Roman Catholic Church was established within the French expatriate community. In 1838 Algeria was designated a diocese under Aix-en-Provence (France), but the church was not allowed to proselytize the Muslims. Missionary activity was only allowed after Charles Lavigerie, a priest with the White Fathers, became bishop of Algiers. The church's spread, however, was much more tied to the arrival of hundreds of thousands of French settlers than to any conversion of the Muslim population.

The Catholic archbishop acquitted himself well during the last years of the struggle for independence, setting the stage for amiable Christian-Muslim relations after 1962. However, the Catholic community

Algeria

Religion	Followers in 1970	Followers in 2010	% of Population	Annual % growth 2000–2010	Followers in 2025	Followers in 2050
Muslims	13,615,000	34,712,000	98.0	1.49	41,784,000	48,284,000
Agnostics	20,000	640,000	1.8	1.49	1,000,000	1,200,000
Christians	105,000	64,600	0.2	3.26	88,700	109,000
Independents	20,500	56,000	0.2	4.15	80,000	100,000
Protestants	4,800	3,700	0.0	–0.25	3,500	3,500
Roman Catholics	76,500	3,100	0.0	–1.49	3,000	3,000
Baha'is	700	3,800	0.0	1.49	6,000	12,000
Atheists	4,000	2,400	0.0	1.49	3,000	4,000
Jews	1,000	600	0.0	–0.85	700	1,000
Total population	**13,746,000**	**35,423,000**	**100.0**	**1.49**	**42,882,000**	**49,610,000**

was gutted by the movement of so many French back to their homeland. The church reoriented itself toward service to the Algerian community through educational and medical institutions. That has been countered by the government policy of Islamicizing all educational efforts, leaving only a minimal Catholic presence.

Short-lived Protestant missions were launched as early as 1830, but permanent work did not begin until the Reformed Church of France arrived with the waves of French settlers beginning in 1873. The church grew in the expatriate community, but it had little impact on the Muslim citizenry. Like the Catholic Church, it was gutted by the massive migrations of the 1960s and had only 17 congregations by the mid-1970s.

In 1881 the founder of the American-based North Africa Mission, Edward H. Glenny, settled in Algiers. The mission found its greatest success among the Kabyle Berbers. Representatives of the British-based Algiers Mission Band, which, like the North Africa Mission, was an independent evangelical group, arrived in 1888.

In 1908, two British women who had been in Algiers as missionaries since 1891 joined the Methodist Episcopal Church (now an integral part of the United Methodist Church), and in 1909 transferred their work to its jurisdiction. Following World War II, additional personnel were sent from the United States, and through the years work was extended to centers across the country. The Methodists opened a hospital in 1966; in 1969, however, most of the missionaries were accused of being agents from the Central Intelligence Agency and expelled from the country.

At the time of Algerian independence, there was a spectrum of Christian groups, the majority of which were various European and North American Protestant/ Free church missionary efforts. Some found a following not so much among the Algerians as among the French Catholics. The Assemblies of God were among the most successful but suffered by the return to France of many members. Most of these churches remained very small, with only one or two centers.

The new government declared Islam the state religion, a provision that stops significantly short of declaring Algeria an Islamic state, and added a provision against discrimination based on religion or race. Christian churches were given freedom to operate but were not allowed to proselytize Muslims. The Jehovah's Witnesses, who had opened work around 1950, were expelled in 1970 due to their proselytizing.

A variety of churches were established to serve other-than-French expatriate communities, including the several Orthodox churches: the Coptic Orthodox Church (Egypt), the Russian Orthodox Church, the Greek Orthodox Patriarchate of Alexandria and All Africa, and the Greek Orthodox Patriarchate of Antioch and All the East. There was also a single congregation of the Coptic Evangelical Church. Unlike the churches based in the French community, these churches were not affected by Algerian independence.

In 1940, many of the Protestant church groups banded together in the Evangelical Mission Council. It was reorganized in 1964 as the Association of Protestant Church and Institutions in Algeria, but many groups withdrew in protest of its relationship to the

World Council of Churches. Much of the work of the council became obsolete when in 1972 the Methodist Church, the Reformed Church, and several other groups merged to form the Protestant Church of Algeria. This church has only eight congregations scattered across the coastal cities of the north but is considered important by European Protestants who wish to maintain a non-Catholic Christian presence in the area. It is a member of the World Council of Churches and retains ties to its parent bodies.

In 2006, Algeria passed a new religious law imposing prison sentences on anyone convicted of attempting to proselytize Muslims to another religion. In the wake of this law, scrutiny on Christians has increased. As of 2008, the Christian community had been reduced to approximately 11,000 people.

With the exception of the Baha'i Faith, which has won a modest number of adherents, few new religions have attempted to settle in independent Algeria.

J. Gordon Melton

See also: Assemblies of God; Baha'i Faith; Coptic Orthodox Church; Greek Orthodox Patriarchate of Alexandria and All Africa; Greek Orthodox Patriarchate of Antioch and All the East; Hanafite School of Islam; Jehovah's Witnesses; Protestant Church of Algeria; Roman Catholic Church; Russian Orthodox Church Outside of Russia; Tijaniyya Sufi Order; United Methodist Church; World Council of Churches.

References

Barrett, David, ed. *The Encyclopedia of World Christianity*. 2nd ed. New York: Oxford University Press, 2001.

Bissio, Roberto Remo, et al. *Third World Guide 93/94*. Montevideo, Uruguay: Instituto del Tercer Mundo, 1992.

Entelis, J. P., and P. C. Naylor. *State and Society in Algeria*. Boulder, CO: Westview Press, 1992.

Lehuraux, L. *Islam et Chrétienté en Algérie*. Alger: Imprimerie Baçonnier, 1957.

Phillips, John, and Martin Evans. *Algeria: Anger of the Dispossessed*. New Haven, CT: Yale University Press, 2008.

Ali ibn Abi Talib

ca. 597–661

Ali ibn Abi Talib was a cousin of the Prophet Muhammad who became his son-in-law by marrying his daughter Fatima. One of Muhammad's first Companions, he was selected as the fourth of the caliphs to lead the early developing Muslims. The events of his caliphate and those following would split the Muslim community into the two major factions that exist to this day: the Sunni and the Shia. The Shia Muslims consider Ali the first imam.

Ali was a native of Mecca and accepted Islam soon after Khadija, Muhammad's wife. He had grown up in Muhammad's household. He proved himself most useful to the cause with his skill and courage at the battle at Badr (624), the first large-scale battle between the Muslims and their opponents at Mecca. The victory was crucial to Muhammad and his followers. Ali was in fact involved in all the battles fought by the Muslims prior to Muhammad's death, except for the expedition against the Byzantine forces known as the Battle of Tabouk.

When Muhammad died in 632, Ali was a popular choice as the first caliph by one group within the growing community, known as the partisans (Shia). They believed that Ali had been appointed by Muhammad during the Farewell Pilgrimage to Mecca shortly before his death. Given the source, they also believed his appointment had divine backing and carried with it an understanding that future caliphs should be sought among Ali's descendants.

The majority of the community did not agree with the partisans and chose Abu Bakr (ca. 573–634), a merchant of relative wealth, as the first caliph. Ali ascended to the majority and recognized Abu Bakr's leadership, which he also did when he was passed over twice more relative to Abu Bakr's successors, Umar (ca. 586–644) and Uthmān ibn 'Affān (ca. 579–656). The third caliph, Uthmān, was murdered. Some accused Ali of being involved in an assassination plot, but in spite of the rumors, he was selected as the fourth caliph.

In part due to the circumstances surrounding his selection, Ali spent much of his caliphate fighting a civil war with Muawiya ibn Abi Sufyan, the leader of the powerful Umayya clan in Mecca, who thought of himself as the rightful caliph. His support dwindled when a faction, the Kharijites (the Exiters), rebelled against him. During the Battle of Siffin (657), Ali agreed to submit his issues with Muawiya to arbitration. At this point, a group of the Kharijites withdrew. They rejected the truce that followed Siffin as wrong. Ali defeated the Kharijites at the Battle of Nahrawan in 658, but three years later one of their number assassinated him at his headquarters in Kufa (in what is now Iraq).

Ali's supporters selected his son Hasan as the new caliph (the second Shia imam), but Muawayya moved against his army and defeated it. Muawayya (r. 660–680) went on to become the next caliph and to found a dynasty that would last for the next 90 years. He set the throne of the Umayyad caliphate in Damascus, Syria, but soon lost much of his support due to his harsh measures.

In 670, Hasan was poisoned. His brother al-Husayn (626–680) succeeded him (the third imam) as the head of what was a relatively small group of followers. In 680, he and his army were defeated at the Battle of Karbala (Iraq). Al-Husayn's death that day is remembered by Shia Muslims on the day of Ashura, a day of mourning on which young men will cut themselves in commemoration of the spilling of Husayn's blood.

Ali was buried secretly, but a century later, one of Ali's descendants, Al-Shaykh Al-Mufid (the sixth imam), revealed the secret location, and Shia generally accept the site known as the Tomb of Imam Ali located in Imam Ali Mosque in al-Najaf, Itaq, a city that grew up because of the location of Ali's burial site. (A minority believe that the true burial site is at the Rawze-e-Sharif, or Blue Mosque, in Mazar-E-Sharif, Afghanistan.)

Ali stands at the beginning of the lineage of imams who led the Shia community. He is venerated as a model of righteousness. Pilgrims, blocked during the reign of Saddam Hussein, continue to flock to al-Najaf, especially on the day of Ashura and the feast day of Ghadir Khumm (the 18th day of the 12th month on the Muslim calendar), which commemorates Muhammad's appointment of Ali as his successor.

J. Gordon Melton

See also: Ashura; Companions of the Prophet; Mecca; Muhammad; Rawze-e-Sharif; Shia Islam.

References

Haeri, Shaykh Fadhlalla, comp. *The Sayings and Wisdom of Imam Ali.* Trans. by Asadullah ad-Dhaakir Yate. London Muhammadi Trust of Great Britain and Northern Ireland, 1992.

Madelung, Wilferd. *The Succession to Muhammad: A Study of the Early Caliphate.* Oxford: Cambridge University Press, 1977.

Jafri, S. H. M. *The Origins and Early Development of Shia Islam.* London and New York: Longman, 1979.

Motahhari, Murtaza. *Polarization around the Character of 'Ali ibn Abi Talib.* Tehran, Iran: World Organization for Islamic Services, 1981.

Shah-Kazemi, Reza. *Justice and Remembrance: Introducing the Spirituality of Imam Ali.* London: I. B. Tauris, 2007.

All Africa Conference of Churches

The All Africa Conference of Churches (AACC) was founded at a gathering of representatives from churches across the continent of Africa in 1963 in Kampala, Uganda. It was created in the crucible of the post–World War II conversations on the end of colonialism and the rise of nationalism that had appeared everywhere. In 1945, the new United Nations organization had in its charter expressed the general principle that all peoples deserved to be self-governing, and this became the focus of anti-colonial debates. In the anti-colonial atmosphere, the many missions established by European and North American churches in Africa moved quickly to place control in the hands of indigenous leadership and move missionary personnel into auxiliary positions. Coming changes in political leadership in the former European colonies would also have the effect of transforming the missions into new autonomous ecclesiastical bodies.

Even before World War II, some new churches founded by former members of the mission churches had appeared. In the post-colonial era, the process of creating new African Initiated Churches would increase significantly.

The All Africa Conference was from its beginning called upon to deal with the issues created by decolonization and nation building, the rise of independent churches, and the need to find a common life among the various divisions of the Christian community. Born in a hopeful time in which the ideal of ecumenical oneness motivated many, the conference soon had to reorient its work around the realities of post-colonial conflicts, government corruption, the rise of dictators, poverty, and disease. The overcoming of poverty and responding to disease has taken a priority position in the conference's life in the new century.

In 2009, the conference reported 139 member churches from 39 nations with a combined membership of 120 million. Most churches based in Africa that are members of the World Council of Churches are also members of the AACC. At its 2002 general assembly, AACC reorganized its structure around a general secretariat that oversees its several program divisions between assembly meetings. Headquarters are located in Nairobi, Kenya.

AACC Secretariat
Waiyaki Way
PO Box 14205
Westlands
Nairobi, Kenya

J. Gordon Melton

See also: African Initiated (Independent) Churches; World Council of Churches.

Reference

Van Beek, Huibert. *A Handbook of Churches and Councils: Profiles of Ecumenical Relationships.* Geneva: World Council of Churches, 2006.

All Ceylon Buddhist Congress

All Ceylon Buddhist Congress (ACBC), known in Sinhala as Samasta Lanka Bauddha Maha Sammelanaya, founded in 1918, has become the primary lay Buddhist organization in Sri Lanka, having as its avowed

Image of UNESCO's World Heritage site, the Golden Temple at Dambulla, Sri Lanka. (Shariff Che' Lah/ Dreamstime.com)

purpose the act of "engaging in the Buddhist tradition" (*yunjatha buddha sasane*) while protecting the rights and dignity of Buddhists.

The predecessor of ACBC was the All Ceylon Young Buddhist Congress (ACYBC; Samasta Lanka Taruna Bauddha Samiti Sammelanaya). In a meeting held at the Colombo Young Men's Buddhist Association (YMBA) on October 18, 1918, the 25 members in attendance decided to establish the ACYBC and to hold its first congress at Ananda College (f. 1895), Colombo. That gathering, held December 20–21, 1919, was chaired by the late statesman Sir D. B. Jayathilaka (1868–1944). Originally the ACYBC was designed to ensure harmony among the various centers of the Young Men's Buddhist Association and to unify their social and religious activities. It subsequently became an organization of indigenous intellectuals such as the late Professor Gunapala Malasekere (1899–1973), who held its presidency from 1940 to 1958 and 1970 to 1973. Although early congresses were exclusively for men, beginning in 1924, with the congress held at Panadura, women also participated. Also in 1924, the chair's speech was delivered in Sinhala (rather than the English that had been used in meetings until that time) by C. W. W. Kannangara (1884–1969). ACBC's influence was extended in 1929 by the appointment of an advisory board of 60 monks, representing the 3 monastic fraternities.

ACBC's history has been punctuated by three prominent achievements. (1) In 1941 (prior to the Buddha Jayanti Tripitaka translation project in 1956), ACBC established a Trust to translate the Tripitaka (Buddhist scriptures of the Pali Canon) into Sinhala, with the aim of reviving Pali literature and the study of Buddhism. By 1967, the Trust had published 10 volumes, including the *Cullavagga*, a volume detailing the rules for Buddhist monks and nuns. (2) In 1950 ACBC hosted the 129 Buddhist leaders (representing 29 countries) who formed the World Fellowship of Buddhists, which was inaugurated on May 25, 1950, at the Tooth Relic Temple in Kandy, Sri Lanka. (3) On December 27, 1953, at the annual meeting of ACBC held at Kegalla, Congress president Professor Gunapala Malalasekere announced the forthcoming appointment of a Buddhist Information Search Committee to investigate the status of Buddhism and Buddhist affairs. The committee was appointed the following April and began a year of collecting data from people in Ratnapura on June 26, 1954. Following the close of its inquiry in May 1955, a 186-page report was presented to the country in a meeting held at Ananda College on February 4, 1956. The Sri Lankan government moved to implement the report by appointing the Buddha Sasana Commission in 1957.

Beginning in the 1940s, ACBC has been actively involved in a variety of social and welfare activities, especially educational projects involving Buddhist children. While maintaining hostels for male and female children, vocational training centers for the youth, homes for elderly adults, a rest house for *bhikkhus* (monks) in Baddegama, and a school and hostel for children of special needs, as well as providing food and medicine for the sick and propagating Buddhism, ACBC has worked on projects across the country aimed at raising the standards of living. Current special projects include the production of Buddhist television dramas and sponsoring the *dharma* publications such as *Dharma to the UK* (2008).

In 1993 the All Ceylon Buddhist Congress celebrated its 75th anniversary, a celebration that included the issuance of a commemorative volume reflecting upon its history and activities. In recent years, the most significant action that the ACBC has undertaken to protect the rights of the Buddhists is the appointment of a 9-member commission to report on "unethical conversions." This report, completed in 2008 by collecting evidence from 348 witnesses, was presented to the Buddhist public on January 6, 2009.

All Ceylon Buddhist Congress
380 Bauddhaloka Mawatha
Colombo 7
Sri Lanka
http://www.acbc.lk

Mahinda Deegalle

See also: World Fellowship of Buddhists; Young Men's Buddhist Association.

References

All Ceylon Buddhist Congress: Diamond Jubilee Celebrations, 1919–79. Colombo: Metro Printers, 1980.

Bond, George. *The Buddhist Revival in Sri Lanka: Religious Tradition, Reinterpretation and Response.* Columbia: University of South Carolina Press, 1988.

Deegalle, Mahinda, ed. *Dharma to the UK: A Centennial Celebration of Buddhist Legacy.* London: World Buddhist Foundation, 2008.

Mutukumara, Nemsiri, ed. *Samasta Lanka Bauddha Maha Sammelanaya: Hattapasvani Jayanti Samaru Sangrahaya* (All Ceylon Buddhist Congress: Seventy-Fifth Anniversary Souvenir). Dehiwala: Srr Devi Mudranalaya, 1993.

Seneviratne, H. L. *The Work of Kings: The New Buddhism in Sri Lanka.* Chicago: University of Chicago Press, 1999.

Alliance World Fellowship

The Alliance World Fellowship is the product of the very successful world mission program launched by the Christian and Missionary Alliance (CMA) following its formation in 1897. Over the next 7 decades, missions were established in more than 50 countries. In the years after World War II, CMA personnel were among the leaders in rethinking the nature of the missionary enterprise, especially in light of the emergence of nations in the Third World. As a number of the CMA missions became autonomous national churches, the Alliance World Fellowship was organized in 1975 as a means of maintaining fellowship and restructuring the relationship among the churches as international partners in mission.

In the partnership model, churches and former missions relate as separate organizational entities, working together as partners. Overseas national churches are seen as independent and autonomous, meaning that they are not related organizationally to the CMA except as equal members in the fellowship.

The Alliance World Fellowship meets quadrennially. It assumes no legislative authority. Programs consist of reports on church work internationally, lectures and discussions, and small group meetings on topics of interest. Worship reflects the multinational participation.

In 2008 the Alliance World Fellowship had 44 member churches from as many nations, representing more than 2 million members.

Alliance World Fellowship
Driemaster 18
Veenendaal, Netherlands 3904 RK
http://www.awf.nu/

J. Gordon Melton

See also: Christian and Missionary Alliance.

Reference

Moore, David H. "How the C&MA Relates to Overseas Church." http://online.cbccts.sk.ca/alliancestudies/ahtreadings/ahtr_s74.html. Accessed October 1, 2001.

Altered States of Consciousness

The question of consciousness is both philosophically and psychologically perplexing. Although consciousness is usually taken to be the a priori of all human experience and knowing, it remains the most elusive human function, defying both certain identification as to its place of origin as well as the nature of its defining substance, if any. Any discussion of altered states of consciousness (ASC) requires a preliminary attempt at delineating of a notion of consciousness.

Most of our attempts to find consciousness, or the source of our awareness, return us to the fundamental "I am," or to the seeming fact that my experiencing self is, apparently, at the center of my conscious experience and therefore I seem to know it (as it knows me) more fundamentally than I know or am capable of knowing anything else. In this view knowing and the known are linked in the very fabric of the act of awareness and the apprehension of what is known and, for human beings, consciousness appears to be the epistemic driver from which all ontological ascriptions derive their origins.

The heart of the problem in studying consciousness seems to be found in the supposed gap that is believed to exist between observer and observed. How can a thing, for example, exist out there in the objective world and also be in my inner experiential world simultaneously? Within science, dualism is not popular because of its implication that there are two parallel ontologies (at least), and science wants to see itself as embracing the whole of reality. David Bohm and a number of other physicists have taken a non-dual position and have developed various models that encompass mind and matter as derived from a single source giving no clear preferential status to either subject or object. Bohm's idea is expressed in his notion of a "Super Implicate Order" in which objective things and their subjective representations emerge as two sides of the same coin from a non-dual, underlying connectedness.

The philosopher John Searle is insistent that we cannot reduce the "subjective ontology" of conscious experience to the "objective ontology" of materialist science. He argues that any attempt to do so obviates

Portrait of late-19th-century philosopher William James. James was not only a pioneer in the study of psychology in the United States but also achieved international fame as a philosopher with his doctrine of pragmatism, a method for determining truth by testing the consequences of ideas. (Library of Congress)

the very essence, or *qualia,* of the subjective world, thereby leaving no consciousness to study. The position taken in this essay follows on from Searle's assertion and William James's *Radical Empiricism* by arguing that consciousness must be understood as being like a Kantian thing-in-itself and thus not directly knowable as either a subjective or an objective entity.

The assumption of a directly apprehensible consciousness as objective neuro-process or as thing-in-itself existing per se is untenable just as it is for all objects of the world. Such objectified inferences are better understood as derived from human experiential knowing wherein some qualia are given objective ontological status while others are understood to be subjective depending on context and learning. From this perspective so-called objective knowledge becomes

intersubjectivity that is mediated through the interpretive experiential frame of language, culture, and other learned signs. This, in effect, was the insightful position taken by James in *Radical Empiricism,* his final statement about consciousness, published around the time of his death in 1910.

For mystics and scientists alike, reality is experiential—the difference between their conceptions is the assignment of ontological status. Both within the scientific, empirical/materialist positions and mystical/ phenomenological views there are no clear-cut agreements on the assignment of ontological status. In general, however, the scientific position is that the ultimate ground is an objective, existent material reality with an ontological status not dependent on consciousness, and for the mystic it is an inner, revealed truth or ontological principle grounded in a transcendental entity and/or consciousness. In the case of the former, consciousness is merely the place where the real world is reflected in neuropsychological processes in order to be known by the observer, but for the latter it can also be the experiential ground of being or reality itself.

In his attempt to resolve this dualism, James argues that "there is only one primal stuff or material in the world, a stuff of which everything is composed, and if we call that stuff 'pure experience,' then knowing can easily be explained as a particular sort of relation towards one another into which portions of pure experience may enter . . . The instant field of the present is at all times what I call the 'pure' experience. It is only virtually or potentially either object or subject as yet. For the time being, it is plain, unqualified actuality, or existence, a simple *that.* In this naïve immediacy it is of course valid; it is there, we act upon it; and the doubling of it in retrospection into a state of mind and a reality intended thereby, is just one of the acts" (James, *Essays,* 23–24).

This seems to be an attempt by James to remove not only Cartesian duality, but any final Kantian thing-in-itself as referent for the experience of objective things or subjective states. Sartre, however, in his classic critique of Husserl's requirement of a "transcendental I" (the phenomenologist's thing-in-itself) as being necessary to achieve the *epochè,* follows a related line of reasoning when he suggests that intentionality is consciousness itself. In arguing this position, he is declaring consciousness to be a "backward cast shadow" of the contiguity of remembered reflected awarenesses experienced as part of self-reflection in the present. Although James seems to put all things, states, and knowledge on the side of experience, Sartre puts them back out onto the object. In either case both positions point us to the unique reality-making quality of intentional conscious experience and appear to suggest that it is here that we should focus our attention in any systematic and scientific exploration of consciousness.

Most of us are aware that there is not just a single, ongoing, homogeneous state of consciousness, sleep being the one most common example of an altered state. Drug-induced experiences, ritually created trance states, the altered awareness induced during prayer and meditation, and spontaneous religio-mystical encounters represent the more exotic end of the spectrum of ASCs known to us, in addition to the more negatively valenced states experienced by individuals undergoing psychotic episodes. Some theorists, including myself, believe that the state of consciousness of the knower is the single most important factor in determining how ontological ascriptions are made and hence what is considered to be real (Nelson 1990).

In the conceptual hands of many scholars and scientists, consciousness is considered to be a thing but yet seems impossible to define without reference to something else. This something else (namely, brain, cosmos, etc.) usually turns out to be, on close inspection, a linguistic metaphor or conceptual analogue. Our language not only derives its implicit epistemic frame from our commonsense notions of time, space, and objects, but language also implicitly feeds these notions back to us through the structuring of our perceptions of the world. Consciousness, rather than being a place or thing, would appear more likely to be a conglomerate of functions or operations and is thus apparently definable more by reference to its states, manifest behaviors, experiential contents, and forms of awareness than by reference to place or things.

To summarize thus far, it is being argued that consciousness, and its objects, are inferential entities derived from the retrospection we call knowing and, in essence, they gain their epistemological status from qualia alone, which must become the focus of any useful consciousness research. Any attempt to reduce or explain consciousness through objective metaphors such as neurophysiological processing or quantum field effects at neural tubules is, in a naive-real sense, attempting to study an object that is being unnecessarily posited. There is little doubt that the explicate metaphor of brain has much to do with the related, but not identical, explication we call consciousness. However, it is usually considered a commission of a category error to superimpose or interchange these metaphoric constructions and, further, naive to fail to recognize that both arise, in the sense of James's radical empiricism, from a human experiential source and only from that source. Thus, the study of consciousness requires that we heed the call of the phenomenological investigators of the first part of the 20th century and return to experience itself.

In order to study ASCs we must start with a consideration of the deployment of attention (and attentional resources) as being the sine qua non of experience's constructional operations. Looking further into this process, it is apparent that the deployment of awareness can be conceived of as generating, in an operational sense, the sum total of experience in the present and itself is set by the degree of self-reflection operating as part of that deployment. Further analysis reveals that the focus and intentional quality of deployment emerges as the result of other operations whose functioning determines the degree of self-reflection occurring at any given moment. In this analysis reality can be understood as a continuous stream of explications unfolding as qualities of conscious awareness generated by the nature and degree of awareness deployment and related self-reflection. The experience of any world is understood herein as an operationally generated metaphoric constellation of concepts working in much the same way as the operations of using a ruler define the concept and hence the knowledge of metric length.

This operational model of consciousness as a self-reflexive "backward cast shadow" is illustrated in Figure 1. From the upper horizontal section of this diagram it can be seen that consciousness is an inferential construct created by intending the contiguity of previous experiential presents (two instances of which

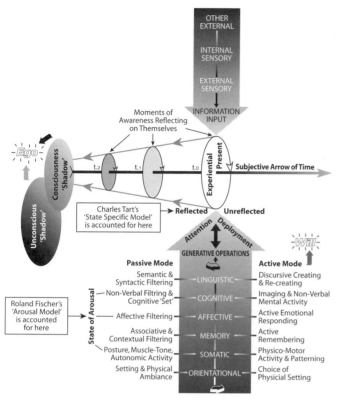

Figure 1

are shown at t-1 and t-2) into an ongoing process that gives the experient the sense that there is a container whose existence is greater than the current moment alone and encloses the objects and reflects the states associated with this collocation of past moments. The current moment is represented by the least shaded oval and the arrow on this oval is intended to denote that the experiential moment is at least partially reflected most of the time, although it is possible that there are moments of awareness that can be totally unreflected. The large, shaded vertical arrows represent, from above, potential sources of informational input into the current moment and, from below, the operations (functions) that determine deployment and quality of attentional resources and thus the ratio of reflected to unreflected experience and thus state of consciousness.

The operational functions that determine state of consciousness and, hence, experiential reality are summarized in Table 1. The fundamental maneuver of the deployment of attention (and hence state of consciousness) is inextricably connected to the process of

Table 1

1. ORIENTATIONAL (Place)—Choice of location and/or creation of explicate self/other forms, in its active mode, and contextual filtering and state maintenance, in its passive mode. Attention is 'directed' by 'significance' and 'meaning' of surrounding forms, ambiance and circumstance (also includes social and cultural shaping and filtering).

2. SOMATIC (Sensory/Motor Operations)—Sensory-motor patterning of 'physical' self and thus active forming of relationship to, and maintenance of the explicate forms of 'self' and 'other' (subject-object dialectic). In the passive form it is the bodily filter determining 'body image' by maintaining self-recreating parameters.

3. MEMORY—This may be the re-enfolding (Bohm 1980) of 'habit patterns' (Sheldrake 1981) into the 'implicate order,' or the unfolding into the 'explicate' in its active form. The associative aspects connect 'habits' in the manner of a holographic recording with a probabilistic relational matrix describing the web of connectedness. In the passive form, this re-determines the state of the system with each emergence of a standard operational configuration. In the active form, this matrix is activated from the 'top' as it were.

4. AFFECTIVE (Affect and Arousal)—In its passive form, it gives 'meaning' and 'reactive' quality to the totality of a given experiential event and, in its active form, it determines what events are 'felt' to be possible. Although affect is generally regarded as a 'by-product' reaction to events for human beings, it is taken here to be like the color we give to a picture and our way of framing it to include and exclude events and things, as well as to determine figure-ground relationships and what 'picture' we choose. Part of this operational system is always active in awareness, but much of it is operative outside of the range of reflective capacity and is in this sense 'unconscious.'

5. COGNITIVE (Conscious Processing)—These are the range of behaviors we label as thinking, remembering, visualizing, conscious attention, etc., in the active mode, and as cognitive 'set,' and overall structure of thought patterning in the passive mode. The experience of 'will' seems most associated with this group of activities, but it is impossible to tell which comes first. 'Will' may be a 'shadow' effect of the active mode like Sartre's transcendental 'ego.' It is with these operations that we associate our choice of *active deployment of attention*. Choice, however, may be an illusion caused by the assignment of initiation of an event to 'self,' but this 'self' is still an operational by-product, determined by the state of the overall system. In either case, we can differentiate an active, as well as a passive deployment of attention.

6. LINGUISTIC (Language and Verbal Operations)—Discursive 'internal dialogue' and external linguistic communication continually re-create the explicate metaphorical forms that constitute the 'picture' of reality. This is the active intra- and interpersonal filtering of experience into culturally- and personally-bound explicate forms (self-cuing). In its passive form, language structure, as an operational connecting grid, filters everything through the shape of syntactic and semantic schema.

conscious awareness reflecting itself. The conglomerate of bodily, emotive, and cognitive operations underlying deployment of attention determines on which aspect, state, or function of consciousness-doings awareness (as experience) intends reflectively. Reflection, and hence deployment of attention, can be passive, as in the sense of a filter whose capacity and form are set as ongoing background states or activities, or it can be active, as in the sense of focused concentration and participation of the experient in consciously manipulating and changing those functions.

In its passive mode, reflection occurs because a system capable of reflective consciousness is itself always at least partially reflected. This state is what defines existence and is the operational explicate metaphor we refer to as our mind-body complex. In its active mode, reflection is seemingly directed by the state of the system and the feedback generated by the background reflexive activity. Underlying the passive mode are a number of sub-operations, which include the perceptual filtering system determined by language semantics and syntax; physico-motor stance or posture (this includes in what place one puts oneself); sensory set and attunement (which varies from modality to modality); and memory, which is activated according to the information flow through the entire experiential matrix. Although we are referring to reflection as being passive here, we recognize that its ongoing activity is implicit to and part of the entire set of the system.

In its active mode, reflexive conscious experience is similar, but it gives the impression of emanating from some source such as a will. Although this will seems, experientially, to be an active agent coming from an active self, it is a projected shadow of the doing of the active mode of reflection. In other words, there is no existent will or doer behind the activity, only the doing in a mode that gives the impression, as part of its cognitive form and involvement, that it emanates from a source beyond itself. In this active mode, language, through the inner discursive dialogue, becomes a labeling and unfolding activity that creates and maintains the explicate form and is directly involved in those activities that generate the sense of will. This active attention mode also determines what aspect, or aspects, of sense experience one emphasizes or attends to.

Since the stability of a particular state of consciousness (SoC) is dependent on the dominance of a given constellation of reflective/deployment operations, then, for example, if discursive internal dialogue is de-emphasized, the whole system will tend to seek a new steady-state. In fact, the interconnectedness of all the operations, as depicted in Figure 1, when disturbed in any aspect, will tend to cause a shift and reassembly of the whole dynamical system. Because of the stochastic nature of this entire implicate/explicate functioning, this occurs in such a manner that the functional form of the re-assembly into any given new stable state is not entirely predictable. This change, as in Tart's model of states of consciousness, Fischer's arousal concept, and Katz's cognitive/affective re-interpretation, causes a shift in overall arousal and hence the perceived intensity and quality of events thus leading to an altered state of consciousness experience.

Probably the most written about and intense ASC experienced is the classical mystical encounter. In my retrospective study of individuals' recalled experiences, the rearranging of the constellation of driving operations appears to cause a very significant alteration in their functional relationships that leads to profound alterations in perception and knowing. It is this epistemic reframing that then leads to the remaking of ontological ascriptions and a sense that one has seen past the veil and penetrated to the core of existence.

I would argue that it is this apparent ontic shift that generates in our knowing a sense of having penetrated to a deeper level of reality. There is no doubt that the experient finds this encounter to be profoundly moving, because of the revelatory quality of revised knowing and, as a result of this feeling of having penetrated beyond the usual reality, this experience is often followed by a re-evaluation of values, relationships, behavior, and lifestyle. William James's report of George Fox's vision and revelation while crossing a field on his way to Litchfield is a wonderful example of the alteration in the way of knowing (and what is therefore perceived and known) that contributed to Fox's capacity to see the world anew and thereby to bring the force of his revelation into the founding and development of the Quakers. I would argue that it is particularly those types of ASCs in which the constellation of operations is altered sufficiently to give the sense that one is seeing a new level of reality, or that one is being cast across an ontic divide, that create the most intense impact and thus often lead to a reframing of meaning and value that is religious in character.

Although the term "altered state of consciousness" was most often associated with drug-induced experiences in the recent past, there is little doubt that these changes in conscious functioning have contributed profoundly to the creative unfoldment of human individual life and culture. Mainstream science's refusal to deal with this topic as anything more than categorizations, such as anomalous experience and psychopathology, has been a sad omission in our attempts to understand the universe and its origins in our collective knowing.

Peter L. Nelson

See also: Fox, George; Friends/Quakers; Western Esoteric Tradition.

References

Bharati, Ahehananda. *The Light at the Center: Context and Pretext of Modern Mysticism.* London: East-West Publications, 1976.

Bohm, David. *Wholeness and the Implicate Order.* London: Routledge & Kegan Paul, 1980.

Broad, Charles D. *Perception, Physics, and Reality.* Cambridge: Cambridge University Press, 1914.

Carroll, J. B., ed. *Language, Thought and Reality: Selected Writings of Benjamin Lee Whorf.* Cambridge: MIT Press, 1956.

Fischer, R. "On Creative, Psychotic and Ecstatic States." In *The Highest State of Consciousness,* edited by John White, 175–194. New York: Anchor Books, 1972.

Husserl, Edmund. *Ideas: General Introduction to Phenomenology.* Trans. by W. R. Boyce-Gibson. New York: Collier-Macmillan, 1962.

James, William. *Essays in Radical Empiricism and a Pluralistic Universe.* Gloucester, MA: Peter Smith, 1967.

James, William. *The Varieties of Religious Experience.* New York: The Modern Library, 1936.

Katz, S. T. "Language, Epistemology and Mysticism." In *Mysticism and Philosophical Analysis,* edited by S. T. Katz, 22–74. London: Sheldon Press, 1978.

Nelson, Peter L. "The Technology of the Praeternatural: An Empirically Based Model of Transpersonal Experiences." *Journal of Transpersonal Psychology* 22 (1990): 35–50.

Reed, Graham F. *The Psychology of Anomalous Experience.* Boston: Houghton Mifflin, 1974.

Sartre, J. P. *The Transcendence of the Ego: An Existentialist Theory of Consciousness.* Trans. by F. Williams and R. Kirkpatrick. New York: Octagon Books, 1972.

Searle, John R. *The Rediscovery of the Mind.* Cambridge: MIT Press, 1992.

Tart, Charles T. *States of Consciousness.* New York: E. P. Dutton, 1975.

Tart, Charles T. "States of Consciousness and State-Specific Sciences." *Science* 176 (1972): 1203–1210.

Amarnath

Amarnath is a mountain cave shrine to the Hindu deity Shiva located about 80 miles from Shrinagar, the capital of Kashmir, India. According to legend, Shiva revealed the secret of immortality to his wife Parvati in the cave at Amarnath. Subsequently, beneath the tiger skin on which Shiva rested, pigeon eggs later hatched. Those who do pilgrimage to this place often report seeing the immortal pigeons incubated by the Lord Shiva himself. Legendary stories also suggest that the first pilgrim to the cave was Maharishi Bhrigu, one of the seven great sages of ancient India. He is considered to be the author of *Bhrigu Samhita*, the classic astrological text written around 3000 BCE.

Entering the leaky cave, one sees at the far end a phallus-shaped ice-covered formation that is often covered with snow. This is considered a "natural" or "self-generated" Shiva Lingam, or phallus, one of the major iconographical representations of the god. To either side of the lingam are two additional ice/snow objects identified as Parvati and Ganesha (Shiva's son usually pictured with the head of an elephant, known as the deity who removes obstacles). Traditionally, the snow lingam forms every lunar month during the bright time of the Moon and dissolves during the dark half of the month. Thus the lingam reaches its greatest

Pilgrims jostle to offer prayers at the stalagmite in the Amarnath cave (seen on far left), which they worship as an incarnation of Shiva, the god of destruction, 150 kilometers (94 miles) from Srinagar, India, July 11, 2003. (AP/Wide World Photos)

size at the full moon and all but disappears during the new moon.

A more modern legend concerns a Muslim shepherd named Buta Malik, who was given a sack of coal by a holy man at this site. Upon his arrival home, the shepherd discovered that the coal had turned to gold. At the same time a Shiva Lingam made of ice had appeared in the famous cave.

The principal pilgrimage to this shrine is on the full moon of the lunar month of *Shravana* (July–August). The full pilgrimage, a widely observed custom since the mid-19th century, takes a total of 40 days, leading the pilgrim from the lowlands at the foot of the mountain upward to the cave and back.

Constance A. Jones

See also: Astrology; Pilgrimage.

References

Harshananda, Swami. *Hindu Pilgrimage Centres.* Bangalore: Ramakrishna Math, 2005.

Hassman, F. M., Yoshiaki Miura, and Vijay Pandita. *Sri Amarnatha Cave, the Abode of Shiva.* New Delhi: Nirmal Publishers & Distributors, 1987.

Singh, Karan. *The Glory of Amarnath.* Bombay: Shanti Svarup Nishat, 1954.

Ambedkar Buddhism

A wave of mass conversions to Buddhism among the so-called untouchable castes in India was set in motion when their leader, Dr. B. R. Ambedkar (1893–1956), publicly went through a Buddhist conversion ceremony in Nagpur, India, on October 14, 1956. From a total number of 180,823 Buddhists in India before this event (1951 census), over the next generation the number rose to 6,431,900 (1991 census), mainly due to these conversions. Several loosely organized local groups of followers together form the movement, which because of a lack of a central overarching organization is here labeled Ambedkar Buddhism. "Neo-Buddhism," which is frequently used in the Western academic literature, is a term that adherents find patronizing and do not use themselves. Geographically the movement is concentrated in Maharashtra, where it started, but a few centers are also found in Western countries, for instance, in Great Britain.

Bhimrao Ramji Ambedkar, "Babasaheb" among his followers, was himself born in an untouchable Mahar caste (consisting of unskilled laborers) in Maharashtra. He received an unusually good education, which included university degrees in law and economics in New York and London. Returning to India in 1923, he started his work of social uplift for the untouchables. He founded three succeeding political parties, and as chairman of the Drafting Committee for the Indian Constitution and as law minister in the first independent government, he secured the political abolishment of untouchability and laid the basis for future schemes of positive compensative discrimination.

Ideologically his aim was to build up a new self-respect among untouchables. This had to be gained by rejecting Hinduism, which to Ambedkar first of all was felt as the religion of caste and untouchability. As part of several campaigns, in 1927 he organized a conference in the town of Mahad, where the Manusmriti, the most prominent of the classical Hindu lawbooks, was burned publicly. By 1935 he had arrived at the conviction that conversion away from Hinduism would be necessary in order to cast off the stigma of untouchability. In 1948 he published his book *The Untouchables,* in which he advanced his theory that the untouchable castes are descendents from the few Buddhists who remained in India when Buddhism was crowded out from the subcontinent during the Hindu revivals in the Middle Ages. Thus, conversion to Buddhism would be a return to the original religion of the untouchables.

In 1955 Ambedkar founded the Buddhist Society of India, whose activities to some extent were hosted by the schools and colleges established by the People's Education Society, another organization founded by Ambedkar in 1945. When he died a few months after his conversion in 1956, the leadership passed on to his son, Yeshwant Ambedkar, but the society remained without a fixed organizational structure. Since that time, it has established itself as a network of more or less independent branches. The geographic centers are in Nagpur, Pune, and Mumbai (where a Dr. Ambedkar Memorial Shrine is situated). Due to the emigration of Ambedkar Buddhists overseas, a few centers have been established in Western countries in recent times.

Ambedkar Buddhism is formed to suit its social purpose. The emphasis is on social ethics, supernatural elements being avoided, in accordance with Ambedkar's understanding of Buddha, expressed in his book *The Buddha and His Dhamma,* published posthumously in 1957. Unlike Theravada Buddhism it is not a monastic religion. The local groups gather in buildings called *viharas* for daily or weekly services, which includes recitation of Ambedkar's books and excerpts from Buddhist canonical literature. Religious veneration for Ambedkar, in such forms as offerings (*puja*) in front of his statue or picture, is also common among the followers. The movement has also published guidebooks for Buddhist ritual, which contain prayers and instructions for weddings, deaths, and other rites of passage. Besides these activities the viharas are used for educational and social purposes.

Apart from Buddha's birthday, the main festivals are the three important dates related to the life of Ambedkar: the Ambedkar Jayanti (his birthday) on April 14, the Dhamma Diksha (the day of his conversion) on October 14, and Ambedkar's death memorial day on December 6.

The movement finds expression in a set of organizations: the Buddhist Society of India, c/o Prof. P. P. Garud, 180/4932, Pant Nagar, Ghatkopar, Bombay 400095, India; the International Buddha Education Institute Buddha Lok, Meerut Road, Hapur 245101 (Ghaziabad), UP, India; Dr. Babasaheb Ambedkar Samarak Samiti, Ambedkar Town Dharaampenth, Nagpur, India; Federation of Ambedkarite Buddhist Organizations, Milan House, 8 Kingsland Road, London E2 8DA, UK.

Ambedkar Buddhism
www.ambedkar.org

Mikael Aktor

See also: Buddhism; Hinduism; Wesak.

References

Ambedkar, B. R. *The Untouchables: Who Were They and Why They Became Untouchable.* New Delhi: Amrit Book Co., 1948.

Ambedkar, B. R. *The Buddha and His Dhamma.* Bombay: Siddharth College Publication I, 1957.

Fiske, Adele. "Scheduled Caste Buddhist Organizations." In *The Untouchables in Contemporary India,* edited by J. Michael Mahar. Tucson: University of Arizona Press, 1972.

Fitzgerald, Timothy. "Ambedkar Buddhism in Maharashtra." *Contributions to Indian Sociology* 31, no. 2 (1997): 225–251.

Zelliot, Eleanor. *From Untouchable to Dalit: Essays on the Ambedkar Movement.* New Delhi: Manohar Publications, 1992.

American Atheists

Among the most important organizations promoting corporate life for professing atheists, American Atheists was founded as the International Freethought Association of America in 1963 by Madalyn Murray O'Hair (1919–1995). Although atheism had been professed by numerous individuals, including prominent cultural and intellectual leaders, it did not take on real organizational life until the 19th century and some difficulty in sustaining stable ideological communities.

O'Hair had filed a lawsuit in the state of Maryland challenging the practice of beginning the day in public schools with prayer and a reading from the Bible. The

An atheist marching in the Minneapolis Gay Pride Parade on June 28, 2009. (Michael Rubin/Dreamstime.com)

suit argued that those practices violated the provisions in the Constitution against the establishment of religion by the state and the principle of separation of church and state. She later instituted a second (unsuccessful) suit calling for the end of tax exemption for church-owned property. The Supreme Court's agreement with her in the first suit became the catalyst that led to the founding of the association. By this time she had moved to Hawaii, and subsequently to Austin, Texas, where the association was superseded by the Society of Separationists and several associated organizations, including the Charles E. Stevens American Atheist Library and Archives and Poor Richard's Universal Life Church (chartered by the Universal Life Church). The Society of Separationists evolved into American Atheists, Inc.

Through the 1970s and 1980s, Murray became the most outspoken and famous atheist in North America, and her often abrasive manner created many critics above and beyond those who rejected her atheist perspective. In 1978, a group left her organization to create the rival Freedom from Religion Foundation, and subsequently other similar atheist organizations appeared. One of her sons, William Murray, broke with his mother to become a Christian. Then on September 4, 1995, O'Hair, her son Jon, and her granddaughter Robin Murray O'Hair disappeared. After a few contacts with some of the organization's leaders through that month, they were not subsequently in communication, and several years later it was finally determined that they had been murdered. Meanwhile, in 1996, the organization reorganized, and Ellen Johnson became its new president.

American Atheists advocate a non-Marxist worldview that is free from theism. They suggest that a world without religion would be a better place. Religion is baseless superstition and supernatural nonsense, according to them, and healthy people do not need God. O'Hair and most of the members reject the historicity of Jesus and belief in a life after death. They have been active in civil rights causes and the peace movement, but the absolute separation of church and state is the primary principle out of which they operate.

American Atheists is largely confined to the United States. In 2008 it reported members organized through more than 40 affiliate chapters. American Atheists has helped establish a global atheist network through United World Atheists, which holds a triennial World Atheist Conference.

American Atheists
PO Box 158
Cranford, NJ 07016
www.atheists.org

J. Gordon Melton

See also: Atheism.

References

O'Hair, Madalyn Murray. *Bill Murray, the Bible and the Baltimore Board of Education.* Austin, TX: American Atheist Press, 1970.

O'Hair, Madalyn Murray. *What on Earth Is an Atheist?* Austin, TX: American Atheist Press, 1969.

Flynn, Tom. *The New Encyclopedia of Unbelief.* Amherst, NY: Prometheus Press, 2007.

Wright, Lawrence. *Saints and Sinners.* New York: Random House, 1993.

American Baptist Association

Beginning in the 1850s, the Southern Baptist Convention was the scene of what became known as the Landmark controversy, led by James R. Graves (1820–1893), who attempted to call Baptists back to what he considered the old landmarks of Christianity. Graves believed that the only true Christian churches in the world were the Baptist churches, and that there had been a succession (however thin) of Baptists since the time of Christ and his baptism by John. Such true Baptist churches practiced baptism by immersion, limited Communion to fellow Baptists, and rejected pulpit fellowship with ministers of non-Landmark churches.

Although Landmark ideas found considerable support among Southern Baptists, it was only at the beginning of the 20th century that this perspective took on organizational life. Seceding from the Southern Baptist Convention and the state conventions associated with it, Landmark Baptists formed the East Texas Baptist Convention in 1900. Other state associations followed. A national association was formed in 1905, the General Association of Baptists. The General Association was never able to gain the support of the majority of Landmark congregations, however, and in 1924 a second organization was attempted, the American Baptist Association. Leading in this second organization was Ben M. Bogard (1868–1951), who also founded the Missionary Baptist Seminary attached to the church he pastored, the Antioch Missionary Baptist Church in Little Rock, Arkansas.

Crucial to the Landmark cause had been a criticism of the organization of the Southern Baptist Convention. The Landmark teachers advocated an equal representation of congregations at the convention meetings, irrespective of their size or financial contributions to the Convention. They also challenged the authority of the Foreign Mission Board to appoint and dismiss missionaries. Although the Landmark position allows for associations beyond the local church, the powers of the association are strictly limited. There is no mission board, and the nurturance of missions has been placed in the hands of a committee that works with local churches. Missionaries are sent out by local churches with the approval of the association. In like manner, colleges are established by local churches and recognized by the association.

In 2000, the American Baptist Association reported 275,000 members. The largest group of American Baptists resides in the state of Arkansas, but affiliated churches can now be found across the United States. Its churches support a number of home missionaries, educational facilities, a variety of missionaries in foreign countries, and numerous indigenous Baptist churches around the world. Most ministers are trained in one of the four major seminaries: Missionary Baptist Seminary, Little Rock, Arkansas; Texas Baptist Seminary, Henderson, Texas; Oxford Baptist Institute, Oxford, Mississippi; and Florida Baptist Schools, Lakeland, Florida.

American Baptist Association
4605 N. State Line Ave.
Texarkana, TX 75501
www.abaptist.org

J. Gordon Melton

See also: Baptists; Southern Baptist Convention.

References

Ashcraft, Robert, ed. *History of the American Baptist Association.* Texarkana, TX: Baptist Sunday School Committee, 2000.

Ashcraft, Robert, ed. *Contending for the Faith: An Updated History of the Baptists.* Texarkana, TX: ABA Baptist Sunday School Committee, 2006.

Forman, L. D., and Alta Payne. *The Life and Work of Benjamin Marcus Bogard.* Little Rock, AR: the authors, 1965–1966.

Glover, Conrad N., and Austin T. Powers. *The American Baptist Association, 1924–1974.* Texarkana, TX: Bogard Press, 1979.

American Baptist Churches in the U.S.A.

The oldest Baptist body in the United States, the American Baptists formed as scattered Baptist churches and associations across the country banded together in the early 19th century. Baptists in the United States generally look to Roger Williams (ca. 1603–1684) and the founding of the independent congregation in Providence, Rhode Island, as their beginning. Williams had been a minister among the Massachusetts Puritans (originators of Congregationalism). His colleague John Clarke (1609–1676) began a second church in Rhode Island in 1648. These congregations championed Baptist ideals of adult baptism, congregational autonomy, and separation of church and state.

Baptists, persecuted in England, fled to the American colonies, where they continued to be persecuted until afforded some relief by the Act of Toleration passed in England in 1689. However, it is not surprising to find their second center of emergence to be in Pennsylvania, the colony established to provide a haven for the equally persecuted and despised Friends (Quakers). The Pennepack Baptist Church opened in Philadelphia in 1688, and it was in Philadelphia that the first Baptist association of churches was formed in 1707. The Philadelphia Association was a loose fellowship of independent Baptist congregations whose powers were strictly advisory. It had a role in disciplining ministers (who received ordination in the local congregation) and could set standards for fellowship.

Choir members sing during Easter service in Harlem at Mount Olivet Baptist Church on April 8, 2007, in New York City. (Getty Images)

Among its important actions was the adoption of the London Confession of Faith, which included a Calvinist theological perspective, and a statement about its use as a standard for association membership.

During the 18th century, Baptists emerged throughout the colonies, and numerous associations like the Philadelphia one were established. Also, three main groupings of Baptists appeared. Besides the Calvinists (who accepted an emphasis on God's election and predestination of believers), there were associations of General Baptists (who emphasized the role of free will in God's salvation plan) and Separate Baptists, who emphasized the necessity of the experience of personal salvation known as being born again. General Baptists found their greatest success in the southern colonies, and most eventually converged in the National Association of Free-Will Baptists.

The first national association of Baptists in America was a direct result of the beginnings of world mission in the early 19th century. In order to facilitate

their support of the missionary enterprise, some Baptists created the General Missionary Convention of the Baptist Denomination in America in 1814. The convention met triennially, and any congregation could choose to associate. The organization of the convention led to a major controversy over the role of organizations that appeared to take responsibility for ministry away from the congregation. Those who rejected the idea of such pan-congregational structures withdrew and formed what became known as the Primitive Baptists. Those who accepted the idea of such organizations, as long as they were voluntary and did not infringe upon congregational autonomy, went on to found additional conventions to facilitate education, home missions, and the publication of literature. These additional societies tended to hold meetings at the same time as the meeting of the Triennial Missions Convention.

The next issue to rend American Baptists was slavery. The issue reflected the growing tension in America that eventually led to the Civil War, but it was precipitated within the convention over its refusal to credential any missionary who also happened to own slaves. In 1845, the issue split the convention, with Baptists in slave-holding states forming the Southern Baptist Convention. This separation occurred just as Baptists were in the midst of a concerted effort to convert African Americans in the South, both slave and free. In the years after the Civil War, lacking a national organization, many African American Baptists chose to affiliate with the Triennial Convention rather than the Southern Baptists. The majority of African American Baptists remained in affiliation with the Triennial Convention for a generation, but toward the end of the century many separated over the issue of self-determination to form the National Baptist Convention in the U.S.A. However, many remained in association with the Triennial Convention and today continue to form a substantial portion of the membership of the American Baptists.

Through the 19th century, Baptists associated with the Triennial Convention were content to continue their separate support of the various national organizations, but they finally moved toward a more centralized organization to coordinate the work of the various national and international ministries. In 1907, delegates moved to form the Northern Baptist Convention and to make the various societies its associated agencies. A new level of cohesiveness emerged.

The Northern Baptist Convention was one of the main arenas for the fight between fundamentalists (who demanded a strict adherence to traditional Baptist doctrinal perspectives) and modernists (who sought a revision of Christian beliefs in the light of modern social and intellectual developments). Although fundamentalists appeared to hold a slight majority in the 1920s, by the 1930s the modernists had firmly taken control, and many of the most conservative members and ministers left to found several new Baptist denominations, such as the Conservative Baptist Association.

Fundamentalists had attempted to force the Northern Baptists to adopt the New Hampshire Confession of Faith (an early statement of the Baptist perspective promulgated in 1730). However, in 1922 the convention adopted an alternate position, affirming that "the New Testament is the all-sufficient ground of our faith and practice and we need no other statement." In sub-

sequent years, the convention has not chosen to adopt a distinctive creedal statement, and a wide divergence in doctrinal perspectives is noticeable.

Following World War II, the Northern Baptists changed names twice. In 1950 the convention became the American Baptist Convention and in 1972 took its present name. In 2006, the American Baptist Churches in the U.S.A. reported 1,371,278 members in 5,659 congregations. It supports a number of colleges and eight postgraduate seminaries for the training of ministers. It is a member of the Baptist World Alliance and the World Council of Churches.

As an organization, it traces its origin to the growth of the Protestant Christian missionary impulse in America. From initial support for Adoniram Judson (1788–1850) in India, the Triennial Convention expanded work to Burma (Myanmar). By the time of the break with the Southern Baptists in 1845, the convention supported 111 missionaries in Europe, West Africa, Asia, and the American West. It went on to found missions in countries around the world, most of which in the last half of the 20th century were transformed into autonomous national churches and many of which are profiled elsewhere in this encyclopedia. The American Baptists continue to support many missionaries who are working with partner churches around the world.

American Baptist Churches in the U.S.A.
PO Box 851
Valley Forge, PA 19482-0851
http://www.abc-usa.org/

J. Gordon Melton

See also: Baptist World Alliance; Congregationalism; Friends/Quakers; National Association of Free-Will Baptists; World Council of Churches.

References

Brackney, William H., ed. *Baptist Life and Thought, 1600–1980: A Source Book*. Valley Forge, PA: Judson Press, 1983.

Brackney, William H., ed. *Baptists in North America: An Historical Perspective*. New York: Wiley-Blackwell, 2006.

McBeth, H. Leon. *The Baptist Heritage: Four Centuries of Baptist Witness*. Nashville: Broadman Press, 1987.

Torbet, Robert G. *A History of the Baptists*. Philadelphia: Judson Press, 1963.

Wardin, Albert W., ed. *Baptists around the World*. Nashville and Holman Publishers, 1995.

American Board of Commissioners for Foreign Missions

Organized in 1810 as the missionary arm of the Congregational Churches of New England (now a constituent part of the United Church of Christ), the American Board of Commissioners for Foreign Missions was the first Protestant sending agency to commission missionaries from the United States. It joined in the missionary thrust begun in the previous century by the Moravians and became one of the most important missionary organizations participating in the dramatic 19th-century expansion of Protestantism around the world. Formally incorporated in 1812, it sent its first missionaries to India the very same year. Among the notable personnel to serve in India was Dr. John Scudder (1797–1855), who created the first medical mission in the country.

Possibly the most famous of the American Board efforts was the Hawaiian mission established in 1820 under the leadership of Hiram Bingham Jr. (1831–1908). Hawaii became the launching pad for work throughout the South Seas. Over the next decades work was expanded to Africa and the Middle East.

Periodically through the 19th century, Congregationalists working through the American Board cooperated with other churches of the Reformed tradition, and for a time the American Board became the missionary arm of the American Presbyterians (1812–1870), the Dutch Reformed Church (now the Reformed Church in America) (1826–1857), and the German Reformed Church (now a constituent part of the United Church of Christ) (1839–1866). Although always predominantly a Congregational venture, by the end of the 20th century the American Board returned to its status as an exclusively Congregational agency. It also became more closely tied to the National Council of Congregational Churches. It continued to work with like-minded denominations, and in 1886 the Congregational Church in Canada used the American Board as its missionary arm in Angola. That relationship continued even after the Canadian Congregationalists merged into the United Church of Canada in the mid-1920s. In 1895 the small Schwenkfelder Church channeled its missionary concern through the American Board.

The operation of the American Board was considerably altered by changes in Congregationalism in the United States. In 1931, the Congregational churches united with the Christian Church, one branch of the American Restoration movement, and the American Board absorbed its missionary program (then entirely devoted to Japan). Then in 1961, following the merger of the Congregational-Christian Churches with the Evangelical and Reformed Church to form the United Church of Christ, the various missionary agencies that had served the merging churches joined together to form the United Church Board for World Ministries. The new United Church Board continued the history of the American Board, but it came into existence just as numerous mission churches were in the process of dropping their missionary status and becoming independent churches. The United Church Board assumed some leadership for reorienting the United Church of Christ around the new idea of partnership relationships with Congregational churches in other countries, many of which continued to need both financial and personnel support, even as they dropped their former subordinate status.

In 1995, the United Board of World Ministries of the United Church of Christ and the Division of Overseas Ministries of the Christian Church (Disciples of Christ) merged into a common Global Ministries Board, a reflection of the complete intercommunion the two churches had accepted. The new common board, which officially began to function on January 1, 1996, now carries the history of the former American Board. Many churches around the world owe their beginnings to the efforts of American Board missionaries, and are so identified throughout this encyclopedia.

Global Ministries Board
130 E. Washington St.
Indianapolis, IN 46204
700 Prospect Ave., 7th floor
Cleveland, OH 44115-1100

475 Riverside Dr., 10th floor
New York, NY 10115
http://www.global ministries.org

J. Gordon Melton

See also: Christian Church (Disciples of Christ) in Canada; Dutch Reformed Church; Reformed Church in America; United Church of Canada; United Church of Christ.

References

Mason, Alfred DeWitt. *Outlines of Missionary History.* New York: Hodder and Stoughton, 1912.
Phillips, Clifton Jackson. *Protestant America and the Pagan World: The First Half Century of the American Board of Commissioners for Foreign Missions, 1810–1860.* Cambridge: East Asian Research Center, Harvard University, 1969.
Strong, William E. *The Story of the American Board.* New York: Pilgrim Press, 1910.

■ American Samoa

American Samoa, located in the South Pacific, consists of those islands at the eastern end of the Samoan archipelago, south of Kiribati and west of the Cook Islands. Some 65,000 people (2008) reside on the 77 square miles of land, most of Polynesian descent.

The history of American Samoa is intertwined and identical with that of the nation of Samoa (or Western Samoa) through the 19th century. Then, in 1899, the United States received hegemony over this area by a treaty and in 1900 established a naval dependency centered on Pago Pago, one of the best natural deep-sea harbors in the world. It has proved a strategic location, especially during World War II.

After World War II, American Samoa became a United Nations trusteeship administrated by the United States. Due to economic and other pressures, coupled with the openness of American immigration policy,

People gather for a church service at Holy Cross Catholic Church in the village of Leone in American Samoa, October 4, 2009. (AP/Wide World Photos)

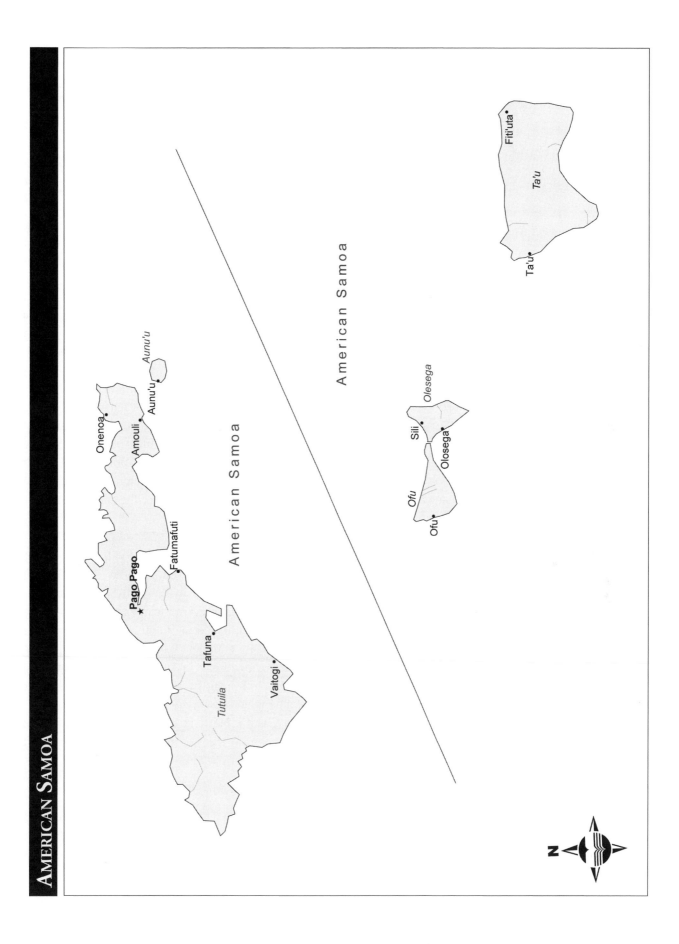

AMERICAN SAMOA

American Samoa

Religion	Followers in 1970	Followers in 2010	% of Population	Annual % growth 2000–2010	Followers in 2025	Followers in 2050
Christians	27,100	69,600	98.3	2.34	88,000	111,000
Protestants	18,900	44,000	62.1	2.04	46,000	57,000
Marginals	2,500	15,500	21.9	1.18	20,000	25,000
Roman Catholics	5,000	15,800	22.3	3.42	21,000	28,000
Agnostics	70	500	0.7	3.56	800	1,000
Chinese folk	0	260	0.4	2.42	400	600
Baha'is	200	180	0.3	–0.43	200	200
Buddhists	0	230	0.3	2.38	400	600
Atheists	10	10	0.0	0.00	30	50
Total population	**27,400**	**70,800**	**100.0**	**2.34**	**89,800**	**113,000**

many Samoans moved to Hawaii and the American mainland. In 1984, the United Nations ruled that independence should be granted, but the islanders have been content with local self-government and their peculiar relationship to the United States. They are considered U.S. citizens, but without the right to vote in the national elections while residing in American Samoa.

Through the 19th century, the missions established in Samoa by the Methodist Church (beginning in 1828), the London Missionary Society (1830), and the Roman Catholic Church (1845) spread across the Samoan archipelago. None of the three missions divided after the eastern islands were separated from the western islands in 1899. They continued to grow and prosper until 1962, when Western Samoa became an independent nation. Almost immediately, the London Missionary Society church became the Congregational Christian Church in Samoa, and in 1964, the Samoa Conference of the Methodist Church in Australia became the Methodist Church in Samoa. The Catholic vicariate that had emerged in 1957 to serve Samoa, American Samoa, and the Tokelau Islands was elevated to a diocese in 1966.

The emergence of Western Samoa as an independent nation eventually affected the major church structures, however, beginning in 1980 with the setting aside of the Congregationalists in the east as the Congregational Christian Church of American Samoa. There have been talks aimed at the reunification of the two churches, but as yet they have not been fruitful. Two years later, the Roman Catholic diocese was divided, and a new Diocese of Samoa-Pago Pago created. Only the Methodist Church has remained as a single body. The Methodists and Congregationalists form the backbone of the National Council of Churches in American Samoa.

Virtually the same array of additional churches has come to American Samoa as established work in Samoa, beginning with the Seventh-day Adventist Church in 1895. These include the Assemblies of God (U.S.), the United Pentecostal Church International, the Church of the Nazarene, and the Jehovah's Witnesses. The single Anglican parish is a part of the Diocese of Polynesia of the Anglican Church of Aotearoa, New Zealand and Polynesia.

The restrictions that had hobbled the work of the Church of Jesus Christ of Latter-day Saints (LDS) under the German rule in Western Samoa were removed following the American takeover. An early center was established at Mapusaga, which became an LDS village, complete with a school and a plantation that provided financial support. Membership at the end of the 20th century was above 12,000 members out of a population of some 40,000.

The Baha'i Faith is also present in American Samoa, though it has not enjoyed the success that it has had in Western Samoa.

J. Gordon Melton

See also: Anglican Church of Aotearoa, New Zealand and Polynesia; Assemblies of God; Baha'i Faith; Church of Jesus Christ of Latter-day Saints; Church of the Nazarene; Congregational Christian Church in Samoa; Congregational Christian Church of American Samoa; Jehovah's Witnesses; London Missionary Society; Methodist Church; Methodist Church in Samoa; Roman Catholic Church; Seventh-day Adventist Church; United Pentecostal Church International.

References

Barrett, David, ed. *The Encyclopedia of World Christianity*. 2nd ed. New York: Oxford University Press, 2001.

Bissio, Roberto Remo, et al. *Third World Guide 93/94*. Montevideo, Uruguay: Instituto del Tercer Mundo, 1992.

Forman, Charles H. *The Island Churches of the South Pacific: Emergence in the Twentieth Century*. Maryknoll, NY: Orbis, 1982.

Shafer, J. Robert. *American Samoa 100 Years under The United States Flag*. Pago Pago: Island Heritage, 2000.

Amish

The Amish are a small conservative Anabaptist group that takes its name from Jacob Amman (b. ca. 1644), a leader among the Swiss Mennonites who insisted upon a strict interpretation of the writings of Menno Simons (1496–1561) (to whom Mennonites look as their founder) and of the Dordrecht Confession of Faith, the common statement of belief among Mennonites. Amman emphasized church discipline and the use of avoidance and the ban to win back erring members. If a church member was put under the ban, the other members were to avoid communications with the person, and the spouse was to neither eat nor sleep with the offender. The advocacy of a ban led to a division among the Mennonites, to which Amman responded by placing all who disagreed with him under the ban. Later attempts at reconciliation failed, and the Amish emerged as a separate group.

Amish farmer harvests wheat with a four-horse team. The Amish, who shun modern technology, preserve traditional forms of farming, such as using animals. (Corel)

The Amish dressed in the common clothing worn by people of the 17th century. One distinctive element in their attire was clothing void of buttons, a fashion that originated from a rejection of the bright buttons worn by the soldiers who had persecuted the Anabaptists. Over the centuries, the clothing was retained in spite of passing styles, and the Amish have become readily identifiable by their distinctive plain garb. The men also continue to keep their hair long and wear beards. The women wear bonnets and aprons.

The Amish began to migrate to America early in the 18th century and were able to maintain their agricultural life for many years in rural Pennsylvania, Ohio, and Indiana. However, during the 20th century the community was under increased pressure to change to accommodate the modern world that now surrounded their communities and the increasing influx of tourists into "Amish country."

Searching for plots of land large enough to support an Amish community has forced their migration to more isolated spots across the United States and Canada, though 80 percent still reside in Pennsylvania, Ohio, and Indiana. There are also a small number in Central America. None remain in Europe. More than half of the estimated 150,000 Amish are members of the Old Order Mennonite Church.

The attempt to lead a separated life has made the Amish the subject of a variety of court actions. They do not use automobiles and wish to travel the public road in their horse-drawn buggies. They advocate education only through elementary school. The Amish are very reluctant to take part in any court proceedings. Several states have passed special legislation to accommodate the buggies, and a U.S. Supreme Court decision in 1972 allowed Amish children freedom not to attend secondary school. The National Committee for Amish Religious Freedom, founded in 1967 at the University of Chicago, attempts to assist the Old Order Amish and related Mennonite groups to continue their way of life in the face of the many rules and regulations that periodically infringe upon their community.

Members of the Old Order Amish generally worship in the homes of the members, each family hosting the congregation on a rotating basis. Some of the smaller splinter groups have built churches.

The Amish are distinguished from the Old Order Mennonites, though they share a number of commonalities—conservative dress and the use of buggies. However, the two groups have a distinct history and differ on a variety of minute points of belief and behavior.

No central address. For information:
c/o Pathway Publishers
Rte. 4
Aylmer, ON
Canada N5H 1R3

J. Gordon Melton

See also: Anabaptism; Mennonites.

References

Denlinger, A. Martha. *Real People: Amish and Mennonites in Lancaster, Pennsylvania.* Scottsdale, PA: Herald Press, 2000.

Hoestetler, John A. *Amish Society.* Baltimore: Johns Hopkins University Press, 1968, 1993.

Kraybill, Donald B., and Carl F. Bowman. *On the Backroad to Heaven: Old Order Hutterites, Mennonites, Amish, and Brethren.* Baltimore: Johns Hopkins University Press, 2001.

Whittmer, Joe. *The Gentle People: An Inside View of Amish Life.* Evansville, IN: Black Buggy Restaurant & General Store, 2006.

Amitabha Buddhist Societies

The Amitabha Buddhist Societies are a set of Chinese Pure Land Buddhist centers associated together under the leadership of the Venerable Master Chin Kung (aka Jing Kong, b. 1927) of Taiwan. The group has developed an extensive educational program that has carried it throughout the Chinese diaspora in Southeast Asia and North America, and made it one of the most important building blocks of Taiwanese Buddhism.

Master Chin Kung was born in China and grew up in Cheino, Fukien. He moved to Taiwan following World War II (1939–1945) and completed his studies toward ordination in 1959. He spent the 1960s lecturing on the Buddha's teachings in Taiwan and abroad. He also founded several Buddhist centers both in Taiwan and around Southeast Asia.

Master Chin Kung created the organizations that formed the nucleus of the network of Amitabha Buddhist Societies: the Hwa Dzan Society of Propagating Teachings, Hwa Dzan Monastery, the Hwa Dzan Buddhist Library, the Hwa Dzan Lecture Hall, and the Corporate Body of the Buddha Educational Foundation. He pioneered the publication in Taiwan of Buddhist materials on audio and video tapes and, through the educational foundation, distributed millions of pieces of Buddhist literature, including his own writings.

Master Chin Kung views Buddhism as an educational endeavor, and defines authentic Buddhism as the "education of understanding the true face of life and the universe" as originally put forth by Shakyamuni Buddha. Pure Land Buddhism is most identified with the popular practice of invoking Buddha Amida's name with the intention of it being the means of allowing the individual to be born in the heavenly realm called the "pure land of bliss." The Pure Land is the central tradition of Chinese Buddhism.

Pure Land Buddhism is based upon five Buddhist texts: The Sutra of Amitabha's Purity, Equality, and Understanding; A Principle Explanation of the Amitabha Sutra; The Chapter of Universal Worthy Bodhisattva's Conduct and Vows; The Sutra on Contemplating Amitabha and His Pure Land; and The Chapter on the Foremost Attainment of Great Strength Bodhisattva through Buddha Recitation. All of these texts are regularly reprinted by the Educational Foundation. The texts also have given rise to four courses offered at the Amitabha centers that lead to an understanding of Buddhism and how to embody it in one's life. The basic course teaches a set of moral principles and the basic practice of reciting Amitabha Buddha's name. Subsequent courses emphasize harmony and self-discipline. A final course centers upon the 10 great vows of bodhisattva conduct: respect for all people, praise for the virtues and kind practices of others, giving, repentance and reform of all one's faults, rejoicing in the virtuous deeds of others, promoting the broad spread of Buddhist teachings, seeking the guidance of the societies' teachers, holding the Buddha's teachings in one's heart, seeking accord with the wishes of people in one's environment, and dedicating the peace gained from practicing to all living beings.

In the 1980s, work expanded to North America, with most support coming from the Chinese American community. The Amitabha Buddhist Society of U.S.A. was founded in 1989 to advocate the Pure Land Study of Buddhism and was able to reach beyond the Chinese-speaking public as English-language translations of Master Chin Kung's writings began to appear in the 1990s.

Centers are now found across Taiwan and in Australia, Singapore, Malaysia, Hong Kong, and the United States.

Amitabha Buddhist Societies
650 S Bernardo Ave.
Sunnyvale, CA 94087

The Corporate Body of the Buddha Educational
    Foundation
11 Fl., No. 55 Hang Chow S Rd., Sec. 1,
Taipei
Taiwan

J. Gordon Melton

See also: Buddha, Gautama; Mahayana Buddhism; Pure Land Buddhism.

References

Amitabha Buddhist Society of U.S.A. http://www .amtb.org.tw/e-bud/e-bud.htm.

Jing Kong. *Buddhism: The Wisdom of Compassion and Awakening.* Taipei, Taiwan: The Corporate Body of the Buddha Educational Foundation, n.d.

Jing Kong. *To Understand Buddhism.* Taipei, Taiwan: The Corporate Body of the Buddha Educational Foundation, 1998.

Jy Din Sakya. *Empty Cloud: The Teachings of Xu Yun.* Taipei, Taiwan: The Corporate Body of the Buddha Educational Foundation, n.d.

T'an Hsu, Grandmaster. *On Amidism.* Taipei, Taiwan: The Corporate Body of the Buddha Educational Foundation, 2001.

Amitabha's Birthday

Amitabha (also known as Amida [Japan]) is a Buddha who rules the spiritual realm known as Sukhavati, the Western Paradise or Pure Land. One of the most popular deity figures in Mahayana Buddhism, Amitabha shows up relatively late in Mahayana's development, the first mention being in the Sutra of the Buddha Amitabha. That sutra seems to have had a Sanskrit origin, but is known today only from its fifth-century Chinese version.

Like the average bodhisattva, Amitabha began life as a human. He is most often identified with Dharmakara, an Indian king who gave up his throne and became a monk. Instead of taking the bodhisattva vow, however, Dharmakara decided to become a Buddha. Following his instructions by the Buddha Lokesvararaja, he made a set of 48 vows through which he laid plans to establish a realm where all souls may reside until they are ready to enter nirvana, in Buddhism the ultimate state of rest for enlightened beings. This realm, Sukhavati, is best understood as a state of consciousness, although in many people's minds it is a kind of heavenly paradise. A practitioner need only recite Amitabha's name at the moment of death, and Amitabha will appear and escort that person to his Western Paradise.

Amitabha thus emerges as one of a small number of the deity figures in Buddhism recognized as a Buddha (as opposed to a mere bodhisattva). A list of other Buddhas would include Maitreya and Baisajya-guru (Medicine Buddha) and of course, Gautama Buddha (the historical Buddha). The majority of the figures worshipped in Mahayana are bodhisattvas.

Calling upon the name of Amitabha was developed as one practice within the T'ian Tai (Tendai in Japan) tradition and then became the central practice that defined the Pure Land tradition as developed by

The Great Buddha of Kamakura, a bronze statue of Amida Buddha. Cast in 1252, it is located on the grounds of the Kotokuin Temple and is the second largest Buddha statue in Japan. (iStockPhoto.com)

Hui-yuan (334–416 CE) and Shan Dao (613–681) in China and Honen (1133–1212) and Shinran (1173–1263) in Japan. In Pure Land settings Amitabha is generally pictured in the center with the bodhisattvas Avalokitesvara (aka Guan Yin) on his left and Mahasthamaprapta on his right. Avalokistesvara is often said to have been born as an emanation from Amitabha's brow. Occasionally, Avalokitesvara is depicted on Amitabha's forehead. The Giant Buddha at Kamakura, so often pictured as a symbol of Japan, is a statue of Amitabha (or Amida).

Belief in Amitabha's Western Paradise has been a powerful force of popular belief and has turned Pure Land Buddhism into the largest of the Mahayana traditions. Entry into the Western Paradise provides the practitioner a short-cut on the road to nirvana. Instead of practicing and constant discipline and looking forward to additional rebirths with more need for exhaustive cultivation, faith in Amitabha allows one to achieve a sort of salvation in this life. Entry into Sukhavati, although still no nirvana, would assure a person of ultimate enlightenment and entry into nirvana.

As a former human, it is appropriate to speak of Amitabha having a birthday. It is celebrated on the 17th day of the 11th month in the lunar calendar. Pure Land Believers celebrate the day with gatherings at Buddhist temples, where they together recite the Amitabha Mantra (in Japan, the *Nimbutsu*).

J. Gordon Melton

See also: Guan Yin's Birthday; Honen; Hui Yuan; Mahayana Buddhism; Pure Land Buddhism; Shan Dao.

References

Boheng, Wu, and Cai Zhuozhi. *100 Buddhas in Chinese Buddhism.* Trans. by Mu Xin and Yan Zhi. Singapore: Asiapac Books, 1997.

Epstein, Ronald, trans. "The Amitabha Sutra." *Vajra Bodhi Sea* 9 (December 1970): 11–21.

Gomez, Luis. "Shinran's Faith and the Sacred Name of Amida." *Monumenta Nipponica* 38, no. 1 (Spring 1983): 73–84.

Hua, Tripitaka Master. *A General Explanation of the Buddha Speaks of Amitabha Sutra.* San Francisco: Sino-American Buddhist Association, 1974.

Ishihara, John. *The Shin Buddhist Doctrines of Amida and the Self in Light of the Christian-Buddhist Dialog: Christ/Amida; Sinner/Bombu.* Claremont, CA: Claremont Graduate School, Ph.D. diss., 1986.

Urakami, Kenjo S. *Amida Buddha and His Pure Land: Three Sutras and One Treatise.* Privately published, 1996.

Vessantara. *Meeting the Buddhas: A Guide to Buddhas, Bodhisattvas, and Tantric Deities.* Birmingham, UK: Windhorse Publications, 1998.

Amritsar

See Golden Temple.

An Najaf

The town of An Najaf in central Iraq south of Baghdad is the site of one of the holiest shrines for Shia Muslims, who constitute the largest segment of the country's population. Its holiness is related to the career of Ali ibn Abi Talib (ca. 602–661), the son-in-law of Muhammad and the fourth caliph to lead the emerging Muslim Empire after the death of Muhammad.

Ali came to his position of power following the assassination of Uthman in 656, and his brief rule would bring to the fore strong disagreement within the Muslim leadership. The minority championed the idea that the family members of Muhammad were the most legitimate rulers in Islam, while the majority supported the historic evolution of the caliphate under the most capable leadership available. Ali represented the minority and after only five years became the victim of an assassination. Following his assassination, those who continued to argue for the leadership of his family would throw their support behind Ali's son Husayn. This group would through time come to constitute Shia Islam.

The sanctity of An Najaf preceded the career of Ali. The Tigris and Euphrates rivers, mentioned in the biblical book of Genesis 2:14 relative to the Garden

Iraqi and U.S. forces near the Imam Ali Mosque in the city of An Najaf during Operation Iraqi Freedom, August 2004. (U.S. Department of Defense)

of Eden, flow through Iraq. Legends had labeled Iraq as the cradle of humanity and designated An Najaf as the burial place of both Adam and Noah. Following his death, Ali was buried in an unknown place. Then, a century after his death, Shia leaders announced An Najaf as the burial place and subsequently erected a shrine over the designated spot. In subsequent centuries, An Najaf became one of its most enduring pilgrimage sites. It attained new stature in the 20th century when the Iranian Shia leader Ayatollah Khomeini (1939–1989) took up residence and directed his efforts against the shah from there.

During the first Gulf War, An Najaf became a center of resistance to Saddam Hussein (1937–2006), who sent government forces in to crush resistance leaders after the war. Sacred sites suffered again when President George W. Bush ordered the invasion of Iraq in 2003. An intense battle was fought to capture the city. Then on August 25 a massive car bomb was set off outside the Imam Ali Mosque. Within a few years celebrations and pilgrimages to the city revived, but further progress has been hindered by the continued fighting following the fall of Saddam Hussein's government as various factions have taken refuge in the city and its most sacred buildings.

J. Gordon Melton

See also: Mosques; Muhammad; Pilgrimage.

References

Jafri, S. Husain M. *The Origins and Early Development of Shi'a Islam.* Oxford: Oxford University Press, 2002.

Nasr, Seyyed Hossein, Hamid Dabashi, and Seyyed Vali Reza Nasr, eds. *Shi'ism: Doctrines, Thought and Spirituality.* Albany: State University of New York Press, 1988.

Tripp, Charles. *History of Iraq.* Cambridge: Cambridge University Press, 2002.

Anabaptism

Anabaptism was a radical Christian renewal movement that emerged in Central Europe simultaneously with the Protestant Reformation. Its name, meaning "re-baptism," was given to it by those who focused upon its demand that its members be baptized when they joined the movement, even though most of them had been baptized as infants. The Anabaptists did not believe infant baptism constituted Christian baptism. In fact, the belief that Christians should not be baptized until they were old enough to understand what Christian commitment entailed and could make a personal confession of faith was merely an outward symbol of the total vision they had for reforming the church as it was then constituted.

Anabaptists, in a sense, began with the Reformation assertion of the Bible as the Christian's authority from which to live and from which to call for reform of the church. The Anabaptists, however, quickly concluded that the Protestants did not go far enough in their reformation program. For Anabaptists, a true reformation would begin with an ideal of restoring New Testament Christianity that would include a break from the control then exercised by the state in church life, an emphasis upon the new birth of believers and their commitment to the disciplines of the Christian life, and the establishment of a church that was composed only of those who confessed faith in Jesus and were ready to live a Christian existence. The acceptance of these principles would have meant a total dissolution of the church as commonly known in the 16th century.

Included in the Anabaptist proposal was the abandonment of the elaborate sacramental system that had developed in Catholicism and that was continued partially by Protestants. They proposed its replacement with two simple ordinances, adult baptism and the Lord's Supper, neither of which carried sacramental implications. The proposal of the Anabaptists was rejected by Roman Catholics and Protestants alike, and both groups persecuted them.

As the movement emerged in the 1520s, its original adherents were known as Swiss Brethren. Over the next several decades, it spread northward in Austria Bohemia and Moravia and the low countries. It rarely had time to formally organize, though a communal branch, the Hutterites, did appear. It finally found an able champion in Holland, Menno Simons (ca. 1496–1561), a former Catholic priest.

The movement built around congregations of committed believers. While acknowledging the state's role in secular matters, it resisted secular authority over the churches. The church was for believers and it exercised its own discipline over the faithful. As state churches were coterminous with the society, they saw no need for evangelism, whereas the Anabaptists were active in calling people to faith and baptizing those who accepted their message.

In their attempt to live by the Bible, many Anabaptists refused to swear oaths, a practice widely used to encourage truth-telling in court and loyalty to the state. Though not their most important difference, this refusal often irritated people in authority with whom Anabaptists had to deal.

Anabaptists survived in the 16th century by moving about and locating pockets of toleration, but most ultimately fled either eastward to the American colonies or westward into Russia. In the late 19th century, many of the Russian Mennonites and Hutterites also moved on to the United States and Canada. During the twentieth century, Anabaptism became a global movement, and as a result of both missionary activity around the world and social work particularly in the areas of disaster relief, community development, and efforts for peace and justice, Mennonites especially have created flourishing communities in the Southern Hemisphere, where the majority of Anabaptists now reside.

J. Gordon Melton

See also: Hutterites; Mennonites; Roman Catholic Church.

References

Estep, William Roscoe. *The Anabaptist Story: An Introduction to Sixteenth-Century Anabaptism.* Grand Rapids, MI: Eerdmans, 1996.

Friedmann, Robert. *The Theology of Anabaptism.* Eugene, OR: Wipf & Stock Publishers, 1999.

Weaver, J. Denny. *Becoming Anabaptist: The Origin and Significance of Sixteenth-Century Anabaptism.* Scottsdale, PA: Herald Press, 2005.

Williams, George Huntston. *The Radical Reformation*. Kirksville, MO: Truman State University Press, 2000.

Ananda Marga Yoga Society

Prabhat Ranjan Sarkar (1921–1990) founded the Ananda Marga Yoga Society in 1955 in the state of Bihar, India. Ananda Marga conceives of itself as "an international socio-spiritual movement involved in the twin pursuit of Self-realization and service to all of creation." Sarkar, better known as Marga Guru Shrii Shrii Anandamurti (meaning "He who attracts others as the embodiment of bliss"), is often referred to by his followers as simply Baba (Father). He is reported to have been an accomplished yogi by the age of four and to have attracted his initial devotees when he was only six. However, he went on to marry and obtain employment with the railway, where he was working when he founded Ananda Marga. During the next 35 years, Sarkar authored more than 250 books as Shrii Shrii Anandamurti. Additional volumes on various topics such as economics, education, social philosophy, and sociology appeared under his given name.

After officially founding Ananda Marga, Sarkar began to train missionaries to spread his teachings, and today Ananda Marga has a complex international organizational structure that divides the globe into eight sectors. It recognizes three levels of membership: (1) *acharyas*, fully committed devotees and teachers who may be deployed to any location in the world; (2) local full-time workers; and (3) *margiis*, initiates who hold jobs outside the movement. The number of active members is not known, but estimates run as high as several hundred thousand.

Ananda Marga involves three distinct dimensions: (1) the practice of ancient Tantra (*tan* is Sanskrit for expansion and *tra* signifies liberation) yoga; (2) meditation; and (3) active engagement in social service toward the goal of realizing a more humane and just world. Acharyas instruct initiates in both yoga and correct methods for meditation. Members of Ananda Marga also follow the Sixteen Points, created by Sarkar, which is an important system of spiritual practices that

Members of the Ananda Marga Yoga Society—which was originally established in India but is now an international movement that combines spirituality and self-development with social activism, meditation, chant, and music—at the site of the Non-Governmental Forum on Women in Huairou District, Beijing, China, September 7, 1995. (AP/Wide World Photos)

helps followers balance the physical, mental, and spiritual parts of their lives.

Sarkar's commitment to a philosophy of "service of humanity" has led to the creation of multiple organizations. The perennial need for disaster relief around the world was addressed by creating the Ananda Marga Universal Relief Team (AMURT) in 1965 and the Ananda Marga Universal Relief Team Ladies (AMURTEL) in 1977. In 1958 Sarkar created Renaissance Universal as a structure to encourage intellectuals to conceive and create programs for improving the human condition. The Education, Relief, and Welfare Section (ERWS) is another organization created for the purpose of propagating Ananda Marga's agenda of social service.

Sarkar was also active in trying to conceptualize and mobilize new ways of educating humankind. In his book *Neo-Humanism: The Liberation of Intellect* (1982), he advocates a form of education that simultaneously develops the physical, mental, and spiritual realms of human existence. At yet another level, Sarkar's philosophy of service to humanity extends Humanism to include animals and plants as well as people. With this belief, Sarkar established a global plant exchange program and also animal sanctuaries around the world.

The political dimension of Sarkar's broad philosophy of social service, called PROUT (Progressive Utilization Theory), was first developed in 1959. It calls for economic democracy and human rights. Sarkar also promoted the creation of a world government with a global bill of rights, Constitution, and justice system.

Sarkar's political activism led Ananda Marga into much controversy in India during the 1960s and 1970s. Sarkar unsuccessfully ran for office in the 1967 and 1969 elections under the Proutist Bloc. At the same time, many began to see the Proutists as a terrorist organization. Both Prout and Ananda Marga were banned in India during the period of national emergency proclaimed by Indira Gandhi, and Sarkar was accused, convicted, and sentenced to life in prison for conspiring to murder former members. He won a new trial in 1978 and was acquitted of the charges.

Ananda Marga and its constituent organizations survived banishment from India and the imprisonment of its founding leader. Since the acquittal, it has recovered slowly in India but experienced international growth. By 2009, it had established centers across southern and eastern Asia, throughout the Americas, and in most European nations. It was also beginning its penetration of sub-Saharan Africa and the Middle East.

Ananda Marga Yoga Society
D41, South Extension Pt 1
N. Delhi 110049
India
www.anandamarga.org

Jeffrey K. Hadden and Angela An

See also: Meditation; Yoga.

References

Anandamurti, Shrii Shrii. *Ananda Marga in a Nutshell.* 4 vols. Calcutta: Ananda Marga Publications, 1988.

Avadhuta, Ácárya Vijayánanda. *The Life and Teachings of Shrii Shrii Ánandamúrti.* Calcutta: Ananda Marga Publications, 1994.

Nabhaniilananda, Dada [Amal Jacobson]. *Close Your Eyes and Open Your Mind: An Introduction to Spiritual Meditation.* Black Forest, South Australia: InterWorld Publications, 2006.

Shrii P. R. Sakar and His Mission. Calcutta: Ananda Marga Publications, 1993.

Way of Tantra: Ananda Marga Yoga Philosophy. Calcutta: Ananda Marga Publications, 1989.

Ancestors

The universality of death and questions surrounding life after death are realities that every religion has to respond to in some way. The issues range from the ultimate questions of death and the final destiny of the deceased to the means used to discern their desires and intentions for the living. Of particular significance for this discussion is the religious framing of the relationships of the departed with their surviving kin, which will be presented through an adaptation of Ninian Smart's dimensions of religion (Smart 1996), including beliefs or doctrines, rituals, stories or narratives, ethical systems, and social institutions.

While the *beliefs* about the ancestors vary, monotheistic religious systems (Christianity, Judaism, Islam) formally acknowledge that life continues after death, but typically teach that the living and the dead are separated with no or only very limited (and exceptional) communication between them. Folk or popular beliefs found at local levels around the world can be at sharp variance with formal religious doctrines about the ancestors. They may come as a result of people carrying prior beliefs into their conversion to a monotheistic faith or through new influences from the outside, especially in our globalized world.

Religious traditions that hold to some form of reincarnation (Hinduism, Jainism, and some varieties

El Dia de Los Muertos celebrations have their roots in pre-Columbian Aztec and other native festivals memorializing departed loved ones. During the holiday (November 1–2), departed friends and family return from the land of the dead to visit with the living. The living prepare special offerings of food and gifts, which are placed on the family altar in the home, in the local parish chapel, or outside the family cemetery. (Zepherwind/Dreamstime.com)

of Buddhism) typically teach that some essence of the dead will be reincarnated in some form according to the karma accumulated in past lives. As a result, they tend to be less concerned with the immediate ancestral connection to the living.

Adherents of localized traditional religions (African traditional religions, Chinese folk religions, Shinto, Latin American tribal religions, Aboriginal religions, Native American religions) typically believe that their ancestors are "living dead" (Mbiti 1995, 25) who are still connected with and concerned about the families they have left behind (Steadman, Palmer, and Tilley 1996).

Despite the variations, one belief commonly seen among those who practice ancestral rituals is the belief that the dead, though spirits, have the same personality characteristics they displayed when alive. Those who

were good and kind in life will be good and kind as ancestors; and those who were impatient or angry prior to death continue to manifest those tendencies as ancestors. Another commonly found belief is that an ancestor's status in the spirit realm is proportional to the status she or he enjoyed while alive. The more respect and honor shown to the ancestors by the living, the greater the respect (and power) the departed will have. Further, ancestors are believed to have access to powers and knowledge not available to the living. It is not surprising that in some respects the status granted to them is an acknowledgment that they hold greater ability to make their wishes known and to punish—or even kill—those who ignore or disobey them.

Ancestral *rituals*, while varying widely, tend to deal with common types of needs found across cultures. The most significant type are the transition rituals that effect their transformation from being dead to being ancestors. Religious specialists (priests, shamans, mediums) typically guide the surviving kin through the rites needed to ensure a successful transition. These may take place anytime from the funeral itself (China) to several months (Shona of Zimbabwe) or even decades (Weyewa of Indonesia) later. These transition rites often include some form of communication with the spirit realm through prayer and/or magical paraphernalia, offerings or gifts given through libations and sacrifices on behalf of the deceased to the spirit realm, or the ritual placement of offerings or gifts of wealth (whether symbolic or literal) that will accompany the dead for their use as currency in the spirit realm. The cost of an appropriate send off can be the equivalent of several years' worth of income—in some cases whole villages band together to share the expenses (the Balinese of Indonesia) in elaborate community-wide celebrations that may take place several years after death.

Once the dead have transitioned to ancestors, ongoing intensification rites are used to maintain the relationship between them and the living. These are often performed by religious specialists in regular cycles (ranging from daily to centennially), including important anniversaries that are significant to the ancestor (birth or death date) or the kin (weddings) as well as special days set aside for death commemorations by the whole society (Chinese Tomb Sweeping Day; Mexican Day of the Dead).

Crisis rituals are employed to deal with a variety of circumstances, such as facing important decisions (marriage proposal, change of job or opportunity), dealing with calamity (illness, drought, infertility), or the presence of omens (abnormal weather, signs that portend impending difficulties). They are performed to acquire ancestral wisdom or pronouncements. In such circumstances, religious specialists lead all or some of the kin through an appropriate divination ritual to determine from the ancestors the cause that led to the crisis at hand and their will in alleviating it.

Stories and other narratives (poetry, proverbs, songs) people tell each other express and reinforce ancestral beliefs. Stories about the ancestors range from the legends of the deeds of the ancestors found in religious scriptures to traditional folk tales rehearsed to children and personal and family stories that are passed on from generation to generation. They include such things as accounts of the dead communicating with the living, tales of the afterlife, and anecdotes of what happens to those who refuse to participate in the rituals and traditions.

Ethical systems for respecting the ancestors and how the living are to continue relating to them are found everywhere that ancestors are recognized. Teachings about respect of ancestors provide boundaries for acceptable and unacceptable behavior. For example, in settings influenced by Confucian values, obligations of filial piety are interwoven into social institutions and children are trained from their earliest days to observe them closely. Doctrines about the ancestral enforcement of social order serve to enforce good behavior. Followers of localized traditional religions know that the ancestors look out for them, but also observe and punish violations of proper social behavior. Society-wide rituals of ancestral commemoration concretize and perpetuate respect for the ancestors and adherence to social roles among the participants. Stories told in family settings teach the listeners about the wisdom of the ancestors and how the living are wise to attend to them in times of crisis or important decisions. In many African societies, for example, important family decisions are best made in consultation with the ancestors—just as would have happened when they were alive.

The ancestors are commemorated through *art* and *material expressions* in ways that convey values and beliefs and maintain their connection to the living. Symbolic mourning apparel, grieving performances, burial paraphernalia from urns to elaborate coffins, and memorials from tombstones and mausoleums all express values and ideals about the ancestors. All of these, together with beliefs, rituals, stories, and ethics are the grid through which the *experiences* of the living are linked emotionally in their hearts of the ancestors.

Ancestral beliefs and practices are inherently *social* and more specifically kin-focused. With the exception of heroes and special leaders, ancestors are remembered primarily by the relatives who actually knew them. These memories are integrally important for their social identity, especially if their ancestors were respected in the larger society. The social institutions, including educational, economic, and political systems and means by which people associate and organize themselves within their societies, are all utilized to reinforce ancestral ideals. Beliefs about the ancestors are communicated through religious teachings and stories. Participating in ancestral rituals with kin binds the living to each other. Those who refuse to participate in the rituals (for example, because of religious conversion) jeopardize not only themselves, but the entire family. Ancestral ethics—including participation in the rituals—are taught and reinforced by responsible members of the society.

Christian Responses to Ancestors Christian responses to ancestral beliefs and practices have varied. By and large, and following biblical prohibitions (Leviticus 19:31; 20:6, 27; Deuteronomy 18:9–14), Christians have denounced the belief that the living should attempt any contact with the dead. It should be noted that while the whole variety of beliefs and practices have often been inappropriately lumped together and labeled "ancestral worship," the reality is that "worship" is rarely the correct term to describe the beliefs and practices seen in many parts of the world. A critical element has been whether Christians have understood exactly what the local ancestral beliefs entail, and to what extent it is possible to separate honoring (which is biblically commanded), venerating, and worshipping (biblically prohibited) the ancestors.

Among Catholics, from the early 1600s the Rites Controversy pitted those who felt the practices were simply honorable social customs against those who saw them as outright worship. The conclusion, finalized in a papal bull in 1742, was that ancestral rites were incompatible with the Christian faith, and Catholic missionaries were required to take an oath prohibiting the practices in China (Luttio 1994, 302–303). Over the course of the 20th century, and especially since Vatican II, however, this attitude has been reconsidered and contemporary Catholics in a variety of locations have incorporated ancestral practices into their faith.

Protestant Christian missionaries, on the other hand, have been fairly consistent in requiring new converts to cease ancestral rites and in many cases to denounce traditional beliefs. As with the Catholics, over the 20th century the traditional approach was challenged, and questions of how to appropriately honor parents have continued to be asked, particularly in Asian (Ro 1985) and African (Mbiti 1990; Gehman 1999) settings.

A. Scott Moreau

See also: Chinese Religions; Native American Religion: Roman Catholicism; Roman Catholic Church.

References

Brandt, Newton. "The Living Dead and the Living God: Christ and the Ancestors in a Changing Africa." *Journal of Theology for Southern Africa* 130, no. 3 (2008): 119–120.

Chambert-Loir, Henri, and Anthony Reid. *The Potent Dead: Ancestors, Saints and Heroes in Contemporary Indonesia.* London: Allen & Unwin, 2003.

Frazer, James G. *The Belief in Immortality and the Worship of the Dead. I; The Belief among the Aborigines of Australia, the Torres Straits Islands, New Guinea and Melanesia.* London: RoutledgeCurzon, 2003.

Friesen, Steven J. *Ancestors in Post-Contact Religion: Roots, Ruptures, and Modernity's Memory.* Cambridge: Distributed by Harvard University Press for the Center for the Study of World Religions, Harvard Divinity School, 2001.

Gehman, Richard J. *Who Are the Living-Dead?: A Theology of Death, Life after Death, and the Living-Dead.* Nairobi: Evangel Publishing House, 1999.

Gutschow, Niels, and Axel Michaels. *Handling Death: The Dynamics of Death and Ancestor Rituals among the Newars of Bhaktapur, Nepal.* Wiesbaden: Harrassowitz, 2005.

Hozumi, Nobushige. *Ancestor-Worship and Japanese Law.* Honolulu, Hawaii: University Press of the Pacific, 2003.

Hsu, Francis L. K. *Under the Ancestors' Shadow; Chinese Culture and Personality.* New York: Columbia University Press, 1948.

Hume, Lynne. *Ancestral Power: The Dreaming, Consciousness and Aboriginal Australians.*

Melbourne; Lancaster: Melbourne University Press; Gazelle, 2002.

Janelli, Roger L., and Ton-hui Im. *Ancestor Worship and Korean Society*. Stanford: Stanford University Press, 1982.

Luttio, Mark D. "The Chinese Rites Controversy (1603–1742): A Diachronic and Synchronic Approach." *Worship* 68, no. 4 (1994): 290–313.

Mbiti. John S. *African Religions and Philosophy*. 2nd rev. and enl. ed. Portsmouth, NH: Heinemann, 1990.

McAnany, Patricia A. *Living with the Ancestors: Kinship and Kingship in Ancient Maya Society*. Austin: University of Texas Press, 1995.

Newell, William H., ed. *Ancestors*. The Hague: Mouton, 1976.

Ro, Bong R. *Christian Alternatives to Ancestor Practices*. Taichung, Taiwan, ROC: Asia Theological Association, 1985.

Smart, Ninian. *Dimensions of the Sacred: An Anatomy of the World's Beliefs*. Berkeley: University of California Press, 1996.

Steadman, Lyle B., Craig T. Palmer, and Christopher F. Tilley. "The Universality of Ancestor Worship." *Ethnology* 35, no. 1 (Winter 1996): 63–76.

Wulfhorst, Ingo. *Spirits, Ancestors and Healing: A Global Challenge to the Church; a Resource for Discussion*. Geneva, Switzerland: Lutheran World Federation, 2006.

Ancient and Mystical Order Rosae Crucis

The Ancient and Mystical Order Rosae Crucis (AMORC) has been a successful purveyor of Western Esotericism to middle America since its founding by H. Spencer Lewis (1883–1939) in 1915. Many leading members of contemporary Esoteric orders were members of AMORC during their early spiritual training. Such new religious movements as Scientology, the Mayan Order, Astara, Silva Mind Control, the Holy Order of MANS, and the Order of St. Germain can be viewed as direct or indirect offshoots of AMORC.

AMORC's origins are in New York City, where Lewis, a former ad man, began dabbling in French Eso-

teric groups and lore in the years between 1909 and 1914. From 1915 to 1939, Lewis formally established the order and moved its headquarters to Tampa, Florida; San Francisco, California; and finally San Jose, California. He spent these years elaborating a spiritual pedigree for the group that included many of the major figures and Esoteric fraternities of both Western civilization and the alternative reality tradition. Prominent figures in this illustrious lineage included Moses, Jesus, Solomon, the German Rosicrucian Fraternity of Pennsylvania, the Ordo Templi Orientis, the Knights Templar, the Essenes, Christian Rosenkreutz, Paracelsus, The Tibetan Great White Brotherhood Lodge, and Theosophy. Although challenges to this mythic history (and thus AMORC's legitimacy) were formidable during the 1920s and 1930s—particularly from the writings of R. Swinburne Clymer of the Fraternitas Rosae Crucis—Lewis's order survived its early controversies and played a key role in spreading the doctrines of Western Esotericism and mysticism in the United States through its ubiquitous advertising and numerous publications.

AMORC represents itself as a nonsectarian, nonreligious school of spiritual initiation whose members devote themselves to the investigation, study, and practical application of natural and spiritual laws. The order's stated purpose is to further the evolution of humanity by helping develop the individual's full potential. By exploring the spiritual side of human nature and learning to work with the universal laws governing human behavior, members are prepared for cosmic initiation into the Great White Brotherhood. This brotherhood is described in AMORC's literature as a group of men and women who have attained high spiritual development and who work behind the scenes to guide humanity's evolutionary growth.

The teachings of AMORC cover such areas of knowledge as metaphysics, mysticism, psychology, and occult science. The emphasis in all these teachings is on personal mastery of outer conditions through mental imaging and practical, daily application of lofty esoteric truths. The order distributes its lessons to members through a correspondence course developed by Lewis's son and successor, Ralph Maxwell Lewis (1902–1987). The younger Lewis moved AMORC away from its earlier emphasis on theurgy and "old occultism" and focused attention on psychological, metaphysical, and mystical approaches to spiritual development. The correspondence course has a scientific style that includes practical experiments.

AMORC's present North American headquarters, Rosicrucian Park, is in San Jose, California. The complex was established in 1927 and houses an acclaimed Egyptological and science museum, a planetarium, and a temple designed after the ancient Egyptian temple of Dendera. The park has been a major tourist attraction in San Jose since the 1930s. The order's present imperator is Christian Bernard (1953–), the son of the prominent French Esoterist, Raymond Bernard (1921–). Bernard was formally installed as imperator on August 7, 1990. He has subsequently dissolved the original Grand Lodge corporate entity and reincorporated the order in Quebec, Canada.

In 1990, the order claimed 250,000 members. By 1998, this number had fallen to 200,000. It is likely this loss of membership stems from a leadership battle fought out in the courts in 1990. Following the death of Ralph Lewis in 1987, Gary Lee Stewart (1953–), who had begun his career as a clerk in AMORC's adjustments department, became imperator. Stewart had impressed Lewis during a stint as a motoring missionary and was designated his successor. Stewart soon made waves among the order's older leadership as he began to implement his vision of a revitalized Rosicrucian Order that took an active role in feeding starving Africans, fighting for human rights in Central America, and saving the Amazon rain forest. Following the creation of a $3 million trust account in Andorra and the securing of a $5 million loan using Rosicrucian Park as collateral—all to fund his initiatives—Stewart was charged by AMORC's board of directors with embezzlement and abuse of power, and forced from office in April 1990. Stewart denied the charges and countersued AMORC for $31 million, alleging that the board had violated state law and its own constitution in firing him. In November 1990, Stewart lost his legal bid to win back his job. He has since become the head of an AMORC-derived order, the ConFraternity Rosae + Crucis, that works with original AMORC lessons and rituals and claims a worldwide membership. It is likely this splinter group has siphoned off many of the 50,000 members AMORC has lost since the 1990s.

Other AMORC splinter groups have appeared in Ghana and Norway.

AMORC now has about 40 meeting sites in the United States and Canada, and Grand Lodges in England, Australia, New Zealand, Germany, Spain, France, Greece, Holland, Italy, Sweden, Czechoslovakia, Japan, Nigeria, Mexico, and Brazil. It claims members in more than 100 countries worldwide. AMORC derives its income mainly from the sale of books, paraphernalia, and annual dues paid by its international membership.

Rosicrucian Order, AMORC
1342 Naglee Ave.
San Jose, CA 95191
http://www.amorc.org/

Phillip Charles Lucas

See also: Western Esoteric Tradition.

References

Bernard, Raymond. *Mysteries of the Tradition: Ancient and Modern.* www.fghoche.com/tribunes/intereng.htm. Accessed April 17, 2009.

Lewis, Ralph M. *Cosmic Mission Fulfilled.* Kings-port, TN: Kingsport Press, Inc., 1979.

Lewis, H. Spencer. *Rosicrucian Questions and Answers.* San Jose, CA: Supreme Grand Lodge AMORC, 1969.

Ancient Church of the East

In 1972, the Apostolic Catholic Assyrian Church of the East, whose headquarters had been in the United States for more than three decades, experienced a schism in Iraq, where the largest number of its members reside. The dissenting group rejected several changes introduced into the Assyrian church, including the adoption of the Gregorian calendar. This group reorganized in 1968 under Mar Thoma Darmo (d. 1969). He was succeeded by Mar Addai II (b. 1950), elected in 1970 and consecrated as the church's new patriarch in 1972.

The new church was also recognized by the government as the official continuing body of the Church of the East, whose history can be traced to the spread of Christianity into the region in the second century.

The Ancient Church of the East is like its parent body in belief and practice, the only distinction being in its administration. The schism spread through the whole of the Church of the East, and dioceses were soon established in Syria, the United States, and Germany (and now in Denmark). Church members in the West showed strong support of the war on Iraq initiated by the United States in 2003, but within Iraq, the church has suffered greatly as a minority group in the war's aftermath.

Ancient Church of the East
c/o Patriarch Mar Addai II
PO Box 2363
Baghdad
Iraq
www.atour.com/~maraddi

J. Gordon Melton

See also: Apostolic Catholic Assyrian Church of the East.

References

Coakley, J. F. *The Church of the East and the Church of England.* Oxford: Oxford University Press, 1992.

Orthodoxia. Regensburg, Germany: Ostkirchliches Institut, issued annually.

Roberson, Ronald G. *The Eastern Christian Churches—A Brief Survey.* 5th ed. Rome: Edizioni Orientalia Christiana, Pontificio Istituto Orientale, 1995.

Andhra Evangelical Lutheran Church

The Andhra Evangelical Lutheran Church (Andhra Suvesesha Lutheran Sangham) represents the first American Lutheran entrance into foreign missions. In 1842 the Ministerium of Pennsylvania, the original Lutheran organization in the United States (now a constituent part of the Evangelical Lutheran Church in America), sent C. F. Heyer (1793–1873) to begin work among the Telegu-speaking residents of Guntar, some 200 miles north of Madras, India. In 1850, the work

begun in 1845 by the Norddeutsche Mission based in Bremen, Germany, was integrated into Heyer's prior effort. The mission spread through the state of Andhra Pradesh.

In the second generation the education emphasis of the mission emerged with the founding of a Bible training school at Rajamunsry (later Luthergiri Seminary). Today the church supports a law school and a set of secondary schools across Andhra Pradesh. About the same time Dr. Anna S. Kugler, a pioneer medical missionary, arrived to establish the first of what later became a set of nine hospitals opened by the mission. The hospital became the keystone in a far-reaching public health program. She was soon joined by Catherine Fahs, who opened the church's nursing school.

The church is headed by its general synod and president. The first Indian president, elected in 1944, signaled the transfer of the church to indigenous leadership. Women have also played a central part in the church's extensive development. They are organized into more than 800 *sanajams* (sections) and have developed a unique evangelism technique—Bible teams. Each team consists of a Bible teacher, a public health nurse, an educator, and a social worker. The teams have established social centers that reach out to villages. They have also established ashrams in which women of different castes come together for education and sharing.

The women's program is integrated into an extensive social service program run by the church as a whole, which also includes efforts initiated by the Lutheran World Federation. Efforts have been made to assist residents to build fireproof housing, hostels have been opened, and cyclone relief provided. The overall aim has been to assist people to become self-supporting. Problems that demand the church's attention have multiplied as modernization spreads through India, disrupting traditional patterns.

In 2008, the church reported 800,000 members, making it one of the largest Lutheran churches in Asia. It now supports the interdenominational Andhra Christian Theological College at Secunderabad, where most of the ministers receive their training, and Andhra Christian College (founded by Lutherans). The church has entered into the Christian ecumenical community in India; it did not participate in the founding of the

Church of South India but does share full pulpit and altar fellowship with it. It is one of 11 churches that make up the associated United Evangelical Churches in India, through which it is a member of the World Council of Churches and the Lutheran World Federation. The church also retains its long-standing special relationship with the Evangelical Lutheran Church in America.

Andhra Evangelical Lutheran Church
PO Box 205
Brodie Pret
522 002 Guntir
Andhra Pradesh
India

J. Gordon Melton

See also: Evangelical Lutheran Church in America; Lutheran World Federation; United Evangelical Lutheran Church in India; World Council of Churches.

References

Neill, Stephen. *A History of Christianity in India, 1707–1858*. Cambridge: Cambridge University Press, 1985.

Swavely, C. *Mission to Church in Andhra Pradesh, India: The Andhra Evangelical Lutheran Church, 1942–1962*. New York: Board of Foreign Missions of the United Lutheran Church in America, 1962.

Swihart, Altman K., ed. *One Hundred Years in the Andhra Country*. Madras, India: The Diocesan Press, 1942.

■ Andorra

Andorra is one of several postage-stamp countries that can still be found across Europe. Known officially as the Principality of Andorra, it consists of 180 square

Sant Joan de Caselles Church, Andorra. The Romanesque church was built between the 11th and 12th centuries and is located near the village of Canillo. (Claudio Giovanni Colombo/Dreamstime.com)

ANDORRA

Andorra

Religion	Followers in 1970	Followers in 2010	% of Population	Annual % growth 2000–2010	Followers in 2025	Followers in 2050
Christians	24,200	69,000	92.2	1.99	66,200	56,200
Roman Catholics	23,400	66,000	88.3	1.94	63,500	53,300
Marginals	60	600	0.8	2.17	800	1,000
Independents	0	200	0.3	19.42	250	300
Agnostics	100	4,100	5.5	2.20	5,000	5,500
Muslims	0	700	0.9	6.20	1,500	2,000
Hindus	0	350	0.5	4.01	600	800
Atheists	50	300	0.4	1.49	400	400
Jews	70	250	0.3	2.03	300	300
Baha'is	0	100	0.1	−2.15	250	400
Total population	**24,400**	**74,800**	**100.0**	**2.03**	**74,300**	**65,600**

miles in the Pyrenees Mountains, bounded on the north by France and on the south by Spain. There is a local council that governs the 83,137 residents (2007), but it is officially a suzerainty of 2 princes, the president of the French Republic and the bishop of the Roman Catholic Diocese of Urgel (in Spain).

The Roman Catholic Church is the dominant religious body, having a history in the area that dates to the beginning of the seventh century CE. The Andorran parishes are part of the Diocese of Urgel.

The religious homogeneity of Andorra has been challenged in the decades since World War II by the entrance of both the Jehovah's Witnesses and the Seventh-day Adventist Church. The Witnesses initiated work around 1960. The Adventist work is part of the SDA Spanish Union of Churches organized in 1903.

J. Gordon Melton

See also: Jehovah's Witnesses; Roman Catholic Church; Seventh-day Adventist Church.

References

Eccardt, Thomas M. *Secrets of the Seven Smallest States of Europe: Andorra, Liechtenstein, Luxembourg, Malta, Monaco, San Marino, and Vatican City*. New York: Hippocrene Books, 2005.

Galinier-Pallerola, J. *La religion populaire en Andorra: XVIe–XIXe siècles*. Paris: Editions du centre national de la recherche scientifique, 1990.

Leckey, Colin. *Dots on the Map*. London: Grosvenor House Publishing, 2006.

Angels

Angelic figures are present in a wide variety of religious systems. Three features commonly characterize them: they are considered as (1) semi-divine figures that make up the divine court; (2) individual custodians of humans or other natural ambits, especially the heavens, fire, air, and the like; (3) messengers of God, or intermediaries between God and humans. It may be said, therefore, that the nature of angelic beings varies considerably from religion to religion, principally in accordance with their respective understanding of God, of the world, and of human beings. The present entry will consider the nature and action of angels in a variety of such religions.

The term "angel" derives from the Greek *angelos*, already used by Homer, which means "messenger" or "envoy." Augustine says that "the term 'angel' designates the assignment, not the nature. If we ask what the nature is, we may say 'spirit,' if we ask what task they carry out, we must say 'angel'" (*Enn. in Ps.*, 103, 1:5).

Some of the earliest references to angels may be found in Babylonian or Assyrian religious documents (Di Nola 1970; M. Leibovici in *Génies*, 87ff.), which are for the most part polytheistic. Many Mesopotamian divinities have ministers, *sukkal*, in their service, some of whom are referred to in the Hebrew scriptures. The sukkal of the god Anu include Ninshubur, the latter's wife, and their ample progeny, and also Papsukkal, messenger of the god Ilbaba. The sun-god Šamas has his own sukkal, whereas the god Nabû is considered the sukkal of all the gods, a title attributed likewise to the god Nusku, the sublime messenger of Bêl (or Baal). Babylonian religion gives considerable space to angels charged with the custody of individuals, this meaning coming close to the biblical Hebrew term *malākh*, "messenger." However, such angels should be considered properly speaking as personal divinities who look after humans during their lifetime but abandon them when they sin or are defiled. Such angels may protect not only individuals but groups of people (Dhorme 1910, 198–202). The distinction may also be found between the "good demon," *šedu damqu*, and the evil one, *šedu limnu* (Furlani 1928, 335ff.). Many texts and icons refer to angels who protect temples and holy places with arms uplifted in prayer, called *kuribu*, from which the Hebrew term *cherubim* is derived.

A significant relationship between Hebrew (and Christian) angelology on the one hand, and Zoroastrian (Iranian, or Persian) angelic beings, on the other, has often been noted (Dumézil 1945; Widengren 1965; M. Hutter in *Angels*, 21–34). The latter are called *ameša spenta*. This association may be due to the fundamental monotheism of both systems (God as the *Ahura Mazdāh*). In any case, the ameša spenta are considered as spirits destined to preside over the good elements of nature (light, fire, water, etc.). They are often presented as hypostases, or manifestations of the divine substance. Other angelic figures in Zoroastrian

Michael the Archangel, painted by a pupil of the Byzantine artist Theophanes the Greek. Michael is an important angel in the Jewish, Christian, and Islamic traditions. In Christianity, he is often associated with military activity and is the protector of soldiers. (Corel)

religion include the *yazata*, adorable or venerable ones, and the *fravaši*, present in the immortal souls of humans as protectors.

For Egyptian religion (D. Meeks in *Génies*, 13ff.; B. Schipper in *Angels*, 1–20), demons are considered as inferior, subterranean divinities (*achu*). Some well-intentioned demons are spoken of, but for the most part they are considered hostile and dangerous, normally bringing chastisement and calamity. On account of this, magic and exorcism were common in Egyptian religious practice.

Roman religious life, drawn principally from Etruscan and Greek religious practice (W. Speyer in *Angels*, 35–47), gives special importance to protecting spirits of nature (Pan, the nymphs), alongside the veneration given to illustrious personages and heroes. Likewise the dead (*numi*) are said to protect the home, as do the *Penati*, the *Lari,* and the *Geni.*

Greek religious forms, especially demonism, provide many elements that clarify our understanding of the action and nature of angelic beings (Dodds 1951; Reale 1997). The Greek notion of *daimōn* (which means "to divide") is ambivalent in meaning, usually taking on a negative and dramatic connotation. Nonetheless, interesting elements may be found that are similar to earlier religious forms. In Homeric texts there is a close parallelism between the terms *daimōn* and *theos*, which supports the notion of the divinization of the demonic forces (Nägelsbach 1861). Later writers present daimōnes in the following five ways. (1) They may be divinized souls of one's ancestors, who, having passed into a realm of perfect happiness, protect humans and provide them with well-being and riches: thus Hesiod (*Op.* 122ff., 251ff.) and Socrates (Plato, *Cratylus* 397f.). (2) Some daimōnes are presented as divine or semi-divine beings, intermediaries and messengers between superior gods and humans: thus Plato's *Eros* in the *Convivium* (202c). According to Hesiod, there are four kinds of rational beings: gods, demons, heroes, and humans (Plutarch, *De def. orac.* X). (3) Daimōnes may also be considered as personified energies acting within humans as protectors, especially in philosophers (Plato, *Cratylus* 397f.; Xenophanes, *Memor. I,* 1:2). Menander says openly that "at birth a good daimōn takes its place alongside each man, to initiate him in the mysteries of life" (550k). (4) The daimōn is frequently termed *agathon daimōn*, the good spirit, fecund and powerful, a notion later rejected by Christianity. (5). Finally, daimōnes may be considered as personified powers in charge of nature. Heraclitus said that "everything is full of souls and demons" (Diog. Laert., *Heracl.* VI). The Pythagoreans claimed that "the air is full of souls; that is what we call daimōnes and heroes, who communicate dreams, sickness and health to humans" (Diog. Laert., *Pyth.* XIX).

The presence of what may be termed "angels" is an integral part of Indian religious traditions, those of Hinduism, Buddhism, and Jainism (J. Varenne in *Génies*, 263ff.). According to the *Bhagavad-Gita* (17, 2:4),

Hinduism's most sacred text, religious faith, though one, has three qualities (*guna*): *sattva* (goodness, purity, essentiality), *rajas* (passion, existence), and *tamas* (heaviness, passivity, and darkness), that are, respectively, under the protection of the gods, of the genies, or of the demons. Angelic figures (called *nat*) are also to be found in Birmanian religions (D. Bernot in *Génies*, 303ff.), in other Southeast Asian practices, mainly (though surprisingly) linked with Buddhism (P.-B. Lafont in *Génies*, 363ff.), in Tibet (I. Martin du Gard in *Génies*, 393ff.), and in China (K. Schipper in *Génies*, 412ff.).

Angels are present extensively throughout the entire Bible (Daniélou 1951; Faure 1988; Giudici 1985; Lavatori 2000; Marconcini 1991; Tavard 1968). "Almost all the pages of the sacred books give witness to the existence of the angels and archangels," observed Gregory the Great (*Hom. 34 in Ev.*, 7). The early Hebrew scriptures refer frequently to the angel of Yahweh, who reveals the divine will to humans as the "external soul" as it were of the Divinity. Often assuming a human form, God's angel is seen to be exceptionally majestic and beautiful. It is not clear, however, that this angel may be considered as a creature distinct from God, a manifestation (or theophany) of the Divinity. The distinct existence of angels, however, is affirmed in the Bible by the fact that their principal task is one of praising and glorifying God (Psalms 102:20; 148:2). Besides, they are meant to look after humans, as may be seen especially in the book of Tobit (*Angels*, 227–290) and the Psalms (91:11–12). Angels care not only for individuals but for communities and entire nations (Daniel 10:13–21; Revelation 2–3). "Angels have been present since creation and throughout the history of salvation, announcing this salvation from afar or near and serving the accomplishment of the divine plan: they closed the earthly paradise; protected Lot; saved Hagar and her child; stayed Abraham's hand; communicated the law by their ministry; led the People of God; announced births and callings; and assisted the prophets, just to cite a few examples. Finally, the angel Gabriel announced the birth of the Precursor and that of Jesus himself" (CCC 332).

Likewise they are present at every stage in the life of Jesus Christ: "From the Incarnation to the Ascen-sion, the life of the Word incarnate is surrounded by the adoration and service of angels. When God 'brings the firstborn into the world, he says: "Let all God's angels worship him"' (Heb 1:6). Their song of praise at the birth of Christ has not ceased resounding in the Church's praise: 'Glory to God in the highest!' (Luke 2:14). They protect Jesus in his infancy, serve him in the desert, strengthen him in his agony in the garden, when he could have been saved by them from the hands of his enemies as Israel had been. Again, it is the angels who 'evangelize' (Luke 2:10) by proclaiming the Good News of Christ's Incarnation and Resurrection. They will be present at Christ's return, which they will announce, to serve at his judgment" (CCC 333). From the very beginning, angels are present in the life of the church, especially so in its liturgy and evangelizing mission (Act 5:19f.; 8:26–29; 10:3–12; 12:7–15; 27:23f.). Besides, there are also fallen angels (Satan and his cohorts) who, though created good, sinned and now induce humans to committing evil (Matthew 16:23; Luke 10:18; John 8:44f.; Revelation 12:10).

Reflections on angelic nature were common from the fourth century on, and especially during the Middle Ages (the Cappadocian fathers, Pseudo-Dionysius, Thomas Aquinas). The role of the angels has always been important for Christian spirituality and social life. Although devotion to them waned somewhat in modern times, a considerable comeback may be detected in recent decades (U. Wolff in *Angels*, 695–714). The following three points have been consistently taught by the Christian church: first, that angels are creatures in the fullest sense of the word (Lateran Council IV, 1215), and therefore play no substantial role in the work of creation; second, that all angels and all angelic activity are inferior and subject to Jesus Christ (Colossians 1:16; Hebrews 1:14; G. Gäbel in *Angels*, 357–376), for they are all "his angels" (Matthew 25:31); third, the veneration of images of the angels, as long as it is contextualized Christologically, is legitimate (Nicaea Council VII, 787).

Islamic teaching about angels, especially in the Koran, may be summed up as follows: "nothing can be known or done without the involvement of angels" (H. Kassim in *Angels*, 645–660; see also Eickmann 1908; Faure 1988, chapter 6). The existence and activity of angels enter into the very definition of Islamic faith, alongside the divine unity, the mission of the prophet Muhammad, the revealed books, and the day of the resurrection. The Koran distinguishes between three types of invisible beings: the *malā'ika* (angels), the *ğinn* (genies), and the *šayāṭīn* (demons), who differ from one another by grade only, although the latter can reproduce. According to the Koran (55:15), angelic substances have received life, the word, and intelligence from God; their very nature is burning and luminous. Subject to the divine will, they are nourished by contemplating God. They are involved in every aspect of human life: spiritual, psychical, corporeal, vegetative, and mineral; they are the very soul of nature, revealing through it divine mercy and power.

In Islam, angels carry out roughly the same functions as are found in the Bible. Among other things, they register human actions like scribes (82:10ff.), with justice and understanding, and after death present humans before the divine tribunal (50:16ff.). Within the spiritual world, angels are distributed among the seven heavens, glorifying God and singing his praise (74:31). Four mysterious beings are present before the divine throne; they are sometimes represented in the form of a man, a bull, an eagle, and a lion, as in the Bible (Ezekiel 1:10; Revelation 4:7), and identified with the four archangels Gabriel, Michael, Seraphiel, and Azrahel (or 'Isra'īl). Gabriel, called the great law and the holy spirit, is the guardian of paradise, the supreme messenger (18:19ff.), who appeared to Muhammad. Michael, who is indescribable, is the master of knowledge and sustainer of the body. Azrahel, who sees all creatures, is the angel of death (32:11), because he stops all movement and separates souls from bodies; humans' appointment with him is inexorable. God is praised incessantly by the *cherubim*. The angel Isrāfīl introduces the breath of the Spirit, *Ruh*, into creation (70:4; 78:38; 97:4). Although most angels obey God and praise him, Islam also speaks of fallen angels, belonging to the category of the *šayāṭīn*. The best known is Iblīs (15:30ff.), who can tempt humans, also sexually (22:52f.). Besides, the Koran refers to primordial spiritual beings similar to humans, the *ğinn*, closely associated with Allah, though considered as deriving from ancient Arabic paganism.

Although the very nature of Islam meant that idolatry was totally excluded in the veneration of angels, for many centuries, angels played an exceptionally important role in Arabic philosophy, spirituality, and mysticism, especially in the area of epistemology. In a strictly hierarchic world, God made himself known by illumination through the angels. Their role is not only theoretical, in that they reveal divine knowledge, but also saving, because they intervene directly on the soul. This may be seen, for example, in the works of Avicenna and Ibn 'Arabī, who place considerable emphasis on the role of angels in the creation of man and the material world. Specifically, the archangel Gabriel is the holy spirit from whom emanates our soul, projecting into it the form that makes possible our union with him, playing a role that medieval philosophy attributes to the agent intellect. The angel appears thus as the transcendent personality of human individuality. The mystical spirituality of Islam is based on these reflections.

Paul O'Callaghan

See also: Augustine of Hippo; Jainism; Muhammad; Thomas Aquinas; Zoroastrianism.

References

Angels: The Concept of Celestial Beings: Origins, Development and Reception. Ed. by F. B. Reiterer, K. Schopflin, and T. Nicklaus, Deuterocanonical and Cognate Literature Studies Yearbook, 2007. Berlin; New York: W. de Gruyter, 2007.

Catechism of the Catholic Church (CCC). 2nd ed. Washington, DC: U.S. Catholic Conference, 2000.

Daniélou, J. *Les anges et leur mission d'après les pères de l'Église.* Paris: Desclée, 1951.

Dhorme, P. *La Religion Assyro-Babylonienne: Conférences données à l'Institut Catholique de Paris*, Études Palestiniennes et orientales. Paris: Librairie V. Lecoffre; J. Gabalda & C.ie, 1910.

Di Nola, A. M. *Angeli e angelologia.* In *Enciclopedia delle religioni* 1, cols. 346–355. Firenze: Vallecchi, 1970.

Dodds, E. R. *The Greeks and the Irrational.* Berkeley: University of California Press, 1951.

Dumézil, G., *Naissance d'archanges. (Jupiter, Mars, Quirinus, III): Essai sur la formation de la théologie zoroastrienne.* Paris: Gallimard, 1945.

Eickmann, W. *Die Angelologie und Dämonologie des Korans im Vergleich zu di Engel und Geisterlehre der Heiligen Schrift.* Leipzig, 1908.

Faure, P. *Les anges.* Paris: Cerf; Fides, 1988.

Furlani, G. *La religione babilonese e assira.* Bologna: N. Zanichelli, 1928.

Génies, Anges et Démons. Egypte - Babylone - Israël - Islam - Peuples altaïques - Inde - Birmanie - Asie du Sud-Est - Tibet - Chine. Paris: du Seuil, 1971.

Giudici, M. P. *Qui sont les anges.* Paris: Nouvelle Cité, 1985.

Lavatori, R. *Gli angeli.* 2nd ed. Torino: Marietti, 2000.

Marconcini, B., A. Amato, C. Rocchetta, and M. Fiori. *Angeli e demoni: il dramma della storia tra il bene e il male.* Bologna: Dehoniane, 1991.

Nägelsbach, K. F. *Homerische Theologie.* Nürnberg: Geiger, 1861.

Reale, G. *Eros, demone, mediatore.* Milano: Rizzoli, 1997.

Tavard, G., A. Caquot, and J. Michl. *Die Engel,* Handbuch Der Dogmengeschichte. Bd. 2, Der Trinitarische Gott, Die Schöpfung, Die Sünde; 0002b. Freiburg i. B. etc.: Herder, 1968.

Thomas Aquinas. *Summa Theologiae I*, qq. 54–64, 98–103.

Widengren, G. *Die Religionen Irans.* Stuttgart: W. Kohlhammer, 1965.

Angkor Wat

Angkor Wat is an ancient Buddhist temple complex located in northern Cambodia, some 100 miles north of Phnom Penh. The buildings of Angkor Wat were originally constructed to promote a purely Hindu belief system, and signs of Buddhism only appear at a later time. Hindu carvings that remain include dancers (*apsaras*) performing for the king, Suryavarman II (1113–1145). History of the region dates to the Funan period of Southeast Asian history (third to sixth centuries CE), the Funan state covering much of what today is Vietnam and Cambodia. During the Funan era, both Hinduism and Buddhism entered the Khmer region. The ruling elite tended to practice Hinduism, while the populace followed Buddhism. Jayavarman II (ca. 802–850), Cambodia's first ruler, began his rule with a ceremony that centered on the installing of the phallic emblem of the Hindu deity Shiva (a linga) north of Angkor on Mount Kulen. The act was a declaration of independence not only from the Vietnamese farther south along the Mekiong River, but from the Javanese who had become influential in the region.

Gradually, over the next centuries, a new, syncretic religion that combined the two religions began to form. This religion evolved as the Khmer kingdom began to expand. It also became common for new rulers to build both a new capital city and a new royal temple, which to a large extent accounts for the abundance of ruins in the immediate area of Angkor Wat. The Khmer kingdom finally fell in the 15th century.

In the ninth century, as Cambodia began to differentiate itself as a separate nation, a new dynasty of Angkor monarchs arose. Jayavarman II, the founder of the dynasty, promoted the cult of the *deva-raja* (god-king). In this concept the king was not only a *chakravartin,* an ideal universal ruler, whose rule is marked by ethical and benevolent leadership, he also acted as the highest priestly figure. Under a later ruler, Jayavarman VII (1181–1219), this concept evolved into the cult of the Buddharaja, a Buddhist-oriented king.

Angkor Wat began as a monastic complex built during the 12th century just outside of Suryavarman II's capital of Yasodharapura. It was constructed facing the capital, which was located to its west. The previously built temples had been oriented north-south. Multiple rings of galleries surround a central temple, with each ring representing a different level of spiritual cultivation. The first gallery is open, made of columns. The second gallery is closed. The third level of gallery is a portico. And the inner temple is enclosed by walls. The inner temple symbolizes Mount Sumeru, which in Buddhist cosmology sits at the center of the universe. The three rings were connected with the levels of achievement of Vajrayana (Tantric) Buddhism.

The Khmers abandoned the Angkor site in 1432, for reasons not yet clear. General knowledge of its existence was gradually lost, though a few local people continued to use it. It was "re-discovered" by French explorers in 1850 and restoration began in 1860. Henri Mouhot wrote the first detailed description of the Ang-

Ruins of a temple at Angkor Wat in Cambodia. Built during the height of the Khmer Empire during the 12th century CE, Angkor Wat was dedicated by the king Suryavarman II to the Hindu god Vishnu. (Corel)

kor Wat complex. It appears that the moat around the complex had been a significant factor holding back the encroaching jungle.

A large range of Hindu and Mahayana/Vajrayana deities were worshipped at Angkor. These included Garuda, the mythical bird from Hindu mythology, and Hevajra, a Vajrayana Buddhist deity. Laksmi, a Hindu deity, was also worshipped in a form very similar to the Buddhist Padmapani. The Buddha Maitreya and Prajnaparamita were also worshipped. Finally, Lokesvara, a form of Avalokitesvara, the Buddhist god of compassion, was identified with the figure of Jayavarman VII, the builder of a nearby complex at Angkor Thom. After Jayavarman's death, worship at Angkor Wat shifted from Vajrayana to the Theravada Buddhism that continued to dominate Cambodian religion.

Angkor Wat and its neighboring sites can be compared to the Javanese site Borobudur. Both sites were constructed around a terrace pyramid with a central temple representing Mount Sumeru. In Agnkor Wat's case the three elements of the universe are the ocean, represented by the surrounding moat; Mount Sumeru, the central temple; and the surrounding mountain ranges, the walls around the temple.

The complex of buildings at Angkor Wat extends over 500 acres. It is one of the wonders of the ancient and Buddhist world. In 1992 the United Nations Educational, Scientific, and Cultural Organization added it to the list of World heritage sites.

J. Gordon Melton

See also: Tantrism; Theravada Buddhism.

References

Long, Mark. "In Pursuit of Sacred Science. Part I. Architectural Survey of Borobudur's Summit." http://www.borobudur.tv/survey_1.htm. Accessed May 15, 2009.

MacDonald, Malcolm. *Angkor and the Khmers.* Singapore: Oxford University Press, 1987.

Porceddu, Laura. "Angkor Wat, Cambodia." In *Encyclopedia of Monasticism,* edited by William M. Johnston, 26–28. Chicago and London: Fitzroy Dearborn, 2000.

Swearer, Donald K. *Buddhism and Society in Southeast Asia.* Chambersburg, PA: Anima Books, 1981.

Anglican Church in Aotearoa, New Zealand, and Polynesia

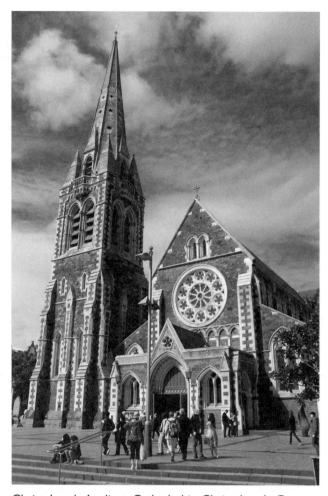

Christchurch Anglican Cathedral in Christchurch, Canterbury, New Zealand, 2008. (Tupungato/Dreamstime.com)

The Anglican Church in Aotearoa, New Zealand, and Polynesia, the representative of the Anglican Communion in New Zealand and a number of the islands of Polynesia, had its beginning in the spread of the Church of England into the South Pacific. Having been previously established in Australia, the Church of England had its beginning in New Zealand when the Reverend Samuel Marsden (1764–1838) reached an 1814 agreement with the Nga Puhi Maori chief for the settlement of three missionary families. The missionaries settled at Oihi in the Bay of Islands about 100 miles north of present-day Auckland. Missionary activity subsequently spread southward throughout the islands under the general guidance of the Church Missionary Society, assisted by early converts among the Maori who became effective evangelists. The first bishop, George Augustus Selwyn (1809–1878), arrived in 1842. The church was set apart in 1857 as an autonomous province, and by the end of the next decade five dioceses had been designated.

Several decades of post–World War II consideration of the diverse makeup of the church led to the adoption of a new constitution in 1992. The church came to see itself as a confluence of three streams of culture—Maori, Polynesian, and European—each of which continue to express their own unique *tikanga* (a

Maori term roughly translated "way" or "style"). The church is no longer seen as an extension of European Christianity into the islands, but a shared and cooperative venture of the three tikangas. With the new constitution, the church adopted its present name. Aotearoa, the name for New Zealand most common among the Maori, has gained increased popularity as a designation for the country.

The adoption of the new constitution in 1992 had its greatest impact in the reorganization of that segment of the church serving the Maori people, the Te Pihopatanga o Aotearoa. In 1928, Te Pihopatanga o Aotearoa was established with a bishop of Aotearoa acting as suffragan to the bishop of Waiapu. In 1978 it became a semi-autonomous body and granted representation in the General Synod. In 1992, Te Pihopatanga o Aotearoa was divided into five Hui Amorangi (or regional bishoprics), and four additional bishops were consecrated to serve along with the bishop of Aotearoa.

Today, the headquarters of the church may be reached through its presiding archbishop, Most Reverend W. B. Turei. The church is an integral part of the larger worldwide Anglican Communion and remains at one with its in doctrine and practice along with the changes wrought by the effort to create a distinctively New Zealand church. Just prior to the adoption of the new constitution, in 1989 the church issued its own revised Prayer Book (which contains the liturgy for its public services of worship). Females were ordained to the priesthood in 1977, and in 1990 the Reverend Dr. Penny Jamieson was ordained as bishop of Dunedin, becoming in the process the first woman diocesan bishop in the Anglican Communion.

Under Bishop Selwyn, the province cooperated with the church in Australia in the development of the Melanesian Mission, which took Anglican missionaries initially to the Solomon Islands. The New Zealand Church later gained hegemony over Anglican work elsewhere in the South Pacific. Today this work survives as the Church's Polynesia Diocese, whose bishop resides in Fiji. The diocese includes Fiji, Samoa, Tonga, and the Cook Islands.

The church is a member of the World Council of Churches. With some 650,000 members, it remains the largest religious body in New Zealand. It supports an Internet site, given below, and each diocese has a linked home page.

Anglican Church in Aotearoa, New Zealand, and
    Polynesia
The Office of the General Synod
200 St. Johns Road
Meadowbank, Auckland
PO Box 87188
Meadowbank, Auckland 1742
New Zealand
www.anglican.org.nz

J. Gordon Melton

See also: Church Missionary Society; Church of England; World Council of Churches.

References

The Church of England Yearbook. London: Church Publishing House, published annually.

Lineham, Peter. "New Zealand Religious History, a Bibliography." 2005. http://www.massey.ac.nz/~plineham/RelhistNZ.htm.

Lineham, Peter, and Allan K. Davidson, eds. *Transplanted Christianity.* Palmerston North, NZ: Department of History, Massey University, 1997.

Morrell, W. P. *The Anglican Church in New Zealand.* Dunedin: Church of the Province of New Zealand, 1973.

Van der Bent, Ans J., ed. *Handbook/Member Churches/World Council of Churches.* Geneva: World Council of Churches, 1985.

Anglican Church in Japan

The Anglican Church in Japan (Nippon Sei Ko Kai), a church in the Anglican tradition, only came into existence in 1887, but its history begins earlier. The very first Christian missionaries allowed into Japan following its opening to the West in the 1840s were John Liggins (1829–1912) and Channing M. Williams (1829–1910), two American Episcopalians who arrived in May 1859 from their former posting in China. Their arrival had been made possible by the demands of the American government that Japan cease its isolationist policies toward the West. Although Liggins was soon forced to retire due to health problems, Williams remained to build the mission. He led in the founding of Saint Paul's University and Saint Luke's Hospital of Tokyo.

The work pioneered by the Episcopal Church was supplemented in 1869 by the entrance of personnel from the Church Missionary Society, representing the Church of England, and the Women's Missionary Union opened the Doremus Girls' School in Yokohama in 1871. The Society for the Propagation of the Gospel in Foreign Parts arrived a short time later. Gradually the Japanese government allowed the missionaries to spread from their original confines in Yokohama and Nagasaki.

The British and American missionaries united in 1887 to form the Japan Holy Catholic Church (Nippon Sei Ko Kai). Channing M. Williams was selected as the first bishop. The first Japanese bishops were consecrated in 1923. In 1940, the Japanese government demanded that all non-Catholic Christian churches unite in the United Church of Japan. The Japan Holy Catholic Church refused the union and had to operate underground for the duration of the war. It reemerged with the declaration of religious freedom in 1945.

The church is led by its bishops and the biennial general synod. The synod selects the Executive Provincial Standing Committee, which administers the church between general synod meetings. The general synod also elects the primate from among the active bishops. The primate serves a two-year term, with the possibility of being reelected, and is the chair of the House of Bishops. There are currently 11 dioceses.

In 2005, the church reported 57,000 members in 315 congregations. The church supports Central Theological College in Tokyo and Bishop Williams Theological school in Kyoto. It also supports an expansive system of parochial schools that includes five junior colleges and five universities.

The church's refusal to join the United Church did not reflect its overall ecumenical spirit. It is a member of the worldwide Anglican Communion, the World Council of Churches, and the National Christian Council of Japan.

Most Reverend Christopher Ichiro Kikawada
Holy Catholic Church in Japan
65 yarai-cho
Shinjuku-ku, Tokyo 162
Japan
http://www.nskk.org (Japanese and English)

J. Gordon Melton

See also: Anglican Communion/Anglican Consultative Council; Church Missionary Society; Episcopal Church; Society for the Propagation of the Gospel in Foreign Parts; United Church of Christ in Japan; World Council of Churches.

References

Koshiishi, Samuel Isamu. "The Nippon Sei Ko Kai Today and Its Future Task." In *Anglicanism: A Global Communion,* edited by Andrew Wingate et al. London: Mowbrays, 1998.
Van Beek, Huibert. *A Handbook of the Churches and Councils: Profiles of Ecumenical Relationships.* Geneva: World Council of Churches, 2006.

Anglican Church of Australia

The British established their first settlement, built around a military post and a penal colony, at Botany Bay. A Church of England chaplain, Richard Johnson, accompanied the initial wave of settlers. Other chaplains came as the settlement grew, and as additional settlers arrived, Anglican parishes were created. In 1824, the church in Australia was incorporated into the Diocese of Calcutta (India) as an archdeaconry. The first Australian bishop, whose diocese covered all of the subcontinent and Tasmania, was consecrated in 1936. Tasmania became a separate diocese in 1842, and three additional dioceses were created in 1847. By 1872, when the General Synod met for the first time, the number of dioceses had increased to 10. The work grew as the population grew, and by the middle of the 20th century there were more than 20 dioceses. Also included in the Australian jurisdiction was Papua New Guinea.

Anglican work in Australia remained a part of the Church of England through 1961. Then in 1962 the dioceses and the several state governments of Australia approved the constitution of the Church of England in Australia. In 1977 the work in Papua New Guinea was set apart as a separate province. The present name of the church was adopted in 1981.

A General Synod, which meets at least every four years, is the primary legislative body of the church, and a primate is selected from among the bishops. The Most Reverend Dr. Philip Aspinall, the archbishop of Brisbane, was elected primate of the Anglican Church of Australia in 2005.

The Anglican Church of Australia has reported a membership of 3,881,000 (2005). The church is an ecumenically oriented body. It remains in full communion with the Church of England and participates in the worldwide Anglican Communion. It is also a charter member of the World Council of Churches.

Anglican Church of Australia
St. Andrew's House, Ste. 101
Sydney Square
PO Box Q190, QVB Post Office
Sydney, NSW 1230
Australia
www.Anglican.org.au

Mt. Rev. Dr Phillip Aspinall, Primate of Australia
C/o St Martin House
373 Ann St.
Brisbane QLD 4000

J. Gordon Melton

See also: Anglican Communion/Anglican Consultative Council; Church of England; World Council of Churches.

References

Bentley, Peter, and Philip J. Hughes. *A Yearbook of Australian Religious Organizations*. Kew, Victoria, Australia: Christian Research Association, issued annually.

Breward, I. *A History of the Australian Churches*. St. Leonards, Australia: Allen and Unwin, 1993.

Frame, Tom. *Agendas for Australian Anglicanism*. Hindmarsh, South Australia: ATF Press, 2007.

Frame, Tom. *Anglicans in Australia*. Seattle: University of Washington Press, 2008.

Hilliard, David. *Godliness and Good Order: A History of the Anglican Church in South Australia*. Adelaide, Australia: Wakefield Press, 1986.

Anglican Church of Canada

The Anglican Church of Canada is the name given in 1955 to the Canadian branch of the Anglican Communion. As with other Anglican churches, its distinguishing characteristics are episcopacy, meaning that most operations come under the authority of bishops elected for geographical dioceses and the use of authorized liturgical texts for congregational worship. The ACC has its own governance independent of any other Anglican body, but it aims to maintain certain "bonds of affection" with other Anglican provinces, and it has representation on certain advisory groups of the worldwide Anglican Communion. The ACC is the third largest religious denomination in Canada. In the 2001 Canadian census, 2,035,495 persons identified themselves as Anglicans, and in that year the ACC counted about 642,000 members.

Its history begins when worship and ministry according to the Church of England were provided for English explorers, soldiers, settlers, and fishing fleets into what is now Canada, at least as early as the 1570s. In 1699 the bishop of London sent a minister to the townsfolk of St. John's, Newfoundland, and over the following decades a few other parishes were created in Quebec and Nova Scotia. A much more substantial Anglican presence in the future Canada followed the American Revolution, when English-speaking refugees began flooding north from the United States. British and colonial governments made sure that Anglican churches were provided for them. Mission societies connected with the Church of England, particularly the Society for the Propagation of the Gospel in Foreign Parts, raised most of the money for church buildings and clergy salaries in these newer provinces of British North America (BNA), and they recruited and oversaw most of the missionaries. In addition, the Crown made large grants of land to the Church of England. The first overseas diocese of the Church of England was Nova Scotia (1787), but BNA bishops had little freedom of action given the authority exercised by the mission societies, the Colonial Office, and the colonial governments.

Statutes establishing the Church of England were enacted successively in Nova Scotia (1758), New Brunswick (1784), and Prince Edward Island (1803). Well into the 19th century, the Church of England was also commonly referred to as the established church elsewhere in BNA, even if it could not legally enforce its pretensions. The government gave the Church of England financial help, appointed its chief ministers, and granted it certain legal privileges. In return, the church undertook to form citizens in Christian and civic virtues, including loyalty to the British Crown, and to provide various social services, including primary, secondary, and university education. But between about 1825 and 1860, most Anglican privilege was dismantled in BNA. Most educational systems were taken over by the government, statutes of establishment were repealed, and the church's landed endowment was seized.

As a result, the Church of England in BNA gradually developed voluntary instruments of self-government and financial self-support. Starting with the Diocese of Toronto in 1853, Anglicans began governing themselves through synods, or church assemblies of clergy and lay representatives. Through their synods they elected their own bishops and developed church constitutions and regulations without interference from England. Imperial judicial rulings in the early 1860s severed most connections between colonial Anglican churches and the British Crown. The church in Canada became legally just one religious denomination among others.

Meanwhile, in the Northwest (the area between and above the Rocky Mountains and the Great Lakes), which was owned by the Hudson's Bay Company, Anglican chaplaincies to settlers and missions to Native peoples began in 1820. They were sponsored largely by the Church Missionary Society (CMS), which had a policy of developing indigenous leadership. In 1850 Henry Budd became the first Canadian Native person to receive Anglican ordination. Synodical government was developed there in 1869. The CMS withdrew after World War I.

With the birth of the dominion of Canada in 1867, its acquisition of the Northwest in 1870, and the completion of a transcontinental railway in 1885, Canadian Anglicans determined to create a national church structure. The Church of England in Canada was formed in 1893 under the authority of a General Synod comprising the bishops and elected representatives of the clergy and laity. The national leader, who is elected by General Synod, is called the primate. The national church assumed responsibility for foreign and domestic missions, among other things. In 1918 General Synod approved the first specifically Canadian Anglican order of worship, called the Book of Common Prayer (Canada).

The constituting document of the Anglican Church of Canada (ACC) is the very brief Solemn Declaration of 1893, which affirms the determination of the ACC to maintain the doctrine, sacraments, and discipline commanded by Christ in scripture and as set forth in the Book of Common Prayer and the Thirty-nine Articles of the Church of England. It particularly affirms the authority of the canonical scriptures as containing all things necessary to salvation. However, no member or minister of the ACC is required to agree with the Solemn Declaration, and the ACC has no formal confessional statement. Its authorized liturgical texts, to which its clergy are obliged to conform when they lead worship, are usually seen as implying the doctrinal norms of the denomination. Either the Apostles' Creed or the Nicene Creed is recited in most services of worship. In principle, Canadian Anglicans accept a wide spectrum of theological beliefs, but tensions and disagreements sometimes result in schisms and secessions. A current presenting issue is the blessing of same-sex unions or marriages. The theological center of gravity in the ACC is liberal.

Since the 1960s, weekly Holy Communion (or Holy Eucharist) has become the norm in the large majority of Anglican churches. Two authorized liturgical texts are in use. The Book of Common Prayer (Canada) of 1959 uses 16th-century English and reflects the theology of the Protestant Reformation. The Book of Alternative Services of 1985, which is much more common, uses updated language and reflects the theology of the ecumenical Liturgical movement of the 20th century. Since 1967, the ACC has welcomed all baptized Christians to receive communion. In practice many Anglican churches invite unbaptized religious seekers to receive communion as well.

Women were initially ordained to the priesthood in the ACC in 1976, and female clergy now make up about 16 percent of active clergy. The first woman to be ordained bishop was Victoria Matthews, in 1994.

The ACC reached a peak of church attendance, church-building, and financial resources in the early 1960s. Published statistics suggest a significant decline since then. The church is a member of the World Council of Churches.

Until its demise in the late 1960s, the residential school system for Native peoples was the largest single item in the church's national budget, although the expenses were almost entirely reimbursed by the government of Canada. The failures and abuses of this system resulted in the filing of more than 1,000 lawsuits against the ACC by former inmates in the 1990s. In 2003 the ACC reached an agreement with the government of Canada with the effect of capping its liability from this litigation, thus averting possible bankruptcy. An estimated 25 percent of First Nations people and 85 percent of Inuit are Anglican. The first Anglican bishop of Aboriginal ethnic identity was elected in 1989. In 2007 Mark MacDonald took office as the first national Aboriginal indigenous bishop.

The church has its headquarters in Toronto. Its current primate is the Most Reverend Fred Hiltz. It supports an Internet site, given below.

Anglican Church of Canada
80 Hayden Street
Toronto, ON M4Y 3G2
Canada
www.anglican.ca

Alan L. Hayes

See also: Anglican Communion/Anglican Consultative Council; Church Missionary Society; Society for the Propagation of the Gospel in Foreign Parts; World Council of Churches.

References

Carrington, Philip. *The Anglican Church in Canada: A History*. Toronto: Collins, 1963.
Grant, John Webster, gen. ed. *A History of the Christian Church in Canada*. Toronto: McGraw-Hill Ryerson, 1972.
Hayes, Alan L. *Anglican Controversy and Identity in Canada*. Urbana: University of Illinois Press, 2004.
Knowles, Norman. *Seeds Scattered and Sown: Studies in the History of Canadian Anglicanism*. Toronto: Anglican Book Centre, 2008.
Journal of the Canadian Church Historical Society. Various issues.

Anglican Church of Hong Kong and Macao

Anglicans arrived in Hong Kong with the British, and the first church was opened in 1842. The cornerstone for St. John's Cathedral was laid five years later. The work grew, along with a set of parochial schools, and was for many years integrated into the larger work in mainland China. Hong Kong was the center of the Diocese of Victoria, which included China and Japan, but through the years, as the work was divided, its episcopal territory was reduced accordingly. Missionaries were received into the diocese not only from the Church of England, but from Anglican churches in North America, Australia, and New Zealand.

The work in Hong Kong and Macao was dramatically altered during the 1940s, first by the Japanese invasion and occupation and then by the Chinese Revolution and the expulsion of all foreign missionaries in 1950. Outside of Hong Kong and Macao, all of the Anglican work in China was merged into the Chinese Protestant Three-Self Patriotic movement and the China Christian Council. The work in Hong Kong continued as an extraprovincial diocese.

In 1941, Li Tim Oi, a Chinese lay member of the church, was ordained as a deacon and placed in charge of a church in Macao as its full-time pastor. As travel from Hong Kong became more restricted and a priest could not travel there to deliver the Eucharist, Bishop Ronald Hall ordained her as a priest, the first female priest in the Anglican Communion.

In 1997, in anticipation of the change of government in the two territories, the Diocese of Hong Kong and Macao evolved into the Province of Hong Kong Sheng Kung Hui (aka the Anglican Church of Hong Kong and Macao) with three dioceses—Hong Kong, East Kowloon, and West Kowloon—and the Missionary Area of Macao under the Diocese of Hong Kong. Currently one archbishop and two bishops serve the province.

Anglican Church of Hong Kong and Macao
c/o The Most Reverend Peter Kwong
Bishop of Hong Kong and Macao
Bishop's House
1 Lower Albert Rd.
Hong Kong.

J. Gordon Melton

See also: Anglican Communion/Anglican Consultative Council; Chinese Protestant Three-Self Patriotic Movement/China Christian Council; Church of England; Women, Status and Role of.

Parishoners pray inside St. John's Cathedral in Hong Kong. (Zhudifeng/Dreamstime.com)

References

Hoke, Donald. *The Church in Asia.* Chicago: Moody Press, 1975.

Poon, Michael. "The Theological and Mission Task Facing Hong Kong Anglicans in the Face of Reunification with China after 1997." In *Anglicanism: A Global Communion,* edited by Andrew Wingate et al. London: Mowbrays, 1998.

Anglican Church of Kenya

Evangelical members of the Church of England pioneered an Anglican presence in Kenya. The Church Missionary Society began work in Mombasa in 1844 and built an extensive ministry and educational system over the next century. Work was strongest among the Kikuyu, Luo, and Luhya peoples. The church moved very early to build indigenous leadership, and the first African priests were ordained in 1885. In 1931, the Bible Churchman's Missionary Society added its strength.

Work in Kenya developed under the jurisdiction of the archbishop of Canterbury. The initial Diocese of Mombasa was established in 1926. The first two African bishops for Kenya were consecrated in 1955, just five years before the several dioceses were set apart as the Province of East Africa (including the churches in neighboring Tanzania). The work in Tanzania was separated in 1970 and the Church of the Province of Kenya emerged at that time. The present name was adopted in 1998.

The church has its headquarters in Nairobi. It is led by its archbishop, currently Most Reverend David Gitari. Churches are divided into 27 dioceses. In 2005, the church reported 5 million members in 1,244 parishes. The church is a member of the worldwide Anglican Communion and the World Council of Churches.

In 1999, the church made history as the first Anglican province to appoint a female to the office of provincial secretary, the office responsible for all of the administrative work of the province.

Anglican Church of Kenya
PO Box 40502
Nairobi
Kenya

J. Gordon Melton

See also: Anglican Communion/Anglican Consultative Council; Church Missionary Society; Church of England; World Council of Churches.

References

The Church of England Yearbook. London: Church Publishing House, published annually.

Van Beek, Huibert. *A Handbook of the Churches and Councils: Profiles of Ecumenical Relationships.* Geneva: World Council of Churches, 2006.

Van der Bent, Ans J., ed. *Handbook/Member Churches/World Council of Churches.* Geneva: World Council of Churches, 1985.

Anglican Church of Korea

Reverend Charles John Corfe (1843–1921) was consecrated in London in 1889 as the first bishop for a projected diocese of the Church of England in Korea. He arrived in 1890 and settled in Seoul as an agent of the Society for the Propagation of the Gospel in Foreign Parts. Early work extended to Kyung-gi and Chung-cheong provinces. He also established a set of educational, medical, and social service facilities. Church growth was slow but steady. In the decade between World Wars I and II, missionary work concentrated in the northern half of Korea. In 1939, the church had some 10,000 members.

As a result of the Korean War, the half of the church's property and members located in the People's Republic of Korea was lost. However, the church has continued to expand in the south. In 1965, the first Korean bishop was named as the bishop of Seoul. At the same time, a second diocese was created, which an Anglo bishop continued to serve. In 1974, he completed his period of service and returned. That same year a third diocese was created, and two Koreans were consecrated as bishops. The three Korean dioceses remained under the jurisdiction of the archbishop of Canterbury until 1993. That year, the Diocese of Seoul was elevated to an archdiocese, the first archbishop of Seoul, Most Reverend Simon K. Kim was consecrated, and the church in Korea reorganized as a new province, the Anglican Church of Korea.

The Anglican Church of Korea is headed by Archbishop Kim, who serves both as primate and as bishop of Seoul. The church supports the Anglican University in Seoul, and four religious orders: the Society of the Holy Cross, the Korean Franciscan Brotherhood, the Order of Saint Benedict, and Jesus Abbey, an intentional Christian community in the mountains of Kangwondo. The church is a member of the worldwide Anglican Communion and the World Council of Churches.

Church of Korea
3 Chong-dong, Jung-ku
Seoul 100-120
Republic of Korea
www.skh.or.kr/eindex.htm

J. Gordon Melton

See also: Anglican Communion/Anglican Consultative Council; Church Missionary Society; Church of England; World Council of Churches.

References

Kane, J. Herbert. *A Global View of Christian Missions.* Grand Rapids, MI: Baker Book House, 1971.

Park, I. G. *The History of Protestant Missions in Korea.* Seoul: Yonsei University Press, 1970.

Ward, Kevin. *A History of Global Anglicanism.* Cambridge: Cambridge University Press, 2006.

Anglican Church of North America

Announced at the end of 2008, the Anglican Church of North America is a conservative Anglican jurisdiction that culminates a decade of dissent from the direction taken by the majority of the Episcopal Church and the Anglican Church of Canada since the 1970s. Members have disagreed with decisions made by the church, including the revision of the Prayer Book, the primary volume directing worship, the ordination of women, the loosening commitment to traditional theological affirmations, and, most recently, the ordination of practicing homosexuals to the priesthood and episcopacy.

While the ordination of women caused a number Episcopalians to withdraw and form separate jurisdictions, women have been accepted as priests and even bishops throughout most of the Anglican Communion. However, the growing acceptance of homosexuality and the debates leading to the election of a practicing homosexual as the bishop of New Hampshire in 2003 was seen by many as a far more serious action indicative of the apostate nature of the Episcopal Church. The debate became international as leading Anglican clerics, especially in Africa and Asia, denounced the Episcopal Church's actions and threatened the unity of the Anglican Communion unless the church was disciplined.

The Anglican Mission to the Americas can be traced to 1998 and the assumption of leadership of St. Andrew's Church, an independent Anglican congregation in Little Rock, Arkansas, by Reverend Thomas W. Johnston. When Johnston's status as a priest was called into question, Bishop John Rucyahana of Rwanda stepped in and offered to assume oversight of the church and its priest. The action relative to St. Andrew's church catalyzed some of Rev. Johnston's fellow priests in the First Promise movement, a movement of conservative priests who saw their vows as priests challenged by the actions of the Episcopal Church. At a meeting in Kampala, Uganda, in 1999, they made an appeal to several Anglican bishops for intervention. The primates of Rwanda and Southeast Asia responded and several months later consecrated two American Episcopal priests, Chuck Murphy and John Rodgers, as missionary bishops to the United States. The new bishops established the Anglican Mission to America in 2000 and began the process of gathering priests, laypeople, and congregations into the Mission.

The Mission began with what most of the new Anglican jurisdictions in North America lacked, unquestioned Anglican orders from direct access to the larger Anglican Communion through bishops with unquestioned authority. These bishops were joined by additional colleagues and became even more vocal following the election of Bishop Robinson in 2003. Their dissent continues to threaten the unity of the Anglican Communion and has required the full diplomatic skill of the archbishop of Canterbury to deal with the internal conflict.

The Anglican Mission to America did not immediately attract the attention of the other Anglican jurisdictions, several of which had already become national organizations. It also adopted a position that women would only be ordained to the diaconate, not the priesthood, even though the Province of the Episcopal Church of Rwanda accepted female priests. In 2006, the Mission created a new structure, the Anglican Mission to America, which included two additional jurisdictions, the Anglican Coalition of Canada and the Anglican Coalition in America, both of which do ordain women. The movement in Canada parallel to the Anglican Mission in America had been spurred by a decision in 2002 of the diocese of New Westminster to condone a rite of blessing for same-sex couples.

In June 2006, the work of the Anglican mission in America was supplemented by the action of the archbishop of the Church of Nigeria, who consecrated Reverend Martyn Minns, of Fairfax, Virginia, and the missionary bishop for another new missionary structure, the Convocation of Anglicans in North America (CANA). Prior to his installation, he was joined by Bishop David J. Bena, retired suffragan bishop of the Episcopal Diocese of Albany. In 2007, the Anglican Province of the Southern Cone of America involved itself in the North American situation when it accepted oversight of the Anglican Network in Canada, a relatively small coalition of parishes dissenting from the Anglican Church of Canada. However, the province took on more importance when it accepted oversight of two dioceses that separated themselves from the Episcopal Church.

As the new missionary organizations emerged, they and conservatives still within the Episcopal Church were linked by Common Cause Partnership. By 2008, the Common Cause Partnership included eight such organizations: the American Anglican Council, the Anglican Coalition in Canada, the Anglican Communion

Network, the Anglican Mission in the Americas, the Anglican Network in Canada, the Convocation of Anglicans in North America, Forward in Faith North America, and the Reformed Episcopal Church, the latter being an older Anglican body that had lost its apostolic succession and had increasingly become identified with Protestant evangelicalism.

Meanwhile, in the summer of 2008, conservative Anglican leaders from around the world, including an indeterminate number of bishops, organized the Global Anglican Future Conference (GAFCON), held in Jerusalem, and issued a statement aimed at the 2008 Lambeth Conference calling for reform of the Anglican movement. A statement released on the final day of the conference denounces a false gospel deemed to be present in the Anglican Communion that both denies the uniqueness of Jesus Christ and promotes alternate sexual behavior as a human right. It backed the plans to establish alternate ecclesiastical structures in North America for its conservative constituency. Before the year was out, the Common Cause Partnership announced the results of the deliberations of its member organizations for the creation of a new jurisdiction to be known as the Anglican Church in North America. The new church would immediately become home to some 700 congregations and more than 100,000 members. Through the Anglican churches in Nigeria, Rwanda, and South America it would have access, though of an irregular nature, to the worldwide Anglican Communion. As this encyclopedia goes to press, the new church is still in the process of forming.

Common Cause Partnership
535 Smithfield St., Ste. 910,
Pittsburgh, PA 15222
http://www.united-anglicans.org/

Anglican Mission Center
PO Box 3427
Pawleys Island, SC 29585

J. Gordon Melton

See also: Anglican Church of Canada; Anglican Communion/Anglican Consultative Council; Anglican Province of the Southern Cone of America; Church of Nigeria; Episcopal Church; Province of the Episcopal Church of Rwanda.

References

Hassett, Miranda K. *Anglican Communion in Crisis: How Episcopal Dissidents and Their African Allies Are Reshaping Anglicanism.* Princeton, NJ: Princeton University Press, 2007.

Norman, Edward. *Anglican Difficulties: A New Syllabus of Errors.* New York: Morehouse Publishing, 2004.

O'Donovan, Oliver. *Church in Crisis: The Gay Controversy and the Anglican Communion.* Eugene, OR: Cascade Books, 2008.

Anglican Communion/Anglican Consultative Council

The worldwide Anglican Communion consists of those Christian churches that have developed out of the ministry and mission of the Church of England and that remain in formal community with the church and its primary official, the archbishop of Canterbury. The Church of England traces its beginning to the emergence of Christian communities in the second century CE and the development of the first dioceses by the fourth century; however, the emergence of the modern Anglicanism is generally referred to the definitive events of the 16th century.

Through the 15th century, the British church was part of the larger Roman Catholic Church. However, in the 1530s King Henry VIII (r. 1509–1547) was excommunicated and led in the separation of the church from Roman authority. At the same time, Lutheran and Reformed churches were being formed in several countries of continental Europe. Under Henry's successor, Edward VI (r. 1547–1553), an attempt was made to swing England squarely into the Protestant camp. Under Mary I (r. 1553–1558), an opposing effort was exerted to return the country into the Roman Catholic realm. Under Queen Elizabeth I (1558–1603), a unique mixture of elements of both Roman Catholicism and Protestantism, a *via media*, or middle way, was created. Modern Anglicanism derives from that middle way, which incorporates the Protestant emphasis on biblical authority and limits the number of sacraments to baptism and the Lord's Supper. A number of Roman Catholic beliefs and practices are

Anglican priest at an altar. (Lucian Coman/Dreamstime .com)

Through the 19th century, independent churches, administratively separate but remaining in communion with the Church of England, began to emerge. This process accelerated in the 20th century after World War II. Earlier, as a result of the American Revolution, an independent Episcopal Church had been created in the United States.

In 1867, at the request of Canadian Anglican leadership, the first of what became regular gatherings, the Lambeth Conferences, was hosted by the archbishop of Canterbury. These conferences have continued to be held, roughly every 10 years, and have provided a time for deliberations by the bishops from around the world and the opportunity for them to speak on issues with a united voice.

In 1897, the bishops saw fit to create a more permanent structure to provide for continuity between conferences and created the Consultative Body of the Lambeth Conference. This organization evolved in several steps into the Anglican Consultative Council, with headquarters at Lambeth Palace in London. The Council brings together not only bishops, but presbyters, deacons, laypeople, and youth from the various churches to work on common problems. It meets every two years and is hosted by different Anglican churches around the world.

The Lambeth Conference of 1888 proposed the most commonly cited expression of the Christian faith as espoused by the church of the Anglican Communion, the Chicago-Lambeth Quadrilateral. This documents affirms the faith of Anglicanism to be based upon four pillars: the holy scriptures of the Old and New Testament as the revealed Word of God; the Nicene Creed as the sufficient statement of the Christian faith; the two sacraments of baptism and the Eucharist as administered with the unfailing words and elements used by Christ; and the historic episcopate. This faith finds expression in the Book of Common Prayer, which includes the liturgical text for Sunday worship and the Thirty-nine Articles of Religion.

The Anglican Communion currently consists of more than 40 independent church bodies. Since the 1990s, the communion has been rent with division over the question of homosexuality, brought to the fore by the election in 2003 of an openly practicing gay man as a bishop by the Episcopal Church, the primary An-

specifically rejected in the church's statement of faith (the Thirty-nine Articles of Religion). At the same time, the threefold ministry of deacon, priest, and bishop is retained, as is the emphasis on a formal liturgy and church tradition. The result was a new form of Christian faith.

Beginning in the early 17th century, England began to plant colonies in North America. The colonial enterprise grew to include a large worldwide empire, which included Australia, New Zealand, various South Pacific island groups, a large section of Africa, India, Hong Kong and several South Asian lands, and many Caribbean islands, among other lands. The Church of England established foreign branches in the various British colonies and, beginning with Canada in 1787 and Australia in 1842, supplied them with a resident bishop.

glican body in the United States. The controversy has threatened to divide Anglicans worldwide, though as of 2008 the only schisms have been within the American church.

The Anglican Consultative Council has its headquarters in London, England. Both it and the Anglican Communion are served by the Anglican Communion Secretariat, all three organizations sharing the same building.

Anglican Consultative Council
Partnership House
157 Waterloo Rd.
London SE1 8UT
England
Anglican Communion
www.anglicancommunion.org/site.html

J. Gordon Melton

See also: Church of England; Episcopal Church; Roman Catholic Church.

References

Hasslett, Miranda K. *Anglican Communion in Crisis: How Episcopal Dissidents and Their African Allies Are Reshaping Anglicanism.* Princeton, NJ: Princeton University Press, 2007.

Howe, John W. *Our Anglican Heritage.* Eugene, OR: Wipf & Stock Publishers, 2007.

Neill, Stephen. *Anglicanism.* London: A. R. Mowbrays, 1977.

Ward, Kevin. *A History of Global Anglicanism.* Cambridge: Cambridge University Press, 2006.

Whale, John. *The Anglican Church Today: The Future of Anglicanism.* London: Mowbrays, 1988.

Wingate, Andrew, et al., eds. *Anglicanism: A Global Communion.* London: Mowbrays, 1998.

Anglican Diocese in Angola

The Anglican Diocese in Angola (originally known as the United Evangelical Church–Anglican Communion of Angola) is one of several churches that grew out of the work of Archibald Patterson, an independent Anglican missionary, and Swiss minister Ernest Niklaus, who in 1922 started a mission in the Angolan province of Uige. The work grew through the 1960s as the Igreja Evangélica do Norte de Angola, and Archibald became a beloved figure to many. However, in 1961, when the Civil War broke out, the church faced severe government repression. Church leaders were forced underground or into exile. Only in 1977 was the church able to reorganize, and the name Evangelical Reformed Church of Angola was chosen. At that time a difference of opinion arose on various issues, and a group of 18 ministers under the leadership of the Reverend Domingos Alexandre left to found a separate denomination, the United Evangelical Church of Angola. The United Evangelical Church of Angola (Igreja Evangélica Unida de Angola) is currently headquartered in Luanda, Angola. In the 1980s it was briefly a member of the World Council of Churches, but it is no longer.

In the 1990s, Alexandre left the United Evangelical Church of Angola and founded the United Evangelical Church–Anglican Communion in Angola, which aligned itself with the Archdeanery of Angola of the Church of the Province of Southern Africa. That alignment led in 2002 to the church being formally reorganized as the Angola Diocese of the Church of the Province of Southern Africa. Through its South African connection, the new Anglican Diocese of Angola is a member of both the Council of Christian Churches in Angola and the World Council of Churches.

United Evangelical Church–Anglican Communion in Angola
CP 10341
Luanda
Angola

J. Gordon Melton

See also: Evangelical Reformed Church of Angola; World Council of Churches.

References

The Church of England Yearbook. London: Church Publishing House, published annually.

Van Beek, Huibert. *A Handbook of the Churches and Councils: Profiles of Ecumenical Relationships.* Geneva: World Council of Churches, 2006.

Van der Bent, Ans J., ed. *Handbook/Member Churches/World Council of Churches.* Geneva: World Council of Churches, 1985.

Anglican Province of the Southern Cone of America

Anglican efforts to build a mission in Argentina began in the 1840s, carried out by the South American Missionary Society, an independent sending agency operating within the Church of England. Initial work was begun in 1824 among the Patagonian people in the extreme southern part of Argentina; however, both initial missions failed, and their members died, those of the first mission from starvation, those of the second at the hands of hostile natives. Then, in 1888, Barbrook Grubb moved to the Chaco region in northern Argentina near the Paraguayan border and began a mission among the Native peoples. The work soon spread into Paraguay, where Wilfred B. Grubb began to work among the Lengua people. The society's work spread to Chile at the beginning of the 20th century, when a medical mission was opened among the Mapuche people.

From these modest beginnings, the Church of England was established throughout the southern half of Spanish-speaking South America. The work was inhibited, however, by the policy of the church, articulated forcefully at the 1910 conference on missions at Edinburgh, that South America was not an object of missions for the church, due to the prior establishment of the Roman Catholic Church. Thus the independent work nurtured by the South American Missionary Society and a few congregations established to serve expatriates constituted the extent of the Anglican thrust in the Spanish-speaking countries of the continent.

Over the years, the society's work grew, a number of congregations were formed, and converts were trained and ordained for the ministry. In the decades after World War II, the hierarchy was developed, with dioceses being formed in Argentina (two), Chile, Paraguay, and Uruguay. These were originally under the direct authority of the archbishop of Canterbury, but in 1974 they were reorganized under the Consejo Anglicano Sud-Americano. A separate Diocese of Peru and Bolivia was formed in 1978. The constitution for the new province of the Anglican Church of the Southern Cone of America was approved in 1981, and the church was inaugurated two years later.

The church is led by its primate, currently Most Reverend Gregory James Venables (b. 1949). He leads what has emerged as one of the more conservative branches of Anglicanism, and it has reached out to provide an organizational home within the worldwide Anglican Communion for those bishops and dioceses in the United States that have chosen to separate from the Episcopal Church over the issue of homosexuality. He has most recently supported the move of the various conservative Anglican bodies in North America to form the Anglican Church of North America.

As of 2005, the province reported 22,500 members (exclusive of North America). It is a member of the worldwide Anglican Communion and the World Council of Churches.

Anglican Province of the Southern Cone of America
Casilla de Correo 187
CP 4400 Salta
Argentina

J. Gordon Melton

See also: Anglican Church of North America; Anglican Communion/Anglican Consultative Council; Church Missionary Society; Church of England; Roman Catholic Church; World Council of Churches.

References

Avis, Paul. *The Identity of Anglicanism: Essentials of Anglican Ecclesiology*. Edinburgh: T & T Clark International, 2008.

Kaye, Bruce. *An Introduction to World Anglicanism.* Cambridge: Cambridge University Press, 2005.

Sachs, William L. *The Transformation of Anglicanism: From State Church to Global Communion.* Cambridge: Cambridge University Press, 2002.

Ward, Kevin. *A History of Global Anglicanism.* Cambridge: Cambridge University Press, 2006.

Wingate, Andrew, et al., eds. *Anglicanism: A Global Communion.* London: Mowbrays, 1998.

■ Angola

Angola is a West African country situated between Namibia and the Democratic Republic of the Congo on the continent's Atlantic coast. It is bounded on the east by Zambia. As of 2008, it had an estimated 16 million residents, the great majority consisting of mem-

Pope Benedict XVI holds the pastoral staff as he blesses the faithful during a mass at the Sao Paulo Church in Luanda, Angola, on March 21, 2009. (AP/Wide World Photos)

bers of 3 prominent ethnic groups, the Ovimbundu, the Kimbundu, and the Bakongo.

Angola had become the home of Bantu peoples beginning in the seventh century CE, but over the centuries various groups passed through the area and settled. Much of what is now northern Angola was incorporated into the Kongo kingdom that the Portuguese found when they first moved along the Atlantic coast toward the end of the 15th century. The Portuguese built cordial relations with the Kongo ruler, Manikongo Nzinga Alfonsa (whose lengthy rule lasted from 1505 to 1543). He converted to Christianity, but both the rule of his successors and the positive relations between the inhabitants and the Portuguese were ended by the Portuguese drive for Angola's mineral wealth and slaves.

Late in the 16th century, the Jaga people, staunchly opposed to the Portuguese, gained control in northern Angola and moved southward. In the meantime the Portuguese had established their center near present-day Luanda, but found their attempts to push inward stopped by local resistance. Through the next centuries, they were able to keep a presence along the coast and keep up the slave trade (which involved the selling into slavery of an estimated three million people), but did not establish control over the entire designated colony until the 20th century.

After World War II, a nationalist movement developed, which was met with attempts by Portugal to increase the European presence in the land and to keep Angola from following the trend toward independence that was becoming so much a part of African life. In 1961 Angola was reclassified as an overseas province of Portugal. That same year a civil war began for control. The conflict lasted for 14 years before independence was finally declared in 1975. However, the

Angola

Religion	Followers in 1970	Followers in 2010	% of Population	Annual % growth 2000–2010	Followers in 2025	Followers in 2050
Christians	4,862,000	17,327,000	93.7	2.93	25,828,000	42,365,000
Roman Catholics	2,667,000	11,350,000	61.4	3.27	17,000,000	28,000,000
Protestants	422,000	5,349,000	28.9	4.20	7,900,000	13,000,000
Independents	61,300	662,000	3.6	3.24	1,200,000	2,000,000
Ethnoreligionists	1,213,000	824,000	4.5	1.95	900,000	950,000
Agnostics	5,000	190,000	1.0	7.95	350,000	800,000
Muslims	2,000	110,000	0.6	3.83	180,000	320,000
Atheists	0	38,400	0.2	2.89	60,000	116,000
Baha'is	400	2,000	0.0	2.93	3,500	10,000
Buddhists	400	1,500	0.0	2.93	2,200	4,500
Chinese folk	40	150	0.0	3.03	200	400
Total population	**6,083,000**	**18,493,000**	**100.0**	**2.93**	**27,324,000**	**44,566,000**

several groups that had worked against the Portuguese now began to fight among themselves for control. Only in 1991 was a peace treaty negotiated, and elections were held the following year. One of the losing groups, the União Nacional para a Independence (UNIDA), did not accept the results and renewed the war for another two years. The country now exists under a government of National Reconciliation that emerged out of the 1994 agreement, the Lusaka Protocol. However, many of the UNIDA resisted steps at disarmament, and the civil war resumed and continues as this encyclopedia goes to press.

The effects of a generation of war (following a rather brutal colonial regime) have included deep divisions between various ethnic groups (especially the larger Ovimbundu, Mbundu, and Bakongo peoples), massive displacements of people, and deep economic problems.

Traditional indigenous religions have declined significantly since World War II. In 1950 more than 70 percent of the public still adhered to a traditional religion, but by the end of the century that number had dropped to around 5 percent. Traditional religion was strongest in some of the most rural areas, especially among the Hukwe, Mbukushu, Mbwela, and Kwangali, all relatively small groups. However, about 70 percent of the half-million Chokwe people retain their traditional faith. Traditional beliefs still retain a broader power as particular elements (belief in malevolent

magic, respect for ancestors, and traditional healing practices) survive within various Christian churches.

Christianity, which now claims more than 90 percent of the population, was introduced into Angola in 1491 by the Portuguese. A number of Roman Catholic priests, including Franciscans and Dominicans, established missions. Christianity flourished for a generation and Henrique, the son of Manikongo Nzinga Alfonsa, became the first sub-Saharan African to be consecrated as a bishop. However, the Portuguese authorities undercut the church with the pursuit of the slave trade. Much of the work (including the diocesan structure) was lost in the 16th century.

The Portuguese shifted southward after the founding of Luanda in 1576, and with the help of Jesuits, the church's presence was reasserted. An episcopal see was established, but the Roman Catholic Church made little progress over the next centuries, due to Native resistance to the presence of the Portuguese authorities and the slave trade. A new beginning for the church occurred in 1865 with the assignment of the White Fathers to Angola by the Vatican. By the end of the nineteenth century, real progress was made, though only since World War II has significant progress in the interior been seen. By 1970 there were more than 2.5 million members; that number has jumped to almost 7 million today. With more than 60 percent of the population, the Catholic Church is by far the most dominant force in Angolan religion.

ANGOLA

Very early in their approach to Angola, which only began in the last half of the 19th century, Protestant groups agreed to a noncompetitive approach, and different groups tended to restrict their missionary efforts to specific peoples. The British Baptists arrived initially in 1878 and established work among the Bakongo people near São Salvador. Two years later, missionaries with the American Board of Commissioners for Foreign Missions arrived to work among the Ovimbundu and were joined by Canadian Presbyterians (now an integral part of the United Church of Canada)

in 1886. Their efforts resulted in what is today the Evangelical Congregational Church of Angola.

In 1885, 45 missionaries from the Methodist Episcopal Church (now an integral part of the United Methodist Church) arrived in Angola as one of the first efforts organized by the newly elected bishop, William Taylor. They began work among the Kimbundi people near Luanda. The Christian Brethren established their mission in 1889. Anglicans established work in Angola early in the 20th century. It remained small and for many years was under the Church of the Province of Southern Africa. A separate diocese for Angola was created in the mid-1990s. Also entering in the 1920s and building a successful affiliated mission was the Seventh-day Adventist Church.

Pentecostals appear to have entered Angola in the 1930s with the initial effort by the Church of God International (Cleveland, Tennessee). Spectacular growth has been experienced by the Assemblies of God mission, now known as the Evangelical Pentecostal Mission of Angola. This church is also notable as one of the few Pentecostal churches with membership in the World Council of Churches.

Independent evangelical missions have had an important role in the development of the country. In 1897, the Philafricaine Mission, supported by Swiss Protestants, began work. The South African General Mission (now the African Evangelical Fellowship) launched work in southern Angola along the Kutsi River in 1914. Its efforts have resulted in the formation of the Evangelical Church of South Angola. The 1920s saw the advent of Archibald Patterson, an independent Anglican missionary who started work in the province of Uige in northern Angola. The work prospered until the 1960s, when it was thoroughly disrupted by the civil war. In subsequent years several churches have resulted from the original missionary effort, including the Evangelical Reformed Church of Angola and the United Evangelical Church–Anglican Communion of Angola.

Angola has been notable for its relative lack of African Initiated Churches. The largest is the Kimbanguist Church (the Church of Jesus Christ on Earth by His Messenger Simon Kimbangu), which originated in the neighboring Democratic Republic of the Congo. In spite of being suppressed for a time, it now has more than 300,000 members. During the period of suppression (following Kimbangu's arrest in the Congo), a splinter group, the Tocoist Church, began in Angola. Angola was also the home of several splinter groups of the Apostolic Church of Johane Maranke (based in Zimbabwe).

Christian ecumenical activity began in 1922 with the formation of the Evangelical Alliance of Angola. The alliance was suppressed in 1961. In 1974, several of the more conservative churches formed the Association of Evangelicals in Angola, now associated with the World Evangelical Alliance. Three years later, a number of the older churches formed the Angolan Council of Evangelical Churches (now the Council of Christian Churches in Angola) and affiliated with the World Council of Churches.

Apart from a small community of the Baha'i Faith and some Buddhists affiliated with Soka Gakkai International, there is little visible presence by groups outside of the Christian tradition. There is no Islamic work of note.

J. Gordon Melton

See also: Assemblies of God; Baha'i Faith; Christian Brethren; Church of God (Cleveland, Tennessee); Evangelical Congregational Church in Angola; Evangelical Pentecostal Mission of Angola; Evangelical Reformed Church of Angola; Roman Catholic Church; Seventh-day Adventist Church; Tocoist Church/Church of Our Lord Jesus Christ in the World; United Church of Canada; United Methodist Church; World Evangelical Alliance; World Council of Churches; World Evangelical Alliance.

References

Grohs, G., and G. Czernik. *State and Church in Angola, 1450–1980.* Geneva: Institut Universitaire de Hautes Etudes Internationales, 1983.

Henderson, Lawrence W. *A igreja em Angola: um rio con várias correntes.* Lisbon: Além-Mar, 1990. English edition: *The Church in Angola: A River of Many Currents.* Cleveland, OH: Pilgrim Press, 1992.

Oyebade, Adebayp O. *Culture and Customs of Angola.* Westport, CT: Greenwood Press, 2007.

Santos, A. F. *Liturgia, Cristianismo e sociedade en Angola.* Neves, Angola: Editorial Coloquios, 1968.

■ Anguilla

Anguilla, the most northerly of the Leeward Islands southeast of Puerto Rico in the northeasterly area of the Caribbean Sea, is a British Dependent Territory,

St. Gerard Catholic Church, Anguilla. (Mark Haddock/Dreamstime.com)

having separated from St. Kitts in 1980. Although known from the 15th century by Europeans, Anguilla (together with the associated Sombrero Island) was unattractive for settlement due to limited fresh water reserves, and only in the 19th century did the population begin to increase. Among its few assets are extensive salt deposits. Today, there are still only slightly more than 8,400 (2005) residents on the less than 40 square miles of land on the island. Most residents are the descendents of the African slaves, but there are some white people who descended from a party of Irishmen who landed on the island in 1698, along with a few expatriates from the United States, Canada, and the United Kingdom.

Beginning in 1916, Anguilla was administered as part of a British colony including the Virgin Islands

ANGUILLA

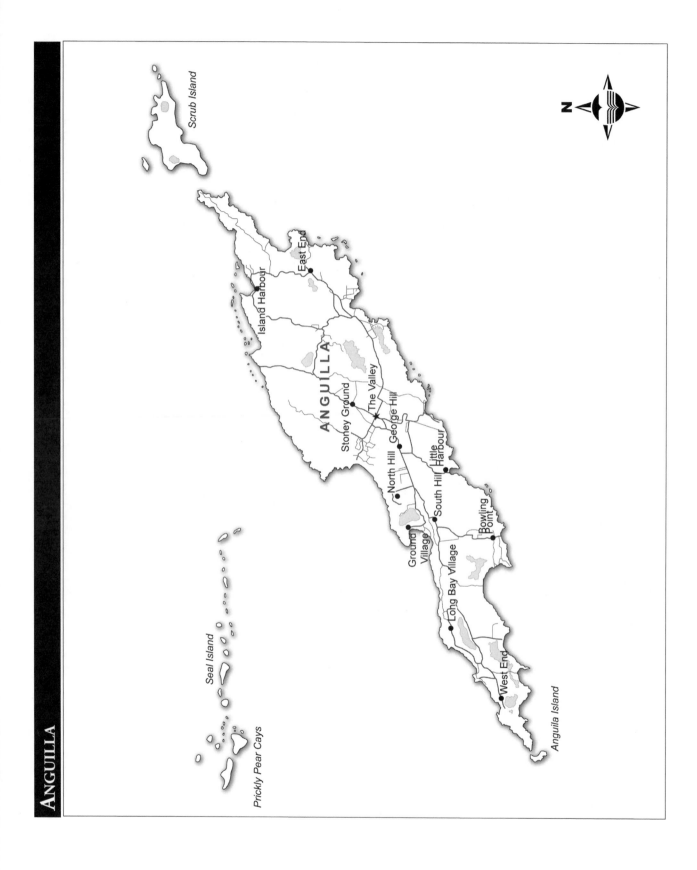

Anguilla

Religion	Followers in 1970	Followers in 2010	% of Population	Annual % growth 2000–2010	Followers in 2025	Followers in 2050
Christians	6,400	11,900	91.1	1.70	14,000	15,400
Protestants	2,500	6,800	51.9	2.14	8,200	9,300
Anglicans	2,800	3,500	26.7	0.60	4,000	4,300
Roman Catholics	100	830	6.3	2.90	1,000	1,300
Spiritists	200	440	3.4	1.73	520	600
Agnostics	0	450	3.4	3.54	600	800
Baha'is	50	140	1.1	1.81	200	300
Muslims	0	70	0.5	1.49	80	150
Hindus	0	50	0.4	1.72	60	70
Jews	0	20	0.2	1.15	30	40
Total population	**6,600**	**13,100**	**100.0**	**1.76**	**15,500**	**17,400**

and St. Kitts. The former separated in 1871. In the 1960s, Anguillans agitated against both their continued colonial status and their ties to St. Kitts; independence was not fully accomplished until 1980. Anguillians are highly religious, which accounted for their great opposition to casino gambling proposals in the 1980s.

Most people in the Leeward Islands consider themselves Christians, although the faith of many is only nominal. It is estimated that more than half the population of Anguilla does not attend church regularly. The most prominent denominations are the Anglican and Methodist churches (each claim about 43 percent of the population).

The Church of England (Anglican) was established on Anguilla at the end of the 17th century, and the British Methodists arrived in 1813. The great majority of the islanders are members of one of these two churches. The Anglican parishes are now part of the Church of the Province of the West Indies and the Methodist churches of the Methodist Church in the Caribbean and the Americas; both are headquartered in Antigua. The Roman Catholic Church established a parish in 1850, which is now part of the Diocese of Saint John's (Antigua).

Other denominations present that arrived during the 20th century are the Church of God (Anderson, Indiana), Church of the Apostolic Faith, Baptist Church, Gospel Halls (Christian Brethren), Jehovah's Witnesses, and Seventh-day Adventists, which constituted the remaining 14 percent of the population.

Clifton L. Holland

See also: Church of God (Anderson, Indiana); Jehovah's Witnesses; Methodist Church in the Caribbean and the Americas; Roman Catholic Church; Seventh-day Adventist Church.

References

Brierly, Peter. *World Churches Handbook.* London, England: Christian Research, 1997.

Dryfoot, Arthur Charles. *The Shaping of the West Indian Church, 1492–1962.* Gainesville: University Press of Florida, 1999; published jointly with The Press University of the West Indies in Jamaica.

Dyde, Brian. *Out of Crowded Vagueness: A History of the Islands of St. Kitts, Nevis and Anguilla.* Northampton, MA: Interlink Publishing Group, 2006.

Holland, Clifton L., ed. *World Christianity: Central America and the Caribbean.* Monrovia, CA: MARC-World Vision International, 1981.

Horowitz, Michael M., ed. *Peoples and Cultures of the Caribbean: An Anthropological Reader.* Garden City, NY: The Natural History Press, 1971.

Petty, Colville L. *A Handbook History of Anguilla.* Anguilla; the author, 1991.

Rogozinski, Jan. *A Brief History of the Caribbean, from the Arawak and Carib to the Present.* Rev. ed. New York: Plume Books/Penguin Group, 1999.

Antarctica

The ice-covered continent of Antarctica is a landmass largely within the Antarctic Circle at the southern most point on the globe. It is completely surrounded by ocean and was uninhabited until the 20th century. Of its 5.4 million square miles of land, only 108 thousand square miles are not covered in ice.

The Antarctic region began to be systematically explored in the 1820s, and by the end of the 1830s it was established that Antarctica was a continent (as opposed to a group of islands connected by ice). Exploration of the interior increased through the first half of the 20th century, and after World War II the continent was targeted for scientific research. Since that time quite a few countries have established year-round stations there, and seven have made formal territorial claims (none of which are broadly recognized). A 1959 treaty (which took effect in 1961) offers a legal framework for the current activities being carried out by the 39 countries that have personnel there.

The Antarctic Treaty freezes the territorial claims that have been made by Argentina, Australia, Chile, France, New Zealand, Norway, and the United Kingdom. Most other nations do not recognize these territorial claims. The United States and Russia have not made territorial claims to date but have reserved the right to make such claims.

The religious life of Antarctica reflects the spectrum of religions from the countries that have sent personnel to the region. There is only one religious structure on the continent, the Chapel of the Snows, a Christian church in which both a Protestant chaplain and a Roman Catholic chaplain conduct services, the largest percentage (68 percent) of the residents being Christian. As might be expected, the second largest group on the continent consider themselves nonreligious.

J. Gordon Melton

References

Barrett, David, ed. *The Encyclopedia of World Christianity*. 2nd ed. New York: Oxford University Press, 2001.

McGonigal, David, and Lynn Woodworth. *Antarctica and the Arctic: The Complete Encyclopedia.* Westport, CT: Firefly Books, 2001.

The World Factbook. Washington, DC: Central Intelligence Agency, 2008. http://www.cia.gov/library/publications/the-world-factbook/geos/ay.html.

Anthroposophical Society

Rudolf Steiner (born 1861 in Croatia, died 1925 in Dornach, Switzerland) was a spiritual and esoteric teacher, scholar, and the founder of the school of spiritual science called Anthroposophy. Anthroposophy is not only an important philosophical/esoteric school in itself but has had direct or indirect impact in such areas as educational philosophy, organic farming, art and architecture, and a number of other human endeavors.

Steiner understood the term "Anthroposophy" to mean "the wisdom of becoming truly human," the knowledge that enables human beings to develop their spiritual faculties and to assimilate the spiritual truths and realities of the cosmos into their consciousness. He felt that attaining the fullest human love and freedom is accomplished through regaining access to the inner reality of the self that humanity has lost in modern civilization.

To this purpose, Steiner, using his reputed spiritual experiences and clairvoyant powers, set out an overarching account of the evolution of consciousness combined with a method of transforming our thinking and way of being.

He wrote some 40 books, beginning in 1891 with his doctoral dissertation, "Truth and Knowledge," and ending with his autobiography written in 1924, the year before his death. However, he was even more prolific in his speaking. It is said that he delivered more than 6,000 lectures, which have been published in 300 volumes.

Early in his intellectual life, Steiner fell under the spell of the great German poet and thinker, Johann Wolfgang Goethe (1749–1852), probably best known in the English-speaking world as a poet and the writer of the play, *Faust.* However, Goethe's brilliant mind

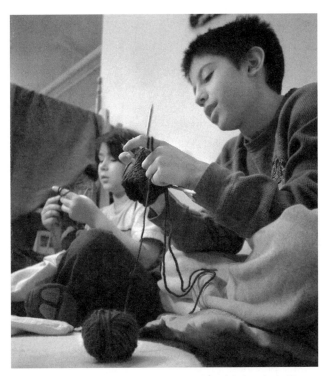

Fifth graders knit during class at Waldorf School in Chicago, January 31, 2005. Rudolf Steiner, the founder of the Anthroposophical Society, started Waldorf schools, which focus on a holistic education using natural materials and progressing with a child's physical development. (AP/Wide World Photos)

wandered over the whole range of human learning and he wrote extensively on scientific subjects as well. Steiner edited Goethe's scientific writings, which see the natural world as a living organic system instead of the blind causal mechanism of dead matter more prevalent in the mainstream scientific models.

Steiner seems to have shown some clairvoyant abilities as a youth but was reluctant to reveal them in a culture that was by and large skeptical of such things. In the early 1900s, when he worked to improve the lot of the German worker, he found himself increasingly at odds with the Marxist and materialist assumptions in the workers' movements. He came to believe strongly that only by bringing the spiritual world into intimate connection with the natural and social world would true human betterment come about.

In 1902, through the connection of some friends, he became involved with the Theosophical movement, believing then that Theosophy was the best way of

understanding his ongoing spiritual experiences. He served as general secretary of the German branch of the Theosophical Society for several years.

However, in 1909, he separated himself from the Theosophical Society because he rejected their claim that Jiddu Krishnamurti (1895–1986) was the coming messiah. His break actually had much deeper roots for Steiner had become convinced that the West could be saved from materialism and spiritual blindness only by drawing upon the resources of Western Christian Esotericism and not by importing Oriental philosophies, however profound.

The foundations of the Anthroposophical movement were actually laid by Steiner's followers in 1913, the year that Steiner laid the foundation stone for the great building called the Goetheanum, which would serve as world headquarters for Anthroposophy. This building was designed to embody Goethe's vision of an organic order. It was made of wood, however, and it was burned down by an arsonist shortly after it was completed. It was then rebuilt in stone.

It would not be until 1923 that Steiner would refound the movement as the General Anthroposophical Society, embracing both inner spiritual work and external practical applications. He became its first leader. The Anthroposophical Society was banned by the Nazis and virtually no Anthroposophist joined the Nazi Party.

A distinguishing mark of the Anthroposophical movement, beginning with Steiner himself, is the readiness to put their principles into practical endeavors. Steiner believed that spiritual principles were directly relevant to modern life and could in practice transform even our everyday living. He was eager to show how different human disciplines and arts could be reworked to make them into spiritual practices.

Steiner freely put himself at the disposal of all who sought his help and guidance. He developed the principles of "eurhythmy" for a dancer, gave public lectures to any who were interested, wrote plays to illustrate Esoteric principles, and wrote extensively on the principles of a just social order during the chaotic years in Germany after its defeat in World War I.

In 1919, Steiner was asked by the owner of the Waldorf Astoria Cigarette Factory to set up a school to help educate the children of his workers, based on his many lectures on child development, curriculum, and pedagogy. This became the model for what became known as "the Waldorf schools," which spread to include more 500 schools around the world, with 90 in the United States. It is the largest non-sectarian private school movement in the world, working to integrate the works of head, heart, and hands to develop each child into a free and responsible adult.

Responding to some farmers who were concerned with the extensive use of chemical fertilizers in modern agriculture, Steiner developed the "biodynamic" methods building on his vision of nature as an organic spiritual and material whole. These methods of organic farming are still studied and utilized today among those who believe that organically grown food is superior.

Steiner was interested in the whole person. Like many esoteric thinkers, Steiner held that the human person was made up of a series of ever more subtle spiritual bodies. He lectured extensively on medicine, particularly homeopathy from an Anthroposophic viewpoint. The Anthroposophical Society continues to work with sympathetic medical professionals to expand the repertoire of medical practice beyond their standard model taught in medical education.

Steiner saw himself as working primarily within the esoteric traditions of Christianity as revealed in the Rosicrucian tradition, alchemy, and the like. He was respectful of but not directly concerned with the institutional Christian church and its exoteric theology. But ever-responsive to those who called upon his help, he agreed to work with a group of ministers and theology students to help renew the institutional church. From this comes the Movement for Religious Renewal, also called the Christian Community. While Anthroposophic Spiritual Science is designed to help individuals in their own spiritual ascent, the central sacrament of the Christian Community, the Act of Consecration of Man, is designed to allow the participant to experience the descent of the divine into an assembled community.

The Society is still headquartered in the Goetheanum in Dornach but has branches in many parts of the world, including the United States. At present, the Anthroposophical Society can be found in 50 countries. It welcomes inquiries, many of its programs are open to the public, and the Anthroposophic Press has made much of Steiner's writings available in careful English translations.

World Headquarters: General Anthroposophical
    Society
Goetheanum
CH-4143
Dornach, Switzerland
Telephone 011-41-61-706-42-42
www.goetheanum.ch

Anthroposophical Society in America
1923 Geddes Avenue,
Ann Arbor, MI 48104-1797
Telephone: 1-888-757-2742 or 313-662-9355
Fax: 313-662-1727
www.anthroposophy.org

Anthroposophic Press
3390 Route 9
Hudson NY 12534
Telephone: 518-851-2054
Fax: 518-851-2047
www.anthropress.org

James Burnell Robinson

See also: Christian Community (Movement for Religious Renewal); Theosophical Society (America); Western Esoteric Tradition.

References

Hemleben, Johannes. *Rudolf Steiner: An Illustrated Biography*. Trans. by Leo Twyman. Vancouver, BC: Sophia Books, 2001.

McDermott, Robert. "Rudolf Steiner and Anthroposophy." In *Modern Esoteric Spirituality*, edited by Antoine Faivre and Jacob Needleman, 288–310. New York: Crossroads, 1992.

Steiner, Rudolf. *The Anthroposophical Movement: Eight Lectures at Dornach, 1923*. London: Rudolf Steiner Press, 1993.

Steiner, Rudolf. *How to Know Higher Worlds: A Modern Path of Initiation*. Trans. by Christopher Bamford. Herndon, VA: Anthroposophic Press, 1994.

■ Antigua and Barbuda

Antigua and its dependencies, Barbuda and Redonda, are small islands located in the Leeward Islands in the northeastern area of the Caribbean Sea, and form an independent state within the British Commonwealth of Nations. Together, the islands now have about 70,000 residents (2008): Antigua has an area of 108 square miles; Barbuda, 62 square miles; and Redonda, less than one-half square mile. Antigua is mountainous and has its highest elevation at Boggy Peak (1,330 feet above sea level).

Antigua and Barbuda were inhabited as early as 2400 BCE by the Siboney Amerindians, but the islands were always rather sparsely populated, primarily due to a lack of fresh water. The Siboney were later displaced by the Caribs, who eventually abandoned the islands. The Spanish first attempted to settle on the islands in the 16th century and the French in the 17th century. After the French settlers departed, the British arrived in 1632 and succeeded in developing a means of saving rainwater. During the 19th century, the colony prospered; settlers created tobacco and sugar plantations and imported slaves from Africa as laborers.

However, slavery was abolished by the British in 1834, although the job limitations left the freedmen in virtual slavery into the next century. Following social and political unrest in the 1960s, a new Constitution was adopted in 1966 that granted the islands self-government, although the United Kingdom remained responsible for the islands' defense and foreign relations. Antigua and Barbuda became an independent nation in 1981, with its capital in St. John's. The new nation adapted a parliamentary system of government.

The nation's economy was initially based on sugar production, which was discontinued in 1972 and later

An Antiguan church in the colonial architecture style. Most Antiguans belong to one of the denominations of Christianity. (Corel)

Antigua and Barbuda

Religion	Followers in 1970	Followers in 2010	% of Population	Annual % growth 2000–2010	Followers in 2025	Followers in 2050
Christians	67,800	81,700	92.8	1.50	93,000	101,000
Protestants	22,100	35,000	39.8	1.44	39,200	43,000
Anglicans	29,500	26,000	29.5	0.66	29,000	31,000
Roman Catholics	6,400	8,900	10.1	2.67	10,500	11,000
Spiritists	700	3,200	3.6	1.58	3,700	4,000
Agnostics	0	1,400	1.6	6.66	1,800	2,600
Baha'is	400	930	1.1	1.57	1,400	2,000
Muslims	300	500	0.6	1.55	700	900
Hindus	0	150	0.2	1.58	200	270
Atheists	0	110	0.1	1.68	180	250
Total population	**69,200**	**88,000**	**100.0**	**1.58**	**101,000**	**111,000**

restarted. Tourism now accounts for the greatest percentage of income. The government encouraged industrialization and a large oil refinery is now in operation.

The original British settlers were affiliated with the Church of England. Anglican chaplains arrived with British occupation and settlement, and the Church of England became the Established Church after the first Anglican priest arrived in Antigua. After 1824, Antigua and Barbuda became part of the Bishopric of Barbados. The Bishopric of Antigua was established in 1842 with responsibility for church matters in Antigua, Aruba, Barbuda, Dominica, Montserrat, Nevis, Saba, St. Barts, St. Eustatuis, St. Martin, and St. Kitts. This geographical area is now part of the Church in the Province of the West Indies and its archbishop resides in Nassau, the Bahamas. The Anglican Church is the nation's largest denomination, with an estimated 32,000 adherents in 2005.

In the middle of the 18th century, both the Moravians (1756) and the Methodists (1760) initiated work on Antigua and Barbuda, and continue to enjoy a sizable following. The Methodist congregations are part of the Methodist Church in the Caribbean and the Americas, headquartered in St. John's, Antigua. The Methodist Church is the nation's third largest denomination, with an estimated 6,930 adherents in 2005. The Moravians are part of the East Indies Province of the Moravian Church, also headquartered on Antigua at Cashew Hill. The Moravian Church has the fourth largest constituency in the nation, with an estimated 5,270 adherents in 2005.

Nathaniel Gilbert was a plantation owner on Antigua who was converted in England through the preaching and teaching of the Reverend John Wesley, and returned to Antigua in 1760 as a Wesleyan Methodist lay preacher. The Wesleyan Methodist Church began work in Antigua in 1786 under missionary William Warrener by the authority of Bishop Dr. Thomas Coke. The Anglican Slave Conversion Society (later known as the Christian Faith Society), under the supervision of the Anglican bishop of London, began work in Antigua in 1798.

During the 20th century a variety of denominations initiated work among the residents of this island nation, including the Roman Catholic Church (now the second largest denomination), the Salvation Army (1904), the African Methodist Episcopal Church, the Christian Brethren, the Church of God of Prophecy, the Church of God World Missions (Cleveland, Tennessee) in 1954, the Southern Baptist Convention in 1964, Baptist International Missions in 1975, the Church of Christ in Christian Union, the Church of the Nazarene, the Seventh-day Adventist Church, and the Wesleyan Church. The Anglicans, Methodists, Moravians, and Salvation Army are affiliated with the Antigua Christian Council, which is in turn associated with the World Council of Churches.

Two marginal Christian groups also have a following: the Church of Jesus Christ of Latter-day Saints (Mormons) was founded in 1984 and now has one church with 181 members (2007); and the Jehovah's Witnesses.

ANTIGUA AND BARBUDA

Although most Antiguans are Christians, there is an outpost of the Ahmadiyya Muslim movement, which has opened a mosque; and there are several spiritual assemblies of the Baha'i Faith. In the 1960s, many residents of African heritage were attracted to the Jamaican Rastafarian movement with roots in Black Judaism, which instilled racial and cultural pride and called for the liberation of black people.

The Constitution provides for freedom of religion, and other laws and policies contributed to the generally free practice of religion. The law at all levels protects this right in full against abuse, by either governmental or private actors. The government generally respects religious freedom in practice.

In 2008, there were no reports of societal abuses or discrimination based on religious affiliation, belief, or practice, and prominent societal leaders took positive steps to promote religious freedom.

According to the 2001 census, 74 percent of the population was Christian. The Anglican Church is the largest religious denomination, accounting for an estimated 26 percent of the population. The Methodist, Moravian, and Roman Catholic churches account for less than 10 percent each. The United Evangelical Association, an organization that includes most independent evangelical churches, claims an estimated 25 percent of the population. The Jehovah's Witnesses number more than 1,000 members. Non-Christians include an estimated 1,000 to 1,500 Rastafarians, more than 200 Muslims, nearly 200 Hindus, and approximately 50 members of the Baha'i Faith.

Clifton L. Holland

See also: Ahmadiyya Movement in Islam; Baha'i Faith; Christian Brethren; Church in the Province of the West Indies; Church of England; Church of God (Cleveland, Tennessee); Church of God of Prophecy; Church of Jesus Christ of Latter-day Saints; Jehovah's Witnesses; Methodist Church in the Caribbean and the Americas; Moravian Church, Eastern West Indies Province; Rastafarians; Roman Catholic Church; Salvation Army; Seventh-day Adventist Church; Southern Baptist Convention; Wesleyan Church; World Council of Churches.

References

Brierly, Peter. *World Churches Handbook*. London, England: Christian Research, 1997.

Dryfoot, Arthur Charles. *The Shaping of the West Indian Church, 1492–1962*. Gainesville: University Press of Florida, 1999; published jointly with The Press University of the West Indies in Jamaica.

Dyde, Brian. *Out of Crowded Vagueness: A History of the Islands of St. Kitts, Nevis and Anguilla*. Northampton, MA: Interlink Publishing Group, 2006.

Holland, Clifton L., ed. *World Christianity: Central America and the Caribbean*. Monrovia, CA: MARC-World Vision International, 1981.

Horowitz, Michael M., ed. *Peoples and Cultures of the Caribbean: An Anthropological Reader*. Garden City, NY: The Natural History Press, 1971.

Rogozinski, Jan. *A Brief History of the Caribbean, from the Arawak and Carib to the Present*. Rev. ed. New York: Plume Books–Penguin Group, 1999.

U.S. Department of State. *International Religious Freedom Report 2008*. http://www.state.gov/g/drl/rls/irf/2008/108510.htm. Accessed August 15, 2009.

Apostles of Infinite Love

The Apostles form an interesting Catholic traditionalist group that sustains Quebec messianism according to which Providence has saved French Canadians from Protestantism, assimilation into Anglo-Saxon culture, and the anticlericalism prevailing in old France. It promises the latter-day triumph of the Quebec Church, which will resurrect Catholicism at large through the pontificate of Gregory.

Father John of the Trinity was born in 1928 at Rimouski, as Gaston Tremblay. He founded a community authorized by Pope Pius XII in 1953. It settled in Saint-Jovite in 1958 as the mother house of the Order of the Mother of God, to fulfill the demands of the Virgin at La Salette in 1846. John met Michel Collin, known as Pope Clement XV (r. 1950–1968), who recognized him as his successor and ordained him priest and bishop in 1962, as well as superior general of his order, the Apostles of Infinite Love. In 1968, John took over the apostolic succession of St. Peter under the name Gregory XVII and was crowned in 1971. His encyclical (1975), *Peter Speaks to the World*, enjoins Christians to unite. He later exposed the apostasy of Pope Paul VI and the Vatican. Strangely enough, he has not been excommunicated by Rome.

The expanding and self-supporting order antagonized the official Church and the surrounding community. From 1966 until 2001, when charges were dropped for lack of evidence, various affairs (mainly about the treatment of resident children) plagued the Apostles. They have had communities throughout North America, but the number of monks, nuns, and lay residents sharply fell to only about 300 followers in the mid-1990s (Cueno 1997, 127).

Expounded in numerous books, John's doctrine upholds that of the pre–Vatican Church, with notable exceptions: ordination of women and married Apostles and the celebration of Mass in French and in English, not in Latin. Based on prayer, work, and discipline, religious rules obey the 33 points dictated by the Virgin at La Salette. Brothers and sisters live in separate quarters. Newcomers share their wealth and belongings.

Gregory looks to the Bible, past prophecies (mostly La Salette, Fatima, Nostradamus), and numerology for the justification of his election and his millenarianism. The Earth is being purged of evil bred by the corrupt Roman clergy and modernism. The church will be born again in glory into a Catholic millennium presided by the grand pontiff, Gregory XVII. Apostates will reappear before a second castigation definitely cleanses the Earth to bring about the end of the world and the resurrection of the true church in Quebec as was announced by Marie in various visions. Gregory also claims Nostradamus predicted the link between his election as pope in 1967 and the rise of the independentist Parti québécois, two signs of divinely protected resistance to assimilation, preparing the gathering of the Christian forces for the final conquest. In this apocalyptic script the gathering of the Jews in the latter-days is replaced by the gathering of the French of the motherland and their diaspora.

Gregory's prophecies relay the social and political mission of the Church of French Canada before its decline in the 20th century. The clergy sublimated the disaster of the English conquest by representing it as desired by God to protect the community from the French revolutions of the 18th and 19th centuries. For him the fight is within Catholicism as well as with Protestantism.

Far from being relegated to a sectarian status in today's Quebec, the Apostles should be regarded as actively participating with about half its population in the province's quest for political and cultural sovereignty. The Apostles' ambition goes even further than this since not only do they envision their Saint Jovite Vatican as the keeper of the traditional values of their province/nation, but also as the savior of the universal church and of the world.

Monastery of the Apostles
PO Box 4478

Mont-Tremblant, Quebec
Canada J8E 1A1
http://www.magnificat.ca/english/index.html
Bernadette Rigal-Cellard

See also: Roman Catholic Church.

References
Major Magnificat publications:

Barette, Jean-Marie. *La Prophétie des Apôtres des Derniers Temps.* S. Jovite: Éditions Magnificat, 1988.

Catéchisme de la doctrine chrétienne catholique, enseignée par Jésus-Christ et les Apôtres. St. Jovite: Éditions Magnificat, 1996.

Coté, Jean. *Père Jean de la Trinité, Prophète parmi les hommes.* (1ère édition: Montréal: Édition Priorité, 1985). St. Jovite: Éditions Magnificat, 1991.

St-Pierre, Catherine. *Tu es Pierre.* St. Jovite: Éditions Magnificat, 1994.

San Pietro, Michel. *Saul, pourquoi me persécutes-tu?* St. Jovite: Éditions Magnificat, 1977.

Specific study:

Rigal-Cellard, Bernadette. "Le futur pape est québécois: Grégoire XVII." In *Missions extrêmes en Amérique du Nord: des Jésuites à Raël,* edited by Bernadette Rigal-Cellard, 269–300. Bordeaux: Pleine Page, 2005.

Studies that briefly present the Apostles:

Cuneo, Michael W. *The Smoke of Satan: Conservative and Traditionalist Dissent in Contemporary American Catholicism.* New York: Oxford University Press, 1997.

Vaillancourt, Jean-Guy et Goeffroy, Martin. "La droite catholique au Quebec: essai de typologie." *Studies in Religion/Sciences religieuses* 25, no. 1(1996): 21–33.

Apostolic Assembly of Faith in Jesus Christ, U.S.A.

This Hispanic denomination traces its origin to the early days of the Pentecostal Revival that broke out in Los Angeles, California, in 1906, but it was not formally organized until 1925 in San Bernardino, California. Its present name was adopted at its legal incorporation in the state of California in 1930. For lack of a denominational structure prior to 1930, the early Hispanic leaders of Oneness ("Jesus Only") Pentecostal churches obtained their ministerial credentials from the Pentecostal Assemblies of the World (PAW). The Apostolic Assembly, early in its development, adopted an episcopal structure of church government.

Among those who attended the famous Azusa Street Apostolic Faith Mission (1906–1913) in Los Angeles were several Mexican believers. Luis López was baptized there in 1909 and before long the mission had produced its first Mexican preacher, Juan Navarro. Evidently, both López and Navarro were Protestants prior to their arrival in Los Angeles, but, upon hearing the Pentecostal message, they were convinced of its truth and received the baptism in the Holy Spirit, as evidenced by speaking in tongues and other signs and wonders. They also accepted the doctrine that they should be baptized or rebaptized only in the Name of Jesus, and that "this is the true baptism that saves." This baptismal practice dates from about 1909, which is several years prior to the controversy that erupted over the "Jesus Only" versus Trinitarian baptismal formula that sharply divided Pentecostals in 1913.

In 1912, soon after 22-year-old Francisco F. Llorente (1890–1928) arrived in San Diego from his home in Acapulco, Mexico, he was converted to Pentecostalism by a group of Anglo-Americans who were followers of the Apostolic Faith (or "Jesus Only" Pentecostals). In 1914 Llorente was instrumental in the conversion and baptism of Marcial De La Cruz; then, together, they traveled throughout Southern California during 1914–1915 and established numerous Spanish-speaking Apostolic churches. These early Mexican Pentecostals differed from other Pentecostals by teaching that their churches should not have women preachers, that women should have their heads covered during public worship services, and that water baptism should be administered only in the Name of Jesus (as in Acts 2:38 and 1 Timothy 2:12).

Beginning in 1916, Navarro, Llorente and De La Cruz received their ministerial credentials from the PAW, and Llorente was named the PAW's "Mexican representative." That event marks the organizational beginning of the Apostolic Assembly as an emergent denomination, with Llorente as its acting bishop (1916–1928).

In 1916–1917, Antonio Castañeda Nava (1892–1999) of Nazas, Durango, Mexico, was converted, baptized in the Holy Spirit, and received a call to the ministry while working in the Imperial Valley of Southern California. He launched a career in evangelism and church planting that led to his being named the second presiding bishop (1929–1950) of the Apostolic Assembly following the sudden death of Llorente in 1928.

Between 1916 and 1919 the Spanish-speaking Apostolic work spread from San Francisco to the Mexican border. Llorente dedicated most of his efforts to ministry between Los Angeles and San Francisco. Although loosely related to the PAW, the PAW leadership exercised no control or supervision of the Spanish-speaking work in California at the time the PAW was formally incorporated in 1919.

In December 1925, the leaders of the Hispanic Apostolic churches (some 23 congregations) in the American Southwest and Baja California met together in San Bernardino, California, for their first general assembly as an organization. Those in attendance chose The Church of the Apostolic Pentecostal Faith (Iglesia de la Fe Apostólica Pentecostés) as the official name of their movement and elected Francisco Llorente as presiding bishop (1925–1928). However, when the new denomination became officially incorporated in California on March 15, 1930, as a nonprofit organization, its name became The Apostolic Assembly of Faith in Jesus Christ and it formally severed its ties to the PAW. The work in Baja California, Mexico, remained under the supervision of the Apostolic Assembly in California until transferred to the supervision of its sister denomination in Mexico, the Apostolic Church of Faith in Jesus Christ (Iglesia Apostólica de la Fe en Cristo Jesús), in 1933. The latter was formally organized in Torreón, Coahuila, Mexico, in 1932, although its first church was formed in 1914 in Villa Aldama, Chihuahua.

Also, the delegates at the first general assembly in 1925 adopted an organizational structure similar to that of Methodism, with an executive board of bishops.

The original officers included the president (pastor general or presiding bishop), executive elder (*anciano ejecutivo*), secretary, and assistant secretary.

The young Hispanic Apostolic Faith movement suffered from the migratory nature of the Mexican American population, mainly composed of agricultural workers that followed the seasonal planting and harvesting of crops in the southwestern states; the lack of literacy and basic education among the Spanish-speaking people; the lack of funds for pastoral salaries and for purchasing land and constructing church buildings; the large-scale movement of migrant farm workers back to Mexico during the Great Depression of the 1930s; and the general lack of experience in organizational development and management.

Also, two divisions affected the new denomination during the 1920s–1930s. In 1926, a small group of pastors, led by José L. Martínez of San Bernardino, revolted against the leadership of Llorente and demanded a doctrinal purification, the purging of the ministry, and a new name for the movement; the requirement concerning tithing was also a major issue in the financial structure of the denomination. The unfortunate result of this conflict was the withdrawal of Martínez and six other pastors, who formed the Apostolic Christian Assembly of the Name of Jesus Christ in 1927. During the late 1930s, a small group of churches in New Mexico, led by Pedro Banderas, left the Apostolic Assembly over disagreements on tithing (ca. 1938) and joined the Pentecostal Assemblies of Jesus Christ, which was created in 1932 by a merger of the Apostolic Church of Jesus Christ and the Pentecostal Assemblies of the World.

During the period 1940–1945, the Apostolic Assembly adopted a pacifist position regarding the bearing of firearms during World War II, and they recommended that if called upon to serve in the armed forces the duty of their members was to obey the draft but to declare themselves as "conscientious objectors" and only serve in a non-combatant role, such as in the medical corps.

The Apostolic Assembly grew slowly during the 1930s and early 1940s, but began a period of expansion following World War II. In 1935, there were a total of 18 churches in California, Arizona, New Mexico, and Texas. In 1946, the Apostolic Assembly agreed to a joint venture with the United Pentecostal Church International and the Apostolic Church of Mexico to evangelize Central America, initially in Guatemala, El Salvador, and Nicaragua. In 1949, the Apostolic Bible Training School was established in Hayward, California, to better prepare Spanish-speaking ministers.

During the 1950s, the denomination divided its work into various districts, each supervised by a bishop who was elected by the majority of the ministers of his district and subject to the approval of the Qualifying Commission, composed of three members of the national board of directors. The ministers of the local congregations were appointed and subject to removal by the district bishop; the local congregations are consulted regarding the matter, but the final decision is made by the bishop. Sometimes the district bishop allows the local church to call its own pastor; however, pastoral changes are normally made at the district conventions or at regional pastors meetings. All church buildings and properties are held in the name of the corporation. The principle of self-support is strongly adhered to and tithing is considered the duty and obligation of every member. In addition, no local church is exempt from sending a tenth of its tithes and offerings to the general treasurer of the Apostolic Assembly. The tithes of the pastors and elders of each district must be sent monthly to the district treasurer for the support of the district bishop and the administration of the district.

During the early 1960s, new Apostolic Assembly churches were established in Washington, Oregon, Iowa, Pennsylvania, and Florida, as well as missionary efforts in Costa Rica, Honduras, and Italy in 1964–1965. By 1966, there were 152 Apostolic congregations with about 8,000 members in 12 states, including new work in Utah, Michigan, and Wisconsin.

By 1980, the Apostolic Assembly had grown to 298 organized churches and 80 missions with about 16,700 members nationally, with the largest concentration of congregations in California (129).

In 1993, the Apostolic Assembly reported 451 organized churches nationally with about 40,600 members, which made it the third largest Hispanic denomination in the United States after the Assemblies of God and the Southern Baptist Convention in terms of Hispanic churches and membership.

In 2004, the annual report listed 52,000 adult baptized members, about 80,000 adherents (adults, adolescents, and children), and 700 organized churches in 44 states distributed among 27 districts in the United States. In addition, there were 19 mission fields in Canada, Mexico, Central America (Honduras, Costa Rica, and Panama), South America (Brazil, Argentina, Uruguay, Chile, Paraguay, Bolivia, Peru, Colombia, and Venezuela), the Caribbean (Dominican Republic and Puerto Rico), and Europe (Italy and Spain). These mission fields reported 19 missionaries, 31,000 adult baptized members, about 50,000 adherents, and 600 organized churches.

As of November 1, 2007, the Apostolic Assembly had 26 districts in the United States and 5 regional mission districts in 20 countries, including 228 affiliated churches in 10 districts in Mexico.

This Hispanic denomination experienced significant growth in membership in the United States between 1996 and 2002. In 2007, it had more than 700 organized congregations with 94,000 members in the United States and more than 690 missionary churches with 36,800 members in 20 countries, including the United States, Central America, South America, Europe, and Africa. Its estimated total membership worldwide is 130,000, and it has 5,500 ordained ministers and deacons.

Since 2002, the *obispo presidente* of the board of directors has been Daniel Sánchez (born in 1939), the current vice president is Bishop Samuel Valverde, and there are six other board members: general secretary, general treasurer, secretary of international missions, secretary of national missions, secretary of Christian education, and secretary of social assistance.

Under the board of directors is the episcopal body, which includes all district supervisors or bishops. Districts generally correspond to state or regional boundaries and are led by a bishop who serves a four-year term. The bishop is assisted by a district secretary and a district treasurer. Bishops may also rely on elders, an elected position for pastors who advise a small group of congregations on behalf of the corresponding district.

During its first 80 years of existence, the Apostolic Assembly has had 8 national leaders or "bishop presidents," who are listed here, with corresponding terms of service in parentheses: Francisco Llorente (1925–1928), Antonio Castañeda Nava (1929–1950, 1963–1966), Benjamin Cantu (1950–1963), Efraín Valverde (1966–1970), Lorenzo Salazar (1970–1978), Manuel Vizcarra (1986–1994), Baldemar Rodríguez (1978–1986, 1994–2002), and Daniel Sánchez (2002–2006, 2006–2010). http://en.wikipedia.org/wiki/Apostolic_Assembly_of_the_Faith_in_Christ_Jesus.

National Headquarters: The headquarters building houses offices for its 8-member board of directors and also for its administrative staff, which is comprised of 15 full-time employees. In addition, it has two conference rooms, a bookstore, a shipping & receiving area, and a warehouse. The Christian bookstore is open to the public.

Obispo Presidente Daniel Sánchez
10807 Laurel Street
Rancho Cucamonga
CA 91730
http://www.apostolicassembly.org/index.aspx
http://www.nationalmissions.org/contact.aspx
Clifton L. Holland

See also: Apostolic Church of Faith in Jesus Christ of Mexico; Pentecostal Assemblies of the World; Pentecostalism; United Pentecostal Church International.

References

Burgess, Stanley M., and Gary B. McGee, eds. *Dictionary of Pentecostal and Charismatic Movements.* Grand Rapids, MI: Regency Reference Library/Zondervan Publishing House, 1988.

Gaxiola, Manuel J. *La Serpiente y la Paloma: Historia, Teología y Análisis de la Iglesia Apostólica de la Fe en Cristo Jesús de México (1914–1994).* 2nd ed. Nacaulpan, México: Libros Pyros, 1994.

Holland, Clifton L. *The Religious Dimension in Hispanic Los Angeles: A Protestant Case Study.* South Pasadena, CA: William Carey Press, 1974.

Holland, Clifton L. "An Update on the National Study of Hispanic Protestant Church Growth in the U.S.A." Unpublished research report. Pasadena, CA: IDEA-PROLADES, 1993. http://www.prolades.com/hispusa.htm.

Martin del Campo, Ismael. *Cosechando en el Field.* Norwalk, CA: Editorial Nueva Visión, 2004.

Martin del Campo, Ismael. "Asamblea Apostólica de la Fe en Cristo Jesús." In *Iglesias Peregrinas en Busca de Identidad: Cuadros del Protestantismo Latino en los Estados Unidos*, edited by Juan F. Martínez and Luis Scott. Buenos Aires, Argentina: Ediciones Kairos and CEHILA, 2004.

Ortega, José A., ed. *Historia de la Asamblea Apostólica de la Fe en Cristo Jesús, 1916–1966.* Mentone, CA: Editorial Committee of the Asamblea Apostólica, 1966.

Torres, Domingo A. "Asamblea Apostólica de la Fe en Cristo Jesús." In *Hacia Una Historia de la Iglesia Evangélica Hispana de California del Sur,* edited by Rodelo Wilson. Montebello, CA: AHET, 1993.

Apostolic Catholic Assyrian Church of the East

Through the second century, the Christian movement spread from Jerusalem and Antioch eastward to Edessa (in eastern Syria) and on to Nisibis and Seludia-Ctesiphon (in present-day Iraq), then a part of the Persian Sassanid Empire. The Sassanid rulers were devoted Zoroastrians, though it was a minority perspective within the empire as a whole, which may account for their allowing Christianity a relative degree of tolerance, at least through the initial decades of their reign. However, during the last decades of the third century persecutions were launched. These coincided with the consecration of the first bishop for the Persian church in Seludia-Ctesiphon in 285. The church, however, appears to have grown even before it had a strong central authority and was noted for the number of Christian who were devoted ascetics.

Real persecutions began during the lengthy reign of Shapur II (309–379) after he concluded that Christians represented a potentially disloyal community, whose real allegiance might turn out to lie with Constantine and the Roman Empire that constantly threatened his western border. The massive, and at times systematic, suppression of the church began in 344 and continued through the end of the century. The church was able to reorganize and rebuild in the fifth century, following the issuance of an edict of toleration by Shah Yazdegerd I around 409. At a synod in 410, the bishops established an independent Church of the East under a *catholicos* (patriarch) who resided at Seludia-Ctesiphon. The church accepted the orthodox confession adopted by the Council of Nicaea (325), but as the century proceeded, it claimed the status of a patriarchate, equal to Constantinople, Jerusalem, and Antioch.

In the fifth century, the Church of the East was swept into the next stage of the Christological controversy, in which the attempt was made to more precisely define the human and divine natures of Christ. The issue was how to defend the complete humanity of Christ without underplaying his divinity, and vice versa. Into this theological morass stepped Nestorius, consecrated as patriarch of Constantinople in 428. In attempting to moderate between the two parties, he attacked a popular phrase describing the Virgin Mary as the "Mother of God." Cyril, the patriarch of Alexandria, accused him of heresy for denying the deity of Christ. The issue came before the Ecumenical Council at Ephesus, which Cyril dominated. The Council excommunicated Nestorius, who accepted exile. The bishops of the Church of the East questioned the legality of the Council's actions and called its manner of acting a disgrace. Although the decrees promulgated by Ephesus were somewhat balanced by the Chalcedonian Council in the next generation, by that time the Persian Church had gone its separate way and came to be identified as the Nestorian Church.

The growth and development of the Church of the East, together with its ever-shifting relationship with the Persian rulers, was abruptly altered by the conquest of Persia by the Muslim Arabs in 644 (when Seludia-Ctesiphon fell). In general, the Islamic rulers appear to have treated the Christians better than had the Zoroastrians. Christians were taxed heavily, but in return were guaranteed the protection of the Islamic state. Through the Muslim centuries, the church maintained its strength in the Kurdish areas of Turkey and northern Iraq.

The 15th century became a period of change for the church. The century opened with the conquest of Baghdad by the Muslim general Tamerlane (1336–1405), operating from his base at Samerkand (in modern-day

Syrian Orthodox worshippers attend services at St. Peter and Paul's Cathedral in Baghdad, Iraq, July 18, 2004. Christians are a minority in Baghdad. (AP/Wide World Photos)

Uzbekistan). The resulting slaughter of Christians led many more Assyrians to flee into northern Iraq. By this time, some additional stability had been introduced into the church by the acceptance of a hereditary episcopacy. Bishops (who were unmarried) tended to pass their position to a nephew. This practice included the church's patriarch, whose position by the middle of the century came to be limited to members of the family of Mar Shimun IV. This practice would ultimately lead to schism.

In 1552, dissenters from Mar Shimun's leadership selected Mar Yohanan Soulaqa VIII as the new patriarch. He established his headquarters at Diyarbakır and then met with Pope Julius III (r. 1550–1555) and entered into communion with the Roman Catholic Church. For the next century the Assyrian Church existed with two patriarchs, the one in the family of Mar Shimun at Alqosh (northern Iraq), and one of the lineage of Mar Yohanan Soulaqa VIII in Diyarbakır

(southeastern Turkey). Then in 1662, Mar Shimun XIII Denha discontinued his relationship with Rome and moved to reconcile with his rival. He subsequently moved his diocesan headquarters to Qochanis (in Turkish Kurdistan). Rome replaced Mar Shimun XIII Denha with a new patriarch who assumed hegemony over the believers still loyal to the Roman Catholic Church. This group of loyalists evolved into the present-day Chaldean Catholic Church.

Early in the 19th century, the family of Mar Shimun IV failed to produce an heir to the patriarchy. The bishops loyal to that lineage shifted their loyalty to the Chaldean Catholic Church. The patriarch at Qochanis assumed hegemony over those Assyrians who did not accept Roman authority and remained independent. Later in the century, in the last stages of the Ottoman Empire, the sultan's army attacked Kurdistan. The Assyrian patriarch, Mar Eshai Shimun XXIII (1908–1975), left Turkey. He returned briefly following World

War I, but after a short stay was again forced to flee. Finally, in 1940, the patriarch relocated to the United States. Many members followed their patriarch to North America, while others resettled in Syria and Iraq.

The Church of the East, although accepted by the Church of England and many Protestant bodies as orthodox in faith and practice, has not been accepted within the larger world of Eastern Orthodoxy, as it still has not affirmed the finding of all of the early Ecumenical Councils, including those that met after the Nestorian controversy ended. The church is a liturgical body with a full sacramental system analogous to that of Eastern Orthodoxy; it is unique in designating the Sign of the Cross, Unction, and "Holy Leaven" as additional sacraments. The idea of holy leaven refers to the belief that a portion of the bread used in the Last Supper of Jesus and the Apostles was brought to the East by the Apostle Thaddeus and that the Eucharistic meals in the church are continuous with the event, a small piece of bread from a Eucharist is incorporated in the bread prepared for the next.

Ecumenically, the church is a charter member of the World Council of Churches, though it has not joined the National Council of the Church of Christ in the U.S.A. A milestone in church relations occurred in 1994 when Mar Dinkha IV met with Pope John Paul II and signed a Common Christological Declaration that affirmed that both churches hold to the same understanding of the nature of Jesus Christ. Both churches continue in dialogue to remove any remaining obstacles to future full communion.

The church is currently led by His Holiness Mar Dinkha IV (b. 1935), the catholicos patriarch. Archbishops are now found in Russia, India, Lebanon, Iraq, and Europe. Bishops reside in Syria, Iran, Australia, New Zealand, Canada, and the United Kingdom. There are three dioceses in the United States. The majority of church members reside in Iraq, where more than 50,000 may be found. In 2005, the church reported 323,000 members worldwide.

In 1968 the church in Iraq experienced a schism, which led to the formation of what became known as the Ancient Church of the East. Both churches have suffered greatly as a result of the Iraq War that began with the American invasion in 2003 and the resulting Shia Muslim-led government.

Apostolic Catholic Assyrian Church of the East
8909 Birch Ave.
Morton Grove, IL 60053

J. Gordon Melton

See also: Ancient Church of the East; Chaldean Catholic Church; Church of England; World Council of Churches.

References

Orthodoxia. Regensburg, Germany: Ostkirchliches Institut, issued annually.

Roberson, Ronald G. *The Eastern Christian Churches—A Brief Survey*. 5th ed. Rome: Edizioni Orientalia Christiana, Pontificio Istituto Orientale, 1995.

Van Beek, Huibert. *A Handbook of the Churches and Councils: Profiles of Ecumenical Relationships*. Geneva: World Council of Churches, 2006.

Van der Bent, Ans J., ed. *Handbook/Member Churches/World Council of Churches*. Geneva: World Council of Churches, 1985.

Apostolic Church

One of the oldest Pentecostal bodies in the United Kingdom, and one of the larger global Pentecostal bodies, the Apostolic Church's beginnings can be traced to the famous revival of 1903–1904, which emerged in Wales in a church at New Quay on Cardigan Bay. Evans Roberts (1878–1949), one of the first people converted in the revival, quickly emerged as an evangelist and the dominant voice. The revival developed some distinctive characteristics, as participants experienced the baptism of the Holy Spirit as a personal empowerment and the gifts of the spirit (prophecy, healing, and the rest) began to appear, though there was no emphasis on speaking in tongues, as in the Pentecostal movement then beginning in the United States.

Pentecostalism was brought to England in 1907 by Anglican priest Alexander A. Boddy (1854–1930), who out of his experience of working in the Welsh revival traveled to Norway and there received the baptism of the Holy Spirit with the accompanying evidence of speaking in tongues. Pentecostalism had been brought to Norway by Thomas B. Barrett (1862–1940), who had himself been in Los Angeles at the services conducted at the Pioneer Pentecostal meetings at the Azusa Street Mission that began in 1906. As the Pentecostal experience spread across Great Britain, independent congregations were formed, and in 1908, the Apostolic Faith Church (named after the work in Los Angeles) was founded in Bournemouth. Among the members of that church were Daniel Powell Williams (1882–1947) and his brother William Jones Williams (1891–1945), both formerly associated with the Welsh revival.

In the second decade of the century, the Apostolic Faith Church (indeed the Pentecostal movement as a whole in Great Britain) experienced a controversy over the gift of prophecy, as a number of people had emerged who spoke inspired prophetic words to the believers. Some accepted the words only as words to inspire the congregation. Others looked to them for guiding and leading the church. Among those congregations that favored the use of prophecy for guidance and leadership was the Penygroes Church in Wales. This church created the office of prophet and called William J. Williams to hold it. His brother was named to the office of apostle. The issue of prophets and apostles came to a head in 1916. The leaders of the Apostolic Faith Church rejected the use of apostles and prophets as leaders, and so, in 1916, many of the congregations that favored this style of leadership withdrew from the church. They were joined by the Burning Bush Assembly in Glasgow, Scotland, in 1922, by which time the initial structure of the Apostolic Church was in place. Other congregations soon aligned themselves with the new church.

The Apostolic Church is similar to other Pentecostal bodies, with the exception of being led by an apostle and a prophet. The church does believe in tithing, which is considered obligatory. In 1922, in response to prophetic guidance, a missionary program was begun, the first missionaries being sent to Argentina. Work subsequently expanded to the United States (1923), Canada (1927), and China (1924). A parallel movement was organized in Denmark in 1924, soon followed by France and Italy, and in the 1930s, Australia and New Zealand. Decade by decade new mission fields have been opened. During the 1990s, work began in Mozambique, Botswana, Indonesia, Singapore, Angola, Chile, Tanzania, and Myanmar.

During the 20th century, much of the mission work of the Apostolic Church outside the United Kingdom evolved into independent national churches, now tied together in a triennial Apostolic World Conference. Autonomous Apostolic churches now exist in Australia, Cameroon, Canada, Denmark, France, Germany, Ghana, Hungary, Italy, Jamaica, New Zealand, Nigeria, Papua New Guinea, Portugal, Switzerland, the United States, Vanuatu, and Nigeria (the largest work). A global membership in excess of four million was reported in 2008.

The primary educational institution of the church is the Apostolic Church School of Ministry (founded in 1933), located at Penygroes, South Wales, the oldest Pentecostal college in Great Britain. In 2008, the church reported 110 congregations in Great Britain. It is active in the Evangelical Alliance UK through which it is related to the World Evangelical Alliance.

PO Box 389
24-27 St. Helens Rd.
Swansea SA1 1ZH
United Kingdom

Apostolic World Conference
c/o The Secretary
216 Beales Lane
Greensborough 3088
Victoria
Australia

J. Gordon Melton

See also: Pentecostalism; World Evangelical Alliance.

References

Hollenweger, Walter J. *Pentecostalism: Origins and Developments Worldwide.* Peabody, UK: Hendrickson, 1997.

Introducing the Apostolic Church: A Manual of Belief, Practice and History. Penygroes, South Wales: Apostolic Church General Council, 1988.

Worsfold, James E. *A History of the Charismatic Movements in New Zealand.* Wellington, NZ: Julian Literature Trust, 1974.

Worsfold, James E. *The Origins of the Apostolic Church in Great Britain.* Wellington, NZ: Julian Literature Trust, 1991.

Apostolic Church of Faith in Jesus Christ of Mexico

The Apostolic Church in Mexico is a sister denomination to the Apostolic Assembly of Faith in Jesus Christ in the U.S.A., and both trace their origins to the early days of the Azusa Street Pentecostal Revival in Los Angeles, California, that began in 1906. Due to a lack of denominational structures prior to the early 1930s, many of the early leaders of Oneness ("Jesus Only") Hispanic Pentecostal churches obtained their ministerial credentials from the Pentecostal Assemblies of the World (PAW), which was organized in Los Angeles in 1906 as an interracial body. Both the Apostolic Church and the Apostolic Assembly, early in their development, adopted an episcopal structure of church government.

In the period 1900 and 1930, hundreds of thousands of people from northern Mexico traveled to the United States to escape the turmoil of the Mexican Revolution (1910–1920) and to find employment, usually in the border states of California, Arizona, New Mexico, and Texas. Many of the migrants traveled north via the Mexican national railroad system that connected to U.S. railroads at Laredo and El Paso, Texas, or at Nogales, Arizona, with connections to major cities in the Southwest, including those in California.

Numerous Mexicans who traveled to Los Angeles came into contact with the early Pentecostal movement and were converted to the Apostolic Faith; eventually they carried the Oneness doctrine back to their homes in Mexico. Between 1914 and 1932, at least 26 Apostolic churches were founded in 12 of Mexico's northern states by migrants who evangelized their hometowns in the border states and then carried the Pentecostal message farther south to Nuevo León, Zacatecas, San Luis Potosí, Tamaulipas, and Veracruz. The first known Apostolic Faith church in Mexico was established in 1914 in Villa Aldama, Chihuahua, by Mrs. Romana de Valenzuela, who traveled to Los Angeles in 1912 as a Congregationalist and returned to her hometown in 1914 as a fervent Oneness Pentecostal.

Many of the early Apostolics in Mexico had close ties to the Apostolic Faith movement in California, which spread among the growing Spanish-speaking population between San Francisco and San Diego during the period 1910–1930. According to Apostolic church historian Manuel J. Gaxiola, the Mexican Apostolic believers in Los Angeles accepted the "Jesus Only" doctrine that they should be baptized (or rebaptized) only in the Name of Jesus, and that "this is the true baptism that saves." This baptismal practice dates to 1909 in Los Angeles, which is four years prior to the controversy that erupted over the "Jesus Only" versus Trinitarian baptismal formula that sharply divided Pentecostals at the Arroyo Seco Camp Meeting in 1913, held near Pasadena, California. In other matters the Hispanic Apostolics had beliefs and practices similar to those of the Pentecostal Holiness denominations in the period 1900–1930.

In the 1930s there were three geographical groupings of Apostolic Faith churches in northern Mexico that were formed by migrants who propagated the Pentecostal message among their families, friends, and neighbors. The first convention of the Church of the Apostolic Faith (present name adopted in 1944) was held in the city of Torreón, Mexico, in August 1932, when 11 pastors from Torreón (Coahuila), Monterrey (Nuevo León), and Nuevo Laredo (Tamaulipas) met to officially organize themselves as a denomination. They elected Felipe Rivas Hernández (1901–1983) as their first "pastor general" (bishop), and he continued to lead the Apostolic Faith movement in Mexico until 1966, when he retired as presiding bishop.

In 1933 Apostolic Faith pastors in the state of Sinaloa, located on the eastern side of the Gulf of California, held their first convention in the town of Flor de Canela. From the founding of the first Apostolic church in Sinaloa in 1925, the Apostolic leaders had maintained a fraternal relationship with the Apostolic Assembly in California, but in 1936 the Sinoloa Apostolics became officially affiliated with the Apostolic association in Torreón.

During the 1920s, Antonio Castañeda Nava (d. 2001) and other Apostolic pastors evangelized and planted churches in the state of Baja California, which were affiliated with the Apostolic Assembly in California until 1937, when they were transferred to the supervision of the Apostolic Church in Mexico under Bishop Rivas Hernández.

During 1928, Nava laid aside his responsibilities in California as pastor general of the Apostolic Assembly and traveled to his hometown of Nazas, Durango, both to see his relatives and to visit the growing number of Apostolic churches in northern Mexico. Navas spent time with Rivas Hernández and his family in Torreón and then traveled with him to preach and teach the Apostolic message among the churches supervised by Rivas, which were located in eight Mexican states. These activities strengthened the status and authority of Rivas in the eyes of other Apostolic leaders and their members throughout northern Mexico. Also, Rivas printed ministerial credentials in the name of the Apostolic Assembly of Faith in Jesus Christ with his headquarters address in Torreón, rather than the U.S. address.

As the authority of Rivas increased, some of his rivals either distanced themselves even farther from his leadership or decided to submit to his authority and work together for the good of the Apostolic ministry in Mexico. In 1931, Rivas became the "official representative" in north-central Mexico of the Apostolic Assembly of California, according to a document signed by Antonio Nava and Bernardo Hernández, pastor general and secretary general, respectively, of the Apostolic Assembly.

However, some of the members of the early Apostolic Faith movement were drawn away by the prophetic witness of two charismatic leaders, known as Saul and Silas, whose real names were Antonio Muñoz and Francisco Flores, respectively, who appeared in northern Mexico in 1924. The bearded and unwashed prophets, with similarities to the biblical John the Baptist, preached a message of repentance and faith, which required people to denounce their old religion and material possessions, and to be rebaptized in the Name of Jesus. Their authority was derived from "special divine revelation" through their own prophecies, dreams, and visions, rather than from the Bible, which was a relatively unknown and unread book in those days in northern Mexico, according to Gaxiola.

The Saul and Silas movement produced a great deal of confusion and dissention within the Apostolic churches during the decade 1925–1935, which caused some Apostolic pastors and church members—including entire congregations—to leave the Apostolic Faith movement.

Such was the case of Felipe Rivas Hernández's (1901–1983) home church in Torreón, Coahuila, where Saul and Silas caused much conflict among Apostolics in 1924–1925. The result was that some Apostolic leaders and church members decided to form another organization in December 1927, known as Consejo Mexicano de la Fe Apostólica (Mexican Council of the Apostolic Faith) under the leadership of Francisco Borrego as pastor general. This group later became affiliated with the Iglesia Evangélica Cristiana Espiritual (Spiritual Christian Evangelical Church) with headquarters in Tampico, Tamaulipas, founded by Joseph Stewart in mid-1926.

As a denomination, the Apostolic Church grew slowly over a large geographical area of northern Mexico during the period 1930–1960. At the general convention in 1940, only 2,113 Apostolics were reported in the whole country, but by 1954 the denomination listed 8,313 members; and in 1960 there were 12,106 members, according to Gaxiola.

During the 1930s, Rivas's influence and authority increased among Apostolics in northern Mexico and was extended to the Pacific states of Sinoloa, Nanyarit, and Jalisco. At the convention in 1934, the Apostolic churches in Mexico began to feel part of a national movement that was separate from the Apostolic Assembly in California but that maintained fraternal ties to the latter as the source of the Mexican Apostolic movement.

Between 1933 and 1937, at least 24 new Apostolic churches were organized in Mexico, almost as many as in the previous period, 1914–1932. During the period 1937–1946, another 96 churches were formed at the national level, which indicates a time of significant growth as an organization.

Apparently, many of the leaders of the Apostolic movement were members of the growing middle class of small businessmen, artisans, shopkeepers, and independent *campesinos* (small landowners rather than landless peasants), who were somewhat independent of the large landowners and the governing class. There was a certain amount of upward social mobility among the leadership ranks of the Apostolic Church based on merit and faithfulness as unpaid church workers. Leadership training was accomplished by pastors who selected and supervised natural leaders, who proved their worth by serving as deacons, evangelists, and assistant pastors in existing churches and by helping to establish new congregations in nearby areas.

In the convention of 1935, Rivas Hernández was recognized (not elected) as pastor general, José Ortega Aguilar (1908–2004) was elected secretary general, and Manuel Tapia was elected treasurer general. In the conventions of 1940 and 1941, the first two posts remained the same and Aurelio Rodríguez was named treasurer general, Maclovio Gaxiola López (1914–1971) was appointed bishop of the Pacific Coast, Felipe S. Coronado became bishop of Chihuahua, and Guadalupe García Enciso became bishop of Durango. In 1942, three pastors were appointed as district supervisors: José Ortega for Coahuila, Nuevo León, Tamaulipas, and northern Veracruz; Donaciano Gaxiloa López for Sinaloa; and Reyes Ruelas for Sonora.

However, it was not until 1945 that the Apostolic Church in Mexico approved its first constitution, which was almost identical to the one adopted by the Apostolic Assembly in California during 1944–1945. The two editorial committees worked together on producing the various drafts and the final copies of the two constitutions, but with slightly different names for the two sister organizations. Mainly, the constitution, which took effect in 1946, formalized and unified an organizational structure that had developed in the two countries since about 1914, while upgrading the requirements and obligations for different church officers at the local, regional, and national levels. It also defined procedures for electing and removing people from office at different levels of leadership, and it sought to prevent the formation of dynasties of church government at the higher levels.

Other important developments occurred during the 1940s and 1950s. The denominational magazine *The Expositor* began to be published in 1943, and two years later the first Sunday school lessons were published on a regular basis. In 1946, the Apostolic Theological Institute was established in Mexico City. In 1948, the Apostolic Church began to send out its first missionaries to Central America: Maclovio Gaxiola to Nicaragua in 1948, Leonardo Sepúlveda Treviño to El Salvador in 1951, and J. Guadalupe Ramírez to Guatemala in 1952. Later, missionaries were sent to Argentina, Colombia, Venezuela, Cuba, and Spain. Maclovio Gaxiola returned to Mexico in the early 1950s and served as supervisor of the Central District, president of the Apostolic Church from 1958 to 1962, treasurer general and bishop of Baja California from 1962 to 1966, and president again from 1966 to 1970.

At the national level, when Maclovio Gaxiola stepped down as presiding bishop of the denomination in 1970, the Apostolic Church reported 459 organized churches and 505 preaching points (*campos blancos*) with 15,244 baptized members and a total church community of about 40,000; also, there were 13 bishops, 446 pastors, 115 assistant pastors, 367 ordained deacons, and 33 evangelists.

The new president of the Apostolic Church for the term 1970–1974 was Maclovio's nephew, Manuel J. Gaxiola, age 43, a graduate of the School of World Mission (Master of Arts in Missiology, 1970) at Fuller Theological Seminary in Pasadena, California, and a representative of the newer generation of trained professionals. Manuel Gaxiola was an innovator who brought many changes to the denomination's operational structure, including a new emphasis on church growth and on improved fraternal relationships with the Apostolic Assembly in Los Angeles, California, and the United Pentecostal Church International in Hazelwood, Missouri. In the convention of 1974, the following statistics were reported: 471 organized churches and 1,131 ministers in 13 districts; although 2 districts did not report their membership, there were a total of 17,161 members in the other 11 districts, or about 19,000 members nationally.

Isidro Pérez Ramírez, a pastor in Tepic, Nayarit, was elected president of the Apostolic Church in 1974 for a term of four years. Manuel J. Gaxiola was chosen to be director of the department of Christian education for this same term, but in 1978 Gaxiola was again elected as presiding bishop (1978–1981). In 1982,

Manuel Rodríguez Castorena was elected as presiding bishop (1982–1986), after having served for eight years as secretary general of the national board of directors.

At that time Manuel J. Gaxiola received a scholarship to continue his education in England, where he received a Ph.D. in theology from the University of Birmingham; he returned to Mexico and, later, served on the board of directors of the Society of Pentecostal Studies (he held several positions, including at least one term as president of that body), and wrote an updated version of *La Serpiente y la Paloma*, a history of the Apostolic Church in Mexico (1994). Gaxiola also served for many years on the board of directors of the Mexican Bible Society, an interdenominational organization involved in Bible translation and distribution. Despite the historical tensions between the Oneness and Trinitarian branches of the Pentecostal movement, and between these two traditions and non-Pentecostals in general, Manuel J. Gaxiola has been one of the bridge-builders of fraternal relationships among Protestants in Mexico and elsewhere, and in so doing helped his denomination achieve a higher level of respect and acceptance in a generally hostile religious environment.

In 1986, Abel Zamora Velázquez was elected as presiding bishop for the term 1986–1990, but he died of cancer in 1987 and was replaced by Miguel Austín Reyes, the former bishop of Chihuahua and secretary of missions and evangelism. From 1958 to 1986 the national offices of the Apostolic Church were in Mexico City, but when Zamora became presiding bishop the offices were moved to Guadalajara, Jalisco. The first headquarters of the Apostolic Faith movement in Mexico were in the city of Torreón, Coahuila, from 1932 to 1958.

Domingo Torres Alvarado served as presiding bishop from 1990 to 1994. Torres was an experienced leader, having served as pastor of several congregations (including two in Mexico City), director of the national literature department, professor in the Apostolic Theological Seminary, secretary of social assistance, secretary of evangelism, and bishop of the District of Tamaulipas. He is also a graduate of the Hispanic Ministries Department at Fuller Theological Seminary in Pasadena, California, where he received the master of arts degree during the early 1980s.

The Reverend Nicolás Herrera Ríos was the presiding bishop for the period 2004–2008, followed by the presidency of the Reverend Félix Gaxiola Inzunza (b. 1954). Gaxiola Inzunza was elected general treasurer in 2004 and assumed his current position in 2008.

In the Apostolic Church, each district is defined geographically, taking into account the number of existing churches, the facility of supervision and communication, the number of members and ministers in the churches, available resources, and the growth possibilities in the communities of the jurisdiction. Each district is supervised and administered by a district board of directors, which has a bishop supervisor, secretary, and treasurer.

Currently, the denomination is organized into 34 districts in Mexico and 6 districts among Hispanics in the United States, in addition to missionary districts in Central and South America and in Europe: http://www.iafcj.org/index.php?uri=distritos. Today, the Apostolic Church of Faith in Jesus Christ is one of the 10 largest Protestant denominations in Mexico.

Currently (2009) it reports 1,394 churches and 151,123 members in Mexico with 201 churches and 6,917 members in the United States.

Avenida Ávila Camacho No. 2336
Col. Jardines del Country
Guadalajara, Jalisco
México CP 44210
http://www.iafcj.org/
http://www.asambleaapostolicamexico.com/
Clifton L. Holland

See also: Apostolic Assembly of Faith in Jesus Christ, U.S.A.; Apostolic Faith; Pentecostal Assemblies of the World; Pentecostalism; United Pentecostal Church International.

References

Burgess, Stanley M., and Gary B. McGee, eds. *Dictionary of Pentecostal and Charismatic Movements.* Grand Rapids, MI: Regency Reference Library/Zondervan Publishing House, 1988.

Castillo de La Torre, J. Pablo. "Historia de la Iglesia Evangélica Cristiana Espiritual." http://members.fortunecity.es/castillojp/iece_historia.html.

Gaxiola, Manuel J. *La Serpiente y la Paloma: Historia, Teología y Análisis de la Iglesia Apostólica de la Fe en Cristo Jesús de México (1914– 1994).* 2nd ed. Nacaulpan, Mexico: Libros Pyros, 1994.

Gaxiola, Manuel J. "Latin American Pentecostalism: A Mosaic within a Mosaic," *Pneuma* 13, no. 1 (1991): 107–129.

Gaxiola, Manuel J. *Mexican Protestantism: The Struggle for Identity and Relevance in a Pluralistic Society.* Ph.D. diss., University of Birmingham, England, 1989.

Gaxiola, Manuel J. "The Unresolved Issue: A Third-World Perspective on the Oneness Question." Paper presented at the 17th Annual Meeting of the Society for Pentecostal Studies, November 13, 1987, Virginia Beach, VA.

Holland, Clifton L. *The Religious Dimension in Hispanic Los Angeles: A Protestant Case Study.* South Pasadena, CA: William Carey Press, 1974.

Ortega, José A., ed. *Historia de la Asamblea Apostólica de la Fe en Cristo Jesus, 1916–1966.* Mentone, CA: Editorial Committee of the Asamblea Apostólica, 1966.

Apostolic Faith

The Apostolic Faith is a relatively small denomination, most notable as the original Pentecostal church that gave birth to the international Pentecost movement. It grew out of the ministry of Charles Fox Parham (1873–1929). Parham was a minister in the Methodist Episcopal Church (now an integral part of the United Methodist Church) who left the Methodists in 1898 and founded a home for divine healing in Topeka, Kansas. In 1900 he opened the Bethel Bible College. Planning to be away over the end-of-the-year holidays, he asked his students to search the Bible while he was gone concerning the baptism of the Holy Spirit. When he returned, as New Year's Eve approached the students reported that the baptism was accompanied with a sign, speaking in tongues. Retiring to the chapel, Parham and the students began to pray for God to baptize them with the Holy Spirit, and Agnes Ozman became the first to experience the baptism and speak in tongues.

Charles Fox Parham (1873–1929), the American preacher who founded modern Pentecostalism. (Mrs. Charles F. Parham. *The Life of Charles F. Parham, Founder of the Apostolic Faith Movement,* 1930)

Over the next years, Parham and his students began to spread the word of the baptism through the American states of Kansas, Missouri, Oklahoma, and Texas.

In 1905, Parham opened a Bible school in Texas. In spite of the racial segregation then the norm in the American South, he allowed an African American preacher, William J. Seymour, to attend the class. The next year, Seymour left for Los Angeles, California, where he became the leader of a small mission that then became the center of a three-year revival during which Pentecostalism spread rapidly across the United States and around the world.

Parham became alienated from the revival, and the revival soon left him behind. He continued to preach in the Midwestern and Eastern United States, though his work was tainted when accusations of immoral behavior were brought against him. In fact, Parham was arrested for sodomy, though no charges appear to have been filed, and it seems that Parham was framed by Wilbur Voliva, the head of the non-Pentecostal Christian Catholic Church. Some colleagues who disliked Parham seized on the opportunity to discredit him.

Those who had responded to his ministry, however, eventually founded the fellowship now known as the Apostolic Faith. In 1950 a Bible school was opened in Baxter Springs, Kansas, and the Apostolic Faith still has its headquarters in Baxter Springs. Its work is confined to the United States. There are an estimated 10,000 adherents.

Apostolic Faith
1009 Lincoln Ave.
Baxter Springs, KS 66713

J. Gordon Melton

See also: Pentecostalism; Seymour, William J.; United Methodist Church.

References

Goff, James R., Jr. *Fields White unto Harvest: Charles F. Parham and the Missionary Origins of Pentecostalism.* Fayetteville: University of Arkansas Press, 1988.

Parham, Charles F. *A Voice of One Crying in the Wilderness.* Baxter Springs, KS: Apostolic Faith Bible College, 1910.

Parham, Sarah E. *The Life of Charles Fox Parham.* Joplin, MO: Hunter Printing Company, 1930.

Apostolic Faith Mission

The Apostolic Faith Mission headquartered in Portland, Oregon, began with the attraction of Florence L. Crawford (1872–1936) to the Pentecostal revival at the Apostolic Faith Mission on Azusa Street in Los Angeles, California, that began in 1906. This original Mission was headed by William J. Seymour (1870–1922), who brought the Pentecostal experience (which included speaking in tongues) from Houston, where he had attended a Bible school headed by Charles Fox Parham (1873–1929). Once the revival began, it continued daily for three years. Crawford testified to a healing of her eyes during these meetings and soon became an assistant to Seymour.

The revival attracted people to California from across North America and around the world. Crawford worked on the *Apostolic Faith*, the tabloid periodical that started to make people aware of what was happening as the message spread. She also began to travel along the West Coast as an itinerant home missionary. As early as December 1906, she made a trip to Portland.

In 1908, having been invited to return to Portland, Crawford left the Los Angeles Mission and relocated permanently to Oregon. With the blessing of Seymour, she brought the Apostolic Faith with her, the work in Portland being seen as an outpost of the original Mission. However, over the next few years, the Portland work became independent of Seymour. It continued the missionary thrust that had become integral to the Pentecostal movement and over the next generation became a global organization. In 1922, the headquarters of the church was established in a new building in downtown Portland, which became known for the large neon sign, "Jesus the Light of the World."

The Apostolic Faith is a Trinitarian Holiness Pentecostal church that stresses the need of a born-again experience of faith, followed by sanctification and the baptism of the Holy Spirit.

Affiliated churches are found in 32 different countries. The majority of its 60,000 members are now outside North America. In 2008, the church reported 54 congregations and approximately 4,500 members in the United States. The largest membership is in Nigeria (20,000 members in more than 600 congregations).

Apostolic Faith Mission
6615 SE 52nd Ave.
Portland, OR 97206
www.apostolicfaith.org

J. Gordon Melton

See also: Parham, Charles Fox; Pentecostalism; Seymour, William J.

References

A Historical Account of the Apostolic Faith. Portland, OR: Apostolic Faith Publishing House, 1965.

The Light of Life Brought Triumph. Portland, OR: Apostolic Faith Publishing House, 1955.

Saved to Serve. Portland, OR: Apostolic Faith Publishing House, 1967.

Apostolic Faith Mission of South Africa

The Apostolic Faith Mission of South Africa is a classical Pentecostal denomination established in 1908 in Johannesburg, South Africa, during the missionary visit of Americans John G. Lake (1870–1935) and Thomas Hezmalhalch, who had arrived from the Azusa Street revival in Los Angeles. The first South African president (1913–1931) was P. L. Le Roux, a graduate of Andrew Murray's Bible school in Wellington, Cape Province. Le Roux had been a missionary among the Zulus for John Alexander Dowie's (1847–1907) Zionist movement, and brought many Zionist churches with him into the AFM. The AFM still practices baptism by threefold immersion, a legacy of Zionism.

In 1919 a large group of Africans left the church as a result of racial disputes. This group became the originators of the Zion Christian Church, the largest African Initiated Church in South Africa. In 1928 a small group left the church as a result of a liturgical dispute, taking the name Latter Rain Church. They were led by a "prophetess," Mrs. Fraser. In 1958 the Pentecostal Protestant Church left the AFM for similar reasons.

Members of an Apostolic Church on the banks of the Emmarentia Dam pray with a minister, in the water, as they prepare for a baptism ceremony in celebration of Easter Sunday, in Johannesburg, South Africa, April 16, 2006. (AP/Wide World Photos)

The AFM is strongly committed to missionary endeavor, and large daughter churches have arisen among the African, Asian, and Coloured (mixed race) populations. Most Asian converts are from Hinduism, most African converts are from tribal religions. In 1996 the previously separated race groups in the South African AFM united formally, bringing together the daughter churches and the white section in a single denominational structure.

As a result of missionary activity from South Africa, autonomous AFM churches exist in most southern and east African countries, as well as in parts of Latin America and South Asia—currently more than 30 countries. They relate under a loose fellowship called AFM International. Major emphases in all areas are evangelization, divine healing, and "separation from the world." Membership currently exceeds 1 million in South Africa, while figures for the rest of Africa are uncertain. The AFM in Africa is a truly indigenous African church, since most of its membership has deep roots in Africa, including the white South Africans, of whom the vast majority are Afrikaners (descendents of Dutch settlers in the 17th century). However, doctrinally and liturgically the church is clearly in the mainstream of Pentecostalism.

The church is organized in each nation on a democratic presbyterian system, with a "call" system operating for pastors (that is, congregations call their pastors rather than accepting a pastor sent by the presbytery). Theological training is at degree level in South Africa and Zimbabwe, but very basic in most other countries. Church headquarters are at Maranatha Park, Lyndhurst, Johannesburg, South Africa.

Mathew Clark

See also: African Initiated (Independent) Churches; Pentecostalism; Zion Christian Church (South Africa, Zimbabwe).

References

Anderson, Allan H. *Bazalwane: African Pentecostals in South Africa*. Pretoria: Unisa, 1992.

Anderson, Allan H. *Tumelo: The Faith of African Pentecostals in South Africa*. Pretoria: Unisa, 1993.

Burger, I. vd M. *Geloofsgeskiedenis van die Apostoliese Geloof Sending van Suid Afrika 1908–1958*. Johannesburg: Evangelie Uitgewers, 1990.

De Wet, C. R. *The Apostolic Faith Mission in Africa: 1908–1980. A Case Study in Church Growth in a Segregated Society*. Ph.D. degree, University of Cape Town, 1989.

LaPoorta, J. J. *Unity or Division? The Unity Struggles of the Black Churches within the Apostolic Faith Mission of South Africa*. Kuils River: Japie LaPoorta, 1996.

Apostolic Sabbath Church of God

At the same time that Johane Marange established his African Apostolic Church of Johane Marange, another enigmatic Shona prophet, Johane (John) Masowe (wilderness, or open place), formerly known by the name Shoniwa (ca. 1915–1973), started the Apostolic Sabbath Church of God, known in Shona as *Vahosanna*, after the frequent calling out of the word by members in church gatherings. He had been a preacher in the Apostolic Faith Mission, a South African Pentecostal church, in 1930, but separated himself from this church soon afterward. He fell sick and dreamed that he had died and risen again as the "Messenger of God," a John the Baptist figure like Marange. He was convinced that he had been sent from heaven to preach to African people. He began to preach that people must leave witchcraft and adultery, destroy all religious books (including the Bible, an injunction that was later lifted), and shun all inventions of the whites. His followers should not carry identification documents, plow their lands, or work for the whites. The biblical prophets would descend from heaven and drive the whites out of the country. He was restricted to his home district and imprisoned for failing to obey the restriction order.

His followers organized themselves into a closed religious community that moved from Zimbabwe in the early 1940s to South Africa, eventually settling in Port Elizabeth in 1947. There they lived in a deprived community of about 1,000 in the slum area of Korsten. The community engaged in various crafts and industries, including basket making, and they were known as the Korsten Basket-Makers. When their company went into liquidation, they began to use the name African Gospel Church, the name of an African Pentecostal church in South Africa. They were declared illegal residents in South Africa under the draconian laws regarding residence, and 1,880 people were repatriated in 1962 to Zimbabwe. Masowe told his people that they were Jews who must return to Israel, and in 1963, some of the Vahosanna began a migration from Zimbabwe, reaching Lusaka in Zambia. Masowe continued to travel and make converts throughout Zambia and soon afterward in Kenya, Tanzania, Mozambique, and the Congo. Only Masowe himself could perform baptisms, but his illness in 1964 left him a recluse in Tanzania for the rest of his life.

In 1972 the name of the church was again changed to Gospel of God Church. Increasing importance was given to a group of nuns, the "wives" of Masowe, also called the Sisters, who would be part of the headquarters, remain celibate, function as ritual singers, and move with the people of God as a guarantee of God's presence and power among them. They constituted the "ark of the covenant" and the "new Jerusalem." By 1975 there were more than 100 Sisters; most were in Lusaka, but some moved to Nairobi. In 1973, Masowe died in Zambia after a long illness, during which he was still planning the next stage of the journey to Kenya, and he was buried at his home in Zimbabwe. Many of the Masowe Apostles and the Sisters have been in Nairobi since 1972, where their somewhat secretive and isolationist lifestyle has brought them into conflict with local authorities. There were claims of half a million Masowe Apostles in 1975, scattered from South Africa to Kenya, but the main body of the church remained in Nairobi in 2009.

Allan H. Anderson

See also: African Apostolic Church of Johane Marange; African Initiated (Independent) Churches; Apostolic Faith Mission.

References

Dillon-Malone, Clive M. *The Korsten Basketmakers: A Study of the Masowe Apostles, an Indigenous African Religious Movement.* Manchester, UK: Manchester University Press, 1978.
Kileff, Clive, and Margaret Kileff. "The Masowe Vapostori of Seki: Utopianism and Tradition in an African Church." In *The New Religions of Africa*, edited by Benetta Jules-Rosette. Norwood, NJ: Ablex, 1979.

Apostolic World Christian Fellowship

Apostolic World Christian Fellowship is a global association that provides fellowship for non-trinitarian (Apostolic or "Jesus Only") churches within the larger world of Pentecostalism. The idea of the fellowship was suggested by Bishop W. G. Rowe in 1970 as a remedy for what he saw as strife and disunity among Apostolic Pentecostal denominations. He served as the organization's first chairman and retired in 1991 after two decades of service. He was succeeded by Bishop Samuel L. Smith.

The fellowship has developed a fourfold program that emphasizes unity in spite of personal and organizational differences, the sharing of successful outreach programs to assist churches in their evangelistic work, activating the laity, and world missions. The fellowship has moved to heal the racial divisions that began to divide Apostolics in the 1920s.

In 2008 more than 180 denominations and organizations were affiliated with the fellowship and worship and outreach efforts are supported in most of the world's countries. Member churches include the Church of the Lord Jesus Christ of the Apostolic Faith, the Pentecostal Assemblies of the World, the True Jesus Church, and the United Pentecostal Church International.

AWCF Headquarters
11 West Iowa Street
Evansville, IN 47711
www.awcf.org

J. Gordon Melton

See also: Church of the Lord Jesus Christ of the Apostolic Faith; Pentecostal Assemblies of the World; Pentecostalism; True Jesus Church; United Pentecostal Church International.

Reference

Apostolic World Christian Fellowship. http://www.awcf.org/. Accessed January 19, 2008.

Ararat, Mount

The 16,946-foot-high Mount Ararat is the higher peak of the Armenian Highland located in easternmost

Snow-covered Mount Ararat towers behind an Orthodox church in Armenia. According to biblical tradition, Noah's Ark came to rest upon Mount Ararat after the flood. (iStockPhoto.com)

Turkey, a mere 10 miles from the Iranian border to the east and 20 miles south of Armenia. It originally took on religious significance as the home of the gods of the pre-Christian Armenian Pagan pantheon. For Jews and later for Christians, however, Ararat became important in the story of the biblical flood. At its conclusion, Noah's ark is said to have landed on the "mountains of Ararat" (Genesis 8:4). That landing place would eventually be identified as the present Mount Ararat. Over the centuries, the Turks began to refer to it as the painful mountain, due to the difficulties reported attempting to climb it. It was not conquered until 1829.

Ararat gained renewed significance in the 20th century as modern critical scholarship of the Bible called the account of Noah into question. Many schol-

ars came to doubt the story of Noah on a variety of rationales, most revolving around the lack of evidence independent of the biblical accounts (be it historical, biological, or geological) that such a flood had occurred. Even the biblical accounts are suspect, as the two retellings of the flood story contradict each other on a variety of key points.

In this context, some began to look to Mount Ararat to supply such evidence. If the flood had actually occurred, possibly remnants of the ark would remain and be preserved in the ice above the tree line on the mountain's slope. That possibility was suggested in the mid-20th century by several people willing to launch expeditions to the top of Ararat. The location of the mountain, however, presented a set of obstacles. Prior to the fall of the Soviet Union, for example, Armenia was a Soviet state. Expeditions to Ararat have tended to bring international sensitivities to the surface whenever outsiders worked on the mountain.

Then in 1955, Frenchman Fernand Navarra announced the discovery of a piece of wood showing human workmanship that had been located some 13,750 feet up the side of the mountain. He returned from his expedition with a small piece of the wood. Fourteen years later, he and others found additional pieces of old wood at two different Ararat sites. He now had enough evidence to write a book, *Noah's Ark: I Touched It*, which sold briskly and was translated into a number of languages. Unfortunately, Navarra's case quickly dissolved when his wood proved to be of recent origin. Some suggested a hoax, going so far as to accuse Navarra of planting the wood on an earlier expedition, then retrieving samples in 1955 and 1969.

While the Navarra case was being resolved, in 1959 a Turkish pilot engaged in a mapping project photographed a "ship-shaped" object, not on Ararat, but on another mountain some miles from Ararat. *Life* magazine published the pictures in 1960, and speculation began to fly as to what the picture actually showed. The picture led immediately to the founding of the Archaeological Research Foundation (ARF), which mounted an expedition for the summer of 1960. The expedition found the object to be a natural formation. No human-made artifacts were found at the site.

While most felt that the site was a dead end, Ron Wyatt, a Seventh-day Adventist from Madison, Tennessee, objected. Though he was unable to visit Turkey until 1977, he kept the possibility that the site was related to the ark alive and put his arguments to paper in a booklet called *Noah's Ark Found*. He claimed to have discovered a number of items, including some stone sea anchors, petrified timbers from the ark (actually retrieved from an Armenian graveyard), the house that Noah built complete with stones with inscriptions describing the flood, and, most important, Noah's grave.

Wyatt used his personal charm to bring *Apollo XV* astronaut Colonel Jim Irwin (b. 1930); Dr. John Morris (b. 1946), head of the Institute for Creation Research, in San Diego; and Marvin Steffins, president of International Expeditions, to his cause. Wyatt founded Wyatt Archaeological Research with a goal of locating a variety of lost biblical sites—Sodom and Gomorrah (two cities destroyed by God for their wickedness), the spot where the Israelites crossed the Red Sea out of Egypt, and the burial place of the lost ark of the covenant below the spot where Jesus was crucified. Details on Wyatt's ongoing claims may be found on the Internet site of Wyatt Archaeological Research. Relative to Noah's ark, he failed to produce results through the 1990s, and subsequently lost the support of most of the people, especially the scholars, who had initially given early, if tentative support. Today few take Wyatt's claims seriously.

In the wake of the falsification of each claim to evidence of Noah's ark, the support of the cause has decreased, though different efforts to locate the ark have continued to the present at Mount Ararat and other nearby locations. None have produced any noteworthy results to date (2009). The record of failures has created a situation such that any discovery of anything claimed to verify the biblical story of Noah and the flood would have to pass a battery of tests verifying its ancient status, while any advocate for such a claim would be under suspicion of fraud.

Mount Ararat is one of the subjects also discussed in the Koran, as Muslims accept Noah as one of the prophets preceding Muhammad. The Koran says that Noah's ark landed in the heights, and some Muslim scholars identify the spot as Mount Judi, another mountain in the Ararat region some 200 miles south of Mount Ararat. It turns out to be the mountain upon which the ship-shaped object was photographed in 1959.

The story of the flood and Noah's ark is one of the most popular of biblical stories and the subject of numerous children's books. As contemporary Christians reach adulthood, it is one of the stories most likely to undercut faith in the authority of the Bible, from a literal perspective. The failure of the search for Noah's ark by conservative Protestant and Free church Christians in the 20th century has been viewed as a step backward in their attempt to defend the inerrancy of the biblical text.

J. Gordon Melton

See also: Creationism; Islam.

References

Amirault. "A Great Christian Scam." http://www .tentmaker.org/Dew/Dew7/D7-AGreatChristian Scam.html. Accessed January 4, 2005.

Bailey, Lloyd R. *Noah: The Person and the Story in History and Tradition*. Columbia: University of South Carolina Press, 1989.

Deal, David Allen. *Noah's Ark: The Evidence*. Muscogee, OK: Artisan, 2005.

Fasold, David. *The Ark of Noah*. New York: Wynwood Press, 1988.

LaHaye, Tim, and John Morris. *The Ark on Ararat*. Nashville: Thomas Nelson Inc. and Creation Life Publishers, 1976.

Navarra, Fernand. *Noah's Ark: I Touched It*. Gainesville, FL: Bridge-Logos Publishers, 1974.

Wyatt Archeological Research. http://www.wyatt museum.com/. Accessed January 4, 2009.

Arcane School

The Arcane School is a Theosophical organization that grew out of the life and experiences of Alice B. Bailey (1880–1949). As a teenager in England, Bailey had been visited by a turbaned stranger, who told her that an important future had been mapped out for her future life. She eventually moved to California and became associated with the Theosophical Society there. She concluded that the stranger who had visited her was Koot Hoomi, one of the Theosophical Masters with whom the Society's founder had claimed to be in contact. She eventually became the editor of the Society's magazine, *The Messenger.* Her husband, Foster Bailey (1888–1977), was the Society's national secretary.

In 1918, Bailey made contact with another Theosophical Master known as Djwhal Khul (D.K.), or the Tibetan. She began to channel material from him that turned into a series of books, the first entitled *Initiation: Human and Solar.* Her channeling eventually led her to separate from the Society and establish the Arcane School in 1923. The Society's leaders had been unhappy with her independent contact with the Masters.

The content of the teachings brought forward by the Tibetan was very much in agreement with Theosophy but also included a vision of a coming New Age and a program by which people could prepare for it. The effort of people in service to the world combined with the power of the Masters, the Spiritual Hierarchy, would bring the reappearance of the Christ. The Arcane School has established meditation groups to channel the energy of the hierarchy to the world. Since the powers from the hierarchy are particularly available at different times of the month and of the year, students of the school gather at the time of the full moon each month, and for three annual festivals—Easter (the celebration of the resurrection of Christ), Wesak (Buddha's birthday), and Goodwill (in June). A program of service has found expression in the New Group of World Servers.

The groups associated with Alice Bailey have been particularly identified with what is termed "The Great Invocation," a prayer that describes the movement of power from the hierarchy to the world as Bailey prescribed. It is frequently repeated in Baileyite gatherings and in various other groups in the Theosophical tradition.

From the point of Light within the Mind of God
Let light stream forth into the minds of men.
Let Light descend on Earth.
From the point of Love within the Heart of God
Let love stream forth into the hearts of men.
May Christ return to Earth.
From the centre where the Will of God is known
Let purpose guide the little wills of men—
The purpose that the Masters know and serve.
From the centre which we call the race of men

Let the Plan of Love and Light work out
And may it seal the door where evil dwells.
Let Light and Love and Power restore the Plan on Earth.

The Arcane School (and the associated Lucis Trust publishing concern) has three major international offices, in London; Geneva, Switzerland; and New York. All three addresses are given below.

In the years after Alice Bailey's death, several of the students in the school left and founded separate parallel organizations, among the more important being Meditation Groups, Inc. (Box 566, Ojai, CA 93023) and the School for Esoteric Studies (58 Oak Terrace, Arden, NC 28708-2820). In the 1980s, one former student of the School, Benjamin Crème, began to announce the imminent appearance of the Christ (identified with the Buddhist Maitreya), from whom he has received a number of messages. He went on to found Share International (Box 41877, 1009 DB Amsterdam, Netherlands) to raise awareness of Maitreya's imminent manifestation and to provide a vehicle of service for those who respond to that message. Share has affiliated groups across North America and Europe as well as Japan, Taiwan, the Philippines, Australia, and New Zealand.

Bailey's teachings had a significant influence on the millennial beliefs that underlay the New Age movement of the 1980s. That movement had looked for the coming of a New Era of peace and wisdom, to be brought about by people channeling the energies of the cosmos into the mundane contemporary world.

Arcane School
Ste. 54, 3 Whitehall Ct.
London
SW1A 2EF
UK

1 rue de Varembe (3e)
Case Postale 31
1211 Geneva 20
Switzerland

120 Wall Street, 24th Fl.
New York, NY 10005
http://www.lucistrust.org

J. Gordon Melton

See also: New Age Movement; Theosophical Society (America).

References

Bailey, Alice. *The Reappearance of the Christ*. New York: Lucis Publishing Company, 1948.

Bailey, Alice. *The Unfinished Autobiography*. New York: Lucis Publishing Company, 1951.

Newburn, Kathy. *A Planetary Awakening: Reflections on the Teachings of the Tibetan in the Works of Alice A Bailey*. Grass Valley, CA: Blue Dolphin Publishing, 2004.

Sinclair, John R. *The Alice Bailey Inheritance*. Wellingsborough, Northamptonshire: Turnstone Press, 1984.

Thirty Years' Works. New York: Lucis Publishing Company, n.d.

Arès Pilgrims

The Arès movement appeared in 1974, following revelations received by a French prophet, Michel Potay (b. 1929). Originally trained as an engineer, then from 1964 a professional occultist, Potay—without giving up his activities in healing and counseling—subsequently converted to Orthodoxy and was ordained a deacon in 1969 in the Église Catholique Orthodoxe de France, an independent Western-rite Orthodox jurisdiction. From 1971, he claimed to be associated with the Living Church, a pro-Communist Russian Orthodox schism launched in the 1920s. In January 1974, Potay and his family settled in Arès, not far from Bordeaux. It was there that Jesus allegedly appeared to him and dictated what became the Gospel Delivered in Arès, first published in 1974.

In 1977, according to Potay, God himself spoke to him from a stick of light. This resulted in a second sacred text, the Book. The two texts form together the Revelation of Arès. Arès Pilgrims see the new revelation as a development within the Abrahamic tradition. They accept the Bible (with the exception of some books) and the Koran, but do not see them as enjoying the same level of authority as the Revelation of Arès. (The Koran is held in high esteem, since it is considered as containing fewer interpolations than the Bible.)

The beliefs of the Arès Pilgrims are monotheistic, but not Trinitarian (Jesus is not considered as God). They aspire to change the world in order to realize the Eden that God originally planned for mankind. If a "remnant" decides to adopt a different behavior, this change can take place; a "small remnant" (that is, the Arès Pilgrims) is called to play a key role in that change, which is not expected in the immediate future, but should take several generations before becoming a reality. It is not uncommon for Arès Pilgrims to engage into grassroots activities with other people involved in various causes in order to contribute to these changes.

The Arès Pilgrims are scattered mainly in France and other French-speaking countries; in addition to a core group of a few hundred people, it can be estimated that 3,000 to 4,000 persons identify more or less with the message. The active ones gather in local groups for missionary activities and various projects, but they have few ritual practices outside of Arès, except for the recitation of the prayer called "Father of the Universe" (a revised version of the Lord's Prayer) four times a day. The pilgrimage to Arès, to the spot where God spoke to Potay, is currently open during three periods of two weeks every summer and offers a major opportunity for gathering. When they enter the House of the Saint's Word, the pilgrims are clothed in white tunics, and they prostrate to the ground, before chanting individually passages from the Bible, the Qu'ran, or the Revelation of Arès, passages that each one chooses. The yearly pilgrimage also offers Potay the opportunity to address the gathered groups of pilgrims.

Arès Pilgrims
c/o Frère Michel Potay
Maison de la Révélation
BP 16, 33740 Arès
France
http://www.freesoulblog.net
http://www.michelpotay.info
http://www.adira.net

Jean-François Mayer

See also: Pilgrimage; Sacred Texts.

References

Mayer, Jean-François. *Michel Potay et la Révélation d'Arès*. Fribourg, Switz.: Les Trois Nornes, 1990.

Mayer, Jean-François. "La 'Révélation d'Arès': naissance d'un pèlerinage dans la France contemporaine." *Social Compass* 48, no. 1 (2001): 63–75.

The Revelation of Arès (French-English bilingual edition). Arès: Maison de la Révélation, 1995.

■ Argentina

This large country is located on the southeastern part of the South American continent, separated from its western neighbor, Chile, by the Andes Mountains. Argentina, with Buenos Aires (current population 12,789,000) as its capital, is bordered by Paraguay and Bolivia to the north, and Uruguay and the Atlantic Ocean on the east. The current population of Argentina is 40,482,000 (2008 estimate) and the national territory includes 1,719,266 square miles.

In 1502, Amerigo Vespucci (1454–1512) commanded the first Spanish ship to arrive at the mouth of the Río de La Plata (the Silver River), and the first attempt at Spanish colonization in Argentina began in 1516. Permanent settlement began in 1536, when Pedro de Mendoza arrived with a large force that was well supplied with equipment and horses. He founded a settlement on the southern bank of the Río de la Plata, called Santa María del Buen Aire (known today as Buenos Aires).

Although the territory of modern Argentina was inhabited by largely nomadic Amerindian groups at the time of Spanish colonization, the influx of the Europeans all but wiped out them out. However, the remnants of these groups survive in the more remote areas along the southwestern Andes Mountains and along the northern border with Bolivia and Paraguay.

Argentina gained its independence from Spain in the period 1810–1816, after the commercial bourgeois of Buenos Aires and its allies ousted the Spanish Viceroyalty of the River Plate, created in 1776 and encompassing what is now Chile, Paraguay, Argentina, Uruguay, and part of Bolivia. Most Argentines (an estimated 86 percent) today are descendants of European immigrants who arrived between 1850 and 1950.

According to the 1895 federal census, the total population of the Republic was 3,945,911, distributed as follows: Argentines, 2,950,384; foreigners, 1,004,527. Of the foreign-born population, 492,636 were Italians; 198,685 Spaniards; 94,098 French; 91,167 Spanish Americans (mainly Bolivians, Chileans, Uruguayans,

Argentina

Religion	Followers in 1970	Followers in 2010	% of Population	Annual % growth 2000–2010	Followers in 2025	Followers in 2050
Christians	22,926,000	37,429,000	91.9	0.96	41,755,000	45,876,000
Roman Catholics	22,432,000	36,311,000	89.1	0.66	40,000,000	43,200,000
Independents	386,000	2,760,000	6.8	3.57	3,500,000	4,250,000
Protestants	583,000	2,500,000	6.1	3.21	3,500,000	4,200,000
Agnostics	210,000	1,352,000	3.3	1.97	2,082,000	2,943,000
Muslims	50,000	800,000	2.0	0.98	1,100,000	1,300,000
Jews	475,000	494,000	1.2	0.15	450,000	400,000
Atheists	140,000	337,000	0.8	1.00	370,000	430,000
New religionists	20,000	104,000	0.3	1.00	120,000	155,000
Spiritists	50,000	91,300	0.2	1.00	100,000	120,000
Ethnoreligionists	75,000	86,500	0.2	0.98	80,000	70,000
Buddhists	10,000	23,400	0.1	0.98	30,000	47,300
Baha'is	5,700	13,400	0.0	0.99	19,000	30,000
Hindus	0	5,800	0.0	1.00	6,500	8,000
Sikhs	500	1,100	0.0	0.99	1,200	1,300
Confucianists	0	500	0.0	0.97	600	800
Chinese folk	0	470	0.0	0.99	600	900
Total population	**23,962,000**	**40,738,000**	**100.0**	**0.98**	**46,115,000**	**51,382,000**

and Paraguayans); 24,725 Brazilians; 21,788 British; 17,142 Germans; 12,803 Austrians; and 1,381 citizens of the United States.

The Roman Catholic Church was established in Argentina with the arrival of Franciscan missionaries in 1536. Their work was supplemented by the Jesuits who arrived in 1586; they were especially active among the Amerindian people. The expulsion of the Jesuits in 1767 placed the Catholic Church in a leadership crisis, which was merely deepened by the social, economic, and political forces that created an independent Argentina in 1816 as part of the United Provinces of South America. The post-colonial ruling elite were both anti-Spanish and anti-clerical. Their opposition to the Catholic Church was manifested in an attempt (ultimately unsuccessful) to establish an independent Argentine Catholic Church. At the end of the 19th century, the country was reported to be 99 percent Catholic, and Catholicism was the state religion.

The Catholic Cathedral of Buenos Aires was erected on the site of the first church in the settlement, built by Don Juan de Garay in 1580. This church and all the others built later depended upon the Catholic authorities of Paraguay until 1620, when Pope Paul V, at the request of King Philip III of Spain, established the Diocese of Buenos Aires. In 1866, the Diocese of Buenos Aires was elevated to an archdiocese.

In January 1910, the Archdiocese of Buenos Aires included 1,700,000 inhabitants, mostly Catholics, located in 130 parishes, with 260 secular priests and 60 religious priests. The male religious communities in the diocese were Franciscans, Dominicans, Fathers of the Sacred Heart, Pallottines, Community of the Divine Word, Passionists, Salesians (since 1896 the Mission of Pampa Central had been entrusted to them), Brothers of the Christian Doctrine, and Marists. Also, there were at least 28 female religious communities in the archdiocese.

Today, there are 14 ecclesiastical provinces (headed by an archdiocese) of the Roman Catholic Church in Argentina, with more than 50 dioceses, headed by the archbishop of Buenos Aires, Cardinal Jorge Mario Bergoglio, S.J. (b. 1936), who is also the president of the Argentine Episcopal Conference.

The patron saint of Argentina, the Virgin of Luján, is honored with a pilgrimage and festival on May 8.

Franciscan church in Salta, northwest Argentina. (iStockPhoto.com)

Her shrine (Basílica Nuestra Señora de Luján) is located 40 miles west of the city of Buenos Aires. Some of the popular folk saints of Argentina are Difunta Correa (María Antonia Deolina Correa, who allegedly died in the 1850s), whose shrine is located in Vallecito, about 37 miles east of San Juan in western Argentina; Gaucho Gil and Pachamama (Mother Earth). Shrines to these folk saints have become major places of pilgrimage where every year thousands of devoted Catholics gather to pay homage.

The Catholic Church was strengthened by a century of heavy immigration (four million arrived between 1850 and 1950) from predominantly Catholic European countries (Italy, Spain, Ireland, and Poland). Affiliated with the Roman Catholic Church in Argentina and with the Vatican are the following Apostolic Exarchates: Faithful of the Oriental Rite (Melkite);

San Charbel in Buenos Aires (Maronite); San Gregorio de Narek in Buenos Aires (Armenian); and Faithful of the Oriental Rite (Ukrainian). Also present is the Priestly Society of Saint Pius X (SSPX), founded in 1969 by Archbishop Marcel Lefebvre in France, which is an international congregation of priests that has establishments in almost every major country. Known as Fraternidad Sacerdotal San Pío X (FSSPX) in Argentina and founded in Buenos Aires in 1978, this controversial religious order represents Traditional Catholics (only use the Tridentine Mass in Latin) who reject the teachings of the Second Vatican Council (1962–1965), which in 1975 resulted in the SSPX no longer being recognized as an organization within the Roman Catholic Church and to the excommunication of Archbishop Lefebvre and four of his bishops in 1988 by the Vatican. The FSSPX headquarters are at the Seminario Nuestra Señora Corredentora in La Reja, Moreno, Buenos Aires.

In addition, there are a number of Eastern Orthodox communities in Argentina, which include the Armenian Apostolic Church (Mother See of Holy Etchmiadzin, Armenia); Greek Orthodox Patriarchate of Antioch and All the East; Orthodox Church of the Ecumenical Patriarchate (Constantinople: Greek Orthodox Archdiocese of North and South America, Parish of Buenos Aires); Autocephalous Orthodox Church in South America (Metropolitan Archdiocese of Brazil, Argentina and Colombia of The Greek Orthodox Church–Old Calendar, headquarters in Rio de Janeiro, Brazil); Russian Orthodox Church (Patriarchate of Moscow); Russian Orthodox Autonomous Church–ROAC, Mission of Our Lady of Vladimir (Diocese of South America under Metropolitan Valentin of Suzdal, Vladimir, Russia); Russian Orthodox Church Outside of Russia–ROCOR (Metropolitan Laurus of New York City); Syriac Orthodox Church of Antioch (Patriarchal-Vicariate of Argentina); and Ukrainian Autocephalous Orthodox Church of North & South America and the Diaspora (under Archbishop Odon of Manizales, Eparch of All Latin America, Spain & Portugal and his superior, Metropolitan Mefodiy of Kyiv & All-Ukraine).

A wave of foreign investment and immigration from Europe after 1850 led to the development of modern agriculture and to a near-reinvention of Argentine society and the economy, which led to the strengthening of a cohesive state. Between 1880 and 1929 Argentina enjoyed growing prosperity and prestige, and became one of the 10 richest countries in the world as a result of an agricultural export-led economy.

Conservative elements, representing the oligarchy, dominated Argentine politics via the National Autonomist Party (1874–1916) through non-democratic methods (electoral fraud and corruption) until 1916, when the centrist Radical Civic Union won the country's first free elections. President Hipólito Yrigoyen Alem (1852–1933), who served two presidential terms (from 1916 to 1922 and again from 1928 to 1930), enacted a series of social and economic reforms, which were most popular with the middle class and provided assistance to family farmers and small businesses. The worldwide economic depression, which began in late 1929, greatly affected the nation's economy and caused much social and political unrest throughout the country. Irigoyen's inability to deal with this growing crisis, combined with increasing levels of violence between left-wing and right-wing elements, prompted the military to remove him from office in 1930, which led to another decade of Conservative rule and to the implementation of more protectionist policies. During World War I and most of World War II, Argentina was politically neutral and became a leading source of food supplies for the Allied Nations.

In the post–World War II period, growing political and social discontent in Argentina led to the presidency of Colonel Juan Domingo Perón (1895–1974) in 1946, under the banner of the Labor Party and with two stated goals: social justice and national economic independence. Perón worked to empower the working class by increasing wages and employment, and to expand the number of unionized workers and of social and educational programs. Labor unions grew from around 500,000 members in 1945 to more than 2 million by 1950, primarily in the General Confederation of Labor (CGT, Confederación General del Trabajo), the nation's principal labor union. Argentina's labor force numbered around 5 million people in 1950, which made it the most unionized nation in Latin America.

This was the first time that Argentina had witnessed the government giving such attention to the working class and the poor, and the oligarchy was

ARGENTINA

San Salvador de Jujuy

Salta

Formosa

San Miguel de Tucuman

Resistencia
Santiago del Estero

Corrientes · Posadas

Catamarca

Santo Tome

La Ribja

Curuzu Cuatia

Cordoba

Santa Fe

San Juan

Parana

Mendoza

Rio Cuarto

San Luis

Resario

Mercedes

Venado Tuerto

San Rafael Renanco

Junin **Buenos Aires**

Realico

General Villegas

La Plata

Telen

A r g e n t i n a

Santa Rosa

Mar del Plata

Bahia Blanca

Zapala

Neuquen

Necochea

Viedma

San Carlos de Bariloche

Esquel Rawson

Comodoro Rivadavia

Las Heras

Puerto Deseado

N

Gobernador Gregores

Puerto Santa Cruz

Rio Gallegos

·Ushuaia

greatly displeased with Perón's policies. Throughout Perón's first and second terms as president, his economic advisors encouraged accelerated industrial and urban development. Perón's administration became increasingly occupied in struggles with the Catholic hierarchy and with his own Peronist movement. Consequently, Perón rid himself of many of his important and capable advisors, while promoting patronage among his strongest supporters.

Perón, an authoritarian populist leader and a nationalist, was intolerant of both left-wing and conservative opposition groups; he faced strong and growing opposition from many sectors, including members of the Catholic hierarchy, the upper class, the armed forces, the universities, the national media and business interests, the Conservatives, the Communists and the Socialists, as well as the U.S. government. Perón was an admirer of Germany's Adolf Hitler, Italy's Benito Mussolini, and Spain's General Franco and their respective fascist regimes. Under Perón's own regime many Nazi war criminals were granted asylum after World War II, and large fortunes were said to be made by Perón and his close associates. However, the Perón administration, surprisingly, was not anti-Semitic, since Argentina accepted more Jewish immigrants from Europe than any other country in Latin America during the postwar years.

Perón's troubles with the Roman Catholic Church finally led to his excommunication by Pope Pius XII on June 15, 1955, following the expulsion of two Catholic priests that Perón believed were behind his recent public image problems. In retribution, Peronist crowds ransacked 11 Catholic churches in Buenos Aires, including the Metropolitan Cathedral. Then, on September 16, 1955, a nationalist Catholic group of high-ranking military officers, from both the army and navy, overthrew Perón in a violent coup; he fled to exile in Paraguay, then to Panama, and eventually to Spain with an estimated fortune of between $100 and $500 million.

Throughout Argentina, Peronism and even the display of Peronist memorabilia was banned by the anti-Peronist government of General Pedro Eugenio Aramburu (r. 1955–1958). Peronists and moderates in the army organized a failed counter-coup against Aramburu in June 1956, but Peronism continued to be a powerful political and social force in the nation. Aramburu's repressive military dictatorship was opposed by the Radical Civic Union (UCRP), the Justicialist Party (Peronist), the Argentine Socialist Party (PSA), the Democratic Progressive Party (PCP), and the Popular Block (PB), which called for immediate and free democratic elections to end the nation's political crisis.

This paved the way for Juan Perón's return to power in 1973, but he only served as president for nine months, until his death in 1974; he was succeeded by his (third) wife and vice president, Isabel Martínez (b. 1931). The resulting conflict between left- and right-wing extremists led to lawlessness and financial chaos throughout the country. President Martínez was not very strong politically, and a military junta led a coup against her in March 1976. The new military government at first brought some stability and built numerous important public works, but its unpopular economic policies led to a sharp decline in living standards and to record foreign debt.

This repressive military dictatorship launched a seven-year campaign against suspected dissidents and subversives, known as The Dirty War (1976–1983), during which many people, both opponents of the government as well as the innocent, were "disappeared" in the middle of the night. They were taken to secret government detention centers where they were interrogated, tortured, and eventually killed. These people are known as *los desaparecidos*. The estimated casualties from this unpopular war range from 10,000 to 30,000 people.

Although the military dictatorship carried out its war against suspected domestic subversives throughout its entire existence, it was ironic that a foreign foe brought the regime to an end. In the early 1980s, it became clear to both the world and the Argentine people that the government was behind the tens of thousands of disappearances. The military junta, which faced increasing opposition over its dismal human rights record as well as growing accusations of corruption, sought to quell domestic criticism by launching a military campaign to regain control of the disputed Falkland/Malvinas Islands, located in the South Atlantic Ocean about 360 miles from the Argentine coast. However, after 72 days of conflict, the British military won the war. This unexpected loss was the final blow

Argentines grieve over the wreckage of a Catholic church burned during an uprising, June 1955. (Hank Walker/Time Life Pictures/Getty Images)

for the disgraced Argentine military regime, and in 1982 it restored basic civil liberties and lifted its ban on political parties. The Dirty War ended when President Raul Alfonsin's (1927–1989) civilian government took control of the country on December 10, 1983.

Unlike its counterparts in Chile and Brazil, the Argentine Catholic Church has, until recently, been known as one of the most politically conservative churches in the region, due to its basic rejection of progressive trends in Latin American Catholicism. This conservatism originated in its preference for strong church-state relations during the colonial era, but these historic ties were exacerbated during the strongman rule of President Juan Perón (1946–1955) of the populist Labor Party. Initially the Catholic Church established a strong relationship with President Perón, but his attempt to consolidate social power through state control of most social institutions and groups conflicted with the Church's own agenda. The Perón government frequently harassed Catholic Action groups that sought to organize Catholic youth and workers to achieve greater social justice. The church-state conflict came to a head in 1955 when the Perón government legalized divorce and prostitution, and expelled two Catholic priests who criticized Perón's morality and leadership. Most Argentine Catholic bishops were strong supporters of the military coup that overthrew Perón that year.

Because the Peronists continued to cause social unrest during the following decades, the Catholic hierarchy actively supported two anti-Peronist military dictatorships, which ruled from 1966 to 1973 and from 1976 to 1983, respectively. During the latter repressive dictatorship, some Catholic priests were known to be present at interrogation and torture sessions conducted by police and military officials. Appeals by the citizenry for Catholic authorities to intervene and denounce human rights abuses and government misconduct were largely ignored. However, since Argentina's return to democratic civilian rule in 1983, the Catholic Church has attempted to repair its tarnished image as a consequence of its support of two repressive military dictatorships and to distance itself from partisan politics.

In addition, several diverse internal tensions arose within the Roman Catholic Church in Argentina during the 1960s and following decades, resulting from challenges posed by the Latin American Bishops Conference in Medellín (Colombia) in 1968, Latin American Liberation Theology, and the Charismatic Renewal movement. These new challenges polarized Catholic bishops, parish priests, religious workers, and the laity into various factions. *Traditionalists* wanted the Church to remain as it was prior to the reforms approved by the Second Vatican Council (late 1960s). *Reformers* supported the Vatican's new modernizing stance; *progressives* who sought to implement the new vision for "a preferential option for the poor" through social and political action aimed at transforming Argentine society and establishing social justice through peaceful democratic means. *Radicals* adopted Liberation Theology, with its Marxist ideology, and advocated violent revolution by the lower and middle classes as a means of overthrowing the oligarchy and creating a Socialist state that would alleviate the suffering of the poverty-stricken masses. *Charismatic agents* sought to renew and transform the spiritual and communal life of Catholics through the power and gifts of the Holy Spirit (including the "baptism of the Holy Spirit and speaking in tongues," healing, and prophecy).

The Catholic Charismatic Renewal (CCR) began in Argentina under the leadership of priest Alberto Ibáñez Padilla as early as 1969, but not without difficulties in gaining the approval of the archbishop of Buenos Aires. It was not until 1973 that the CCR was officially established in Argentina with the proper ecclesiastical approval and administrative controls, which led to a growing withdrawal of Catholics from participation in ecumenical (attended by Evangelicals and Catholics) charismatic groups and activities due to pressure from Catholic authorities.

During the next 25 years, there was a significant spiritual awakening among Roman Catholics in many parts of Argentina due to their participation in CCR activities, such as prayer groups, conferences, healing campaigns, rallies in soccer stadiums, and the like. In 1985, priest Felicísimo Vicente initiated the CCR in his parish, Sanctuary of the Sacred Heart of Jesus in San Justo, which became a center for the CCR in Greater Buenos Aires. Also, priest Darío Betancourt of Colombia played an important role in the growth and development of the CCR in many cities of Argentina, especially between 1985 and 1995. In November 1994, Betancourt was the principal speaker at a CCR rally in Velez Stadium in Buenos Aires attended by an estimated 50,000 people.

Today, freedom of religion is guaranteed for all citizens by the Constitution. The Roman Catholic Church maintains its official status, and adherence to Catholicism is a requirement for eligibility to the offices of president and vice president of the republic. The recent governments have increasingly promoted interfaith dialogue through advisory committees and grassroots initiatives. Diverse religious groups enjoy tolerance and coexistence, but not necessarily equality, in Argentine society.

In 1995, the country was reported to be 88 percent Catholic, the Protestant population was 7 percent, and other religious groups or the nonreligious comprised about 5 percent. However, according to an April 2001 public opinion poll by Gallup-Argentina, only 70 percent claimed to be Catholic, 11 percent were Protestant, 3 percent were affiliated with other religions, and 16 percent reported no religious affiliation (or were non-responsive). The latter category includes those who may believe in God, but do not attend church regularly, as well as agnostics and atheists.

In 1992, the Ministry of Cults and Foreign Affairs listed 2,986 registered religious groups: 1,790 were Protestant groups, about 400 were Catholic or Eastern Orthodox organizations (mainly religious orders and institutions), 382 were listed as "diverse spiritual cults," and 387 were of Afro-Brazilian origin (such as Umbanda and Condomblé).

The early presence of Protestantism in Argentina (1800s) was due in large part to the immigration of English Methodists, Scottish Presbyterians, German and Scandinavian Lutherans, Italian Waldensians, Welsh Protestants, German-Russian and French-Swiss Baptists, Armenian Congregationalists, Dutch Mennonites, and Dutch Reformed, among others. Today, at least nine branches of Eastern Orthodoxy also exist, and there is a small Anglican presence. Missionary efforts by Anglicans (from the Church of England) and Presbyterians (from the Church of Scotland) began in Argentina in 1824, ministering to English and Scottish immigrants in their own languages in Buenos Aires. The Anglican work is now incorporated into the Anglican Province of the Southern Cone. The Methodist Episcopal Board of Missions began work in Buenos Aires in 1836. In the 1850s, Anglican missionaries (later, the South American Missionary Society) began work among the Amerindians in the Patagonian region and later in the Chaco region of northern Argentina. During the late 1800s, new Protestant missionary efforts were begun among the Spanish-speaking population: the Christian Brethren/Plymouth Brethren (1882), Salvation Army (1882), Seventh-day Adventist Church (1894), Christian and Missionary Alliance (1895), South American Evangelical Mission (1895), and Regions Beyond Missionary Union (1899).

The Evangelical Church of the River Plate dates to 1840 with the arrival of German Lutheran and Reformed immigrants in Argentina, Paraguay, and Uruguay. In 1843 the German Evangelical Congregation was founded in Buenos Aires, which was the first German-speaking community in the Río de la Plata region. This became the mother church to scores of other German-speaking congregations in Argentina. Later immigrants from Switzerland, Austria, Russia, Brazil, and Romania joined these congregations because they had in common the German language. In 1899, the German Evangelical Synod of the River Plate was established as part of the Evangelical Church in Germany (EKD), with which it became officially affiliated in 1934. In 1965 the synod approved a new constitution and was renamed the Evangelical Church of the River Plate (IERP), and it became independent of the EKD. Today, about 70 percent of the members live in Argentina and the rest in Uruguay and Paraguay. Twenty-two Lutheran, Reformed, and United regional churches (Landeskirchen) form the Evangelical Church in Germany (Evangelische Kirsche in Deutschland [EKD]).

In 1969 the Instituto Superior Evangélico de Estudios Teológicos (now ISEDET University Institute) was established to train pastors and Christian workers as a joint venture between the Evangelical Church of the River Plate and Methodist, Waldensian, Disciples of Christ, United Lutheran, Danish Lutheran, Reformed, Anglican, and Presbyterian churches.

In 1956, the Evangelical Church of the River Plate became affiliated with the World Council of Churches, as well as a member of the Argentine and Uruguayan Federation of Evangelical Churches. Also, this denomination is a member of the River Plate Lutheran Council, which was created in 1992 as a space for dialogue with churches affiliated with the World Lutheran Federation. Since 1978 it has participated in the Latin American Council of Churches (CLAI), and since 1991 in the World Alliance of Reformed Churches.

Dozens of other Protestant mission agencies arrived during the early 1900s, notably the Southern Baptist Convention (1903), the Christian Church (Disciples of Christ) (1904), the Lutheran Church–Missouri Synod (1905), the Assemblies of God (1914), the Mennonite Church (1917), and the Danish Lutheran Church (1924).

The New Apostolic Church International is hard to classify, but it arrived in South America around 1920 when a number of New Apostolic families from Europe settled near the mouth of the Rio de la Plata in Argentina and Uruguay. The church apostle assigned to South America was the Dutchman Sijtze Faber, who settled in the province of Córdoba, from where he cared for the small group of families. In 1930, when Chief Apostle Helper Franz-Wilhelm Schlaphoff visited South America, it was decided that worship services would be conducted in the local languages. The New Apostolic Church in Argentina has been officially recognized by the state since 1938. This religious group, founded in England in 1830, was originally named the Catholic Apostolic Church. It has roots in Presbyte-

rian, Congregational, and Anglican theology and church polity; it is a pre-Pentecostal body that believes in and practices the charismatic gifts of healing, prophecy, and speaking in tongues. Today its international headquarters are located in Zurich, Switzerland.

In 2000, the estimated size of the non-Pentecostal Protestant denominations in Argentina was as follows: Seventh-day Adventist Church (72,900 members), the Evangelical Baptist Convention (49,700), Plymouth Brethren (Iglesias Evangélicas Cristianas en la República Argentina, 36,500), Evangelical Lutheran Church (Missouri Synod, 22,400), Church of God (Anderson, Indiana, 19,600), and the Anglican-Episcopal Church (12,000). All other non-Pentecostal Protestant denominations had less than 10,000 members each in 2000.

Today, Pentecostals (about 70 percent) outnumber all other Protestants in Argentina, due to substantial church growth resulting from spiritual revivals since the mid-1950s, beginning with the Tommy Hicks Crusade in 1954. The largest Pentecostal denominations in Argentina in 2000 were reported to be the following (estimated membership): National Union of the Assemblies of God (137,000), Vision of the Future Church (led by Omar Cabrera, 132,000), Swedish-Norwegian Assemblies of God (93,700), Italian Christian Assemblies (48,400), Chilean Evangelical Pentecostal Church (40,900), Foursquare Gospel Churches (31,900), Church of God International (Cleveland, Tennessee, 24,500), Christian Pentecostal Church of God (24,100), and the United Evangelical Church of Argentina (23,500). All other Pentecostal groups in Argentina had less than 20,000 members each in 2000.

The Charismatic Renewal movement (CRM), known as Movimiento de Renovación in Argentina, began in 1967 at the home of a Plymouth Brethren businessman, Alberto Darling, located in a wealthy suburb of Buenos Aires, when members of an informal prayer meeting on a Monday night spontaneously experienced glossolalia (speaking in tongues), later identified as the baptism of the Holy Spirit. The weekly meetings continued and grew in attendance as more people came to see what was occurring. At the beginning of 1968, the group leaders rented a larger facility to accommodate 600 to 700 participants.

As the number of charismatic groups multiplied, many Catholics began to participate, along with evangelicals, and experienced the baptism and gifts of the Holy Spirit as well. Some of the early leaders of this movement were Alberto Darling (Plymouth Brethren), Orville Swindall (Plymouth Brethren), Juan Carlos Ortiz (Assemblies of God), Jorge Himitian (Christian & Missionary Alliance), and Keith Benson (Overseas Crusades).

One of the major events that led to the expansion of the Argentine CRM to other countries and continents was an ecumenical conference, later called the first Latin American Renewal Congress, held in 1972 in Buenos Aires. Many Argentine evangelicals and Catholics participated, along with representatives from at least 12 other countries, who became catalysts for the spread of the CRM.

Many Pentecostal leaders credit decades of dictatorial and military misrule, Argentina's Dirty War and its humiliating loss to Great Britain in the War of the Falkland/Malvinas Islands, the people's loss of confidence in traditional religion, and serious socioeconomic problems as factors in creating a spiritual vacuum in the nation and making the Argentine people more responsive to movements of spiritual renewal since the 1950s. These include the mass conversions that took place during the Tommy Hicks Crusade in Buenos Aires in the 1950s; the tens of thousands who participated in the Charismatic Renewal movement in the 1970s and 1980s; and mass evangelistic, healing, and deliverance crusades conducted by Omar Cabrera, Carlos Annacondia, Héctor Gimenez, and others during the 1980s and 1990s, especially among the working class.

According to some sources, the Great Argentine Revival began in 1982 with the first city-wide, interdenominational crusade by former businessman turned evangelist, Carlos Annacondia. Previously, Omar Cabrera, who heads what has been called "the fastest-growing Christian movement in Argentina," founded the Vision of the Future Ministry, with headquarters in Buenos Aires, in 1972; Cabrera is said to have pioneered many of the crusade practices that Annacondia later popularized.

Many of the older Protestant churches had been involved in the multinational Confederation of Evangelical Churches of the River Plate, which was replaced by the Argentina Federation of Evangelical Churches in 1958. Today, the churches associated with the larger Protestant ecumenical community are members of the Argentine Federation of Evangelicals, which is related to the Latin American Council of Churches (CLAI) and the World Council of Churches (WCC). Many of the more conservative evangelical groups are members of the Argentine Alliance of Evangelical Churches, which is affiliated with the World Evangelical Alliance (WEA).

Among the non-Protestant Christian-based groups in Argentina are the Church of Jesus Christ of Latter-day Saints (Salt Lake City, Utah: founded in Argentina in 1925; reported 863 congregations with 363,990 members in 2007), the Reorganized Church of Jesus Christ of Latter-day Saints (Independence, Missouri), Jehovah's Witnesses (1,782 kingdom halls and 131,513 adherents in 2005), The Family (formerly known as Children of God, founded by Moses David), Christian Science (Church of Christ, Scientist), Unity School of Christianity, Light of the World Church (Guadalajara, Mexico), Voice of the Cornerstone Church (Puerto Rico, founded by William Soto Santiago), Growing in Grace Churches (Miami, Florida; founded by José Luís de Jesús Miranda), the quasi-Pentecostal Universal Church of the Kingdom of God, and the God is Love Church (both from Brazil).

The Jewish community of Argentina is the largest in South America and the fifth largest in the world. The first Jews in Argentina were Marranos from Spain, and Sephardic Jews still form a significant and visible portion of the Argentina Jewish community. Jews from Germany, North Africa, and the Balkans began to arrive in large numbers in the 1860s, and the first Eastern European Jews (Ashkenazies) arrived in 1889. Today, more than 300,000 Jews reside in Argentina, about two-thirds of whom live in Greater Buenos Aires. They have their center in the Representative Organization of Argentine Jews. Jews of Iberian origin (an estimated 60,000 to 100,000) have formed the Central Sephardic Community. Eastern European Jews, representing Orthodox Judaism, have formed the Latin American Rabbinical Seminary. Despite a return to democracy and increasing tolerance of religious pluralism since 1983, some anti-Semitism persists in Argentina. In 1994 nearly 100 people were killed when a Jewish community center in Buenos Aires was bombed by terrorists; the perpetrators were never apprehended.

The same migrations from North Africa and the Middle East that brought Jews to Argentina also brought a minority of Muslims, who formed mosques in Buenos Aires (home to one of the largest in Latin America) and Mendoza and have now adopted a missionary stance vis-à-vis the Spanish-speaking population. The country's Muslim population is the largest in Latin America today. Of the 500,000 to 600,000 in the Muslim community, the Islamic Center estimates that 90 percent are Sunni and 10 percent Shia. Also, Subud, a Sufi-related movement founded in Indonesia in the 1920s by Muhammad Subuh Sumohadiwidjojo, has been present in Argentina since 1958, as well as Schools of the Fourth Way (influenced by Georges Ivanovich Gurdjieff and Sufism); both of these groups have a small number of adherents.

Some of the other religions that exist in Argentina today include Buddhism, Hinduism, and the Baha'i Faith. Buddhism entered the country through the immigration of Japanese, which steadily increased during the 20th century. The following Buddhist groups are present in Argentina: Japanese Soto School (Tangen Daisetsu lineage), Soka Gakkai International, International Zen Association (Paris, France), Buddhist Community Seita Jodo-Shinshu Honpa-Honganji, Kagyu Dak Shang Choling, Shobo An Zendo, and the Tzong Kuan Buddhist Temple. Perfect Liberty Kyodan, founded in Japan, also exists in Argentina. Hindu groups include the Brahma Kumaris (Raja Yoga), Vedanta Society (Order of Ramakrishna), Krishnamurti Foundation, Sawan Ruhani Mission (Science of Spirituality), Vaisnava Mission, International Society for Krishna Consciousness (Hare Krishnas), Ananda Marga Yoga Society (The Way of Perfect Happiness), Swami Shivapremananda Foundation (Centro Sivananda Yoga Vedanta), and the Master Ching Hai Meditation Association. The Baha'i Faith has about 6,000 adherents and more than 100 centers in Argentina.

In 2005, the Argentine government reported a population of about 600,000 Amerindian peoples (about 1.6 percent of the total population). Many of them continue to observe traditional animistic religious practices, the most numerous of whom are the Mapuches who dwell along the Chilean border in the southwest.

The Guaraní people (also called Chiriguanos) still inhabit the Corrientes and Entre Rios Provinces of northern Argentina, where shamans are recognized as alternative healers, and the sophistication of Guarani religious thought has been recognized by anthropologists. Also, animistic religion is practiced by Quechua-speaking Bolivians who work on sugarcane plantations in northern Argentina. Overall, about 20 indigenous languages are still spoken in the nation.

Since the mid-1950s, several varieties of Afro-Brazilian religions (animism) have been present in Argentina, including the Center of African Religion (Ile Afonxa Xango e Oxum Leusa), the Xango Aganyu African Temple, and other Candoblé and Umbanda centers. In 2005, there were hundreds of these groups in Greater Buenos Aires.

Western Esoteric groups are commonplace in Argentina, representing Ancient Wisdom and Spiritualist-Psychic-New Age groups. The Panamerican Spiritualist Confederation (influenced by Frenchman Allan Kardec) was founded in Buenos Aires in 1946 and includes affiliated members in Brazil, Colombia, Cuba, Dominican Republic, Honduras, and Mexico. Other groups include Freemasonry (between 1795 and 1802), the Theosophical Society (founded by the Russian Helena Petrovna Blavatsky in New York City in 1875), the Anthroposophical Society (founded by Rudolf Steiner in Germany in 1917), the Basilio Scientific School (co-founded by Blanca Aubreton and Eugenio Portal in Argentina in 1917; named after Portal's father, Pedro Basilio Portal), the True Spiritism Society (founded in 1928 by Joaquín Soriano in Córdova Province, Argentina), Sacred Order of the American Knights of Fire (also known as CAFH, founded by Santiago Bovisio in 1937 in Buenos Aires), Grand Universal Fraternity (founded in Venezuela in 1948 by Serge Raynaud de la Ferriere), the Church of Scientology (founded in Arizona by science fiction writer L. Ron Hubbard in 1952), the Holy Spirit Association for the Unification of World Christianity (followers of Reverend Sun Myung Moon, founded in Korea in 1954), the New Acropolis Cultural Association (founded by Jorge Angel Livraga Rizzi in Buenos Aires in 1957), Siloism (founded in the 1960s by Mario Rodríguez Cobo, known as Silo), Universal Gnostic Movement (founded by Samael Aun Weor in 1977 in Mexico), the Raelian

Movement International (founded in France in 1974 by Claude Vorilhon, known as Rael), and several other flying saucer-extraterrestrial study groups.

J. Gordon Melton and Clifton L. Holland

See also: Ananda Marga Yoga Society; Anglican Province of the Southern Cone; Armenian Apostolic Church (Holy See of Etchmiadzin); Assemblies of God; Baha'i Faith; Blavatsky, Helena P.; Brahma Kumaris; Candomblé; Charismatic Movement; Christian Church (Disciples of Christ); Church of England; Church of Jesus Christ of Latter-day Saints; Church of Scientology; Church of Scotland; Eastern Orthodoxy; Ecumenical Patriarchate/Patriarchate of Constantinople; Franciscans; Greek Orthodox Patriarchate of Antioch and All the East; Gurdjieff, George Ivanovitch; International Church of the Foursquare Gospel; International Society for Krishna Consciousness; International Zen Association; Krishnamurti Foundation; Latin American Council of Churches; Lutheran Church–Missouri Synod; Master Ching Hai Meditation Association; New Acropolis Cultural Association; New Apostolic Church; Pentecostalism; Perfect Liberty Kyodan; Roman Catholic Church; Russian Orthodox Church (Moscow Patriarchate); Russian Orthodox Church Outside of Russia; Salvation Army; Seventh-day Adventist Church; Soka Gakkai International; Steiner, Rudolf; Subud; Sufism; Umbanda; Unification Movement; Vedanta Societies; World Alliance of Reformed Churches; World Council of Churches; World Evangelical Alliance.

References

Brierly, Peter, ed. *World Churches Handbook.* London: Christian Research, 1997.

Calvo, David. "Nuevos movimientos religiosos en la Argentina." In *Nuevos Movimientos Religiosos.* http://www.monografias.com/trabajos11/nuevmov/nuevmov.shtml.

Enns, Arno W. *Man, Milieu and Mission in Argentina.* Grand Rapids, MI: Eerdmans, 1971.

Grimes, Barbara F., ed. *Ethnologue: Languages of the World.* 12th ed. Dallas, TX: Summer Institute of Linguistics, 1992.

Holland, Clifton L. *Toward a Classification System of Religious Groups in the Americas by Major Traditions and Family Types.* San José, Costa Rica: PROLADES, 2008. http://www.prolades.com/cra/clas-eng.pdf. Accessed March 1, 2009.

Monti, Daniel P. *Presencia del protestantismo en el Río de la Plata durante el Siglo XIX.* Buenos Aires: Editorial La Aurora, 1969.

Oro, Ari Pedro, and Pablo Semán. "Pentecostalism in Argentina." "Pentecostalism in the Southern Cone Countries: Overview and Perspectives." *International Sociology* 15, no. 4 (December 2000): 605–627.

PROLADES Religion in the Americas database, "Religion in Argentina." http://www.prolades.com/cra/regions/sam/arg/arg-rd.htm. Accessed March 1, 2009.

Saracco, Norberto, ed. *Directorio y Censo de Iglesias Evangélicas de la Ciudad de Buenos Aires.* Buenos Aires: Fundación Argentina de Educación y Acción Comunitaria, 1992.

Soneira, Adelardo Jorge. *¿Quiénes son los Carismáticos? La Renovación Carismática en la Argentina.* Buenos Aires: CONICET/Universidad de Salvador, 1998.

U.S. Department of State. *International Religious Freedom Report 2007: Argentina.* http://www.state.gov/g/drl/rls/irf/2007/90239.htm. Accessed March 1, 2009.

Villalpando, Waldo Luis, ed. *Las Iglesias del Trasplante: Protestantismo de Inmigración en la Argentina.* Buenos Aires: Centro de Estudios Cristianos, 1970.

Arius

ca. 250–336

Arius was an important Christian teacher who emerged just as the church was ending three centuries of persecution and marginalization and enjoying a position of favor throughout the Roman Empire. As a priest, Arius entered into the ongoing debates over the nature of Jesus as the church attempted to find a way to affirm Jesus' divine nature while maintaining its affirmation of a strict monotheism. Arius championed the position that as the Son of God, Jesus was not God but the first

Portrait of Arius, controversial Christian priest and founder of Arianism. Arius, who formulated the first great heresy that threatened to divide the ancient Christian Church, argued that Jesus was inferior to God the Father. (Library of Congress)

creation of God. His position was condemned by the Council of Nicaea (324), and Arius was sent into exile.

Arius emerges out of obscurity in the second decade of the fourth century when he was ordained as a deacon by Peter of Alexandria (d. 311) and a short time later a priest by Achillas (312). He was put in charge of the Baucalis, a chief church of Alexandria, Egypt. He may have been from Libya and seems to have studied with Lucian of Antioch (ca. 240–312), who had earlier championed the teachings with which Arius would later become identified.

Around 318, he challenged his bishop, the notable Alexander of Alexandria (r. 313–326), concerning the divinity of Christ. Arius maintained that the Son of God was not coeternal nor to be considered of the same substance with God the Father. Instead, there was once a time when he did not exist. For speaking out, Arius (and several other priests) was excommunicated. He left Alexandria and traveled into Syria and Palestine to locate any supporters.

Arius emerged simultaneously with the rise of Constantine and the almost instantaneous change of Christianity's position in the Roman Empire. Christianity began the century as a persecuted minority, the persecution having been particularly acute under Diocletian (r. 303–305). Under Constantine (r. 306–337) Christianity received toleration via the Edict of Milan (313) and then moved into a privileged position as Constantine's power was consolidated. As the controversy around Arius continued, the church's new position allowed it the possibility of calling an international council to resolve the matter. At that Council, held at Nicaea in 325, Athanasius, then the secretary to Alexander of Alexandria, took the lead in opposing Arius's teaching.

By the mid-320s Arius had come to affirm that Jesus Christ as the Son of God and Word (or Logos) of God was not of the same essence (Greek: *ousia*) as the Father. Rather, the Son of God was a created being. As the initial creation of God, the Son existed before all time and God created the world through him. Almost unanimously, the Council of Nicaea condemned Arius's position and issued a creedal statement (later incorporated into the liturgy of the Eastern Orthodox and Roman Catholic churches) that the Son was "Very God of Very God, begotten, not made, being of one substance (*homoousia*) with the Father by whom all things were made."

Following the decision of the Council, Arius was again exiled, and his writings burned. Few of his writings survived, and he is primarily known through the writings about him of those who triumphed at this time. The issue seemed resolved. Alexander of Alexandria died in 327, and Athanasius became the new bishop of Alexandria.

Arius, who had taken refuge in Palestine, however, was soon permitted to return, after reformulating his Christology in a manner seemingly in accord with the new Nicene Creed. Constantine ordered Athanasius to readmit Arius to communion. Athanasius believed that Arius had not disavowed his former position and refused to accept him; Arius was exiled to Germany. Constantine then summoned Arius to Constantinople and after finding the controversial priest to have adjusted his opinions into an acceptable theology, now ordered Alexander, the bishop of Constantinople, to receive Arius back into communion. Alexander objected but finally gave in. The day before Arius was to be readmitted to communion, however, as he was being paraded through the streets with his supporters, he suddenly took ill and died. Some believed that he had been poisoned.

By the time of Arius's death in 336, his views had spread to various places. Especially on the edges of the empire, factions emerged around different opinions over how similar the Son of God was to God the Father. Its growth was lamented by Saint Jerome (ca. 342–420), who complained that the whole world had turned to Arian ideas. The invading Vandals who sacked Rome in 455 were Arian Christians. Their Arian church continued until they were defeated by Belisarius in 534. Meanwhile Arianism spread among the Goths but largely died out following the conversion of the Franks to Catholicism in 496.

Having disappeared by the Middle Ages, Arian Christology was revived in the 16th century by the Unitarians, among whom it retains a significant following to the present. It found a variety of champions in the 19th century as the ability of the church to suppress dissenting opinions waned, among notable Arians being Charles Taze Russell, founder of what became the Jehovah's Witnesses.

J. Gordon Melton

See also: Athanasius; Constantine the Great; Jehovah's Witnesses; Russell, Charles Taze, Unitarian Universalist Association.

References

Barnes, Michel R. *Arianism After Arius: Essays on the Development of the Fourth Century Trinitarian Conflicts.* London: T. & T. Clark Publishers, 1994.

Wiles, Maurice F. *The Archetypal Heresy: Arianism through the Centuries.* Oxford: Clarendon, 1996.

Williams, Rowan. *Arius: Heresy and Tradition.* Grand Rapids: Eerdmans, 2002.

■ Armenia

Following the collapse of the Soviet Union, Armenia became an independent republic in 1991. At that time

Armenian church at sundown. A number of Christian denominations are present in Armenia; the official state church is the Armenian Orthodox Apostolic Church. (Mikle15/Dreamstime.com)

it occupied less than 18,641 land-locked square miles of the southern Caucasus—one-tenth of the land that was known in ancient times as Greater Armenia. The republic shares borders with Turkey to the west, Iran to the south, Azerbaijan to the east, and Georgia to the north. The capital is Yerevan, with the ancient spiritual capital, Etchmiadzin, 12 miles to the west; both offer a clear view of Mount Ararat, which, although located in present-day Turkey, has served throughout the centuries as a potent symbol of Armenian identity. Like its geographical boundaries, the population (estimated at just under three million in 2008) has fluctuated throughout history as a result of invasions, conquests, earthquakes, migrations, deportations, and genocide. Political, military, and economic upheavals and disasters have resulted in an estimated eight million Armenians now living in the diaspora (mainly in the United States, Russia, France, and the Middle East), greatly

Armenia

Religion	Followers in 1970	Followers in 2010	% of Population	Annual % growth 2000–2010	Followers in 2025	Followers in 2050
Christians	858,000	2,550,000	85.4	–0.19	2,610,000	2,280,000
Orthodox	854,000	2,264,000	75.8	–0.43	2,268,000	1,940,000
Roman Catholics	0	235,000	7.9	0.00	270,000	245,000
Independents	2,100	28,000	0.9	6.18	35,000	50,000
Agnostics	964,000	264,000	8.8	–1.36	180,000	90,000
Atheists	580,000	100,000	3.3	–2.46	50,000	30,000
Muslims	107,000	70,000	2.3	–0.42	60,000	45,000
New religionists	3,100	2,000	0.1	–0.43	2,000	2,000
Baha'is	0	1,200	0.0	–0.41	5,000	10,000
Jews	5,000	500	0.0	–0.41	500	500
Total population	**2,518,000**	**2,987,000**	**100.0**	**–0.42**	**2,908,000**	**2,458,000**

outnumbering those living in the republic. The Armenian people in the Caucasus have remained remarkably homogeneous, one reason being the Armenian language and its unique script, but perhaps the most important unifying factor has been the persistence for 1,700 years of the Armenian Apostolic Church (Armenia being the first Christian state), of which 94.7 percent of the population consider themselves to be members as a birthright, even if they rarely enter a church building. Alternative religions found in the republic are almost entirely Christian (mainly Russian Orthodox, and Armenian Catholic and Protestant churches), with a few thousand (1.3 percent) Yezidis and a handful of Muslims, Jews, Pagans, and other faiths. Since 1962, the Armenian Apostolic Church has been an active member of the World Council of Churches.

By 1988 Armenia was enjoying a higher standard of living, better education, and greater freedom than most Soviet Republics. It also had the advantage of its large and supportive diaspora. But its fortunes were to change dramatically. In December 1988 an earthquake in Spitak measuring 6.9 on the Richter scale killed 25,000, injured 15,000, and left 517,000 homeless. This led to the closure of the country's nuclear plant because of fears about its safety, but the acute need for electricity resulted in its being reopened in 1995. Even more disruptive was the war in Nagorno-Karabakh, an Armenian-populated enclave within its neighbor, the predominantly Muslim Azerbaijan, which had long been a bone of contention. The situation erupted in 1988 and in 1993 an economic blockade was imposed

on Armenia by Turkey and Azerbaijan. Fierce fighting ensued, and ethnic cleansing and wholesale migration on both sides resulted in an influx of Armenian refugees from Azerbaijan and an exodus of Azerbaijanis from Armenia. By 1994, when an uneasy cease-fire was agreed to, Karabakh and much of the surrounding territory were in Armenian hands. The country was, however, severely impoverished, and during the 1990s, with limited power and water supplies, its population suffered from extreme hardships, especially during the harsh winters. Although the Karabakh conflict had not been resolved by the end of the first decade of the 21st century, the Republic of Armenia has started to improve its situation, while it is still facing some severe economic and political challenges. On January 25, 2001, Armenia became the 42nd member state of the Council of Europe.

Archaeological sites indicate that the Armenian highlands have been inhabited since the Lower Paleolithic period; hieroglyphs from the Hittite Kingdom record some details of those who lived and fought in the area from the mid-14th century BCE. Present-day Armenians are thought to have emerged as a unique Indo-European linguistic family around 600 BCE, the earliest mentions of Armenians and Armenia occurring, respectively, in 550 and 520 BCE. By 70 BCE, the Armenian King Tigranes II (ca. 95–55) had united an empire stretching from the Caspian to the Mediterranean. As the result of many bloody battles among empires in the region, however, Armenia has found itself under the rule of the Roman, Byzantine, and Ottoman

ARMENIA

empires and Turkey in the west, and Persia, Russia, and the Soviet Union in the east. Nonetheless, it has managed to enjoy brief periods of independence and to remain relatively autonomous, with its own distinct cultural identity.

Little is known about the religion(s) of pre-Christian Armenia, but it seems the elements and some nature gods were worshipped. There then emerged various legendary heroes who have been compared with the gods of the Hittites and Assyrians. Later, a

number of Persian and, still later, Greek divinities were appropriated into the syncretistic Armenian pantheon, with their own, specifically Armenian, names: Aramazd, the creator, had his principal shrine at Ani; Anahit, the goddess of fertility and protector of the Armenians, had one of her chief temples at Erez.

It is said that Christianity was first introduced to Armenia in the second part of the first century by two of Jesus' disciples, Thaddeus and Bartholomew (hence the church's claim to apostolic origins). As elsewhere, the early Christians were persecuted, but around 301 King Tiridates III, having been converted by St. Gregory the Illuminator (whom he had imprisoned for 13 years), declared Armenia a Christian nation. Gregory was consecrated as the first catholicos (as the primates of the Armenian Apostolic Church and some other Eastern churches are called), and a cathedral was erected on the site of a Pagan temple at Etchmiadzin, the present site of the Catholicosate of All Armenians). Paganism was officially abolished, and most of its temples and statues were destroyed; but it continued for centuries, with remnants still surviving in folklore and local customs.

The homogeneous character of the church and the people was greatly strengthened in 406, when Mesrob Mashtotz (361–440) invented a special alphabet, enabling the Bible and other Christian literature to be translated into Armenian, but the church found itself under increasing attack from the Persians, who were trying to convert the Armenians to Zoroastrianism. In 451 the national hero, Vartan Mamikonian (d. 505), was defeated by an overwhelmingly superior force of Persians. The Armenians persisted in their Christianity, however, and in 485 were granted freedom of worship. Another event in 451 that was to contribute to the segregation of Armenian Christians was the Council of Chalcedon, which concluded that the one Person of Christ consists of two natures (divine and human). The Armenians, busily fighting to be Christians rather than Zoroastrians, did not attend the Council. They considered a sharp division between the two natures to be tainted with the Nestorian heresy, to which they were opposed. They were, however, also opposed to a Monophysite doctrine (according to which Christ was seen as having only a divine nature), believing rather that in Christ a divine and human nature was "one nature united in the Incarnate Word." While the fact that it has, historically, differed in its Christology from both Eastern Orthodoxy and the Roman Catholic Church has served to maintain the Armenian Church's separate identity, it has also meant that other Christian churches have not always been as ready to defend it as they might otherwise have been.

Challenges to the monolithic identity of Armenians and the early life of the Armenian church came during the first millennium from numerous heretics such as the Manicheans, Messalians (Euchites), Encratites, Montanists, and Novitianists, and the more specifically Armenian Borborites, Mcłnē, Iconoclasts, and Paulicians, all of whom underwent considerable persecution. Around the ninth century, the Tondrakian movement gained substantial support as a messianic social reformist movement that advocated asceticism and renunciation of material riches; it championed the peasants and poorer classes, causing serious disturbances for almost two centuries. Not surprisingly, it too was persecuted by the Armenian aristocracy and hierarchy of the Apostolic Church.

From the early 11th century Armenia suffered 400 years of invasions and massacres. Some Armenians fled to Persia, Europe, or India; many went to the northeast edge of the Mediterranean where, with the help of the Crusaders, they founded the Cilician Kingdom (1098–1375). The See of the Catholicos of All Armenians was re-established at Sis, the capital of the kingdom. But when in 1441 the Holy See returned to Etchmiadzin, a parallel Cilician Catholicosate continued, leading to an organizational split within the Apostolic Church.

In Cilicia, Catholicism gained the allegiance of a number of upper-class Armenians through intermarriage, educational institutions, and conversion. An Armenian Uniate Order (which uses an Eastern liturgy), the Mekhitarists, was founded in 1701. Although representing less than one percent of Armenians, they maintain important monastic centers of learning on the Venetian island of San Lazzaro, in Vienna, and elsewhere.

The establishment of the Ottoman Empire in 1453 led to four centuries of relative peace and independence, with the Armenian patriarch responsible for the Armenian millet (the millet system being one with semi-autonomous organizations administering various religious communities throughout the empire). However, the internal homogeneity the system offered the Armenian community worked only insofar as the Armenians followed a single religion. In 1830, French pressure resulted in the creation of a separate millet for Catholics; then Protestant missionaries, mainly from America, who were forbidden by law to convert Muslims, concentrated on the Christian Armenians, and, by 1847, a Protestant millet was established.

Toward the end of the 19th century, relations between the Armenians and their Turkish rulers deteriorated. In response to oppression and attacks by Turks and Kurds, small numbers of Armenian revolutionaries banded together; there followed a series of massacres of tens of thousands of Armenians in 1894–1896 and again in 1909. Then, in 1915, Armenians throughout Turkey were systematically murdered or marched into the desert to die. Perhaps half a million survived, thereby contributing to most of the present diaspora; two or three times that number perished as a result of genocidal atrocities.

In 1828 the Ottomans ceded the eastern area of Armenia to Russia; this portion, which roughly comprised present-day Armenia, enjoyed a short-lived independence from 1918 to 1920 before being conquered by the Red Army and becoming part of the Soviet Union. The church in Soviet Armenia suffered from the persecution and many of the deprivations experienced by other Soviet republics but continued to play an important part in the life of the community (although accusations of its being a Communist puppet resulted in a rift between the Catholicosates of Etchmiadzin and Cilicia).

Compared with its immediate neighbors, Armenia has a relatively high standard of human rights. The 1991 Law on Freedom of Conscience and Religious Organizations guarantees freedom of thought, conscience, and religion to everyone, subject only to the protection of public order, health and morality, and the rights and freedoms of other citizens. Although the law affirms the separation of church and state, and maintains that all citizens and registered religious communities have the same rights, the Apostolic Church (defined as the national church) is accorded certain privileges. Proselytizing is forbidden, except by the Apostolic Church, and religious organizations are required to register, a 1997 amendment raising the minimum requirement for registration from 50 to 200 adult members, and banning foreign funding for religions with headquarters outside Armenia. The law also gave the Armenian Church the exclusive right to have chaplains in hospitals, prisons, and the army. In 2000, a Memorandum of Understanding was signed as a preliminary step toward a concordat between church and state that would amend the Constitution by clarifying conditions for church-state collaboration on subjects such as education, social services, state protocol, and the media. Since 2004 "The History of the Armenian Church" has been a compulsory subject in the schools. But while most of the population would seem to endorse the rightness of perceiving the Armenian Apostolic Church as the national church, at the turn of the century only 8 percent were attending church services at least once a week, and when the Armenian Center for National and International Studies (ACNIS) asked 50 intellectuals in 2004 "Which component prevails in the average Armenian's worldview?" 34 percent said it was a Christian worldview, 32 percent Pagan, and 24 percent atheist. When the same group was asked "What is the role of the spiritual world in our life today?" 2 percent estimated "great," 74 percent "small," and 24 percent "none."

By 2004, more than 50 different groupings of religions and religious charitable organizations were officially registered. These included the Armenian Catholic Church, several Armenian evangelical Baptist churches and evangelical Protestants, the Russian Orthodox Church, the Seventh-day Adventist Church, Charismatics, the Apostolic Catholic Assyrian Church of the East, the New Apostolic Church, the Word of Life, the Watchman Nee Memorial Church, Judaism, the Baha'i Faith, the Church of Jesus Christ of Latter-day Saints, and the Pagan Order of Arordy (the "children of Ara," Ara being the principal god in the Armenian neo-Pagan pantheon). There were also a number of ethnically affiliated Orthodox churches (Georgian, Greek, Romanian, Bulgarian), and a few other religions that had not registered for a variety of reasons—for example, most Yezidis and Molokans do not feel the need to register as a religious community; the charter of the Jehovah's Witnesses is deemed to contradict the Constitution; and ISKCON (the International Society of Krishna Consciousness) did not have the necessary 200 members. Some religions function openly without official sanction, while members of other religions, such as the Unification movement, operate in a more or less clandestine fashion as individuals or small communities.

As elsewhere throughout the former Soviet Union, the traditional religions of the new republics have continued to feel the effects of the years of oppression.

State-imposed secularism, the confiscation of property, a shortage of clergy, an atheistically socialized population, lack of experience in teaching and pastoral skills, and other deprivations all took their toll. The arrival of well-trained and prosperous missionaries offering their spiritual (and secular) wares to the recently liberated population was seen as adding insult to injury. In 1992, the two catholicoi issued an official joint statement vigorously objecting to the proselytizing efforts of Armenian Roman Catholics, Mekhitarists, Protestants, various para-church movements, such as Jehovah's Witnesses, Pentecostals, and Mormons, and non-Christian movements such as ISKCON and Transcendental Meditation.

On the whole, the traditional religious communities have continued to practice their beliefs without too much difficulty, but the fortunes of the newer religions have been more mixed. The ISKCON temple in Yerevan has been desecrated more than once. In April 1995 members of a number of minority religions, including Krishna devotees, Baptists, Baha'i, Charismatics, and Jehovah's Witnesses, were threatened, robbed, attacked, and even imprisoned by paramilitary gangs. Krishna devotees were taken, bleeding from the head, to hospitals; members of The Family International were told that if they did not leave Yerevan within the next few hours they would be thrown over the balcony of their fifth-floor Yerevan apartment. They left. Members of an indigenous new religion, the Warriors of Christ, were imprisoned for hooliganism. Such incidents provoked international condemnation and have not been repeated; however, the Warriors of Christ has had its property confiscated and its leader imprisoned on suspicion of swindling—an accusation that the movement hotly denied; there are reports of police standing by and watching while Jehovah's Witnesses have been physically assaulted; some 80 Witnesses were in prison in 2008 for conscientious objection because, although an Alternative Service Law was introduced in 2004, the Witnesses object that it "does not provide for a genuine civilian service as the service is still managed and supervised by the Ministry of Defense."

Armenia entered the 21st century facing acute economic, political, and military challenges, and, as throughout its turbulent history, its national church has continued to play a significant role in the social and political life of its people. As well as being confronted by a multiplicity of internal problems, the republic has to cope with a variety of tensions that are constantly emerging and re-emerging in its relationships with its neighbors, with its diasporic community, and with the Council of Europe over issues related to human rights. How it will develop in an environment of increasing globalization and pluralism remains to be seen.

Eileen Barker

See also: Apostolic Catholic Assyrian Church of the East; Armenian Apostolic Church (Holy See of Etchmiadzin); Armenian Catholic Church; Baha'i Faith; Church of Jesus Christ of Latter-day Saints; Eastern Orthodoxy; Family International, The; International Society for Krishna Consciousness; Jehovah's Witnesses; Molokans; New Apostolic Church; Roman Catholic Church; Russian Orthodox Church (Moscow Patriarchate); Seventh-day Adventist Church; Unification Movement; World Council of Churches; Yezidis.

References

Abrahamian, Levon. 2006. *Armenian Identity in a Changing World*. Costa Mesa, CA: Mazda, 2006.

Bournoutian, George A. *A Concise History of the Armenian People: From Ancient Times to the Present*. Costa Mesa, CA: Mazda, 2006.

Corely, Felix. "The Armenian Church under the Soviet and Independent Regimes, Part 3: The Leadership of Vazgen." *Religion, State, and Society* 26, nos. 3–4 (1998). See also vol. 24, nos. 1 and 4 for parts 1 and 2, 1996.

Dadrian, Vahakn N. *The History of the Armenian Genocide: Ethnic Conflict from the Balkans to Anatolia to the Caucasus*. Providence, RI: Berghahn, 1995.

Hovannisian, Richard. *The Republic of Armenia*. 4 vols. Berkeley: University of California Press, 1977, 1982, 1996.

Nersessian, Sirarpie Der. *The Armenians*. London and New York: Thames and Hudson, 1969.

Tchilingirian, Hratch. "In Search of Relevance: Church and Religion in Armenia since Independence." In *Religion et politique dans le Caucase post-soviétique*, edited by Bayram Balci and

Raoul Mitika, 277–311. Paris: Maisonneuve & Larose, 2007.

Walker, Christopher J. *Armenia: The Survival of a Nation.* 2nd ed. London: Routledge, 1990.

Armenian Apostolic Church (Holy See of Etchmiadzin)

The Holy See of Etchmiadzin is one of the two major existing hierarchical sees (the other being the Great House of Cilicia) of the Armenian Apostolic Church and has jurisdiction over the largest segment of the worldwide Armenian Christian population. Virtually all Armenians are at least nominal Christians, and Christianity has had a profound influence on Armenian culture and life even among the increasing number of secular Armenians. This influence has ancient origins. The presence of Christians in Armenia can be traced back as far as the Apostolic period. According to a tradition, 2 of the 12 Apostles, Thaddeus and Bartholomew, were the first evangelizers of Armenia and were both martyred there. There is historical evidence of a substantial Christian community in Armenia during the first three centuries of Christianity.

Christians remained a persecuted minority in Armenia until the missionary activity of Saint Gregory the Illuminator (240–332). Gregory, a relative of the Armenian king Tiridates III (ca. 238–314), was raised a Christian. The Pagan Tiridates had Gregory imprisoned for nearly 15 years in Khor Virab (deep dungeon) in Artashat, near Mount Ararat. Gregory was eventually released to cure Tiridates of a debilitating illness. Gregory converted the king and royal family to Christianity. Tiridates proclaimed Christianity the state religion of Armenia around 301.

After his ordination, Gregory baptized the king and royal family and was subsequently installed as the first *catholicos,* or chief bishop, of all Armenians, and continued his efforts to evangelize the Armenian people. In particular, Gregory is reported to have had a vision in Vagharshapat (12 miles west of Yerevan, the present-day capital of Armenia) of Christ descending from heaven and striking the ground with a golden hammer. At this spot, the Cathedral of Holy Etchmiadzin (the Only Begotten One Descended) was built.

Etchmiadzin thus became the original See of the Catholicos of All Armenians. With the support of the royal family, Christianity was able to spread quickly throughout Armenia and to permeate all aspects of Armenian life and culture.

The fifth century is significant to the Armenian church for three reasons. First, Saint Mesrop Mashtots (d. 438) invented the Armenian alphabet in 405. Together with the catholicos Saint Sahak I (d. 439) and a number of disciples, Mesrop worked on the translation of the Bible into Armenian. Second, the Persian king attempted to impose Zoroastrianism on the Armenians. The Armenians resisted and, under the command of the general Saint Vardan Mamikonian (d. 451), met the Persian forces in battle at Avarair in 451. Although the Armenian forces were defeated, the resistance continued and, in 484, the new Persian king allowed the Armenians to practice their Christian faith. The war against the Persians remains a defining feature of Armenian religious and national identity. Finally, due to the war, the Armenians were not represented at the Council of Chalcedon (451), one of the international gatherings of bishops of the Christian church at which decisions on essential Christian doctrines were made. The Armenian church later formally rejected Chalcedon. As a result, the church has been isolated from the Eastern Orthodox churches that accepted the Council's ruling, while being in communion with the other non-Chalcedonian or Oriental Orthodox churches. The liturgy and traditions of the Armenian church are nevertheless very similar to those of Eastern Orthodoxy.

The See of the Catholicos of All Armenians is not attached to any particular city. In 485, the see moved to Dvin, near Etchmiadzin. From the 10th to the 12th centuries, it was moved several times to various cities. As a result of invasions in Armenia, many Armenians migrated to Cilicia during the 11th and 12th centuries. In 1116, the see was moved to Cilicia. During the Cilician period, there was increased contact with other churches. Saint Nerses IV Klayetsi (the Gracious) (1102–1173) was a remarkable catholicos who worked for unity with the Roman Catholic and Eastern Orthodox churches.

In 1375, the Armenian Kingdom of Cilicia fell. Many Armenians wished to return the see to Etchmiadzin. The incumbent catholicos, however, did not want

Cathedral in Etchmiadzin, home of the Holy See of Etchmiadzin of the Armenian Apostolic Church. (Haikik/Dreamstime.com)

to leave Cilicia. Instead, a new catholicos was elected at Etchmiadzin in 1441. Henceforth, there have been two Armenian catholicoi, the catholicos of all Armenians in Etchmiadzin and the catholicos of Cilicia.

The church in Etchmiadzin faced various challenges in the ensuing centuries. The church had a political function, since there was no longer an Armenian state. The catholicos of Etchmiadzin had to deal with Persian and later Russian authorities. Various catholicoi of Etchmiadzin, most notably Mkrtich I Khrimian (d. 1906), were influential national leaders.

An attempted genocide of the Armenians by the Ottomans starting in 1915 resulted in the deaths of more than a million Armenians and the creation of a worldwide diaspora. A small fraction of historical Armenia, including Etchmiadzin, became the Soviet Republic of Armenia. The church was severely persecuted under Communist rule. With the fall of the Soviet Union and the restoration of Armenia's independence in 1991, the see has been free to operate its seminary and resume its prominent role in the life of the Armenian people. Catholicos Karekin I (d. 1999) signed a historic common declaration with Pope John Paul II in 1996 articulating the agreements on Christology that have been made by the Armenian church in dialogue with the Chalcedonian churches. The current catholicos, Karekin II, was elected and consecrated in 1999. He has been especially active in rebuilding and restructuring the church in Armenia.

Today, approximately six million Armenians claim adherence to the Armenian Apostolic Church. Half of all Armenians now live outside Armenia. The see of Etchmiadzin has primacy of honor for all faithful of the Armenian church. Only a catholicos can ordain bishops and bless the holy *meron*, or chrism, used in the sacraments of ordination and chrismation. The catholicos has, in addition to his ecclesial functions, an important role as a national figurehead. The catholicos is elected by a delegation of bishops and laypersons. The see has direct jurisdiction over dioceses in Armenia and the former Soviet Union, Europe, North and South America, and Australia. Several dioceses in the Middle East, as well as three dissident dioceses in North America (Eastern United States, Western United States, and Canada) are under the jurisdiction of the see of Cilicia. The Armenian patriarch of Constantinople exercises authority over the Armenian churches of Turkey, while the Armenian patriarch of Jerusalem is the custodian of Armenian churches and holdings in the Holy Land. Both patriarchs, however, are dependent on the catholicos of all Armenians for bishops and the holy chrism.

Armenian Apostolic Church
c/o The Holy See
Etchmiadzin
Armenia
www.etchmiadzin.com

Michael Papazian

See also: Armenian Apostolic Church (See of the Great House of Cilicia).

References

Arpee, L. *A History of Armenian Christianity from the Beginning of Our Own Time.* New York: Armenian Missionary Association of America, 1946.

Gulesserian, P. C. *The Armenian Church.* New York: AMS, 1970.

Papazian, M. B. *Light from Light: An Introduction to the History and Theology of the Armenian Church.* New York: SIS Publications, 2006.

Sarkissian, Karekin. *The Council of Chalcedon and the Armenian Church.* New York: Armenian Church Prelacy, 1965.

Thomson, R. W. *Studies in Armenian Literature and Christianity.* Aldershot, UK: Variorum, 1994.

Armenian Apostolic Church (See of the Great House of Cilicia)

The See of the Great House of Cilicia is one of the two major existing hierarchical sees of the Armenian Apostolic Church (the other being the See of Holy Etchmiadzin). While the see of Cilicia had a smaller jurisdiction than does Etchmiadzin, which most Armenians recognize as the preeminent see of the Armenian church, the historical significance of Cilicia, which is located in Anatolia along the Mediterranean coast, and the important role that the see of Cilicia has had in maintaining the identity and loyalty of Armenians living in oppressive circumstances has given the see considerable prestige and significance.

As a result of invasions of Armenia by the Seljuk Turks in the 11th century, a large number of Armenians migrated to Cilicia. The See of the Catholicos of All Armenians moved to Cilicia in 1116, eventually settling in the city of Sis. This was an especially vibrant period for the Armenian church, in part because the church was now in direct contact with Latin Christians and Crusaders. Many of the Armenian bishops were greatly influenced by Latin Christianity and culture, and even entered into full communion with Rome. Notable clergy in this period were catholicos Saint Nerses IV Klayetsi (the Gracious) (1102–1173), the author of numerous theological works and poems, and Saint Nerses of Lampron (1153–1198), bishop of Tarsus and author of an extensive commentary on the Armenian liturgy. Both men were actively involved in attempts to restore unity with the Greek and Latin churches.

With the aid of Crusaders, the Armenians were able to establish a kingdom in Cilicia. The Armenian Kingdom of Cilicia fell in 1375 to the Egyptian Mamelukes. Many Armenians began to return to Armenia and wanted to return the see to Etchmiadzin in Armenia. The incumbent catholicos, Grigor IX Mousabegyantz, however, did not want to leave Cilicia. Instead, a new catholicos, Kirakos of Virab, was elected at Etchmiadzin in 1441. As a result, there are today two Armenian catholicoi, the catholicos of all Armenians, whose see is at Etchmiadzin, and a catholicos of the Great House of Cilicia. Both catholicoi have the same privileges and authority to ordain bishops and to bless the holy *meron,* or chrism, used in the sacraments of ordination and chrismation. The catholicos of all Armenians enjoys a primacy of honor, though the catholicos of Cilicia has complete authority within the dioceses under his jurisdiction. There are no doctrinal or liturgical disagreements between the two sees. Disagreements over jurisdiction were limited and inconsequential until the political crises of the 20th century.

In 1915, the Ottoman government began a policy of genocide against the Armenians. As a result, Cilicia was effectively depopulated of Armenians. The see of Cilicia went into exile, eventually settling in Antelias, Lebanon, on the outskirts of Beirut. Having lost its traditional dioceses in Cilicia, the see of Cilicia was granted the dioceses of Lebanon, Syria, and Cyprus, formerly under the jurisdiction of the Armenian patriarch of Jerusalem. In 1920, Armenia was forcibly incorporated into the Soviet Union. Thus, the see of Etchmiadzin fell under Communist domination. Because of opposition to Communist influence, several dioceses that had been under Etchmiadzin asked to be taken under the jurisdiction of the see of Cilicia. In 1956, Catholicos Zareh I of Cilicia agreed to extend his jurisdiction over the dioceses of Iran, Greece, and a number of North American parishes that refused to accept the authority of the Etchmiadzin diocese. As a result, there are now rival Armenian dioceses in North America. The Eastern and Western U.S. Prelacies as well as the Canadian Prelacy are the dioceses that are under the jurisdiction of the see of Cilicia. The corresponding Dioceses of the Eastern United States, Western United States, and Canada remain under the jurisdiction of the see of Etchmiadzin. The collapse of the Soviet Union and the restoration of Armenian independence in 1991 were viewed as hopeful signs that the conflict would end. The jurisdictional conflicts, however, have persisted. All recent efforts at unity have been fruitless and the status quo has effectively solidified.

Because it was free of Communist interference, the see of Cilicia was more active in the 20th century than the see of Etchmiadzin. Its seminary has produced clergymen who serve the Armenian church throughout the word. The see publishes a large number of books in Armenian on religious and secular topics. Several of the catholicoi of Cilicia have also been prominent leaders in the ecumenical movement. Catholicos Karekin II (catholicos of Cilicia from 1977 to 1995; as Karekin I, catholicos of all Armenians, 1995–1999) was an observer at the Second Vatican Council and a vice moderator of the World Council of Churches. Catholicos Aram I (catholicos of Cilicia since 1995) served as moderator of the World Council of Churches for two consecutive seven-year terms beginning in 1991.

Armenian Apostolic Church
c/o the Holy See
Armenian Catholicosate of Cilicia
Antelas
Lebanon
www.armenianorthodoxchurch.org

Michael Papazian

See also: Armenian Apostolic Church (Holy See of Etchmiadzin); World Council of Churches.

References

Arpee, L. *A History of Armenian Christianity from the Beginning of Our Own Time.* New York: Armenian Missionary Association of America, 1946.

Gulesserian, P. C. *The Armenian Church.* New York: AMS, 1970.

Papazian, M. B. *Light from Light: An Introduction to the History and Theology of the Armenian Church.* New York: SIS Publications, 2006.

Sarkissian, Karekin. *The Council of Chalcedon and the Armenian Church.* New York: Armenian Church Prelacy, 1965.

Thomson, R. W. *Studies in Armenian Literature and Christianity.* Aldershot, UK: Variorum, 1994.

Armenian Catholic Church

The Armenian Catholic Church, an Eastern-rite church in full communion with the Roman Catholic Church, emerged in the 18th century as the outgrowth of several centuries of missionary activity by Roman Catholics among members of the Armenian Apostolic Church residing in Lebanon. The ancient church of Armenia was separated from the larger body of Christendom in the fifth century following the Council of Chalcedon (451 CE). For a variety of reasons, the Armenian bishops refused to affirm the teachings promulgated by the Council, one of the international gatherings of bishops of the Christian church at which decisions on essential Christian doctrines were made concerning the nature of Christ. The Armenian position has traditionally been

Armenian Supreme Patriarch Karekin I, center, blesses bread and salt during a celebration of the centennial of the Diocese of the Armenian Church of America at a special service at St. Vartan Cathedral in New York, May 3, 1998. Armenian archbishop Khajag Barsamian, left, and Cardinal John O'Connor of New York were among the religious leaders celebrating the 100th anniversary of the arrival of the first Armenian immigrants to the United States and the subsequent founding of the Armenian Church in America. (AP/Wide World Photos)

termed Monophysitism, the doctrine that Christ had only one nature, the divine, even though he took on human form. Chalcedon taught that Christ had both a human and a divine nature. The argument remains an important one in Christian theology, and many within other Christian communities considered the Armenians to be heretics.

After many centuries of independent development, members of the Armenian church came into contact with the Crusaders who passed through Little Armenia (Cilicia), an Armenian land on the southern coast of what is now Turkey. An initial alliance of the church in Cilicia and the Church in Rome was established in

1198. However, the union was unacceptable to the main body of Armenians and was ultimately brought to an end by the Tatar conquest of the area in 1375. The Roman Catholics kept the ideal alive with the publication of a union decree by the Council of Florence in 1439.

Over the next centuries, as opportunities arose, missionary activity was carried out by Catholic priests, and a scattered number of Armenian congregations affiliated with the Roman Catholic Church emerged. Then in 1742, following the conversion of an Armenian bishop, Abraham Ardzivian (1679–1749), to Catholicism, Pope Benedict XIV (r. 1740–1758) established the Armenian Catholic Church as a formal body of believers with Ardzivian as their patriarch. He took the name Abraham Pierre I, and his successors have subsequently included Pierre as part of their religious title. The church continued to use the Armenian liturgy, which had been developed among the Armenian people through the centuries, with some minor adjustments.

The faithful under the new patriarch's jurisdiction resided within the Ottoman Empire, and they became subject to some immediate persecution. The Ottoman authorities wished to relate to their Armenian subjects through one church, the Armenian Apostolic Church, and its bishop in Constantinople. It was not until 1829 that the government recognized those Armenians in communion with Rome. The government allowed the appointment of a second bishop, to reside in Constantinople. Finally in 1867, the two bishoprics were united into a single patriarchal office located at Constantinople.

The church grew substantially for a half century but was decimated by the Turks' wholesale slaughter of Armenians at the end of World War I. Those who died included an estimated 100,000 Armenian Catholics, among them 7 bishops, 130 priests, and 47 nuns. In 1928, the patriarch was relocated to Lebanon. During this same period, many Armenians left their traditional homeland and relocated across Europe, North Africa, Australia, and North and South America. Subsequently dioceses were established in France, the United States, and Argentina.

The church is currently led by His Beatitude Nerses Bedros XIX (b. 1940), who assumed the patriarchal office in 1999. In 2008, there were seven dioceses, including two in Syria and one each in Lebanon, Iraq, Iran, Egypt, and Turkey. The Eparchy of Our Lady of Nareg, established in 2005, includes the nine parishes in the United States and Canada. There are some 376,000 members worldwide, of which 36,000 reside in North America. Following the fall of the Soviet Union, the Vatican moved to strengthen its ties to Armenian Catholics in the former Communist countries and appointed a bishop to oversee their work. The church supports three ordered religious communities, a seminary in Lebanon, and a college in Rome. The church is an active member of the Middle East Council of Churches.

Armenian Catholic Church
rue de l'Hopital Libanais
Jeitaoui, 2400 Beirut
Lebanon
http://www.armeniancatholic.org/

J. Gordon Melton

See also: Armenian Apostolic Church (See of the Great House of Cilicia); Middle East Council of Churches.

References

Liesel, N. *The Eastern Catholic Liturgies: A Study in Words and Pictures.* Westminster, MD: Newman Press, 1960.

Roberson, Ronald G. *The Eastern Christian Churches—A Brief Survey.* 5th ed. Rome: Edizioni Orientalia Christiana, Pontificio Istituto Orientale, 1995.

Arminius, Jacob

1560–1609

Jacob Arminius, a minister/scholar with the Reformed Church of the Netherlands at the beginning of the 17th century, created a form of Calvinist theology that attempted to correct the dominant position of the Reformed Church that Arminius believed made God the author of sin and turned humans into automatons. His position led to the formation of a dissenting group, the Remonstrants, and the calling of the Synod of Dort, which hammered out what became the majority Calvinist opinion on God's sovereignty.

Arminius was born October 10, 1560, in Oudewater, Utrecht, Holland. His father died during Jacob's childhood, and his mother, now responsible for several children, allowed a Catholic priest, Theodorus Aemilius, to adopt Jacob. Aemilius sent the youth to school at Utrecht. He was in his mid-teens when his mother became one of the victims of the massacre at Oudewater following the Spanish conquest of the besieged city in 1575. A short time later he moved to Leiden to major in theology at the university. Following a common practice, he adopted a latinized form of his birth name, Jacob Hermansen, and emerged with the name by which he is commonly known.

Arminius remained at Leiden for six years (1576–1582) just at the time that the Reformed Church was

Jacob Arminius (1560–1609), Dutch clergyman and theologian. (Bettmann/Corbis)

becoming the dominant religious force in the land. Among his teachers was Johann Kolmann, a critic of the more stringent forms of the theology of John Calvin (1509–1564). Its over-emphasis on God's sovereignty tended to make God an authoritative and arbitrary monarch and an executioner. Arminius, nevertheless, moved on to Geneva, where he studied under Theodore Beza (1519–1605), who had assumed Calvin's chair in theology. In 1588 Arminius returned to Holland, where he was ordained as a minister and became the pastor of a Reformed congregation in Amsterdam. He married Lijsbet Reael two years later.

During his years at Amsterdam and beginning in 1603 as a professor of theology at Leiden he assumed the task of refuting the attacks upon Calvinist thought, especially its teaching of predestination by prominent Dutch philosopher/theologian Dirck Volckertszoon Coornhert (1522–1590). However, his study of Coornhert's arguments convinced Arminius of their correctness. Slowly he began to reconstruct his own Calvinist position to accommodate his changing views.

Arminius died at Leiden on October 19, 1609. While he had worked out the major points, what would become Arminian theology would be systematized by his followers and published a year later as the Five Articles of Remonstrance (1610).

The Five Articles affirmed that God had willed the salvation of those whom he knew would turn in faith to him; that Christ died for all; that humans stand in need of salvation; that humans may resist God's grace; and that humans who have been saved are empowered by the Holy Spirit to remain in a state of grace. The position of the Remonstrants would lead to the calling of a synod at Dort, which met in 1618–1619. The Synod of Dort rejected the Arminian position and issued five statements refuting the Five Articles point by point. The position of the Remonstrants stood condemned by the state-related church of the country but was tolerated and allowed to continue to exist by the secular authorities.

In England, Arminius's position would be adopted by the Arminian or Free Will Baptists and a century later by John Wesley, who infused it into the theology of the Methodist movement.

J. Gordon Melton

See also: Calvin, John; Methodism; Reformed Churches in the Netherlands (Liberated); Remonstrant Brotherhood; Wesley, John.

References

Bangs, Carl. *Arminius*. Nashville: Abingdon Press, 1971.

Curtiss, George L. *Arminianism in History: Or the Revolt from Predestinationism*. Nashville: Carnston & Curtis, 1894.

McKinley, O. Glenn. *Where Two Creeds Meet: A Biblical Evaluation of Calvinism and Arminianism*. Kansas City, MO: Beacon Hill Press, 1959.

Muller, Richard Alfred. *God, Creation, and Providence in the Thought of Jacob Arminius*. Grand Rapids, MI: Baker Book House, 1991.

Pinnock, Clark H. *The Grace of God, the Will of Man: A Case for Arminianism*. Grand Rapids, MI: Zondervan, 1989.

Army of Mary

The Army of Mary is a large splinter Catholic group, founded by the Canadian mystic Marie-Paule Giguère, which separated itself from the mainline Roman Catholic Church in the first decade of the 21st century. Marie-Paule Giguère was born in Sainte-Germaine-du-Lac-Etchemin (Quebec) in 1921 and married Georges Cliche (1917–1997) in 1944. Although Marie-Paule had five children, her marriage was not happy. Georges was a spendthrift, unfaithful, and an alcoholic. Counseled by a number of Catholic priests, Marie-Paule left him in 1957. She started hearing the "internal voice" of Jesus Christ and the Virgin Mary as a teenager, and eventually they asked her to write a voluminous spiritual autobiography, *Vie d'Amour* (*Life of Love*), the 15 volumes of which were published between 1979 and 1994.

Marie-Paule first "heard" a reference to the Army of Mary, a "wonderful movement" that she was called to lead, in 1954. It was officially established on August 28, 1971. A priest from the Catholic diocese of Rimouski (Quebec), Father Philippe Roy (1916–1988), joined the movement in 1972 and eventually became its general director. Following a request by Monsignor Jean-Pierre van Lierde (1907–1995), a prelate in the Vatican's Roman Curia and a friend of Marie-Paule, the archbishop of Quebec, Maurice Cardinal Roy (1905–1985; not a relative of Father Philippe Roy) officially recognized the Army of Mary as a Catholic lay association in 1975. In 1976, a popular French author of texts on prophecy, Raoul Auclair (1906–1997), after having read the manuscript of *Vie d'Amour*, decided to become a member of the Army of Mary. In 1978, he moved from France to Quebec, where he became the editor of the movement's magazine, *L'Etoile*. In the years that followed, the Army of Mary gathered thousands of followers in Canada (and hundreds more in Europe).

The Community of the Sons and Daughters of Mary, a religious order including both priests and nuns, was established in 1981, with Pope John Paul II (1920–2005) personally ordaining the first Son of Mary as a priest in 1986. Several other ordinations followed, and a number of Catholic dioceses throughout the world were happy to welcome both the Sons and the Daughters of Mary to help them in their pastoral work. After her husband's death in 1997, Marie-Paule herself became a Daughter of Mary and was subsequently elected superior general of the congregation. A larger Family of the Sons and Daughters of Mary also includes lay organizations, such as the Oblate-Patriots, established in 1986 with the aim of spreading Catholic social teachings, and the Marialys Institute (created in 1992), which gathers Catholic priests who are not members of the Sons of Mary but who share their general aims.

The Army of Mary's success has always been accompanied by conflicts with members of the Catholic hierarchy. Liberal Catholic bishops in Quebec regarded the movement as suspiciously archconservative. After Cardinal Roy's death, his successor Louis-Albert Cardinal Vachon (1912–2006) proved to be as hostile to Marie-Paule's visions and revelations as Roy had been sympathetic. Vachon regarded some of the visions as of dubious orthodoxy. He focused on certain writings by Raoul Auclair (according to which the Immaculate existed as a spiritual being since before the creation, later to descend into the Virgin Mary) and on other writings by a Belgian member, Marc Bosquart, who had moved to Quebec and had written two books claiming that the Immaculate was now mystically inhabiting Marie-Paule. Although the Army of Mary maintained that these were Bosquart's personal opinions, rather than teachings of the movement itself, Vachon proceeded to withdraw the official recognition of the Army of Mary as an official Catholic organization. The case went to Rome, and in 1987 the Congregation for the Doctrine of Faith judged Bosquart's opinions as "seriously erroneous." Although the Army of Mary promptly withdrew Bosquart's books from circulation, skirmishes with Catholic bishops in Quebec continued, while some English-speaking Canadian bishops, and certain bishops in Italy, were still prepared to accept both the Sons and Daughters of Mary and the Army of Mary itself into their dioceses.

Finally, on March 31, 2000, the Vatican Congregation for the Doctrine of Faith sent a note to all Canadian bishops stating that Marie-Paule's *Vie d'Amour* contained doctrinal errors and that further action needed to be taken. In 2001, the National Conference of Canadian Bishops published a statement saying that the Army of Mary should no longer be regarded as a Roman Catholic organization. Subsequent attempts at reconciliation did not prove fruitful, and in 2006–2007 a priest of the Army of Mary, Father Pierre Mastropietro, was first acclaimed Universal Father of a Church of John and then proceeded to perform acts normally reserved in the Roman Catholic Church to the pope. He canonized Raoul Auclair as a saint, issued bulls and doctrinal definitions, and authorized the ordination of new priests (without the sanction of any Catholic bishop in good standing). Although the Army of Mary insisted on the distinction between a mystical Church of John (led by Mastropietro, aka Padre Jean-Pierre) and the (apparently still recognized as valid and existing) Church of Peter (led by Benedict XVI), the Vatican could not tolerate the new situation and with a declaration dated July 11, 2007, moved to excommunicate both Mastropietro and all the members of the Army of Mary recognizing him as Universal Father and participating in his ceremonies. The Army of Mary is now regarded by Rome as a separated, schismatic group, although several Canadian bishops have declared that they still hope that a dialogue with this large movement of some 5,000 members may be maintained.

Army of Mary
Centre International de l'Armée de Marie
Spiri-Maria
155 Route de la Grande-Ligne
Lac-Etchemin, Quebec G0R 1S0
Canada
http://www.communaute-dame.qc.ca
Massimo Introvigne and PierLuigi Zoccatelli

See also: Roman Catholic Church.

References

Giguère, Marie-Paule. *Vie d'Amour*. 15 vols. Limoilou, Quebec: Vie d'Amour, 1979–1994. Volumes 1–3, 5, and 7–15 have been translated into English as *Life of Love*. Limoilou, Quebec: Vie d'Amour, 1979–1987. See also the five volumes *Appendices*. Limoilou, Quebec: Vie d'Amour, 1992–1993.

Introvigne, Massimo. "En Route to the Marian Kingdom: Catholic Apocalypticism and the Army of Mary." In *Christian Millenarianism: From the Early Church to Waco,* edited by Stephen Hunt. London: Hurst, 2001.

Arnold, Gottfried

1666–1714

Gottfried Arnold was a Lutheran Pietist and pioneering Christian church historian who attempted to write a more balanced history of Western religion. In his mature years he moved toward a more mystical and esoteric faith that incorporated elements of Gnosticism.

Arnold was born in Annaberg, Saxony (Germany), the son of a school teacher. He studied at the Gymnasium at Gera before entering the University of Wittenburg in 1682. He majored in theology and church history and became acquainted with Philip Jacob Spener (1635–1705), then serving as the court chaplain at Dresden at the behest of the elector of Saxony. Spener had emerged as the leader of a movement to bring a more personal faith and life into the German Lutheranism (now the Evangelical Church in Germany) and had met with much negative response from people who had charged him with doctrinal deviance and disturbing church order. However, he had also gained some degree of popular support. With Spener's help, Arnold received an appointment as tutor at Quedlinburg, Saxony-Anhalt. While there, Arnold would write his first book, a life of Christ that gained a popular response and went through multiple editions.

The biography of Jesus also earned Arnold an appointment as the professor of church history at Giessen; however, he found that he disliked the academic life, especially the school's internal politics, and in 1698, after only a year, he resigned and returned to Quedlinburg. While at Geissen, however, he had begun to work on what would prove his most significant work, the *Unparteyische Kirchen- und Ketzer-historie (An Impartial History of the Church and of Heresy)*. The two-volume tome, published in 1699 and 1700, departed from the standard approach of church histories, which traced the development of the orthodox churches and treated dissenting groups as deviating heresies.

Arnold assumed a more modern position that attempted to understand the various different movements that had arisen through the centuries of church life and avoid the common apologetic position assumed by most historians.

His work called attention to a variety of different movements right up to his own day and included treatments of the post-Reformation Rosicrucians and Theosophists such as Jacob Boehme. He made the study of heretical movements a legitimate topic for academic research and in his overall perspective anticipated the approach that has become dominant in contemporary religious studies.

Critics immediately accused Arnold of demonstrating a high degree of sympathy for heretics, at times treating them more kindly than the orthodox church and its clergy. Arnold had accused some of his colleagues of subverting the historical task in favor of biased apologetics and neglecting the task of understanding the dissident movements throughout the church's history. He concluded that church authorities created heresy by assuming a defensive posture when attacked. Arnold, like many on the edge of or outside the established churches of his day, concluded that the Constantinian transformation of the church into a body aligned with government to have been a disaster.

Arnold posited the existence of a True Church composed of all those who have received the baptism of the Holy Spirit, the touch of God that converts the soul. God, in the form of wisdom, comes to dwell in the heart. In tracing the history of the True Church, many of the heretical groups, most of the Gnostic and Esoteric tradition, are considered as being within the lineage. In the orthodox church, the members of the True Church and others worship side by side, the unconverted being unaware of the True Church members in their midst.

While most contemporary church historians disapproved of Arnold's history, he would find enough of a positive response, primarily among the Free churches, to keep it from disappearing and it would in the next century influence the German Enlightenment. It would, for example, receive positive reviews from the likes of Goethe (1749–1832), the main literary figure of the German phase of the Enlightenment.

Arnold's next book, *Geheimniss der göttlichen Sophia* (*The Mystery of the Divine Sophia*), would reveal that he had in fact absorbed some of the perspective of the heretics about which he had earlier written. He developed a mystical theology that focused on a female image of wisdom (*sophia*). Wisdom was equated with the Word (John 1:1), the intelligence of God, that was spoken by God before creation. Sophia is communicated to those who are ready to receive her. She is hidden from those religious officiants who have no contact with her. She is the same when she appears whether to Protestants, Catholics, or heretics. Those who have come into contact with wisdom share the same truth and form an invisible communion, the communion of the saints. This communion would eventually extend to all.

Soon after publishing his book on Sophia/wisdom, Arnold married and in 1701 accepted a pastorate. He suppressed his mystical and esoteric views. His later writings tend to concentrate on practical theology. He identified with mainstream Lutheran Pietism, and from this perspective authored a number of hymns that were accepted within the Lutheran Church. He died on May 30, 1714, at Perleberg. His works emerged within the larger Pietist world that included the Church of the Brethren and the Mennonites, both of whom he influenced. At the same time, he stepped within the realm of the more radical mystical and Esoteric thinkers who were continuing the Western Esoteric tradition and surviving on the less-monitored edges of the established churches.

J. Gordon Melton

See also: Brethren; Evangelical Church in Germany; Gnosticism; Lutheranism; Mennonites; Western Esoteric Tradition.

References
Arnold, Gottfried. *Unparteyische Kirchen- und Ketzer-historie* (An Impartial History of the Church and of Heresy). Frankfurt, 1699–1700.

Deghaye, Pierre. "Gottfried Arnold." In *Dictionary of Gnosis & Western Esotericism*, edited by Woulter J. Haanegraaff, 103–105. Leiden: Brill, 2005.

Dörries, Hermann. *Geist und Geschichte bei Gottfried Arnold*. Göttingen: Vandenhoeck & Ruprecht, 1963.

Roberts, Frank Carl. *Gottfried Arnold as a Historian of Christianity: A Reappraisal of the Unparteyische Kirchen- und Ketzerhistorie.* Ph.D. diss., Vanderbilt University, 1973.

Stoffer, Dale R. "The Ecclesiology of Gottfried Arnold." *Brethren Life and Thought* 28 (Spring 1983): 91–100.

Stoffer, Dale R. "Gottfried Arnold's View of the Christian Life." *Brethren Life and Thought* 26, no. 4 (1981): 237–246.

Stoffer, Dale R. "The Life and Thought of Gottfried Arnold." *Brethren Life and Thought* 26, no. 3 (1981): 135–151.

Aro gTér

The mass exodus of Tibetans to India and the West after the Chinese occupation of 1959 has brought with it an extraordinary wealth of ideas and new possibilities. The development of the diaspora has coincided with a new kind of global culture, marked by affordable access to international travel and the opportunity to publish books inexpensively. The last decade of the 20th century saw the process accelerated with the development of Internet technology. One of the most important causes for the development of Tibetan Buddhism in the West is, however, socio-cultural. A profound dissatisfaction with conventional Christian forms and the absence of other significant philosophical movements has created a space in which Tibetan Buddhism has found a niche. The materialist dialectic embodied in the Cold War did not address spiritual concerns.

Within this Tibetan Buddhist niche there are many kinds of Tibetan Buddhism. Some kinds emphasize the study of traditional materials with an emphasis on Tibetan or Sanskrit texts. Some have resident Tibetan lamas, teaching either in English or with a translator. Most groups that have been established for more than a few years include older Western students as teachers. Very few expect Western students to become monks or to wear traditional Tibetan dress.

A group that places great importance on Western teachers is the Aro gTér. It was founded in the early 1980s by a Westerner who has adopted the name Ngak'chang Rinpoche. He was born in Germany in 1952 and raised in England. In 1989 he was awarded a doctorate in Tibetan Tantric Psychology from the University of West Bengal (Shantiniketan) by one of his main teachers, the rNying ma lama 'Chi med Rig 'dzin Rinpoche. The Aro gTér philosophy emphasizes family life and the formulation of traditional teachings in a new way to suit Western culture. Their principal practices are Tantrism and Dzogchen (rDzogs chen), a meditation technique, and the organization is divided into three regions, or Confederate Sanghas, in the United Kingdom, the United States, and continental Europe.

They have a program of apprenticeship, which is a training period of seven years followed by discipleship. Apprenticeship is described in these terms: "The apprenticeship programme offers access to a system of teaching which is both traditional and highly untraditional. It is traditional in that its teachings and practices have their origin in a specific Tibetan lineage—the Aro gTér lineage of Khyungchen Aro Lingma. It is untraditional in that its approach to those teachings and practices is deliberately and specifically offered in a Western context by Western Lamas. This approach is based upon the use of contemporary non-academic language."

Aro gTér
c/o Aro Books, Inc.
PO Box 330
Ramsey, NJ 07446
www.aroter.org

Diana Cousens

See also: Nyingma Tibetan Buddhism; Tantrism; Tibetan Buddhism.

References

Ngak'chang Rinpoche. *Wearing the Body of Visions.* Ramsey, NJ: Aro Books, 1995.

Ngak'chang Rinpoche with Khandro Déchen. *Spectrum of Ecstasy: Embracing Emotions as the Path.* Ramsey, NJ: Aro Books, 1997.

Arsha Vidya Gurukulam

Arsha Vidya Gurukulam was founded at Saylorsburg, Pennsylvania, in 1986, by Swami Dayananda Saraswati, who had been a disciple of Swami Chinmayananda (1916–1993), famous as an authority on the scriptures of India and founder of a teaching mission to the West. Swami Dayananda seemed destined to be the teacher's successor as head of Chinmaya West, but in 1982 he left the organization in part to lead what he considered a more simple life as a teacher rather than an administrator of a growing institution.

Swami Dayananda emerged in the 1970s teaching a course on Advaida Vedanta, a monistic form of Hindu thought that views reality as one, and all distinctions as illusion. Important to the advaida approach is a understanding of the self (*atman*) as identical with God (*Brahman*). Advaida negates *dvaida*, which means "two." Thus advaida means "that which is nondual." It reveals that there is nothing other than the One, a whole without parts. Enlightenment is a shift in understanding concerning the Whole that is best brought about through the study of sacred texts.

Dayananda's teaching career has included both an intensive study of classical Hindu literature that undergirds the more than 20 books he has authored. He continues to teach intensive courses on Vedanta at Saylorsburg and its two sister ashrams in India, one at Coimbatore, established in 1990, and one at Rishikesh. These ashrams are distinctive in that they are not dominated by a contemplative atmosphere but attempt to create a more academic environment. The primary goal is the acquisition of knowledge about Vedanta. Residents spend much time in the study of the ancient Sanskrit texts. Spiritual practice is centered on the 30-minute period of meditation each morning. Mastery of the sacred scripture is seen as the more reliable means to overcome ignorance and appropriate direct knowledge of the Absolute.

Through the years Swami Dayananda has trained a number of students who have themselves gone on to establish their own ashrams following the traditions they have learned at Arsha Vidya Gurukulam. Included are Swami Viditatmananda, founder of Adhyatma Vidya Mandir in Gujarat; Swami Vagishananda, founder of the Education for Living program in London, England; and Gambhira Chaitanya who teaches in Argentina and Brazil. The staff of teachers at the three ashrams oversees a year-round program of instruction that also includes classes on hatha yoga and ayurveda medicine.

Arsha Vidya Pitham
PO Box 1059
Saylorsburg, PA 18353
www.arshavidya.org

J. Gordon Melton

See also: Enlightenment; Meditation; Rishikesh.

References
Dayananda Saraswati, Swami. *Exploring Vedanta.* Chennai, India: Arsha Vidya Centre, 2007.
Dayananda Saraswati, Swami. *The Sadhana and the Sadhya (The Means and the End).* Rishikish, India: Sri Gangadhareswar Trust, 1984.
Dayananda Saraswati, Swami. *The Value of Values.* Chennai, India: Arsha Vidya Centre, 2007.
Jordens, J. T. F. *Dayananda Saraswati: Essays on His Life and Ideas.* New Delhi: Manohar Publishers and Distributors, 1998.
"Swami Dayananda Renounces Chinmaya Mission West: Changes and Challenges Ahead." *New Saivite World* (Fall 1983).

Art of Living Foundation

Ravi Shankar (b. 1956, honored with the title of Sri Sri), who is not to be confused with the famous Indian musician, was born in 1956 in southern India. His life is totally dedicated to what he defines as the "re-evaluation of human values." In 1982 he founded the Art of Living Foundation in the United States. This educational organization, which refuses to be labeled a religious organization, was created to assist all members of society, regardless of their socio-cultural context, in reaching their full human potential. The International Association for Human Values (IAHV), with main offices in Geneva, Switzerland, and with three national chapters (United States, India, and Canada) embodies the common objective of all of the initiatives promoted and inspired by Ravi Shankar. Since November 1996, the Art of Living Foundation has been a nongovernment organization (NGO), with the status of consultant to the Economic and Social Council (ECOSOC) of the United Nations, offering educational programs, practical tools, and experience-gaining processes for stress management, problem solving, health

Founder of the Art of Living Foundation Sri Sri Ravi Shankar, center, arrives for Shivratri and the silver jubilee celebration of the foundation in Ahmadabad, India, February 16, 2007. (AP/Wide World Photos)

improvement, and living life with greater joy and enthusiasm. According to the foundation, more than a million people in 98 nations around the world have participated in these programs.

The Art of Living Foundation has affiliate offices on all of the continents and manages three main international centers: Bangalore (India), St. Mathieu du Parc (Quebec, Canada), and Bad Antogast (Oppenau, Germany). The "5 H Program" is a volunteer-operated initiative of the International Association for Human Values and offers social and community development programs that focus on five objectives: Health, Homes, Hygiene, Harmony amidst Diversity, and Human Values. In 1992, Ravi Shankar created the Prison SMART

(Stress Management and Rehabilitative Training) Foundation, whose activities are aimed at those people involved in the justice system. The foundation also organizes a series of specific training programs, which include the ART Excel (All 'Round Training for Excellence) program and the Corporate Executive Program (for corporate training).

Although Ravi Shankar draws from a spiritual patrimony of Indian origin, he also borrows from humanity's various religious and spiritual traditions, which he sees as having a universal relevance. According to the Art of Living, there are seven levels to human existence: body, breathing, mind, intellect, memory, ego, and self. In the teaching of Ravi Shankar, health is not seen simply as the absence of illness, but rather as consisting of the harmony of these seven levels. The Art of Living emphasizes the importance of learning special techniques for preserving or reestablishing this harmony. These techniques, which use breathing as the main tool, are applied at two levels. The first consists in different types of *pranayama* (from the Sanskrit; it literally means "to direct or store vital energy"), in which it is believed that inhalation coincides with taking in energy and exhalation coincides with the elimination of toxins from the body. The purpose of the pranayama is to keep the mind calm and lucid, to increase lung capacity, and to energize the entire organism. The second application is *sudarshan kriya* (from the Sanskrit, it literally means "purifying action that permits a clear vision of your own nature"), which again works with breathing in its twofold nature: the intake of vital energy and the release of toxins. The sudarshan kriya starts a self-healing process, making it possible for the individual to enjoy great benefits. The final purpose of these techniques is the revitalization of the seven levels and the resynchronization of the first six with the "self." When the body is charged with energy and the seven levels are in harmony, the natural and spontaneous response is for the individual to express the fundamental human values that represent the true human nature, a state of things that the Art of Living perceives as its objective.

Another tool used by the Art of Living is *Sahaj Samadhi* meditation. Meditation is defined as a state of being in which the individual effortlessly enters into contact with the most profound part of him or herself—"the Self"—the essence of the human soul by using a method that dates back to the ancient Vedic tradition, being the oldest, indeed the eternal scripture, according to Hindu belief. In addition to teaching these techniques, Ravi Shankar makes use of other tools, including a learning system aimed at integrating healthy and effective life principles into one's own daily life and at recognizing the mechanisms of the human mind that generate stress and uneasiness; the techniques are then used for self-liberation from stress and uneasiness.

There is no central headquarters for the foundation; of the international centers, the most important is in Bangalore.

Art of Living Foundation
c/o Ved Vignan Mahavidya Peeth-Bangalore
Prashant Rajore
21st km
Kanakapura Rd.
Udayapura, Bangalore, Karnataka 560 062
India

The International Association for Human Values (IAHV)
2 Ave.
Pictet Rochemont, CH-1207
Geneva
Switzerland
http://www.iahv.org/.
http://us.artofliving.org/index.html.

Andrea Menegotto

See also: Meditation; Yoga.

References

Menegotto, Andrea. "Arte di Vivere." In *Enciclopedia delle religioni in Italia,* edited by Massimo Introvigne et al. Torino, Italy: Elle Di Ci, 2001.
Shankar, Sri Sri Ravi. *God Loves Fun.* Santa Barbara, CA: Art of Living Foundation, 1996.

■ Aruba

Aruba, an independent island nation in the Caribbean Sea near the northern coast of Venezuela, is an autonomous member of the Kingdom of the Netherlands. Its 74 square miles of land is inhabited by about 103,065 residents (2009).

Aruba was originally settled by the Caiquetios people. They were the unfortunate victims of contact with Europeans, and through the 1600s were conquered; many were sold into slavery by the Spanish. The few Spanish settlers who occupied the island began to raise horses and cattle, which for many years formed the base of the island's economy.

The island came under Dutch control as a result of the Treaty of Westphalia in 1648, when Aruba was grouped together with nearby Curaçao and Bonaire as the Netherlands Antilles. Through the next century, because of the low need for labor, few slaves were

The Catholic chapel of Alto Vista sits on the site of the first Roman Catholic church in Aruba. (iStockPhoto.com)

imported. People of African descent constituted about 12 percent of the population when freedom was granted in the 19th century.

Life on Aruba changed dramatically at the end of the 1920s with the discovery and development of the oil fields. Many expatriates, mostly U.S. citizens, settled there. Through the last half of the 20th century, Arubans agitated for freedom from the Netherlands Antilles, which was governed from Curaçao, and then for independence as a nation. The former status was granted in 1986, but in 1990 Aruba withdrew its petition for independent nationhood and remains an autonomous member of the Kingdom of the Netherlands.

Languages spoken are Papiamento (a Spanish-Portuguese-Dutch-English dialect), 66.3 percent; Spanish, 12.6 percent; English (widely spoken), 7.7 percent; Dutch (official), 5.8 percent; other, 2.2 percent; unspecified or unknown, 5.3 percent (2000 census). The ethnic composition of the population was mixed white/

Caribbean Amerindian 80 percent, and other 20 percent.

When the Dutch took control of the West Indies (includes the Windward Islands, Leeward Islands, and what later became known as the Dutch Antilles), they expelled the Spanish Catholic missionaries. However, the Jesuit priests were allowed back in 1705. Subsequently, the Roman Catholic Church became and has remained the dominant religion of Aruba; it claims about 75 percent of the residents. The Dutch introduced the Reformed Presbyterian tradition to the Antilles, and it continues as the United Protestant Church, combining both Reformed and Lutheran traditions.

In 1654, when the Dutch lost their foothold in Brazil, they evacuated the Jewish community, which had been centered in Racife and which feared the impending arrival of Portuguese rule. Most of the Brazilian Jews were taken either to New Amsterdam (New York) in North America or to Curaçao. Some of the

ARUBA

Aruba

Religion	Followers in 1970	Followers in 2010	% of Population	Annual % growth 2000–2010	Followers in 2025	Followers in 2050
Christians	55,000	98,700	95.8	2.64	99,000	92,200
Roman Catholics	48,000	81,500	79.1	2.26	79,300	70,700
Protestants	2,200	9,700	9.4	3.77	12,000	13,000
Independents	230	1,900	1.8	5.28	2,400	3,000
Agnostics	650	1,800	1.7	2.64	3,000	5,000
Spiritists	350	1,200	1.2	2.64	2,000	2,500
Muslims	50	380	0.4	2.62	800	1,200
Chinese folk	200	220	0.2	2.62	400	500
Jews	250	180	0.2	2.71	300	400
Buddhists	200	170	0.2	2.62	300	400
Atheists	100	120	0.1	2.71	600	900
New religionists	0	120	0.1	2.55	200	300
Baha'is	50	150	0.1	2.71	400	600
Total population	**56,800**	**103,000**	**100.0**	**2.64**	**107,000**	**104,000**

Curaçao Jews eventually moved to Aruba but abandoned the island in the 19th century. A new start for the Jewish community was made in 1924, and now a small community of about 35 families resides there. The community dedicated a new synagogue in 1962.

Also, early in the 20th century, a community of Muslims was formed in Curaçao, consisting of emigrants from Syria, Lebanon, and Surinam. Later, members of this community moved to Aruba.

Throughout the twentieth century a variety of Protestant churches arrived in Aruba, including The Evangelical Alliance Mission (TEAM), which came in 1931 and sponsors a broadcasting station, Radio Victoria; and the Seventh-day Adventist Church, which came a few years previously and has the third-largest membership on the island. Other Protestant denominations are the Assemblies of God, the Baptist Church, Christian Churches/Churches of Christ, and a few other Pentecostal groups.

The Jehovah's Witnesses arrived on Aruba in the early 1940s; officials reported 10 churches with 766 members in 2008. The Church of Jesus Christ of Latter-day Saints (Mormons) organized its first congregation in 1986; the following year, portions of the Book of Mormon were translated into the local language, Papiamento, and published. Officials reported three churches with 458 members in 2007, with all church services conducted in Papiamento since 2003.

According to the 2000 census, the religious affiliation of the Aruban population was Roman Catholic, 80.8 percent; evangelical, 4.1 percent; older Protestant denominations, 2.5 percent; Jehovah's Witnesses, 1.5 percent; Methodist, 1.2 percent; Jewish, 0.2 percent; other, 5.1 percent; and none or unspecified, 4.6 percent.

J. Gordon Melton and Clifton L. Holland

See also: Assemblies of God; Church of Jesus Christ of Latter-day Saints; Jehovah's Witnesses; Jesuits; Pentecostalism; Reformed/Presbyterian Tradition; Roman Catholic Church; Seventh-day Adventist Church.

References

Brada, W. M. *Kerkgeschiedenis.* Curaçao: Paulus Drukkerij, 1946.

Brierly, Peter. *World Churches Handbook.* London: Christian Research, 1997.

Central Intelligence Agency. *The World Factbook.* Washington, DC, 2009. https://www.cia.gov/library/publications/the-world-factbook/geos/aa.html.

Dryfoot, Arthur Charles. *The Shaping of the West Indian Church, 1492–1962.* Gainesville: University Press of Florida, 1999; published jointly with The Press University of the West Indies in Jamaica.

Horowitz, Michael M., ed. *Peoples and Cultures of the Caribbean: An Anthropological Reader.* Garden City, NY: The Natural History Press, 1971.

Rogozinski, Jan. *A Brief History of the Caribbean, from the Arawak and Carib to the Present.* Rev. ed. New York: Plume Books–Penguin Group, 1999.

Arunachala

Arunachala (Sanskrit) or Tiruvanamalai (Tamil), is a sacred mountain in southern India located approximately 100 miles southwest of Madras. The mountain is considered to be the largest Shiva Linga in the world (his sexual organ being a prominent symbol of Shiva). The origins of the mountain's veneration predate the history of the area. At its base is a large temple complex ranging over 25 acres that dates to the early years of the Common Era. Its massive towers were erected in stages from the 10th to the 16th centuries.

Through the year, pilgrims engage in a practice called *Arunachala giri valam* (circling Arunachala), considered to be a simple and effective form of yoga. The circumambulation is done barefoot, as wearing shoes on the mountain is considered a sacrilege. Shiva worship is especially highlighted at the beginning of winter each year, when for a 10-day period during the Hindu month of Kartikai, Arunachala hosts the Deepam festival to celebrate Shiva's light. The festival culminates with a huge bonfire on top of the mountain that can be seen for miles in all directions.

Arunachala's profile was significantly increased in the West during the mid-20th century as the popular guru Sri Ramana Maharshi (1879–1950) received visitors at his home on the mountain. Maharshi's first Western disciple was Frank Humphreys, who wrote articles about him in the *International Psychic Gazette*. These articles prompted Western esoteric teacher Paul Brunton (1898–1981) to visit Arunachala in 1931. Brunton then authored two widely circulated books, *A Search in Secret India* and *A Message from Arunachala*, about his encounters with Maharshi. These books made the mountain (and Maharshi) globally famous, and through the last half of the 20th century, it was the goal of numerous Western spiritual seekers.

Among the most famous seekers who found their way to Arunchala was Abhishiktananda (Henri Le Saux) (1910–1973), a Roman Catholic priest who emerged as a leading voice in Christian-Hindu dialogue in the mid-20th century. A North American-based movement centered on Maharshi and his writings, the Arunchala Ashrama has two lead ashrams in New York and Nova Scotia and a number of affiliated centers across the continent.

J. Gordon Melton

See also: Devotion/Devotional Traditions; Yoga.

References

Abhishiktananda. *The Secret of Arunachala: A Christian Hermit on Shiva's Holy Mountain.* New Delhi: Indian Society for Promoting Christian Knowledge, 1997.

Brunton, Paul. *A Message from Arunachala.* London: Rider and Company, 1936.

Brunton, Paul. *A Search in Secret India.* London: Rider and Company, 1934.

Skandananda. *Arunachala: Holy Hill.* Madras, India: Weldun Press, 1980.

Arya Samaj

Arya Samaj is a sectarian philosophy within Hinduism that challenges Brahmanism. Its early leaders attracted followers from late 19th-century, north Indian communities at a time of traumatic social and economic transformation under British rule. Converts are actively sought by Samaji communities. Today, Arya Samaj centers are found all over the world.

Founded in 1875 in colonial India, the Arya Samaj (noble soul), formerly known as Arya Pratinidhi Sabha, is a reformist Hindu sect that synthesizes ancient orthodox ritual practice with modern notions of social organization and interaction. Arya Samajis reject much of Hinduism's *sanatan dharma* (for example, idol worship, *puja*) and instead have made the Vedas their preeminent sacred texts. Havan (an ancient fire ceremony) is their central ritual practice, and they promote 10 basic principles: (1) God is the original source of all that is true; (2) God is a single, eternal, fully conscious being; (3) the Vedas are the books of all true knowledge; (4) all people should be ready to accept truth; (5) all acts should be performed with righteousness and duty; (6) Samajis should promote good to the whole world through physical, spiritual, and social progress of all humans; (7) all interactions should be regulated by love and due justice in accordance with the dictates of righteousness; (8) realization and acquisition of knowledge (*vidyaa*) should be promoted for all; (9) Samajis should strive for the upliftment of all and not be satisfied with only personal development; and (10) while the individual is free to enjoy individual well being, everyone should dedicate themselves to overall social good.

Most of these principles support a strong, anti-caste, universalizing sentiment of social service. Moreover, they introduced a ceremony for conversion called *shuddhikaran* (purification) that ritually cleansed converts so that they could be absorbed or reabsorbed into the Hindu fold. Despite this ceremony, and promotion of fundamental principles of social justice, many Samaji communities were unable to forget a convert's caste background, thus making it difficult for individual converts to be absorbed socially into the group. For this reason, especially in the first half of the 20th century, proselytization efforts focused on entire (usually endogamous) groups.

Mul Shankara (1824–1883), founder of the Arya Samaj, was born a Brahmin, reared with an orthodox Brahmin education in Gujarat, and went on to take the vows of a *sannyasi* (a follower of the renounced life) in 1848 with the Sarasvati Dandi Order of Yogis. As

The Arya Dewaker temple in Paramaribo, Suriname, is the largest Hindu temple in Suriname and is a center of the Arya Samaj sect. (Feije/Dreamstime.com)

a sannyasi, he took a new religious name, Dayananda Sarasvati, and wandered the length and breadth of India for the next 12 years, eventually settling in Mathura to study under the Vedic scholar Virajananda. In the context of colonial India's emerging social and political consciousness and nationalism, Dayananda preached a message of gender equality and social liberalism (strongly anti-caste) through Vedic interpretations, a message that was often in conflict with other emerging sectarian philosophies of the time. His abrasive and polemic style did not endear him to many who cherished traditional Hinduism, but there were others who found his message liberating. Thus the Arya Samaj grew as an organization, particularly in the Punjab, where it remains an important sect to this day.

Members of the group continue to engage in proselytizing its universalizing message of spiritual truth and social reform, a practice that has taken the organization and its philosophy around the world. Countries of the Indian diaspora, in particular (for example, Guyana, Trinidad and Tobago, Canada, Kenya, and many more), have numerous, registered centers for worship, but the worldwide number of adherents is difficult to assess. Trinidad (in the eastern Caribbean) is particularly notable for having the first woman to become a Hindu priest (*pandit*). Indrani Rampersad was inducted as a *pandita* of the Arya Pratinidhi Sabha.

Arya Samaj
Sarvdeshik Arya Pratinidhi Sabha
Dayanand Bhawan
Asaf All Road
New Delhi
India
www.whereisgod.com
http://aryasamaj.com

Carolyn V. Prorok

See also: Hinduism; Women, Status and Role; Yoga.

References

Gupta, Shiv Kumar. *Arya Samaj and the Raj, 1875–1920.* New Delhi: Gitanjali Publishing House, 1991.

Lajpat Rai, Lala. *The Arya Samaj: An Account of Its Origin, Doctrines, and Activities.* New Delhi: Reliance Publishing House, 1991.

Llewellen, J. E. *Legacy of Women's Uplift in India: Contemporary Women Leaders in the Arya Samaj.* London: Sage Publications, 1998.

Yoginder, S. S. "The Fitna of Irtidad: Muslim Missionary Response to the Shuddhi of Arya Samaj in Early Twentieth Century India." *Journal of Muslim Minority Affairs* 17, no. 1 (1997): 65–83.

Ascension Day

The Feast of Ascension is a Christian holiday that commemorates the bodily ascension of Jesus into heaven as recorded in Acts 1:1–11. Until recently this holy day fell on the sixth Thursday after Easter Sunday, the traditional 40 days between the resurrection and ascension in the biblical narrative. However, some Roman Catholic provinces have moved the celebration to the following Sunday to facilitate the obligation of the faithful to receive Mass as part of the feast.

Writing in the fifth century, Augustine (354–430 CE) claimed that the feast had apostolic origins and it is evident that by this time the day was universally observed in the church. The ascension emphasizes the entrance of Jesus into God's heavenly presence. He is there concealed from sight but will return again (cf. Acts 1:11 and Colossians 3:3). The event further affirms that Jesus Christ, the head of the church, precedes believers into the heavenly kingdom so that members of his Body may live in the hope of one day being with him forever. Finally, the Feast of Ascension celebrates that having entered the sanctuary of heaven once and for all, Jesus now intercedes as Mediator.

Ascension Day practices include a three-day "Rogation" period preceding the feast to invoke God's mercy. The actual feast itself includes a procession of torches and banners symbolizing Christ's journey to the Mount of Olives and entry to heaven, the extinguishing of the Paschal Candle, and an all-night vigil. White is the liturgical color of Ascension Day. The prayers and liturgy often include a Blessing of Beans and Grapes as part of the Mass in Commemoration of the Dead as the first fruits of the resurrection. In some churches the scene of the ascension is re-enacted by elevating the figure of Christ above the altar through an opening in the roof of the church. The feast is followed by an "Afterfeast" of eight days when hymns and readings carry on the theme.

In some countries, including Austria, Belgium, Croatia, Denmark, Finland, France, Germany, Iceland, Indonesia, the Netherlands, Norway, Sweden, and Switzerland, Ascension Day is a public holiday. Germany also holds its Father's Day on the same date.

The Eastern Orthodox churches calculate the date of Easter differently, so its Ascension Day will usually be a week to a month later than in Western traditions. The earliest possible date for the Eastern feast is May 14, and the latest possible date is June 17. Some of the Oriental Orthodox Churches, however, observe Ascension on the same date as the Western churches. Some Protestant churches, especially the Anglicans, observe Ascension Day and/or Ascension Sunday, but most do little more than pay lip service to the day. It is not observed in most Free churches and post-Protestant groups, which have largely abandoned the traditional liturgical calendar.

Kevin Quast

See also: Augustine of Hippo; Easter; Eastern Orthodoxy; Liturgical Year; Roman Catholic Church.

References

Jones, Chelsyn, Geoffry Wainwright, and Edward Yarnold, eds. *The Study of Liturgy.* Rev. ed. Oxford: Oxford University Press, 1992.

"Ascension of Christ." In *The Oxford Dictionary of the Christian Church,* edited by F. L. Cross. New York: Oxford University Press, 2005

Duchesne, Louis. *Christian Worship: Its Origin and Evolution.* London, 1903, 491–515.

Wynne, John. "Feast of the Ascension." In *The Catholic Encyclopedia.* Vol. 1. New York: Robert Appleton Company, 1907.

Asceticism

The word "asceticism" derives from the ancient Greek *askēsis* and was associated with the training of athletes and soldiers. In time, the term acquired metaphorical usage in relationship to any kind of disciplined program of training. The term *askeō* in ancient Greece at first meant to adorn or to demonstrate artistic skill; later it acquired the meaning of putting virtue into practice. Bodily training for athletes was considered the askēsis of the body, easily applied to spiritual asceticism as to be trained in taming the passions and the senses, controlling thoughts, and restraining impulses while pursuing virtue. The principle that a divine quality is gained through ascetical struggle is explicitly affirmed in Aeschylus's play *Agamemnon*, where it is a decree of Zeus that in this age wisdom be obtained by suffering, almost against the hedonic inclination of the human will. The Apostle Paul applies this to his own experience in Acts 24:16, "I train myself" by taking pains to have a clear conscience before God and man; it is close to the idea of conscience and obligations toward others (cf. 1 Corinthians 9:25–27). His contemporary in Alexandria, Philo, saw Jacob's wrestling with the angel (Genesis 32:25) as an archetype of ascetic practice. The early church readily embraced Philo's ideas in this as in other areas. Origen in particular, in his "Exhortation to Martyrdom," sees the fulfillment of ascetic self-discipline in contempt for death and perseverance unto the end in the faith. Monasticism took the meanings of askesis from Philo and from the church's experience with martyrdom to create a community within which the practices would become a basis for a daily life ordered toward the battle against evil impulses and in favor of acquiring the virtues. Many of the practices associated with monasticism were already present in the Jewish priestly temple regulations and military traditions. Early Christian monasticism adopted this understanding of its own program designed to perfect the life promised in the sacrament of baptism. Asceticism in various forms can be found in most religions, with varying emphasis placed on purification, penitence, spiritual and mental training, and acquisition of supra-normal powers.

Ancient Indian asceticism took the form of bodily and mental disciplines (Sanskrit: *tapas*) as a means for gaining unusual powers and magical abilities (*siddhi*). This aspect of the practice of yoga seems to be in harmony with earlier shamanic practices that link self-mortification, fasting, sensory restriction, and mental focus with acquiring powers to diagnose and heal. Asceticism may have been practiced by persons as long ago as the pre-Aryan Harappan civilization in northwestern India. Some of the less-discussed statuary from these archaeological sites are clearly representative of yogic postures, which require a long and disciplined apprenticeship to perfect. The Vedic civilization seems to have taken up several themes from the Harappan, including asceticism. Ascetic practices were understood to bring about the acquisition of spiritual power, either from within the possibilities of the body-mind complex, or as boons wrested from the deities. By undergoing trials, initiation, training by a master, and retreat practice in solitude, a disciple might first of all begin to encounter spiritual entities opposed to his spiritual development. Typically, these entities attempt to dissuade the ascetic from commitment to mental focus, chastity, fasting, and sensory restrictions. In time, following the recitation of appropriate mantras in large numbers, a desired deity (*ista-devata*) may appear to the yogin offering various spiritual boons. Depending on the instructions of the guru, these boons might be welcomed, or postponed until better gifts were acquired. The main idea is that asceticism is not primarily practiced to make reparation for one's negative previous actions (although purification is, in fact, part of the process); rather, tapas per se is a method for acquiring spiritual, or even magical powers more or less reluctantly conceded by a deity. Japanese and Thai cultures similarly venerate ascetics, whether Buddhist, Shinto, or shamanic, for these very powers are sources of healing, exorcism, reversal of ill fortune, and divination for those in need.

Religious asceticism takes a variety of forms. Fasting is practiced in Judaism, Christianity, and Islam, in accordance with the values of ancient Middle Eastern cultures. For Judaism and Islam, as for lay Christianity, asceticism is not a full-time way of life but is confined to certain periods such as Yom Kippur, Lent, or Ramadan in which repentance and spiritual purification are emphasized. Christian monasticism sought to make asceticism a way of life within which salvation

A Hindi ascetic Sadhu sits still while practicing yoga in Pashupatinath, Nepal, 1999. (Attila Jandi/Dreamstime.com)

would be pursued with rigor and regularity. The monasticism of the early desert hermits was characterized by heroic and even competitive ascetic feats such as lengthy fasts, prayer while immersed in cold water, recitation of the entire book of Psalms as the core daily prayer practice, combating sleep by limiting the time of rest or dividing the night into periods of sleep interrupted by prayer, and interpersonal forms of asceticism such as submission to one's spiritual master in strict obedience.

Ascetic discipline of this kind leads to the more advanced practices associated with the cultivation of the virtues. The monastic tradition emphasized the Pascal dimension, that is, death and resurrection, of the Christian's incorporation into Christ. Thus, asceticism became a pattern of training requiring free, affective, and faithful decisions to die to (that is, mortify) one's

passions, emotions, and desires in order to be open to receiving the grace of new life in Christ. The goal of asceticism in early monasticism was defined by John Cassian as "purity of heart," a state of psychological freedom from the passions (Greek: *apatheia*), indispensable for further growth in holiness. As various monastic rules evolved and revived between the fourth and the 13th centuries, a variety of religious orders emerged, each with its own characteristic way to sustain the ongoing practice of self-denial within the framework of community life in pursuit of holiness.

Refraining from bodily pleasures and sensory input is characteristic of the various monastic systems of asceticism. For example, Hatha Yoga *niyamas* are techniques that require restraint of the senses and of the mind itself, in pursuit of the goal of perfect quieting of the fluctuations of the mind (*citta-vritti-nirodha*). Buddhist and Catholic Benedictine monasticism organizes the day into a regulated round of ascetic observances to which the *bhikshu* or monk is to adhere, ideally, for life. Most of the ascetic traditions affirm that self-denial for its own sake carries serious risks. Only if one's goals are truly spiritual, open to transcending the demands of the isolated self, is asceticism considered a fruitful path within the sphere of embodied human life. The mental dimension of asceticism, in which the mind settles into one-pointed attention and readily sets aside distracting thought-impressions, is in some ways more demanding and difficult to attain than bodily self-control. In each religious system, the final salvific or liberative goal partly moderates and reshapes the basic practices involving bodily, sensory, and mental restraint.

Priestly and warrior asceticism seems to be the origins of celibacy, whether temporary, periodic, or permanent. David adhered to the practice of chastity required of priests ministering in the temple and warriors during a campaign (1 Samuel 21:4–5). Men must be sexually pure in order that their religious rites, including battle understood as a sacred rite, might be acceptable to God, who is "holy," that is, "set apart." This is already part of the ethos that we find in the biblical book of Exodus (19:15). The Jewish sect identified as the Essenes, mentioned by Josephus, Philo, and Pliny the Elder, may have had some more advanced members who practiced celibacy, in contrast with the practice of mainstream Judaism. The New Testament encourages celibacy, both in the writings of the Apostle Paul (1 Corinthians 7:1, 7–8) and in the Christian Gospels (Matthew 19:10–12; 19:29; Luke 18:29), as a sign of the life of the world to come (Matthew 22:30–31). The discipline set in motion toward acquiring Christian moral perfection is understood to be responding in human gestures to the gift of divine grace, on the basis of models found in scripture. Thus, although the early Christian priesthood was not universally celibate, in time the notion of purity derived from the chastity required of priests serving in the temple in Jerusalem came to be applied to all bishops and, later, to all priests of the Latin Church (though not to the parish clergy of the Eastern Christian churches). Christian priesthood and monastic life explored various psychologically astute ways of overcoming sexual temptation by cultivating specific virtues, nurturing the habit of prayer, regulating the body through vigils and fasting, and the like. Ascetical theology in this way takes moral theology in the direction of actual practice in both body and mind, and links it to priestly service to the community of the faithful; for those drawn to the way of spiritual perfection, mystical theology builds on ascetical theology to open the way to contemplation and transforming union, neither of which are even possible without moral and ascetical discipline.

In some cultures, the rewards to be gained through asceticism are of such great value that forms of self-torture may be readily embraced. Some Native American rituals involve forms of self-torture involving bodily piercing (the Sundance ritual) and tearing of the flesh; pre-Columbian Mesoamerican practices included piercing the tongue or the genitals. Ritual circumcision of the male prepuce or of parts of the female sexual organs is widespread in parts of Africa and Central Asia. Voluntary genital mutilation is still practiced by sacred transvestites in India, as it was among devotees of the Mother Goddess in ancient Syria. Archaic cultures still surviving in many parts of the world make use of initiation rituals involving physical and mental trials including isolation, fasting, painful exercises, humiliations, and vigils, to admit youths to the ways of the community or tribe. Jain ascetics begin their monastic commitment with the ritual gesture of pulling out five handfuls of hair from their heads. Even Buddhist monks and nuns, usually held to a "middle way" of moderate asceticism, practice painful rituals such as the burning of a number of cones of incense on the head at the time of monastic ordination. As a sign of particularly intense commitment, Chan Buddhists ritually burn off a finger. In times of social crisis, some Buddhist monks have undergone self-immolation, as in Vietnam to protest the fratricidal war of the 1950s and 1960s.

Buddhist asceticism was originally designed as a middle way between undignified hedonism and severe self-deprivation. The Visuddhimagga by Buddhaghosa, a master of Theravada Buddhism, counsels a life of restraint within which the depths of meditation can be explored consciously over many years of commitment. Mahayana Buddhism similarly employs a systematic approach devised on the basis of the earlier practices by Asanga in the late fourth century CE in the Bodhisattvabhūmi. For Asanga's system, "knowing the measure of food" (moderate fasting) and embodying compassion set in motion a process by which the current corrupt condition of the human body-mind complex can be reversed permanently through the attainment of full and perfect enlightenment. Both Theravada and Mahayana Buddhism continued to esteem (with cautionary advice to the over-zealous) the early Buddhist ascetical practices known as the *dhutagunas:* begging one's food, wearing clothes made of rags from a dust heap, dwelling in a forest, dwelling in cremation grounds, living out in the open, dwelling in solitude, sleeping in a sitting posture, and the like. Each of these practices was meant to enhance the degree of commitment to the path to enlightenment for an advanced practitioner.

Francis V. Tiso

See also: Benedictines; Exorcism; Lent; Mahayana Buddhism; Martyrdom; Monasticism; Paul; Ramadan; Theravada Buddhism; Yoga; Yom Kippur.

References

Barry, William A., and William J. Connolly. *The Practice of Spiritual Direction*. New York: Seabury Press, 1982.

Bernard, Charles André. *Teologia Spirituale*. Torino, Italy: Edizioni Paoline, 1987.

Bernard of Clairvaux. *Sermons on Conversion.* Kalamazoo, MI: Cistercian Publications, 1981.

Bhagat, M. G. *Ancient Indian Asceticism.* Delhi: Munshiram Manoharlal, 1976.

The Book of the Discipline (Vinaya-Pitaka). Trans. by I. B. Horner. London: The Pali Text Society, 1983.

Chadwick, Owen, ed. *Western Asceticism.* Philadelphia: Westminster John Knox Press, 1958.

Eliade, Mircea. *Yoga: Immortality and Freedom.* Trans. by Willard R. Trask. Princeton, NJ: Princeton University Press, 1969.

Hariharānanda Āranya, Swami. *Yoga Philosophy of Patañjali.* Trans. by P. N. Mukerji. Albany: State University of New York Press, 1983.

Merton, Thomas. *Contemplative Prayer.* New York: Herder and Herder, 1969.

O'Flaherty, W. D., ed. *Hindu Myths: A Sourcebook Translated from the Sanskrit.* Middlesex, UK: Penguin Books, 1975.

Palmer, G. E. H., Philip Sherrard, and Kallistos Ware, eds. *The Philokalia: The Complete Text.* London: Faber and Faber, 1981.

Peifer, Claude J. *Monastic Spirituality.* New York: Sheed and Ward, 1966.

Singh, Jaideva. *Śiva Sūtras: The Yoga of Supreme Identity.* Delhi: Motilal Banarsidass, 1982.

Varenne, Jean. *Yoga and the Hindu Tradition.* Chicago: University of Chicago Press, 1976.

Ashoka

ca. 304–232 BCE

The Indian King Ashoka (aka Asoka), born several centuries after Gautama Buddha, emerged in the third century BCE as one of the most important Buddhists of all time, both for his work in spreading the religion and in leaving written records of his effort.

As is the case with many of the famous persons of the ancient world, many details of Ashoka's life are missing and others highly disputed. In Ashoka's case, the date of his birth is disputed by scholars, though most believe he was born in about 304 BCE. His grandfather Chandrgupa (ca. 340 BCE–ca. 290 BCE) had founded and established the Mauryan dynasty and succeeded in bringing together most of the Indian subcontinent. Ashoka came to the throne following the death of his father, Bindusara (ca. 320 BCE–ca. 272 BCE). His kingdom was headquartered in Magagha (Bihar and Jharkhand). As king he was also known as Devanampiya Piyadasi (Beloved-of-the-Gods, He Who Looks On with Affection).

As a young military leader, Ashoka expanded the kingdom of his grandfather and father, eventually unifying much of what is modern India (as well as Pakistan and Afghanistan), but in 262 BCE he found himself deeply affected by the suffering he had caused through his war to conquer the rebellious state of Kalinga (the modern state of Orissa). Though a Buddhist, the horror of the war challenged his faith and the largely nominal commitment he had held. He now took his Buddhism seriously and began to integrate Buddhist principles into his regime. In his attempt to live the Eightfold Path, he initiated a series of good works that included the building of hospitals, digging wells, and improving travel facilities.

Ashoka would build what are believed to be the first major Buddhist monuments. He also oversaw the third Buddhist Council, held at Pataliputra. Throughout his empire, he ordered the building of inscribed pillars that commemorated the establishment of the Buddha's Dharma (teachings). He sent his son Mahinda to Sri Lanka to introduce Buddhism and then sent his daughter Sanghamitta to further the work. As a gift, she brought a cutting from the Bodhi Tree, the tree under which Buddha had sat when completing his search for enlightenment. Many also credit him with gathering the relics of the Buddha, which had been distributed following the Buddha's death, and redistributing them within the much larger Buddhist world of the third century.

Ashoka ruled for 38 years, dying in 232 BCE. He later came to be seen as the *carkravartin*, the ideal ruler who causes the wheel of the law to turn, that is, one who promotes the spread of the Buddha's Dharma.

Following the conquest of much of India by the Muslims and the suppression of Buddhism, memory of Ashoka faded and then largely disappeared. Then in the 19th century, European scholars began to read widely in Indian literature where they found a variety of references to a capable if ruthless prince who came to power over the bodies of his own brothers but who then experienced a dramatic conversion to Buddhism and afterward ruled justly and facilitated the spread of Buddhism. Further study led to their identifying the king Ashoka mentioned in the literature with a King Piyadasi named in the texts of many edicts that had been carved into various stone monuments. Finally in 1915, a stone monument with Ashoka's name was discovered. When assembled, Ashoka's edicts came to comprise the earliest decipherable corpus of written documents from India. Through the 20th century, the details of his career have slowly been compiled.

By the middle of the twentieth century, Ashoka's career had become well known in India. The Ashoka Chakra (or wheel of Ashoka), depicted on many of the objects now known to have come from his kingdom, was placed in the center of the flag of India. The Ashoka Chakra is also found on the base of the Lion Capital initially erected by Ashoka at Sarnath. The Lion from the capital was also adopted by India as its national emblem.

Edward A. Irons

See also: Buddha, Gautama; Sarnath.

References

Dhammika, Ven. S., *The Edicts of King Asoka: An English Rendering.* Kandy, Sri Lanka: Buddhist Publication Society, 1993. Posted at http://www.cs.colostate.edu/~malaiya/ashoka.html.

Hultzsch, Eugene, trans., *The Inscriptions of Asoka.* Vol. 1. Delhi: Indological Book House, 1969.

Smith, Vincent Arthur. *Asoka, the Buddhist Emperor of India.* Charleston, SC: BiblioLife, 2009.

Strong, John S. *The Legend of King Asoka: A Study and Translation of the Asokavadana.* Princeton, NJ: Princeton University Press, 1983.

Thapar, Romila. *Asoka and the Decline of the Mauryas.* Delhi, NY: Oxford University Press, 1997.

Wheeler, Mortimer. *Early India and Pakistan to Ashoka.* New York: Praeger, 1959.

Ashura

Ashura, an important religious holiday for Muslims, occurs on the 10th day of Muharram, the first month of the Islamic calendar. The day had been acknowledged by Arabs prior to the emergence of Islam as a day for fasting and was identified with Yom Kippur (Day of Atonement) by Jews. Muhammad (d. 632) initially identified it as a day of fasting for Muslims. Sunni Muslims see it as a day to remember Moses, who is believed to have fasted on that day as he remembered God's liberation of the people of Israel from Egypt. Islamic tradition has associated this important day with biblical events recognized by Jews and Christians, including the day when Noah's ark landed after the flood and the day when Jonah was freed from the fish that had swallowed him.

Though Muhammad fasted on this day, the Ashura fast would later be superseded by the month of fasting during Ramadan. Thus the Ashura fast was downgraded to a voluntary (rather than mandatory) event in the Sunni Muslim community.

For Shia Muslims, however, Ashura has taken on an altogether different significance. On this day in the year 680, Husayn ibn Ali, the grandson of the Prophet, along with male members of his family and some close companions, died at the hands of the forces of the Islamic Umayyad caliph Yazid (r. 680–683) in the desert of Karbala, Iraq. Husayn's mutilated body would be buried in what is now a shrine in Karbala, while his sister Zaynab in Kufa and daughter Fatimah al-Kubra were taken prisoner and carried to Damascus. This event would become one of the most important events recounted by Shia Muslims concerning their origins and is integral to understanding their distinctiveness over against the Sunni Muslim community. It also led to Shia Muslims placing a high value on martyrdom. Commemoration of the event is traced to Zaynab and the prisoners in Damascus. Subsequently, pilgrims began to arrive in Karbala, and over the centuries annual commemorations evolved.

Shia Muslims begin their celebration of Ashura with 10 days of mourning for the death of Husayn that start with the arrival of the month of Muharram. Activities expressive of mourning become visible throughout the Shia-dominated areas of the Middle East, especially Iran, Iraq, and Azerbaijan, other countries with strong Shia communities from Lebanon to India, and throughout the Shia diaspora worldwide. Mourners gather to sing, conduct street processions, and stage

Afghan Shiites during an Ashura procession in a mosque in Kabul, Afghanistan, January 18, 2008. Ashura marks the Shiite Muslims' commemoration of the seventh-century killing of their most revered saint, Imam Hussein, the grandson of Prophet Muhammad and a symbol of martyrdom for Shiites. (AP/Wide World Photos)

morality plays. Theatrical performances reenact the events of the Karbala tragedy.

Ashura is not a day of joy or celebration but a day for mourning, remembrance, and repentance. Public lamentations can reach a frenzy on Ashura itself, especially in Iraq, as the day is frequently marked by young men beating their breasts with chains and/or slashing their heads to draw blood in commemoration of the spilling of Husayn's blood as he died. In Iran and areas where Persian influence is strong, people engage in the *rowzeh khani* (called a *qiraya* "reading" in Arabic-speaking Iraq). The word *rowzeh* is traced to a book of stories about Karbala, *Rawdat al-shuhada* (*The Garden of the Martyrs*), written by Husayn Waiz Kashifi around 1503, at the time of the rise of the Shia Safavid dynasty in Iran. The rowzeh khani includes lamentations, moving oratory, and readings about the events that transpired at Karbala.

The fact that Ashura commemorates a battle between two communities that live close to each other has allowed Ashura to become the occasion for violence, especially as Shia believers, always a minority in the Muslim world, assert themselves in the face of the larger Sunni community. Many Sunnis consider the Shias to be heretics. In 1884 in Trinidad and Tobago, 22 people were killed in what became known as the Hosay (Husayn) Massacre, when Shia Muslims attempted to commemorate Ashura against the orders of British authorities. In the 1930s, as part of his program to modernize Iran, Reza Shah Pahlavi (r. 1925–1941) found himself in conflict with the Iranian clergy as he introduced Western clothing. He later banned the gathering for Ashura as being too politically volatile. Ashura was also banned for a number of years in Iraq during the regime of Saddam Hussein, who privileged the minority Sunni community over the Shia majority.

The celebration of Ashura made a quick comeback after his fall in 2003.

J. Gordon Melton

See also: Calendars, Religious; Shia Islam; Yom Kippur.

References

Aghaie, Kamran Scot, ed. *The Women of Karbala: Ritual Performance and Symbolic Discourses in Modern Shii Islam.* Austin: University of Texas Press, 2005.

Ayati, Ibrahim. *Probe into the History of Ashura.* Jamaica, NY: Imam Al Khoei Islamic Center, 1985.

Chelkowski, Peter, ed. *Taziyeh: Ritual and Drama in Iran.* New York: New York University Press, 1979.

Pinault, David. *The Shiites: Ritual and Popular Piety in a Muslim Community.* New York: St. Martin's Press, 1992.

Toufic, Jalal. *Ashura: This Blood Spilled in My Veins.* Saucilito, CA: Post-Apollo Press, 2005.

Assemblies of God

The General Council of the Assemblies of God (AG), the largest white and Hispanic Pentecostal denomination in the United States, was organized in 1914 by a broad coalition of ministers who desired to work together to fulfill common objectives, such as providing for accountability, ministerial training schools, and credentialing missions agencies. Formed in the midst of the emerging worldwide Pentecostal revival, the Assemblies of God quickly took root in other countries and formed indigenous national organizations. The AG is a constituent member of the World Assemblies of God Fellowship—one of the largest Pentecostal fellowships in the world.

The Assemblies of God was founded at Hot Springs, Arkansas, April 2–12, 1914. The roots of the AG can be traced to radical evangelicals in the Wesleyan wing and especially the Reformed wing of the 19th-century Holiness movement. In addition to the historic truths of the Christian faith, these Holiness forerunners of the AG subscribed to three distinctive beliefs: they believed in sanctification, or full consecration, as a work of grace subsequent to conversion, referred to later in the century as baptism in the Holy Spirit; they believed in divine healing; and they preached the urgent need to evangelize the world before the imminent premillennial return of Jesus Christ. Classical Pentecostalism arose from this background; its beginning generally dates to a revival on January 1, 1901, under the leadership of Charles F. Parham (1873–1929) at his Bethel Bible School in Topeka, Kansas. Parham taught that glossolalic utterance, or speaking in tongues, signified that the prophesied outpouring of the Holy Spirit (Joel 2:28–29) had now come, that it (not Holiness sanctification) verified the reception of Spirit baptism, and that it provided linguistic expertise and spiritual empowerment for God's end-time missionaries. Parham's identification of tongues-speech as the evidence of Spirit baptism became an important identity marker within classical Pentecostalism. Subsequent Pentecostal revivals, notably in Houston, Los Angeles, Chicago, Zion, Illinois, Nyack, New York, and elsewhere, also strongly impacted those who formed the AG.

Concerns about doctrinal stability, legal recognition, overseas missions, ministerial training, and spiritual unity led more than 300 largely independent Pentecostals to gather in Hot Springs, Arkansas, in 1914 to establish the AG. Preferring to be identified as a "cooperative fellowship" rather than as a denomination, the council did not adopt a creedal statement until 1916 ("Statement of Fundamental Truths"), when a schism occurred over the nature of the Godhead, a schism that resulted in the withdrawal of "Jesus Name" or "Oneness" believers. A constitution and bylaws came later in 1927. From the beginning, the AG embraced conservative evangelical doctrines, with the addition of a distinctively Pentecostal spirituality emphasizing baptism in the Holy Spirit with the "initial physical evidence," as it was called, of speaking in tongues and the restoration of the charismatic gifts of the Spirit, as enumerated by Saint Paul (1 Corinthians 12:8–10), for the life and mission of the church. The most recent exposition of AG theology appears in the 1995 edition of *Systematic Theology,* edited by Stanley M. Horton (b. 1916).

Organizationally, the AG adopted a mixed congregational/presbyterial church polity. This polity allows

Service of the Assemblies of God. (General Council of the Assemblies of God)

for a measure of local church sovereignty, under the oversight of the General Council, the highest governing body, made up of all ordained ministers and lay delegates from the churches, which meets biennially. Two smaller bodies, the General Presbytery and the Executive Presbytery, also administer the denomination and its many programs. The general officers include the general superintendent, assistant general superintendent, general secretary, and general treasurer; other top leaders include the executive directors of AG World Missions and AG U.S. Missions. Ministerial training is provided through regional and national institutions of higher education (Bible institutes, colleges, universities), as well as through the Assemblies of God Theological Seminary and the nontraditional program of Global University, both located in the headquarters city of Springfield, Missouri. The Gospel Publishing House serves as the denominational publishing arm and the weekly *Pentecostal Evangel* as its official magazine.

Aggressively evangelistic, the AG included 30 missionaries on its roster in 1914. By 2008, 2,098 missionaries served in 213 nations, in ministries of gospel proclamation and compassion, in association with fraternally related constituencies numbering more than 61 million people. Central to its concept of missionary work have been the priorities of establishing self-supporting, self-governing, and self-propagating indigenous churches and providing leadership training. In the United States, the AG lists 34,177 credentialed ministers, 12,377 churches, and an overall constituency of 2,899,702. It also holds membership in the National Association of Evangelicals, through which it is related to the World Evangelical Alliance. The Flower Pentecostal Heritage Center, located in the national headquarters complex, houses a museum and archival resources.

Assemblies of God
1445 Boonville Ave.
Springfield, MO 65802
www.ag.org

Gary B. McGee and Darrin J. Rodgers

See also: Holiness Movement; Parham, Charles Fox; Paul; Pentecostalism; World Evangelical Alliance.

References

Horton, Stanley M., ed. *Systematic Theology.* Springfield, MO: Gospel Publishing House, 1995.

McGee, Gary B. *People of the Spirit: The Assemblies of God.* Springfield, MO: Gospel Publishing House, 2004.

McGee, Gary B. *This Gospel Shall Be Preached: A History and Theology of Assemblies of God Foreign Missions to 1959.* Springfield, MO: Gospel Publishing House, 1986.

McGee, Gary B. *This Gospel Shall Be Preached: A History and Theology of Assemblies of God Foreign Missions Since 1959.* Springfield, MO: Gospel Publishing House, 1989.

Wilson, Everett A. *Strategy of the Spirit: J. Philip Hogan and the Growth of the Assemblies of God Worldwide, 1960–1990.* Irvine, CA: Regnum Books International, 1997.

Assemblies of God in Brazil

Pentecostalism in Brazil began with the immigration of two Swedes to Belém in 1910. Daniel Berg (b. 1885) was a Baptist who moved from his native Sweden to the United States in 1902. In 1909, while visiting his homeland, he received the Pentecostal baptism of the Holy Spirit with the accompanying evidence of speaking in tongues. Upon his return to America, he joined the congregation led by Pentecostal pioneer William H. Durham (1873–1912) in Chicago. There he met Gunnar Vingren, who had a dream that the pair should go to Brazil as missionaries. Once settled in Belém, they began to spread the Pentecostal message among the Baptists of the city.

As they mastered the language, the pair began to travel across Brazil, first in the north and then in the 1920s in the south. The Assemblies of God emerged as the result of their work. As early as 1913, the initial missionaries (to Portugal) were commissioned. Subsequently, missionary work was launched in French Guiana, Bolivia, Colombia, Canada, the United States, Ecuador, Paramaribo, Mozambique, and East Timor. The church had some 400,000 members by 1940. It surpassed the million mark in the early 1960s. By the 1970s the Assemblies were the largest Protestant church in the country and the only one with congregations in all of the states of Brazil. By the end of the century, it had more than six million members and a constituency more than twice that number.

The church has an extensive website, given below, through which it may be contacted. Its publishing house is located at Av. Brasil, 34.401, Bangu, Rio de Janeiro RJ, CEP 21851-000, Brazil. It has rejected membership in the World Council of Churches.

www.admb28.hpg.ig.com.br/setor28.htm

J. Gordon Melton

See also: Pentecostalism; World Council of Churches.

References

Albanez, Miguel Angelo. "Introduction to the History of the Pentecostal Movement in Brazil." Th.M. thesis, Fuller Theological Seminary, 1996.

Conde, Emilio. *Historia das Assembleias de Deus no Brasil.* Rio de Janeiro: Assembleias de Deus, 1960.

Dantas, Elias. "O Movimento Pentecostal Brasileiro: Sua Historia e Influencia Sobre as Denominacoes Traditionais no Brasil." Th.M. thesis, Fuller Theological Seminary, 1988. (Portuguese, with summary in English)

Endruveit, Wilson Harle. "Pentecostalism in Brazil: A Historical and Theological Study of its Characteristics." Ph.D. diss., Northwestern University, 1975.

Assemblies of God Incorporated

Pentecostalism arrived in the United Kingdom in 1907 at a time when the British empire spanned the globe. Though there were 19th-century stirrings of revivalism, the particular configuration that came to be called Pentecostalism comprised a belief in the imminent return of Christ, a belief in the outpouring of the Holy

Spirit as a vital experience of the contemporary church, an acceptance that such an experience was often marked by speaking in tongues after the pattern of Acts 2:4, and an expectation that miraculous healing—divine healing—would occur in evangelism and in the church as a consequence of the operation of the Spirit. In short, evangelistic revivalism was formalized and strengthened by openness to an experience of the Spirit and a criterion established by which the Spirit could be discerned. The arrival of Pentecostalism in Britain led to the establishment of the first organized Pentecostal missionary agency, the Pentecostal Missionary Union (PMU), in 1909, and then by 1924 to the formation of four Pentecostal denominations (that is, denominations in which Pentecostal phenomena were written into the founding tenets of these churches), of which British Assemblies of God is the largest. It was the particular gift of several leading British Assemblies of God ministers to formulate an exposition of the books of Acts and 1 Corinthians in a way that came to have something of a standard form that, from the 1930s to the 1960s, was acceptable to wide swathes of global Pentecostalism.

The United Kingdom comprises a group of islands located off the northwest coast of Europe. During the 19th century and the first part of the 20th century it was the center of the largest empire ever established, and this fact facilitated the spread of Protestant and, later and to a lesser extent, Pentecostal mission.

The United Kingdom has a population of 60.9 million, with the greatest density being around London and the southeast of the country (http://www.statistics.gov.uk). Post-1945 citizens of many countries previously within the empire had a right to settle in Britain. Immigration to Britain from countries has changed traditional demographic features so that 13 percent of the UK population is now non-white. The non-white populace is unevenly distributed with the result that parts of Britain (for example south of the Thames in London or areas of Bradford) are almost entirely black or Asian in character. The 2001 national census revealed that more than 71.6 percent of the country classified itself as Christian, 15.5 percent described themselves as having no religion, and the next largest group was Muslim with 2.7 percent of the total (http://www.statistics.gov.uk/cci/nugget.asp?id=293). These figures disguise the fact that the United Kingdom is profoundly secular in terms of its culture and in terms of predominant lifestyles. The mass media generally support a secular agenda though Christmas and Easter are recognized and the queen, as titular head of state, is also head of the Church of England and observes her religious duties punctiliously. Secularism is promoted by a vocal minority, and the Muslim community—because it is younger than the host community—will become proportionately more numerous as the 21st century proceeds.

The Assemblies of God Incorporated (AGI) was originally named Assemblies of God in Great Britain and Ireland (AGGBI). When Ireland became a separate grouping, the remaining churches, now covering England, Wales, and Scotland, altered their name, partly in response to British charity law. The AGGBI was founded from independent Pentecostal or revivalistic congregations in the United Kingdom, many of which were the product of the Welsh Revival of 1904. In response to an invitation from the Anglican clergyman Alexander Boddy, T. B. Barratt arrived in Sunderland in the north of England to hold a series of meetings for several weeks. At these there was speaking in tongues, which Boddy took to be an indication that a new move of the Holy Spirit was about to sweep the church. He arranged a series of annual conventions (1908–1914) in Sunderland, England, which rapidly took on an international character and helped to spread Pentecostalism into both Germany and The Netherlands. In addition he founded a magazine, *Confidence*, by which he propagated news of the Pentecostal outpouring and gave order and stability to the exercise of charismatic gifts. Boddy was no pacifist whereas many of those who were to become leaders in the post-1918 Pentecostal movement in Britain were.

Among these was John Nelson Parr (1886–1976), who called a gathering at Aston, Birmingham, in February 1924. Parr assured those present that "the autonomy of the local assembly would be strictly observed." He had in mind a British fellowship based on the pattern of the General Council of the Assemblies of God, which had been formed in the United States in 1914. The union of assemblies that was envisaged was to operate at three levels. First, assemblies would adhere to the same fundamental truths. Second, assemblies should maintain fellowship through District

Presbyteries. Third, a General Presbytery would be set up, composed of local pastors and elders.

The Assemblies' statement of fundamental truths followed basic evangelical tenets regarding the Trinity, the authority of the Bible, and the need for a personal experience of conversion. They also believed water baptism should be by total immersion and that healing from illness is provided for by the death of Jesus on the cross (the atonement). In common with many other Pentecostal denominations, they agreed that spiritual gifts and miracles should be expected in the modern era and that speaking in tongues (*glossolalia*), as described in the New Testament, is the initial evidence of the baptism of the Holy Spirit, a divine experience given to empower the ordinary believer for Christian service.

A second meeting was held in Highbury, London, in May 1924 with 80 people present, among them Donald Gee (1891–1966) and the Carter brothers, John (1893–1981) and Howard (1891–1971), all of whom had been pacifist. As a consequence of an invitation, 37 assemblies in England and one in Belfast joined immediately and 38 from Wales and Monmouth joined in August, accepting the pattern that had been worked out at the Aston meeting.

At the end of 1925 several senior members of the Pentecostal Missionary Union (PMU) resigned. The remaining members, who were by now representatives of the AGGBI, took responsibility for the whole enterprise, and the two bodies merged. This provided British Assemblies of God with a ready-made missionary work, which has continued to be active, first in specific fields in China, India, and Congo, where missionaries were already supported, and later in a less organized way in 30 countries of the world, often by providing teaching and other support for indigenous churches.

The number of assemblies (or congregations) in Britain increased from 140 in 1927 to 200 in 1929. It has continued a steady growth, and by the mid-1950s there were more than 500. At the end of the century, there were around 630. More significant than this growth against a background of growing secularism, however, was the writing, preaching, and teaching of Donald Gee and, to a lesser extent, Howard Carter. Gee clarified understandings of gifts of the Spirit (tongues, prophecy, healing, and so on) and showed

how these gifts might be related both to Pentecostal ecclesiology and to Pentecostal ministry. In essence, he showed how spiritual gifts might function in congregations where divisions between clergy and laity could be broken down because every member might be endowed with spiritual power. He also demonstrated how ministerial gifts (apostles, modern-day prophets and evangelists, and others) might function collaboratively and in relation to local congregations. In this way, he anchored Pentecostal experience in a rational exposition of the New Testament and removed many of the unpredictabilities that had attended Pentecostalism up until that point.

By the 1960s, the Pentecostal movement, and British Assemblies of God, was in need of refreshment. Many of its leaders were approaching old age. Quite suddenly and unexpectedly, the Charismatic movement burst on the scene. This was a new move of the Spirit during which Pentecostal phenomena like tongues and healings began to occur in the mainline or non-Pentecostal denominations. In some respects Pentecostal and Charismatic congregations became indistinguishable. Even so, British Assemblies of God was in need of "Another Springtime" (the title of a sermon preached at the General Conference by Donald Gee in 1960), and many attempts were made to secure this, mainly by reforming the intricate and increasingly complex constitution.

Tensions between reformers and conservatives in the 1970s led by the end of the 1980s to a simplified constitution; this appeared to encroach on local church autonomy, since it gave authority to regional and national superintendents. A policy of regionalization grouped congregations together into 12 larger blocs and also allowed for the delegation of business matters to smaller subgroups of ministers. Efforts to combine reforms with an emphasis on creating new churches in Britain were partly successful, but it was difficult to accelerate growth at home while maintaining overseas efforts.

In the late 1990s the General Superintendency and the National Leadership Team ensured that local projects and departmental structures—particularly in education, training, and church planting—were coordinated, and ambitious targets for growth were set for the internationally proclaimed "Decade of Evangelism."

At the same time expansion of facilities permitted a full range of degree courses to be offered at Mattersey Hall, the denominational theological college.

Since then, and following the failure to reach targets for growth set at the start of the Decade of Evangelism, further changes have been made. Many of these culminated in a revision of the constitution, which in 2007 concentrated power in the hands of the general superintendent. However, in 2008 he resigned. Although there remains a National Leadership Team that is affirmed at annual conferences, it is difficult to interpret these events as anything but a power struggle that has diminished the original vision of Pentecostalism and that may result in the dismemberment of the organizational structure and the formation of looser networks of ministers. There is a precarious balance within church groupings that value the spontaneity of spiritual gifts while also recognizing elected national officers. The balance is resolved by muting one or the other sides of the balance.

Currently AGI has six areas or departments for the general office to coordinate: *Joy* magazine, the Children's Department, the Church Planting Department, the Social Concern Department, World Ministries, and Youth Alive. The AGI also supports theological training at Mattersey Hall in north Nottinghamshire. The agreed mission of AGI is to reach every man, woman, and child with the message of Christ's love.

Assemblies of God
PO Box 7634
Nottingham
NG11 6ZY
UK
www.aog.org.uk

William K. Kay

See also: Charismatic Movement; Pentecostalism.

References

Dayton, Donald W. *Theological Roots of Pentecostalism*. Peabody, MA: Hendrickson, 1987.

Gee, Donald. *Concerning Shepherds and Sheepfolds*. London: Assemblies of God Publishing House, 1930.

Gee, Donald. *Concerning Spiritual Gifts*. London: Assemblies of God Publishing House, 1928.

Gee, Donald. *Wind and Flame*. Nottingham, UK: Assemblies of God Publishing House, 1967.

Kay, William K. *Inside Story*. Mattersey, UK: Mattersey Hall Publishing, 1990.

Kay, William K. *Pentecostals in Britain*. Carlisle, UK: Paternoster, 2000.

Massey, R. *A Sound and Scriptural Union: An Examination of the Origins of the Assemblies of God in Great Britain and Ireland, 1920–25*. Ph.D. diss., University of Birmingham, 1987.

Assemblies of God in Great Britain and Ireland

See Assemblies of God Incorporated.

Assemblies of Yahweh

The Assemblies of Yahweh emerged in the 1980s as the largest of the groups of the Sacred Name movement, a faction within the larger Adventist movement in the United States. The Adventist movement had originated in the 1830s around the prediction of founder William Miller (1782–1849) that Christ would return in 1843–1844. When Christ failed to appear, the movement split into three major segments, each of which spawned a number of individual churches. One faction took the name Church of God and was distinguished by its acceptance of sabbatarianism (worship on the Sabbath or Saturday rather than Sunday). In the 1930s, the idea that Yahweh, God's name in Hebrew (the original language of the Jewish Bible/Christian Old Testament), was significant and that it and Yahshua (rather than Jesus) should be used within the Church of God (Seventh Day) began to gain currency. The use of the Sacred Names was often aligned with the demand that the church revive the observance of the ancient Jewish festivals.

In 1937, Elder C. O. Dodd founded *The Faith*, a periodical supporting the cause of the Jewish festivals. By the early 1940s, he had begun to argue for the Sacred Name cause in *The Faith* and to print supportive material through the Faith Bible and Tract Society. Over the next generation a small number of Sacred Name congregations formed in various parts of the United

States. Into this situation in the 1960s came Jacob O. Meyer, a former member of the Church of the Brethren who had been converted to the Sacred Name Cause and affiliated with a small congregation in Hamburg, Pennsylvania. In 1964 he moved to Idaho to become the assistant editor of the *Sacred Name Herald,* one of several periodicals serving the loosely organized movement.

In 1966 Meyer returned to Pennsylvania and began an independent radio ministry. By 1968 his ministry had grown to the point that a magazine, *The Sacred Name Broadcaster,* was launched, and in 1969 he founded the Assemblies of Yahweh. By the end of the century, some 70 congregations had been formed. There are affiliated assemblies in some 50 countries, with offices for the global work located in the United Kingdom, the Philippines, and Trinidad.

Apart from the use of the Sacred Names, the Assemblies of God have developed other unique beliefs. Meyer asserts that if one is to understand the scriptures, the Old Testament must be allowed to supply the basis of faith. He denies the doctrine of the Trinity and believes that all the Jewish commandments must be followed (including the Jewish festivals) with the exception of the animal sacrifice ordinances. Women in the Assemblies dress modestly and cover their heads during worship services. Worship without using the words "God" and "Jesus" has made much of the traditional Christian literature unacceptable to the Assemblies, and, to fill the vacuum, Meyer has led in compiling a Sacred Name hymnal and translation of the Bible.

The Assemblies of Yahweh sponsor the Obadiah School of the Bible, also in Bethel, Pennsylvania. It is headed by the directing elder (Meyer) and the ordained elders (all male). There are also a number of senior missionaries and missionaries (who may be female). The primary spread of the Assemblies has come in response to its expansive radio ministry, which is broadcast in some 70 countries.

Assemblies of Yahweh
PO Box C
Bethel, PA 19507
www.assembliesofyahweh.com

J. Gordon Melton

See also: Church of the Brethren.

References

Meyer, Jacob O. *The Memorial Name—Yahweh.* Bethel, PA: Assemblies of Yahweh, 1978.

Psalms, Anthems. Spiritual Songs for the Assemblies of Yahweh. Bethel, PA: Assemblies of Yahweh, n.d.

The Sacred Scriptures, Bethel Edition. Bethel, PA: Assemblies of Yahweh, 1981.

Associated Churches of Christ in New Zealand

The Associated Churches of Christ in New Zealand (also known as Christian Churches New Zealand) is one product of the Restoration movement, which emerged on the American frontier early in the 19th century. In the attempt to "restore" the true church of the apostolic era of the Christian movement, ministers such as Barton W. Stone (1772–1844) and Alexander Campbell (1788–1866) left their connection with the Presbyterians in an expressed desire to be known simply as Christians. It was their belief, in spite of the many denominations they saw around them, that the church was essentially one, and they desired to find an expression of that unity. The Restoration movement is generally dated from Barton Stone's ministry at Cane Ridge, Kentucky, in 1801. Campbell and his father, Thomas Campbell (1763–1854), arrived in the United States later in the decade.

The Campbells began to advocate reform in the 1820s, during which time they were most closely associated with the Baptists, but by the 1830s the Campbellites, as they were called, were a distinct body. The Stone and Campbell movements united in 1832. Through the rest of the century, the movement expanded, based on a conservative Free Church theology (which resembled that of the Baptists in many ways). Like the Baptists, the movement rejected the idea of sacraments and practiced two ordinances, baptism and the Lord's Supper. However, it was identified by its desire to overcome denominational differences.

In the late 19th and early 20th centuries, the movement fell victim to a variety of differences, some related to American sectionalism, some to relative degrees of affluence. A key factor was the desire of some in the congregationally organized movement for more centralized control over various denominational ministries, including publications and missionary work. During the last decades of the 19th century, the congregations in the northern states moved toward a degree of centralization. Local churches also began to install church organs in their sanctuaries. Churches in the southern states (which came to be known as the Churches of Christ) tended to reject both tendencies and gradually broke fellowship with the northern churches, which came to be known as the Christian Church (Disciples of Christ). A third group, which rejected any centralization, but was open to some practices such as instrumental music in their congregations, became known as the Christian Churches and Churches of Christ.

In 1840, the first Restoration church was founded in New Zealand by Scottish minister Thomas Jackson at Nelson. Its existence was noted in both American and British periodicals associated with the movement later in the decade. The spread of the church through the islands was somewhat dependent on migration from Great Britain. Eventually three conferences (Auckland, Middle District, and South Island) facilitated cooperative action among the congregations, and in 1901, for the first time, a national conference was convened. The national conference has been held annually since 1921 and has become the means of establishing a variety of cooperative ministries. As early as 1906, missionary work in what is now Zimbabwe was launched, and work was added later in Vanuatu. In 1927 a theological college was opened, though it has since closed.

During the last decades of the twentieth century, the churches experienced a steady membership decline. In 2006, the Churches of Christ reported 33 congregations and some 1,800 members. It is a member of the World Council of Churches. It is also related to the larger community of the Churches of Christ, Christian Churches and Churches of Christ, and the Christian Church (Disciples of Christ), through the World Convention of Churches of Christ.

Associated Churches of Christ in New Zealand
PO Box 30 896

Lower Hutt
New Zealand-Aotearoa
www.churchesofchrist.org.nz

J. Gordon Melton

See also: Baptists; Christian Church (Disciples of Christ); Christian Churches and Churches of Christ; Churches of Christ in Australia; World Convention of Churches of Christ; World Council of Churches.

References

Davidson, Allan K. *Christianity in Aotearoa: A History of Church and Society in New Zealand.* 2nd ed. Wellington: Education for Ministry, 1997.

Van der Bent, Ans J., ed. *Handbook/Member Churches/World Council of Churches.* Geneva: World Council of Churches, 1985.

Association for Research and Enlightenment

The Association for Research and Enlightenment (ARE) was founded in 1931 as the vehicle for presenting the work and teaching of American seer Edgar Cayce (1877–1945) to the public. Cayce was one of the more notable psychics of the 20th century, who during the 1920s developed a reputation for being able to diagnose the illness of those who came to him and prescribe for their conditions. He later became known for his giving what were termed "life readings." While in a trance state, he would offer observations on an individual's previous embodiments on Earth and how experiences from these past lives affected that individual's present existence. These life readings were recorded by a stenographer and later transcribed. By the end of Cayce's life, records of more than 14,000 readings had been compiled.

In 1948, three years after Cayce died, The Edgar Cayce Foundation was chartered as a sister organization. It now has formal ownership of the transcriptions of the readings, the related documentation, and the facilities in Virginia that house ARE. ARE is a membership organization that disseminates material derived from the readings, holds conferences related to the

Portrait of American psychic Edgar Cayce (1877–1945), founder of the Association for Research and Enlightenment. (Used by permission–Edgar Cayce Foundation– Virginia Beach, VA)

teachings, and promotes study groups in which people around the world may become familiar with and appropriate the teachings for their own lives.

ARE became more than a small organization of Cayce associates under the leadership of Cayce's son Hugh Lynn Cayce (1907–1982), who oversaw the production of a number of commercially published books about his father and the perspective that emerged from the readings (more than 300 such books having been written to date). ARE became prominent as the New Age movement developed in the 1970s and in subsequent decades has become a global organization. Writers associated with the Association continue to mine the vast set of readings for inspiration.

In 1997 ARE had 40,000 full members and served many more who were attracted to the teachings. Cen-

ters are now operating in more than a dozen countries (including Poland, Germany, France, England, Sweden, and Japan), and study groups are found in more than 50 countries. ARE supports an Internet site at http:// www.edgarcayce.org/, and many of the national affiliates also have sites. Related facilities include Atlantic University (which offers degrees in transpersonal psychology), the Cayce-Reilly School of Massotherapy, the Health and Rejuvenation Research Center, and the Edgar Cayce Institute for Intuitive Studies. ARE is presently led by Charles Thomas Cayce (b. 1942).

Like many groups in the Western Esoteric tradition, ARE considers itself a spiritual but not a religious group, and notes that a number of people who are otherwise members of various religious communities participate in its activities.

Association for Research and Enlightenment
Atlantic Avenue at 67th St.
Box 595
Virginia Beach, VA 23451

J. Gordon Melton

See also: Reincarnation.

References

Bro, Harmon Hartzell. *A Seer out of Season: The Life of Edgar Cayce.* New York: New American Library, 1989.

Cayce, Edgar, and Charles Thomas Cayce. *My Life as a Seer: The Lost Memoirs.* New York: St. Martin's Press, 2002.

Cayce, Hugh Lynn, ed. *The Edgar Cayce Reader.* 2 vols. New York: Bantam Books, 1982.

Kirkpatrick, Sidney D. *Edgar Cayce: An American Prophet.* New York: Riverhead Trade, 2001.

Smith, Robert A. *Hugh Lynn Cayce: About My Father's Business.* Norfolk, VA: Donning Company, 1988.

Association of Baptist Churches in Rwanda

The Association of Baptist Churches in Rwanda emerged as a result of war in the Congo, which in 1964 forced a Baptist pastor and some missionaries into neighboring Rwanda. In 1966 they formally began work in northern Rwanda, which was officially registered the following year. The church, with roots in the Conservative Baptist Foreign Mission Society, grew steadily from its evangelistic endeavors and soon developed a parallel primary educational program and sponsorship of several health clinics. Finding themselves working in a poverty-ridden area, the church initiated a variety of programs to assist people in the formation of small businesses. The church continues the conservative Calvinist theology of its Baptist forebears.

By 2005, the church had grown to include more than 250,000 members. In 2001 it joined the World Council of Churches and is also a member of the Baptist World Alliance.

BP 217
Kilgali
Rwanda

J. Gordon Melton

See also: Baptist World Alliance; World Council of Churches.

Reference

Van Beek, Huibert. *A Handbook of the Churches and Councils: Profiles of Ecumenical Relationships.* Geneva: World Council of Churches, 2006.

Association of Evangelical Reformed Churches of Burkino Faso

The Association of Evangelical Reformed churches of Burkino Faso dates to 1977, when a pastor of the Assemblies of God working in the country left to begin independent evangelism. He subsequently studied at the Theological Institute of Porto Novo in Benin, where he became attracted to the Reformed Presbyterian tradition. He focused evangelistic efforts in the rural northern part of Burkino Faso and the initial fruits of his labors were formally organized in 1986 as the Association of Evangelical Reformed Churches. The association operates out of the tradition as expressed in the ancient Ecumenical creeds and the Reformed creeds of the 16th century.

The association has developed its work in some of the poorest sections of Burkino Faso. Thus, along with its evangelism it had initiated a variety of efforts, including the creation of new water resources, for improving the conditions among the people with whom it has found a home.

By 2006, the association had welcomed some 39,000 members who worship at its 9 churches and 3 evangelistic stations. It also supports several schools, medical clinics, and an orphanage. It joined the World Council of Churches in 2005. It is also a member of the World Alliance of Reformed Churches and the All Africa Conference of Churches.

Association of Evangelical Churches of Burkino Faso
01 BP 3946
Ouagadougou 01
Burkino Faso

J. Gordon Melton

See also: All Africa Conference of Churches; Assemblies of God; World Alliance of Reformed Churches; World Council of Churches.

Reference

Van Beek, Huibert. *A Handbook of the Churches and Councils: Profiles of Ecumenical Relationships.* Geneva: World Council of Churches, 2006.

Association of German Mennonite Congregations

The Mennonite movement in Germany originated out of the Anabaptist movement that emerged in southern Germany and German-speaking Switzerland during the early years of the Protestant Reformation. The most tragic incidents in Anabaptist history occurred in Germany, where the millennial movements led by Thomas Müntzer at Mühlhausen (1524) and then Jan Matthys of Leiden at Münster (1534–1535) both turned into open warfare. These incidents increased the pressure on the adherents, who had already been feeling the ire of both Protestants and Roman Catholics on religious grounds. The Anabaptists rejected infant baptism and with it the idea of a general population that was Christian, whose members lived in a Christian state led by

Menno Simons (1492–1559) was a Dutch Catholic priest who, influenced by Lutheranism, converted to Anabaptism. He became an Anabaptist leader in Holland and northwest Germany, and his followers would later become known as "Mennonites." (Getty Images)

Christian rulers. They sought a church separate from state authority, one composed only of those who had experienced regenerating faith and chose freely to join the fellowship and live under its discipline.

In Holland, Menno Simons (1492–1559) became the spokesperson of the movement and developed its theology, distinguishing it from the theology of the Protestants and Catholics on the one hand and that of the radical Münsterites on the other. He reformed the movement and spearheaded its spread, especially into northwestern Germany. Emden was an early Mennonite center, and strong communities emerged at Hamburg and Lübeck. As early as 1623, Duke Friedrich invited them to settle in Friedrichstadt. They also later found refuge on the estates of other sympathetic noble families. They developed in strength in the Palatinate in southern Germany after 1664, where the elector Karl Ludwig issued a letter of toleration. While successfully finding refuge in various places, the Menno-

nites always lived under the threat that the current ruler of the territory in which they resided might change his opinion—or that a new ruler might not be as open-minded. When a more tolerant situation was discovered, they frequently migrated.

The Mennonites were especially influenced by the Pietist movement, which originated in the late 17th century. The Pietists shared an emphasis on personal religion and faith that resonated with Mennonite emphases. While helping to revive some Mennonite congregations, Pietism also led to many rejoining the established church.

The Mennonite emphasis on peace and their refusal of military service led to conflict with Friedrich Wilhelm (1620–1688) and thus created an openness in the 1760s to the invitation given by Catherine the Great of Russia (r. 1762–1796) to German Mennonites to relocate to Russia. Between 1762 and 1772, some 100 Mennonite colonies were founded in Russia, further depleting the German community. Already, in the 1680s, the first moves of European Mennonites to Pennsylvania (then a British colony) had begun. The Palatinate Mennonites joined the move in the first decade of the 18th century. In the next century, the thrust of Mennonite history was transferred from Europe to North America.

Through the 19th century, the German Mennonite movement developed as two separate communities, a more urbanized community in the northwest and a more rural community in the south. Education became an issue. Although some leaders were trained in the Mennonite seminary in Holland, most attended the Pietist and, in the 19th century, Baptist schools in Germany. A large Mennonite boarding school, the Weierhof, developed in the Palatinate. It produced the most important Mennonite leader of the early 20th century, Christian Neff (d. 1946), a pioneer advocate of Mennonite unity. During his half century of leadership, the German Mennonite community experienced a revival. They supported world missions through the Mennonite Missionary Association, a Dutch sending agency. They developed a relief agency to assist Mennonites trapped in the Soviet Union (1924), and they opened a new Bible study center at Karlsruhe.

Many German Mennonites died during World War II. Others who originally lived east of the Oder-

Neisse Line were displaced westward. They recovered with assistance from North America and by the 1960s appeared to have revived. In 1952, the European Mennonite Evangelism Committee was established as a joint effort by German, Swiss, French, and Dutch Mennonites; it continued the efforts of the Mennonite Missionary Association established by the Dutch church in the previous century. Through the committee, work was supported in Indonesia and Africa.

Today, the Association of German Mennonite Congregations (Vereinigung der Deutschen Mennonitengemeinden) has its headquarters at the Ökumenisches Institut, Plankengasse 1, D-69117 Heidelberg, Germany. There are approximately 20,000 members. The Association is a member of the World Council of Churches and cooperates with the Mennonite World Conference.

There are also several other smaller Mennonite bodies in Germany. In the 1990s, the German Mennonite community was suddenly swelled by the addition of some 77,000 Mennonites who moved from the Volga Region in Russia to Germany. Some joined the several older groups and others formed new groups reflective of the various divisions that had emerged in Russia since the 18th century.

J. Gordon Melton

See also: Anabaptism; Mennonite World Conference; Mennonites; World Council of Churches.

References

Dyck, Cornelius J. *An Introduction to Mennonite History*. Scottsdale, PA: Herald Press, 1967.
The Mennonite Encyclopedia. 5 vols. Scottsdale, PA: Herald Press, 1955–1959.
Mennonite World Handbook: Mennonites in Global Mission. Carol Stream, IL: Mennonite World Council, 1990.

Association The Church of God

The Association The Church of God is a product of the spread of the modern Pentecostal movement in Latin America. It was formed in 1952 by the coming together of three Pentecostal congregations and subsequently has spread to every part of the county. It stands out from the larger segment of the Pentecostal movement by its commitment to ecumenical relationships. It was a founding member of the Latin American Council of Churches and also joined the Evangelical Pentecostal Commission of Latin America. In 1980 it joined the World Council of Churches.

The Association is Pentecostal in faith and practice but has also developed a strong commitment to human rights and the creation of a more humane, just, and responsible society. To that end its has established a variety of service centers (from soup kitchens to clothes banks and literacy services).

By 2006, the Association reported 8,000 members in its 70 congregations. It sponsors Emmanuel Seminary for the training of its pastors.

Association The Church of God
Miralla 453
1408 Buenos Aires
Argentina

J. Gordon Melton

See also: Latin American Council of Churches; Pentecostalism; World Council of Churches.

Reference

Van Beek, Huibert. *A Handbook of the Churches and Councils: Profiles of Ecumenical Relationships*. Geneva: World Council of Churches, 2006.

Astrology

Astrology can be roughly defined as an umbrella term denoting any one of several systems of divination that attempt to uncover information that is otherwise hidden or difficult to access by examining the position and motion of various heavenly bodies. Unpacking this definition reveals that the term covers a quite diverse set of practices and beliefs. Diviners have scrutinized the movements of the heavens over the last several thousand years in a variety of historical and cultural contexts. They have had very divergent reasons for performing divination. They have speculated on the modus operandi of their art in very distinct ways, placing it within a Christian, hermetic, secular, magical,

Chart of the zodiac used by medieval astronomers and navigators to determine locations, 1544. (Library of Congress)

occultist, Jungian, or other framework. Even if we restrict ourselves to the contemporary period in the West, there is a remarkable pluralism of aims, attitudes, and approaches. Astrological charts are consulted in order to gain insight into one's personality, predict the future course of events, determine the most auspicious moment for initiating various ventures, assess the compatibility of couples, increase one's chances of succeeding as a stock market investor, foresee political events, and for many other purposes. And whereas consultations with an astrologer will typically have such a divinatory purpose, astrology can also be encountered in the shape of sun sign predictions in newspapers, magazines, and the Internet, where its function is at least as much to entertain as to serve as a method of divination.

Practitioners can also have different opinions regarding the technical details invoked in the actual process of astrological divination: how many planets should be included; what significance, if any, should be attributed to the so-called astrological houses, and what method should be used in calculating these; should asteroids be considered significant; should midpoints between astrological objects be included in the chart; how should the influence of various factors be weighted

in the overall interpretation of a chart; what status should be accorded such non-Western systems as Vedic astrology; and so on. The present article can do no more than provide basic information on some of the types of astrology that will be most familiar to people in Western countries: natal (birth chart) astrology, sun sign astrology, and the concept of astrological ages, followed by a very brief exploration of the role of astrology in the contemporary West.

The birth chart, in contemporary natal astrology, is a symbolic map of the heavens, as seen from the perspective of one specific human being at the time of birth. More specifically, it is generally plotted as a circle, with the place on Earth where this individual is born placed in the middle. On the circumference are the signs of the Zodiac (Aries, Taurus, Gemini, Cancer, Leo, Virgo, Libra, Scorpio, Sagittarius, Capricorn, Aquarius, and Pisces), each of which is allotted one 30 degree segment of the circle. Due to an astronomical phenomenon known as the precession of the equinoxes, the positions of the astronomical constellations and the astrological signs bearing the same names do not correspond to each other.

The planets of the solar system are placed in the chart in the position where these appear against the backdrop of the astrological Zodiac. For astrological purposes, the list of planets includes the Sun and Moon. When plotted in this way, some planets will form angles to each other that are of particular interest to astrologers: they can overlap (astrologically speaking, form a conjunction), stand opposite to each other, or form a 90 degree angle (a square) or a 60 degree angle (a trine). Usually, astrologers will accept some degree of departure from these "ideal" angles, so that a distance of, for example, two or three degrees between two planets will still be seen as a conjunction. Finally, complex methods of calculation will divide charts into 12 sectors of unequal size, the houses.

In contemporary, psychologizing interpretations of astrology, each element of the chart will typically be associated with certain dynamics of the personality. The planets are often interpreted as symbols of the basic expressions of the human being: the conscious ego (the Sun); emotions and intuition (the Moon); aggression and assertiveness (Mars); the intellect (Mercury); responsibility, control, and inhibition (Saturn);

adventurous individualism (Uranus); deep-seated impulses from the unconscious (Pluto); and so forth. The signs of the Zodiac are the various ways in which such drives are acted out, for instance, with serious commitment and service to others (Virgo), with extroversion and self-centeredness (Leo), with liveliness and a quest for a diversity of experience (Gemini), or with a forceful drive (Aries). The houses are arenas of human activities in which these expressions are acted out: the realm of material possessions (second house), communication (third house), creativity and children (fifth house), or career (tenth house). These various elements of a person's character can to varying extents complement or stand in tension with each other, depending on the angles formed by the planets.

Many symbols have a range of standard interpretations in the astrological literature, as even this overly simplistic set of key-words should be able to convey. The task and challenge of the astrologer is to be able to formulate a narrative that—in the perspective of the person whose chart is being read—makes sense. Due to the sheer mass of information in a chart, and the many ways of interpreting any given set of symbols, these narratives can differ substantially from each other, and any example of how a particular element of a chart will be understood by the astrologer can only represent one option among many. Even within the work of one specific astrologer one finds a range of possible interpretations: the chart element "Saturn in Gemini and the third house" can, according to Jungian astrologist Liz Greene, be linked to a blockage (Saturn) in the intellect's (Mercury) ability to grapple with the new and unexplored (Gemini), but can also manifest as an inhibition in one's ability to speak of things that truly matter to oneself.

Astrologers will attempt to predict future trends by one of two main techniques. The method of astrological transits interprets the movements of astrologically significant objects over time, typically the angles formed between planets at the moment of divination and the moment of birth. If, say, Saturn has made a full circle around the chart and is now located at the same place as one's natal Saturn, this can be interpreted as a sign of entering a new phase in life. The other common technique, astrological progressions, involves symbolically calculating the chart for a new time, for example, bringing the chart one day forward for each year of a person's life. In order to assess trends for an individual at age 30, a chart would be constructed for a point in time 30 days after the birth of that person.

Compared to the many complexities of natal astrology, sun sign astrology is quite simple. This form of astrology is based on the premise that people born with the Sun in a particular zodiacal sign will undergo broadly similar events at a given point in time. Sun sign astrology is a fairly recent innovation and is generally attributed to the astrologer R. H. Naylor (1889–1952), who began writing sun sign columns in the *Sunday Express* in 1930. Since then, sun sign columns have become a ubiquitous part of popular culture. Precisely because of its simplicity, sun sign astrology is not only the form of astrology most widely known to the general public, but also a version of astrology that many who practice natal astrology consider crude and simplistic.

Beside such astrological practices that involve character analysis and predictions for individual people, the astrological concept perhaps most familiar to the general public is that of astrological ages, and in particular the Age of Aquarius. Due to the precession of the equinoxes mentioned above, the distance between astronomical constellations and astrological signs steadily increases, at a speed of roughly one sign each 2,160 years. Such a period of over two millennia is known as an astrological age, and many astrologers have suggested that we will either soon be leaving one such age (the Age of Pisces) or have already entered the next (the Age of Aquarius). Each age is said to be marked by certain overarching characteristics, for instance, the Age of Pisces by the dominance of Christianity (since the fish is a common symbol for that religion) and the Age of Aquarius by a more individualistic spirituality. During the spiritually adventurous 1960s it was commonly asserted that the transition into the Age of Aquarius was taking place.

Astrology occupies an ambiguous position in contemporary society. Surveys suggest that roughly a quarter or more of the population of various countries in Europe and North America profess at least a modicum of belief in astrology, and an even larger number of people read sun sign columns for their entertainment. Open support for astrology has been most noticeable in the various groups of the Western Esoteric tradition, especially Wicca. At the same time, astrology is excluded from the institutional pillars of society and is regularly characterized by skeptical voices as superstitious or pseudoscientific. When astrology does enter core social institutions, for example, in political decision making in the Reagan years or in a few university settings in the early 21st century, the response from non-astrologers has generally been very negative.

One reason for the lack of acceptance of astrology in core sectors of Western societies is the incompatibility of the astrological worldview with widespread assumptions inherent in the natural sciences and the failure of astrology to pass scientific testing. Numerous experiments have been carried out in order to determine whether astrological methods can assess personalities or predict events better than chance, and generally speaking these tests suggest that under controlled conditions astrologers fare no better than if they had proceeded via random guesswork. The disparity between the popular support for astrology and the apparent failure of astrology to live up to its promises has occasioned considerable hostile coverage by skeptics. Some astrologers have countered by attempting to support the empirical validity of their craft, for example, by citing the research of Michel Gauquelin (1928–1991), who by means of large statistical samples attempted to study the possible relations between birth times and subsequent careers. He thus claimed that there was a correlation between a time of birth with a rising or culminating Mars and a later athletic career. For the ordinary user of astrological services, however, scientific legitimacy appears to be a tangential issue, and personal experience of a good match between the astrologer's interpretation and one's personal self-perception is the main source of legitimacy.

Olav Hammer

See also: Astrology, Hinduism; Western Esoteric Tradition; Wiccan Religion.

References

Curry, Patrick. *A Confusion of Prophets: Victorian and Edwardian Astrology*. London: Collins & Brown, 1992.

Munk, Kirstine. *Signs of the Times: Why do Modern People Use Astrology?* London: Equinox, (forthcoming).

Stuckrad, Kocku von. *History of Astrology: From Earliest Times to the Present*. London: Equinox, 2005.

Astrology, Hindu

Astrology as it developed in ancient and medieval India continues to be a major influence on the ways that Hindus interpret and attempt to manage important events in their lives. Traditional manuscript texts on what is called *jyotisa* contain theories about heavenly bodies along with reports from observations of the night sky that involve a combination of mathematics, astrology, and astronomy as one interconnected domain of knowledge. Many of the *jyotihsastra* texts that are known to have survived into the modern period were preserved to provide a source of proprietary knowledge and power by generations of descendents, in particular, kin groups that specialize in astrological consultation.

The history of astrology as a human enterprise is as yet an incomplete story, and how much of Hindu astrology originated in India without any outside influence is highly controversial. David Pingree, on the one hand, has argued that Greek mathematics and Babylonian concepts greatly influenced astrology as it has been practiced in India and that since ancient times there has been considerable traffic in traditional knowledge across central and southern Asia between what nowadays are the nations of Iran and India. Subash Kak, on the other hand, has argued that Vedic ritual practice indigenous to India prior to the rise of classical Hinduism provided the necessary and sufficient conditions to stimulate the research that produced Hindu astrological and astronomical knowledge. He proposes that Hindu and Babylonian astrology each emerged independently. In India, intense popular controversy about the origin and nature of astrology erupted in 2001 when the University Grants Commission published guidelines for establishing university departments of Vedic astrology and funding to teach it as an approved school subject.

Whatever their origins, Western and Hindu astrology are different in their details, and the most obvious difference is in the zodiac. A zodiac in astrology is an imaginary arc through the sky that encircles the Earth and appears to move in an east to west direction. An obvious difference between Hindu and Western astrology is that the Western system uses a tropical zodiac that takes the springtime or vernal equinox as its starting point in Aries. Although the night sky has changed (due to what is called the precession of equinoxes) in the centuries since simple observation established that conjunction, it continues to be the formal starting point for the Western zodiac as a symbolic system rather than as a contemporary fact of observation. Hindu astrology uses a sidereal zodiac that is based on where constellations are physically located when they are actually viewed in the night sky. Hindu astrology like Western astrology divides its zodiac into 12 parts, each identified by a sign. But the names and significance of the signs in the system are different, additional heavenly bodies are identified and accorded significance, and the Moon and its relation to the Sun's ecliptic or pathway through the zodiac have a major role in Hindu astrology and in the traditional Hindu calendar system, too. That makes the rising sign or ascendant (the sign on the eastern horizon at the time of birth) a crucial factor in the construction of an individual's horoscope and in calculating the influences on one's life.

Like life in family or society, life in relation to astrological forces requires that many influences must be taken into account, and that is neither easy nor simple. Ideally one would seek a trusted trained advisor and return for repeated consultations as life-circumstances change. Crucial developmental stages (birth, youth, adulthood, marriage, death), key beginnings (new job, new business, new home), and key seasonal activities (plowing and planting) can benefit from correct timing in order to increase prospects for a successful outcome. Much of the information needed for accurate calculation and timing is widely available in published annual almanacs, but for most Hindus the printed page is no substitute for a professional counselor who knows how to select appropriate data and apply it to particular people and situations in order to achieve an auspicious result. Anyone who has experienced a tax audit will appreciate the value of a skilled accountant, and in Hindu society the astrologer is thought to have similar specialized knowledge about how to avoid the dire consequences that can follow ill-considered or ill-timed action.

An unfortunate and inaccurate stereotype represents Hindus as fatalistic in contrast to people of other geographic regions, or ethnic backgrounds, or religious persuasions that are imagined to be enterprising and optimistic in outlook. Astrology, in fact, can be taken as evidence that in richly diverse Hindu cultures there are traditional resources for many kinds of life-enhancing strategies that contrast with a passive capitulation to karmic forces that would overwhelm one and make one powerless to alter the destiny established by a relentless fate. Astrological prediction functions alongside a large number of readily available and widely encouraged traditional strategies for improving and transforming oneself and the world. These would include making vows and undertaking fasts, appealing to great beings in the form of holy men or temple deities, experiencing spirit-possession and using other methods of divination, making donations to worthy sacred institutions, and making pilgrimages. All of these tend to be motivated by short-term pragmatic aims as well as long-term transcendental purposes. Thus, astrology can be an important and positive resource for Hindus.

Gene R. Thursby

See also: Astrology; Hinduism; Pilgrimage; Spirit Possession.

References

Chenet, Francois. "Karma and Astrology: An Unrecognized Aspect of Indian Anthropology." *Diogenes* 33 (1985): 101–126.

Kak, Subash C. "The Astronomy of the Age of Geometric Altars." *Quarterly Journal of the Royal Astronomical Society* 36 (1995): 385–395.

Kent, Eliza F. "'What's Written on the Forehead Will Never Fail': Karma, Fate, and Headwriting in Indian Folktales." *Asian Ethnology* 68, no. 1 (2009): 1–26.

Pingree, David. "Astronomy and Astrology in India and Iran." *ISIS* 54, 2 (1963): 229–246.

Pugh, Judy F. "Into the Almanac: Time, Meaning, and Action in North Indian Society." *Contributions to Indian Sociology* 17, no. 1 (1983): 27–49.

Athanasius

ca. 296–373

Athanasius of Alexandria, a Christian bishop and theologian, is remembered as one of the major shapers of the orthodox Christian tradition by his defense of what became the accepted solution to the problems of the trinitarian nature of God and the divinity of Jesus. The Athanasian position would be embodied in the Nicene Creed, the most ubiquitous statement of Christian faith since the fourth century.

The early years of Athanasius, including the date of his birth are shrouded in obscurity, but it is generally believed that he was born shortly before 298 CE. In later years, it would be charged that he was underage when in 328 he was consecrated a bishop, it being required that a person reach his 30th birthday before his consecration. He emerged from obscurity when he served as Alexander's secretary during the Council of Nicaea (324–325), the first of the great ecumenical councils at which the important questions before the whole of the church were debated and decided. At this Council, the position of Bishop Arius, that Jesus was not God, but a little less than God, was declared to be heretical. In 328, Alexander died and Athanasius was chosen as his successor.

As bishop, Athanasius inherited an immediate problem—a schism that focused on Meletius of Lycopolis (fl. 310) who argued for severe treatment of believers who had denied their faith during times of persecution. Athanasius opposed Meletius, arguing for a more lenient and forgiving stance toward the lapsed. The position assumed added importance when the bishops supporting Meletius aligned with the Arians in the East.

Athanasius, however, soon emerged as the champion against Arius, who did not go away after Nicaea and who continued to enjoy strong support in various parts of the church and the ear of the emperor in Constantinople. Athanasius's first writing, written at this time, was his *Against the Heathen*, which presented his apology against Pagan practices. Also, at this time he penned his singularly most important work, *The Incarnation of the Word of God*, which discusses the doctrine of God's entering the world to bring salvation to humankind. The latter work attacks Arianism and

Athanasius, also known as Saint Athanasius, was one of the most important Christian theologians of the fourth century CE. (Library of Congress)

set the direction of the future development of orthodox theology in the major doctrines of creation, salvation, the Triune God, and the incarnation of the Logos (Word).

In the meantime, Bishop Athanasius had more immediate problems to handle. His fellow bishops charged him with mistreatment of both the Meletians and the Arians and, following a council at Tyre in 335, deposed him from office. They followed with accusation against him to the emperor and later that year after a meeting with the emperor, Constantine (272–337), banished Athanasius to Trier in far-off Germany. During these years he stayed in touch with his flock in a set of letters, in which he involved himself on the question of the dating of Easter, a controversy that would remain open for centuries.

Athanasius was not allowed to return until Constantine died, but his situation remained in flux. The new emperor Constantius II (r. 337–361) renewed the exile and Athanasius left for Rome, where he enjoyed the protection of Constans (r. 337–350), the other son of Constantine who reigned as emperor of the West. Athanasius found broad support in Rome but could not return to Alexandria until Gregory of Cappadocia (r. 339–346), who had in Athanasius's absence assumed the bishop's chair, died.

When Athanasius finally returned to his post in Alexandria in 346, he had had only a brief reprieve before threats on his life forced him to flee to Upper Egypt, where he found refuge within the strong monastic community. He would be exiled again (362–364) by the emperor Julian (r. 360–363), an exile continued by Julian's successor Valens (r. 364–378). However, when he returned in 366, he was able to remain in Alexandria until his death in 373. At that point he had been the bishop over Alexandria for some 45 years.

Throughout his mobile life, Athanasius wrote numerous works, many continuing the debate with the Arians. He also found time to write a life of the monastic pioneer Antony, a book that pioneered a pattern of writing hagiographies, lives of the saints, so popular in the Eastern Church. The nature of his life required him to write many letters. One memorable epistle penned in 367 is noteworthy as including the first known listing of the books of the New Testament that included all those books now accepted as the New Testament. Athanasius's writings are available in multiple sites on the Internet.

Athanasius has been declared a Doctor of the Church by the Roman Catholic Church, while the Eastern Orthodox churches consider him as one of the four Great Doctors of the Eastern Church. He is also venerated as a saint, but with different feast days set by the Roman Church (May 2), Eastern Orthodox churches (January 18), and the Coptic Orthodox Church (May 15).

Because Athanasius was an Egyptian, the Coptic Church has a special place for him in their history. Following Athanasius's death, his body was buried in Alexandria but at a later date was taken to Rome. In an act of ecumenicity, during the visit of Pope Shenouda III (r. 1971–) to Rome, Pope Paul VI (r. 1963–1978) gave him some relics of Athanasius, which are now in the Coptic cathedral in Cairo.

J. Gordon Melton

See also: Arius; Cathedrals—Christian; Constantine the Great; Eastern Orthodoxy; Relics; Roman Catholic Church.

References

Anatolios, Khaled. *Athanasius: The Coherence of His Thought.* New York: Routledge, 1998.

Arnold, Duane W.-H. *The Early Episcopal Career of Athanasius of Alexandria.* Notre Dame, IN: Notre Dame University Press, 1991.

Barnes, Timothy D. *Athanasius & Constantius: Theology and Politics in the Constantinian Empire.* Cambridge: Harvard University Press, 1993.

Brakke, David. *Athanasius and Asceticism.* Baltimore: Johns Hopkins University Press, 1998.

Kannengieser, Charles. *Arius and Athanasius: Two Alexandrine Theologians.* Brookfield: Gower, 1991.

Pettersen, Alvyn. *Athanasius.* London: Geoffrey-Pettersen, 1995.

Rubenstein, Richard E., *When Jesus Became God: The Epic Fight over Christ's Divinity in the Last Days of Rome.* New York: Harcourt Brace & Company, 1999.

Atheism

Atheism (literally "without theism") refers to a spectrum of belief systems that do not include a belief in a deity. In the modern West, dominated by Christian theism, atheism has often been defined in relation to Christianity as "denial" of belief in God. While on a practical level atheism is frequently in debate with theistic beliefs and often contrasted with them, atheists contend that atheisms are belief systems that have been constructed apart from any affirmation of God or a deity. Atheisms do not in and of themselves deny God. Rather they find no rationale for such an additional affirmation. Many atheists find no meaning in the term "God."

There have been thinkers throughout history who have proposed ways of thinking about the world that were nontheistic, and while atheism is often seen as a nonreligious way of viewing the world, several prominent religious systems (notably Jainism and Theravada

Buddhism) are also atheistic. Most modern Western atheists trace their beliefs to Baron d'Holbach (1723–1789), who authored a series of works, most published anonymously, that denounced the Roman Catholic Church. In 1772 the first openly atheist book, written by him, *The System of Nature*, appeared. His books denounced what he saw as the erroneous systems of the past and advocated a new order in which a nature-based ethical system would be operative.

In the 19th century, several atheist systems gained widespread support and became the basis of a developing organizational life. Most widely held was Marxism, as developed by Karl Marx (1818–1883), Friederich Engels (1820–1895), and their followers. Marxist thought, in its several variations, has offered a complete worldview without God that is basically antireligious. Marx attacked religion for defending oppressive socioeconomic systems and drugging the masses of humanity into accepting their exploited state. No form of atheist thinking has been so successful in perpetuating itself as has Marxism, which rose to a position of dominance in the Soviet Union, the countries of Eastern Europe, and many Third World nations through much of the 20th century, and still is the controlling philosophy in the People's Republic of China. Marxism also continues to be espoused by some Western intellectuals, though its support in academia has measurably declined since the dissolution of the Soviet Union at the end of the 1980s.

In its rise to political dominance, Marxism has developed an extremely poor record in human rights, and many Western atheists have attempted to separate themselves from it. They instead follow a lineage of atheists that includes such notable writers as Revolutionary philosopher Thomas Paine, poet Percy Shelley, popular lecturer Robert G. Ingersoll, 19th-century Freethought movement leader Robert Bradlaugh of the National Secular Society (in Great Britain), and a spectrum of 20th-century thinkers and organizations. These organizations and individuals (many of whom have edited periodicals) have been known as defenders of free speech and advocates of a variety of liberal political causes, including those related to sexual education and birth control. In the 20th century, prominent atheist spokespersons included Joseph Lewis (1889–1968) of Freethinkers of America; Charles Lee Smith (1887–1964) of the American Association for the Advancement of Atheism; and R. M. Bennett, editor of the *Truth Seeker*. A variety of intellectuals identified with atheism would include Ludwig Feuerbach, Auguste Comte, Bertrand Russell, Clarence Darrow, and John Dewey. Contemporary atheists have attempted, with some success, to identify atheism as the chosen worldview of the majority of contemporary academics, especially scientists.

Since World War II, non-Marxist atheism has appeared under a variety of guises, including Humanism (a nontheistic system that emphasizes human values and ethics), Secularism (which offers a worldview apart from any reference to the sacred), and Rationalism (emphasizing the essential role of reason in establishing a worldview). Humanism has developed both as a religious system and a nonreligious alternative to religion. Atheism as an organized alternative to religion received a significant boost from Madalyn Murray O'Hair (1919–1995), who in 1963 organized American Atheists, one of the largest atheist organizations ever created. Her acerbic personality eventually led to the organization's splintering, and her own life was ended in 1995 when she, along with her son and granddaughter, was murdered. However, American Atheists had a definite impact in raising the profile of atheism within American culture.

Although North American atheist groups are among the best organized in the world, other nonreligious and atheist groups, not associated with the spread of Marxism, have appeared in other countries, including the Atheist Foundation of Australia, the Mexican Ethical Rationalist Association, the Finnish Freethought Union, the Union Rationaliste (France), the International League of Non-Religious and Atheists (Germany), the Deutscher Freidenker Bund (Germany), the Union degli Atei e degli Agnostici Razionalisti (Italy), the Portuguese Freethought Association, the Forbundet for Religionfrihet, and the World Union of Freethinkers (Belgium). Some of these groups are members of the International Humanist and Ethical Union.

Though still a minority belief system, atheism had a significant impact on the intellectual climate in the 20th century and is especially important in the political arena in many countries such as France and the former Communist countries of Europe. Contemporary atheists have identified themselves with such causes as the separation of religion and the state, the fight against prescientific and pseudoscientific thinking, and the promotion of ethical systems apart from religious foundations.

As the 21st century began, the atheist community, most notably in the English-speaking world, has been energized by a new movement generally referred to as neo-Atheism, built around the writings of the likes of Richard Dawkins, Sam Harris, and Christopher Hitchens. The neo-Atheists have become known not so much for any new perspectives as for their aggressive stance relative to traditional atheist positions. They pointedly denounce religion and champion Darwinian evolution. While their assertiveness has been rejected by some atheists, most appear to appreciate the attention to their position that the neo-Atheists have brought.

J. Gordon Melton

See also: American Atheists; Freethought; Humanism; International Humanist and Ethical Union; Jainism; Theravada Buddhism.

References

Bradlaugh, Charles. *A Plea for Atheism*. London: Freethought Publishing Co., 1864.

Dawkins, Richard. *The God Delusion*. Boston: Houghton Mifflin Harcourt, 2006.

Hitchens, Christopher. *God Is Not Great: How Religion Poisons Everything*. Toronto: McClelland & Stewart, 2007.

Johnson, B. C. *The Atheist Debater's Handbook*. Buffalo, NY: Prometheus Books, 1982.

O'Hair, Madalyn Murray. *What on Earth Is an Atheist?* Austin, TX: American Atheist Press, 1970.

Stein, Gordon, ed. *An Anthology of Atheism and Rationalism*. Buffalo, NY: Prometheus Books, 1980.

Athens

Athens, the capital of the modern state of Greece, has a unique place in the religious world, which can be divided into three overlapping periods. Athens emerged on the world scene as a hill-top fortification that subsequently expanded into the adjacent Attica Basin. The basin, which is home to the modern city, is surrounded on three sides by four large mountains. To the southwest is the Saronic Gulf, which opens onto the Mirtoan Sea.

The Pagan Era Athens began to be able to challenge Sparta's leadership among the city-states of the Greeks in the sixth century BCE. Following the overthrow of an unpopular dictator in 510, the new leader Cleisthenes reorganized the city as a democratic state. Democratic Athens then established its status throughout the region by defeating Persian invaders twice, in 490 and 480 BCE. The latter victory at the Battle of Salamis followed on the heels of two losses by the Spartans and the evacuation of Athens. Following their victory, Athens organized most of Greece's city-states into the Delian League, which it dominated. Riding high through the remainder of the century, Athens began to see the end of its dominance when it was defeated in the lengthy Peloponnesian War in 404 BCE. In 338, Philip of Macedonia formally ended Athenian independence and absorbed it into the kingdom of Macedonia soon to be inherited by Alexander the Great. Athens would remain a wealthy city but would not regain its independence for two millennia.

Dominating ancient Athens was a large flat-topped rock that rose some 500 feet above sea level in the middle of the Attica Basin. Its flat top had a surface area of more than 3,000 square feet. The first temple dedicated to Athena Polias (Protectress of the City) was erected on the Acropolis in the sixth century BCE. Its exact placement is unknown, though pieces of it have survived. Toward the end of the century a second temple, the Archaios Naos (Old Temple) was erected. It served as the primary worship site for the city until after the 490 victory at Marathon. This older Parthenon was constructed on the southern part of the Acropolis. It was still unfinished when the city was evacuated and sacked by the Persians in 480. Both it and the Archaios Neos were burned. The religious remnants of the building were ceremoniously buried.

During the period of leadership under Pericles (460–430 BCE), the rebuilding that had been pursued since recovering from the two Persian Wars would give

The Acropolis in Athens, Greece. Situated in a defensive position on a limestone outcrop, the Acropolis was the site of important civic and religious structures, notably a temple to the goddess Athena. (Fabio Cardano/Dreamstime.com)

the Acropolis its familiar shape. Pericles entrusted the building of the Parthenon, the most important temple, to the architects Ictinus and Phidias. Additional prominent structures included the Propylaea; the small Ionic Temple of Athena Nike; and the large Erechtheum, a temple on the northern edge of the Acropolis with areas sacred to Athena Polias and Poseidon Erechtheusa, which included shrines to a variety of legendary Athenian heroes. Behind the Propylaea, Pericles saw to the placement of a large bronze statue (some 30 feet high) of Athena holding a lance and a giant shield.

The Acropolis functioned as the Athenean center for the worship/acknowledgment of the Greek pantheon, which was built around 12 major deities and a number of lesser ones. Athens was a site sacred to Athena, from which it took its name, but also made space for the worship of Poseidon, the god of the sea and of earthquakes, both of which played significant roles in Athenian life. Although the Acropolis was the major Pagan center, numerous smaller temples were scattered around the city.

Rome conquered Greece in 146 BCE and during the next centuries a synthesis of Greek and Roman religion occurred as architectural styles were blended and the Roman deities identified with their Greek equivalents. Athena was identified with Minerva and Poseidon with Neptune. This compatible form of Paganism would remain dominant even as the Roman Empire suffered its ups and down for the next five centuries. Then in the fourth century CE the empire would make a sudden shift. Christianity, which had been pres-

ent in Athens since the middle of the first century CE, suddenly became the new religion of the empire under Constantine I, and life would change in Athens.

The Christian Era   The beginning of Christianity in Athens is described in the book of Acts in the New Testament. The Apostle Paul arrived in the city (ca. 521 CE) and delivered his famous address on the "Unknown God" to a group of Athenian intellectuals on the Areopagus or Hill of Ares, a hill in the city northwest of the Acropolis that took its name from the story of the Greek gods holding a trial there for the murder of Poseidon's son.

Paul established the first church in Athens, but Christianity remained a minority faith until the fourth century. Christianity in Athens emerged in its new role as the majority religion under the authority of the archbishop of Constantinople, who led what would become known as the Ecumenical Patriarchate. Eastern Orthodoxy would become the new dominant faith. Christianity's replacement of Greek Pagan religion was punctuated by Emperor Theodosius's declaration of Christianity as the official religion of his empire (394) with a parallel outlawing of the worship of the Pagan deities, and Justinian's declaration outlawing the study of the ancient Greek philosophers. For a time, during the Byzantine period, the Parthenon was turned into a church, which like Justinian's church in Constantinople was named Hagia Sophia (Holy Wisdom).

The weakening of the Byzantine Empire as the Ottoman Empire arose led to Greece's being pulled from Constantinople's control. Various powers fought for land, and during the Fourth Crusade (1204) Athens fell to Otho de la Roche (d. 1234) from Burgundy. His son Guy de la Roche was named Duke of Athens by the king of France. Athens remained under French and then Italian control until 1456, when three years after the fall of Constantinople the Ottoman forces overran the city. Though ruled by Roman Catholics, the city remained Orthodox. The authorities of the Duchy of Athens used the Acropolis as its administrative center and the Parthenon as its cathedral.

The Muslim Era   The major change that came with Ottoman rule in Greece was the imposition of the tax common to non-Muslims in Muslim lands. The tax was paid to support the government and the army that protected the empire. Non-Muslims were, in return, exempt from army service. At the same time, the Ottomans supported the Christian establishment and allowed its patriarchs to exercise significant authority within the overall Ottoman structure. The Christians in Athens remained under the authority of the ecumenical patriarch. Greek clergy received their salary from the state.

Life in Athens was relatively stable until the 17th century, when Athens became the victim of the conflict between the Ottomans and Venice. The Ottomans attacked Vienna in 1683. In response, a European coalition captured the Peloponessos and attacked Athens. The Ottoman forces retreated to the Acropolis. They had used the Parthenon to store munitions with the idea that the Venetians would not attack the monument. The Venetians, aware of the munitions, fired on the hill. The explosion destroyed the Parthenon. The Venitians took the city, but then abandoned it. Much of the population left with them and Athens was largely deserted for several years. It was only repopulated when the Ottoman authorities offered amnesty and significant tax breaks.

Toward the end of the 18th century, Europeans rediscovered Athens as a rich artistic, intellectual, and cultural resource. This interest led to the collecting of artistic treasures and their movement out of the country, the most infamous incident being the removal of statues originally on the façade of the Parthenon by Lord Elgin (1801–1802). These artifacts remain on display at the British Museum.

Independence   In 1821 the Greeks revolted and attempted to assert their independence. After some success, they were finally defeated in 1827. However, in October 1827, the major European powers intervened and destroyed the Ottoman fleet. Greece was suddenly able to emerge as an independent country. The last of the Turkish troops left the Acropolis in March 1833. The European powers named Otto (1815–1867), the 16-year-old son of King Ludwig of Bavaria, as the first king of Greece, and in 1834 his capital was established in Athens, then a small city of a mere 10,000 residents. The University of Athens opened in 1837.

Greek independence came at a price to the Ecumenical Patriarchate. It had sided with the Ottomans during the revolution. Christians of the new country declared their autonomy from the church hierarchy in Constantinople, urged on by the regents who acted for Greece's teenage ruler. The action would not be recognized as such by the Patriarchate until 1850, when it issued a decree normalizing relationships between the two churches. Agreements between the Church of Greece, now led by the archbishop of Athens and all Greece, and the Ecumenical Patriarchate spelled out the boundary of their territory and detailed their special connections.

In 1842, Annunciation Cathedral, the seat of the archbishop of Athens, was dedicated by King Otto and his wife. It now houses the body of Gregory V the Ethnomartyr, the patriarch of Constantinople who was executed by the Ottoman sultan following the outbreak of the Greek Revolution in 1821. Mahmud held him responsible for not keeping the people of his jurisdiction pacified. His body was thrown into the Bosphorus but retrieved by Greek sailors and brought to Athens. Other notable churches in Athens include the Church of Agii Theodori, now believed to be the oldest Christian church in the city; the Church of the Holy Apostles, an 11th-century structure noted for the Byzantine frescoes on its interior; and the Church of Panagia Gorgoepikoos or Agios Eleftherios, a well preserved 12th-century church near the cathedral and known as the Little Metropolis. It was built from a variety of blocks taken from earlier buildings.

Just outside Athens is the monastery of Daphni. The site was originally a temple to Apollo and named for the many daphnia laurels that were considered sacred to him. The temple was destroyed by the Goths in 395 CE. The interior of the monastery's church is decorated with some of Greece's finest Byzantine mosaics, most notably the representation of the Christos Pantokrator (Christ in Majesty) above the altar. This monastery was named to the UN Educational, Scientific and Cultural Organization (UNESCO) World Heritage list in 1990.

Throughout the whole of the Pagan and Christian eras, there was a Jewish presence in Greece that expanded under Alexander the Great and his successors. Further expansion was caused by Jews leaving Palestine during the Maccabean revolt (168–135 BCE). The pioneering Christian Apostle Paul visited many of the Jewish communities on his travels through Greece in the middle of the first century CE. Jews resided in Greece through the remaining Pagan era, the centuries of Byzantine rule, and under the Ottomans. The main community was at Thessaloniki. The small community at Athens had a synagogue, but it was destroyed in the fifth century and not rebuilt.

The years of Ottoman rule were notable as the time of gradual dominance of the Jewish community by the many Sephardic Jews who had arrived in Greece after being expelled from Spain in the 1490s. The 19th and 20th centuries proved complete disasters for the Jews. Many were killed during the Greek Revolution in the 1820s, as they had a reputation for having supported Turkish rule. Then early in the 20th century there was a mass migration into Greece of Greeks who had formerly resided in Turkey, followed by a massive effort to have the Jewish community assimilate.

The Jews in Athens finally built the Ioanniotiki Synagogue in 1903. The Sephardic community built the larger Beth Shalom Synagogue in the 1930s. As World War II began, the Italians occupied Athens while the Germans occupied the northern part of Greece. The result was the complete destruction of the community in Thessaloniki and the death of the great majority of Greek Jews, some 75,000 of an estimated 80,000. However, in Athens, the archbishop led an effort to protest action against the Jewish community. In their protest document, they cited the "unbreakable bonds between Christian Orthodox and Jews." Most of the small community of Jews in Athens survived.

Today an estimated 5,000 Jews remain in Greece, of which 3,000 reside in Athens. The rabbis of the two Athens synagogues serve most of the Jews scattered around the countryside.

The last decades of the 20th century were marked by an effort to recover the history and restore as far as possible the Acropolis. This effort has been marked by a generation of archaeological excavations, the development of an Acropolis Museum, the return of many items taken away from the site, and the rush to block the effects of significant pollution in Athens. It was declared a World Heritage Site by UNESCO in 1987 and formally proclaimed as the pre-eminent monument on the European Cultural Heritage list of monuments in 2007.

In 1897, the city of Nashville, Tennessee, had a full-scale replica of the Parthenon built as part of its celebration of the centennial of the state of Tennessee. Originally intended as a temporary structure, public response was such that it was not torn down after the exposition. In 1920, the city voted for the resources to have the building reconstructed of modern permanent materials. It was reopened in 1931. Among the features of the refurbished building were the replicas of the pediments, based on molds of the Elgin marbles, and painted as they are believed to have been in ancient Greece.

In 1897, the front of the original replica building was the site of a large mega-statue of Athena, now destroyed. In 1982, the city commissioned Alan LaQuire to reproduce the statue of Athena that had once been inside the original Parthenon. Its appearance could be derived from its picture on ancient coins and surviving small reproductions of it. The final reproduction was completed in 1990 and its gold gilding added in 2002. It stands 42 feet, 10 inches, and is the largest piece of indoor sculpture in the Western world; it is now the largest statue of a Pagan goddess. The statue's right palm is the pedestal for a 6-foot statue of the god Nike.

J. Gordon Melton

See also: Hagia Sophia; Paul.

References

Beard, Mary. *The Parthenon*. Cambridge: Harvard University Press, 2003.

Ehrlich, Frederick. "Jews in Greece." In *Encyclopedia of the Jewish Diaspora: Origins, Experiences and Culture*, edited by W. Avrum Ehrlich, vol. 3, 855–857. Santa Barbara, CA: ABC-Clio, 2009.

"A History of Athens." Anagnosis Books. http://www.anagnosis.gr/index.php?pageID=54&la=eng. Accessed May 15, 2009.

Freely, John. *Strolling Through Athens.* London: Penguin, 1991.

Georgakas, Dan. "Safe Havens: Sheltering Jews during the German Occupation of Greece." *Odyssey* (July–August 1995): 38–42.

Georgiou, Lolita. *The City of Athens: A Journey into the Past.* Trans. by Judy Ayer-Giannakopoulou. Athens: Trochalia, 1993.

The Parthenon. Nashville: Board of Parks and Recreation, Centennial Park, [2007].

Travlos, John. *Pictorial Dictionary of Ancient Athens.* London: Thames and Hudson, 1971.

Athos, Mount

Mount Athos, the most famous Orthodox monastic center in the world, is located on Halkidki Peninsula, south and east of Thessaloniki, Greece. In the pre-Christian era, the region was considered the home of the gods, Mount Olympus being only some 60 miles away. Christian tradition, however, speaks of the Virgin Mary visiting the area accompanied by the Apostle John. Mount Athos began to draw Christian ascetics in the sixth century and monks several centuries later. In 1060, the emperor in Constantinople decreed that the peninsula would be a male-only area, thus setting conditions allowing it to become a primary center of Christian monasticism. Subsequently, monasteries were constructed to house monks from the variety of nationalities who had heard about the life being developed by the residents. They set in place the mount's continuing status as a male-only domain. By 1500 the population of monks had reached around 20,000.

Mount Athos became the primary center for the practice of Hesychasm, a system of prayer advocated by St. Gregory Palamas (1296–1359), a monk at Athos before becoming bishop of Thessalonica in 1349. He-

Hilandar, a Serbian Orthodox monastery on Mount Athos in Greece, was founded in 1198. Mount Athos is an important pilgrimage destination for Orthodox Christians and is the site of a number of monasteries. Only males (whether humans or animals) are allowed on Mount Athos. (Mladen Prokic/Dreamstime.com)

sychasts believe it is possible to see the very uncreated Light of God, and to that end follow a devotional pattern of activity that includes asceticism, detachment, submission to a spiritual guide, and constant prayer. They believe that contemplation of the Light is the true purpose of humanity, an experience they see recounted in the transfiguration event from the Christian Gospels (Matthew 17:1–6). Dedicated Hesychasts were known to sit all day in a chosen spot while repeating silently the prayer, "Lord Jesus Christ, have mercy on me."

As the Hesychast approach was popularized, it provoked a major and lengthy controversy in the Orthodox Church. Critics accusing the Hesychasts of pantheistic heresies, including the error of dividing God (who could not be seen) from his Light (which could be seen). Argument continued through the 14th century and even became the focus of several church councils. In the meantime, the Roman Catholic and Greek Orthodox churches went their separate ways. This proved decisive, as the opposition to the Hesychasts was successfully identified with the Roman Catholics. The Hesychasts finally won the debate and the theological presuppositions upon which the practice at Athos was built were accepted as Orthodox, even though the practice itself remained primarily confined to the monasteries. Hesychast practice retains its popularity at Athos.

Today, male visitors are allowed on the peninsula, and annually tens of thousands arrive for brief visits. Some come merely as tourists, others to visit the particular monasteries, a few of which possess items known for their miracle-working powers, or to visit with a particular monk who serves as a spiritual counselor. At least three of the monasteries claim a fragment of the True Cross (upon which Jesus was crucified).

About 3,000 monks are permanent residents on Athos at present. There are a few hermits, but overwhelmingly the monks reside in one of 20 monastic communities.

J. Gordon Melton

See also: Asceticism; Devotion/Devotional Traditions; Eastern Orthodoxy; Monasticism; Pilgrimage; Relics.

References

Bryer, Anthony, and Mary Cunningham. *Mount Athos and Byzantine Monasticism*. Aldershot, UK: Ashgate Publishing, Very Fine/Fine, 1998.
Kadas, Sotiris. *Mount Athos: An Illustrated Guide to the Monasteries and Their History*. Athens: Ekdotike Athenon, 1989.
Valentin, Jacques. *The Monks of Mount Athos*. London: Andre Deutsch, 1960.

Atisha

Atisha, an Indian Buddhist teacher instrumental in the second transmission of Buddhism to Tibet, originally traveled to Western Tibet in the 11th century. Though Atisha is of immense importance to the movement of Buddhism to a place of dominance in Tibet, little is known of his life, including the facts relative to his birth and death.

The initial move of Buddhism into Tibet led to a period of opposition under King Langdarma. His persecution of Buddhism in the ninth century had initiated a period of decline. His reign was followed by a period of favor in the next century. The rulers of Western Tibet sent Tibetans to India to recover the Buddhist tradition. Some 21 were sent, of which 2—Rinchen Zangpo and Lekpe Sherab—returned in 978 and launched a time of revival through their new translations of Buddhist texts. The pair examined the older texts, still used by the surviving Nyingma practitioners, and deleted anything they deemed not originating in India. The effect of their work was the exclusion of anything perceived integrated into the teachings from pre-Buddhist Tibetan sources (primarily from Tibetan indigenous religions).

Building on the 10th-century revival, Lkhalama Yeshe-o, the king of Western Tibetan, invited Atisha, a scholar from Vikramashila University in Bengal, to his land. While in Tibet, he wrote the *Bodhipathapradipa* (*Lamp for the Path of Enlightenment*), a summary of Tantric Buddhist teachings, for which he is most remembered. This book gained an extensive audience, as it presented Buddhism in a manner that made it relatively easy for the practitioner to appropriate Buddhist teachings along a graded path of attainment leading to enlightenment. Atisha subsequently spent his life engaged in the spread of a reformed path of Tibetan Buddhism.

In 1056, Dromtonpa, a disciple who had accompanied Atisha on the journey from India, established Rva-sgreng monastery as a disseminating point for Atisha's new way. The creating of the monastery is now considered the founding date of the Kadampa School of Tibetan Buddhism. That tradition would eventually be absorbed into the Gelug School headed by the Dalai Lama.

Geshe Kelsang Gyatso (b. 1931), a contemporary Gelug-pa monk who had developed several differences with the leadership of the Dalai Lama, founded the independent New Kadampa tradition. In so doing, he called upon the original reformist ideals of Atisha's Kadampa School to counter what he saw as changes initiated by the Dalai Lama in the years since the widespread movement of Tibetans outside their homeland.

J. Gordon Melton

See also: Dalai Lama III, Sonam Gyatso; New Kadampa Tradition–International Kadampa Buddhist Union; Nyingma Tibetan Buddhism.

References

Atisha. *Lamp for the Path to Enlightenment.* Commentary by Geshe Sonam Rinchen. Ithaca, NY: Snow Lion Publications, 1997.

Coleman, Graham, ed. *A Handbook of Tibetan Culture: A Guide to Tibetan Centres and Resources throughout the World.* Boston: Shambhala, 1994.

Lharmpa, Khenchen Thrangu Rinpoche Geshe. *The Seven Points of Mind Training.* Delhi: Sri Satguru Publications, 2002.

Sarkar, Anil Kumar. *The Mysteries of Vajrayana Buddhism: From Atisha to Dalai Lama.* Colombia, MO: South Asia Books, 1993.

Augustine of Hippo

354–430

Augustine of Hippo, the bishop of Hippo (now Annaba, Algeria) and one of the foremost theologians of Western Christianity, developed the theology of the post-Constantinian church in the wake of the councils at Nicaea (325) and Constantinople (381). A prolific writer, he is remembered most for his works such as *The City of God*, his autobiographical *Confessions*, *On Christian Doctrine*, and *On the Trinity*. His thought dominated Catholic thinking until the emergence of Thomas Aquinas (ca. 1224–1274) and became a principal source for the prominent ideas of the Protestant Reformation. He is recognized by the Roman Catholic Church as both a saint and a Doctor of the Church.

Augustine was born in 354 CE in Tagaste, Numidia, a Roman province in what is now Algeria. His mother Monica was a Christian, but during the first phase of his life he identified with his Pagan father, Patricius. He had a good education that began with his parents initially sending him to Tagaste to study and later his receiving the patronage of Romianus, who underwrote his education at Madaura and Carthage.

While at Carthage, he was attracted to Manicheanism and its strong dualistic views of good and evil, and took the initial steps to formally convert. He then

Portrait of Saint Augustine of Hippo, a bishop (396–430 CE) and one of four principal saints of the Catholic Church. Augustine's influence extended from late antiquity into the early Middle Ages and beyond. (Library of Congress)

moved to Rome to complete his studies before, with the assistance of his Manichean acquaintances, getting an appointment in Milan as a professor of rhetoric at the court of the youthful emperor Valentinius II (r. 375–392) in Milan. His mother arranged a marriage with a wife appropriate to Augustine's projected successful secular career.

Internally, as he rose to prominence as a young scholar, Augustine was undergoing a significant transformation. He had found the thought of the Manicheans ultimately unsatisfying and found his way to Christianity through an association with Ambrose, the bishop of Milan, and his teacher, Simplicianus. His conversion culminated in an experience in a local garden where he heard the voice of a child telling him several times to "Take and read!" the Bible. The key text he read was Romans 13:13, which called into question his current life. He renounced his past, including his sexual infidelities, and also resigned his teaching post in the imperial court. He was baptized in 387. He moved back to Africa and, inspired by the Egyptian hermit Antony, announced plans to found a monastic community. However, on a visit to Hippo while making his way back to Tagaste, he was named a priest. He settled in the city and was elected its bishop in 395. During his tenure as bishop, Augustine would be called upon to assume leadership during two of the Christian movement's most important controversies.

Through the fourth century, Donatism had grown strong. The movement developed as a result of the period of intense persecution during the reign of Roman Emperor Diocletian (303–305). During this time, many Christians suffered martyrdom for refusing to hand over the Christian scriptures to be burned or to offer sacrifices to the Roman deities. Those who saved themselves by handing over their copies of the scriptures, making a libation to a deity, or simply hiding were considered to have betrayed the cause by the Donatists. The majority party wanted to quickly rehabilitate those who lapsed during the persecution. The more rigorous, who took their name from Donatus (d. 355), the bishop of Carthage, saw those who had betrayed the scriptures or waivered in their faith as traitors to the church who needed to undergo significant penance, during which time they would be without benefit of the sacraments. Priests among the betrayers should cease serving the sacrament. Those who had received baptism from a *traditor* priest needed to be rebaptized. By this means, the church would remain pure and undefiled.

Augustine offered a broad refutation of the Donatist position. He noted that the sacraments are administered by Christ, thus they have never depended on the spiritual or immediate moral condition of the priest officiating at worship. Augustine's position would later be codified as the principle of *ex opera operato* (Latin for "from the deed done"), meaning that a sacrament (especially baptism and the Eucharist) were valid without regard to the status of the priest.

Augustine's most controversial moment relative to the Donatists came in his agreeing to secular actions against the Donatist faction. In 405, he went against his earlier stated opinion that no one should be coerced into the Catholic communion (*Letters* 34) when he sanctioned an imperial Edict of Unity that removed the legal standing of the Donatists. Then, seven years later, he offered his acquisition to the government's use of force to suppress the Donatists. His actions would later be cited as precedent for the use of force to suppress heretics in the Middle Ages.

Pelagius (ca. 354–ca. 430), a British unordained monk/theologian, denied that all humans inherited sin from Adam and are thus in need of grace because their will had been warped. He felt that humans had a choice and could choose good over evil. To Pelagius, Adam's sin was a pattern followed by many but was not humanity's inheritance. Pelagius attended and was examined by two church councils in the East that found him sound in theology. However, Augustine believed his ideas heretical and mobilized the leadership in the Western church, especially Pope Zosimos (r. 417–418), to have him condemned.

While battling the Donatists and Pelagians, Augustine's own background kept ongoing issues with Manicheanism before him. The Manicheans, as presented in Augustine's works, believed that good and evil were opposing and enduring forces in the universe, with good siding with the human spirit and evil with the body. Augustine, building on a more Hebraic view of creation, asserted that God had created the world and pronounced it good. All of the material world, in both its material and spiritual aspects, was created good. Evil entered the world through the disordered will of humans (and of angels). He also asserted the doctrine of what he termed "original sin," the idea that humans are born in sin inherited from Adam.

One of Augustine's last controversies would be with the Pelagian Julian, bishop of Eclanum, in central Italy. Julian attacked Augustine by tying him to his Manichean past, but Augustine both answered Julian's charges and pushed back on the Pelagian issues with which he was more than familiar. Julian was forced into exile in 418 and the church formally condemned his teachings at the Council of Ephesus in 418.

Augustine emerged toward the end of the first century following Christianity's coming out of three centuries of persecution and marginalization. He bequeathed to the church his expansive vision of the process of salvation that would remain dominant into the Middle Ages, inspired the development of a large order of monks and nuns, and expounded on themes (grace, predestination) that would come to the fore again in the 16th-century Protestant Reformation. Few if any theologians have been as influential through the centuries of the Christian West.

J. Gordon Melton

See also: Thomas Aquinas.

References

Brown, Peter. *Augustine of Hippo*, 2nd ed. Berkeley: University of California Press, 2000.

TeSelle, Eugene. *Augustine the Theologian*. New York: Herder and Herder, 1970.

Wills, Gary. *St. Augustine*. New York: Viking Penguin, 1999.

van der Meer, Fredrik. *Augustine the Bishop*. New York: Sheed and Ward, 1962.

Augustinians

The Augustinians are a set of Roman Catholic religious orders that trace their history to the 11th century. The Canons Regular of St. Augustine (or simply, Augustinian Canons) is one of the oldest orders in the church, having its origin in the 11th century in northern Italy and southern France among young men who sought a life of poverty, chastity, and obedience. They received official approval in the Lateran synods of 1059 and 1063 and soon became known as Canons Regular. As Canons, members live together as a community. Some congregations of Canons Regular also take a vow of stability, with members taking an additional vow relative to the place where they join the order.

The Canons Regular became established in France when William of Champeaux (ca. 1070–ca.1120) retired from public life, became a Canon, and established St. Victor's Abbey in Paris. The abbey's school later evolved into the University of Paris. Meanwhile, British Canons had charge of maintaining the famous shrine of Our Lady of Walsingham in the centuries prior to the Protestant Reformation of the 16th century.

The Order of Hermits of St. Augustine (Augustinian Friars) is a religious order of men founded in Tuscany. It began as several independent groups of hermit monks. In 1243, Pope Innocent IV (1243–1254) issued the bull *Incumbit nobis* calling on these communities to unite themselves into a single religious order under the Rule of Saint Augustine. The following year, these hermits held a founding chapter in Rome under the guidance of Cardinal Richard Annibald and put the pope's guidance into effect. Then in 1256 Pope Alexander IV (r. 1254–1261) issued the bull *Licet ecclesiae catholicae* of Pope Alexander IV (r. 1254–1261), which confirmed the union of 1244 and recognized it as the Order of Hermits of Saint Augustine. The Order of Hermits is one of several mendicant orders originating in 13th-century Europe. It contrasts with the Canons Regular in that its members moved about to serve the people where they lived and worked, especially in the new emerging urban centers.

Both the Canons Regular and the Friars draw upon the writings of Saint Augustine of Hippo (354–430) who left three documents relative to organizing the monastic life: the Order for a Monastery, the Precept, and *Letter* 211. As a Christian layperson, he had lived in a small informal monastic-like community in his hometown in North Africa, which provided the experience upon which his rule was later constructed. Relative to most other monastic rules, the Rule of Augustine has proved very flexible and adaptable to different ways of life.

The Augustinians grew in numbers through the 15th century but suffered losses through the 16th century as countries they had spread into became Protestant (England, the German states). The order of Canons Regular was known for its support of the papacy and included among its members Pope Adrian IV (r. 1154–1159, the only pope from England), the mystic Thomas à Kempis (ca. 1380–1471), the Christian Humanist scholar Desiderius Erasmus (1466–1536), the theologian Giles of Rome (1243–1316), and the pioneering geneticist Gregor Johann Mendel (1822–1884). Martin Luther (1483–1536), the leader of the Reformation, was an Augustinian friar. Augustinians served as papal chaplains from 1352 to 1991.

At the same time, the Rule of Saint Augustine proved attractive and was adapted by a variety of different orders, including the Servites, Victorines, Premonstratensians, and Assumptionists, and women's orders such as the Ursulines and Visitation Sisters.

The Augustinian Order was brought to the United States by Matthew Carr in 1796. Augustinians later founded Villanova University (1842) near Philadelphia. In the new century, they remain active in Europe, North and South America, and the Philippines. There are some 3,000 friars worldwide and 1,500 nuns in enclosed convents.

J. Gordon Melton

See also: Augustine of Hippo; Luther, Martin; Monasticism; Servites, Order of; Ursulines.

References

The Augustinians (1244–1994): Our History in Pictures. Roma: Pubblicazioni Agostiniane, Via Paolo VI, 1995.

Gavigan, John. *The Augustinians from the French Revolution to Modern Times.* Villanova, PA: Augustinian Press, 1989.

Gutierrez, David. *The Augustinians in the Middle Ages.* Villanova: Villanova University Press, 1984.

Hackett, Michael Benedict. *A Presence in the Age of Turmoil: English, Irish and Scottish Augustinians in the Reformation and Counter-Reformation.* Villanova, PA: Augustinian Historical Institute, Villanova University, 2002.

Martin, Thomas S. *Our Restless Heart: The Augustinian Tradition.* Maryknoll, NY: Orbis Books, 2003.

Rano, Balbino. *Augustinian Origins, Charism and Spirituality.* Ed. by John Rotelle. Villanova, PA: Augustinian Press, 1995.

Aum Shinrikyô/Aleph

Aum Shinrikyô is a Japanese new religion founded by the partially blind, charismatic Asahara Shôkô (b. 1955). Originating in 1984 as a yoga and meditation group, it developed millennial orientations and taught that a final confrontation between good and evil would occur around the end of the 20th century. Asahara claimed his sacred mission was to lead the forces of good in this final encounter, which would destroy the corrupt material world and bring about a new spiritual realm on Earth.

Aum taught that humans were weighed down by negative karma but that this could be eradicated through religious austerities. If they did eradicate it, they could attain enlightenment and rebirth in higher realms; if not, they would be reborn in lower realms. Asahara was regarded as an enlightened guru whose words expressed supreme truth and to whom followers had to show absolute obedience. Disciples were expected to perform arduous ascetic tasks, and those who succeeded were granted holy names and special ranks in the movement, which became intensely hierarchical.

Aum attracted a highly dedicated but limited following among young Japanese, who renounced the world and left their families to join its commune at Kamikuishiki in Yamanashi prefecture (about two hours outside Tokyo) and follow Asahara. It also aroused opposition from the families of devotees who objected to their offspring severing all familial ties in this way, and from the media, which portrayed the disciples' devotion to their leader in a negative light. A campaign was organized against Aum, to which the movement reacted with hostility and intolerance, branding all who opposed it as enemies of the truth who were unworthy of salvation. Such aggressive responses provoked further opposition and increasingly led Aum into conflict with the outside world—a conflict that took on, in Asahara's mind, the nature of a final confrontation between good and evil, in which he declared that anyone who opposed Aum was an enemy of the truth who deserved to be punished with death.

Ultimately these doctrines were used to legitimate the killing of others in the name of truth and in order to further Aum's mission on Earth. This turn to violence was spurred by widespread public rejection of Aum in Japan, by internal fragmentation and tensions, and by its failure to expand overseas; apart from a brief period of success in Russia, it failed to gain a secure footing outside Japan. The violence was also fueled by Asahara's increasing paranoia, as he came to regard every sign of opposition to Aum as evidence of a conspiracy against the movement. Eventually he came to envision his movement as under siege from a world conspiracy that included the U.S. and Japanese

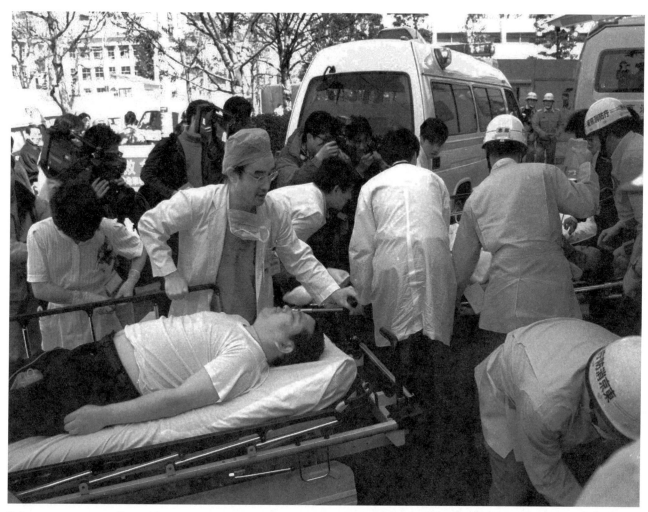

Subway passengers affected by nerve gas released in central Tokyo subways by Aum Shinrikyô are carried into St. Luke's Hospital, March 20, 1995. The incident killed 12 people and sickened more than 5,500 others. (AP/Wide World Photos)

governments and others, such as the Jews and the Freemasons, who planned to destroy him and Aum so as to enable the forces of evil to triumph.

Proclaiming that Aum had to fight against such evil, that the world merited punishment for its sins, and that only devout Aum followers were worthy of salvation, Asahara set the movement on a collision course with society. From the early 1990s Aum began to manufacture biological and chemical weapons to fight against its enemies and to strike out at individual opponents and the wider public. This culminated in its March 1995 nerve-gas attack on the Tokyo subway, which killed 12 and injured thousands of commuters. This attack was followed by massive police intervention, the arrests of most of Aum's hierarchy, and nu-

merous trials in which senior figures in the movement have been charged with murders and other crimes. As of the beginning of 2009, several had been sentenced to death and executed, while Asahara has been convicted, exhausted his appeals, and awaits execution.

The movement continues to exist, however, although it has severed formal ties with Asahara and has changed its name to Aleph in order to emphasize this severing. It retains almost 1,000 followers (down from around 10,000 at its peak), who continue to believe that the world is evil, and that the only way to liberation is through meditation and renunciation. They also continue to venerate Asahara as the spiritual master who taught them the way of liberation. Aleph's continuity of belief with Aum has led to a continuation of suspicion in Japan. It is thus kept under very close scrutiny at all times by the authorities, who have passed laws especially for this purpose.

www.aleph.to/index_e.html

Ian Reader

See also: Meditation; Yoga.

References

Asahara, Shoko. *Supreme Initiation: An Empirical Spiritual Science for the Supreme Truth.* New York: AUM U.S.A., 1988.

Asahara, Shoko. *The Teachings of the Truth.* 3 vols. Shizuoka, Japan: Aum Publishing Co., 1992.

Lifton, Robert Jay. *Destroying the World to Save It: Aum Shinrikyô, Apocalyptic Violence, and the New Global Terrorism.* New York: Metropolitan Books, 1999.

Reader, Ian. *Religious Violence in Contemporary Japan.* Richmond, UK, and Honolulu: Curzon Press and University of Hawai'i Press, 2000.

Shimazono Susumu. "In the Wake of Aum: The Formation and Transformation of a Universe of Belief." *Japanese Journal of Religious Studies* 22, nos. 3–4 (1995): 343–380.

Watanabe Manabu. "Reactions to the Aum Affair: The Rise of the Anti-Cult Movement in Japan." *Bulletin of the Nanzan Institute for Religion and Culture* 21 (1997): 32–48.

Aumist Religion

The Aumist Religion is a relatively new faith community, founded in 1969 by Gilbert Bourdin (1923–1998), best known as His Holiness Lord Hamsah Manarah. It considers itself a Religion of Unity, representing a synthesis of all the religions and spiritual movements of the planet, and became well known in the late 1990s due to its conflicts with the French government.

Bourdin was born into a traditional Roman Catholic family but was attracted by mysticism and occult sciences when he was young. He investigated a wide spectrum of Western initiatory paths (Kabbalah, alchemy), and studied the "philosophical" principles of Freemasonry, Rosicrucianism, Loges Martinistes, and Saint-Graal. In India, he stayed with the renowned yogi Swami Sivananda, founder of the Divine Life Society, from whom he received initiation into the renounced life of a *sannyasi*, on February 13, 1961, at Rishikesh. Sivananda gave Bourdin the name Hamsananda Sarasvati.

During his numerous trips, Lord Hamsah Manarah was also initiated into Jainism, Sufism, various branches of Hinduism and Buddhism, and several African religions. The titles of *acharya* and *mahacharya* (a teacher who preaches what he has himself accomplished) were given to him in stages by Jainist and Hindu masters. He also received the title of *adinath*, first master or patriarch, with the implication that he is a divine incarnation.

After his long initiatory pilgrimage, which included the visitation of many of the world's holy sites, in 1969 Lord Hamsah Manarah settled on a mountain over the small village of Castellane in the Alps of Haute-Provence, France. This place corresponded to one he had seen in a dream. As news of his presence spread, many journeyed to meet him. As some who were attracted to him decided to stay on the mountain, an ashram emerged, and plans for a city began to be projected. Included in the city were temples and statues from different religions, including the largest Buddha in Europe (69 feet), a giant figure of Christ (56 feet), and one known as the Cosmoplanetary Messiah (108 feet). In 1990, Lord Hamsah Manarah revealed to the world that he was the Cosmoplanetary Messiah, that is, the messiah for whom all the traditions wait.

Lord Hamsah Manarah devoted almost two decades of his life to leadership of the community and the creation of Aumism, writing some 22 books. His final years were, however, caught up in problems with the French government, which, in the wake of the deaths of members of the Solar Temple in 1994, began a crusade against various minority religions in the country. The Aumist Religion was singled out for special attention and efforts were made to destroy the city. Following the leader's death in 1998, a controversy ensued over the final resting place of his body. Various forces have attempted to have the sacred statues demolished and the community scattered.

Aumism sees itself as the synthesis all the religions and spiritual movements of the planet. Aumists pray equally to Buddha, Allah, Christ, and Mother Nature. The Aumist also feels a harmonious relationship with all people, all races, all classes, and all traditions, and the religion does not demand that members give up their prior faith in order to become Aumist (though acknowledging Lord Hamsah Manarah and his teachings contradicts the teachings of many religions).

The name Aumism is derived from the sound OM, considered to be the root of all the sacred sounds found in every tradition (Amen, Amin, and so on). According to Aumists, the benefits from repeating "Om" are vast. Aumists also repeat various other mantras (words of power) for collective and individual ascent.

Aumists believe in reincarnation according to the Law of the Evolution of the Souls. A vegetarian diet is recommended, although it is not demanded. Aumism is opposed to drugs, suicide, and sexual deviations (that is, polygamy and homosexuality).

The Aumist Religion has its headquarters at the Holy City of Mandarom Shambhasalem, Haute-Provence, France, where some 50 monks and nuns reside. The movement has been formally organized into a church, with priests, priestesses, and bishops. The community expects Lord Hamsah Manarah to reincarnate, and they believe that they will be able to recognize him in much the same manner that Tibetans recognize the next incarnation of a lama. In the meantime, leadership has passed to a group of high priests. Priests and priestesses oversee five sacraments: Baptism, Confirmation, Renovation, Marriage, and Transition.

One becomes an Aumist through Baptism, that is, the transmission of the sound OM. Those who pursue their spiritual path within the movement may associate with the Initiatory Order of Triumphant Vajra, and become Knights. The Initiatory Order is structured in 22 degrees, with each degree corresponding to a particular spiritual journey of prayer and study. Knights may also enter the priesthood. Both men and women, married and unmarried, may become priests. Married priests belong to the outside branch. Unmarried priests may join the renunciate monastic branch and live in the Holy City.

Centroms, as places for prayer are called, serve as local centers for Aumists. Centroms are located across France (about 100), in most European countries, and in primarily French-speaking lands in Africa, Oceania, the Indian Ocean, and Canada. In Canada, where the Aumist Religion has a considerable following, an ashram has been established. Aumists from around the world come to the Holy City for various events and seminars. There are approximately 1,000 Knights and thousands of Aumists in the world.

Aumisme
Cité Sainte de Mandarom
La Baume 04120
Castellane
France
www.aumisme.org (in French)

James R. Lewis

See also: Divine Life Society; Freemasonry; Solar Temple, Order of the.

Reference

Manarah, S. Hamsah. *Aumism: The Doctrine of the Golden Age.* Castellane, France: Editions du Mandarom, 1999.

■ Australia

The continent of Australia has been inhabited for at least 50,000 years. The original inhabitants possibly found their way to the continent from Indonesia, located to its north. It is located between the Indian Ocean to its west and the Pacific Ocean to its east. Today, its 2,941,299 square miles of land, which includes the island of Tasmania off the southern coast, is home to 21,007,310 people (2008).

At some undetermined point the Aboriginal people emerged as a distinctive ethnic grouping; they developed more than 260 languages, a variety of cultures, and a number of related religious perspectives. They were a semi-nomadic people whose existence was tied to the land that they revered. Aboriginal religions included a series of stories related to the creation of the world out of preexisting substance by the Ancestors. They were also marked by a set of rituals that integrated them into the natural world as the seasons changed and the process of obtaining food and shelter continued.

Nan Tien Temple complex, Sydney, Australia, one of the largest Buddhist temples in the Southern Hemisphere. (Rorem/Dreamstime.com)

Though the Spanish first sighted Australia in 1606, European settlement did not begin until 1788, when the first group of British colonists arrived, most as prisoners. Their arrival at Botany Bay (Sydney) serves to divide Australian history into two eras. A period of aggressive settlement of particularly the southeastern coast followed. Efforts to establish European hegemony cost the Aboriginal people an estimated 80 percent of their population. More prisoners were sent, the largest number coming in 1830, when some 58,000 arrived. No additional prisoners were sent after 1840. Further periods of population expansion followed gold discoveries in 1851 and 1892. Though most settlers were of European background, significant numbers came from Italy, Greece, Germany, the Netherlands, and the southern Balkans.

Six British colonies were established on the continent. In 1901, they were reorganized as autonomous states (including Tasmania), associated together as the independent Commonwealth of Australia. Women were granted the vote the following year. Areas remaining outside the commonwealth were added in 1911.

The Aboriginal population suffered from the attempts of Europeans to claim ownership of the land. Those who survived this process of displacement had their culture and way of life disrupted. Although Aboriginal life and religion survives, it does so primarily in the less hospitable rural areas away from the more populated coasts and river valleys.

Christianity was introduced to Australia by Church of England ministers serving as chaplains of the original penal colony. Neither the prisoners nor the soldiers sent to guard them were particularly responsive to the church's ministrations. The Reverend Samuel Marsden oversaw the church's development beginning in 1793. His hegemony extended to Tasmania and other British settlements in the South Pacific. In 1823, Australia was placed within the geographically impossible Diocese of Calcutta, and it was not until 1832 that a bishop arrived in Australia. Over the next decade five dioceses were carved out.

The Anglican Church developed sporadically as British settlement evolved and the colony prospered. As early as 1826 a mission among the Aboriginal people was launched, though its progress was slow. The church's attempts to build settled Christian congregations and communities clashed with the Aboriginal nomadic life.

In January 1, 1962, the church became autonomous as the Church of England in Australia, assuming its present name, Anglican Church in Australia, in 1981. Once claiming more than half of the population as members, the church declined as a percentage of the population through the 20th century. In the 1980s it was replaced by the Roman Catholic Church as the largest religious group in the country.

Among the first settlers were Irish political prisoners, who formed the core from which the Roman Catholic Church in Australia grew. Immigrants from predominantly Catholic countries led to further expansion, and in the 20th century a number of Australians converted to the church. Irish priests arrived in 1803

Australia

Religion	Followers in 1970	Followers in 2010	% of Population	Annual % growth 2000–2010	Followers in 2025	Followers in 2050
Christians	11,826,000	15,816,000	74.1	0.95	16,917,000	18,020,000
Roman Catholics	3,038,000	5,552,000	26.0	0.69	5,600,000	6,000,000
Anglicans	3,775,000	3,900,000	18.3	–0.16	3,900,000	4,100,000
Protestants	1,911,000	2,400,000	11.2	0.04	2,700,000	2,900,000
Agnostics	561,000	3,540,000	16.6	1.42	4,670,000	6,100,000
Buddhists	12,000	500,000	2.3	3.09	750,000	1,000,000
Muslims	25,000	480,000	2.2	3.78	700,000	1,200,000
Atheists	200,000	380,000	1.8	0.80	500,000	600,000
Hindus	5,000	180,000	0.8	8.42	220,000	300,000
Jews	62,500	104,000	0.5	1.19	120,000	130,000
New religionists	10,000	96,000	0.4	2.35	120,000	170,000
Chinese folk	5,000	80,000	0.4	2.40	130,000	160,000
Ethnoreligionists	5,000	62,000	0.3	2.94	80,000	100,000
Confucianists	0	50,000	0.2	2.44	90,000	130,000
Sikhs	3,000	35,700	0.2	8.21	50,000	70,000
Baha'is	9,100	20,000	0.1	2.05	25,000	34,000
Spiritists	0	6,300	0.0	1.30	7,000	8,500
Daoists	0	4,500	0.0	0.92	4,800	5,500
Zoroastrians	0	2,400	0.0	3.89	2,500	2,500
Jains	0	1,600	0.0	12.42	2,000	4,000
Total population	**12,724,000**	**21,358,000**	**100.0**	**1.20**	**24,388,000**	**28,034,000**

and have dominated the clergy over the years. The first bishop was consecrated in 1834, and the hierarchy expanded nationally in the 1840s.

Protestantism began with Presbyterian settlers, who built an initial church in 1809. The first Baptist church followed in 1813, but membership growth was extremely slow during their first generation. Methodism also emerged as a visible community in the second decade of the century, and in 1815 the first minister arrived from England to travel among them. Over the century the Methodists emerged as the second largest group in the colony.

Through the 19th century a variety of British and American groups established work, including the London Missionary Society, the Salvation Army, the Churches of Christ (associated with the American group known as the Christian Church [Disciples of Christ]), the Lutherans, and the Seventh-day Adventist Church. In 1977, the Congregationalists (resulting from the London Missionary Society's work), the Methodists, and the majority of the Presbyterians united to form the Uniting Church of Australia, the third largest group in the country. Some 30 percent of the Presbyte-

rians formed as the Presbyterian Church of Australia (Continuing).

Through the 20th century, groups representing the entire spectrum of Christianity emerged in Australia. Greek immigrants created a large Orthodox community under the jurisdiction of the Ecumenical Patriarchate of Constantinople, with an archbishop in Sydney. Pentecostalism grew steadily over the century, though membership is scattered among a number of both local and imported groups. Several new churches, such as the Christian Life Churches International and Christian Outreach Centres, have come on strong as a result of the late 20th-century Charismatic movement.

The Jewish presence in Australia became visible in 1817, when a small group formed a burial society (it being common for a cemetery to be the first communal structure created by a newly established Jewish community). A congregation was founded in Sydney in 1828 and an initial synagogue opened in 1844. Meanwhile worshipping communities emerged in Melbourne, Ballarat, Geelong, and Adelaide. By the beginning of the 20th century, Jews had spread across the

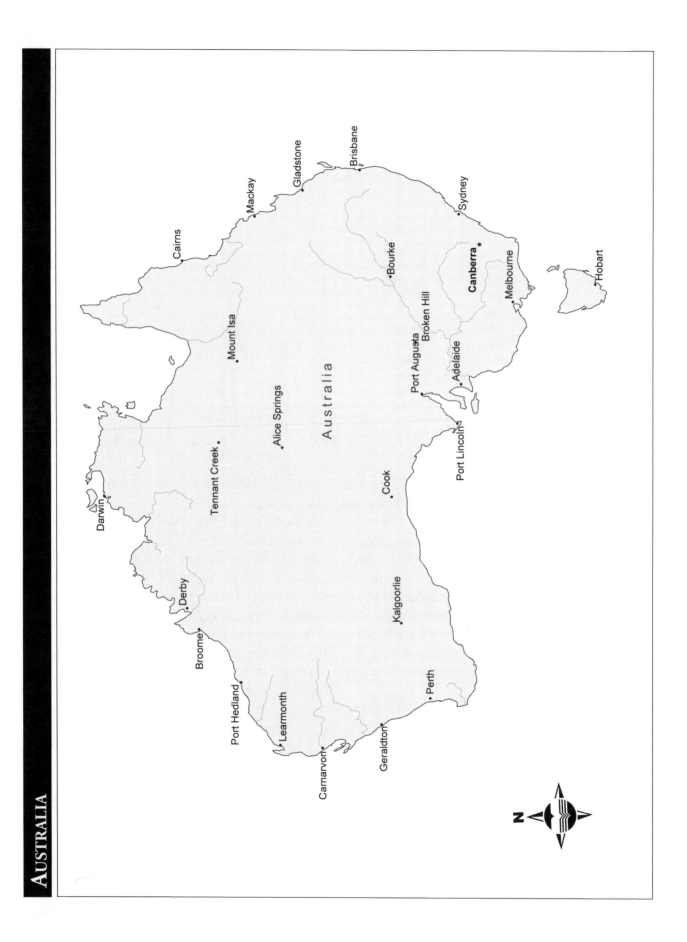

continent, and many had risen to positions of prominence in the business and government community.

Today there are more than 90,000 Jews in Australia, more than half of whom reside in Melbourne. Community affairs are cared for by the Executive Council of Australian Jewry, also headquartered in Melbourne. The majority of religious Jews can be found in the Ashkenazi and Sephardic Orthodox synagogues, though there are various forms of Reform Judaism, united by the Australian Federation for Progressive Judaism.

Buddhism grew during the 20th century, primarily by the arrival of tens of thousands of immigrants from China, Thailand, Tibet, and Japan. Since World War II, a strong Western Buddhist community has emerged, and a variety of Buddhist ecumenical structures now attempt to bridge the language and cultural barriers that separate the different Buddhist groups. The Buddhist Council of New South Wales carries an extensive directory of Buddhist centers on its Internet site at www.buddhistcouncil.org/. In 2001, the United Vietnamese Buddhist Congregation in Australia hosted the meeting of the World Buddhist Sangha Council's international conference.

The first Muslims in Australia came from Afghanistan in the 1860s, and by the census of 1911, there were some 4,000 residing in Australia. The community declined through the 1930s but then grew slowly through the middle of the century. It has more than doubled since 1971, primarily from immigration, and now numbers in excess of 200,000. Muslims form a very diverse community, coming from all parts of the Muslim world, including Bosnia and Africa. The majority of Muslims are united in the Australian Federation of Islamic Societies. While the great majority of Muslims are mainstream Sunnis and Shiites, there is a small group attached to the Ahmadiyya Muslim movement and groups of Druze in Adelaide and Sydney. There is a small following of the Naqshbandiyya Sufi Order and a equally small number of Westerners associated with the Australian center for Sufism in Sydney.

The religions of the Indian subcontinent (Sikhism, Hinduism, Jainism) also came to Australia in the 19th century, but not in great numbers. Growth was limited by immigration restrictions through much of the 20th century. During the last decades of the 20th century, however, tens of thousands arrived from India and Sri Lanka. The 1991 census reported more than 40,000 Hindus, most from India, but an almost equal number arriving from Fiji.

Mingled with the Hindu immigrants were a variety of Indian spiritual teachers (gurus), most of whom simply visited Australia as part of their work in spreading their movements internationally, and a few of whom resided in Australia. At the same time, Australian spiritual seekers traveled to India in search of spiritual enlightenment. Possibly the most famous of these is John Mumford, who as Swami Anandakipila has become a major force in spreading the Tantric teachings of the International Yoga Fellowship Movement among Westerners.

As an English-speaking country, Australia has been the home of Western Esoteric groups since the mid-19th century. Spiritualism thrived, and both the Theosophical Society and the Liberal Catholic Church had major centers in the cities. In the last half of the 20th century, Australia became the home to the same spectrum of Esoteric, Occult, Wiccan, and New Age groups that are now found across North America and Europe. A variety of Japanese new religions also found an initial base in the country's Japanese community.

J. Gordon Melton

See also: Aboriginal Religions (Australia); Ahmadiyya Movement in Islam; Anglican Church in Australia; Buddhism; Charismatic Movement; Christian Church (Disciples of Christ); Christian Outreach Centre; Church of England; Druze; Ecumenical Patriarchate/Patriarchate of Constantinople; Hinduism; International Yoga Fellowship Movement; Jainism; Liberal Catholic Church; London Missionary Society; Methodism; Naqshbandiyya Sufi Order; New Age Movement; Pentecostalism; Presbyterian Church of Australia (Continuing); Reform Judaism; Roman Catholic Church; Salvation Army; Seventh-day Adventist Church; Spiritualism; Sufism; Theosophical Society (Adyar); Uniting Church in Australia; World Buddhist Sangha Council.

References

Breward, I. *A History of the Australian Churches.* St. Leonards, Australia: Allen and Unwin, 1993.

Carey, Hiary. *Believing in Australia: A Cultural History of Religions.* Sydney: Allen & Unwin Academic, 1997.

Coucher, P. *Buddhism in Australia, 1848–1988.* Sydney: New South Wales University Press, 1988.

Drury, Nevill, and Gregory Tillett. *Other Temples, Other Gods: The Occult in Australia.* Sydney: Hodder and Stoughton, 1982.

Gillman, I. *Many Faiths, One Nation: A Guide to the Major Faiths and Denominations in Australia.* Sydney: Collins, 1988.

Humphries, R. A., and R. S. Ward, eds. *Religious Bodies in Australia: A Comprehensive Guide.* Wantirna, Australia: New Melbourne Press, 1995.

Piggin, S. *Evangelical Christianity in Australia: Spirit, Word, and World.* New York: Oxford University Press, 1996.

Saeed, Abdullah. *Islam in Australia.* Sydney: Allen & Unwin Academic, 2003.

■ Austria

Church at Heilingenblut, Austria, with Mount Grossglockner in the background. (Dan Breckwoldt/Dreamstime .com)

During the last centuries of the pre-Christian era Austria was mainly inhabited by Celtic tribes who venerated Celtic gods, an observation deduced from theophoric elements in personal names, and also from epigraphical sources. Then in 15 and 9 BCE, the main areas of Austria became the provinces Noricum and Pannonia of the Roman Empire, thus bringing not only Roman gods to Austria, but also the gods of various Eastern religions, which then flourished within the Roman Empire. The more famous deities, Mithras, Jupiter Dolichenus, and Isis, were partly identified with local Celtic gods. During the fourth century CE, Christianity came to Austria, mainly via Aquileia in Italy; the most famous missionary in these early times was Severin (d. 487). His biography, written by his disciple Eugippius, details the spreading of Christianity along the River Danube and to the Alps and also reports on the decline of social structures due to the migration of nations that had brought non-Christian Slav people to the southern and eastern parts of the Alps, people who began to replace the Celtic and Roman population. Some Germanic tribes, who were Arians, also lived in the area of modern Austria. In the next century Bavarians migrated to the north of Austria.

In 696, Rupert of Worms founded the Diocese of Salzburg, which became the starting point for the organization of the Catholic Church in Austria. Bishop Virgilius of Salzburg (745–784), one of Rupert's successors, came from Ireland as one among the Irish and Scottish monks and missionaries who then were active in Austria. Through the beginning of the 10th century, Christianity spread and developed a stable organization, but migrating Avars and Hungarians gave this growth a setback, which lasted until the early years of the regency of the counts of Babenberg (976–1246). Beginning in the 11th century, the restoration of Christianity led to the founding of parishes all over Austria and to the creation of new dioceses at Gurk (1072) and

Austria

Religion	Followers in 1970	Followers in 2010	% of Population	Annual % growth 2000–2010	Followers in 2025	Followers in 2050
Christians	7,239,000	6,708,000	79.5	−0.06	6,328,000	5,662,000
Roman Catholics	6,613,000	5,800,000	68.7	−0.60	5,483,000	4,827,000
Protestants	455,000	340,000	4.0	−0.83	280,000	250,000
Orthodox	62,300	178,000	2.1	0.95	205,000	230,000
Agnostics	145,000	1,173,000	13.9	2.87	1,445,000	1,729,000
Muslims	18,000	400,000	4.7	1.31	650,000	900,000
Atheists	50,000	120,000	1.4	7.96	145,000	145,000
Buddhists	1,000	11,400	0.1	1.58	15,000	18,500
Jews	10,000	8,100	0.1	−0.16	8,000	8,000
Hindus	0	7,200	0.1	0.44	12,000	15,000
New religionists	2,000	5,100	0.1	0.41	6,500	10,000
Chinese folk	0	3,600	0.0	0.44	5,200	3,500
Baha'is	2,000	2,600	0.0	0.45	4,000	6,000
Confucianists	0	1,500	0.0	0.44	2,000	800
Sikhs	0	1,300	0.0	0.44	1,500	2,000
Ethnoreligionists	0	300	0.0	0.47	500	100
Total population	**7,467,000**	**8,442,000**	**100.0**	**0.44**	**8,622,000**	**8,500,000**

Seckau (1218). At the same time monastic life was reorganized, and a number of new monasteries were founded (primarily by Augustinians, Benedictines, and Cistercians). Thus during the 11th, 12th, and 13th centuries Christianity at last became the dominant religion all over Austria, professed by all except the Jews, whose historical beginnings in Austria date to the early 10th century. The Jewish community centered on Vienna. During the 13th century, Jews lived throughout the city, though the more concentrated Jewish community was renowned in Middle Europe until the Jews were expelled from (or suffered martyrdom in) Vienna in 1420–1421.

From the beginning of the reign of the Hapsburg dynasty (1276–1918), Austria's rulers involved themselves in Catholic concerns; they led in the founding of the faculty of theology at the University of Vienna in 1365 and in establishing Vienna as the center of a new diocese in 1468. At the end of the Middle Ages, such state-church connections were not only of benefit to the Roman Catholic Church. From the early years of the Protestant Reformation we find members of the Evangelical Church of the Augsburg and Helvetic Confessions in Austria who could openly practice their religion, though their protected status ended in 1620 with the coming of the Counter-Reformation, led by

the Society of Jesus (the Jesuits) and the Capuchins. The strengthening of the Catholic Church also created a new cultural impact with the Baroque period, which can only be understood as a result of a widespread feeling of triumph after the Thirty Years' War (1618–1648) and the defeat of the Turkish Muslims before the walls of Vienna (1683). The Baroque era placed a strong Catholic stamp on Austrian history for more than a century and a half.

This Catholic dominance was somewhat affected during the later 18th century, when the emperor Joseph II dissolved a number of the Catholic monasteries not directly engaged in social or educational activities and also extended toleration to the Evangelical and Orthodox churches; Byzantine Orthodox Christians had settled in Austria during the course of the 18th century as merchants. Also the Jews now found themselves in a better situation again, and the revived Jewish community of Vienna became famous as a center for printing Hebrew books. In the early 19th century the *haskalah* movement, the Jewish Enlightenment, prospered in Vienna.

The proliferation of Christian denominations and sects in Austria can be traced to the second half of the 19th century. In 1867 religious freedom was granted to all inhabitants by the Fundamental Law of the State,

AUSTRIA

and in 1874 another law opened the possibility for religious communities to obtain official acknowledgment by the state. The Roman Catholic Church, the Evangelical Church, and the Jewish community were the first three religions to attain this status, with the Old Catholic Church of Austria following in 1877. Islam was acknowledged in 1912 as a result of the Muslim community in Herzegovina then being part of the Austrian monarchy. The Roman Catholic Church remained the dominant religion, although after World War I, with the end of the Austrian monarchy, the new government established a policy of separating state and church. In 1933, the Republic of Austria ratified a concordat with the Holy See.

The Nazi occupation and World War II brought significant change to Austria. In the years following the war, the Catholic Church, which presently reports 6 million members, holds the allegiance of only 75 percent of the total population, a significant decline since 1945, when more than 90 percent of the Austrian population were Catholics. The Jewish community, which had 180,000 members in 1938, was decimated by the Nazi terror, and as the new century begins only some 8,000 Jewish people reside in Austria. Since the 1960s a growing number of Muslim people have migrated to Austria, in the early years mainly as guest workers from Turkey and Yugoslavia. The 1980s saw refugees from Iran and various Arabic countries settle in Austria, and in the 1990s Bosnian Muslims sought shelter in Austria. To a minor degree also native Austrians have converted to Islam, so that presently there are about 400,000 Muslims living in Austria.

In 1983 Austrian Buddhists also became acknowledged as an official religion by the state. The Buddhist community is estimated to include approximately 12,000 with a Western and 5,000 with an Asian ethnic background. The Catholic Bishops' Conference has taken the lead in interfaith dialogues and has founded and financed an institution to pursue dialogue with the non-Christian religions in Austria. Protestant Christian churches initiated a new phase of ecumenical activity in 1958 with the formation of the Ecumenical Council of Churches in Austria; the Roman Catholic Church has freely cooperated in ecumenical endeavors since the Second Vatican Council (1962–1965). An additional important ecumenical activity began in 1964 with the founding of Pro Oriente, an organization that concentrates upon theological dialogues with the pre-Chalcedon churches and the Christological issues that divide these churches. Several churches in the Middle East did not accept the doctrines of the Council of Chalcedon (451 CE), now considered the Orthodox position on the divine and human natures of Christ. Two non-Chalcedonian churches, the Armenian Apostolic Church, with 3,000 members, the Coptic Orthodox Church (3,000 members), and the Syriac Orthodox Church of Antioch (also 3,000 members) now have legal acceptance as official religions in Austria. At the same time, other churches have also received legal status, including the Church of Jesus Christ of Latter-day Saints (4,000 members), the United Methodist Church (1,100 members), and the New Apostolic Church (5,000 members). Also more than 20,000 members of the Greek Orthodox Church (under the authority of the Ecumenical Patriarchate) reside in Austria.

Discussions on religious freedom and the acceptance of minor religions, called new religions, led in 1998 to new state legislation for some minority religions as religiöse Bekenntnisgemeinschaften. Although they now are acknowledged as juridical communities, they do not get the same support by the state as the older religious communities, whose juridical status is based on the legislation of 1874. At present, only 11 communities have been accepted as Bekenntnisgemeinschaften: the Baha'i Faith, the Hindu community, the Christengemeinschaft (a Christian community with an Anthroposophical background), the Seventh-day Adventist Church, a group of Pentecostal communities, a group of independent churches, the Baptist Church, the Mennonites, the ELAIA Christian community, and the Jehovah's Witnesses.

The Jehovah's Witnesses have about 25,000 members in Austria; all the others report between 1,000 and 5,000 members. During the last years of the 20th century there was a significant discussion about the different levels of status of religions, which some viewed as a sign of injustice and denial of religious freedom. Some have also seen it as problematic that the smaller new religions (each having less than 500 to 1,000 members) are frequently spoken of in the public and presented in the media as (destructive) cults. Therefore, in July 2008, the Jehovah's Witnesses successfully fought a lawsuit with the European Court of Human Rights at Strasbourg against the Republic of Austria because of this religious discrimination. So in the near future it is to be expected that the legal situation of religious communities in Austria has to be subject to some juridical changes.

Buddhism in Austria. www.buddhismus-austria.org
Islam in Austria. www.islam.at
Christian churches in Austria. www.kirchen.at

Manfred Hutter

See also: Anthroposophical Society; Armenian Apostolic Church (Holy See of Etchmiadzin); Augustinians; Baha'i Faith; Benedictines; Church of Jesus Christ of Latter-day Saints; Cistercians; Ecumenical Patriarchate/Patriarchate of Constantinople; Evangelical Church of the Augsburg and Helvetic Confessions in Austria; Jehovah's Witnesses; Jesuits; Mennonites; New Apostolic Church; Old Catholic

Church of Austria; Roman Catholic Church; Seventh-day Adventist Church; United Methodist Church.

References

Leeb, Rudolf, ed. *Geschichte des Christentums in Österreich. Von der Antike bis zur Gegenwart.* Vienna: Ueberreuter, 2003.

Bundespressedienst, ed. *Religionen in Oesterreich.* Vienna: 1997.

Glaser, F. *Fruehes Christentum im Alpenraum.* Regensburg: Pustet, 1997.

Religions in Austria. Austria Documentation. Vienna: Federal Press Service, 1990.

Schoen, D. *Orientalische Kulte im roemischen Oesterreich.* Vienna: 1988.

Austrian Buddhist Association

A small number of Buddhists in Austria founded a Buddhist society in Vienna in 1947 under the then operative law that gave religious communities the possibility of forming a society; this juridical status still did not put the groups that chose it on a level with religious communities like the Old Catholic Church of Austria or the Church of Jesus Christ of Latter-day Saints. Further efforts to improve the status of the society led eventually in 1983 to the foundation of the Austrian Buddhist Association (German: Osterreichische Buddhistische Religionsgesellschaft), which then gained full legal recognition by the Austrian republic as one of the official religions in Austria. The Association is also a member of the European Buddhist Union and serves as a regional center of the World Fellowship of Buddhists.

The Association is an umbrella organization covering different Buddhist groups and individual Buddhists alike. At the end of 2000, 12 groups were formally members of the Association, while about 10 other Buddhist groups had not applied for membership. In 2000, discussions began concerning the possible affiliation of the Austrian branch of Soka Gakkai International, which became a full member of the Association; other groups joined as well, so at the moment the Austrian Buddhist Association has 23 member groups. Slightly more than 2,000 individuals have also joined the Association, a low percentage of the estimated 17,000 Buddhists now living in Austria and practicing their religion in various groups and communities.

The Association is headed by a board of five people who serve as official representatives of the Association in relation to the Austrian republic. Of greater importance in administering the affairs of the Association, however, is the Council of the Sangha (German: *Sangharat* [community]), consisting of the five people on the board and representatives of all the Buddhist groups and communities who have joined the Association. The main aims of the Association are to promote knowledge of Buddhism to the general public, to serve as representative for public or administrative institutions, and to provide religious instruction in public schools to all pupils who are Buddhists. Another important organizing body within (and partly parallel to) the Association are the three Buddhist communities for the northeastern, southern, and western areas of Austria. These three communities were established in 1997 as a result of the increase of the number of Buddhists in Austria, in order to serve better their religious needs. These communities help different groups or individuals in their respective areas to organize meetings, to promote the teachings of the Buddha, or to encourage all to lead a Buddhist way of life. In 2003, the Association could establish the first Buddhist cemetery in Austria as a separate area within the public central cemetery in Vienna; this is esteemed as an important event for the Buddhist community because at the cemetery they now can conduct funeral rites for deceased members in a better way.

The Association is not related to a specific Buddhist school or tradition but creates a network and structures for cooperation among the various Buddhist groups. Though not an official journal of the Association, the quarterly journal *Ursache und Wirkung* focuses on the same aims and has since 1991 covered all topics concerning Buddhism in Austria. The journal has an Internet site at www.ursache.at.

Austrian Buddhist Association
Osterreichische Buddhistische Religionsgesellschaft
Fleischmarkt 16

A-ł 1010 Vienna
Austria
www.buddhismus-austria.at

Manfred Hutter

See also: Church of Jesus Christ of Latter-day Saints; European Buddhist Union; Old Catholic Church of Austria; Soka Gakkai International; World Fellowship of Buddhists.

References

Hutter, Manfred, ed. *Buddhisten und Hindus in deutschsprachigen Raum.* Frankfurt: Peter Lang, 2001.

Österreichische Buddhistische Religionsgesellschaft, ed. *OBR Newsletter.* Vienna [available free online: www.buddhismus-austria.at].

Riedl, Peter, ed. *Buddhismus in Osterreich.* Vienna: Ursache und Wirkung Zeitungsverlag, 1998.

Usarski, Frank. "Buddhismus in Österreich." In *Handbuch der Religionen. Kirchen und Glaubensgemeinschaften in Deutschland. 5,* ed. Michael Klocker and Udo Tworuschka. *EL.* München: Olzog, 2001.

Autumn Equinox

See Fall Equinox.

Avebury

Avebury, one of England's most spectacular megalithic sites, is primarily formed by stone circles, both around 340 feet in diameter. At one time in the center of the southernmost circle there was a single stone surrounded by a rectangle of smaller stones. A cove of unknown purpose anchored the center of the northern circle. The site has been inhabited for more than four millennia, its oldest part dating to approximately 2600 BCE.

The entire Avebury site, some 2,500 feet in diameter, remains one of the largest in the United Kingdom. It is bounded by the large circular embankment that surrounds the two inner circles. Immediately inside the embankment is a ditch and on its inner edge was a circle of some 100 stones, only a few of which remain in place. The larger site was constructed in stages from the center outward. Among the latest additions was the double line of stones (referred to as West Kennet Avenue) that lead from Avebury to another site about a mile away to the south. Avebury is older than Stonehenge and most of its stones show little sign of having been reshaped before being put in place. Avebury is located in Wiltshire, some 90 miles west of London. Today, a village is located inside the embankment and a modern road transverses the circle entering and exiting through the breaks in the embankment.

Using the technology available to them, the people who constructed Avebury consumed a considerable percentage of their resources above what was required to simply survive over a number of decades. The inner circles had 46 stones between them, some rising as much as 20 feet in the air and weighing upwards of 40 tons.

Through the centuries of the Common Era, the site fell into disuse, especially with the spread of Christianity. Beginning in the 14th century, records indicate efforts to remove the stones and use the land within the embankment for farming. The large stones were pulled down and used for houses and other structures. Study of the site began in the early 18th century by Dr. William Stukeley (1687–1765), who made the first detailed measurements along with a set of drawings. Unfortunately, Stukeley was unable to prevent further destruction of the site.

Since World War II, study (both amateur and professional) of Avebury, now a protected archaeological site, has flourished. Some have picked up Stuckey's observation that the wider ground plan of Avebury represented a serpent passing through a circle (an alchemical symbol). A number of researchers integrated the data on Avebury into the growing acknowledgment that many of the megalithic sites were involved with the observation of the heavens by the ancient residents of England and suggested that the stone alignments marked cyclical movements of the Sun and Moon and possibly other planetary bodies. Engineer Alexander Thom (1894–1985) suggested the builders had a sophisticated knowledge of the Moon's movements. These observations, of course, intimated that lunar activity played an

The Neolithic archaeological site of Avebury in England is known for a quarter-mile-wide circle of megaliths built within a raised earth mound. Some scholars believe the site had significance in fertility rituals, while human remains discovered at the site suggest it may have been a burial ground. (Corel)

important role in ancient British religion. Thom and others have also emphasized the connections of Avebury with additional nearby sites expressive of the megalithic culture such as Silbury Hill, West Kennet Long Barrow, Windmill Hill, and the Sanctuary.

Additional students of the megalithic culture have employed a variety of more questionable methodologies to arrive at observations that expand the knowledge of the site not available from normal scientific methodology. Some have, for example, attempted to tease information from ancient folklore and popular legends, while a few have used various psychic arts from clairvoyance to dowsing. One popular theory ties Avebury into a system of ley lines, a system of straight lines believed to connect various sacred sites across England and Europe. Conclusions drawn from these studies rest upon the evaluation of the methodology and the presence of independent verification. Such speculation has additional significance, however, as

it attempts to tie the religion of ancient Britons into modern alternative Esoteric and Pagan religions. While many tourists visit Avebury out of historical interest, many Pagans and New Agers visit on spiritual pilgrimage, and together have made Avebury one of England's top tourist stops.

J. Gordon Melton

See also: Pilgrimage; Stonehenge.

References

Burl, Aubrey. *Prehistoric Avebury.* New Haven, CT: Yale University Press, 2003.

Gillings, Mark, and Joshua Pollard. *Avebury.* London: Duckworth Publishers, 2004.

Miller, Hamish, and Paul Broadhurst. *The Sun and the Serpent.* Hayle, Cornwall, UK: Pendragon Press, 1990.

Thom, Alexander. *Megalithic Sites in Britain.* Oxford: Oxford University Press, 1967.

■ Azerbaijan

Azerbaijan, a small country on the Caspian Sea, emerged in the fourth century BCE as several peoples residing in the region united and proclaimed their independence from Persia, which had recently been overrun by Alexander the Great. The name Azerbaijan is a derivative of the name of one of these peoples, the Atropatene. The eastern border of this central Asian nation is located on the Caspian Sea. It is otherwise bounded by Iran, Armenia, Georgia, and Russia. Its 33,243 square miles of territory is inhabited by 8,177,717 people, most of a Turkic and Islamic heritage.

In the seventh century CE, the area that now constitutes Azerbaijan was incorporated into the Arab kingdom and the peoples of the region united by the imposition of Islam. As the division developed between Sunni Islam and Shia Islam, Azerbaijan became part of the Shiite world. In the 11th century, the Turks occupied the land, and the Turkish language came into common usage. Modern Azeri is a dialect of Turkish, and it is also the case that Azeri identity developed in this period, tied to both the country's unique language and Shia Islam.

Beginning in the 16th century, Azerbaijan became the target of expansionist dreams of its neighbors, Turkey and Persia, and in the 18th century, Russia. Russia was granted northern Azerbaijan in 1828. The country became increasingly prized for its rich oil deposits. In 1920, all of the country was incorporated into the new Soviet Union and then joined with Armenia and Georgia into a Transcaucasian Federated Soviet Republic.

The Muslim Azeris and the Christians of nearby Armenia have a long rivalry. In 1918, while an independent Azerbaijan nation briefly existed, Azeris carried out a massacre of Armenians residing in their country. Then in 1988, as the Soviet Union was in its last phase, the Armenians who controlled the province of Nagorno-Karabakh revolted, and in 1991, when the cease-fire was negotiated, a strip of land connecting the province to Armenia was in Armenian hands. To the present, that section of Armenia (though a matter of ongoing dispute) divides Azerbaijan into two geographically separated territories. As a result of the loss to Armenia, the Azeris carried out a retaliatory persecution of Armenians living in the remaining part of the land. Many left the country at this time.

The majority of Azeris are Shia Muslims, the remainder being Sunni Muslims, primarily of the Hanafi School of Islam. The Shiites are closely related to the Iranians who share the same faith, especially to the large Azeri-speaking community in northern Iran. Sunni Islam was introduced in the 19th century with the encouragement of Russian authorities, who facilitated Hanafi imams' relocation to the northern part of the land. At the same time, members of the Naqshbandiyya Sufi order entered the region, as did members of the Qadrriyya. Both became the source of anti-Russian agitation.

Azerbaijan

Religion	Followers in 1970	Followers in 2010	% of Population	Annual % growth 2000–2010	Followers in 2025	Followers in 2050
Muslims	3,153,000	7,623,000	87.9	0.69	8,623,000	8,712,000
Agnostics	1,000,000	720,000	8.3	−1.40	500,000	282,000
Christians	263,000	280,000	3.2	1.25	344,000	371,000
Orthodox	250,000	260,000	3.0	0.96	300,000	300,000
Independents	0	10,000	0.1	6.61	25,000	40,000
Protestants	1,000	7,000	0.1	5.40	15,000	25,000
Jews	5,000	28,000	0.3	0.51	25,000	20,000
Atheists	750,000	17,000	0.2	0.61	10,000	10,000
Baha'is	500	2,000	0.0	0.49	3,000	6,000
New religionists	1,000	1,500	0.0	0.52	2,800	3,100
Total population	**5,172,000**	**8,671,000**	**100.0**	**0.51**	**9,508,000**	**9,404,000**

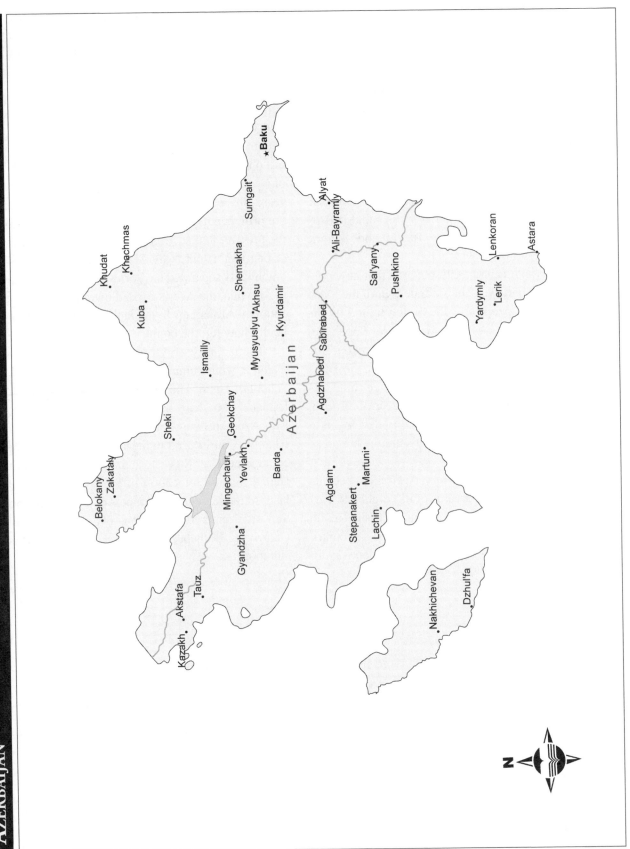

However, during the years of Soviet rule, secularization proceeded, and in the 1990s, a secular government, based to some extent on the Turkish model, was instituted. There is no state religion in contemporary Azerbaijan. Islam revived in the 1980s, but not to the extent of being strong enough to impose an Islamic theocracy on the emerging state. The strongest Muslim political party, the Azerbaijan Islamic Party, has as its major ideological thrusts anti-Semitism and anti-Turkism, Turkish thought being seen as a hindrance to uniting Azeris around Islam.

Soviet authorities attempted to suppress Islam and closed numerous mosques during the 1930s. A few were allowed to reopen in the 1940s, but only 11 were in operation as changes began to occur in the 1980s. Also, in the 1940s, the government created the Muslim Spiritual Board of Transcaucasia, based in Baku, as an administrative body over the Muslim community throughout the Caucasus region. During the period when the Soviet Union was led by Leonid Brezhnev and then by Mikhail Gorbachev, the freedom for Islamic practice increased. In the 1980s, Allashukur Humatogly Pashazade was named sheikh ul-Islam, that is, head of the Muslim Spiritual Board. The board continues as the Supreme Religious Council of the Caucasus Peoples in independent Azerbaijan. It oversees one seminary for the training of imams.

Christianity reached the Caucasus by the end of the first century CE and was well established by the third century. It became the dominant religion in the northern half of the country in the fifth century but was displaced in the seventh century by Islam.

Two main forms of Christianity survive to the present. The Armenian Apostolic Church survives primarily among the Armenian people who reside within Azerbaijan, and the Russian Orthodox Church grew significantly among the Russians who moved into the area beginning in the 18th century. The strength of the Armenian church was dramatically reduced by the incorporation of Nagorno-Karabakh into Armenia. An estimated 2 percent of the population is ethnically Russian.

Prior to both Christianity and Islam, Zoroastrianism had been established in Azerbaijan. Zoroaster was born in the seventh century BCE in what is now Azerbaijan. His faith spread southward and later became the dominant religion of Persia. The Surakhany Temple on the Apsheron Peninsula near Baku remains a sacred site acknowledged by Zoroastrians. With the arrival of Islam, Zoroastrian power was broken, and in the eighth century many believers moved to India, where they remain as a recognizable group, the Parsis. Most Zoroastrian activity today originates from outside of the country.

The Molokon movement, a Free church group that developed in the Volga River valley, moved southward into the Caucasus during the 19th century. In 1873, Vasili V. Ivanov-Klyshnikov (1846–1919) moved to Azerbaijan from Georgia. He was a Molokon who had become a Baptist, and he began to gain converts, primarily among Molokon Russians. A congregation was established in Baku around 1880. The Baptists survived the Soviet era, and at the end of the 1990s, there were six congregations that had united as the Union of Evangelical Christians-Baptists, which is associated with the Euro-Asian Federation of Unions of Evangelical Christians-Baptists that provides fellowship for Baptists throughout the countries of the former Soviet Union.

J. Gordon Melton

See also: Armenian Apostolic Church (Holy See of Etchmiadzin); Hanafite School of Islam; Molokons; Naqshbandiyya Sufi Order; Qadiriyya Sufi Order; Russian Orthodox Church; Shia Islam; Union of Evangelical Christians—Baptists of Russia.

References

Alstadt, Audrey L. *The Azerbaijani Turks: Power and Identity under Russian Rule.* Stanford, CA: Hoover Institution Press, 1992.

Barrett, David, ed. *The Encyclopedia of World Christianity.* 2nd ed. New York: Oxford University Press, 2001.

De Waal, Thomas. *Black Garden: Armenia and Azerbaijan through Peace and War.* New York: New York University Press, 2004.

Swietochowski, T. *Russian Azerbaijan, 1905–1920: The Shaping of a National Identity in a Muslim Community.* Cambridge: Cambridge University Press, 1985.

B

Baal Shem Tov

1698–1760

The modern Hasidic movement, the mystical branch of Orthodox Judaism, is generally traced to the Baal Shem Tov ("Master of the Good Name"/the "Besht"). Known for his positive piety and knowledge of the secret names of God, he would inspire many, including a small number of teachers who carried on his emphases. The movement would grow strong until it was almost destroyed by the Nazi onslaught during World War II.

The person who came to be called the Baal Shem Tov was born Israel ben Eliezer in Akop, Poland, on what in the Jewish calendar was Elul 18, 5858 (1698). His father, a rabbi, and his mother were relatively poor. They both died before he was of school age and he was raised by the townspeople. Little is known of his early years other than the fact that he was a fairly good student. He also had a tendency to simply disappear from the village to wander in the nearby Carpathian Mountains.

Reputedly, amid his wanderings he met a member of the Tzadikim Nistarim, a secret order whose members roamed the countryside visiting Jewish communities; they spread a simple piety and encouraged those who felt the sting of persecution. Subsequently, Israel went to live with one of the order's members, Reb Meir. Meir was known as a *tzaddik* (a teacher with mystical knowledge). In 1712, after several years under Meir's tutelage, Israel became a full member of the Tzadikim Nistarim.

Israel came out of relative obscurity in 1716 when he assumed duties as the *bahelfer* (assistant to the religious teacher) in the town of Broady, also in southern Poland. His primary duties included the instruction of the children. At the same time he began to lobby his fellow members of Tzadikim Nistarim that they assume responsibility for education in Jewish communities where it was lacking. The order responded by building schools and providing teachers to lead them.

In 1719 he moved back to Akop as the *shamash* (caretaker) for the synagogue. His duties were light and he used the opportunity to spend long hours in the study of the Torah. He also married, though his wife died a few years later. During the Akop years, he succeeded to the leadership of the Tzadikim Nistarim and benefited from the arrival in town of the son of Rabbi Adam Baal Shem. The rabbi's son brought with him some texts on the Kabbalah and introduced this mystical system that had come to the fore during the Middle Ages within the European Jewish community. The teachings resonated with Israel's own natural piety and striving for spiritual enlightenment.

Following the death of Rabbi Adam's son and his own wife, Israel left Akop, met and married the woman who became his second wife, and eventually settled again in Brody. Here in 1724, he had the life-changing experience that would determine his future. He was visited by the spirit of Ahiya of Shilo, the ancient prophet who had lived during the reign of King David (ca. 1037–967 BCE). He moved into the mountains and lived for the next 10 years in seclusion. His time was spent in studying the Torah, mastering the Kabbalah, and continuing in contact with the spirit of Ahiya of Shilo. The decade culminated on his birthday in 1734 in his receiving a revelation of his future mission. He was to leave home and become a teacher. Having mastered the mystical arts, he was now known as the Baal Shem Tov. He and his wife moved to Meziboz, where he soon attracted a number of students drawn to his emphasis on individual piety and joyfulness over traditional study and ascetic practices. He had a broad appeal as he claimed that faith was accessible to all.

In Meziboz, the Baal Shem Tov established the basic elements of Hasidism, including a focus on developing a religious spirit. He emphasized *devekut*, the cleaving to God both in worship and in one's daily life over against traditional emphases on knowledge of the Talmud and appreciation of physical pleasures as creations of God. He saw life centered on worship of God in everything individuals do and prayer as the personal mystical experience of the Almighty. To experience oneness with God produces joy and leads to a joyfulness in the performance of the commandments. Joy is often expressed in dancing.

As the Baal Shem Tov's reputation as a magnetic teacher and a worker of miracles spread, along with his openness to all people (not just his students), the number of devotees grew. The Hasidic movement he launched would over the next two centuries come to encompass approximately half of European Jewry. He died at Meziboz on Sivan 6, 5520 (1760). The only negative events in his last year concerned charges of heresies by the more conservative rabbinical leaders, the *mitnagdim*, who accused him of assuming messianic pretentions. These charges made little impact upon the movement he founded.

Today, all of the several dozen Hasidic groups that have emerged in the post-Holocaust Jewish community trace their lineage to the Baal Shem Tov, primarily through his primary pupil and successor, Rabbi Dovber of Meziboz (ca. 1710–1772).

J. Gordon Melton

See also: Hasidism.

References

Amos, D. Ben, and J. R. Mintz, eds. *In Praise of the Baal Shem Tov.* Lanham, MD: Jason Aronson, 1994.

Buber, Martin, and Maurice Friedman. *The Origin and Meaning of Hasidism.* New York: Horizon Press, 1960.

Rabinowicz, Tzvi. *Chassidic Rebbes: From the Baal Shem Tov to Modern Times.* New York: Feldheim Publishing, 1989–2002.

Schochet, Jacob Immanuel. *Rabbi Israel Baal Shem Tov: A Monograph on the Life and Teachings of the Founder of Chassidism.* Toronto: Lieberman's Publishing House, 1961.

◆ Baha'i Faith

Historical Background   The Baha'i Faith is a religion that began in Iran in 1853. Its founder was Mírzá Husayn-'Alí (1817–1892), known as Bahá'u'lláh. Worldwide membership in the Baha'i Faith has grown to more than five million, and the Faith has emerged as the most geographically widespread religion in the world after the Roman Catholic Church.

The Baha'i Faith arose from the Bábí Faith, a religion that briefly flourished in Iran in the 1840s. It was established by 'Alí-Muhammad of Shiraz (1819–1850), who in 1844 took on the title of the Báb (the gate) and who declared himself to be the fulfillment of Islamic prophecies. The Twelver Shia Islam that dominates Iran expected the return of the 12th imam (a messianic figure), and the expectation peaked among some Shiites in 1844. The Báb initially hinted that he was merely a gate to the 12th imam, but gradually made explicit a claim to be the 12th imam himself. He also penned mystic commentaries on the Koran, whose style and content signified a claim to divine revelation.

Among the early converts to the Bábí movement was Mírzá Husayn-'Alí, a nobleman born in northern Iran whose father was a palace official. As the Bábí leadership was executed, one after another, his role in the movement grew in importance. In the summer of 1848 he assembled a gathering of the remaining Bábí leaders at which he gave each a title; he took on the title of Bahá'u'lláh (the glory of God), one subsequently endorsed by the Báb. Before his execution, the Báb recognized Bahá'u'lláh's teenage half-brother Yahyá (1831–1912) as a figurehead leader of the Bábí community, though he gave Yahyá no explicit authority. Considering that Yahyá was completely unknown in the Bábí community and was still a youth living in Bahá'u'lláh's household, the appointment was probably made to allow Bahá'u'lláh to run the Bábí movement with a minimum of government interference.

In August 1852 a group of Bábís attempted to assassinate the king, resulting in a severe government-sponsored pogrom against the remaining Bábís. Bahá'u'lláh was arrested and imprisoned for four months.

When the Iranian government released Bahá'u'lláh from prison, they banished him from Iran. Hence he departed for Baghdad, a city in the Ottoman Empire frequented by many Iranians intent on performing pilgrimage to the Shiite shrines nearby. The next 10 years were highly productive ones, in which Bahá'u'lláh penned several of his most important works: *The Hidden Words* (a collection of ethical and mystical aphorisms), *The Seven Valleys and Four Valleys* (two works about the mystic journey of the soul, in dialogue with Sufi concepts), and the *Book of Certitude* (a work delineating basic theological concepts and principles of personal spiritual development through commentary on passages from the Bible and the Koran). His efforts to revitalize the Bábí community of Baghdad and to revive the Iranian Bábí community were so successful that the Iranian government requested that the Ottomans move him farther from Iran. On the eve of his departure for Istanbul, in April 1863, Bahá'u'lláh publicly declared to his companions and close associates that he was the prophetic teacher the Báb had prophesied.

The latter work specified that upon Bahá'u'lláh's passing, his eldest son, 'Abbás, was to become his successor; other tablets praised 'Abbás as the exemplar of Bahá'u'lláh's teachings and the official interpreter of Bahá'u'lláh's revelation. Consequently, when Bahá'u'lláh passed in 1892, at age 75, 'Abbás, age 48, was quickly acknowledged by all as the rightful head of the Baha'i Faith. He took the title of 'Abdu'l-Bahá, meaning "servant of Bahá," to underline his subservience to his father's legacy. An attempt by one of 'Abdu'l-Bahá's half-brothers to form a rival Baha'i movement garnered virtually no support and died out, though it did cause Ottoman officials to look at all Baha'is with suspicion and to renew 'Abdu'l-Bahá's confinement within the city of Acre. The decade of confinement ended in 1908, when the Young Turks Revolution toppled the Ottoman sultan and converted Turkey into a secular republic.

From 1892 to 1908, 'Abdu'l-Bahá was free to receive visitors and communications, including cablegrams. The spread of the Baha'i Faith to the United States and subsequently to Europe, Hawaii, Australia, and Japan resulted in a diverse group of pilgrims entering Acre—still a prison city—to meet 'Abdu'l-Bahá and receive his wisdom. When 'Abdu'l-Bahá's confinement permanently ended in 1908, he considered travel. In 1910 he visited Egypt and in 1911 he traveled to Europe to meet and encourage that continent's fledgling Baha'i communities. In 1912 he traveled to North America, arriving in early April (just two weeks before the sinking of the *Titanic*, a ship many Baha'is had urged him to take because of its reputation for safety). His nine-month journey extended as far south as Washington, as far north as Montreal, and as far west as Los Angeles. He gave hundreds of speeches to thousands of people gathered in churches, synagogues, and theosophical lodges. He spoke to the annual Lake Mohonk Peace Conference and the fourth annual national conference of the National Association for the Advancement of Colored People (NAACP). The result was hundreds of newspaper articles, almost all favorable. He left North America in December 1912, spending the winter and spring visiting Baha'is from London to Budapest before returning to Palestine months before the beginning of World War I. A contemplated trip to India was rendered impossible by the war and his age. He passed away in November 1921 at age 77.

Like his father, 'Abdu'l-Bahá wrote a will, in which he named his eldest grandson, Shoghi Effendi Rabbani, to be his successor and *valí amru'lláh* (Guardian of the Cause of Allah). As a result, aside from a few small efforts to split the Baha'i community (none of which garnered more than a few hundred followers or lasted more than a generation), the Baha'is unitedly accepted Shoghi Effendi as their new head. 'Abdu'l-Bahá's will also specified the system whereby Baha'is would elect nine-member local spiritual assemblies (governing councils of local Baha'i communities) and delegates who would elect nine-member national spiritual assemblies. The will also specified that the members of all national spiritual assemblies would serve as the delegates to elect the Universal House of Justice, the supreme worldwide Baha'i governing body.

'Abdu'l-Bahá's will asserted that while the Guardian had the power to interpret authoritative Baha'i texts, the Universal House of Justice had the authority to legislate on matters about which the texts were silent.

Shoghi Effendi's sudden death, without a will, in November 1957 plunged the Baha'i world community into a crisis, because it deprived the community of its international leadership and raised the specter of schism. But Shoghi Effendi had begun a 10-year plan for expansion of the Baha'i Faith in 1953 that provided the Baha'is with clear goals until April 1963. He had also appointed a series of individuals as Hands of the Cause of Allah (a position created by Bahá'u'lláh). In October 1957 he raised their total number to 27 and termed them "the Chief Stewards of Baha'u'llah's embryonic World Commonwealth, who have been invested by the unerring Pen of the Center of His Covenant with the dual function of guarding over the security, and of insuring the propagation, of His Father's Faith" (Shoghi Effendi, *Messages to the Baha'i World,* 127). 'Abdu'l-Bahá's will had also given the Hands clear authority. Consequently the Baha'is of the world turned to the Hands, who coordinated the Baha'i Faith until the completion of Shoghi Effendi's 10-year teaching plan. One effort by a Hand of the Cause, Charles Mason Remey, to claim leadership of the Baha'i community garnered support from several hundred persons, but subsequently the Remeyite movement split into at least four factions.

In April 1963 the Hands oversaw the election of the Universal House of Justice (they voluntarily disqualified themselves as members). Subsequently the Universal House of Justice has been elected every five years by the members of all the national spiritual assemblies, who either send their ballots by mail, or gather in Haifa, Israel, to cast their ballots in person. The Universal House of Justice has overseen continued expansion of the Baha'i community and coordinated translation of more Baha'i texts into English and other languages (including the *Kitáb-i-Aqdas*); it was also responsible for a great increase in the public visibility of the Baha'i Faith worldwide.

In 1888 two Lebanese Christians became Baha'is in Egypt and in 1892 immigrated to the United States. One of them, Ibrahim George Kheiralla (1849–1929), was responsible for converting the first Americans in

The Baha'i House of Worship at New Delhi, commonly called the Lotus Temple. (Arvindimg/Dreamstime.com)

1894. From a small group in Chicago, by 1900 the United States had four Baha'i communities of 50 or more believers, plus scattered Baha'is in 23 states. By 1899 the Faith was also introduced from Chicago to Ontario, Canada; Paris, France; and London, England. A convert in Europe in turn took the Baha'i Faith to Hawaii in 1901, and two Hawaiian Baha'is took it to Japan in 1914. In 1910 a pair of American Baha'is circled the globe westward, visiting major Baha'i communities in every country where the religion could be found. By 1921 other American Baha'is had settled in Mexico, Brazil, Australia, New Zealand, and Korea.

'Abdu'l-Bahá was so impressed by the American Baha'i community that he sent them a series of 14 tablets from 1914 to 1916 entitled *The Tablets of the Divine Plan,* in which he enjoined them to spread the Baha'i religion to every nation and island on the globe.

He enumerated hundreds of places where there should be Baha'i communities, all of which subsequently became missionary goals. In the 1920s Shoghi Effendi gave the American Baha'is the chief responsibility for establishing Baha'i elected institutions, and he patterned such bodies in Europe, Asia, and Australasia on the American model.

In 1937, the North American Baha'is having finally established firm local and national spiritual assemblies, Shoghi Effendi gave them a Seven Year Plan (1937–1944) calling for them to establish at least one local spiritual assembly in every state in the United States and one in every province of Canada, to establish the Baha'i Faith in every country in Latin America, and to complete the exterior of the Baha'i House of Worship in Wilmette, Illinois. In spite of World War II, every goal was achieved, and many Latin American nations had local spiritual assemblies as well as small groups of Baha'is in 1944.

In 1946, Shoghi Effendi launched a second Seven Year Plan (1946–1953) that called for creation of a separate national spiritual assembly for Canada (the Canadian Baha'is having shared a national assembly with the United States all that time), a single national spiritual assembly for all of South America, another for all of Central America, and re-establishment of the Baha'i Faith in war-ravaged Western Europe.

By 1953 there were 12 national spiritual assemblies worldwide: one in Italy and Switzerland, one in Germany and Austria, one in Egypt and Sudan, one in Australia and New Zealand, one in India and Burma, the four aforementioned in the Americas, the United Kingdom, Iran, and Iraq. Shoghi Effendi gave plans to all 12 of them for the period 1953–1963. Among the goals were to more than double the number of countries, islands, and significant territories in which the Baha'i Faith was established and to raise the number of national spiritual assemblies to 57. Except for a national spiritual assembly in one Islamic country, all the goals were achieved by 1963. The United States achieved perhaps a third of the goals, while expanding the number of American Baha'is from 7,000 to 10,000.

The decade 1963–1973 saw the fruits of the effort to spread the Baha'i Faith widely but very thinly around the world. Latin American Baha'is settling in Bolivia reached out to the rural population, and tens of thousands became Baha'is; the Bolivian Baha'i community is still the largest in Latin America, with a university and a radio station to serve its members and the citizenry. In the United States, door-to-door teaching brought 10,000 to 15,000 rural African Americans into the Baha'i Faith in South Carolina, North Carolina, and Georgia in the years 1969–1972. At the same time an unusual receptivity swept the college population, no doubt stimulated by the Vietnam War and the civil rights movement. By 1974 the United States had 60,000 Baha'is. Subsequent conversion has been supplemented by immigration (some 12,000 Iranian Baha'is and perhaps 10,000 Southeast Asian Baha'is have settled in the United States since 1975), with the result that in 2001 the United States had 142,000 Baha'is and nearly 1,200 local spiritual assemblies. The National Spiritual Assembly of the Baha'is of the United States owns retreat and conference centers in five states; publishes a children's magazine, a monthly newspaper, and a quarterly scholarly periodical; operates a radio station in South Carolina; runs a senior citizens' home and two institutions for economic development and public health; and employs some 200 staff.

Expansion of the American Baha'i community in the last 25 years has also allowed resources to be channeled in several new directions. The Baha'i community has been able to sustain much greater commitment to the abolition of racism, the establishment of world peace, and the development of society. One result has been greater media attention. The larger community also produced an expanded book market that stimulated writers and scholars, so that Baha'i literature greatly expanded in scope and depth. Cultural expressions of the Baha'i Faith, such as operas and "Baha'i gospel" music, developed and have become much more sophisticated. Now more than a century old, the American Baha'i community is an indigenous American religion, with fifth- and sixth-generation members.

Beliefs and Practices The Baha'i Faith possesses authoritative texts from the Báb, Bahá'u'lláh, 'Abdu'l-Bahá, Shoghi Effendi, and the Universal House of Justice. In all cases a sharp distinction is made between written and oral statements by the head of the Faith: the former are binding if they can be authenticated; the latter are not binding unless they were committed to writing and subsequently approved by the head of the Faith.

The authoritative texts also are hierarchically ranked in importance. Those by the Báb and Bahá'u'lláh are the most important, because both individuals are considered Manifestations of God and thus mouthpieces of divine revelation. Their writings are considered the word of God. Because Bahá'u'lláh often abrogated specific laws of the Báb, the latter are not binding on Baha'is. 'Abdu'l-Bahá is not considered a Manifestation of God, but his writings come from an individual whose spiritual rank is considered unique in human history (above that of an ordinary human being but below that of a Manifestation); hence his writings possess a sacredness and are considered part of Baha'i scripture. Shoghi Effendi, on the other hand, occupies a rank even farther from that of a Manifestation, and his writings, though binding and authoritative, occupy a less sacred place in the hierarchy of Baha'i scripture. The writings of the Universal House of Justice are also binding and authoritative but, like papal encyclicals, would not be considered scripture.

A significant feature of Baha'i authoritative texts is their sheer volume; 15,000 documents by Bahá'u'lláh, 27,000 by 'Abdu'l-Bahá, and more than 17,500 by Shoghi Effendi. No official estimate of the quantity of writings of the Universal House of Justice is known, but when one considers that the 9-member body employs a large secretariat to research and draft responses, the rumored estimate of 250,000 letters composed since 1963 may be approximately correct. To date, perhaps 5 percent of Bahá'u'lláh's corpus has been translated into English; much more of 'Abdu'l-Bahá's writings have been translated into English, but the old translations have not been checked for accuracy, updated, or even completely collected together. The Baha'i World Centre has been computerizing the Baha'i authoritative texts in their original languages and their translations for some 20 years.

Baha'i teachings are often summarized as the unity of God, the unity of religion, and the unity of humankind. If one adds teachings about the creation of a Baha'i community and about the personal spiritual life, one has a useful division of Baha'i teachings.

Bahá'u'lláh describes God as an unknowable essence—in other words, ultimately God is beyond human ken and reckoning. Bahá'u'lláh's view, however, is not that humans can know nothing about God; on the contrary, even though the divine has an unknowable essence, it also has attributes such as mercy, justice, love, patience, self-subsistence, might, and knowledge that we can experience and know. By developing these qualities in their own souls, humans guide and foster their personal spiritual development and prepare themselves for the next life, in which spiritual growth occurs continuously and primarily through God's grace. Experiencing God's attributes in creation is the basis of nature mysticism; Bahá'u'lláh says that all created things reflect divine attributes (a concept that is also fundamental to Baha'i environmental ethics). Bahá'u'lláh notes, however, that the perfect reflector of divine attributes on this plane of existence is the Manifestation of God, a rare figure who receives divine revelation and guidance and manifests them perfectly in the language of his or her culture and through his or her own life and actions. In an epistemological sense the manifestation *is* God, because in the mortal plane she or he is the only perfect source of knowledge of the divine. Bahá'u'lláh identifies Abraham, Moses, Jesus, Muhammad, Zoroaster, the Báb, and himself as Manifestations and suggests that Adam, Noah, the founder of the Sabaean religion, Salih, and Hud were also Manifestations (the last three are figures mentioned in the Koran as well). To this list 'Abdu'l-Bahá adds Buddha and Shoghi Effendi adds Krishna, raising the total to 14. Bahá'u'lláh also states that many Manifestations lived so long ago that their names have been lost; 'Abdu'l-Bahá stresses that humanity has always received divine guidance through Manifestations.

The Baha'i recognition that the majority of the world's major religions were established by Manifestations is the basis of the Baha'i concept of the unity of religion. Bahá'u'lláh and 'Abdu'l-Bahá both state that all religions are based on a divine revelation (either directly or by borrowing divine ideas from previous religions) but add that, while all religions share certain basic ethical and metaphysical principles, they also differ because the revelation had to be tailored to the

Inspirational prayers, music, and readings create an uplifting atmosphere at the Hush Harbor devotional meetings in the New York Baha'i Center. (Baha'i World News Service)

social and cultural context in which it was expressed. Bahá'u'lláh and 'Abdu'l-Bahá also criticize the learned and clergy of all religions for misunderstanding and distorting the original teachings. The bewildering diversity of the world's religions—especially in ritual and practice—is attributed to differing cultural contexts and interpretations. Baha'i scholars have just begun to research issues that arise from the Baha'i approach to religion, such as the relationship of the Baha'i Faith to Buddhism (which fits the Baha'i model of a religion the least), and to Sikhism, Jainism, and Chinese religions (which have no Manifestations recognized by the Baha'i Faith). Interfaith dialogue is also affected by the Baha'i concept of Manifestation, for it implies that the latest Manifestation— Bahá'u'lláh—is in some sense the most important. Bahá'u'lláh states that God will continue to send Manifestations to humanity in the future, but the next one

will come only after the lapse of 1,000 years (which is the time given the Baha'i Faith to develop itself and mature).

Bahá'u'lláh emphasizes that human beings are the "waves of one sea," "the leaves of one branch," and "the flowers of one garden," images that emphasize the overriding unity of all human beings. Shoghi Effendi notes that the oneness of humankind is the watchword and pivot of the Baha'i teachings. Although this teaching can be seen as similar to Paul's words that Christians are "baptized into one body, whether we be Jews or Gentiles, whether we be bond or free" (1 Corinthians 12:13), Bahá'u'lláh and 'Abdu'l-Bahá strongly emphasized the implications of this principle: that all persons are equal before God and therefore must have basic equality in human society; that men and women are equal; that races are equal and must be reconciled and united. In his visit to the United States in 1912,

'Abdu'l-Bahá insisted on all Baha'i meetings being open to blacks as well as whites and encouraged an African American man, Louis Gregory, to marry an English woman, Louise Matthew. American Baha'i communities began the struggle to integrate themselves ethnically and racially as early as 1908, and women were first elected to Baha'i local and national governing bodies as early as 1907 (in 2001 they constitute the majority of the membership of American local spiritual assemblies and four-ninths of the membership of the national spiritual assembly).

In addition to its implications of unity, the oneness of humanity also is understood to imply the need to establish a global governing system. Bahá'u'lláh called on all kings and rulers to end war, limit armaments, and meet in an international summit to establish common treaties and institutions. He said that an international language and script should be selected to supplement local languages and allow easy world communication. The Baha'i texts also call for an international system of weights and measures, a world currency, an elected world legislature, an international collective security arrangement, and global measures to ensure universal education and health care, to create equitable access to resources, and to diminish the extreme imbalances of wealth and poverty. Indeed, the Baha'i authoritative texts include an extensive critique of existing social norms and a vision for creating a just, unified world.

The Baha'i community consists of all persons who have accepted Bahá'u'lláh and have requested membership in the body of his followers. It is conceived of as an evolving entity destined to reflect Bahá'u'lláh's teachings ever more perfectly and to embrace an ever-larger segment of humanity. The chief goal of the Baha'i community is to achieve ever-greater unity.

Baha'is strive for spiritual unity through various means. Baha'i gatherings begin with prayer. Discussion about any matter is conducted according to the principles of consultation, whereby individuals are encouraged to be frank but tactful in expressing themselves; should listen carefully and avoid offending or feeling offended by others; where ideas, once expressed, belong to the group and thus can be modified or rejected by all present, including the person first proposing the idea; where decisions ideally should be unanimous, but can be carried by a majority; and where the results of consultation must be trusted and not undermined by subsequent dissent, noncooperation, or backbiting. Consultation is simultaneously a set of principles of behavior, a collection of attitudes toward people and ideas, and a culture of discourse to model and perfect.

In addition to the Baha'i governing institutions, the Baha'i texts describe the creation and development of Baha'i communities. Baha'i community life centers on the institution of the feast, a gathering once every Baha'i month (which lasts 19 days) wherein the Baha'is worship together, consult on local community activities, and socialize. The feast also provides the principal opportunity for local spiritual assemblies to share their ideas and plans and receive feedback from the local members. In addition to feasts, Baha'is attend firesides (gatherings, usually in people's homes, to introduce the Baha'i Faith to others), deepenings (meetings to study Baha'i texts and principles together), children's classes (the equivalent of Sunday school), adult classes, and devotional meetings (sometimes held weekly on Sundays). Particularly important are Baha'i holy days, nine of which are observed every year. In addition to the Baha'i New Year's Day (March 21), they commemorate events in the lives of the Báb and Bahá'u'lláh. Supplementing the nine holy days on which Baha'is should suspend work are two holy days connected with the life of 'Abdu'l-Bahá (on which Baha'is can carry out their occupations) and Ayyám-i-Há, a four- or five-day period of service, merrymaking, and gift giving (February 26 through March 1; Ayyám-i-Há is necessary to bring the total days in the Baha'i calendar from 361 to the number of days in a solar year). Every Baha'i holy day is accompanied by a gathering that is open to the public.

In the United States, most local Baha'i communities meet in the homes of the members, but rented and purchased Baha'i Centers are becoming much more common. The United States has only one Baha'i House of Worship, located in Wilmette, Illinois, outside Chicago. It is a national House of Worship and does not serve a particular local Baha'i community. It hosts daily worship programs, holy day observances, and a variety of classes, special gatherings, and interfaith activities.

No account of Baha'i teachings would be complete without an exploration of the devotional life of the individual. The Baha'i scriptures state that the purpose of life is "to know and worship" God and to "carry forward an ever-advancing civilization," thus embracing both a vertical relationship with one's Creator and a horizontal relationship with one's fellow humans. Rather than stress an instant of personal salvation, like some Christian groups, or a moment of enlightenment, like some Buddhist groups, the Baha'i scriptures stress ongoing personal transformation based on internalization of the Baha'i revelation and its expression in service to others. Bahá'u'lláh called on Baha'is to build their prayer life on the pillar of daily obligatory prayer; he gave three prayers among which Baha'is choose one to say daily. (Baha'is also can choose among hundreds of prayers penned by Bahá'u'lláh, the Báb, and 'Abdu'l-Bahá on a variety of subjects, such as forgiveness, assistance, healing, and grief; they rarely pray spontaneously in their own words.) Bahá'u'lláh ordained the repeating of the phrase *Alláh-u-Abhá* (God Is Most Glorious) 95 times each day as the basis for one's meditative and contemplative life. He established a period of fasting (from sunrise to sunset, for 19 days from March 2 through March 20; in that period Baha'is abstain from eating, drinking, and tobacco) as a mild ascetic practice, granting exceptions to those under age 15 or over age 70, the ill, travelers, women who are pregnant, menstruating, or nursing, and anyone performing heavy labor. He enjoined the practice of reciting the word of God twice daily in order to connect the believer to the revelation.

The horizontal dimension of the devotional life has various aspects. Bahá'u'lláh says Baha'is should be "anxiously concerned with the needs of the age you live in, and center your deliberations on its exigencies and requirements" (*Gleanings from the Writings of Bahá'u'lláh,* selection CVI). Baha'is are thus encouraged, individually and collectively, to improve the world around them.

Robert Stockman

See also: Abraham/Abram; Asceticism; Bahá'u'lláh; Birth/Ascension of Bahá'u'lláh; Birth of the Báb; Devotion/Devotional Traditions; Moses; Muhammad; Sacred Texts; Shia Islam.

References

'Abdu'l-Bahá. *Some Questions Answered.* Wilmette, IL: Baha'í Distribution Service, 1981.

The Báb. *Selections from the Writings of the Báb.* Haifa: Baha'í World Centre, 1978.

Bahá'u'lláh. *The Kitáb-i-Aqdas: The Book of Certitude.* Trans. by Shoghi Effendi. London: Baha'í Publishing Trust London, 1961. Various additional editions.

Collins, William P. *Bibliography of English-language Works on the Babi and Baha'i Faith, 1845–1985.* Wilmette, IL: Baha'i Publishing Trust, 1991.

Hatcher, William S., and J. Douglas Martin. *The Baha'i Faith: The Emerging Global Religion.* San Francisco: Harper and Row, 1984.

Perkins, Mary, and Philip Hainsworth. *The Baha'i Faith.* London: Ward Lock Educational, 1980.

Smith, Peter. *The Babi and Baha'i Religions: From Messianic Shi'ism to a World Religion.* Cambridge: Cambridge University Press, 1987.

Universal House of Justice. *The Promise of World Peace.* Haifa, Israel: Baha'i World Centre, 1985.

■ Bahamas

The Bahamas, an archipelago that stretches from near the southeastern coast of Florida to the Turks and Caicos in the Caribbean Sea, consists of 700 islands and cays, many quite small. However, the total land area is 5,380 square miles. The islands are coral formations and the highest point on any of them is only 400 feet above sea level. The country has an area of 13,939 square miles (land and maritime).

The nation's population in 2009 was estimated at 340,000, including those residing on the islands illegally, and its citizens comprise an independent state within the British Commonwealth of Nations. The country is ethnically diverse and includes a Haitian minority of legal and illegal immigrants estimated at 40,000 to 60,000 persons and a white/European minority that is nearly as large. The ethnic composition of the Bahamas today is 85 percent black, 12 percent white, and 3 percent Asian and Hispanic (2000 census).

Christopher Columbus's (1451–1506) first sight of land on his historic 1492 voyage to the New World

Bahamas

Religion	Followers in 1970	Followers in 2010	% of Population	Annual % growth 2000–2010	Followers in 2025	Followers in 2050
Christians	165,000	315,000	91.8	1.25	360,000	403,000
Protestants	85,800	209,000	60.9	1.30	240,000	270,000
Roman Catholics	33,200	51,000	14.9	0.52	55,000	58,000
Anglicans	30,000	48,700	14.2	0.30	55,000	61,000
Agnostics	2,600	19,000	5.5	2.06	26,000	32,000
Spiritists	1,700	6,500	1.9	1.30	7,500	9,000
Baha'is	230	1,400	0.4	1.30	2,000	3,000
Atheists	0	700	0.2	1.29	900	1,200
Jews	300	300	0.1	1.29	300	300
Hindus	0	100	0.0	1.29	200	400
Chinese folk	0	100	0.0	1.33	300	500
Total population	**170,000**	**343,000**	**100.0**	**1.30**	**397,000**	**449,000**

was San Salvador Island in the Bahamas, which was originally the home of the Arawak Amerindian people. Unfortunately, this first contact with Europeans proved disastrous, and the Arawak were soon obliterated by a combination of warfare and diseases to which they had no immunity during attempts by Spanish forces to enslave them.

The Spanish did not colonize the Bahamas, as they were looking for lands rich in gold and none was found there. However, the Bahamas were later colonized by British privateers, who preyed on Spanish ships that were loaded with gold from its American colonies and preparing to cross the Atlantic Ocean.

England first staked a claim on the Bahamas in the form of a land grant in 1578. However, no attempt was made to colonize the islands until they were granted to Sir Robert Heath in 1629. The first settlement was on Santa Catalina Island, now called New Providence, in 1630. Other settlers came in gradually, among them the Puritan Eleuteran Adventurers who settled on New Providence in 1947, which was used by many buccaneers as a base of operations. The buccaneers of many nationalities so harassed Spanish shipping that the Spanish raided Santa Catalina Island in 1641; they retained possession until 1666, when the English regained control. In 1717, the Bahamas became a British Crown colony. The buccaneers were brought under control by the first British governor, Captain Woodes Rogers, a former pirate himself.

In the 1640s, the British began serious settlement in the Bahamas and developed a plantation culture, which required more laborers. To fill that need, the British imported African slaves, whose descendants constitute the majority of the population today. Slavery was abolished in the British-controlled Caribbean in 1838.

The economy was based principally on fishing and salvaging the remains of the numerous shipwrecks that occurred in the shallow Bahamian waters. Poor soil brought failures to any large-scale plantation operation. The Bahamas had periods of prosperity as a center of Confederate blockades during the U.S. Civil War (1861–1865) and as a base for U.S. Prohibition-era rum-runners (1920–1933).

Since World War II, the Bahamas have been an attractive tourist resort area, and tourism is the mainstay of the economy. U.S. citizens account for more than 75 percent of all foreign visitors. Banking and finance constitute the economy's second most important sector. The Bahamas' status as a tax haven and its system of banking regulations have led to its growth as an international banking center. The Bahamas have become an important transshipment point for oil going to North America. Other industries include pharmaceuticals, cement, and rum and liquor distilleries (mainly rum made from sugarcane).

The Bahamas became independent from Great Britain on July 10, 1973, but have remained part of the

BAHAMAS

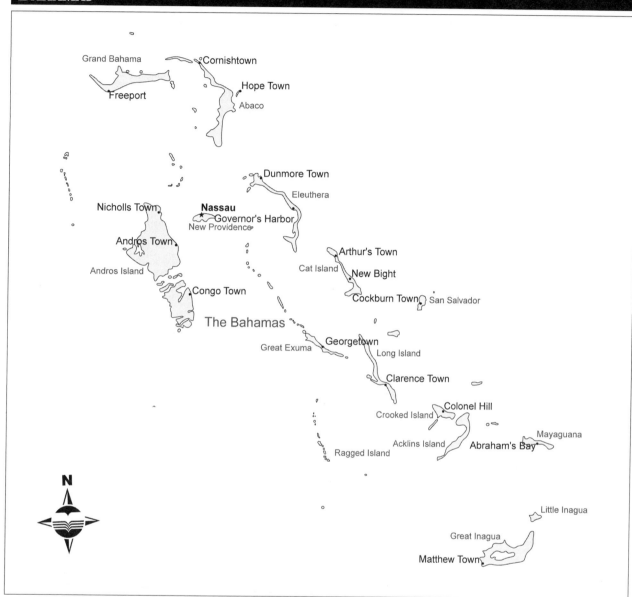

Grand Bahama
Cornishtown
Hope Town
Freeport
Abaco

Dunmore Town
Eleuthera
Nicholls Town
Nassau
Governor's Harbor
New Providence
Andros Town
Andros Island
Arthur's Town
Cat Island
New Bight
Congo Town
Cockburn Town
San Salvador
The Bahamas
Georgetown
Great Exuma
Long Island
Clarence Town
Colonel Hill
Crooked Island
Mayaguana
Acklins Island
Abraham's Bay
Ragged Island

Little Inagua

Great Inagua
Matthew Town

N

British Commonwealth of Nations. The head of state is Queen Elizabeth II, who is represented by a governor-general, whom she appoints. The current head of government is Prime Minister Hubert Alexander Ingraham (2007). Legislative powers are vested in the Parliament, consisting of an elected 38-member House of Assembly and an appointed 16-member Senate. The Progressive Labor Party controls the politically stable Bahamian government.

Overview of Religious Development For the first 200 years of British dominance of the Bahamas, the Church of England was the only organized religious group. Its hegemony was not disturbed until the arrival of the Methodists in 1786. During the 19th and 20th centuries, however, it lost substantial ground, as more and more religious groups, primarily from the United States, established congregations. Today, the Anglican Diocese of the Bahamas is part of the Church in the

Province of the West Indies, whose archbishop currently resides in Nassau. There are more than 41,000 adherents and 100 churches served by 40 priests in the Anglican Diocese of Nassau and the Bahamas.

According to the 2000 census, the religious affiliation of the Bahamian population was Baptist 35.4 percent; Anglican 15.1 percent; Roman Catholic 13.5 percent; Pentecostal 8.1 percent; Church of God 4.8 percent (no differentiation was made between the various Church of God organizations); Methodist 4.2 percent; other Christian 15.2 percent; none or unspecified 2.9 percent; and other 0.8 percent.

The first recorded Protestant worship service in the Bahamas was conducted by the Eleutheran Adventurers, who were Puritan separatists from the Church of England and came seeking freedom of worship. They landed on a Bahamian island in 1648, which they named Eleuthera; they initially conducted worship services in a cave, presumably building a chapel later. An Anglican chapel was built in Nassau in 1724, and the Anglican Church was the Established Church in the Bahamas between 1734 and 1869. The Wesleyan Methodist Church was established by Freemen in 1786, and effective Methodist missionary work was begun in 1800. No permanent Roman Catholic work was started until 1866.

Wesleyan (British) Methodists expanded into the Caribbean after the American Revolutionary War (1775–1783), when Methodists in the United States became independent of British Methodism. As with the Anglican Church, the Methodist constituency in the Caribbean was strengthened by British Loyalists who left the former British colonies in North America and settled in the Bahamas.

In 1786, Joseph Paul, a former slave from the Carolinas, arrived in the Bahamas. He is considered one of the founders of Methodism in the Bahamas. In 1800, the Reverend William Turton of Barbados came as the first Methodist minister. The Bahamas came under the jurisdiction of the British Methodist Church through the Methodist Missionary Society, which sent its first missionary to the Bahamas in 1848. The Methodist community in the Bahamas received a new injection of energy in 1877 with the arrival of missionaries from the African Methodist Episcopal Church, a predominantly black U.S. denomination. In 1968, the Bahamian Methodists joined the Conference of the Methodist Church in the Caribbean and the Americas. In 1973, this denomination reported more than 3,300 members and an estimated community of 7,400 in the Bahamas.

Among the 20th-century arrivals were missionaries representing the Baptists with ties to the British Baptist Union, who are now organized as the Bahamas National Baptist Missionary and Education Convention. Baptist work started in 1780 with the preaching of Frank Spence, a former slave. In 1790, a group of free slaves, including Prince Williams, arrived in an open boat from St. Augustine, Florida, and started preaching among the Bahamians. He built a small chapel and started what is known as Bethel Baptist Church in 1801; Sambo Scriven was its first pastor and Prince Williams was his assistant. In 1833, Mr. and Mrs. Joseph Burton arrived as missionaries of the Baptist Missionary Society based in London. The Burtons founded almost 100 churches in the islands. The Bahamas National Baptist Missionary and Education Convention is reported to be the largest religious community in the islands, with an estimated constituency of 51,900 among 330 churches in 2005, which surpassed the Anglican community of an estimated 29,900 adherents in 2005. Today, there are at least eight Baptist associations and several independent Baptist churches in the Bahamas.

The Roman Catholic Church began its ministry in the Bahamas in 1866, but it was not until 1960 that the first diocese was organized. The Prefecture Apostolic of Bahama was established in 1929, under the Archdiocese of New York; and the Vicariate Apostolic of Bahama Islands was created in 1941. The Diocese of Nassau was established in 1960 under the Archdiocese of Kingston in Jamaica. The *1980 Catholic Almanac* reported 26,340 Catholics (about 12 percent of the population) in the Bahamas. This figure is considerably less than the statistics reported in 1968: 34,000 Catholics (28 percent of the population).

In 2002, the Archdiocese of Nassau (established in 1999) reported that 15.4 percent of the Bahamian population was Roman Catholic (adherents). Patrick Christopher Pinder was named its archbishop in 2004, at which time the archdiocese reported 30 parishes served by 29 priests (15 diocesan and 14 religious

Greek Orthodox church in Nassau, Bahamas. (Jkerrigan/Dreamstime.com)

priests). Also, there were 14 male religious and 28 female religious workers, along with 13 permanent deacons. This archdiocese has two suffragan dioceses: Hamilton in Bermuda (1967) and Turks and Caicos (1984).

Today, more than twenty Protestant denominations operate in the Bahamas, most affiliated with U.S.-based church bodies. Although many unaffiliated Protestant congregations are almost exclusively black, most mainstream churches are integrated racially.

The Seventh-day Adventist Church first arrived in the Bahamas in 1909 and developed a strong following. This denomination had an estimated 21,700 adherents in 2005. Also present are the following Free church denominations: Baptist International Missions (6,130 adherents in 2005), the Church of God (Anderson, Indiana—about 10,000 adherents in 2005), the Christian Brethren (known as Open Brethren), Exclusive Brethren, Christian Churches/Churches of Christ, the Evangelical Church in the West Indies (founded by

West Indies Mission, now World Team), the Presbyterian Church, the Salvation Army, and other small groups.

The Pentecostal movement had a constituency of about 24,000 adherents in 2005; it is represented by the Assemblies of God, the Church of God (Cleveland, Tennessee), the Church of God of Prophecy, and smaller groups. Pentecostal influence began in 1909 when a black couple from the Bahamas was converted in Florida and brought back the Pentecostal message. Along with a retired Methodist minister, they were the founders of the Church of God (Cleveland, Tennessee) in the Bahamas. In 1980, this denomination reported 57 affiliated congregations in the Bahamas.

In 1928, the first Assembly of God was founded in the city of Nassau. The Bahamian Council of the Assemblies of God was organized in 1955. In 1980, there were 17 Assemblies of God churches with more than 2,400 adherents; in 2005, there were an estimated 30 churches with 4,800 adherents, which did not indicate much growth compared to what this denomination has reported in many other countries.

The Bahamas Christian Council, affiliated with the World Council of Churches, includes a spectrum of churches, from Lutherans and Pentecostals to Greek Orthodox and Roman Catholics.

Non-Protestant marginal Christian bodies include the Jehovah's Witnesses that arrived in 1926 (officials reported 31 churches with 1,658 members and had an estimated 4,195 adherents in 2008); and the Church of Jesus Christ of Latter-day Saints (Mormons), founded in 1979, with 3 churches and 820 members in 2007.

Myalism and Obeah are reportedly practiced in secret by some Bahamians, especially those who are not active members of Christian churches. Myalism is an African-derived belief system that developed among blacks in the British West Indies during the slavery period. Obeah is the specific practice of "black magic," or witchcraft by sorcerers, known as "obeah-men." A small number of Bahamians and Haitians, particularly those living in the Family Islands, practice Obeah, which has similarities to Vodou in Haiti.

Reportedly, there are numerous independent spiritualist practitioners in the Bahamas, who advertise themselves as energy healers, psychic mediums, spiritual teachers, and/or spiritualist ministers.

There are several thousand Rastafarians in the Bahamas. In May 2006, IRASCOM International (Bahamas Chapter) in conjunction with RAS (Rastafari Association of Students) Bahamas held a national conference in Nassau, New Providence Island. The purpose of this rally was stated as follows: "We seek, at this gathering, to determine whither we are going and to chart the course of our destiny as sons and daughters of Rastafari here in The Commonwealth of The Bahamas Islands. It is no less important that we know whence we came. An awareness of our past is essential to the establishment of our personality and our identity as Africans."

There is a small Jewish community in the Bahamas centered at Freeport, as well as several spiritual assemblies of the Baha'i Faith. Some members of the small, resident Guyanese and Asian Indian populations in the Bahamas practice Hinduism and other South Asian religions.

The Bahamian Constitution provides for freedom of religion, and other laws and policies contribute to the generally free practice of religion. The law at all levels protects this right in full against abuse, by either governmental or private actors. The government generally respects religious freedom in practice.

In 2008, there were no reports of societal abuses or discrimination based on religious affiliation, belief, or practice. More than 90 percent of the population professes a religion, and anecdotal evidence suggests that most attend religious services regularly.

Clifton L. Holland

See also: African Methodist Episcopal Church; Assemblies of God; Baha'i Faith; Bahamas National Baptist Missionary and Education Convention; Christian Brethren; Church in the Province of the West Indies; Church of England; Church of God (Anderson, Indiana); Church of God (Cleveland, Tennessee); Church of Jesus Christ of Latter-day Saints; Evangelical Church of the West Indies; Jehovah's Witnesses; Pentecostalism; Rastafarians; Roman Catholic Church; Salvation Army; Seventh-day Adventist Church; Spiritualism; Vodou; Witchcraft; World Council of Churches.

References

Barrett, Leonard E., Sr. *The Rastafarians.* Boston: Beacon Press, 1997.

Barry, C. J. *Upon These Rocks: Catholics in the Bahamas.* Collegeville, MN: St. John's Abbey Press, 1973.

Brierly, Peter. *World Churches Handbook.* London: Christian Research, 1997.

Craton, Michale. *A–Z of Bahamas Heritage.* Oxford: Macmillan Caribbean, 2007.

Dryfoot, Arthur Charles. *The Shaping of the West Indian Church, 1492–1962.* Gainesville: University Press of Florida, 1999; published jointly with The Press University of the West Indies in Jamaica.

Fernández Olmos, Margarite, and Lizabeth Paravisini-Gebert, eds. *Sacred Possessions: Vodou, Santería, Obeah and the Caribbean.* New Brunswick, NJ: Rutgers University Press, 1997.

Horowitz, Michael M., ed. *Peoples and Cultures of the Caribbean: An Anthropological Reader.* Garden City, NY: The Natural History Press, 1971.

Prozan, V. M. "A Religious Survey of the Bahama Islands, British West Indies." M.A. thesis, Columbia Bible College, 1961.

Rogozinski, Jan. *A Brief History of the Caribbean, from the Arawak and Carib to the Present.* Rev. ed. New York: Plume Books–Penguin Group, 1999.

Thompson, J. K. *The Rise of the Seventh-day Adventist Church in the Bahamas and the Cayman Islands.* Nassau, Bahamas, 1992.

U.S. Central Intelligence Agency, *The World Fact Book* (2009). www.cia.gov/library/publications.

U.S. Department of State. *International Religious Freedom Report 2008.* http://www.state.gov/g/drl/rls/irf/2008/108512.htm.

Williams, C. *The Methodist Contribution to Education in the Bahamas (circa 1790-1975).* Gloucester, UK: A. Sutton, 1982.

Wooly Days website. "Rastaman Political Vibration" (February 24, 2007). http://nebuchadnezzarwoollyd.blogspot.com/2007/02/rastaman-political-vibration.html.

Bahamas National Baptist Missionary and Education Convention

The Baptist Church came to the Bahamas in 1780 in the person of Frank Spence, an African American who had left slavery to join the British during the American Revolution. He had left the South during the war and finally made his way to Long Island, New York, from which he was transported to Nassau. He began preaching and by the 1830s oversaw a chapel that could hold some 900 worshippers. Other Baptist preachers with a similar story also found their way to the islands.

In 1833, the Baptist Missionary Society (supported by British Baptists) arrived, and the members were appalled by the conditions they found. They took control of two congregations, dissolved them, and reconstituted them by accepting only the minority who had maintained what they considered a moral life. In the process one of the congregations broke with the missionaries and founded the independent Native Baptist Church. Through the decades additional schisms rent the growing church.

Crucial to the growing movement, the National Baptist Convention, U.S.A., a large African American denomination, took an interest in the Bahamas and began supporting the work. Their entrance into the field coincided with the lessening of the Baptist Missionary Society's presence, which was completely withdrawn in 1931. The National Baptists encouraged the Bahamians to unite and in 1935 inspired the formation of the Bahamas Baptist Missionary and Educational Convention, which brought six different groups together. The Southern Baptist Convention added its support to that of the National Baptists.

The new Convention launched an educational program in 1943 with the founding of Jordan Memorial School. Jordan Memorial has recently merged with a second school, founded in 1961, to become the Jordan-Prince Williams Baptist School. The Convention also oversees the Bahamas Baptist Bible Institute and the Bahamas Baptist College. (The institute had begun in 1953 as an effort of two Southern Baptist missionaries.)

In 1971, Baptists adopted a new constitution in an effort to bring greater unity to the movement, with the former association that constitutes the Convention retaining a considerable amount of power in managing the affairs of the churches associated with it.

In 2007 the Convention reported some 75,000 members in 270 churches, making it the largest religious group in the islands. It is a member of the Baptist World Alliance.

Bahamas National Baptist Missionary and
    Educational Convention
PO Box N-4435
Nassau
Bahamas

J. Gordon Melton

See also: Baptist World Alliance; National Baptist Convention, U.S.A.; Southern Baptist Convention.

References

Canzoneri, Antonina. "Early History of the Baptists in the Bahamas." *Journal of the Bahamas Historical Society* 4 (October 1982): 9–16.

Symonette, Michael C., and Antonina Canzoneri. *Baptists in the Bahamas*. El Paso, TX: Baptist Publishing House, 1977.

Bahá'u'lláh

1817–1892

Mírzá Husayn-'Alí of Núr, titled Bahá'u'lláh, was the founder of the Baha'i Faith. Born on November 12, 1817, in Tehran, Iran, he was the son of Khadijih Khánum and Mírzá Buzurg, a prominent aristocrat and government official. He married just before his 18th birthday to Ásíyih of Yálrúd, called Navváb; as was fitting of Persian aristocrats of the day, he later married twice more. He had 14 children, of whom 8 survived to adulthood.

In 1844 Bahá'u'lláh accepted the claims of 'Alí-Muhammad of Shiraz, titled the Báb, to be a divine messenger, becoming a member of the Bábí religion. He soon emerged as a prominent Bábí leader. For his prominence in the Bábí community, Bahá'u'lláh was tortured and imprisoned, and his property was confiscated. While confined in an underground dungeon in late 1852, Bahá'u'lláh had a vision of a "maid of heaven," which symbolically marked the beginning of his ministry.

In early 1853 he was exiled from Iran to Baghdad. There, he set about to rebuild the Bábí community, which had been decimated by severe persecution. Difficulties prompted him to retreat to the mountains of Kurdistan for two years. Back in Baghdad in March 1856, Bahá'u'lláh began to compose treatises. *The Seven Valleys* and *The Four Valleys* provided mystic insights into the journey of the soul; *The Hidden Words* consisted of spiritual and ethical aphorisms; *Gems of Divine Mysteries* explored various theological and mystical subjects; the *Book of Certitude* expounded on biblical and Koranic doctrines. In none of the books did Bahá'u'lláh make an explicit claim to divine revelation, but he frequently alluded to a divine source to his knowledge.

Bahá'u'lláh's emergence as the central figure in a reviving Bábí community prompted the Iranian government to ask the Ottoman Turkish government to remove him farther from their borders, so in the spring of 1863 Bahá'u'lláh was summoned to Istanbul, the imperial capital. In late April, before a gathering of his closest followers in a garden named Ridván (paradise), Bahá'u'lláh proclaimed that he was "he whom God shall make manifest" the divine messenger promised by the Báb. The event marked the official beginning of his ministry.

After some months in Istanbul, Bahá'u'lláh was further exiled to Edirne, a city in European Turkey. For four years Bahá'u'lláh composed scores of epistles and treatises, generally referred to by Baha'is as tablets, including the first of a series of letters to monarchs proclaiming his divine mission. The vast majority of Bábís, hearing about his claims and reading his writings, became Baha'is. This aroused the jealousy of his half-brother Yahyá (1831–1912), who was the symbolic head of the Bábí community, and he tried to poison Bahá'u'lláh. The rupture split Bahá'u'lláh's family in half and aroused the ire of the Turkish government, who exiled Bahá'u'lláh and the majority of his followers to the pestilential prison city of Akka on the Palestinian coast. Yahyá and most of his small band of followers were sent to Famagusta, Cyprus.

In Akka, Bahá'u'lláh and his followers were confined to prison for more than two years. Three died of illness, but gradually conditions improved and they were allowed to rent houses within the city walls. In 1877 Bahá'u'lláh was permitted to leave the city and rent various residences outside the walls, but he remained an exile the rest of his life and died outside Akka on May 28, 1892, at age 74.

The Akka period was Bahá'u'lláh's most prolific from a literary point of view. He rarely wrote; usually he chanted a text as it came to him and a secretary, who had developed a form of Arabic shorthand, wrote it down, then transcribed it and presented the draft to Bahá'u'lláh for correction. In Akka he completed his series of epistles to monarchs, including a second tablet to Napoleon III predicting his downfall and a tablet to Pope Pius IX abolishing the clergy and proclaiming himself the return of Christ. In 1873 he revealed the Kitáb-i-Aqdas, or Most Holy Book, which delineated the Faith's laws of prayer, fasting, and personal conduct, defined its main holy days, and outlined its organization. A series of works elaborated on the Aqdas and enunciated principles of social reform such as collective security, the need for a world governing system, the selection of an international auxiliary language, the obligation to educate all children, the spiritual importance of work, and the importance of consorting with all peoples in friendliness and fellowship. Altogether, Bahá'u'lláh composed some 15,000 works, mostly letters to individuals; they have been collected by the Baha'i World Center in Haifa, Israel, have been indexed, and are being translated. Many were in reply to letters brought to Bahá'u'lláh by Baha'i pilgrims, who carried his responses home and disseminated them.

In many tablets Bahá'u'lláh made it clear that after his death his eldest son 'Abbás, titled 'Abdu'l-Bahá (1844–1921), was to succeed him as head of the Baha'i Faith. Consequently the Faith's unity was preserved upon Bahá'u'lláh's passing. Today his tomb, in northern Israel, is a center of Baha'i pilgrimage.

Robert Stockman

See also: Baha'i Faith; Birth/Ascension of Bahá'u'lláh.

References

Bahá'u'lláh. *Selected Writings of Baha'u'llah.* Wilmette, IL: Baha'i Publishing, 2005.

Cedarquist, Druzelle. *The Story of Baha'u'llah, Promised One of All Religions.* Wilmette, IL: Baha'i Publishing, 2005.

Momen, Moojan. *Bahá'u'lláh: A Short Biography.* Oxford: Oneworld Publications, 2007.

■ Bahrain

Bahrain is an island nation consisting of one large island (30 by 9 miles) and 32 smaller islands located in the Persian Gulf, with a total land area of 256 square miles. Several of the islands lie just off the coast of Qatar. Of the 718,306 residents (2008), approximately a third are expatriates working in the petroleum industry or business attracted to the country because of its

View of Bahrain's Al Fateh Mosque, the nation's largest religious edifice, located in the city of Juffair. The building also houses Bahrain's National Library. (iStockPhoto.com)

Bahrain

Religion	Followers in 1970	Followers in 2010	% of Population	Annual % growth 2000–2010	Followers in 2025	Followers in 2050
Muslims	209,000	661,000	83.4	2.14	788,000	928,000
Christians	8,200	73,500	9.3	4.04	108,000	142,000
Roman Catholics	1,800	45,000	5.7	6.15	65,000	80,000
Independents	1,800	11,000	1.4	1.50	17,500	28,000
Anglicans	2,500	5,600	0.7	0.74	6,000	7,500
Hindus	2,400	50,000	6.3	0.68	63,000	80,000
Agnostics	0	3,200	0.4	2.41	6,000	9,000
Baha'is	300	1,800	0.2	2.19	2,400	5,000
Buddhists	0	1,500	0.2	2.20	2,600	4,000
Jews	150	800	0.1	2.21	1,000	1,500
Atheists	0	260	0.0	2.18	500	1,000
New religionists	0	200	0.0	2.12	400	800
Ethnoreligionists	0	200	0.0	2.12	500	800
Total population	**220,000**	**792,000**	**100.0**	**2.20**	**972,000**	**1,173,000**

oil wealth. Bahrain has been important over the centuries as a trading center in the flow of goods between India and Mesopotamia. It gained additional importance in the 20th center as a source of oil. Christians arrived in the islands quite early and during the third century CE a bishopric was established. The Christian movement was overwhelmed and largely displaced by Islam. Islamic culture flourished from the 11th through the 15th centuries.

Then in 1507 the Portuguese arrived and brought Catholicism with them. However, a century later Christianity was again displaced when Persians (Iranians) drove the Portuguese out. The Persians ruled the land for a century but were then driven out by Sheikh al-Khalifah, who assumed power in 1782. He established a dynasty that has continued to rule into the 21st century. Though still ruled by this dynasty, from 1861 to 1971 Bahrain existed as a British Protectorate, the arrangement having begun due to fear that Persia might attempt to assert its hegemony over the island state. Since 1971, the country has existed as a fully independent nation.

Islam is the religion of Bahrain and is supported by legal structures, including laws against proselytization. However, the Muslim community is divided fairly equally between Sunni and Shia Islam, the latter enjoying a dominant role outside the urban areas. Divisions within the Muslim community are largely along national lines, there being many people from neighboring lands residing in Bahrain. The community has been especially influenced by the Wahhabi Sunni Muslims who dominate Saudi Arabia, especially since the opening in 1986 of the superhighway that connects the capital, al-Manamah, with the Arabian peninsula.

The Christian community had a third beginning in Bahrain in 1889 when representatives of the Arabic Mission of the Reformed Church in America began work concentrated in education and medical assistance. This effort exists today as the National Evangelical Church of Bahrain, which has four congregations. Amy Elizabeth Wilkes, the first Anglican in Bahrain, was sent by the Church Missionary Society in 1895 to work in Baghdad. However, she met and married Samuel Zwemer, the head of the Reformed work, and settled in Bahrain to assist him with what was known then as the American Mission. Only in the 1930s did enough Anglicans reside in Bahrain to organize a separate Anglican parish, and it was not until 1951 that a chaplain was secured. St. Christopher's Church (now St. Christopher's Cathedral), was dedicated two years later. The Anglicans, primarily expatriate British residents, now have the largest number of members among the small Christian community. The several congregations in Bahrain are part of the Diocese of Cyprus and the Gulf of the Episcopal Church in Jerusalem and the Middle East. The Roman Catholic Church created a

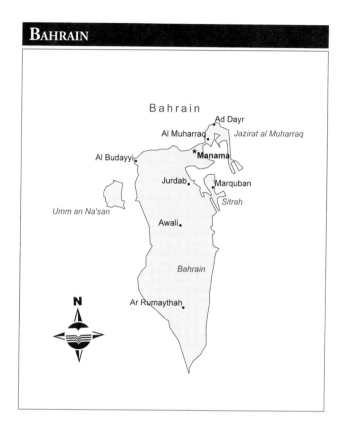

BAHRAIN

Bahrain

Ad Dayr
Al Muharraq
Jazirat al Muharraq
Al Budayyi
★Manama
Jurdab
Marquban
Sitrah
Umm an Na'san
Awali
Bahrain
N
Ar Rumaythah

See also: Baha'i Faith; Church of South India; Episcopal Church in Jerusalem and the Middle East; Mar Thoma Syrian Church of Malabar; Reformed Church in America; Roman Catholic Church; Shia Islam; Wahhabi Islam.

References

Barrett, David, ed. *The Encyclopedia of World Christianity*. 2nd ed. New York: Oxford University Press, 2001.

Bissio, Roberto Remo, et al. *Third World Guide 93/94*. Montevideo, Uruguay: Instituto del Tercer Mundo, 1992.

Horner, N. A. "Present-Day Christianity in the Gulf States of the Arabian Peninsula." *Occasional Bulletin of Missionary Research* 2 (April 1978): 53–63.

Love, Life & Light of Bahrain. 3 vols. Bahrain: Miracle Publishing, 2004.

Bailey, Alice Ann

1880–1949

Alice Ann Bailey, a prominent Theosophical teacher and founder of the Arcane School, was born June 16, 1880, in Manchester, England. She had a rather confined childhood. Religiously, she was raised as a devout member of the Church of England, but at the age of 15 had a life-changing experience. One Sunday, as she was in her room at home, a stranger, dressed in a business suit but wearing a turban, entered and sat beside her. He confided to her that she had an important future mission to fulfill and that she should prepare herself for it. She initially thought that the person was Christ.

After completing finishing school, she worked for the YWCA in India. While there she met her first husband, John Evans. They moved to the United States, where he studied for the Episcopal Church ministry. After his ordination, they moved to California. They had three children, but their marriage experienced a variety of troubles. They separated in 1915 and were formally divorced four years later.

In 1915, Alice initially encountered the Theosophical Society. She visited the Society's headquarters in

prefecture for Arabia in 1875 that included Bahrain in its assigned territory, but it was not until 1938 that its first (and only) parish was opened in al-Manamah. The parish is part of the present vicariate of Arabia, and its priests and religious also serve the Catholic community of Oman.

Given the size of the Christian community, it is extremely diverse, consisting almost totally of expatriates from different countries who have been allowed to bring their religion with them. The largest groups, from India, support the Mar Thoma Syrian Church, the St. Thomas Evangelical Church, the Church of South India, and the Orthodox Syrian Church of India, among others. A variety of small evangelical groups also operate within the Indian, British, and American expatriate communities. Although no Arab Bahrainis are openly Christian, observers suggest that there are many secret Christians who have quietly responded to the many radio broadcasts beamed into Bahrain from other countries.

Even smaller than Christianity in Bahrain, Hinduism has several thousand adherents and the Baha'i Faith several hundred, also all expatriates.

J. Gordon Melton

Los Angeles, where she was startled to find a picture of a man in a turban, the same person who had appeared to her in England when she was 15 years old. She later learned that picture showed someone named Koot Houmi, one of the Ascended Masters that had communicated with the Society's founder Helena P. Blavatsky. She joined the Society and become an active member. Through it, she met her future husband, Foster Bailey.

During her early years with the Society, she was contacted by another of the Ascended Masters, Dwjhal Khul, usually referred to as D.K. or simply The Tibetan. Bailey began to channel writings from the Tibetan, and these writings, received over many years would be compiled into some 19 books. The first book, *Initiation: Human and Solar*, was initially well received by the Theosophical Society's membership, but the Society's international president Annie Besant (1847–1933) rejected it. She was skeptical of writings received independently from the Masters (a major issue in her earlier break with one of Theosophy's co-founders, William Q. Judge). Soon after the book appeared, both Alice and her future husband were soon dismissed from their positions in the Society.

Alice and Foster married in 1921. They subsequently founded the Lucis Trust to publish and the Arcane School to disseminate the writings of The Tibetan. The teachings articulated in his books continued the Western Esoteric tradition (with a dash of Hinduism and Buddhism) initially articulated by Madame Blavatsky. The Tibetan emphasized the Divine Plan for humankind's evolution, the role of karma and reincarnation, and further contact with the spiritual hierarchy. Bailey was unique in introducing a set of three ceremonies to be observed annually, as well as a ritual to be observed monthly at the full moon, all of which were designed to assist the spiritual hierarchy in implementing the plan for humanity.

Alice Bailey led the Arcane School until her death on December 15, 1949, in New York City, where she had established Arcane School headquarters in the shadow of the United Nations. Following her death there were several schisms in the school, over which Foster had assumed control. Today, the Arcane School continues as an international organization perpetuating Bailey's teachings and practices. There are also several smaller additional groups.

J. Gordon Melton

See also: Arcane School; Besant, Annie; Blavatsky, Helena B.; Theosophical Society (American).

References

Bailey, Alice A. *The Externalisation of the Hierarchy.* New York and London: Lucis Publishing, 1957.

Bailey, Alice A. *Initiation, Human and Solar.* New York and London: Lucis Publishing, 1922.

Bailey, Alice A. *The Reappearance of the Christ.* New York and London: Lucis Publishing, 1948.

Sinclair, John R. *The Alice Bailey Inheritance.* Wellingborough, England: Turnstone Press, 1985.

Thirty Years Work the Books of Alice A Bailey and the Tibetan Master Djwhal Khul. New York and London: Lucis Publishing, 1957.

■ Bangladesh

After existing for several decades as the eastern half of Pakistan, what became the new nation of Bangladesh separated from Pakistan and became an independent nation in 1971. Its 52,000 square miles of land is home to 153,546,896 people. The development of the country has been hindered by flooding, with approximately a third of the land going under water each year during the rainy season.

Though one of the newer nations of the world, Bangladesh traces its history to the ancient kingdom of Banga and to the story of India recorded in the *Mahabharata*. In the 17th century, the British named the area of present-day Bangladesh and the section of India to the west, Bengal. In 1947, England divided the area into West Bengal (dominated by Hindus) and East Bengal (dominated by Muslims). East Bengal then became East Pakistan at the time the new nation of Pakistan was created. Through the 1950s and 1960s, the people of East Pakistan felt that it was being treated as the lesser partner in the new nation, and in 1971 they broke free. Bangladesh (literally, the land of the Bengali-speaking people) also differed linguistically

Bangladesh

Religion	Followers in 1970	Followers in 2010	% of Population	Annual % growth 2000–2010	Followers in 2025	Followers in 2050
Muslims	54,278,000	148,078,000	88.9	2.03	184,575,000	228,477,000
Hindus	14,500,000	15,600,000	9.4	0.89	17,700,000	20,700,000
Buddhists	450,000	1,065,000	0.6	1.91	1,320,000	1,630,000
Ethnoreligionists	300,000	862,000	0.5	1.98	950,000	1,150,000
Christians	249,000	859,000	0.5	2.14	1,253,000	1,784,000
Roman Catholics	120,000	320,000	0.2	2.00	450,000	600,000
Independents	51,000	340,000	0.2	3.11	500,000	700,000
Protestants	76,300	195,000	0.1	0.90	300,000	480,000
Agnostics	20,000	123,000	0.1	1.99	160,000	250,000
Sikhs	6,000	27,100	0.0	1.91	30,000	43,000
Atheists	10,000	13,000	0.0	2.03	20,000	30,000
Baha'is	3,200	10,300	0.0	1.91	15,000	20,000
Zoroastrians	200	350	0.0	1.92	400	700
Jews	0	190	0.0	1.96	200	200
Total population	**69,817,000**	**166,638,000**	**100.0**	**1.91**	**206,024,000**	**254,084,000**

from West Pakistan, where Urdu and Punjabi were the dominant languages.

Hinduism flourished in the area for centuries, but in the 13th century Muslims from Afghanistan swept across the lands immediately south of the Himalayas, and Muslim rule was established in Banga. Various dynasties came and went prior to the 17th-century arrival of the Portuguese, the first Europeans in the area. They were followed by the Armenians, French, and British. The British expanded their trade through the 18th century to the point that, following the Battle of Plassey in 1757, it was able to take control of the region, later incorporating it into India. The people of East Bengal participated in the move to free India from British rule, thus setting the stage for the events that led to the reestablishment of the nation in 1971.

In the years following the Muslim conquest, Islam replaced Hinduism as the primary religion and today claims more than 80 percent of the population. Most follow the Sunni Hanafite School of Islam, but there is a significant Wahhabi minority and some followers of Shia Islam (most of whom trace their ancestry to Persia). The Ahmadiyya Muslim movement, condemned as not Muslim in Pakistan, as well as Subud (an Indonesian Sufi movement), has also established a presence in Bangladesh. The Baha'i Faith, a new religion from Iran with roots in Shia Islam, began to spread in

Bangladesh after being initially established among Iranian expatriates.

In 1975, the government declared Bangladesh an Islamic state. Though making up more than 80 percent of the population in Bangladesh, Muslims have been mild in their treatment of members of other faiths, especially Christians, Hindus, and Buddhists. Various interfaith efforts, such as the Bangladesh Buddhist Christian Hindu Unity Council, have made important contributions to social unity.

Roman Catholicism was introduced into the area in the 16th century by the Portuguese, but it was not until 1886 that it had grown to the point that a diocese could be erected. It found particular strength among descendants of those Portuguese who had intermarried with native Bengalis.

British Baptist William Carey, at the behest of the Baptist Missionary Society, initiated one of the great thrusts of Christian missionary history with his arrival in Bengal in 1793. The effort radiated out from Calcutta, by 1795 was in East Bengal, and by 1816 had been established in Dhaka. This work was incorporated into the Bengal Baptist Union. The Union's work in East Bengal emerged, after several name changes, as the Bangladesh Baptist Sangha. Australian Baptists working along parallel lines built, beginning in the 1880s, what became the Bangladesh Baptist

Thousands of Muslim pilgrims crowd a train in Tongi, 15 kilometers (10 miles) north of Dhaka, December 30, 1996, to return home after a three-day Islamic festival. At least 2 million Muslims prayed for the unity of the Islamic Ummah. (AP/Wide World Photos)

Fellowship. Its efforts were increased by the merger with separate work initiated by New Zealand Baptists and missionaries of the Southern Baptist Convention. Carey is also remembered for doing the first translation of the Bible into Bengali.

Anglicans initiated work on the Indian subcontinent in the 17th century primarily to serve those involved in trade with the East India Company; however, it was not until early in the 19th century that missionaries settled in East Bengal. About this same time, 1817, Presbyterians from the Church of Scotland launched a mission. In 1924, the Church of England mission, the Presbyterians, and the Congregationalists of East Bengal joined the United Church of North India. Shortly thereafter the Anglicans withdrew from the United Church in order to form the Anglican Church in India, later known as the Church of India, Pakistan, Burma,

and Ceylon. Those two churches (along with various Methodist and Baptist bodies) began what proved to be a 40-year negotiation process. In the 1970s, they finally created two churches, the Church of Pakistan and the Church of North India. The Church of Pakistan was no sooner created than the war that led to the establishment of Bangladesh as a separate nation occurred. Thus in 1971, the Diocese of Dhaka was set apart as the Church of Bangladesh.

Also entering East Bengal in the 19th century were the Lutherans. The present Bangladesh Evangelical Lutheran Church was initiated by Norwegians, with later assistance from Denmark and the United States. Several Holiness and Pentecostal bodies initiated work early in the 20th century, and the number of American missionary groups has grown considerably since World War II.

BANGLADESH

Among the more interesting Christian churches in the country are the indigenous churches, such as the Bengal Evangelistic Mission (which dates to 1833) and the All One in Christ Fellowship. The Jehovah's Witnesses entered East Bengal in the 1930s, and the Church of Jesus Christ of Latter-day Saints in the 1980s.

Christian ecumenism is focused in the Bangladesh National Council of Churches, founded in 1954 as the East Pakistan Christian Council. It cooperates with the World Council of Churches. More conservative evangelical denominations are united by the Evangelical Fellowship of India, which in turn is related to the World Evangelical Alliance.

Although the country is predominantly Muslim, there is a significant Hindu and Buddhist presence in Bangladesh. Since the independence of Bangladesh, there has been a tendency of Hindus (drawn from across the spectrum of Bengali Hinduism) to migrate to India. During the same period, the International Society for Krishna Consciousness, an American Hindu body with Bengali roots, has established work in Bangladesh. Buddhists tend to be concentrated in the easternmost part of Bangladesh, among various peoples residing east of Chittagong.

In the rural areas of the country, there are still peoples who follow traditional indigenous religions that are part of neither Hinduism nor Buddhism.

J. Gordon Melton

See also: Ahmadiyya Movement in Islam; Baha'i Faith; Bangladesh Baptist Sangha; Church of Bangladesh; Church of England; Church of Jesus Christ of Latter-day Saints; Church of North India; Church of Pakistan; Church of Scotland; Hanafite School of Islam; International Society for Krishna Consciousness; Jehovah's Witnesses; Shia Islam; Southern Baptist Convention; Subud; Wahhabi Islam; World Council of Churches; World Evangelical Alliance.

References

Baum, R. A. *Islam in Bangladesh*. International Studies in Sociology and Social Anthropology, vol. 58. Leiden: E. J. Brill, 1991.

Biswas, S. *Religion and Politics in Bangladesh and West Bengal: A Study of Communal Relations*. Tokyo: Institute of Developing Economies, 1993.

Khan, A. K. *Christian Mission in Bangladesh: A Survey*. Leicester, UK: Islamic Foundation, 1982.

Roy, A. *The Islamic Syncretistic Tradition in Bengal*. Princeton, NJ: Princeton University Press, 1983.

Uddin, Sufia M. *Constructing Bangladesh: Religion, Ethnicity, and Language in an Islamic Nation*. Chapel Hill: University of North Carolina Press, 2006.

Bangladesh Baptist Sangha

British Baptists began their missionary enterprise in Bengal, north of Calcutta. The work quickly spread to East Bengal. They had little success among the Hindu and Muslim communities, but found a ready audience among various peoples in the backcountry, especially among the hill people east and south of Chittagong in the southeastern part of East Bengal. The work in Bengal grew up as a single mission, and that mission was reorganized in 1935 as the Bengal Baptist Union.

In East Bengal, a number of primary and secondary schools were established as well as a hospital at Chandraghona in 1907. Pastors are trained at the Pastors Training School at Dhaka, and through the College of Christian Theology, a cooperative project with several other Protestant groups.

In 1947 East Bengal left the nation of India and became part of Pakistan. In 1956, following the renaming of East Bengal as East Pakistan, the Bengal Baptist Union divided, and East Bengal was set apart as the Baptist Union of Pakistan. At that time East Bengal became a separate field for the missionary work of the Baptist Missionary Association representing the Baptist Union of Great Britain. East Pakistan separated from Pakistan and became the state of Bangladesh in 1970–1971. Subsequently the Baptist Union of Pakistan was renamed the Bangladesh Baptist Sangha.

In 2008 the Sangha reported 17,144 members in 347 congregations. In the new century, the Baptists remain the largest Protestant group in Bangladesh, and the Bangladesh Baptist Sangha (also known as the Communion of Baptist Churches in Bangladesh) is the largest of the several Baptist churches. It is a member of the Baptist World Alliance.

Bangladesh Baptist Sangha
33, Senpara Parbatta
Mirpur-10, Dhaka 12 16
Bangladesh

J. Gordon Melton

See also: Baptist Union of Great Britain; Baptist World Alliance.

References

Ahmed, R. *Islam in Bangladesh: Society, Culture and Politics*. Dhaka: Bangladesh Itihas Samiti, 1993.

Soddy, Gordon. *Baptists in Bangladesh*. Khulnu, Bangladesh: Literature Committee, National Council of Churches, Bangladesh, 1987.

Baptist Association of El Salvador

Baptist work in the small Central American nation of El Salvador began relatively late, in 1911, but built upon earlier work by independent evangelicals with Baptist leanings. Since the late 19th century, Protes-

Parishioners pray on May 20, 2005, in the central church of the Biblical Tabernacle Baptist in San Salvador, at the beginning of an 18-hour prayer vigil to demand the freedom for Minister Edgar Lopez Bertrand. (AP/Wide World Photos)

The work matured to the point that the Baptist Association of El Salvador was founded in 1934. The American Baptist Home Mission Society continued its support, though in 1941 the seminary it had established was moved to Nicaragua. The Southern Baptist Convention added its support in 1974 through the assignment of a missionary couple to develop the literature ministry. They opened a bookstore, which cooperates with various Baptist groups in the country. The British Baptist Union, through the Baptist Missionary Association, added its support to the Nicaragua Association in 1988.

In 2005, the Baptist Association of El Salvador reported 5,927 members in 57 churches. Not a part of the Association is the 5,000-member independent Baptist Church in San Salvador, which claims to be the largest Baptist congregation in Latin America. The Association is a member of the Baptist World Alliance and since 1991 of the World Council of Churches.

Baptist Association of El Salvador
Av. Sierra Nevada 922, Apartado 347
San Salvador
El Salvador

J. Gordon Melton

See also: American Baptist Churches in the U.S.A.; Baptist World Alliance; World Council of Churches.

References

Beers, G. Pitt. *Ministry to Turbulent America.* Philadelphia: Judson Press, 1957.

Kirkwood, Dean R. *Renewal amid Revolution.* Valley Forge: International Ministries, American Baptist Churches of the U.S.A., 1980.

Van Beek, Huibert. *A Handbook of the Churches and Councils: Profiles of Ecumenical Relationships.* Geneva: World Council of Churches, 2006.

Baptist Bible Fellowship International

The Baptist Bible Fellowship International grew out of the World Baptist Fellowship, which in turn had arisen within the Southern Baptist Convention. At the height of the fundamentalist-modernist controversy in

tant distributors of Christian literature had traveled the country, and several autonomous missions had been established. In 1911 the American Baptist Home Mission Society (now an integral part of the American Baptist Churches in the U.S.A.) adopted William Keech, formerly superintendent of the British and Foreign Bible Society in Central America, to lead its work, and the Society found its first group in adopting the mission in Santa Ana already begun by Percy T. Chapman and his wife. Chapman quickly extended the work by organizing groups that had emerged from the distribution of Christian literature. The Woman's American Baptist Home Mission Society added their strength to the work and began to found elementary schools.

Statue of J. Frank Norris, Dallas, Texas. (J. Gordon Melton)

the 1930s, J. Frank Norris (1877–1952), pastor of the First Baptist Church of Fort Worth, Texas, emerged as a leading conservative fundamentalist voice. As pastor of a 28,000-member parish, he began to accuse the leadership in the convention of tendencies toward Modernism (deviation from traditional Christian beliefs in response to modern changes) and cooperation with various ecumenical structures. As early as 1924, he was excluded from the Texas Baptist Convention, and then in 1931 he resigned from the Southern Baptist Convention and formed the Premillennial Fundamental Missionary Fellowship to raise money for fundamentalist missionaries in China.

Once separated from the Southern Baptists, Norris set about the task of building the fundamentalist cause nationally, and the Missionary Fellowship evolved into the World Baptist Association. The flamboyant and somewhat autocratic Norris drew many conservative pastors to his cause and trained others at the Arlington Baptist College. He also ultimately pushed away many of his followers by his manner.

In 1948, the aging Norris, who had also become pastor of a second church in Detroit, Michigan, turned the church congregation in Texas over to G. Beauchamp Vick (1901–1975). Two years later, Vick and Norris clashed at the annual meeting of the World Baptist Association, and Vick withdrew and with his supporters founded the Baptist Bible Fellowship. Also formerly the president of Arlington Baptist College, Vick quickly moved to found the Baptist Bible College in Springfield, Missouri, and the *Baptist Bible Tribune*. With Norris's death two years later, the Baptist Bible Fellowship emerged as the most vital force in the continuing fundamentalist cause within the American Baptist community. It immediately gained support in the South and Midwest, and by the mid-1970s had become a national body. It also developed an aggressive evangelism and missionary program, and it became known for the large Sunday schools developed by its leading congregations.

In 1997 the Baptist Bible Fellowship International reported 1,700,000 members in 4,500 churches in the United States. In addition it supports more than 750 missionaries in 70 countries. Besides the original Baptist Bible College (and its associated Baptist Bible Graduate School of Theology), the Fellowship supports five additional colleges. The Fellowship is not a member of any ecumenical groups. One of the Fellowship's former ministers, Jerry Falwell (1993–2007), left to become one of America's leading televangelists in the late 20th century and founder of Liberty University and Liberty Baptist Fellowship.

The Fellowship's leaders follow a premillennial dispensational theology of the kind exemplified in the *Scofield Reference Bible* and the teaching of Irish theologian John Nelson Darby (1800–1882), founder of the Plymouth Brethren movement.

Baptist Bible Fellowship International
PO Box 191
Springfield, MO 65801
www.bbfi.org

J. Gordon Melton

See also: Darby, John Nelson; Southern Baptist Convention.

References

Bartlett, Billy Vick. *A History of Baptist Separatism.* Springfield, MO: the author, 1972.

Falwell, Jerry. *The Fundamentalist Phenomena.* Garden City, NY: Doubleday, 1981.

Baptist Convention of Haiti

Formed in 1964, the Baptist Convention of Haiti inherited the work of various Baptist bodies, including the American Baptist Churches in the U.S.A. and the Southern Baptist Convention in northern Haiti. The work dates to the 1815 arrival of famed African American minister Thomas Paul (1773–1831) who was sent to Cap Haitien from Boston, Massachusetts. He stayed only six months and was greatly hindered by his inability to speak French, but he left a small core group that would later be served by successive missionaries, many sponsored by the Baptist Free Missionary Society. Jean Jacques Lillevoix, ordained in 1852, was the first Haitian pastor.

The churches of the Convention follow the Baptists in belief and practice. Its conservative theological orientation is reflected in its membership in the Council of Evangelical Churches of Haiti. Local churches are autonomous but associated together in the delegated general assembly, which meets annually. In the 1990s, the Convention became open to female pastors and subsequently sanctioned the ordination of the first woman minister in 1998. The Convention supports the Christian University of Northern Haiti, which includes the Baptist Theological Seminary of Haiti, and sponsors a variety of educational and social service centers.

Second grade students eat during lunchtime at Nosirel Lherisson, a private Baptist school in the slum of Bel-Air in Port-au-Prince, Haiti, on September 25, 2006. (AP/Wide World Photos)

By 2005, the Convention reported 82,000 members in 110 congregations. It joined the World Council of Churches in 2005. It is also a member of the Baptist World Alliance.

J. Gordon Melton

See also: American Baptist Churches in the U.S.A.; Baptist World Alliance; Southern Baptist Convention; World Council of Churches.

References

Schweissing, Dan. "A History of American Baptist Missions in Haiti." http://haitianministries.blogspot.com/2008/06/history-of-american-baptist-missions-in.html. Accessed January 9, 2009.

Van Beek, Huibert. *A Handbook of the Churches and Councils: Profiles of Ecumenical Relationships.* Geneva: World Council of Churches, 2006.

Baptist Convention of Hong Kong

Even before China ceded Hong Kong to Great Britain in 1842, Baptists had begun to use it as an entry point for missionary activity farther inland. In 1836, John Lewis Shuck (1814–1863) arrived in Macao (a Portuguese colony since 1557) and moved on to Hong Kong in 1842. He opened the first Baptist church on Queen's Road, but after two years he moved to Canton. He had been joined in Hong Kong by William Dean, who opened the Tie Chiu Baptist Church. These two congregations were the first Baptist churches around the entire Pacific basin. The island remained the headquarters for American Baptists until 1860, when a shift was made to Swatow. Through the years, Baptist work in Hong Kong was kept alive even without missionary support and was eventually incorporated into the larger China mission of the Southern Baptist Convention (SBC) in 1881. In 1938 the Hong Kong Baptist Association was formed. The first Baptist missionaries (from the SBC) were stationed in Macao in 1910.

Hong Kong took on added importance following the Chinese Revolution and the expulsion of missionaries from China. Many moved to Hong Kong, which became the vital center of Baptist work. A number of primary schools were created, and Hong Kong Baptist Theological Seminary (1951) and Hong Kong College (now University) (1956) were established. The association matured into the Hong Kong Baptist Convention and grew into one of the strongest bodies in the territory.

In the 1990s, the Convention reported a membership of more than 45,000. It operates Baptist Press, which serves churches throughout Southeast Asia. The Convention is a member of the World Baptist Alliance.

Baptist Convention of Hong Kong
73 Waterloo Rd., 1st Floor
Kowloon
Hong Kong

J. Gordon Melton

See also: Baptists; World Baptist Alliance.

Reference

Wong, Paul Tat-Keung. *The History of Baptist Missions in Hong Kong.* Ph.D. diss., Baptist Theological Seminary, 1974.

Baptist Convention of Kenya

Missionary representatives of the Southern Baptist Convention arrived in Kenya in 1956, with the transfer of three families from their mission in Nigeria. Work was begun in Nairobi and Mombasa, and soon followed in the Nyeri region. The new mission found an immediate response, and the first church was formally initiated just two years later. The Shauri Mayo section of Nairobi became an early center of activity with the formation of a business college and community center.

Growth had proceeded to the point that the Nairobi Baptist Association was formed in 1961. The Southern Baptists continued to offer support in the form of both finances and personnel. Other local associations followed, and they joined together to form the Baptist Convention of Kenya in 1971. The Convention supports two secondary schools, a nonresidential theological college, and an effective correspondence course, the Bible Way, which has enrolled more than 150,000 Kenyans, including some 2,000 in the prison system. A coordinated evangelistic program is reaching out to the diverse language groups of the country. In one of its more successful campaigns in and around Mombasa in 1990, 84 new congregations were established.

The Baptist Convention joined the National Christian Council of Kenya but withdrew over differences of opinion with its stances. The Nairobi Baptist Convention has remained a member of the Council. The Convention has also withdrawn fellowship from the original Baptist congregation, the Nairobi Baptist Church, because of the latter's practice of open Communion.

In 2008 the Baptist Convention of Kenya reported 700,000 members in 3,000 churches. It is a member of the Baptist World Alliance.

Baptist Convention of Kenya
PO Box 14907
Nairobi
Kenya

J. Gordon Melton

See also: Baptist World Alliance; Southern Baptist Convention.

Reference

Saunders, Davis Lee. *A History of Baptists in East and Central Africa.* Th.D. diss., Southern Baptist Theological Seminary, 1973.

Ebenezer Baptist Church, built in 1852, on Corn Island, Nicaragua. (Rjlerich/Dreamstime.com)

Baptist Convention of Nicaragua

In the 1840s, the Moravians opened work along the Miskito Coast, an area along the eastern coast of Nicaragua that at the time had existed for many years as a semi-autonomous region under the leadership of a local ruler loosely aligned to the British. In 1850, the Clayton-Bulwer Treaty assigned this land to Nicaragua as a protectorate, though it was many years before any effective authority was established in the area.

Baptist work began from Belize, where the Baptist Missionary Society (BMS) had been working since 1822. In 1850 the BMS withdrew from Belize and liquidated its property. Thus it was that in 1852 a young missionary, Edward Kelly (d. 1914), was free to come to Corn Island on the Miskito Coast. His work was interrupted in 1865 when a hurricane hit the coast and destroyed the chapel that had been built. After being

away for more than a decade, he returned in 1880 and devoted the rest of his life to the mission.

In 1916, the American Baptist Home Mission Society (ABHMS) (now an integral part of the American Baptist Churches in the U.S.A.) held a significant conference in Panama on the need for missions in Latin America. This conference led directly to the expansion of Baptist work to the larger Spanish-speaking part of Nicaragua. The Woman's American Baptist Home Mission Society adopted Eleanore Blackmore, already working in Nicaragua, and in 1917 the ABHMS sent George H. Brewer, who organized a church in Managua in 1918. The work had a slow but steady growth. The Woman's Society founded schools and a hospital, and later a college was opened in Managua. In 1941, the Central American Seminary, originally opened in El Salvador, was moved to Nicaragua.

The mission matured into the Baptist Convention of Nicaragua (Convención Bautista de Nicaragua) in 1937. It continued to be supported by American Baptists, and Southern Baptists added their support in 1990 with the assignment of Jim and Viola Palmer to Nicaragua. The Palmers had previously worked in Honduras.

The Convention faced a serious challenge during the Sandinista era (1979–1990), as it attempted to remain politically neutral while extending freedom to its members to hold conflicting political views. In 1992 the Convention experienced sudden growth from the incorporation of 12 churches that previously comprised the Miskito Baptist Association, an independent work built by Nicaraguan native Denis Centero.

In 2005, the Convention reported 25,000 members in 170 churches. It is a member of the Baptist World Alliance and the World Council of Churches.

Baptist Convention of Nicaragua
Aopartado postal 2593
Managua
Nicaragua

J. Gordon Melton

See also: American Baptist Churches in the U.S.A.; Baptist World Alliance; World Council of Churches.

References

Beers, G. Pitt. *Ministry to Turbulent America.* Philadelphia: Judson Press, 1957.

Kirkwood, Dean R. *Renewal amid Revolution.* Valley Forge: International Ministries, American Baptist Churches of the U.S.A., 1980.

Van Beek, Huibert. *A Handbook of the Churches and Councils: Profiles of Ecumenical Relationships.* Geneva: World Council of Churches, 2006.

Baptist Convention of Ontario and Quebec

The Baptist Convention of Ontario and Quebec (also known as Canadian Baptists in Ontario and Quebec) unites Baptists in east-central Canada in a voluntary association that facilitates mutually supported ministries and allows their speaking with one voice to the larger culture. The Convention was the result of a union in 1888 of the Regular Baptist Missionary Convention of Ontario, the Canada Baptist Missionary Conference of the East, and the Baptist Foreign Missionary Society of Ontario and Quebec. It had been a turbulent courtship with open and closed Communion, support of educational institutions such as McMaster College, and the role of the various societies being large issues.

At least 6 Baptist missionary societies from the new United States were involved in outreach in the colonies of Lower Canada (Quebec) and Upper Canada (Ontario) with at least 25 missionaries active before 1820. In 1794, Elisha Andrews (1768–1740) baptized at least 30 people and a Baptist church was formed at Caldwell's Manor. By 1800 there were some eight churches in the Canadas. In 1802, three churches in the Bay of Quinte area formed the Thurlow Association. The War of 1812 with its loyalty issues, the coming of the Scotch Baptists to the Ottawa River Valley, and the immigration of Baptist leaders from England all led to a lessened influence from the United States.

In 1927 doctrinal differences articulated by the fundamentalist preacher T. T. Shields (1873–1935) resulted in the current Fellowship of Evangelical Baptist Churches in Canada emerging from the Baptist Convention of Ontario and Quebec. This controversy and the eventual withdrawal of Shields and 70 of 490 churches and 8,500 of about 60,000 members is probably the most discussed incident in Canadian Baptist history.

In 1944, the Baptist Convention of Ontario and Quebec was a founding member of the Baptist Federation of Canada (Canadian Baptist Ministries since 1995) and the Canadian Council of Churches. It has 360 churches and 17 associations and is a partner with Baptist Women of Ontario and Quebec. McMaster Divinity College is its seminary. The Baptist Convention of Ontario and Quebec is a covenanting partner in Canadian Baptist Ministries and a member of the Evangelical Fellowship of Canada and Canadian Council of Churches.

Baptist Convention of Ontario and Quebec
100-304 The East Mall,
Etobicoke, ON
Canada M9B 6E2
http://www.baptist.ca/

Robert S. Wilson

See also: Canadian Baptist Ministries.

References

Bentall, Shirley. *From Sea to Sea: The Canadian Baptist Federation; 1944–1994*. Mississauga, ON: Canadian Baptist Federation, 1994.

Grant, John Webster. *The Church in the Canadian Experience*. Vancouver, BC: Regent College, 1998.

Priestley, David. "Introduction." In *Memory and Hope: Strands of Canadian Baptist History*, by David Priestly. Waterloo, ON: Wilfred Laurier University Press, 1996.

Renfree, Harry. *Heritage and Horizon: The Baptist Story in Canada*. Mississauga, ON: Canadian Baptist Federation, 1988.

Wilson, Robert S. "Patterns in Canadian Baptist Life," Global Baptist History, Papers Presented at the Second International Conference on Baptist Studies, Wake Forest University, July 19–22, 2000, *Baptist History and Heritage* 36, nos. 1–2 (Winter–Spring 2001).

Wilson, Robert S. "History of Canadian Baptists." In *Baptist History Celebration, 2007: A Symposium on our History, Theology, and Hymnology*. Springfield, MO: Particular Baptist Press, 2008.

Zeman, Jarold K. ed. *Baptists in Canada, Search for Identity Amidst Diversity*, Burlington, ON: G. R. Welsh, 1980.

Zeman, Jarold K. ed. *Costly Vision: The Baptist Pilgrimage in Canada*. Burlington, ON: G. R. Welsh, 1988.

Baptist Convention of Western Cuba

During the late 19th century, many Cubans came to the United States. Albert J. Díaz, who had joined a Baptist church in New York City, returned to his native land in 1882 and the following year organized the first Baptist congregation in the country in Havana. Word of what he had accomplished found its way to several Baptists in Key West, Florida, who in turn recommended that the Southern Baptist Convention send some missionaries to Havana to offer Díaz some sup-

port. Díaz himself came to Key West in 1885 and was ordained as a minister. Upon his return he reorganized his congregation as a Baptist church and led them to baptism in the harbor at Havana. Shortly thereafter, F. W. Wood moved from Florida to Cuba under the auspices of the Jamaica Baptist Missionary Society and began work in Cienfuegos. The Southern Baptists began giving support in 1886.

In 1886 the Spanish authorities granted some degree of religious toleration, which allowed Díaz to purchase a cemetery plot and a former theater as the new Baptist headquarters. The work continued to develop across the island during the Spanish American War (when Díaz was imprisoned) and the establishment of the independent Cuban government with an American-style Constitution. In the midst of these momentous occurrences, the Southern Baptists quietly worked out an agreement with the American Baptist Home Mission Society (now part of the American Baptist Churches in the U.S.A.) to divide the island. The American Baptists assumed responsibility for the eastern half and the Southern Baptist Convention for the western part (including Havana).

In 1901, the Southern Baptists sent C. D. Daniel to Havana as superintendent over the Baptist work. Taking this as a vote of no confidence, Díaz resigned. Four years later Daniel led in the formation of the Baptist Convention of Western Cuba. The same year Nathaniel McCall arrived to found the Colegio Bautista and commence theological training in Havana. He soon succeeded Daniel as head of the Convention and continued to lead it for the next 42 years. He was succeeded by Herbert Caudill.

In 1959, Fidel Castro came to power. He has headed a regime that has been generally hostile to religion, but the Baptist Church has been able to survive, though the government has nationalized its many schools. Many of the missionaries left in 1961 when Castro openly declared the Marxist base of the new government. Then in 1965 he arrested Caudill and 47 other leaders of the Baptist Convention of Western Cuba. Most were sentenced to prison for currency violations and cooperation with the Central Intelligence Agency. Caudell was allowed to leave the country in 1969. Cuban Baptists emerged from this experience both self-supporting and self-governing.

In the freer religious atmosphere generated in Cuba in the 1990s, the Baptists have experienced remarkable growth. In 2006 the Baptist Convention of Western Cuba reported 16,687 members in 209 churches. Like its counterpart in eastern Cuba, it has joined the Baptist World Alliance.

Baptist Convention of Western Cuba
Zulueta No. 502, Esq. Dragones
Habana 2
Cuba

J. Gordon Melton

See also: American Baptist Churches in the U.S.A.; Baptist World Alliance; Southern Baptist Convention.

References

Greer, Edward. "History of Southern Baptist Mission Work in Cuba, 1886–1916." M.A. thesis, University of Alabama, 1963.

Ramos, Marcos A. *Protestantism and Revolution in Cuba.* Coral Gables, FL: North-South Center for the Research Institute for Cuban Studies, University of Miami, 1989.

Baptist Union of Denmark

Baptist life in Denmark was deeply rooted in German Baptist work. Julius Köbner, the son of a Jewish rabbi, was converted to Christianity in 1826. Ten years later he was baptized by J. W. Oncken (1800–1884), the founder of the German Baptist movement. He became a close associate and assisted in the founding of the seminary in Hamburg and the spread of the Baptist movement throughout Europe.

In the late 1930s, Köbner established contact with some informal Bible study groups in Copenhagen, and toward the end of the 1830s he traveled to Denmark with Oncken and baptized 11 people. They formed the first Baptist church in Denmark in 1839. One of their number, Peder C. Monster, was arrested (on laws passed several centuries earlier against the Anabaptists) and later deported. Later Köbner returned to pastor the church. In 1849, the Union of Associated Churches of Baptized Christians in Germany and Denmark was formed. That same year, the laws governing religion were relaxed in Denmark, and the Baptists experi-

enced some religious freedom as a "tolerated" group. The Baptists could not, however, own property or solemnize weddings for their members, a privilege only granted in 1952.

In spite of obstacles, including the loss of many members to the Church of Jesus Christ of Latter-day Saints and the migration of a fourth of their members to the United States, the movement slowly grew. In 1888, it separated from the German Union and formed the Baptist Union of Denmark. By this time the group had built a relationship with American Baptists and accepted the New Hampshire Confession of Faith as their doctrinal statement. Their ministers were increasingly trained in the United States. By the end of the century, the Baptists had 28 churches. In 1906 they joined the Baptist World Alliance. In 1918 they created their own seminary.

In the decades since World War I, the Danish Baptists have become a more ecumenical church. They have absorbed elements of Lutheranism into their doctrine, they practice open Communion (meaning that non-Baptists may receive the Lord's Supper at their churches), and have accepted individuals from infant-baptizing traditions without rebaptizing them (the common standard in Baptist churches being a nonrecognition of infant baptism). They have been members of the World Council of Churches since its beginning in 1948, and they have also participated in the Lausanne Movement, a confessional movement of conservative evangelical Christians.

Danish Baptists have been active in foreign missions since 1928, when they began work in Burundi and Rwanda. They have continued in the last generation as a cooperative partner with the new postcolonial Baptist churches in Africa. In the 1990s, Knud Wümpelmann became the first Dane elected as president of the Baptist World Alliance. In 2005, the Union reported 20,000 members in 50 congregations.

Baptist Union of Denmark
c/o Reverend Ole Jørgensen, Gen. Sec.
Købnerhus
Lærdalsgade 5, 1
DK-2300 København S.
Denmark

J. Gordon Melton

See also: Baptist World Alliance; Church of Jesus Christ of Latter-day Saints; World Council of Churches.

References

Hylleberg, Bent, and Bjarne Moller Jorgesen. *Et kirkesamfund bliver til: Danske baptisters historie gennem 150 år*. Brabde, Denmark: Føltveds Forlag, 1989.

McBeth, H. Leon. *The Baptist Heritage: Four Centuries of the Baptist Witness*. Nashville: Broadman Press, 1987.

Parker, G. Keith. *Baptists in Europe: History & Confessions of Faith*. Nashville: Broadman Press, 1982.

Rushbrooke, J. H. *The Baptist Movement in the Continent of Europe*. London: Kingsgate Press, 1923.

Van Beek, Huibert. *A Handbook of the Churches and Councils: Profiles of Ecumenical Relationships*. Geneva: World Council of Churches, 2006.

Baptist Union of Great Britain

Baptists emerged in the context of British Puritanism, the continued effort to reform the Church of England, to "purify" it of all elements seen as unscriptural. During the Elizabethan era, some concluded that the Church of England could not be purified and that Christians should separate from it and organize congregations where proper belief prevailed and proper worship occurred, conclusions that gave them the name of Separatists. They believed that the church should be free of entanglement with the state and composed of those who actively professed the faith. Robert Browne (1550–1633) became a popular spokesperson for this position.

As the movement progressed, the logic of the Separatists led to several other conclusions, among them the belief that the local church should be the basic unit of organization of the church. The local church should be composed of baptized adult believers, and the proper biblical mode of baptism should be full immersion. The Separatists' emphasis on correct baptism later gave them their name. Their emphasis on the local church

meant that the development of church associations was a relatively low priority. The focus on the local church, each headed by a pastor with distinctive background and training, also allowed a variety of theological perspectives to arise.

The Baptists emerged within the context of the Reformed theology of John Calvin (1509–1564) (while rejecting the presbyterian polity he advocated) and the assertion of God's sovereignty and a belief in predestination. Reformed theology tended to affirm that God both foreknew and elected, or chose, those who would be saved. This view emphasized the need for those who knew themselves to be the elect, to be saved Christians, to organize themselves into pure congregations. Dissenting from this view were those identified with Dutch theologian Jacob Arminius (1560–1609), who affirmed that Christ died for all and left some room for human freedom. The Arminians asserted that any who responded in faith to Christ would be saved. This latter view emphasized the need for evangelism and calling people to have faith. John Smyth (ca. 1570–1612) was an early Separatist identified with this position.

These two positions came to be identified with the Particular (Christ died for the elect) and General (Christ died for all) Baptists, and they were expressed in a set of confessions, brief summaries of their theological perspective. The most important of the confessions were, for the General Baptists, the Orthodox creed of 1678, and for the Particular Baptists, the Second London Confession of 1677 (revised and reissued in 1689). Crucial for the development of the Baptist position was Andrew Fuller (1754–1815). Raised as a Particular Baptist, Fuller faced the problem of the movement's inward direction. He came to believe that the neglect of the example of the Apostles, who were continually presenting the claims of Christ to unbelievers, was wrong. He led in the development of a theology that wedded the Particular position with a strong emphasis upon evangelism. Fuller's moderate Calvinism eventually largely replaced the more stringent Calvinism that had previously dominated the Particular Baptists, though the older position was continually revived.

Given the emphasis upon the local church, it is not surprising that the Baptist movement could exist for centuries without national organizations and the

Young people celebrate during a Leading Edge retreat, a program sponsored by the Baptist Union of Great Britain. (Baptist Union of Great Britain)

development of denominational structures. More informal groupings had been able to meet the demands of the early generations. As early as the 1640s, Particular Baptists had formed regional associations, and pastors had met together for fellowship and theological discussions. There had even been national conventions. The motivation for a more stable national organization appears to have been a response to the success of the missions program. The need to undergird the missionary enterprise became a pragmatic rationale for the congregations' drawing together in unity. Such a call was issued in 1811 by Joseph Ivimey (1773–1834).

The model for Ivimey was the very successful Baptist Missionary Society (BMS), formed in 1792 as the Particular Baptist Society for the Propagation of the Gospel among the Heathen. The moderate Calvinism of Andrew Fuller (1757–1815) provided the theological foundation, and a booklet by William Carey (1761–1834), *An Enquiry into the Obligations of Christians to use means for the Conversion of the Heathen* (1792), the inspiration. Fuller became the first secretary of the BMS, which was headquartered in Kettering, where he pastored a church. Carey was sent to India as the Society's first missionary, and a new era in Protestant missions was launched.

The meeting in response to Ivimey's call was held at the London church pastored by John Rippon (1751–1836) in 1812. That meeting issued a more formal call to Baptist churches to send representatives to a meeting the next year, a meeting in which a Union was to be formed. The Union would support missions, Sunday schools, preaching in more rural parts of the country, and the raising of funds for the construction of new church buildings. Forty-six ministers met to form the Union. The new Union initially involved only a minority of Baptists, Fuller being among those who refrained from participation. He felt that it would compete for attention with the BMS.

The Union grew by steps through the 19th century. It underwent several reorganizations, but operated in the shadow of the BMS through its first 50 years. In the meantime, the General Baptists had pioneered organizational life as early as 1770 with the formation of the New Connection of General Baptists, inspired by the work of Dan Taylor (1738–1816), a pastor who came to the Baptists from the Methodists, with whom they shared a similar theological perspective. Also inspired by the missionary endeavor, but cut out from participation in the BMS, they formed the Foreign Mission Baptist Mission in 1816 and patterned it on the BMS organizationally.

Through the 19th century the distinctions between General and Particular Baptists were softened. General Baptist congregations participated in both the New Connection and the Baptist Union and the doctrinal basis of the Union was modified to downplay Particular distinctions. Beginning in 1870, a growing number of leaders concluded that the two groups should unite. That merger occurred in 1891. The General Baptist structures were dissolved, and their substance incorporated into the Union.

The creation of the new Union in 1891 seemed also to mark a turning point in Baptist life in England. The Baptist denomination had arrived at the point of being established as a national organization. It tended to turn its attention away from evangelism and growth stopped. The growth that did occur through the first half of the 20th century came from the mission field. Through the 19th century, the Union cooperated with the BMS in the development of an extensive international Baptist movement. Baptist churches emerged throughout the British colonies and beyond, and growth continued through the middle of the 20th century. However, the last half of the century was characterized by the maturing and independency of the mission churches and the reorientation of the Baptist Union to life in a worldwide Baptist ecumenical fellowship, most clearly epitomized in the Baptist World Alliance.

In 2005, the Baptist Union of Great Britain reported 141,918 members and 2,092 churches. It was a charter member of the World Council of Churches.

Baptist Union of Great Britain
Baptist House
PO Box 44
129 Broadway
Didcot, Oxfordshire OX11 8RT
United Kingdom
www.baptist.org.ik

J. Gordon Melton

See also: Baptist World Alliance; Church of England; World Council of Churches.

References

McBeth, H. Leon. *The Baptist Heritage: Four Centuries of the Baptist Witness.* Nashville: Broadman Press, 1987.

Parker, G. Keith. *Baptists in Europe: History & Confessions of Faith.* Nashville: Broadman Press, 1982.

Robinson, H. Wheeler. *British Baptists: An Original Anthology.* Manchester, NH: Ayer, 1980.

Underwood, A. C. *A History of the Baptists.* London: Carey Kingsgate Press, 1947.

Van Beek, Huibert. *A Handbook of the Churches and Councils: Profiles of Ecumenical Relationships.* Geneva: World Council of Churches, 2006.

Baptist Union of Hungary

Baptist work in Hungary dates to 1842 and a fire that swept through Hamburg, Germany. In the wake of the fire, carpenters from the large German-speaking community in Hungary came to Hamburg to assist in the rebuilding process. While there they encountered the members of the Baptist church headed by John G. Oncken (1800–1854). Five of the carpenters were baptized in 1845 and upon their return home formed a tract society to distribute Christian literature. Their activity was limited, given the country's law regulating religious activity outside the Roman Catholic Church.

Authorities disbanded the first congregation that had formed in Budapest in 1846. In the 1860s, one of Oncken's assistants, G. W. Lehmann, made contact with the believers and while in Budapest held a midnight baptismal service in the Danube.

It was not until the 1870s, however, that a second congregation emerged. Oncken sent a new missionary, Heinrich Meyer, who formed a church in Budapest in 1874. He also discovered in Mahaly Kornya and Mihaly Toth two capable local workers. Kornya baptized more than 11,000 people in the next 35 years. During this early stage, the work was conducted in German and primarily reached German-speaking Hungarians. Their work spread throughout Hungary, then part of the Hapsburg Empire, which included Transylvania (now in Romania) and parts of Slovakia and Serbia. Finally in 1893, two Hungarians, Lajos Balogh and Andreas Udvarnoki, completed studies at the seminary in Hamburg and began to build the church among Hungarian-speaking people. In 1905, the Hungarian-speaking work was organized as a separate Union that received state recognition (leaving the German-speaking Baptists separated without such recognition). Only after World War I and the disruption of the Austrian hegemony in Hungary did the two groups come together as the Union of Hungarian Baptist Churches (Magyarországi Baptista Egyház). They were helped by the Southern Baptist Convention and German American Baptists, and in 1920 opened a seminary.

Following World War II, Hungary came under the rule of a Marxist government, though its attitude toward religion was milder than that in neighboring Warsaw Pact countries. The church negotiated its position with the government and survived with a minimum of persecution. Beginning in 1955, the Union operated for a time under the name Hungarian Baptist Church. In 1967 it revised its doctrinal statement, adopted in 1902 from that of the German Baptists. The new statement affirms biblical authority, declaring that the Bible was written by divinely inspired men and compiled by the church under the guidance of the Holy Spirit. The Bible has thus been saved from essential error. The confession goes on to affirm the major Christian doctrines and speak of the religious life.

The Baptist Union emerged from the fall of the Marxist government at the end of the 1980s with the need to face the changes brought about by the new freedom. Among its first projects was the founding of an International Baptist Lay Academy, which attracts students from both Hungary and the neighboring countries. The church reported 11,400 members in 240 churches in 2005. It is a member of the Hungarian Evangelical Alliance, the Baptist World Alliance, and, since 1956, the World Council of Churches.

Baptist Union of Hungary
Aradi ut. 48
1062 Budapest
Hungary

J. Gordon Melton

See also: Baptist World Alliance; Southern Baptist Convention; World Council of Churches.

References

McBeth, H. Leon. *The Baptist Heritage: Four Centuries of the Baptist Witness.* Nashville: Broadman Press, 1987.

Parker, G. Keith. *Baptists in Europe: History & Confessions of Faith.* Nashville: Broadman Press, 1982.

Rushbrooke, J. H. *The Baptist Movement in the Continent of Europe.* London: Kingsgate Press, 1923.

Westin, Gunnar. *The Free Church through the Ages.* Nashville: Broadman Press, 1958.

Van Beek, Huibert. *A Handbook of the Churches and Councils: Profiles of Ecumenical Relationships.* Geneva: World Council of Churches, 2006.

Baptist Union of New Zealand

The Baptist movement came to New Zealand with the original British settlers at the end of the 19th century. The Baptists worshipped with other denominations until enough arrived that separate churches could be formed, with lay leadership. It was not until 1851, however, that the first ordained minister arrived, Reverend Decimus Dolamore, who founded a church in Nelson. Among the additional ministers that found their way to the islands was Thomas Spurgeon, the son of the famous British preacher Charles H. Spurgeon (1834–1892). Others were trained in the school founded by Spurgeon, and they gave the New Zealand Baptists a decidedly conservative Reformed theological perspective. The movement continued to grow as immigration from England persisted.

Dolamore's early suggestion that a national association be created was ignored. Churches were scattered over the islands and had quickly developed an appreciation of their independency. Initial organization was centered on the Canterbury Baptist Association, created by six congregations in 1873. The Association developed a plan of training and sending out lay preachers to form new churches. The Association's success gave support to those desiring a larger union. Charles Dallaston called a meeting in Christ Church in 1880 to consider a national organization. The Baptist Union of New Zealand was formed in 1882, with 22 of 25 churches participating. Two years later the Canterbury Association disbanded and turned its periodical, the *New Zealand Baptist,* over to the Union.

The Union emerged with a broad program for missions, Christian education, and ministerial development but was slowed by lack of resources. Its first program was a mission among the Maori people, the indigenous people of the islands. Thomas Spurgeon emerged as the leading minister, and he traveled the islands holding evangelistic services. Growth was aided by the development of an extensive Sunday school program for children and youth.

The New Zealand Baptists struggled to establish their identity. Many Baptists stayed with the original churches in which they had worshipped before Baptist churches had been founded. Also they experienced direct competition from the Plymouth Brethren, who had similar organization and doctrine, but were known for their unique premillennial eschatology. Brethren founder John Nelson Darby had developed a method of Bible interpretation that divided Bible history into various eras, or dispensations, and saw the return of Christ as the next item on God's agenda for humankind. This dispensationalism, as it was called, appealed to ministers of a conservative Reformed theological background.

The Union ended the 19th century on a down note, being strongly affected by the bad economic times and the migration of many of its members to Australia or back home to England. However, in the 20th century they were able to reverse the trend and begin an era of growth. The Baptist Missionary Society of New Zealand was formed in 1885 and sent their first missionary to India. Over the 20th century India became the focus of their foreign missionary work.

Through the early 20th century, the Union struggled with a leadership spread along a theological spectrum and faced criticism from its most conservative leaders. However, a long history of interaction with other churches led gradually to the emergence of an ecumenical perspective in which Baptists, while asserting their unique identity, nevertheless saw themselves as a part of the larger Protestant camp. They joined the New Zealand Council of Churches in 1941 and applied for membership in the World Council of Churches while that organization was still in its formative stages. The maturing of the church was further reflected in the change in missionary policy in 1967. The Indian mission was at the time in the process of being turned over to indigenous leaders. The "Other Avenues of Services" policy suggested that in the future New Zealand Baptists would operate through centers sponsored by other bodies.

In 2005, the Baptist Union of New Zealand reported 42,800 members in 256 churches.

Baptist Union of New Zealand
PO Box 97-543
South Auckland Mail Centre, Auckland
New Zealand

J. Gordon Melton

See also: World Council of Churches.

References

McBeth, H. Leon. *The Baptist Heritage: Four Centuries of the Baptist Witness*. Nashville: Broadman Press, 1987.

"Our Story." History Churches of New Zealand. www.baptist.org.nz. Assessed March 1, 2009.

Tenson, Paul, et al. *A Handful of Grain: The Centenary History of the Baptist Union of New Zealand*. 4 vols. Wellington, NZ: New Zealand Baptist Historical Society, 1982–1984.

Van Beek, Huibert. *A Handbook of the Churches and Councils: Profiles of Ecumenical Relationships.* Geneva: World Council of Churches, 2006.

Baptist Union of South Africa/Baptist Convention of South Africa

Within South Africa, Baptists trace their origins to the arrival of the 1820 British settlers and the German settlers of 1857–1858. Baptist churches were formed first in the Eastern Cape and later in other parts of Southern Africa. This meant that Baptists, along with other denominations, were inextricably caught up in the processes of imperialism, colonialism, and, later, apartheid.

The first Baptist church in South Africa was established at Salem on the Assegai Bush River, followed by a church in Grahamstown (1823). Other English, German, and, later, Afrikaans Baptist churches were established in the following years. These were originally in the Eastern and Western Cape as well as in Natal. Subsequently, with the discovery of diamonds and gold, churches were established in the interior of the country. Limited support was received from churches in England and Germany, especially in the provision of ministers. In 1877, the Baptist Union was formed.

As a result of an agreement between the London Missionary Society and the Baptist Missionary Society, to the effect that the former would work in Southern Africa and the latter north of the Limpopo River, no Baptist missionaries were sent from overseas to South Africa. Mission work among the indigenous African inhabitants was first started by the German Baptists at Tschabo in 1870. The South African Baptist Missionary Society was only formed in 1892 to promote evangelism among the black population. These efforts were severely hampered by black anger and suspicion as a result of the occupation of previously Xhosa-owned land by white settlers and, equally, by lack of enthusiasm on the part of white Baptist settlers for missionary work as a result of the ongoing border wars. Later, the National Black American Baptists also engaged in mission work in the Eastern Cape.

In 1927, the Baptist Union grouped all the black churches into the Bantu Baptist Church. In 1966, the Bantu Church dissolved and was superseded by the Baptist Convention of South Africa. Ostensibly, this grouping existed under the Baptist Union umbrella, but it enjoyed no real equality and perpetuated the separation between white and black Baptists. Separate assemblies, ministerial rolls, theological education, and pension policies, together with subsequent general conformity with apartheid, served to entrench, within Baptist circles, the social stratification of the country as a whole. In 1987, the Baptist Convention declared itself an autonomous group, exposing the fiction of the Baptist "union," and severed its remaining institutional ties with the Baptist Union (though some black churches did remain within the Union).

Both the Baptist Union and the Baptist Convention of South Africa are members of the Baptist World Alliance. The Baptist Union and the Baptist Convention are the two largest Baptist groups in the country, though small compared to the Methodists and Anglicans (Church of the Province of South Africa), but they are not the only groups. Other Baptist groups include the Afrikaans Baptist Churches and two Indian Baptist groups. All five of these groups formed the South African Baptist Alliance in 2001. In 2008, the Baptist Union reported 52,000 members in 681 churches and the Baptist convention 24,000 members in 154 churches.

Baptist Convention of South Africa
Box 93521
Yeoville 2143
South Africa

Baptist Union of Southern Africa
Private Mailbag X45
Wilropark 1731
South Africa

Louise Kretzschmar

See also: Baptist World Alliance; London Missionary Society.

References

Hudson-Reed, Sydney. *By Taking Heed: The History of the Baptists in Southern Africa, 1820–1977.* Roodepoort, South Africa: Baptist Publishing House, 1983.

Kretzschmar, Louise. *Privatization of the Christian Faith: Mission, Social Ethics and the South*

African Baptists. Legon, Ghana: Asempa Press, 1988.

Baptist World Alliance

In 1904, Archibald T. Robertson (1863–1934), a professor at the Southern Baptist Theological Seminary in Louisville, Kentucky, wrote a brief article suggesting a conference of Baptists from around the world. The article was sent to a host of global contacts, and amid the many positive responses was that of J. H. Shakespeare, the editor of the *Baptist Times and Freeman* in London. Shakespeare and several prominent British Baptists extended an invitation to meet in London in the summer of 1905. Representatives from 23 countries gathered for the week of July 11–19, 1905, and formed the Baptist World Alliance. The word "alliance" was chosen deliberately to communicate to Baptists that the new organization had no plans to assume the functions normally assumed by Baptist unions, associations, or conventions.

The new organization set as its goals to promote fellowship between the world's Baptists; to offer inspiration; to speak on issues of mutual concern, such as religious freedom and world peace; and to coordinate the distribution of relief funds in response to emergencies. That the promotion of religious liberty was its first priority reflected in part the problems that Baptists were experiencing in extending their fellowship into predominantly Roman Catholic areas.

Shakespeare became the first general secretary, and his 20 years of service gave the Alliance its early direction. The Alliance was headquartered in London and projected plans for meetings every five years.

The Alliance headquarters remained in London until 1941, when the German attack on London forced it to move to the United States, a move that became permanent. A European headquarters was established in London after the war but later moved to Copenhagen, Denmark. Membership grew annually and increased markedly through the late 20th century as missions matured into autonomous churches. The Alliance identified (without formal affiliation) with the new World Council of Churches, though it has included many conservative Baptist bodies for whom the Council was much too liberal. Additionally, many Baptists rejected fellowship with various groups that have affiliated with the Council, such as the Orthodox churches. The Southern Baptist Convention, the largest Protestant body in the United States, prominent in its absence from American and world ecumenical structures, has nevertheless remained a prominent force in the Alliance.

The Alliance operates through a set of regional Baptist fellowships, including the North American Baptist Fellowship, with whom it shares office space in Virginia. In the year 2009, the Alliance reported 213 member Baptist associations and unions with a combined 37 million members.

Baptist World Alliance
6733 Curran St.
McLean, VA 22101
www.bwanet.org

J. Gordon Melton

See also: Baptists; Southern Baptist Convention; World Council of Churches.

References
Baptists Together in Christ 1905–2005. Birmingham, AL: Samford University Press, 2005.
McBeth, H. Leon. *The Baptist Heritage: Four Centuries of the Baptist Witness*. Nashville: Broadman Press, 1987.
Tiller, Carl W. *The Twentieth Century Baptist: Chronicles of Baptists in the First Seventy-Five Years of the Baptist World Alliance*. Valley Forge, PA: Judson Press, 1980.

Baptists

The Baptists are a Protestant church tradition whose theological origins (as seen in beliefs such as believer's baptism, freedom of religion, and separation between church and state) can be traced back to the 16th-century Anabaptists, who rejected infant baptism and held that adults should be rebaptized (whence Anabaptist), once they became believers. Historically, however, they are more closely linked to the 17th-century English Puritan Separatists.

Alexa Heichelheim, 17, is baptized by Pastor Kelley Vaughan during a Seaside Baptist Church Easter sunrise service on the beach on April 12, 2009, in Jamaica Beach, Texas. (AP/Wide World Photos)

Although this development of a middle way eventually led to the main body of English Christians being incorporated into the Church of England, those who were called Puritans by their enemies, including those later known as Congregationalists and Presbyterians, demanded further purification of the church. They wished to move the church more clearly into the Protestant camp and change its government from rule by the monarch and the bishops appointed by the monarch to a congregational or presbyterian (rule by elders) system, though they still assumed that there would be only one church and that there would be an intimate tie between the church and state. Those who were called Separatists by their enemies, including the Baptists, while largely sharing the Protestant theology of the Congregationalists and Presbyterians, called for a more radical solution. They did not want to wait for the government to reform the church; they wanted to separate from the established church and form their own congregations, consisting only of true Christian believers, immediately. The Baptists also taught believer's baptism and stressed liberty of conscience and separation between church and state, refusing to accord to the state the authority to suppress "false" religious beliefs.

Following his acceptance of (adult) believer's baptism, the former Separatist John Smyth (d. 1612) formed a Baptist church in the Netherlands (1609) while in exile from England. He is generally considered the founder of organized Baptists in England. Another erstwhile Separatist and member of Smyth's church, Thomas Helwys (ca. 1550–ca. 1616), returned home and established the first Baptist church in England in 1612. English Baptists largely espoused 17th-century radicalism, with its resistance to royal authority, and they participated in the English Civil War of 1642–1648. During the 18th century, they experienced religious decline, and they both benefited from and contributed to the evangelical revival of the 19th century. Along with other groups such as Presbyterians, Congregationalists, Quakers, and Methodists, they were termed Dissenters, or Nonconformists, since they refused to conform to the established (Anglican) Church.

The first German Baptist church was established in Hamburg in 1834. Along with German Baptists, the English (and some American Baptists) were involved in advancing Baptist work on the continent of Europe. European Baptists, through missionary work and colonial settlement, established many churches in other parts of the world, especially in Africa, Australia, and Asia.

Also in the 17th century, some Baptists immigrated along with the Puritans to North America from both England and the Netherlands. The first Baptist church in America was established by Roger Williams on Rhode Island in 1639, and Baptist churches later spread across what became the United States of America. Today, Baptist churches are prominent in the United States, with the Southern Baptist Convention and the American Baptist Churches being two of the largest groups. As a result of the Great Awakening, a revival of religious life that affected a large part of the American colonies in the 18th century and the missionary movements of the 19th and 20th centuries, Baptist churches were established in many other parts of the world, including Africa, Asia, and Latin America.

Today, Baptists form one of the largest Protestant communions in the world, with approximately 42 million baptized members and a Baptist community of about 100 million. The Baptist World Alliance (BWA) is an international fellowship of 188 national unions or conventions from across the world. The major foci of the BWA are fellowship, justice, evangelism, and aid (relief and development).

Along with other Christian traditions, Baptists share a faith in the Triune God, commitment to the gospel of Jesus Christ, belief in the authority of the Bible, the priesthood of all believers, the church as a community of believers, and the importance of mission. In addition, certain principles are stressed by Baptists, although specific interpretations of these principles may differ. Baptists practice believer's baptism (as opposed to infant baptism) because of their understanding of Christian faith as centered in personal, conscious, and committed discipleship. They stress regenerative church membership and congregational (as opposed to episcopal or presbyterian) church government. Some Baptists speak of the autonomy of the local church, others of the interdependence of Baptist churches.

Baptists believe in the separation of church and state because of their conviction that religious belief cannot be compelled; thus, they strongly support religious freedom and resist religious persecution. Different understandings of the Baptist principle of the separation of church and state throughout Baptist history have led some Baptists to neglect social involvement, while others have been leaders in social renewal and transformation. With respect to war and political involvement, Baptists in different contexts and periods have sometimes been pacifists and, at other times, participated in both revolutionary movements and wars. Unlike some denominations, Baptists do not adhere to a definitive doctrinal creed, but they do espouse an acceptance of the authority of the Bible and basic Christian beliefs, together with the above-mentioned Baptist principles.

Louise Kretzschmar

See also: American Baptist Churches in the U.S.A.; Baptist World Alliance; Southern Baptist Convention.

References

Cook, Henry. *What Baptists Stand For*. London: Carey Kingsgate, 1961.

Leonard, Bill J. *Baptist Ways: A History*. Valley Forge, PA: Judson Press, 2003.

Macbeth, Leon. *The Baptist Heritage: Four Centuries of Baptist Witness*. Nashville: Broadman Press, 1975.

Stanley, Brian. *The History of the Baptist Missionary Society, 1792–1992*. Edinburgh: T. & T. Clarke, 1992.

Torbet, Robert G. *A History of the Baptists*. Philadelphia: Judson Press, 1950, 1975.

Wardin, Albert W., ed. *Baptists around the World*. Nashville: Broadman and Holman Publishers, 1995.

■ Barbados

Barbados, the most easterly of the Windward Antilles, is an island 166 square miles in size, located to the north of Venezuela. The highest point is Mount Hillaby at 1,105 feet, which is located toward the center of the island. Interestingly, there are no rivers on the island as the rainwater percolates quickly through the soil to form numerous underground channels.

The country is home to 284,589 (July 2009) people, of which 90 percent are descendants of African slaves brought to the island as laborers on British sugar plantations; 4 percent are white; and the remaining 6 percent are Asian and mixed race. The capital and largest city is Bridgetown, with a population of 96,578 (2006). About 40 percent of the population is urban.

Barbados was discovered by the Portuguese in 1536 and named after the "bearded" fig trees found there. The island was settled in 1627 by the British and remained under British administration until November 30, 1966, when Barbados became an independent nation within the British Commonwealth of Nations. The official language is English.

The head of state is the British monarch, represented by a governor-general. There is a bicameral Parliament: a 21-member designated Senate and a 24 member elected House of Assembly, which elects the prime minister.

Barbados was originally home to the Arawak Amerindians and was one of the few islands in the Caribbean not taken over by the Carib. The Spanish first landed there in the early 1500s and repaid the kindness of the Arawak people with a wholesale massacre. When the British returned a century later, they found the island uninhabited. Looking for farmland rather than mineral wealth, they settled the land and established a plantation system based on sugarcane, which required the importation of large numbers of slaves from West Africa. Although slavery was abandoned in 1834, universal voting rights were not extended to all citizens regardless of race until 1951.

Historically, the Barbadian (or Bajans) economy has depended on sugarcane cultivation and related activities. However, in recent years the economy has diversified into light industry and tourism, with about three-quarters of GDP and 80 percent of exports attributed to the services sector. Since 2003, the economy has rebounded due to increases in construction projects and tourism revenues. This reflects the success of the high-end economic sector, which will likely face declining revenues with the current global economic downturn.

Currently, the nation enjoys one of the highest per capita incomes in the West Indies. Offshore banking and information services are important sources of foreign exchange and thrive from being in the same time

Barbados

Religion	Followers in 1970	Followers in 2010	% of Population	Annual % growth 2000–2010	Followers in 2025	Followers in 2050
Christians	235,000	284,000	95.5	0.35	287,000	253,000
Protestants	50,600	100,000	33.7	1.46	110,000	110,000
Anglicans	90,000	85,600	28.8	–0.19	80,000	65,000
Independents	8,900	16,000	5.4	2.04	20,000	21,000
Agnostics	2,400	5,100	1.7	2.38	5,400	6,000
Baha'is	1,300	3,600	1.2	0.38	4,000	5,000
Muslims	400	2,300	0.8	0.39	3,200	4,000
Hindus	100	980	0.3	0.38	1,200	1,400
Atheists	0	700	0.2	0.39	900	1,200
New religionists	50	480	0.2	0.38	600	800
Buddhists	0	120	0.0	0.35	150	200
Spiritists	0	60	0.0	0.34	90	100
Jews	30	40	0.0	0.58	40	40
Ethnoreligionists	0	30	0.0	0.68	50	80
Total population	**239,000**	**297,000**	**100.0**	**0.38**	**303,000**	**272,000**

St. James Parish Church, Barbados. Located near the island's first settlement, it is one of the oldest surviving churches in Barbados. (Ramunas Bruzas/Dreamstime.com)

zone as Eastern U.S. financial centers and from having a relatively highly educated workforce. The government continues its efforts to reduce unemployment, encourage direct foreign investment, and privatize state-owned enterprises.

Religious affiliation in 2000 (census) was reported as follows: Protestant, 63.4 percent (Anglican 28.3 percent, Pentecostal 18.7 percent, Methodist 5.1 percent, other 11.3 percent); Roman Catholic, 4.2 percent; other Christian, 7 percent; other religions, 4.8 percent; none or unspecified, 20.6 percent.

The 1980 census reported the following statistics on religious affiliation: Protestant, 67 percent (Anglican 40 percent, Pentecostal 8 percent, Methodist 7 percent, other 12 percent), Roman Catholic, 4 percent; other religions, 9 percent; none, 17 percent; unknown or unspecified, 3 percent.

By comparing data from 2000 with 1980, it is obvious that the Anglicans have greatly declined during this period, the Methodists have slightly declined, the Roman Catholics have remained at the same level, other religions have increased, and none/unspecified remains constant. Most growth has occurred among Pentecostals, from 8 percent in 1980 to 18.7 percent in 2000.

In addition to the more established denominations, the island's villages contain numerous independent store-front churches that cater to the lower class who face the constant struggles and difficulties of everyday life amid acute poverty.

Barbados is often portrayed as having a highly religious society because of the large variety of religious groups present. Normally, women make up the majority of those active in religious groups, while few men

BARBADOS

are in attendance. Many of the religious groups are fundamentalist and revivalistic, and preach a strict moral code that does not have much appeal to the island's young people or to the male population in general.

During the late 1990s, Barbados reportedly had 1,769 local churches that represented more than 100 denominations and independent religious groups.

The Church of England was established with the arrival of the first British settlers in 1626. The Church of St. Michael was dedicated in 1665 in Bridgetown. In 1795, the Anglican Slave Conversion Society (later known as the Christian Faith Society) was established under the bishop of London. The Church Missionary Society, led by evangelical Anglicans, began work in

Barbados in 1794, which later resulted in the formation of the Barbados Society for Promoting Christian Knowledge and the founding of schools for the colored (mixed race) and black population. The Diocese of Barbados was created in 1824, which included the Windward and Leeward Islands, along with Trinidad-Tobago and Guyana. This jurisdiction is now an integral part of the Anglican Church in the Province of the West Indies, whose archbishop currently resides in Nassau, the capital of the Bahamas. About 28 percent of all Barbadians considered themselves Anglicans in 2000, compared to 40 percent in 1980. There are about 60 Anglican churches in Barbados.

The non-conformist Moravians and Methodists came to Barbados in 1765 and 1788, respectively. The Moravians developed a special interest in evangelizing and defending the black plantation workers. They established their first mission at Sharon in St. Thomas Parish. The Moravians are part of the Moravian Church, Eastern West Indies Province, with headquarters in Antigua. After the U.S. Revolutionary War, British Methodists redirected some of their energy away from their former work in North America to evangelization in the Caribbean. The Barbadian Methodists are part of the Methodist Church in the Caribbean and the Americas, with headquarters in Antigua.

Beginning in the late 19th century and continuing through the 20th century, numerous mainline U.S. Protestant and Free church denominations began mission work in Barbados. Among the earliest to arrive was the African Methodist Episcopal Church (1897), which a decade previously had opened work in the Bahamas. Among the most successful of the new missionary efforts was the Church of God (Cleveland, Tennessee), which sent its first missionaries to the island in 1936 and founded the New Testament Church of God. Other Pentecostal denominations include the Apostolic Faith Mission, Church of God of Prophecy, the Pentecostal Assemblies of Canada, and the Pentecostal Assemblies of the World. The Wesleyan Holiness tradition is represented by the Church of the Nazarene, the Wesleyan Holiness Church (whose work had been initiated by the former Pilgrim Holiness Church), the United Holy Church of America, the Bible Missionary Church, and the Salvation Army.

Other Free church denominations include Barbados Baptist Convention (1972, affiliated with the Southern Baptist Convention), the National Baptist Convention (1975), Baptist International Missions (1979), the Barbados Christian Mission (an independent Baptist denomination), Brethren Assemblies (Plymouth Brethren), the Christian Churches/Churches of Christ, and the Seventh-day Adventists.

Some of the Protestant churches are members of the Barbados Christian Council, which is related to the Caribbean Conference of Churches (CCC), and through that organization to the World Council of Churches (WCC). Evangelical denominations such as the Worldwide Church of God have united in the Barbados Evangelical Association which is related to the World Evangelical Alliance.

The Roman Catholic Church had a late start in the West Islands, which were under British control, and it was not until 1839 that the first Vicarate Apostolic was established with a bishop headquartered in Port of Spain, Trinidad. Although the first Catholic church was constructed on Barbados between 1840 and 1848, Catholics have remained a small minority. Barbados had the smallest number of Roman Catholic adherents in the Windward Islands (10,000) in 1980, with only 6 parishes, 9 priests, and 5 schools.

Other Religions Post-Protestant Christian groups include the Christadelphians; the Jehovah's Witnesses (30 churches with 2,430 members in 2008); the Church of Jesus Christ of Latter-day Saints (founded in 1978, reported 4 churches with 696 members in 2007); the Unity School of Christianity; and the Church of Christ, Scientist.

Myalism and Obeah is reportedly practiced in secret by some Barbadians, especially those who are not active members of Christian churches. Myalism is an African-derived belief system that developed among blacks in the British West Indies during the slavery period; Obeah is the specific practice of "black magic," or witchcraft, by priests, known as "obeahmen."

The Spiritual Baptists—known as "tieheads" in Barbados in reference to the brightly colored cloths they wear tied around their heads—practice a hybrid religion of mixed African and Protestant belief systems. This Afro-Caribbean tradition was brought to

Barbados from Trinidad in 1957 by "archbishop" Granville Williams. The Spiritual Baptist movement originated in Trinidad and Tobago during the early 20th century as a spirit-possession religion that is "Baptist" in name only. Its members believe themselves to be possessed by the Holy Spirit and are led to hand clap, foot stomp, dance, sing, or, most characteristically, shout. They came to be known as "shouters" by their early detractors. One of the movement's prominent churches is the Jerusalem Apostolic Spiritual Baptist Church in Earling Grove. There are an estimated 10,000 Spiritual Baptist adherents on the island.

Rastafarianism was introduced to Barbados in 1975 from Jamaica. The Rastafarian movement began with the teachings of Marcus Garvey, who founded the Universal Negro Improvement Association in the 1920s. Rastafarians live a peaceful life, needing little material possessions and devoting much time to contemplating the holy scriptures. They reject the white man's world as the new age Babylon of greed and dishonesty. The proud and confident Rastas stand up for black rights and are identified by their long hair, knotted in dreadlocks in the image of the Lion of Judah. The movement spread quickly in Barbados and was very attractive to the local black youths, who saw it as an extension of their adolescent rebellion from school and parental authority. With it came some undesirable elements (vagrancy, loose morals, use of marijuana and alcohol, etc.), but true Rastas stand for "peace and pride and righteousness." Also, there is an Ethiopian Orthodox Church on Hastings Main Road, Christ Church.

Reportedly, there are numerous independent spiritualist practitioners in the Bahamas, who advertise themselves as energy healers, psychic mediums, spiritual teachers, and/or spiritualist ministers.

Barbados has one of the oldest Jewish communities in the Western Hemisphere, a community formed in 1650 by refugees from Brazil who escaped when the Portuguese retook land seized by the religiously tolerant Dutch. The Jewish community existed quietly on Barbados through the 18th century, with 275 Jews residing in Barbados in 1715. In 1820, Barbados became the first British colony to remove all political restrictions from the Jews. The Jewish community declined through the early 20th century, as many moved away to escape the poor economy. However, in 1932, when only one practicing Jew was left on the island, another group of Jewish immigrants arrived from Europe. The community grew and prospered, so that in 1987 they were able to reopen the old synagogue in Bridgetown, built in 1654, which is the second oldest synagogue in the Western Hemisphere (only the one in Curaçao is older). The synagogue is now a Barbados National Trust protected building and an active synagogue.

Buddhism is represented by the Tara Kadampa Buddhist Centre in Saint George, and by a Nichiren Daishonin group. The Baha'i Faith came to Barbados in the 1960s and established a string of spiritual assemblies throughout the Windward Islands. There are more than 800 Muslims on Barbados, who are served by the Islamic Teaching Centre in Christ Church and by the Juma Mosque in Bridgetown. There are about 500 Hindus (mostly from East India), with the majority residing in Bridgeport, who are served by Sanatan Dhuram Maha and the Sathya Sai Baba Centre.

Clifton L. Holland

See also: African Methodist Episcopal Church; Apostolic Faith Mission; Baha'i Faith; Caribbean Conference of Churches; Christadelphians; Church in the Province of the West Indies; Church of England; Church of God (Cleveland, Tennessee); Church of God of Prophecy; Church of Jesus Christ of Latter-day Saints; Church of the Nazarene; Ethiopian Orthodox Tewahado Church; Free Churches; Jehovah's Witnesses; Methodist Church in the Caribbean and the Americas; Moravian Church, Eastern West Indies Province; National Baptist Convention of America; New Kadampa Tradition–International Kadampa Buddhist Union; Pentecostal Assemblies of Canada; Pentecostal Assemblies of the World; Rastafarians; Roman Catholic Church; Salvation Army; Sathya Sai Baba Movement; Spirit Possession; Spiritual Baptists; Spiritualism; World Council of Churches; World Evangelical Alliance; Worldwide Church of God.

References

Barrett, Leonard E., Sr. *The Rastafarians.* Boston: Beacon Press, 1997 (first published in 1988).

Blackman, F. *Methodism: 200 Years in Barbados.* Bridgetown, Barbados: Caribbean Contact, 1988.

Brierly, Peter. *World Churches Handbook.* London, England: Christian Research, 1997.

Campbell, P. F. *The Church in Barbados in the Seventeenth Century.* St. Michael, Barbados: Barbados Museum and Historical Society, 1982.

Dryfoot, Arthur Charles. *The Shaping of the West Indian Church, 1492–1962.* Gainesville: University Press of Florida, 1999; published jointly with The Press University of the West Indies in Jamaica.

Fernández Olmos, Margarite, and Lizabeth Paravisini-Gebert, eds. *Sacred Possessions: Vodou, Santería, Obeah and the Caribbean.* New Brunswick, NJ: Rutgers University Press, 1997.

Glazier, Stephen D. "Spiritual Baptists." In *Encyclopedia of African and African-American Religions,* edited by Stephen D. Glazier, 315–319. New York: Routledge, 2001.

Hill, B. *Historic Churches of Barbados.* Bridgetown, Barbados: Art Heritage Publications, 1984.

Holland, Clifton L., ed. *World Christianity: Central America and the Caribbean.* Monrovia, CA: MARC-World Vision International, 1981.

Horowitz, Michael M., ed. *Peoples and Cultures of the Caribbean: An Anthropological Reader.* Garden City, NY: The Natural History Press, 1971.

Maynard, G. O. *A History of the Moravian Church: Eastern West Indies Province.* Port of Spain, Trinidad: Yuille's Printerie, 1968.

Newton, Melanie J. *The Children of Africa in the Colonies: Free People of Color in Barbados in the Age of Emancipation.* Baton Rouge: Louisiana State University Press, 2008.

Pariser, Harry S. *Explore Barbados.* 3rd ed. San Francisco: Manatee Press, 2000.

Religion in Barbados. http://www.funbarbados .com/ourisland/religion/.

Taylor, Patrick, ed. *Nation Dance: Religion, Identity and Cultural Difference in the Caribbean.* Bloomington: Indiana University Press, 2001.

U.S. Central Intelligence Agency. *The World Fact Book.* http://www.cia.gov/library/publications/the-world-factbook/goes/bb.html.

Basel Mission

The Basel Mission, officially the Evangelische Missionsgesellschaft in Basel, one of the leading missionary societies that facilitated the phenomenal spread of Protestant Christianity around the world in the 19th century, was a product of the spread of Pietism and the British Evangelical Awakening in Central Europe. Christians from various denominations found new spiritual life as a result of the movement, one result of which was the desire to spread the Christian message around the world. The Mission began to support a school for the training of missionaries and sent out its first missionaries under the auspices of some of the older missionary societies, particularly the Church Missionary Society, which shared similar roots in the Evangelical Awakening.

In 1922, the Basel Mission sent out its first missionaries under its own direct sponsorship. They took up work in Russia. Work spread to Ghana, India, Hong Kong, and southern China within the first generation. Work expanded in Africa after Germany established new colonies in the 1880s, but then shrank following the loss of those colonies following World War I. In fact, it lost all of its work for a short period as a result of its identification with Germany (even though it was based in Switzerland), but regained many of its posts during the 1920s.

The work grew considerably during the 1940s, and as World War II approached, structural changes were made to prevent the kind of disruption that had occurred during World War I. The German part of the society was set apart as a separate German branch with headquarters at Stuttgart. The Swiss branch was thus able to continue with little disruption through the war years.

Over the years, support for the Mission had come from a variety of sources, though Reformed churches in Germany and Switzerland provided the bulk of the support, and the missionaries tended to be in the Reformed tradition. The establishment of an exclusively Swiss branch of the Mission gave it an even more Reformed outlook, as it relied heavily upon support from the Swiss Protestant Church Federation.

In the postwar years, the Mission has had to respond to the changing face of Protestantism worldwide, especially the maturing of missions into independent churches. One symbol of this change was the alignment of the Mission with the other mission organizations that constituted the Swiss Mission Council and the German Mission Council and the alignment of both these councils with the World Council of Churches. Most recently, the Basel Mission merged with four other missionary organizations to create Mission 21.

Mission 21 continues an active international program supporting the indigenous churches that grew out of its earlier missionary activity.

Mission 21
Missionsstrasse 21
Postfach, 4003 Basel
Switzerland
www.mission–21.org (German only)

J. Gordon Melton

See also: Church Missionary Society; World Council of Churches.

Reference

Mission 21 (in German). www.mission–21.org. Accessed March 1, 2009.

Basilica of Our Lady of Peace of Yamoussoukro

The Basilica of Our Lady of Peace located in Yamoussoukro, Cote d'Ivoire, is one of largest Christian churches in the world. It was initiated and financed by Felix Houphouet-Boigny (1906–1993), the first president of Cote d'Ivoire. Though distinct, the church to some extent is modeled on St. Peter's with the inclu-

Cattle are herded past the Roman Catholic Basilica of Our Lady of Peace in Yamoussoukro, Ivory Coast, on March 12, 2003. (AP/Wide World Photos)

sion of a courtyard surrounded on either side by a curved colonnade.

Cote d'Ivoire was officially a French colony from 1893 to 1960. Houphouet-Boigny, leader of the Parti Democratique de la Cote d'Ivoire (PDCI), assumed the presidency of the newly independent country and retained his post until his death in 1993. In 1983, Houphouet-Boigny oversaw the movement of the official capital from Abidjan on the coast, to Yamoussoukro, located in the center of the country. About the same time he announced plans to build the new church, and his efforts were blessed two years later, when on August 10, 1985, Pope John Paul II arrived to bless the building's cornerstone. As the economy of the country deteriorated, however, the pope questioned his support of the construction effort and only reluctantly returned for the consecration of the building on September 10, 1990.

The completed basilica emerged as one of the tallest religious structures in the world. The cross on the dome reaches upward of 518 feet (12 feet shy of the Ulm Cathedral in Germany, which is the tallest church in the world; St. Peter's reaches 434.7 feet high). Thus, Our Lady of Peace is the tallest Roman Catholic church in the world and the tallest church in Africa. There is some dispute as to whether it or St. Peter's Basilica is the larger church. The *Guinness Book of World Records,* for example, lists it as the largest church in the world, with a total enclosed area of 322,917 square feet, compared to St. Peter's with 163,182.2 square feet. St. Peter's appears to have a larger enclosed area in its main sanctuary, accommodating 30,000, while Our Lady of Peace can accommodate 18,000. The piazza in front of the church can accommodate 30,000 people and is slightly larger than the piazza in front of St. Peter's. It remains difficult, however, to obtain comparable figures between the two churches.

While outsiders argued whether a poor country should be putting so much into such an expensive building, especially one in the new capital that has remained largely uninhabited, a public controversy erupted inside the country over the erecting of a building with public money that would be serving only the 20 percent of the population that were Roman Catholic. To respond to the criticisms of the other religious com-

munities, the president also saw to the erection of a Protestant Temple and an impressive national mosque in Yamoussoukro.

J. Gordon Melton

See also: Roman Catholic Church.

References

Edwards, John M. "West Africa's Capital of Ghosts." Salon Wanderlust. http://www.salon.com/wlust/feature/1998/05/05feature.html. Accessed May 15, 2009.

Fuchs, Regina. *Ivory Coast.* Edison, NJ: Hunter Publishing, 1991.

Hebblewaite, Peter. "Ivory Coast's Basilica May Turn into White Elephant." *National Catholic Reporter* (March 30, 1990).

Basilica of the National Shrine of Our Lady of Aparecida

The story of Our Lady of Aparecida begins in October 1716, when three fishermen were plying their trade on the Paraiba River in Brazil. They were having a bad day but found in their fishless nets a small headless terracotta statue of the Virgin Mary that they dubbed "Nossa Señora Aparecida." They cast their nets again and the head soon appeared and shortly thereafter the needed catch of fish was made. The occasion of their fishing that day was the expected arrival of a nobleman, Dom Pedro de Almedida, Count of Assumar, who was passing through the area. The people of Guarantinqueta had decided to hold a feast in his honor.

The statue would later be identified as the product of Frei Agostino de Jesus, a monk from Sao Paulo known for his sculpture. The image, less than three feet tall, was sculpted around 1650. After the head was reattached, it remained in the possession of one of the fishermen, Felipe Pedroso. Neighbors began to visit his home and reports of a number of answered prayers began to circulate. As the statue's fame grew, Pedroso's family constructed a chapel and then in 1734 the local priest had a larger chapel built. The chapel

Basilica of the National Shrine of Our Lady of Aparecida in Aparecida, Brazil. (Gilvan Oraggio/Dreamstime.com)

sufficed for a century, but in 1834 it was replaced by a large basilica.

The new basilica was finished just as the doctrine of the Immaculate Conception (referring to the birth of the Virgin Mary without original sin) was beginning to develop. It would be declared a dogma of the Roman Catholic Church in 1854. In the new basilica, the statue was identified as Our Lady of the Conception. The 1854 pronouncement suggested the crowning of statues of Mary was an appropriate way to venerate the Virgin. The coronation of the statue at the basilica occurred in 1904, the 50th anniversary of the pronouncement on the Immaculate Conception. The statue was now referred to as Nossa Senhora da Conceição Aparecida (Our Lady of the Conception who Appeared), and as Our Lady of the Conception who Appeared, the Virgin Mary was designated the principal patroness of Brazil by Pope Pius XII in 1930.

In the decade after World War II, the continued increase in people making pilgrimages to view Our

Lady who Appeared placed the issue of a new larger facility before local officials. Thus a new larger basilica was inaugurated. It proved a spectacular effort. The main worship area was designed with a floor plan shaped like a Greek cross (with the four arms of equal length), 568 feet long and 551 feet wide. The central dome reached 230 feet in the air. It can accommodate 45,000 worshippers at any given time.

The finished church turned out to be the second largest Catholic place of worship in the world, second only to St. Peter's Basilica in Vatican City. (Some consider the Basilica of Our Lady of Peace of Yamoussoukro, Cote d'Ivoire as the second largest church.) In 1980, Pope John Paul II visited Brazil and consecrated the church, then nearing completion. Four years later the National Conference of Bishops of Brazil declared it to be the largest Marian Temple in the world.

Once in place in the new basilica, the small statue has been in the news but once. In 1995, on October 12, the annual feast day of Our Lady of Aparecida, a minister of the Igreja Universal do Reino de Deus/Universal Church of the Kingdom of God, the largest Protestant denomination in Brazil with an expansive television broadcast ministry, spoke against the veneration of the Virgin. Declaring it no saint, he kicked a model of the statue of Our Lady of Aparecida. The public outrage was such that the minister had to leave the country for a time.

In 1928, Guaratinqueta, the town in which the shrine basilica was located was renamed Aparecida. It is located between São Paulo and Rio de Janeiro. The church currently (2009) receives more than six million visitors annually and has become the single most popular pilgrimage site in all of Latin America. Since she was named patroness of Brazil, more than 300 parish churches and 5 cathedrals have been named after Our Lady who Appeared.

J. Gordon Melton

See also: Basilica of Our Lady of Peace of Yamoussoukro; Mary, Blessed Virgin; Roman Catholic Church; Universal Church of the Kingdom of God.

References

Cruz, Joan Carroll. *Miraculous Images of Our Lady.* Rockford, IL: Tan Books and Publishers, 1993.

"Marian Titles in the Popular Religiosity of Latin America." The Marian Library/International Marian Research Institute, Dayton, Ohio. http://campus.udayton.edu/mary/resources/english.html. Accessed May 15, 2009.

Batak Christian Community Church

The Batak Christian Community Church (GPKB) was formed in 1927 when a group of ministers and churches withdrew from the Rhenish Mission (now known as the Protestant Christian Batak Church), which had been working for many years among the Batak people of Sumatra, Indonesia. The new church established a presbyterial-synodal polity. The synod operates as the church's governing body. It calls pastors, appoints them to churches, and pays their salaries. The chair of the synod is designated as the church's *ephorus*, or bishop. The church has a Lutheran theological per-

spective, inherited from the German Lutheran Church through the Rhenish Mission.

The church chose the name Gereja Punguan Kristen Batak (Batak Christian Community Church) and is generally designated by the acronym of its Indonesian name, GPKB. Relative to its parent body, it is a small church with around 20,000 members in 41 congregations (2005). It is based among the Batak people but has extended its mission beyond the Batak population to include, for example, the Maya-Maya people in the northern part of the island. It operates two Bible schools for training lay evangelists. Ministers complete their theological work at one of several schools operated by other churches, including that of their parent body.

After World War II, the church reestablished relations with the Rhenish Mission, now known as the United Evangelical Mission, and with the Lutheran Church of Australia. It is also a member of the Lutheran World Fellowship, the Community of Churches in Indonesia, and, since 1975, the World Council of Churches.

J. Gordon Melton

See also: Lutheran World Federation; Protestant Christian Batak Church; Rhenesh Mission; World Council of Churches.

References

Bachmann, E. Theodore, and Mercia Brenne Bachmann. *Lutheran Churches in the World: A Handbook.* Minneapolis, MN: Augsburg Press, 1989.

Van Beek, Huibert. *A Handbook of the Churches and Councils: Profiles of Ecumenical Relationships.* Geneva: World Council of Churches, 2006.

Bear Butte

Bear Butte is a mountain on the western edge of the Black Hills in South Dakota. It is geologically unique, a laccolith, formed by the solidifying of molten magma. Its uniqueness was recognized by the first peoples who moved in and through the area and artifacts discovered by archaeologists suggest its early use as a ritual site.

A sign stands in front of Bear Butte near Sturgis, South Dakota, on August 7, 2006. Bear Butte is a land mass that juts above the prairie where some American Indians come for prayer and religious ceremonies. (AP/Wide World Photos)

In the centuries prior to their contact with European Americans, the Cheyenne and Lakota peoples had designated the mountain as the site for their important religious ceremonies. The Cheyenne people, in particular, recognized Bear Butte as the place where Sweet Medicine, a Cheyenne prophet, had had his encounter with the Creator, Maheo, the Four Sacred Persons, and the Sacred Powers during which he was empowered and received a set of spiritual teachings. After his encounter, he returned to his people and lived among them for the equivalent of four lifetimes. He emerged as a young adult each spring, aged through the summer, fall, and winter, and then returned to youth to begin the process over as the next spring arrived. He taught them the various ritual and sacred ways and gave them the Four Sacred Arrows, the most sacred objects of the Cheyenne.

For the Lakota, the mountain became the site of vision quests, fasting, and prayers, and a place to feel the direct connection with the Creator. Numerous Lakota spiritual leaders spent time there.

The mountain became a site of contention as white people moved into the area and especially after gold was discovered in the Bad Lands. Prospectors looked to the mountain as their guide to the gold deposits. Later, access to the mountain emerged as a matter of contention following the government's restrictions of the Lakota to their reservations. Then, in the 20th century, the mountain started to draw individual Native Americans from across the western United States and Canada who chose it as their place for vision quests and spiritual retreats. Simultaneously the government was making plans for developing the area, in the wake of the 1961 designation of the mountain and the surrounding land as a state park by the state of South Dakota. While cutting off commercial development in the park itself, the park drew tourists by the thousands and targeted land immediately adjacent to the park as prime areas for commercial development. Then in 1980 the U.S. Department of the Interior issued mining leases in the Black Hills and shortly thereafter opened the area for nuclear power plant development. More recently, the growth of tourist activity in the summer months has added noise pollution to the list of concerns by those who view the mountain primarily as sacred space.

In the 1970s, Frank Fools Crow (ca. 1891–1989), a Lakota ceremonial chief, and others of the Lakota and Cheyenne peoples filed a suit that contended that the development of tourist facilities and the resulting tourist traffic around Bear Butte violated their religious freedom by destroying the sanctity of the area. The courts initially ruled against the Native plaintiffs and the case was appealed, but the court of appeals sustained the lower courts and the Supreme Court refused to hear the case. Thus the mountain remains a spot of contention between Native Americans, who wish to reserve the mountain for their sacred activities, and the government, which maintains that its responsibility is to facilitate access for all people who wish to use it for recreational purposes.

J. Gordon Melton

See also: Lakota, The; Native American Religion: Roman Catholicism.

References

Hirschfelder, Arlene, and Paulette Molin. *Encyclopedia of Native American Religions*. New York: Facts on File, 2000.

Odell, Thomas Edward. *Mato Paha; the Story of Bear Butte, Black Hills landmark and Indian shrine. Its scenic, historic, and scientific uniqueness.* Spearfish, SD: the author, 1942.

Oehlerking, Jerry. "The Dick Williams Story: If Bear Butte Would Speak." *South Dakota Conservation Digest* (March–April 1977): 22–25.

Bektashi Order (Bektashiye)

The Bektashiye is a Turkish Sufi brotherhood active today mainly in the Balkans and, though officially banned, in its traditional homeland Turkey. The Bektashis claim patronage of Haji Bektash Veli, a legendary 13th-century figure who, according to Bektashi tradition, traveled from Horasan in eastern Iran to Anatolia as follower of the famous Sufi sheikh Ahmad Yasawi (d. 1166). Haji Bektash was likely involved in the Sufi-led Babai Rebellion against the Seljuk Turks in 1240 in southeastern Anatolia. Following the suppression of the revolt, he settled in a small, central Anatolian village now known as Hacıbektaş. Historical traces connect the Babai Rebellion with the Kizilbash ("Redhead") movement, which organized several regional uprisings against Ottoman rule in the early 16th century. Since the early 20th century, in the context of Turkish nationalism, Kizilbash groups began to be called "Alevi," a label sometimes also applied to the Bektashis. Bektashis and Alevis share part of their history and even more so rites and beliefs, but are different in regard to their social organization, their ethnic composition, and their socio-economic position in Ottoman and Turkish societies. In the modern context, Bektashism has been closely associated and shaped by nationalist movements in Albania and Turkey.

The Bektashiye took on its characteristic feature as a Sufi order in the early 16th century under the leadership of Balim Sultan (d. 1516), possibly appointed as head of the Sufi lodge of Hajibektash by Sultan Bayezid II. Balim Sultan, honored by the Bektashis as their "second master," formalized the rules and structures of the order. He brought together Anatolian dervishes of different traditions (such as Kalenderiye, Haydariye, and Yeseviye) who united in their adoration of Haji Bektash. It is quite possible that the institutionalization of the Bektashis as a *tariqat* (Sufi brotherhood) was politically motivated. Its goal might have been to bind and de-radicalize those parts of the rural Anatolian population who supported and venerated the shah of Persia as their *pir* (religious leader). The Anatolian adherents of the shah, the Kizilbash, were considered a severe political threat to Ottoman hegemony over Anatolia.

Though historically still quite obscure, there are circumstances indicating that the division of the Bektashiye into the two branches of the Babayan and Celebiyan was a product of Balim Sultan's innovations. Due to the reforms he introduced, especially celibacy as a condition for members initiated in the higher ranks of the tariqat, he can be regarded as the founder of the Babayan branch of the Bektashiye. Whereas the

Celebi, spiritual leader of the Celebiyan, legitimized his position by claiming direct descent from Haji Bektash, the Babayan branch insisted on Haji Bektash's celibacy and established the principle of leadership qua election. While the Celebiyan do not bear the formal characteristics of a Sufi brotherhood, but are integrated into the rural Kizilbash-Alevi milieu, the Babayan branch is clearly recognizable as a tariqat.

The hierarchy of the Babayan-Bektashi in its classical form is structured in accordance with the spiritual level of its adherents. The order is led by the elected *dedebaba*, followed by the *dedes* (or *khalifes*) and the *babas*. Traditionally, the babas acted as principals of the dervish lodges, and the primary function of the dede was to keep the various lodges in contact with the center in Hacıbektaş, residence of the dedebaba. The adherents who are not yet initiated and live worldly lives outside the lodge are called *ashik*, while the initiated ones are called *muhip*. After several years of service in the lodge, the muhip may obtain the status of a fully initiated dervish—provided he meets the requirement of celibacy. Low-ranked Bektashis owe obedience to high-ranked Bektashis, who are their guides (*mürshid*) on the mystic path. The vow to celibacy required for initiation into the closer circles of the Bektashiye led to speculations about Christian monastic influences and distinguishes it from other Sufi brotherhoods, which generally encourage their disciples to get married and live in the world.

According to the doctrine of *dört kapı* (Four Gateways) at the heart of Bektashi as well as Alevi belief, the first station of the mystical path is the *şeriat kapısı* (Gateway of the Law), which relates to the exoteric meaning of the religious law. It is followed by the *tarikat kapısı* (Gateway of the Path), entered by a candidate with his initiation into the ritual community. The third station, *marifet kapısı* (Gateway of Knowledge), marks the achievement of mystical experience and knowledge. As metaphor for the achievement of the mystical union with God, the ultimate goal of the Sufi path, the *hakikat kapısı* (Gateway of Truth), refers to the highest level of spiritual maturity.

In contrast to adherents of orthodox Sunni and Shia Islam, the Bektashis typically not only reject the religious duties of Islam, but also perceive God as immanent, manifesting himself in nature and human beings, especially in the human face. The Bektashis themselves link the pantheistic element in their philosophy with the ideas of the famous mystic Ibn ʿArabî (d. 1240), while their conception of God's manifestation in the human derives from the strong influence of the Hurufi sect, which emerged in 15th-century Persia.

With regard to their rites and doctrines, the Bektashis have over time appropriated a broad range of cultural and religious traditions. They belong to those branches of Muslim mysticism that did not follow Islamic law consequently but also cultivated beliefs and practices from outside the Islamic tradition, be it of pre-Islamic Central Asian—as the national Turkish narrative holds—or other, such as Christian, origins. Notwithstanding its non-Muslim elements, Bektashi terminology is highly influenced by Shia mythology and Sufi Muslim ideas. The Bektashis' astonishing ability to integrate foreign religious conceptions may be explained by the fact that the brotherhood has kept a relative distance to the more legalist Islam of the urban elites and has tended to be closer to rural culture, where the boundaries between religious tradition were less clearly defined.

The most important rite of the Bektashis (as well as Alevis) is the so-called Celebration of Communion (*ayin-i cem*). Central to the celebration is the recollection of mythical events of early Shia history and the praising of its martyrs. The recollection is accompanied by the music of the *saz* (a traditional stringed instrument) and mourning hymns. Especially in Ottoman times the (regional) use of alcohol during the ritual communion, the participation of women, and its celebration at night provoked severe criticism from Sunni Muslims, who accused Bektashis and even more so Alevis of celebrating orgies in their gatherings.

The early history of the order is still quite obscure. From the rise of the Ottoman Empire in the 14th century, Bektashi dervishes, as well as adherents of similar traditions that later submerged in the Bektashi tradition, were at the forefront of Ottoman expansion and contributed actively to the Islamization of new territories, mainly in the Balkans. Their close relations with the Ottoman elite forces, the Janissaries, made them a sort of army clergy. In 1826, their institutional relationship with the Ottoman Empire came to an abrupt end when the Janissaries, whom the sultan accused of leading a conspiracy, were dissolved, and the closely related Bektashi Order disbanded. Many of its lodges were destroyed or transferred to the strictly Sunni Naqshbandiyya tariqat, and many highly ranked Bektashis were killed or fled to Albania; by the mid-19th century; however, the order had succeeded in reestablishing itself as a semi-legal organization. Since the second half of the 19th century, some of its social elites developed close relationships to Freemasonry, and subsequently to the emerging Turkish nationalist movement. Still, they were not able to escape the Turkish ban of all Sufi orders in 1925. Thereafter, Bektashis in Turkey had to leave their lodges and could continue their practices only in secrecy. Albania, already the stronghold of the brotherhood, became a refuge for high-ranked Bektashis fleeing Turkey—despite the fact that since the last decades of the 19th century, Albanian and Turkish Bektashis had already parted ways due to their involvement and appropriation of the respective nationalist projects and highly different political and societal circumstances. This alienation deepened when the Turkish Bektashis loosened the rule of celibacy after the closure of the dervish lodges, a measure severely criticized by the Albanian Bektashis.

Today, the order is strongest in Albania, where the Bektashi Order was rehabilitated as an officially recognized religion after the downfall of the Communist regime in 1990. Bektashi convents are found in the Balkans (Albania, Macedonia, and Kosovo), but there is also one in the U.S. state of Michigan. The traditional mother lodge of the brotherhood in Hacıbektaş was converted by the Turkish state into a museum in 1964. Following the Balkans, Turkey is still home to the largest numbers of people associating with Bektashism, even if this association is often of more ideal than institutional nature. The order is relatively secretive and keeps its distance from mainstream Sunni and Shia Islam. For a list of Babayan Bektashi centers and some contact addresses, see the website at http://www.bektashi.net/.

Markus Dressler

See also: Alevism; Naqshbandiya Sufi Order; Shia Islam; Sufism.

References

Birge, John Kingsley. *The Bektashi Order of Dervishes*. 1937; rpt.: London: Weatherhill, 1994.

Dressler, Markus. "Alevīs." In *Encyclopaedia of Islam*, 93–121. 3rd ed. Leiden: Brill, 2008.

Küçük, Hülya. *The Role of the Bektashis in Turkey's National Struggle. A Historical and Critical Study*. Social, Economic and Political Studies of the Middle East and Asia 80. Leiden: Brill, 2002.

Mélikoff, Irène. *Hadji Bektach: un mythe et ses avatars. Genèse et évolution du soufisme populaire en Turquie*. Islamic History and Civilization, Studies and Texts 20. Leiden: Brill, 1998.

Popovic, Alexandre, and Gilles Veinstein, eds. *Bektacchiyya. Etudes sur l'ordre mystique des Bektachis et les groupes relevant de Hadji Bektach*. Istanbul: İsis, 1995.

■ Belarus

An Eastern European country, formerly a part of the Soviet Union, the land-bound Belarus is bounded on the west by Poland and Lithuania, on the south by Ukraine, on the north by Latvia, and on the east by Russia. It is home to 9.7 million residents. The Belarusians form a distinct Slavic ethnic group and speak a distinct language, though one closely related to Polish and Russian. Ethnic Belarusians make up more than 80 percent of the country.

The territory of the present country of Belarus was settled around the first century CE by several Slavic peoples and centuries later participated with Slavic peoples in adjacent lands to form Kiev Rus, the state that eventually gave rise to the modern countries of Russia, Ukraine, and Belarus. The differentiation of the three cultures and languages occurred gradually through the 14th, 15th, and 16th centuries. In 1569, Belarus was incorporated into Poland, and their cultural identity was further forged in the attempt to resist the imposition of the Roman Catholic Church. However, in 1596 the Belarusian Orthodox Church became an Eastern-rite Roman Church.

In the 1790s, Russia completed its annexation of Belarus, and the Orthodox Church was reestablished. At this time, authorities also forbade the use of the term "Belarusian." Belarus became an important part of the Russian Empire, and the key railroad line connecting Moscow to Poland passed through Minsk and Brest.

Belarus

Religion	Followers in 1970	Followers in 2010	% of Population	Annual % growth 2000–2010	Followers in 2025	Followers in 2050
Christians	5,418,000	7,020,000	73.7	–0.15	6,798,000	6,011,000
Orthodox	4,554,000	5,215,000	54.7	0.00	5,043,000	4,451,000
Roman Catholics	810,000	1,040,000	10.9	–0.61	1,040,000	900,000
Protestants	23,300	220,000	2.3	1.91	220,000	240,000
Agnostics	2,208,000	2,127,000	22.3	–0.91	1,608,000	750,000
Atheists	1,403,000	327,000	3.4	–3.94	200,000	120,000
Jews	9,000	26,100	0.3	–0.52	20,000	15,000
Muslims	2,000	27,000	0.3	–0.60	40,000	60,000
Buddhists	0	1,300	0.0	–0.91	1,500	3,000
Ethnoreligionists	0	500	0.0	–0.52	600	800
Baha'is	0	100	0.0	–0.39	200	400
Total population	**9,040,000**	**9,529,000**	**100.0**	**–0.52**	**8,668,000**	**6,960,000**

Belarus became a pocket of discontent at the beginning of the 20th century. At the end of World War I, an independent Belarus was proclaimed, but it dissolved when Poland and the Soviet Union split the land in two. The Polish part of Belarus was incorporated into the Soviet Union in 1937. Finally, in the wake of the dissolution of the Soviet Union, in 1991 Belarus emerged as an independent country.

In 989, Vladimir (ca. 958–1015), the ruler of the Kiev Rus, converted to Orthodox Christianity, and the process of Christianization of the Slavic people, including the Belarusians, began. It was largely completed over the next centuries. A form of Orthodox Christianity utilizing the Slavonic language came to dominate in the region.

In the 14th century, Lithuania expanded to include the Belarusians, and the Lithuanians brought Roman Catholicism with them. Several orders, including the Franciscans, began work among the people, and the Catholic Church began to draw away believers from Orthodoxy. This initiated a centuries-long struggle between the two churches. That struggle had a major turning point in 1596, when Bishop Ipaci Pocei (1541–1613) led in a union of the Orthodox and Catholic factions by convincing the Orthodox leaders to form a Uniate church. The Orthodox kept their liturgy and many of their customs but united with Rome theologically and administratively. Thus the Greek Catholic Church came to dominate in Belarus.

Following the Russian takeover a century later, authorities suppressed the Roman Catholic Church, both the Latin rite and the Greek rite, and imposed the Russian Orthodox Church on Belarus. Believers in the western part of the country, especially those of the Latin rite of Polish background, resisted the Russification and remained loyal to Rome. Their position was supported between 1921 and 1939 when Western Belarus was again part of Poland. However, the Greek rite was almost totally suppressed.

Both the Orthodox and Catholic churches suffered during the Soviet era, but both were able to revive in the 1990s. The Greek Church essentially started over in 1990. It currently has a dozen parishes in the major cities of the county served by six priests and one deacon. Seminarians are in training and will be immediately put into service as new parishes emerge across the country.

In 1989, the Russian Orthodox Church in Belarus was designated as a semi-autonomous Belarusian Exarchate. The 10 dioceses include approximately half of the 10 million citizens of the country. In 2006, Archbishop Tadevush Kandrusievich (b. 1946) succeeded Cardinal Kazmierz Swiatek (b. 1914) as archbishop of the Minsk-Mogilev Archdiocese. Archbishop Kanrusievich now heads the approximately 400 Roman Catholic parishes, with adherents making up an estimated 10 to 20 percent of the population.

In 1997, the government established the State Committee on Religious and National Affairs (SCRNA)

Belarusians dance around a fire during the Ivan Kupala festival, a night-long celebration marking the summer solstice and the feast of St. John the Baptist. The late June holiday is generally marked with bonfires and the wearing of flowered garlands. (AP/Wide World Photos)

to oversee the various religions and denominations. The government, while professing to treat all religions as equal before the law, has shown distinct bias in favor of the Orthodox Church, which receives various financial advantages. The country's president has declared the preservation and development of the Orthodox Church to be a moral goal of the country. The Roman Catholic Church, as the second largest religious organization, has seen itself in a struggle for equal treatment by the government.

Lutheranism spread to Lithuania in the 1540s and from there found its way to the cities of Belarus. Following close behind were representatives of the Reformed tradition. Beginning in the 1570s, however, Polish Unitarianism, that is, Socinianism, spread into Belarus, and all three variations on Protestant Christianity competed with each other and found their pock-

ets of strength. While facing various problems, the Reformation churches survived into the 20th century, but during the Soviet era they disappeared. In 1992, the first congregation of the Belarusian Evangelical Reformed Church was founded in Minsk as a self-conscious attempt to revive the Reformed tradition. Lutheranism also revived in the 1990s; in 1997 there were 4 parishes and 10 parishes by the end of the century. The constituting Synod of the Belarusian Evangelical Lutheran Church took place on December 2, 2000, in Viciebsk.

Baptists began work in Belarus in 1877, when Dmitri P. Semenstov, who had become a Baptist while living in Odessa, returned to his home village of Usokh. He built up a small following, which constituted the first (and for some years the only) Baptist congregation in the country. In the meantime, Baptists began to

BELARUS

arrive in Belarus from their center in St. Petersburg. A second congregation was organized in 1912 under the leadership of B. S. Cheberuk. Through the early 20th century various other Protestant and Free churches emerged, including the first Pentecostal churches and a few Methodist churches.

The annexation of Belarus to Russia in 1937, the attempts to suppress religion by the Marxist government, and World War II led to numerous changes in the ensuing years. The Baptists joined with other Evangelicals in the All-Union Council of Evangelical Christians-Baptists in 1944. Pentecostals merged into the Union in 1945. Even earlier, in 1937, the Methodists had disbanded the Russian Mission and advised all the members to join the Baptists or one of the other Free churches. What is now the Union of Evangelical Christians-Baptists experienced continued suppression through the 1960s but found some relief in the 1980s and enjoyed significant growth through the 1990s. When allowed, the Pentecostals pulled away and formed their own church. The Pentecostal Union, with more than 16,000 members, is the largest evangelical church in Belarus. The Seventh-day Adventist Church also had established work in the country, which was organized into the Belarus Conference in 1978.

Some religions are viewed as traditional, including Russian Orthodoxy, Roman Catholicism, Judaism, and Islam (as practiced by a small community of ethnic Tatars with roots in the country dating back to the 11th century); some are viewed as nontraditional, including some Protestant and other faiths; and some are viewed as sects, including Eastern religions and other faiths. The authorities deny permission to register legally at the national level to some faiths considered to be non-traditional, and to all considered to be sects. Without legal registration, it is extremely difficult to rent or purchase property in order to hold religious services.

Jews appear to have first settled in Belarus in the 15th century and were identified with the Lithuanian segment of the population. Through the next century communities sprang up in most of the larger towns and cities. They periodically faced attempts to force them to convert to Christianity and often had to pay taxes at a much higher rate than Christians. At the time of the Russian annexation of all of Belarus in 1939, there were more than 400,000 Jews living there. During the time that the Germans occupied the territory of the Soviet Union, approximately three-fourths of the Jewish population (including those trapped in Belarus) were massacred. After the war, less than 100,000 could be found in Belarus. In 1989 there were some 112,000 Jews in Belarus, but over the next 3 years almost 50,000 migrated to Israel and elsewhere. Migration to Israel continued through the 1990s, but some 40,000 Jews remain in the country, and synagogues remain open throughout Belarus.

There is a small Islamic community in Belarus, which dates to the 11th century when Tatars settled there. Today some 100,000 Muslims reside in 25 communities throughout the country, which are organized through the Islamic Association of Belarus.

Like Judaism, Islam is considered a traditional religion of Belarus by the government. In stark contrast are the new religions that have entered the country over the last generation, especially during the 1990s. The International Society for Krishna Consciousness, the Unification Church, and the Church of Scientology have opened centers. Buddhism has entered into the country through the Diamond Way Kagyu Karma Tibetan lineage under Ole Nydahl. The Church of Jesus Christ of Latter-day Saints opened work in Minsk at the beginning of 1994. Although these newer religions in Belarus represent only a small percentage of the population, they have introduced the country to the world's contemporary religious pluralism.

J. Gordon Melton

See also: Baptists; Church of Jesus Christ of Latter-day Saints; Church of Scientology; Diamond Way Buddhism; Franciscans; Free Churches; Greek Catholic Church; International Society for Krishna Consciousness; Lutheranism; Roman Catholic Church; Seventh-day Adventist Church; Unification Movement; Union of Evangelical Christians-Baptists of Russia.

References

Plotky, Serhi. *The Origins of the Slavic Nations: Premodern Identities in Russia, Ukraine, and Belarus.* Cambridge: Cambridge University Press, 2006.

Rigsby, J. "Standing Room Only: Christian Resurgence in Belarus." *Christian Century* 111 (July 17–August 3, 1994): 709–711.

The World Factbook. Washington, DC: Central Intelligence Agency, 2008. https://www.cia.gov/library/publications/the-world-factbook/geos/bo.html.

■ Belgium

The area covered by the present-day Federal Kingdom of Belgium has found itself under the rule of various European powers and empires during its history, being used as a pawn on the international political chessboard.

Christianity was gradually introduced into the country at the end of Roman rule, but evangelism did not really start until the sixth and seventh centuries, when missionaries such as Eloi, Aubert, Amand, and others came into the area from present-day France. At that time, the local population still worshipped Gallo-Roman and Germanic deities. In the eighth century, monasteries enjoyed exceptional prosperity and became centers of intense agricultural and economic activity. The Roman Catholic Church dominated social and political life throughout the Middle Ages.

In the 15th century, the Belgian territories fell under the rule of the House of Burgundy and later, the Austrian Habsburgs. In the 16th century, Charles V, grandson of the Habsburg Archduke Maximilian of Austria and son of Joanna of Aragon, inaugurated Spanish rule

Roman Catholic Cathedral of Our Lady, Antwerp, Belgium. Roman Catholicism has played an important role in Belgium's history and remains a significant force in the country. (Jchambers/Dreamstime.com)

over the Low Countries. Initially encompassing present-day Belgium, Luxembourg, and The Netherlands, the Low Countries progressively became part of a wider empire, which included German and Austrian territories, a part of Italy, the Iberian Peninsula, and recently discovered territories in Central and South America. Under Charles V's rule, and despite his own role as staunch defender of the Catholic Church, the Protestant Reformation was introduced into Belgium by the Lutherans, Anabaptists, and Calvinists. The first decrees curbing heresies were passed in the 1520s. The Inquisition raged over the Low Countries; with the encouragement of Charles V, it was carried out by civil courts, but clerics of the Catholic Church were also involved in the proceedings as experts. In 1523, two Lutherans were burned at the stake in Brussels as the Inquisition's first martyrs. Thousands of heretics or suspected heretics were tortured, hanged, drowned, decapitated, burned, or buried alive. Many Protestants fled the country and settled in Germany, England, or the New World. One of the villages they founded was on the island of Manhattan, the current location of New York City.

Charles V's son and successor, Philip II, retained the policy of supporting the Inquisition. In 1565, 2,000 noblemen requested the then governor of the Low Countries, Margaret of Parma, to put an end to the Inquisition and establish freedom of religion. Encouraged by this defiance, Protestants set out to destroy images, paintings, and statues in Catholic churches, an uprising called the iconoclast fury. A number of Calvinist noblemen set up an army to obtain freedom of religion but were defeated by Spanish troops in 1567, north of Antwerp. In the same year, Philip II sent the duke of Alba to the Low Countries to stamp out Protestantism for good. The earls of Egmont and Hoorne, leaders of the rebellion, were decapitated; around 1,100 death sentences were pronounced, and the total possessions of about 9,000 people were confiscated. By 1585, the Catholic Counter-Reformation had been successful in the southern part of the Low Countries (present-day Belgium), but war continued with the northern provinces (mainly the present-day Netherlands), which eventually managed to become independent, serving as a refuge for persecuted Protestants from the southern provinces.

Until the beginning of the 18th century, the area now called Belgium remained under Spanish rule (a rule challenged by the kings of France) and so also under the influence of Roman Catholicism. However, from 1640 on, the Roman Catholic Church faced an internal conflict between Jansenists and Jesuits. At its origin was the publication in 1640 of the book *Augustinus*, written by the late bishop of Ypres, Corneille Jansen (1585–1638); the book's interpretation of the teachings of Saint Augustine (354–430) was close to Protestant ideas of the time. The Jansenist movement inspired by the book survived in the country until around 1725–1730.

Belgium

Religion	Followers in 1970	Followers in 2010	% of Population	Annual % growth 2000–2010	Followers in 2025	Followers in 2050
Christians	8,914,000	8,636,000	82.1	–0.10	8,445,000	8,105,000
Roman Catholics	8,655,000	7,750,000	73.7	–0.33	7,600,000	7,200,000
Protestants	77,000	130,000	1.2	0.89	140,000	170,000
Marginals	50,500	58,400	0.6	–0.66	60,000	100,000
Agnostics	477,000	1,200,000	11.4	4.88	1,350,000	1,450,000
Muslims	90,000	390,000	3.7	0.51	600,000	700,000
Atheists	100,000	212,000	2.0	0.39	250,000	270,000
Jews	40,000	27,900	0.3	0.40	28,000	30,000
Buddhists	4,000	24,800	0.2	0.47	30,000	40,000
Confucianists	1,000	9,000	0.1	0.40	10,000	11,700
Sikhs	0	5,300	0.1	0.40	6,000	7,000
Spiritists	800	4,100	0.0	0.50	5,000	6,400
Hindus	0	3,200	0.0	0.40	4,000	4,500
Baha'is	1,800	3,000	0.0	4.02	4,000	6,500
Ethnoreligionists	500	3,500	0.0	0.40	4,000	4,700
New religionists	2,100	2,200	0.0	0.40	4,400	5,800
Jains	0	900	0.0	0.50	1,200	1,500
Zoroastrians	10	20	0.0	0.00	50	100
Total population	**9,632,000**	**10,522,000**	**100.0**	**0.40**	**10,742,000**	**10,643,000**

In the 18th century, the area now called Belgium was under Austrian rule, with the exception of a few years of French occupation. In 1781, the Austrian Habsburg emperor, Joseph II, published an Edict of Tolerance, which recognized freedom of worship and established that all citizens, whatever their religion, would have equal access to public jobs. He also attacked the privileges of the Catholic Church, dissolving hundreds of convents, replacing all episcopal seminaries with one general seminary under his authority and limiting the number of processions, and the like. These measures caused widespread opposition among the clergy.

In 1789, the French Revolution abolished absolute monarchy and the privileges of the Catholic Church in France. Six years later, the French Republic opened war against the Austrian Empire, annexed the Belgian territories, and converted them into nine French administrative divisions to be ruled according to the French law and Constitution. Many churches were closed or desecrated, abbeys were burned down, and hundreds of nonjuring priests were deported. To restore religious peace, Napoleon reestablished freedom of worship for

the Catholic Church and concluded a concordat with the Vatican.

After the fall of Napoleon in 1815, Britain, Austria, Prussia, and Russia agreed to include the (predominantly Catholic) Belgian territories in the (Protestant-dominated) Kingdom of the Netherlands, to protect themselves against France. Through various repressive measures, the new sovereign, William I, tried to bring the Catholic Church to its knees, quickly alienating his new Catholic subjects in the process. He closed Catholic schools, expelled the Christian Brothers, left three of the five dioceses vacant, and broke off concordat negotiations with the Holy See. All the minor seminaries were closed, and candidates for the priesthood had to attend a state-run college. It was in this context that unionism, a political coalition between Catholics and anticlerical liberals formed to drive out the Dutch, began to take shape in the 1820s.

In September 1830, the Belgians rebelled against Dutch rule and gained independence under the protection of England and France. A parliamentary monarchy was created, and Leopold I, a German Lutheran, was chosen as the first king. The Belgian Constitution

BELGIUM

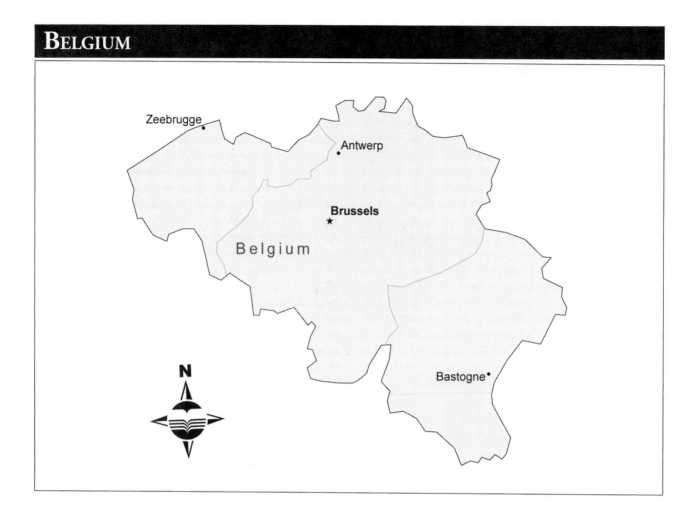

of 1831 guaranteed complete freedom of worship, including the right of each religious body to select its own officials without state interference. Freedom of education was also recognized.

Catholicism, Protestantism (about 5,000 members, only 2,000 of whom were Belgians), and Judaism (with then about 1,000 members) enjoyed de facto state recognition. They were followed by Anglicanism (only a few hundred members) in 1835. The state did not endorse the theological claims of any religion but afforded a privileged status to all of them on the basis of their social utility, providing for the payment of the salaries and retirement pensions of their clergy and chaplains, the maintenance of their places of worship, and other material advantages.

In 1846, the Catholic-Liberal political alliance disintegrated. During the next 30 years, bitter political battles took place between Catholics and Liberals, especially over Catholic and public school issues.

Under Leopold II (1865–1909), Protestantism's various denominations experienced some significant growth. The Salvation Army opened a mission in 1889. In 1904 the first Baptist church was established. In 1899 the (Dutch-speaking) Reformed churches were created.

World War I (1914–1918) slowed down the expansion of Protestantism, but this conflict also drew the attention of British and American Protestants to Belgium. A number of missions, which had helped war victims and Belgian troops under siege, opened several churches after 1918. The American evangelists Ralph and Judith Norton founded the Belgian Evangelical Mission and a Biblical Institute in 1919. The Jehovah's Witnesses movement also started in the 1920s. British and American Methodists created the Methodist Mission in 1922. In 1923, a Swedish couple began to spread Pentecostal teachings, but it was only in the aftermath of World War II (1940–1945) that the Pentecostal denomination emerged under the name of Assemblies of God. Between the two World Wars, a number of Protestant denominations progressively joined the main branch of Protestantism that had been recognized just after the creation of the Belgian state.

Since 1945, evangelical and Pentecostal churches have grown rapidly, in particular in the last few decades because of the immigration from Africa. Their followers now number more than those of the historical Protestant churches. Inevitably, the merging process continued after World War II and led in 1978 to the creation of the United Protestant Church of Belgium (EPUB/VPKB). In 2003, a major merger brought together the EPUB/VPKB and most of the evangelical and Pentecostal churches. The new official interlocutor of the Belgian state is now named Administrative Council of the Protestant and Evangelical Religion (CAPCE).

The influx of peoples from Central and Eastern European countries along with Muslim countries has opened the door to both Eastern Orthodoxy and Islam in Belgium. Islam (then numbering about 250,000 adherents) was recognized by the state in 1974. Most Muslims come from North Africa (the Malekite School of Islam) and from Egypt and Turkey (the Hanafite School of Islam). Orthodoxy enjoyed state recognition in 1985. Orthodox Christians then numbered about 40,000 and are affiliated with either the Greek Orthodox Church (under the Ecumenical Patriarchate) or the Russian Orthodox Church. Secular Humanism was recognized by the state as a worldview in 1994 and enjoyed the same material advantages as state-sanctioned religions. Buddhism is in the process of being recognized by the state as a worldview. Various Hindu denominations have set up a common platform to apply for state recognition. Jehovah's Witnesses, who number about 40,000, have never applied for a similar status.

Secularization of society is progressing constantly. Out of a population of 10.5 million inhabitants, only about 45 percent still identify themselves as of Catholic culture (only 7 percent regularly attend religious services). About 10 percent are indifferent to religion, agnostic, or atheist. About 4 percent are of Muslim culture. Protestants number about 150,000; Orthodox 70,000; Jews 50,000; Anglicans 11,000; Buddhists and Hindus 10,000; and Mormons 4,000.

In 1997, a parliamentary commission on cults issued a report listing 189 religious movements suspected of being "harmful cults." Most of them were new religious movements that settled in Belgium in the second half of the 20th century, but there were more than 20 Christian evangelical and Pentecostal-oriented groups mentioned, and even some Roman Catholic movements such as the Charismatics. Since the publication of that report and the creation of an observatory on cults, many communities of faith or belief have regularly complained in international fora about religious intolerance and discrimination by public institutions and non-state actors, including the media. The Anthroposophic Society, the Universal Church of God, and Sahaja Yoga have won several cases in court against the Belgian state or its institutions on the grounds of defamation.

Willy Fautré

See also: Assemblies of God; Ecumenical Patriarchate/ Patriarchate of Constantinople; Hanafite School of Islam; Jehovah's Witnesses; Jesuits; Malikite School of Islam; Roman Catholic Church; Salvation Army; United Protestant Church of Belgium.

References

Braekman, Emile. *Le protestantisme belge au 16me siècle.* Carrières-sous-Poissy, France: Editions La Cause, 1997.

Braekman, Emile. *150 ans de vie protestante en Belgique.* Brussels, Belgium: Bulletin VIII-7 de la Société d'histoire du protestantisme belge, 1980.

Hasquin, Hervé. *La Wallonie, son histoire.* Brussels, Belgium: Editions Luc Pire, 1999.

Jansen, H. P. H. *Prisma Kalendarium. Geschiedenis van de Lage Landen in jaartallen,* Utrecht, Nederland: Uitgeverij Het Spectrum, 1995.

■ Belize

Belize, known as British Honduras from 1862 until 1973, is located on the southeastern part of the Yucatan Peninsula on the Caribbean coast between Mexico to

Belize

Religion	Followers in 1970	Followers in 2010	% of Population	Annual % growth 2000–2010	Followers in 2025	Followers in 2050
Christians	116,000	279,000	91.2	2.41	352,000	437,000
Roman Catholics	74,500	237,000	77.5	2.51	300,000	360,000
Protestants	15,100	80,700	26.4	3.31	100,000	125,000
Anglicans	16,000	10,000	3.3	−1.47	10,000	10,000
Baha'is	2,900	7,500	2.5	2.41	10,000	13,000
Hindus	0	6,200	2.0	2.41	9,000	12,000
Jews	1,400	3,100	1.0	2.41	3,600	4,500
Spiritists	1,400	2,900	0.9	2.40	3,600	4,500
Agnostics	100	2,200	0.7	2.41	4,500	7,500
Ethnoreligionists	1,000	1,900	0.6	2.41	1,500	1,200
Muslims	0	1,600	0.5	2.42	2,500	4,000
Buddhists	0	1,500	0.5	2.40	2,000	3,000
Atheists	0	70	0.0	2.34	100	200
Total population	**123,000**	**306,000**	**100.0**	**2.41**	**389,000**	**487,000**

the north and Guatemala to the west and south. The area of the country is 8,867 square miles, and it had an estimated population of 312,000 in 2008. The growing Mestizo community now comprises 48.7 percent of the nation's population. The Creole community, composed of English-speaking persons of African or mixed African and European ancestry, has declined to 24.9 percent. The Mayan community continues to be about 10 percent of the population. The Garinagu (singular Garifuna) community, also known historically as the Black Carib, constitutes about 6 percent. The remaining 10 percent of the population includes Europeans, East Indians (Hindus), Chinese, Middle Easterners (mainly Lebanese and Jews), and North Americans.

The Euro-North American population of Belize includes many Mennonites who arrived in the 1950s and 1960s by way of Canada, the United States and Mexico. Also, there is a sizeable community of people who identify as East Indian, some of whose ancestors came to Belize from Jamaica in the 1850s, others from various Caribbean countries in the 1880s, and still others from India during the 1950s.

About 50 percent of the population claimed adherence to the Roman Catholic Church in 2000 (census), while Protestant groups accounted for about 36 percent; adherents to "other religions" were 4.6 percent; and those who reported "no religion" or provided "no answer" were 10 percent. The government of Belize actively promotes a spirit of religious tolerance. The Constitution provides for freedom of religion, and other laws and policies contribute to the free practice of religion.

The fact that Belize's literacy rate is 94 percent reflects the nation's commitment to providing basic education for its citizens. The church-administered school is the foundation for the country's education system, and this system of government-subsidized church-run schools dates to 1816 when the Anglican Church organized and managed the first public school. Historically, three denominations have administered most of the country's public schools (Anglican, Roman Catholic, and Methodist churches), although today other denominations are also operating public schools with government subsidies, including the Mennonites, Seventh-day Adventists, Belize Baptist Association, Church of the Nazarene, Gospel Missionary Union, Assemblies of God, the Salvation Army, Christian Brethren, Church of God in Christ, and others.

This small nation (about the size of Massachusetts) has more historical ties to the Caribbean than to the rest of Central America. The first European settlers in the region of modern Belize were called Baymen, who settled in the Belize City area in the 1650s. They were mainly English buccaneers and pirates in the Bay of Honduras who were trying to outmaneuver the Spanish rulers in Mexico and Central America.

BELIZE

The British and Spanish engaged in frequent disputes over the territory of Belize, even after the 1763 Treaty of Paris established the former's rights to cut logwood in Belize. The Baymen were chased out of the territory by the Spaniards no less than four times between 1717 and 1780. Treaties in 1783 and 1786 gave the Baymen more security; but only after the Battle of St. George's Caye in 1798, when the Baymen and their armed slaves defeated—with the help of several British naval commanders—a Spanish naval force from Mexico, did the Baymen have full control of their settlement, which was affirmed by its admission to British colonial status in 1863 as the Colony of British Honduras. The anniversary of this famous battle is now a national holiday in Belize.

It was the Baymen who established the slavery system in Belize in order to provide a workforce for the logwood trade. The imported African slaves, acquired mainly from the British-controlled areas of the Caribbean, were not allowed to own land and had to depend on their slave masters for all their supplies, but they could associate with each other. Before the arrival of 2,207 slaves and freedmen (former slaves) from the Misquito Coast in 1787, the Baymen of Belize numbered fewer than 800 and had no more than 2,600 slaves. Slavery was abolished in the British Empire in 1838.

After the independence of Central America from Spanish rule in 1821, the British government claimed the right to administer part of the Caribbean coast of Central America, from Belize in the north to Nicaragua in the south, where British colonies had previously been established. In 1862–1863, Great Britain formally declared Belize a Crown colony, subordinate to the colonial government of Jamaica, and renamed it British Honduras.

The Great Depression of the 1930s caused a near-collapse of the colonial economy and a series of public demonstrations and riots in 1934 marked the beginning of an independence movement in Belize. After World War II, the colony's economy again stagnated, especially after Britain devalued the British Honduras currency in 1949. This situation led to the creation of the People's Committee, which demanded independence from Great Britain. In 1964, British Honduras became a self-governing colony, was renamed Belize on June 1, 1973, and gained full independence from the United Kingdom in 1981. Today, it is a constitutional monarchy and a member of the British Commonwealth of Nations.

Belize is the only country in Central America where English is the national language and Protestantism has been the dominant religion. However, due to the large-scale immigration of Spanish-speaking peoples from Mexico, Guatemala, Honduras, and El Salvador during the 19th and 20th centuries, the size of the Spanish-speaking population had increased to about half of the nation's total population in 2000 and the size of the Roman Catholic population has grown correspondingly.

The Roman Catholic Church   Although the Roman Catholic Church was not officially present in British Honduras until 1851, when the first Catholic missionaries arrived, by 1860 the Catholic community in Belize City accounted for 15 percent of the total population. However, the growth of the Catholic Church in Belize prior to 1900 occurred chiefly among the Amerindian, Mestizo, and Garifuna peoples in rural areas, and not among the Creoles in Belize City. Even as the early Protestant denominations in Belize mainly grew from the influx of Afro-European immigrants (called West Indians or Creoles) from the British-controlled islands of the Caribbean, so also the Catholic Church there increased principally due to the influx of Mayan refugees from Mexico's Yucatán Peninsula who settled in the northern lowlands of Belize during the late 1840s, as well as from the immigration of other Amerindian and Mestizo peoples from Guatemala after 1850.

The missionary zeal of the early Jesuits (Society of Jesus) from Jamaica, England, and Italy prior to the 1890s, and of the American Jesuits from the Society of Jesus' Missouri Province since 1893, has strengthened the position of the Roman Catholic Church in Belize, especially among the Mestizos, Amerindians, and Garifuna. The Vicariate Apostolic of British Honduras was created in 1893, but it was not until 1956 that a Bishopric was organized there. The Jesuits, aided by other religious orders, established schools and social ministries, in addition to parish churches, throughout the country among the various ethnic groups.

There were few, if any, Roman Catholics among the early settlers of Belize. In 1837, Belize became part of the new Vicariate of Jamaica, with the Very Reverend Benito Fernández (a Spanish Franciscan), as its first vicar (1837–1855). In 1848 the mission received its first notable influx of Catholics, mainly from Mexico's Yucatán Peninsula; about 7,000 Mestizos took refuge in British Honduras to escape the so-called Caste War of Yucatán (1847–1901). This war was an uprising by ethnic Mayans against the Mestizo population of European descent (called *Yucatecos*) for political and economic control of the Yucatán Peninsula, which was an ancient center of Mayan civilization (ca. 500–1546 CE).

Some Jesuits who passed through the colony in 1850 were asked by the newly arrived Catholics from Mexico to have priests sent to them. As a result of their intervention, the vicar apostolic of Jamaica (Bishop Benito Fernández) visited Belize, accompanied by Friar James Eustace DuPeyron (a Jamaican Jesuit) who built the first Catholic church in 1851. This is considered the founding date of the Belize Catholic Mission. The Very Reverend James Eustace DuPeyron, S.J., became head of the Vicariate of Jamaica in 1855. He visited the Belize Catholic Mission several times until 1871, when he resigned his office and was succeeded by the Very Reverend Joseph Woollett, S.J.

Later, because of the difficulty of communication between Jamaica and British Honduras, the latter territory was separated from the Vicariate of Jamaica. This led to the establishment of the Prefecture Apostolic of British Honduras in 1888, which was headed by the Reverend Salvatore di Pietro (d. 1898) (a Sicilian Jesuit) from 1869, with several interruptions, until 1893, when he was appointed the vicar apostolic of British Honduras and consecrated bishop. He was succeeded in 1898 by the Reverend Frederick Charles Hopkins (1844–1923), an English Jesuit. In 1925, the name of the diocese was changed to the Vicariate Apostolic of Belize and was administered under the Metropolitan Archdiocese of Kingston in Jamaica.

A few months after the consecration of Bishop di Pietro in 1893, the Belize Catholic Mission was removed from the care of the English province of the Society of Jesus, and attached to the Missouri Province. This resulted in more priests coming to serve in the Belize Mission, and new residences were built for them. Ten years previously, in January 1883, several Sisters of Mercy had come to Belize from New Orleans and had opened a convent for girls. A school for boys was established in 1887 by the Reverend Cassian Gillett, an English Jesuit; this institution was replaced nine years later by St. John Berchmans' College, established in 1896. In May 1898, the Sisters of the Holy Family (an Afro-American religious order) arrived from New Orleans and began a teaching ministry in Dangriga among the Garifuna.

In 1900, most of the Catholic population of the vicariate was scattered throughout the territory in small villages. There were few roads at the time; communication was by boat via the waterways or on horseback through the dense tropical bush. The diversity of language presented another obstacle because the population was (and still is) very heterogeneous; most lived in conditions of poverty.

Diverse tensions arose within the Roman Catholic Church in Central America during the 1960s and following years, because of challenges posed by the Second Vatican Council (1962–1965), the Conference of Latin American Bishops held in Medellín (Colombia) in 1968, Latin American Liberation Theology, and the Catholic Charismatic Renewal movement. These powerful new currents polarized Catholic bishops, priests (diocesan and religious), lay brothers and sisters (members of religious orders), and the laity in general into various factions. *Traditionalists* wanted the church to remain as it was prior to the reforms approved by the Second Vatican Council (mid-1960s), with an emphasis on apostolic authority, orthodox theology, the sacraments, and personal piety. *Reformers* generally supported the church's modern, post-Second Vatican Council stance of modernization and toleration of diversity based on its official social doctrine. *Progressives*, inspired by reforms approved at the Second Vatican and Medellín conferences, sought to implement the new vision for "a preferential option for the poor" through social and political action aimed at transforming society and establishing greater social justice through peaceful democratic means. *Radicals* adopted the Marxist-inspired Liberation Theology and advocated violent revolution by the people as a means of overthrowing Central American dictatorships and creating Socialist states that would serve the poor, marginalized masses. *Charismatic agents* sought to transform the spiritual and communal life of Catholics by means of the power and gifts of the Holy Spirit (including the "baptism of the Holy Spirit and speaking in tongues"), rather than by political and social activism.

Today, the Diocese of Belize City-Belmopan is subordinate to the Archdiocese of Kingston (Jamaica) and a member of the Antilles Episcopal Conference. Bishop Dorick Wright replaced Bishop O. P. Martin as head of the Diocese of Belize City-Belmopan in January 2007. In 2006, the diocese had a total of only 13 parishes, served by 17 diocesan and 13 religious priests, in addition to 16 religious brothers and 49 religious sisters (nuns) in Belize. The cathedral of the diocese is Holy Redeemer Catholic Church in Belize City (first built in 1858, rebuilt several times, and consecrated as a cathedral in 1894); and Our Lady of Guadalupe Cathedral in Belmopan is the co-cathedral of the diocese.

Catholics predominate in every administrative district, with the exception of the District of Belize, where 55 percent of the population is Protestant and largely Creole. As the Mestizo and Amerindian segments of the population increase during coming years, along with a corresponding decrease in the proportion that is Creole, the size of the Catholic Community will tend to increase as well.

The Protestant Movement Protestant missionary efforts were first begun in British Honduras by the Anglican Church (also known as the Church of England), which is now part of the Church in the Province of the West Indies. This jurisdiction includes the Caribbean islands as well as Guyana and Surinam, with headquarters in Nassau, in the Bahamas. Anglican chaplains were first sent to the colony of British Honduras in the 1770s by the Society for the Propagation of the Gospel in Foreign Parts to attend to the spiritual needs of the British colonists and military garrison concentrated in Belize Town, a former pirate enclave at the mouth of the Belize River, probably founded in 1638.

Until the 1860s the Anglican Church (supported by the British colonial government) dominated the religious life of the colonists, which was centered in Belize Town as St. John's Anglican Cathedral, built in 1815. The size of the Anglican community in Belize has gradually increased over the years, mainly due to natural population growth. From about 12,000 adherents in 1936, the number of Anglicans increased to 17,783, according to the 1970 census. In 1980, there were about 16,894 adherents, scattered among 26 organized parishes and mission stations, and the Anglican Church operated 23 primary schools and 2 secondary schools in Belize. However, according to the 2000 census, there were a total of 12,386 Anglican adherents in Belize, which means that many former Anglicans may have joined other churches or reported "no religion."

During the early 1800s, groups of English nonconformists or dissenters (meaning non-Anglicans) began arriving in British Honduras, which led to a progressive erosion of Anglican influence even though it was the established church. English Baptist and Methodist missionaries were sent to the colony in 1822 and 1824, respectively, and Scottish Presbyterian laymen began work in Belize Town in 1825. St. Andrews Presbyterian Church was formally established in the 1850s. By 1856, the Protestant community of Belize Town, where most of the inhabitants of the colony resided, included 2,500 Anglicans, 500 Methodists, 500 Baptists, and 200 Presbyterians, in addition to 1,000 Roman Catholics and 2,260 "others" in a total population of about 7,000 people.

The origin of British Methodist work in Belize is attributed to a British merchant, William Jeckel, who arrived in the early 1800s and was instrumental in organizing Methodist societies in Belize Town, Burrell Boom, and Freetown. In 1824, Jeckel requested help from the Wesleyan Methodist Missionary Society in England, which soon sent three missionaries to the colony. In 1829, Methodist work consisted of one small chapel in Belize City and a few preaching points along the inland rivers. According to Kenneth Grubb (1937), the British and Foreign Bible Society began colportage work in the colony in 1819 with the help of the Methodists.

Early Methodist missionary endeavors in Belize were plagued by sickness and death, storms and fires, staff shortages and financial hardships, and membership growth and decline for more than a century. In 1913, the British Methodist District of the Wesleyan Methodist Church consisted of 2,000 communicant members and was served by 9 ministers, including 3 native Belizeans.

After the withdrawal of the Wesleyan Missionary Society from the western Caribbean in 1930, the British Honduras District was under the supervision of the Methodist Church in Jamaica from 1932 to 1952. In 1967, the Belize–Honduras District became a founding member of the autonomous Methodist Church in the Caribbean and the Americas, with headquarters in St. Johns, Antigua, in the West Indies. In 1960 there were 1,800 communicant members among the 15 Methodist congregations in Belize; in 1978, 22 churches were reported with about 1,700 communicant members; and in 2000 the situation was about the same.

The London-based Baptist Missionary Society began work in Belize City in 1822, with the arrival of Mr. and Mrs. Joseph Bourne, not to serve the spiritual needs of the English colonists but to Christianize their slaves and freedmen. In 1832, the population of the colony of Belize totaled about 4,550, which included 2,100 slaves, 2,200 free African people, and fewer than 300 whites.

The Baptists shared a similar history of trials and tribulations with the Methodists, in an inhospitable climate that caused much sickness and death among the early missionaries. Bourne organized the First Baptist Church in 1825 and served a small congregation of 20 members until leaving the colony in 1834. Another Englishman, Alexander Henderson, arrived in late 1834 to continue the work of evangelism among slaves, soldiers, and discharged prisoners in the poorer sections of Belize Town.

Henderson was assisted by other missionaries from England during the 1840s, but not without controversy. Because Henderson practiced closed Communion (only baptized Baptists could receive the Lord's Supper), several new recruits from the Baptist Missionary Society refused to work with him. Henderson was forced to resign from the Mission in 1850, but he soon organized the Independent Baptist Mission of Belize with the support of most of his former members. Consequently, the Baptist Missionary Society decided to abandon Belize, recalled its missionaries, and sold its properties, leaving Henderson as the uncontested leader of the Baptist movement. In 1850, Baptist work in Belize included 2 organized churches,

7 preaching stations, 3 day schools, 5 Sunday schools, and about 230 baptized members. Henderson pioneered the founding of the Queen Street Baptist Church in 1850, which he pastored from 1850 to 1879.

During the late 1830s, a young English seaman, Frederick Crowe (1819–1846), became interested in Henderson's work, was converted to Christianity, and joined the Baptist Church. Crowe, with some formal education in English and French, became a teacher in the Baptist school and, later, served as an evangelist and missionary with the Belize Baptist Mission. Between 1841 and 1846, Crowe was a traveling agent for the British Honduran Bible Society; in 1843, he became the first Protestant missionary to work in Guatemala. Although Crowe was expelled from Guatemala by the government in April 1846, he and Henderson, together with other helpers, distributed at least 2,000 Spanish and 500 English New Testaments during the mid-1840s in both countries.

Following Henderson's retirement in 1879 due to failing health, Baptist work was carried on by laypeople until the arrival of missionary David Waring from England in 1881. Waring continued the work begun by his predecessors, including outreach to the Yucatecan Maya in the north and the Garifuna in the south, as well as supporting Baptist work in the Bay Islands of Honduras, begun by Mr. and Mrs. John Warner in 1849. Waring sought assistance from the Jamaican Baptist Missionary Society, which sent James Bryant to Belize in 1886. When Waring returned to England in 1888, Bryant was placed in charge of the Belize Baptist Mission.

Encouraged by Bryant, the Jamaican Society was invited to assume responsibility for the Belize field. Soon thereafter, Mr. and Mrs. Charles Brown arrived from Jamaica along with their nephew, Robert Cleghorn, to administer the work in Belize, which began to prosper under the new leadership. By 1901, the Baptist Mission reported 353 baptized members and 1,324 adherents among 9 organized congregations, along with 6 schools and more than 600 children enrolled. After Brown's retirement in 1901 due to poor health, Cleghorn became the head pastor and superintendent of the Baptist Mission in a distinguished career that ended in 1939, after celebrating his 50th year of service in Belize. To commemorate the occasion, Cleghorn wrote

A Brief History of Baptist Missionary Work in British Honduras (1822–1939).

Two major events occurred that seriously affected Baptist Mission work, as well as that of all Protestant Churches in Belize. The first was World War I, from 1914 to 1918. Many young men from Belize served with British troops during the war, only to return home restless and unsettled to face unemployment and economic decline in the colony. Consequently, many Belizeans immigrated to other countries, mainly the United States, hoping to improve their socio-economic status. This trend was accentuated by the combined impact of the Great Hurricane of 1931 that brought death and destruction, and the Great Depression of the 1930s that created economic disaster in Belize.

Not much is known about Baptist work in Belize between 1940 and 1960, but in 1960 the Conservative Baptist Home Mission Society (from the United States) was invited to work with the Belize Baptist Mission. The N. T. Dellingers arrived soon thereafter to supervise the work and rebuild the ministry. By 1978 there were 6 organized churches and 330 baptized members, mainly among the Creoles. Several missionaries associated with the Southern Baptist Convention arrived in Belize in 1977 to begin work in the interior and to assist with Baptist work in Belize City. The independent Big Falls Baptist Church was organized in 1975 by missionary Mike Willis, and Outreach For Belize was established in 1977 by an independent Baptist missionary, John Collier. Missionaries associated with Baptist Bible Fellowship arrived in 1979 and began an independent ministry. In 2000, there was a total of 25 Baptist congregations in Belize with about 2,500 baptized members. According to the 2000 census, there were 8,077 Baptist adherents.

The Seventh-day Adventist Church entered Belize in the early 1900s as an extension of its work in Honduras that began in 1887. The Adventist Mission in British Honduras was officially organized in 1922. The two countries were separated administratively in 1930. By 1960, the Adventist community in Belize numbered 1,050; it grew to about 2,500 in 1970, and increased to about 12,000 in 1978. Adventist work was centered in the districts of Belize and Corozal. In 2000, the Adventists reported 48 congregations and 10,700 members, which made it the largest Protestant denomination in Belize in terms of communicants. The 2000 census reported 12,160 Adventist adherents.

The Church of the Nazarene began work in Belize in the 1930s as an extension of their work in Guatemala, after two Mayan Indian lay preachers walked more than 60 miles from their home in the Petén of Guatemala to Benque Viejo on the border to evangelize and start new churches in British Honduras. In 1931 the Mission Council of the Church of the Nazarene decided to enter Belize as a new field of service, and eventually sent two veteran, elderly, single female missionaries to work in Benque Viejo, located in Cayo District. By 1955, 11 Nazarene missionaries were serving in Belize, assisted by 22 national workers, who served 10 organized churches with about 450 members and 300 children enrolled in 6 Nazarene schools. In 1966, there were 16 churches and 11 missions. During the 1960s work began among East Indians, Garifuna, Kekchí, and Mopan-Maya near Punta Gorda in the Toledo District. The Nazarene High School was established in 1964 in Benque Viejo and later was moved to Belize City. Also, the Nazarenes began a program of Theological Education by Extension (TEE) throughout Belize in several languages: English, Spanish, and various Amerindian dialects. In 2000, the Nazarenes reported 28 congregations with 1,820 members; the 2000 census reported 6,117 Nazarene adherents.

The Gospel Missionary Union (GMU), an independent Holiness mission that has been renamed Avant Ministries (Kansas City, Missouri), sent their first missionaries to Belize in 1955, the Gordon Lee family, who established the Yarborough Bible Church in Belize City in 1956. The GMU acquired a 20-acre tract of land about 30 miles from Belize City in 1956, where they opened a camping-conference center and a Bible school, known as Carol Farm. Outreach began among the Yucatec-Maya in 1960 in Orange Walk District, and a Christian bookstore was established in Belize City in 1962. In 2000, the GMU reported 17 congregations with about 940 members.

Several Anabaptist-Mennonite groups began arriving in Belize in the late 1950s from northern Mexico, and by 1978 there were at least a dozen Mennonite agricultural colonies in the country, mainly composed of Old Colony Mennonites (Reinlanders), Kleinegemeinde Mennonites ("The Little Brotherhood"), and Sommerfelders who spoke Low German. After Hurricane Hattie devastated parts of Belize in 1961, a number of Mennonite agencies arrived to provide disaster relief, including the Beachy Amish and the Eastern Mennonite Board of Missions and Charities. In 1969, the Mennonite Central Committee established the Mennonite Center in Belize City to assist the Mennonite colonies both economically and socially.

By 1978, the Belize Evangelical Mennonite Church had been organized with 5 congregations and 122 communicant members among Creoles, Mestizos, Mayans, and Garifuna. In addition, 10 distinct Mennonite communities reported 37 organized congregations and about 1,900 communicant members. Overall, in 1978, the total Mennonite community in Belize numbered about 2,800, and most of them resided in agricultural colonies at Spanish Lookout, Blue Creek, and Shipyard. In 1987, the total Mennonite membership was 2,236 in 37 congregations, with a total community of about 3,286 people. According to the 2000 census, the total Mennonite community in Belize numbered 9,497 adherents; however, the *Global Anabaptist Mennonite Encyclopedia Online* only reported 3,575 members in 40 congregations in 2003.

Other non-Pentecostal groups in Belize include the Salvation Army (1913), Christian Brethren (1949), National Presbyterian Church of Mexico (1958), independent Christian Churches/Churches of Christ (1969), Friends/Quakers (1975), Congregational Methodist Church (2002), Gospel Outreach Ministry International (1991), Mission to the World/Presbyterian Church in America (1996), the Methodist Protestant Church, and dozens of other small denominations and independent churches.

Although there were few Pentecostal churches in Belize in 1960 (the oldest are the Pentecostal Christian Assembly in Roaring Creek Village, founded in 1912; and City Mission International Pentecostal Church in Belize City, founded in 1938), since that time the Pentecostal movement has experienced substantial growth throughout the country. From 5 organized churches and about 200 members in 1960, the Pentecostals grew to 67 congregations and 1,656 baptized members in 1978. According to the 1980 census, Pentecostal adherents numbered 3,237 and represented 2.3 percent of the na-

tional population. According to the 2000 census, there were 17,189 Pentecostal adherents in Belize, which represented 7.4 percent of the national population.

In 1978, the largest Pentecostal denomination in the country was the Kekchí and Mayan Churches of Belize, founded in 1968, which reported 15 congregations and 750 members. The Church of God (Cleveland, Tennessee) arrived in 1944 and by 1978 there were 22 churches and 610 members among Creoles and Mestizos.

The Assemblies of God of Jamaica (Evangel Temple in Kingston) sent the Reverend and Mrs. Malchus B. Bennett to Belize in September 1946 to begin missionary work among the Creoles. By 1949, several small congregations had been established in Belize City, Sand Hill, Stann Creek, and Corozal. The arrival in 1951 of the Reverend and Mrs. Walter Clifford, who previously had served as missionaries in India and Ceylon for 20 years with the Assemblies of God (Springfield, Missouri), brought experience and encouragement to the work in Belize. Later in 1951, the Cliffords established a Bible Institute in Belize City to train Christian workers. The mother church in Belize City, Bethel Temple, opened a primary school in 1953 under the administration of the Cliffords.

In 1960, the Assemblies of God in Belize reported only 3 churches with a total of 90 baptized members. However, the work was hindered by internal controversies in 1955 with Malchus B. Bennett and in 1969 with Lloyd Wright that led to the formation of two rival groups with a combined membership in 1978 of only a few hundred members. These divisions led to demoralization and decline in the work of the Assemblies of God in Belize: some of the talented Belizean and Jamaican pastors went to the United States and others became separatists; the number of national workers declined from 11 in 1969 to 4 in 1971; and the number of adherents declined from 480 in 1969 to 149 in 1971.

In 1978, missionary Edward Fairbanks, affiliated with the Assemblies of God Division of Foreign Missions, reported 6 organized churches and 17 preaching points, with a total of only 96 baptized members. The Council of the Assemblies of God of Belize was reorganized in 1980, under missionary superintendent Alver Rance who coordinated church work in English and Spanish. In 1985, the Assemblies of God reported 41 churches and 16 preaching points, but with only about 1,000 members; in 1998, there were a total of 47 churches; and in 2001, there were 54 churches and 14 preaching points, served by 27 ordained pastors and 30 Christian workers.

In 2002, the Belize Assemblies of God established a camp and conference facility, Green Pastures Retreat Center, which has become a place of ethnic unity that depicts the uniqueness of its multicultural ministry in Belize. In 2003, this denomination reported 81 churches, missions, and preaching points, comprised of English, Spanish, Chinese, and Mayan believers.

The Church of God in Christ (COGIC) traces its origin in Belize to 1953–1955, when Malchus B. Bennett left the Assemblies of God and became affiliated with the COGIC, an Afro-American denomination with headquarters in Memphis, Tennessee. However, after 25 years of labor, only 5 churches and 2 missions had been established by the COGIC, with 540 members, by 1978. The mother church in Belize City, Calvary Temple, operates a large primary school under the supervision of Bishop Bennett.

Other smaller Pentecostal denominations include the Pentecostal Church of God of America (1956), Church of the Lord Jesus Christ of the Apostolic Faith Church (1957), Elim Fellowship (1967), Shield of Faith International Mission (1983), Calvary Commission (1984), United Pentecostal Church International (1984), Full Gospel Grace Fellowship (1989), International Pentecostal Holiness Church (2000), Church of God of Prophecy, Resurrection Churches and Ministries, and Youth With A Mission (YWAM).

The Belize Association of Evangelical Churches (BAEC), previously known as The Protestant Council, was formed in the late 1960s or early 1970s with seven affiliated denominations. Despite many difficulties it survived, and in 1982 it was renamed the BAEC. It had more than 30 members in November 2008 and was led by its president, the Reverend Eugene Crawford, who is affiliated with the Central Assembly of God in Belize City.

Many Christian groups are associated through the Belize Council of Churches (CCC), which in turn is related to the Caribbean Council of Churches and the World Council of Churches (WCC), or to the Belize

Association of Evangelical Churches (BAEC). The BCC was founded in 1978 as the Belize Christian Council; it was previously called the Belize Social Council, founded in 1957 with eight member institutions as an interfaith organization, which became the BCC in 1981.

Historically, the majority of Protestants in Belize have been Anglicans and Methodists, although most are non-communicants, which reflects an attitude of religious indifference or nominalism. However, the proportional decline of Anglican and Methodist adherents in the total population was offset by the growth of other Protestant denominations between 1970 and 2000, based on an analysis of the corresponding census data.

Overall, according to the 2000 census, the largest group of Protestant adherents was Pentecostal (7.4 percent of the national population) followed by Anglican (5.3 percent), Adventist (5.2 percent), Mennonite (4.1 percent), Baptist (3.5 percent), Methodist (3.5 percent), and Nazarene (2.6 percent); all other Protestants adherents were 4.2 percent.

Other Christian Groups According to the 2000 census, "other religions" in Belize had a total of 10,677 adherents (4.6 percent of the national population), among which were the following non-Protestant Christian groups: Maronite Christians (Eastern-rite believers who recognize the authority of the pope in Rome) among the Lebanese; a Greek Orthodox Church in Santa Elena, Cayo District; and a significant presence of Jehovah's Witnesses (42 churches, 1,561 members, and 3,366 adherents in 2005) and of the Church of Jesus Christ of Latter-day Saints (Mormon missionary work began in 1980), which reported 12 churches and 3,430 adherents in 2008. There are small communities of Christadelphians, Unity School of Christianity, and The Family International (formerly known as the Children of God).

Other Religious Groups Non-Christian religions (2000 census data) include Hinduism (367 among East Indians); Islam (243 adherents, including Black Muslims); Garifuna religion; Myalism (the old tribal religion of the Ashanti adapted to the Caribbean context), Obeah (witchcraft), and Rastafarianism among the Creole population.

Traditionally, most of the Asian Indian immigrants were Hindus, although some were Muslims. Today, the Asian Indian heritage persons—whose ancestors arrived during the 19th century—live in villages scattered all over Belize; their ancestors intermarried with the local people and lost their language and original religions during subsequent generations. They live in reasonably compact rural communities and number between 10,000 and 15,000, which is more than 5 percent of the population of Belize. The newer Asian Indian Diaspora in Belize consists of "People of Indian Origin" (known as PIOs) who arrived in the country during the 1950s, when Belize was still a British colony. The PIOs maintain close and regular contact with India through frequent trips to visit friends and relatives in their homeland.

The Islamic community of Belize is estimated at 2,794 (2008) and represents about one percent of the total population; the community is led by the Islamic Mission of Belize (IMB), headquartered in Belize City. As the only recognized Islamic organization in Belize, the IMB's Islamic center has a prayer hall and a primary school.

There is a small Jewish community (less than 1,000) and a yet smaller Baha'i Faith community (205 adherents) that add to Belize's pluralistic religious life.

Among practitioners of Amerindian religions and Popular Catholicism there are "specialists" who practice witchcraft (*brujería*), shamanism (*chamanismo*), and folk healing (*curanderismo*). Three of the Amerindian peoples in Central America that survived the ravages of colonization are the Kekchí, Mopán, and Yucatán Maya in Belize, which today number around 25,000. Most Mayans are nominal Catholics who also maintain native animistic religious beliefs and practices. Most Garifuna today are marginal Christians (Catholics or Protestants) who still maintain their traditional cultural and religious beliefs and practices based on animism. "Popular religiosity" (syncretistic) is practiced by a majority of the Catholic Mestizo population.

Clifton L. Holland

See also: Assemblies of God; Baha'i Faith; Baptists; Caribbean Conference of Churches; Christadelphians; Christian Brethren; Church of England; Church of God (Cleveland, Tennessee); Church of God in Christ; Church of God of Prophecy; Church of Jesus Christ of Latter-day Saints; Church of the Nazarene; Family International, The; Garifuna Religion; International Pentecostal Holiness Church; Jehovah's Witnesses; Jesuits; Maronite Catholic Church; Mennonites; Methodist Church in the Caribbean and the Americas; Rastafarianism; Roman Catholic Church; Salvation Army; Seventh-day Adventist Church; Society for the Propagation of the Gospel in Foreign Parts; Southern Baptist Convention; Unity School of Christianity/Association of Unity Churches; Witchcraft; World Council of Churches.

References

Barry, Tom. *Belize, A Country Guide.* Albuquerque, NM: The Inter-Hemispheric Education Resource Center, 1989.

Cleghorn, Robert. *A Brief History of Baptist Missionary Work in British Honduras (1822–1939).* London: The Kingsgate Press, 1939.

Crowe, Frederick. *The Gospel in Central America.* London: Charles Gilpin, 1850.

Dayfoot, Arthur Charles. *The Shaping of the West Indian Church, 1492–1962.* Gainesville: University Press of Florida, 1999.

Fernández Olmos, Margarite, and Lizabeth Paravisini-Gebert, eds. *Sacred Possessions: Vodou, Santería, Obeah and the Caribbean.* New Brunswick, NJ: Rutgers University Press, 1997.

Findlay, George G., and W. W. Holdeworth. *The History of the Wesleyan Methodist Missionary Society.* Vol. II. London: The Epworth Press, 1921.

Gingerich, Melvin, and John B. Loewen. "Belize." In *Global Anabaptist Mennonite Encyclopedia Online.* 1987. http://www.gameo.org/encyclopedia/contents/B4459.html. Accessed March 7, 2008.

Gonzalez, Nancie L. *Sojourners of the Caribbean: Ethnogenesis and Ethnohistory of the Garifuna.* Urbana: University of Illinois Press, 1988.

Grimes, Barbara F., ed. *Ethnologue: Languages of the World.* 12th ed. Dallas, TX: Summer Institute of Linguistics, 1992.

Holland, Clifton L., ed. *World Christianity: Central America and the Caribbean.* Monrovia, CA: MARC-World Vision, 1981.

Holloway, Clinton J. "The Stone-Campbell Movement in Belize" (February 2005). http://www.worldconvention.org/country.php?c=BZ.

PROCADES. *Directory of Churches, Organizations and Ministries of the Protestant Movement in Belize.* San José, Costa Rica: The Central America Socio-Religious Studies Program (PROCADES), 1982 (revised version, March 1990).

PROLADES-RITA Database: "Ethnic and Religious Diversity in Belize." http://www.prolades.com/cra/regions/cam/bel/bel-docs.htm.

Smith, Norma O. "A Short History of the Assemblies of God of Belize," a translation and enlargement of the work of Louise Jeter Walker (June 27, 2001: 34 pages).

U.S. Department of State. *International Religious Freedom Report 2008: Belize.* http://www.state.gov/g/drl/rls/irf/2008/108514.htm.

Waddell, David Alan Gilmour. *British Honduras: A Historical and Contemporary Survey.* London: Oxford University Press, 1961.

Benares

Benares, also known as Varanasi (from the two rivers, Varana and Asi, between which the city is located) and Kashi, is thought by many to be the oldest continuously inhabited city in the world, while even the more skeptical agree that the area has been inhabited for more than 2,500 years. The city is located southeast of Lucknow, on the banks of two of the tributaries of the sacred Ganges River. Legends attribute the founding of the city to the deity Shiva who subsequently lived

Hindu people taking a ritual bath in the holy Ganges River in Varanasi (commonly known as Benares), North India, January 15, 2010. (Eddy Van Ryckeghem/Dreamstime.com)

there for a period of time. Pilgrims believe that bathing in the Ganges, and/or dying in what they consider Shiva's hometown, releases them from the cycle of rebirths (reincarnation). Serving the dead has become integral to the city's routine. Last rites for the dead are performed almost daily. Cremation grounds are found in the heart of the city.

Buddhists also connect Varanasi to their origin. The city is less than 10 miles from Sarnath to which Gautama Buddha journeyed shortly after finding enlightenment. It was in Sarnath that he delivered his first sermon.

More recently, Benares was deeply affected by the era of Muslim rule. In the middle of the 17th century, the Mughal Emperor Aurangzeb (r. 1658–1707) attained the throne. During his half-century reign he sanctioned the wholesale destruction of Hindu temples as part of a general policy of suppression of Hindu worship. Benares suffered greatly during this time and, as a result, few of the present Hindu structures in Varanasi predate the 18th century, when Hindu control was reasserted in the region. However, beginning with the return of Hindu rule, some 1,500 temples, palaces, and shrines have been constructed. Among the oldest is the Vishwanath Temple, rebuilt in 1777 by Ahilya Bai Holkar (1725–1795), queen of the Malwa kingdom, on the same site of what had been the principal Shiva temple during the millennium prior to Aurangzeb. The temple roof and altar area are heavily decorated with gold. Among the modern structures is the Bharat Mandir, dedicated to "Mother India," a 20th-century temple opened by Mahatma Gandhi. It contains a large decorative marble map of India.

In spite of the many temples, the essential religious life of Benares is found along the ghats, the stairways that lead down to the river's edge, where the holy men gather, the faithful come to take their symbolic baths, and the bodies of the deceased are cremated.

J. Gordon Melton

See also: Devotion/Devotional Traditions; Reincarnation; Sarnath; Temples—Hindu.

References

Eck, Diana. *Benares: City of Light*. Princeton, NJ: Princeton University Press, 1982.

Gutschow, Neils. *Benares: The Sacred Landscape of Varanasi*. Stuttgart-Fellbach, Germany: Edition Axel Menges, 2006.

Medhasananda, Swami. *Varanasi at the Crossroads: A Panoramic View of Early Modern Varanasi and the Story of its Transition*. Calcutta: Ramakrishan Mission Institute of Culture, 2002.

Singh, Birendra Pratap. *Life in Ancient Varanasi: An Account Based on Archaeological Evidence*. New Delhi: Sundeep Prakashan, 1985.

Sinha, Kunal. *A Benarasi on Varanasi*. New Delhi: Bluejay Books, 2004.

Bene Israel

In the 18th century, the Jewish community in the West discovered the existence of a group of people in India who called themselves Bene Israel (Children of Israel). They described themselves as descendants of Jews who had left Palestine prior to the building of the Second Temple and settled in India following a shipwreck near Konkan, an area on the western coast of India. Seven men and seven women survived and became the parents of a new tribe. They settled in the village of Navgon and adapted to Indian life, including the caste system. They eventually became a caste within Indian culture and were responsible for the pressing and production of oil. As they grew, members of the Children of Israel moved to other towns along the Konkan coast. In the 20th century, many of the members of the community rose to prestigious positions requiring professional acumen.

Over the centuries they forgot Hebrew and many elements of the tradition, but they still continued various Jewish traditions. They observed the Sabbath and refused to work on that day. They circumcised their children and retained elements of the biblical dietary laws. They observed Jewish holidays, all dating to the time prior to the building of the Second Temple.

In the 19th century, the Jews residing in the Portuguese settlements in southern India (Chochin) made contact with the Bene Israel and facilitated a revival of Jewish tradition among them. Through the Jews of Cochin, the West learned of the Bene Israel's existence. Meanwhile, some soldiers serving with the British in

Aden, Yemen, opened a prayer hall and made contact with the Yemenite Jewish community. Subsequently, some Yemenite Jews moved to India and assumed a role in ritual practice for the Jewish community, especially in the circumcision of males and the butchering of meat. The first synagogue was built among the Bene Israel in 1796 by Samuel Divekar, following what he considered his fated survival while a prisoner of war. Subsequently other synagogues have been built.

The Bene Israel experienced a noticeable revival in the early 1800s, when Christian missionaries turned their attention to them. The missionaries, hopeful of new converts, translated the Bible into Marathi and created a Hebrew-Marathi grammar. Their efforts produced few fruits, as the Bene Israel used their contacts with the missionaries to reach out to the European Jewish community in Europe for additional support.

The Bene Israel have a set of unique beliefs and practices. The Malida is a thanksgiving ceremony performed in the home as the men sit around a plate of spices, rice, and flowers. It includes a song praising Elijah as the precursor of the Messiah. Elijah is believed to have visited them on the occasion of the shipwreck that first landed them in India. They also do not eat beef, a custom they have developed out of deference to their neighbors, who are Hindu. They do maintain a kosher diet, but it is less strict than among Orthodox Jews in the West. There are no rabbis, and worship is led by the members.

There are two main groups within the community. Those born of two Jewish parents are called Gora, and those who lack a Jewish mother, Kala. The Kala are not allowed to participate in some practices, such as the blowing of the shofar, as they are considered less than complete Jews.

In the 1950s, there were an estimated 30,000 in the Bene Israel community, but through the last half of the century the majority migrated, most to Israel, but others to England, Australia, and the United States (where a synagogue serving some 350 members has been opened in New York City). As of 2008, only some 5,000 remain in India. Those who remain live primarily in Thana, a Mumbai (Bombay) suburb. In Israel, Bene Israel centers can be found in Ashdod, Lod, Ramle, and Beersheba (among others). Significant recognition of their presence came in 1962, when the Orthodox Chief Rabbinate of Israel decreed that marriage of other Jews with the Bene Israel was permitted. Two years later the Israeli prime minister affirmed that the government of Israel regards them as Jews in every respect; hence, the Bene Israel may move to Israel under the Law of Return.

Council of Indian Jewry
c/o The Jewish Club
Jeroo Building, Second Floor
137 Mahatma Gandhi Rd.
Bombay 400023
India

J. Gordon Melton

References

Isenberg, Shirley. *Israel's Bene Israel: A Comprehensive Inquiry and Sourcebook.* Berkeley: J. L. Museum, 1988.

Katz, Nathan. *Who Are the Jews of India?* Berkeley: University of California Press, 2000.

Strizower, Schifra. *The Bene Israel of Bombay.* New York: Schocken Books, 1971.

Benedictines

One of the most historically important and widespread orders of the Roman Catholic Church, the Benedictines are distinctive in part for their decentralized structure. Lacking the strong hierarchy present in orders such as the Jesuits, the Benedictines are often described as a confederation of monasteries and congregations that follow the Rule of St. Benedict.

Saint Benedict of Nursia (ca. 480–ca. 547) is considered the father of Western monasticism. After experiencing several aspects of the monastic life, Benedict founded a monastery at Monte Casino, and it is to him that the popular code that still guides Benedictine life is ascribed, an ascription that is somewhat in doubt due to the general lack of information about Benedict's life. The rule was but one of several that circulated in the next centuries, from which the various monastic communities could choose. It was championed by Pope Gregory the Great (ca. 540–604), and was the discipline accepted by Augustine of Canterbury (d. 604) and those who helped him establish Chris-

Baroque death circular (rotulus) depicting hiking monks with the Benedictine Monastery in Scheyern, Upper Bavaria, in the background, ca. 1754. The tradition of dispatching a "rotulus" (circuit in roll form) to monasteries was part of prayer fraternization and served not only to announce the death of a monk, but to introduce the monastery visually. (Getty Images)

tianity in England. Through the seventh century, those who followed the rule assisted the spread of Christianity in northern Europe. The Benedictine monk Ansgar began the evangelization of Scandinavia in 826.

Through the remainder of the first Christian millennium, the rule accompanied the spread of monasticism throughout Europe. The decentralized nature of the Benedictine life, however, allowed its subversion by local rulers and its weakening by lax monks. In the 10th century, the first of several important reform movements began at Cluny (in western France) under William of Aquitaine (935–963). A new evangelistic zeal accompanied the Cluniac reforms and led to the fur-

ther spread of Christianity into the more remote corners of Europe from Norway to Bohemia. Further new orders inspired by the rule emerged in the 11th, 12th, and 13th centuries, including the Camoldolese, Celestines, and Olivetians. At the same time the Benedictines experienced new levels of corruption stemming from their incorporation into the system of feudal land ownership.

Attempts at reform that began in the 14th century culminated in the 15th century in the introduction of a new structure, the congregation, an association of monasteries in a region or country. Through the century, for example, all the monasteries in Italy were united in the Cassinese Congregation, headquartered at Monte Cassino. Soon national congregations had arisen from Poland and Hungary to Spain and Portugal. The Council of Trent (1545–1563) ordered every monastery to affiliate with a congregation.

The modern world was not kind to the Benedictines. The Reformation destroyed Benedictine monasticism in Great Britain, Scandinavia, Holland, and northern Germany, and it faced severe reduction in Switzerland, France, and Belgium. It recovered during the 17th century, only to be devastated by the Enlightenment, which led to further closing of centers in France, Switzerland, and even Italy. Early in the 19th century, all the monasteries in the German states of Baden, Bavaria, Württemberg, and Prussia were closed. Those in Spain and Portugal were lost in 1834–1835.

After reaching its low point in the first half of the 19th century, Benedictine monasticism experienced a revival that has carried it into the present time. Besides recovering in areas where it had formerly existed across the European continent, it gained new life by expansion to America in 1846. Then in 1888 Pope Leo XIII (r. 1878–1903) reestablished the Collegio Sant'Anselmo as an international training center for Benedictine monks and in 1893 created a new office, the abbot primate, as the head of all the confederated congregations. In 1952, Pope Pius XII approved a new code, the Lex Propria, which governs the confederation.

The current abbot primate of the Benedictines is Notker Wolf, O.S.B. (b. 1940), who was elected to office in 2000. Though he is responsible for the global concerns of the order, his actual job is limited in that he does not have administrative powers over the various monasteries associated with the order. The monasteries have congregational autonomy and some relate directly to their local bishop rather than the order as such. Thus, the abbot primate is more like the leader of a loose association than a superior general of a typical Roman Catholic religious order.

Quite apart from the monasteries and congregations of male Benedictines, there are a number of female monasteries that are associated together in federations that are also a part of the Benedictine Confederation. Female Benedictines trace their lineage to Saint Benedict's sister Saint Scholastica and enjoy a history as long and expansive as that of their male counterparts. Also part of the confederation are the oblates, men and women living a secular life in the world according to the spirit of the Rule of Saint Benedict. Oblates tend to be attached to the particular monastery close to their place of residence.

At present there are some 250 Benedictine monasteries (of monks) worldwide, grouped in 21 congregations. There are some 350 monasteries for nuns (those who take solemn vows), grouped in 24 federations. In addition there are some 600 houses of sisters (who take simple vows), also grouped in federations.

Benedictine Confederation of Congregations
Badia Primaziale Sant'Anselmo
Piazza Cavalieri di Malta, 5
I-00153 Roma, Italia
http://ww.osb.org

J. Gordon Melton

See also: Jesuits; Roman Catholic Church.

References

Butler, Dom Cuthbert. *Benedictine Monachism: Studies in Benedictine Life and Rule*. London: Longmans, Green, 1924.

De Waal, Esther. *Living with Contradiction: Introduction to Benedictine Spirituality*. Harrisburg, PA: Morehouse Publishing, 1998.

McQuiston, John. *Always We Begin Again: The Benedictine Way of Living*. Harrisburg, PA: Morehouse Publishing, 1996.

Rippinger, Joel. *The Benedictine Order in the United States: An Interpretive History*. Collegeville, MN: Liturgical Press, 1990.

Swan, Laura. *The Benedictine Tradition*. Collegeville, MN: Liturgical Press, 2007.

Bengal Orissa Bihar Baptist Convention

The Bengal Orissa Bihar Baptist Convention began as a missionary thrust of American Free Will Baptists. The first missionaries arrived in the late 19th century in the area where the states of Bengal, Orissa, and Bihar come together. Besides English, other languages spoken include Bengali, Hindi, Oriya, and Santali, as well as some Telegu. By 1911 the missionaries had founded 23 churches with 1,600 members. In that year, in America, the Free Will Baptists in the northern United States merged into the Northern Baptist Convention (now the American Baptist Churches in the U.S.A.), and they brought the Indian mission with them.

The mission grew slowly during the 20th century, hindered to some extent by the multilingual nature of the work, which has made the development of leadership difficult. The largest growth has been among the Santali-speaking people. The primary projects supported by the church are the Balasore Industrial School and several secondary schools at Balasore and Bhimpore.

In the 1990s the church reported 9,500 members in 170 churches. It has been a member of the World Council of Churches since 1965.

Bengal Orissa Bihar Baptist Convention
Sepoy Bazatr
Midnapore
West Bengal, 721 101
India

J. Gordon Melton

See also: World Council of Churches.

References

Van Beek, Huibert. *A Handbook of the Churches and Councils: Profiles of Ecumenical Relationships*. Geneva: World Council of Churches, 2006.

Wardin, Albert W., ed. *Baptists around the World*. Nashville: Holman Publishers, 1995.

■ Benin

Benin is a West African nation located between Nigeria and Togo, with a costal outlet to the Atlantic through the Bight of Benin. It has a land area of approximately 43,000 square miles. The 8.5 million inhabitants come from more than 60 different native peoples who inhabited the land prior to the present state of Benin being designated by the arrival of Europeans. The most important of these groups were the Fon (39 percent), Adja (15 percent), Yoruba (12 percent), and Bariba (9 percent). The Yoruban culture reached into Benin from the city of Ifa, now in neighboring Nigeria. The Fon settled in central Benin along the Okpara and Ouémé rivers. In the 17th century, the Ewe people (related to the Yoruban) developed two states, the Hogbonu, centered on present-day Porto Novo, and Abomey. In the 19th century, the Fon emerged with an expansive empire that moved east and west from Abomey into traditional Yoruban territory, and established Ouidah as a major port of call for European slave traders.

The British upset the structure of Benin society by banning the slave trade in 1818, though some illegal traffic continued into midcentury. Many Yorubans passed through Ouidah on their way to Cuba, one of the last American countries to drop slavery. In 1890 the French attempted to occupy Benin and in 1891 defeated the primary Fon army. The defeated ruler, Benhanzin, kept up a resistance until 1894 and is remembered today as a national hero. In establishing colonial rule, the French destroyed the economic basis of Fon culture in palm oil and other agricultural products. During their 70-year rule of Dahomey, as it was then called, the French ran the colony into bankruptcy.

Benin became an independent republic in 1960. The country went through two decades of political instability and a change of government every year or two. A more stable government was elected in 1980s, and it was helped by improved sugar production and the discovery of oil off the coast. Optimism was dimmed by the encroachments of the Sahara into the northern part of the country. A new president, elected in 1991, abandoned the Marxism of his predecessor, and the country has been making a transition to democracy.

A Guardian of the Night dancer in Fouditi, Benin. Voodoo is widely practiced in Benin, and during the dance ceremony the voodoo priest first lifts the costume to show there is no one inside; after prayers, the costume begins to shake and dance, an indication that the Guardian of the Night spirit has entered the costume. After the ceremony, the priest again lifts the straw, showing no one inside. (Corel)

Traditional religion has remained strong in Benin. The Yoruban faith is built around veneration of and possession by the deities, the Orisha. Knowledge of the will of the deities is sought by the use of oracles. Among the Fon, the deities are referred to as the Vodoun. The Yoruban faith was exported to the Caribbean, especially Cuba, and has become the basis of contemporary Santeria.

Islam has come into Benin from two directions. In the north it has been introduced among the Fulani, Dendi, and Bariba peoples from Niger and in the south among the Yoruban from their own people in Nigeria.

Benin

Religion	Followers in 1970	Followers in 2010	% of Population	Annual % growth 2000–2010	Followers in 2025	Followers in 2050
Ethnoreligionists	1,909,000	3,513,000	35.6	1.54	3,551,000	3,238,000
Christians	515,000	3,872,000	39.2	4.33	6,840,000	12,340,000
Roman Catholics	394,000	2,180,000	22.1	4.18	3,800,000	7,200,000
Independents	37,400	920,000	9.3	3.54	1,500,000	2,700,000
Protestants	52,600	770,000	7.8	5.79	1,500,000	2,400,000
Muslims	399,000	2,450,000	24.8	4.50	4,000,000	6,800,000
Agnostics	600	18,000	0.2	3.27	30,000	60,000
Baha'is	3,400	12,000	0.1	4.41	25,000	40,000
Atheists	0	4,600	0.0	3.27	10,000	20,000
New religionists	1,000	1,600	0.0	3.27	4,000	8,000
Total population	**2,828,000**	**9,872,000**	**100.0**	**3.27**	**14,460,000**	**22,506,000**

The great majority of the Muslims are of the Malekite School of Islam, but both the Tijaniyya and Qadiriyya Sufi Order are active. Approximately 17 percent of the population are Muslims. The Muslim-inspired Ahmadiyya Muslim movement has also opened centers, and the Baha'i Faith has a small presence.

As early as 1689, Portuguese Roman Catholics opened a chapel at Ouidah, and both French and Portuguese priests served the small Catholic community into the 19th century. Active missionary work began in the interior in the 1860s under the African Missions of Lyon. In 1883 a prefecture was erected, and steady growth followed. A seminary was opened in 1913, but the first African priest was not ordained until 1928. The Archdiocese of Cotonou was erected in 1955, and the first African archbishop consecrated in 1860. The Roman Catholic Church is strongest among the Fon, Mina Adja, and Gun peoples.

British Methodists, in the person of famed African missionary Thomas Birch Freeman (1809–1890), arrived in Dahomey in 1843, and a small work was started. It grew in spite of the opposition of the local king, but very slowly. It gained members as French influence increased in the area during the last third of the 19th century. Through the first half of the 20th century, the Methodist work was tied to that in neighboring Togo. It has more recently been separated both from Togo and from the Methodist Church in Great Britain as the Protestant Methodist Church in Benin. It is the largest Protestant body in the country. The other major Protestant churches (Presbyterian, Lutheran, Baptist, Congrega-

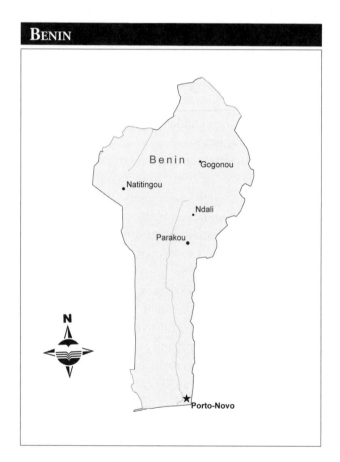

tional) have not established work in Benin, and there is no national Protestant ecumenical organization.

Benin was an early scene for the spread of African Initiated Churches (AICs). Possibly the first was the African Union Mission, a branch of the United Native African Church, a schism of the Church Missionary

Society (Anglican). The church appears to have arrived in Dahomey in 1895, only four years after its establishment. Through the 20th century, other AIC bodies arrived, including the Cherubim and Seraphim (1933); the Heavenly Christianity Church (Église du Christianisme Céleste du Bénin), which originated in Benin in 1947 and late reemerged in Nigeria as the Celestial Church of Christ; and the Église Apostolique du Togo et Bénin, founded as the Divine Healers Church in 1951 in Togo.

The Sudan Interior Mission launched work among the Bariba people from a station in Kandi. Missionaries from the Assemblies of God, a Pentecostal church from the United States, arrived in Benin in 1938. They began work in the northern part of the country among the Somba and Pillapila peoples, and the church quickly became the major Christian body challenging the spread of Islam. The Jehovah's Witnesses established their initial work in 1935.

Benin has not been a major target of new religious movements (Eastern or occult), though the number of African Initiated Churches grew through the last half of the 20th century.

J. Gordon Melton

See also: African Initiated (Independent) Churches; Ahmadiyya Movement in Islam; Assemblies of God; Baha'i Faith; Celestial Church of Christ; Cherubim and Seraphim/Eternal Sacred Order of the Cherubim and Seraphim; Ife; Jehovah's Witnesses; Malikite School of Islam; Methodist Church; Protestant Methodist Church in Benin; Qadiriyya Sufi Order; Roman Catholic Church; Santeria; Tijaniyya Sufi Order.

References

Decalo, Samuel. *Historical Dictionary of Benin.* Metuchen, NJ: Scarecrow Press, 1995.

Merlo, M. C. "Les sectes du Dahomey." In *Devant les sectes nonchrétiennes.* Louvain, Belgium: Desclée de Brouwer, 1961.

Roese, Peter M. *A Popular History of Benin: The Rise And Fall Of A Mighty Forest Kingdom.* New York: Peter Lang, 2004.

The World Factbook. Washington, DC: Central Intelligence Agency, 2008. http://www.cia.gov/library/publications/the-world-factbook/geos/bn.html.

■ Bermuda

Bermuda comprises a set of 150 small coral islands in the Atlantic Ocean due west of the U.S. state of Georgia. The total available land is slightly more than 20 square miles. Some 66,500 people live on Bermuda, over half being of African heritage.

Bermuda was uninhabited until 1609, when some British immigrants on their way to America settled there after being shipwrecked. These original inhabitants encouraged others to join them, and in 1684 a government was organized under the British Crown. Over the next decades an agricultural economy developed, and, as with many lands settled by Europeans, it depended on slaves imported from West Africa. At the time slavery was discontinued in the 1830s, the majority of the population on the 20 inhabited islands was of African descent. In 1968, the colony was given a level of local autonomy, and since that time the majority party in the Parliament names the prime minister. The governor is appointed from London.

The original settlers were Anglicans. Though Presbyterians arrived a few years later and eventually became the largest church in the colony, the Church of England regained its majority status early in the 1700s and has remained the largest religious body in Bermuda to the present. St. Peter's Church in St. George's, constructed in 1612 by Governor Richard Moore, is the oldest Anglican church in continuous use in the Western Hemisphere. It was also the meeting place of the first General Assembly (forerunner of Bermuda's Parliament) on August 1, 1620. The Anglicans have unique status as an extra-provincial diocese directly under the archbishop of Canterbury. Enlarging the Anglican community is the Reformed Episcopal Church, a 19th-century group that broke from the Episcopal Church in the United States and opened work in Bermuda around 1890.

Presbyterians from the Church of Scotland arrived in 1612. Christ Church in Warwick is believed to be the oldest Presbyterian church in the British colonies. Methodists arrived in the 18th century and settled in Hamilton. The Methodist community was enlarged by the establishment of work by the African Methodist Episcopal Church, which emerged through the 20th century as the second largest Protestant church in the

Bermuda

country. Because of the country's relative closeness to the United States, a number of Christian groups, representative of the broad spectrum of Christianity, expanded to Bermuda through the 20th century. Bermuda, as a loyal British colony, developed a special relationship to Canada in the decades after the American Revolution. The religious expression of that relationship is found in the congregations in Bermuda with direct ties to the United Church of Canada, the Pentecostal Assemblies of Canada, and the Presbyterian Church in Canada.

The Roman Catholic Church developed from a small presence in the 19th century to become the sec-

ond largest religious body in Bermuda by the middle of the 20th century. Also a part of the country's Canadian ties, the work existed as an outpost of the Diocese of Halifax (Nova Scotia). In 1953 it was made a prefecture and three years later a vicariate. Finally, in 1957 the Diocese of Hamilton was created as a suffragan, subordinate to the Diocese of Kingston (Jamaica).

As Bermuda has attracted members of many Christian groups, so it has drawn to it adherents of a variety of other religions. There exist presently in the islands small communities of Jews, Baha'is, Muslims, Rosicrucians, Subud, Rastafarians, and Hindus. The Jewish

Bermuda

Religion	Followers in 1970	Followers in 2010	% of Population	Annual % growth 2000–2010	Followers in 2025	Followers in 2050
Christians	49,600	57,900	89.1	0.25	55,800	50,200
Protestants	11,600	20,600	31.7	0.98	21,000	20,000
Anglicans	22,000	14,000	21.5	−1.28	12,000	10,000
Roman Catholics	7,500	9,400	14.5	−0.05	9,600	9,000
Agnostics	1,000	4,000	6.2	3.72	6,500	8,000
Spiritists	1,000	1,800	2.8	0.41	1,800	1,800
Baha'is	100	450	0.7	0.40	600	800
Buddhists	50	330	0.5	0.45	500	600
Atheists	0	240	0.4	0.45	400	700
Chinese folk	10	140	0.2	0.45	200	300
New religionists	20	60	0.1	0.35	100	150
Muslims	0	40	0.1	0.52	80	150
Jews	20	20	0.0	−1.98	20	20
Total population	**51,800**	**65,000**	**100.0**	**0.41**	**66,000**	**62,700**

community meets in a metaphysical church, the Unity Foundation of Truth. There is a congregation of both the United Church of Religious Science and of the Church of Christ, Scientist in Hamilton. Given the relative smallness of the country, most new groups have had difficulty establishing more than one or two centers of worship in what has become a highly competitive atmosphere.

J. Gordon Melton

See also: African Methodist Episcopal Church; Church of Christ, Scientist; Church of England; Church of Scotland; Episcopal Church; Pentecostal Assemblies of Canada; Presbyterian Church in Canada; Rastafarians; Roman Catholic Church; Subud; United Church of Canada.

References

Barrett, David, ed. *The Encyclopedia of World Christianity*. 2nd ed. New York: Oxford University Press, 2001.

Bissio, Roberto Remo, et al. *Third World Guide 93/94*. Montevideo, Uruguay: Instituto del Tercer Mundo, 1992.

Craven, Wesley Frank. *An Introduction to the History of Bermuda*. Hamilton: Bermuda Maritime Museum Press, 1990.

Besant, Annie

1847–1933

Annie Besant was an English Socialist reformer and advocate of atheism who was converted to Theosophy after reading the works of Helena P. Blavatsky (1831–1891) and later succeeded to the presidency of the Theosophical Society, which she subsequently headed for a quarter of a century. She emerged as an influential figure in the growth of Western Esotericism and in the knowledge and appreciation of Hinduism in the West.

Besant was born Annie Wood in London; her parents were from Ireland and in the middle class. Her father died when she was a child, and her mother raised her in a very religious environment. At the age of 20 she married Frank Besant, an Anglican minister-school master. They had two children. In 1873 she left her husband and with her children began to live on her own. A primary cause of the separation was her increasing religious skepticism. The couple would be legally separated in 1878.

Once on her own, she began to write about her skeptical views. She met the atheist/freethinker Charles Bradlaugh (1833–1891), joined the National Secular Society, and began to lecture on feminist issues. She and Charles Bradlaugh subsequently formed

Portrait of Annie Besant, late 19th and early 20th-century British reformer and author. After escaping an unhappy and unsuccessful marriage, Besant became a leading reformer and spokesperson for the working class in Great Britain and for women, in particular. (Library of Congress)

the Freethought Publishing Company. In 1877, she and Bradlaugh were arrested for selling birth control materials (considered obscene at the time) in London's slums. They were initially convicted, but the verdict was later overturned. The trial substantively moved public attitudes on the issue. In 1888 she coordinated a strike of female laborers in a match factory. The strike turned public attention to the cruel and unsafe labor conditions under which unskilled female factory workers were forced to operate. By this time she had established herself as one of England's leading orators, a forthright skeptic, and passionate advocate for women's rights. During the 1880s, she also became a friend of George Bernard Shaw (who had been drawn to her by her speaking ability and considered her Britain's and perhaps Europe's greatest orator). Through

him she initially developed an interest in Socialism and became a member of the Fabian Society.

Then, in 1888, she read Blavatsky's recently published text, *The Secret Doctrine.* It changed her life. She found in the revelations of Theosophy answers to questions she had been asking but that had been left unanswered by Christianity and more recently Socialism and Freethought. She then resigned from the National Secular Society, renounced Socialism, and threw her impressive set of skills into the cause of Theosophy, just at the moment when the movement needed someone who could defend it from the waves of scandal that had befallen it, most notably the charges of fakery that had been leveled at Blavatsky.

Blavatsky died just a few years after Besant arrived on the scene, but in spite of her inexperience within the organization, in 1891, Besant became head of the Esoteric Section of the Theosophical Society and became powerful within the organization. She made a triumphal tour of the United States during which time she addressed the World Parliament of Religions in Chicago. She survived the attack on her authority by William Q. Judge (1851–1896), one of the society's co-founders, who felt he should have become head of the Esoteric Section, and the loss of most of the American membership who broke with Besant. She moved to India, which became her home and the international headquarters of the Theosophical Society. In 1907, Henry S. Olcott (1832–1907), the third co-founder and the president of the Society, died, and she became the new president, a post she would hold until her death. As the successor to H. S. Olcott she presided over a time of rapid global expansion of the Society.

Besant replaced Olcott's emphasis on Buddhism with an emphasis on Hinduism, with which Theosophy shared a far greater resonance. She also developed a relationship with Charles W. Leadbeater, a former Anglican priest. She admired his explorations of the Esoteric realities that she herself yearned for but only lightly experienced. Leadbeater greatly expanded Theosophical Esoteric literature and later became a bishop of the Theosophically oriented Liberal Catholic Church. Leadbeater was also a pedophile and became a major problem for Besant, who was forced to banish him from Theosophical headquarters in India.

Leadbeater had discovered the boy Jiddu Krishnamurti and convinced Besant that he was the coming World Teacher, a messianic personage that would also be explained in terms of the Buddhist expectations of Maitreya the Future Buddha and the Second Coming of Jesus Christ (Maitreya and Jesus were somewhat identified in the thought of the Liberal Catholic Church). In 1909 she organized the Order of the Star in the East to serve as a vehicle for the promotion of Krishnamurti as the coming World Teacher. In the 1920s, as Krishnamurti matured and began to travel as a lecturer, both the Theosophical Society and the Order greatly expanded.

Besant encountered a major problem in 1929. Krishnamurti, increasingly skeptical of the expectations that had grown around him, announced his disbelief, resigned from the Order and the Society, and broke with Besant. The move proved devastating. The Order soon disbanded, and membership in the Society dropped. A few months later, the stock market crashed and the Society's membership worldwide plunged. It never returned to the level it had reached prior to Krishnamurti's withdrawal.

Though caught up in the Esoteric teachings and practices of Theosophy, Besant never lost her drive for social reform and the uplifting of women. Once established in India, she led the society in the founding of schools across the country, including some of the first for women. She emerged as a champion for Indian independence from British rule and served a term as president of the Indian National Congress (1917). Her social and political work in India has given her a favored spot in Indian history.

Besant remained president of the Theosophical Society until her death in Madras, India, on September 23, 1933.

J. Gordon Melton

See also: Atheism; Blavatsky, Helena P.; Krishnamurti Foundations; Liberal Catholic Church; Theosophical Society (American); Western Esoteric Tradition.

References

Bennett, O. *Annie Besant*. London: Hamish Hamilton, In Her Own Time Series, 1988.

Besant, A. W. *The Ancient Wisdom*. London: Theosophical Publishing House, 1910.

Besant, A. W. *Autobiography*. Adyar, India: Theosophical Publishing House, 1939.

Besant, A. W. *Esoteric Christianity*. New York: J. Lane, 1902.

Besant, A. W. *Theosophical Lectures*. Chicago: Theosophical Society, 1907.

Nethercot, A. H. *The First Five Lives of Annie Besant*. Chicago: University of Chicago Press, 1960.

Nethercot, A. *The Last Four Lives of Annie Besant*. Chicago: University of Chicago Press, 1965.

Wessinger, Catherine. L. *Annie Besant and Progressive Messianism (1847–1933)*. Lewiston, NY: Edwin Mellen Press, 1988.

Beta Israel

Beta Israel, the Jewish community of Ethiopia, was present in the fourth century CE, when most Ethiopians became Christian. They were among a variety of people who declined the new faith. They identified themselves as Jewish, and over the years continued to practice their faith.

The origin of Beta Israel is lost to history, and a variety of explanations have been offered as to how a large community of Africans devoted to the Torah and Jewish belief and practice could have arisen. The community itself tends to favor a Yemeni origin. In the fifth century BCE a kingdom was established in Yemen that included much of Ethiopia. The founding of this kingdom is attributed to Menelik, the son of the queen of Sheba who is mentioned in the Hebrew Bible (1 Kings 10). Whatever the exact origin, the existence of the Yemenite kingdom for many centuries provided numerous opportunities for Jews and Judaism to enter Ethiopia and for a community of Jewish believers to emerge.

The existence of Beta Israel became known outside of the region in the 14th century, a time of conflict between Muslims (who wished to expand into Ethiopia) and the Christian nation centered at Axum. Over the century of ongoing conflict, Beta Israel was involved as a balancing power between the two groups, frequently changing sides as their interest demanded. As a minority group, however, they found that each wave of fighting tended to decrease their numbers and take from their land. They survived largely because they commanded high ground (which is more easily defended) in the Semien Mountains. However, between the 13th and the 17th centuries, their numbers are estimated to have declined from one million to 200,000.

A new era for Beta Israel began early in the 19th century, when Anglican and Protestant Christians discovered their existence and launched a mission to convert them. This campaign led to the alerting of some European Jewish leaders to the existence of a Jewish community in Africa, and in 1868 Joseph Halevy, a professor from the Sorbonne who had worked in Yemen and agent for the Alliance Israelite Universelle in France, visited the community. It was one of Halevy's students, Jacques Faitlovitch (1881–1955), who placed the Ethiopian community on the agenda of world Jewry. After his first visit in 1904, he spent the rest of his life assisting them educationally and helping European Jews to view Beta Israel as brothers and sisters. He became an Israeli citizen and launched a drive to have them recognized under the Israeli law of return, which would allow them to immigrate to Israel. His efforts were picked up and carried forward by the American Association for Ethiopian Jews and the British-based Falasha Welfare Association (Falasha being a popular designation for Ethiopian Jews during the 20th century).

In spite of Faitlovitch's efforts the Beta Israel community continued to decline during the 20th century. By the 1970s only some 30,000 remained. Various successive governments, especially that of Emperor Haile Selassie (1892–1974) who assumed the throne in 1948, found reasons to attack them. Their situation did not improve under the Marxist regime that followed. That regime forbade the practice of Judaism, and members of the Beta Israel were imprisoned on various charges, such as being "Zionist spies." Jewish religious leaders, called *kesim* (singular *kes*), experienced a new level of government harassment. Their situation became increasingly acute in the mid-1980s during the Ethiopian civil war.

Religiously, the Beta Israel have followed an archaic form of Judaism under the leadership of a high priest. They have the Hebrew Bible, but have been unfamiliar with the later written commentaries on the Torah that were compiled as the Talmud. Thus they inherit a system of belief and practice that reflects their own appropriation of the scriptures and has not reflected the ongoing developments elsewhere in the Jewish world. They have a system of dietary laws and emphasize the keeping of the Sabbath. One practice that they have altered as a result of the contact with Faitlovitch was the sacrificing of a lamb at Passover, which they gave up at his request. Both the questions concerning their origins and the nature of their practices made it more difficult for their advocates to interest important Jewish leaders in their situation.

The efforts to sway Orthodox Judaism to recognize Beta Israel led to the 1973 decree by Ovadia Yossef, the Sephardic chief rabbi in Israel, that the Ethiopian Jews should be allowed to immigrate to Israel under the law of return. He voiced an interesting notion that they were descendants of the ancient tribe of Dan. Two years later, his Ashkenazic counterpart, Rabbi Shlomo Goren, who led the Ashkenazi (European) Jewish community, lent his support to the Beta Israel cause. Shortly thereafter the Israeli Parliament consented. A few Beta Israel arrived in Israel in the 1970s, but it was not until the crisis of 1985 that Israel undertook Operation MosesThree and airlifted some 15,000 Jews to Israel. Hundreds more arrived a short time later under Operation Sheba. Then both Ethiopia and Sudan (where many had fled), closed their borders, and an additional 15,000 Falasha found themselves stuck in refugee camps. Only in 1991 was Israel allowed to assist these additional Jews (Operation Solomon).

Today, most members of Beta Israel reside in Israel. The Israeli government and social service agencies assisted their resettlement, the development of new means of support, and adjustment to a new homeland. Although some 80,000 Beta Israel have moved to Israel (and have grown over the decades to more than 100,000), an estimated 20,000 remain in Ethiopia, many in Addis Ababa and others in the countryside that has been their traditional homeland. The exact count has been made more difficult by the emergence since the 1990s of new groups of people who claim Jewish ancestry. Termed the Falasha Mura, these newer converts have not been given the same status as the Beta Israel.

The flow from Ethiopia to Israel has been steady since 2005, the Israeli government having set an immigration quota of 300 per month. Efforts to assist the Beta Israel remaining in Ethiopia are being spearheaded by the North American Conference on Ethiopian Jewry (NACOEJ), 132 Nassau St., 4th Fl., New York, NY 10038. Up-to-date information is posted on their website at http://www.circus.org/Old%20NACOEJ%20 Site/nacoej.htm.

Israel Association for Ethiopian Jews
5 Even Israel St.
Jerusalem
Israel
94228
www.ahava.com/iaej/

Association of the Ethiopian Family and Child in
    Israel (ALMAYA),
PO Box 5668
Shaul Hamelech St. 89/42
Beer-Sheva
Israel
84152

J. Gordon Melton

See also: Orthodox Judaism.

References

Avraham, Shmuel, with Arlene Kushner. *Treacherous Journey: My Escape from Ethiopia.* New York: Shapolsky Publishing, 1986.

Gruber, Ruth. *Rescue: The Exodus of the Ethiopian Jews.* New York: Atheneum, 1987.

Herman, Marilyn. "Songs, Honour and Identity: the Beta Israel (Ethiopian Jews) in Israel." Ph.D. diss., Oxford University, 1994.

Messing, Simon D. *The Story of the Falashas: "Black Jews" of Ethiopia.* Brooklyn, NY: Balshon Printing and Offset Co., 1982.

Rapoport, Louis. *The Lost Jews: Last of the Ethiopian Falashas.* New York: Stein and Day, 1983.

■ Bhutan

Bhutan is a small country of 18,000 square miles sandwiched between India and Tibet (China). It is home to

A dancer in Bhutan performs an ancient ritual to celebrate the life of Buddhist mystic Guru Rinpoche during the Paro Tsechu (religious festival) in The Kingdom of Bhutan in the Land of the Thunder Dragon high in the Himalayas on March 23, 2005. (Mrallen/Dreamstime.com)

682,000 people (2008), about half of whom are of Bhote ethnicity, the Tibetan group from whom the country derives its Westernized name. The largest minority group are Nepalese.

Although known as Bhutan to the outside world, it is known as Druk-Yul (the land of the Thunder Dragon) by its citizens. The traditional religion of the area was the Bon religion, a shamanistic faith that has survived to the present by incorporating Buddhist elements. However, in the 12th century CE a religious revolution occurred, as the Drukpa Kagyu branch of Tibetan Buddhism gained dominance. The Kagyu tradition had originated in the 11th century through the synthesizing work of the accomplished teacher Tilopa (988–1069). He was followed by a succession of teachers: Naropa (1916–1100), Marpa (1012–1097),

BHUTAN

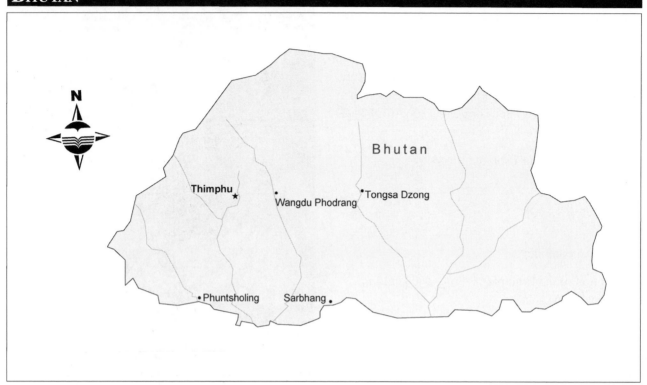

Bhutan

Religion	Followers in 1970	Followers in 2010	% of Population	Annual % growth 2000–2010	Followers in 2025	Followers in 2050
Buddhists	208,000	451,000	66.0	2.66	543,000	621,000
Hindus	72,000	185,000	27.0	2.66	222,000	253,000
Ethnoreligionists	14,000	30,000	4.4	2.66	30,000	30,000
Christians	950	8,900	1.3	2.66	12,700	17,000
Independents	500	5,800	0.8	2.51	8,000	11,000
Protestants	200	2,100	0.3	4.77	3,500	4,500
Roman Catholics	250	1,000	0.1	0.00	1,200	1,500
Muslims	3,000	7,200	1.1	2.66	8,500	10,000
Agnostics	0	1,000	0.1	2.67	1,500	2,000
Baha'is	100	760	0.1	2.68	1,000	1,700
Total population	**298,000**	**684,000**	**100.0**	**2.66**	**819,000**	**935,000**

Milarepa (1052–1135), and Gampopa (1079–1153). Among several subschools that originated under Gampopa's students was the Pagtu Kagyu, begun by Pagtu Dorje Gyalpo. Drukpa Kagyu was begun by one of Pagtu's disciples, Lingje Repa.

Although it was the dominant religion in Bhutan, Drukpa Kagyu continued to struggle with Bon and other rival groups for several centuries; then in the 17th century the nation of Bhutan was united around Drukpa Kagyu by Lama Ngawang Namgyal (who was both the spiritual leader and secular ruler). The religion lent its name to the country and has since that time been integral to its life and structure. The country existed as a theocracy until 1907, when the rule of the *shabdrungs* (as Namgyal and his successors were known) was overthrown and an hereditary monarchy established by Ugen Wangchuch. Today, the Buddhist leadership appoints two of the nine members of the council that assists the ruler, and a large number of Buddhist monks serve in the Tsongu, the national consultative assembly.

The majority of Bhutan's citizens are Tibetans and Butias. However, approximately 25 percent are Nepalese, most of whom are Hindus. Though there is legal recognition of the Nepalese, considerable friction exists between the two communities. The 1990s were marked by the "bhutanization" program and the attempt to have the Dzong language be used throughout the land. Rejection of the effort by the Nepalese occasionally led to violent exchanges between protesters and the authorities. The Ammasese also exist as a second significant Hindu ethnic group.

Bhutan has severe laws against proselytizing, which have significantly blunted efforts of Christians to launch work within the country. Openings have been found among Bhutanese who were living across the border in India. The Scandinavian Alliance Mission began work in 1892. Its missionaries were soon joined by representatives of both the Sental Mission, a work among the Sental people initiated by the Northern Evangelical Lutheran Church, and the Church of Scotland mission. The Church of Scotland established several schools in Western Bhutan and its successor, the Church of North India, is the only Protestant group both resident and working in Bhutan. A variety of evangelical groups, such as the Assemblies movement started by Bhakt Singh, have been working along the Indian border for several decades, but with little visible result.

Catholicism has also spread among the ethnic Indians of Bhutan, though membership is still measured in the low hundreds. Most of these are workers in the several Catholic-run schools. Work has been incorporated in the Diocese of Tezpur in India. The single parish is located in Puntsholing, a border community.

Lopen Karma Phuntsho

See also: Bon Religion; Church of North India; Church of Scotland; Milarepa; Naropa; Tibetan Buddhism.

References

Barrett, David, ed. *The Encyclopedia of World Christianity.* 2nd ed. New York: Oxford University Press, 2001.

Bartholomew, Terese Tse, and John Johnson, eds. *The Dragon's Gift: The Sacred Arts of Bhutan.* Chicago: Serindia Publications, 2008.

Bissio, Roberto Remo, et al. *Third World Guide 93/94.* Montevideo, Uruguay: Instituto del Tercer Mundo, 1992.

Chakravarti, B. *A Cultural History of Bhutan.* 2 vols. Chittaranjan: Hilltop, 1979, 1980.

Dorji, C. T. *History of Bhutan Based on Buddhism.* Thimphu, Bhutan: Sngay Xam in collaboration with Prominent Publishers, 1994.

Frey, K. "Studies in Bhutanese History Dealing with the Structural Organization of the Bhutanese Theocracy." *Tibetan Review* 18, no. 4 (1983): 15–22.

Bible Sabbath Association

The Bible Sabbath Association was founded in 1943 by several Sabbatarians (people who believe that the Jewish Sabbath rather than Sunday is the proper day for Christians to set aside for worship) who had a felt need for mutual support as they made their way in the Christian world that was oriented on Sunday. At the time of the Association's founding, many countries (especially the United States) still had a number of laws restricting Sunday activities and allowed discrimination against those who kept the Sabbath.

The Sabbatarian perspective had been discussed during the early centuries of the church as it separated from Judaism. It reemerged in the 1550s among the British Reformers, and an initial book offering it support was published in 1595. An early Sabbatarian Baptist church was founded in England in 1617, and the idea was brought to the American colonies in 1664. About the same time, Sabbatarianism appeared among the German Pietists.

Sabbatarianism was the exclusive possession of the Baptists until the middle of the 19th century, when Ellen G. White, the founder of the Seventh-day Adventist Church (SDA), injected it into the scattered Adventist movement, which was still trying to recover from the nonappearance of Jesus in 1844. The issue split the Adventists, but the SDA emerged as a successful movement and in the 20th century spread worldwide. Less successful was the Church of God Adventist group, which accepted Sabbatarianism but not the other unique ideas of Ellen G. White. They splintered into numerous small groups, many also adhering to the idea of the "Sacred Names," that is, that the personages generally referred to as God and Jesus should more properly be called Yahweh and Yahsua.

Finally, in the 20th century, Sabbatarianism found a home among the many splinter groups of the Church of Jesus Christ of Latter-day Saints.

The Bible Sabbath Association has included members from all the modern Sabbatarian churches. Primarily concerned with groups in the United States and with removing what it felt were discriminatory regulations that directly affected them, the Association has in recent decades reached out to Sabbatarian congregations that have emerged around the world in the developing pluralistic culture. Among its most valuable activities is the periodic publication of a directory of Sabbatarian groups worldwide.

Bible Sabbath Association
RD 1, ox 22
Fairview, OK 73737
www.biblesabbath.org

J. Gordon Melton

See also: Church of Jesus Christ of Latter-day Saints; Sabbatarianism; Seventh-day Adventist Church; White, Ellen G.

References

Dellinger, George. *A History of the Sabbath Resurrection Doctrine.* Westfield, NJ: Sabbath Research Center, 1982.

Directory of Sabbath-Observing Groups. Fairview, OK: Bible Sabbath Association, Revised periodically.

Haynes, Carlyle B. *From Sabbath to Sunday.* Washington, DC: Review and Herald Publishing Association, 1928.

Bilal

d. ca. 641

Bilal ibn Rabah was an African of Ethiopian ancestry who became an early convert to Islam and was later chosen to be the first person to call the faithful to prayer. He became particularly important as an African among the Companions of the Prophet Muhammad as Islam spread in sub-Saharan Africa.

Bilal was born a slave in Mecca, his owner being a powerful member of the dominant Quraysh tribe (of which the Prophet Muhammad was also a member, though of a different clan). Muslim sources indicate that he converted to Islam very early, long before his owner, who remained an adherent of the pre-Islamic Arabian polytheistic religion. Bilal's owner tortured him in an effort to make him denounce his Muslim faith. Bilal is said to have responded by crying, "One, one!" an affirmation of his faith in Allah, the one God.

Another of Muhammad's companions, Abu Bakr, learned of Bilal's plight and arranged for his freedom by swapping one of his slaves for him. Bilal was thus able to join the Hijra, the move by Muhammad and his Companions from Mecca to Medina in 622 CE. In Medina, Muhammad appointed Bilal as the *muezzin*, the first man appointed to the duty of calling the Muslim community to prayer. It appears that the honor fell to Bilal because of his powerful and melodious voice. For a time, he also served as Muhammad's personal attendant. He later participated in the Muslim conquest of Syria and resided there for the rest of his life. His career is remembered with a shrine in the cemetery of Damascus.

Bilal is possibly, next to the prophet, the most famous African Muslim. A number of organizations, including uplift and charitable organizations and missionary efforts operating in predominantly Christian areas, are named for him. He enjoys a prominent place in the story of Islam's first generation.

He is also especially honored among African American Muslims. Warith Din Muhammad (1933–2008), who succeeded to leadership of the nation of Islam movement and led it to adopt orthodox Muslim belief, called the members of the former Nation of Islam mosques Bilalians, and he changed the name of the movement newspaper to *Bilalian News.*

J. Gordon Melton

See also: Mecca; Medinah; Muhammad; Nation of Islam.

References

Abdul-Rauf, Muhammad. *Balal ibn Rabah: A Leading Companion of the Prophet Muhammad.* Indianapolis: American Trust Publications, 1977.

Craig, H. A. L. *Bilal.* London: Quartet Books, 2007.

Longs, Martin. *Muhammad: His Life Based on the Earliest Sources.* New York: Inner Traditions International, 1983.

Birth

Birth could be considered the first rite of passage in the human life cycle and many religious traditions practice ceremonies marking the entry of new human life into the world. Important religious considerations relative to birth include beliefs about the unborn child, rituals of pregnancy and childbirth (including ritual pollution of the mother), and ceremonies that welcome the newborn into the religious community.

The Origins of the Child Within the Abrahamic religions, a child is considered to be a gift from God, created by God in his own image, and thus the life of the fetus is sacred. However, traditions differ as to when they believe that the embryo acquires a soul. Within Jewish law, an embryo is considered "mere fluid" for the first 40 days; after 40 days, the unborn baby is considered part of the mother's body until labor has begun. The Roman Catholic Church states that life begins at conception and abortion, for any reason, is prohibited; many Protestant denominations concur with this teaching, but most Protestants dissent and will allow abortions in a limited set of circumstances. Islamic scholars and schools of thought differ as to when the fetus is believed to have gained a soul; 120 days after conception is perhaps the most widespread belief, while others hold it occurs at the moment of conception or 40 days after conception.

The Hindu traditions contain different beliefs concerning the entry of the soul into the fetus. Many Hindus believe that the soul and matter that make the fetus are joined at conception. Other sources state that the soul enters the fetus at four months or at seven months. The fetus is considered not as a developing person but as already a person, as the embodied soul has lived many times previously. Some believe that in the ninth month, the fetus has awareness and can remember past lives, but this memory is eradicated in the birth process. Most Sikhs believe that life begins at conception and that a child is a gift from God.

Pregnancy and Birth Rituals Few religious traditions prescribe rituals to be performed during pregnancy. In Hindu traditions, life cycle rituals (*sanskars* or *samskaras*) do begin during pregnancy. Hindu customs and ceremonies differ between communities, but some Hindus hold ceremonies at three and seven months of pregnancy. *Punsavana sanskar* is a ceremony held at three months to promote the protection and strong physical growth of the fetus. In some communities, this might include a prayer for the birth of a son. *Simantonnyana sanskar*, which loosely translates as "satisfying the cravings of the mother," is a celebration sometimes held seven months into pregnancy and includes prayers for the health of mother and baby, with the mother receiving gifts from her female friends and relatives. The emphasis of this ceremony is on the mental development of the baby, which is believed to be connected to the mother's mental and emotional health during pregnancy.

During labor, followers of the Abrahamic religious traditions might recite prayers. Muslim women, for instance, might repeat the Profession of Faith (*shahadah*) during labor and continue to say the formal daily prayers until they start to bleed during labor, whereas Sikh families might recite from the *Guru Granth Sahib*.

Some religious communities might encourage a natural approach to birth, possibly encouraging homebirth and eschewing such things as pain-killing drugs. There are a number of small Christian churches emphasizing faith healing that advocate church leaders rather than medical practitioners supervising births. There also exist Christian intentional communities, such as Rose Creek Village in the U.S. state of Tennessee, where a number of female members are trained midwives and thus able to deliver babies in the community. Also advocating natural childbirth is The Farm, a spiritual intentional community founded in 1971 and also based in Tennessee. The Farm Midwifery Center, run by members of the community who are qualified midwives, claims to teach "a holistic approach to

The circumcision of Christ, after Bellini. (Getty Images)

natural childbirth" and holds midwifery workshops open to those outside the community. There are numerous teachers who combine religious beliefs and practices and/or alternative medical therapies with teachings about childbirth. In the United Kingdom some of the most well known include Dr. Yehudi Gordon and Janet Balaskas, pioneers of the Active Birth movement, and Dr. Gowri Motha, founder of the Jeyarani Gentle Birth Method. In the United States, Gurmukh Kaur Khalsa, founder of the Golden Bridge spiritual village, offers pre- and post-natal yoga classes. Kaur teaches kundalini yoga, pioneered by Harbhajan Singh Yogi Bhajan (1929–2004), founder of the Sikh Dharma and its educational branch 3HO (Healthy, Happy, Holy Organization).

The Church of Scientology is one of a few religions whose theology incorporates a suggested birth practice. Scientologists believe that words spoken dur-

ing times of stress can be stored in the "reactive mind" as engrams, or blockages, and adversely affect the individual later in life, preventing the person from living up to her or his full potential. It is believed that words spoken during a child's birth can create these engrams in the new baby. For this reason, Scientologists may choose to have a "Silent Birth" in which words are avoided as much as possible by all present. It is believed that this will create an atmosphere of maximum benefit to both the mother and baby. The mother might also refuse pain-killing drugs, in line with the drug-free lifestyle advocated by the church.

Purity and Pollution of the Mother   In many religions, issues of purity and pollution surround the woman in labor and the new mother. Within the Abrahamic religions, these are largely derived from the prescriptions in the book of Leviticus, which state that uterine blood, whether from menstruation or childbirth, is ritually impure. Both menstruating women and those bleeding postnatally are thus subject to various restrictions/exemptions, including visiting the mosque/synagogue, having sexual intercourse with their husbands, and saying the daily prayers in the case of Islam. For strictly observant Orthodox Jews, the husband is prohibited from having any physical contact with his wife during menstruation and labor after there has been any blood loss, including holding her hand and passing objects directly to her. The prohibition against touch lasts until the woman has had seven days without blood loss and has been to the *mikvah*, a ritual bath traditionally attached to a synagogue. Leviticus also stipulates different periods of impurity depending on whether a woman has given birth to a boy or a girl (she is considered to be unclean for 40 days after having a boy and twice as long after having a girl).

While the main Christian traditions do not follow the laws of Leviticus, the descriptions of Mary's presentation at the temple 40 days after Jesus' birth (celebrated annually in the festival of Candlemas), has influenced the practice of "churching" within Christianity. Within Catholicism, it is a blessing given by the church to women as a thanksgiving for their recovery from childbirth. Traditionally, in the ceremony, the woman is led into the church from the vestibule by the priest and receives a blessing by the altar, indicating the return of the woman to the church. The practice was also adopted by the Anglican Church although its popularity sharply declined in the 1960s. Today the Anglican Church is more likely to include the whole family in a service called "Thanksgiving for the Gift of a Child," which can be either a private celebration of birth or adoption, or a public celebration held during the main Sunday service. This service is sometimes performed as a preliminary to the baptism of an infant into the church, but it does not, by itself, mark initiation into the Christian faith.

In Hindu traditions bodily emissions are generally considered to be polluting and women do not attend the temple while bleeding. Five or six weeks after the birth, the mother and baby may have a ritual wash before attending the temple for a blessing. In contrast, Guru Nanak, founder of the Sikh religion, was explicitly concerned with eradicating inequalities between genders; according to Sikh doctrine, women who have just given birth are not considered to be polluting (although cultural factors may also be relevant).

Welcoming the Baby Many religious traditions perform ceremonies to welcome the baby into the community. In the Jewish tradition circumcision is performed on male children in remembrance of the covenant that God made with Abraham. The circumcision is traditionally performed on the eighth day after birth in the ceremony called the *brit milah* by a specially trained circumciser, the *mohel*. During the ceremony, the baby is held on the lap of the *sandek*, a close male friend or relative. The baby boy is also given his name during this ceremony. A baby girl is traditionally given her name the first time her father is called for public reading of the Torah after her birth. Liberal Jews might hold a ceremony to mark the birth of a daughter, called the *simhat bat* or *brit habat*.

Within Islam, the baby is welcomed into the faith as soon as he or she is born, when his or her father whispers the Muslim call to prayer (*adhaan*) into the right ear. For many Muslims, it is important that these are the first words that the baby hears as they are the introduction to the Muslim faith. Within Islam, circumcision is performed primarily for reasons of physical cleanliness and there is no formal religious ceremony. Although circumcision can be performed any time before puberty, traditionally it is performed on the seventh day after birth in combination with a number of other ceremonies, including the naming of the child and the shaving of the baby's head (to symbolically remove the impurities of birth and to show that the child is the servant of Allah). The baby's hair is weighed and the equivalent weight in silver given to charity. The *aqeeqah* ceremony in which sheep are slaughtered (or ordered from the butchers) and the meat distributed to friends, relatives, and the poor might also be performed on the seventh day after birth.

The main Christian traditions practice the sacrament of infant baptism (sometimes called christening), usually in the first few months of life, whereby the parents dedicate the child to their faith. Godparents are chosen who will support the child in the Christian faith. A significant act within this ceremony is the priest marking the sign of the cross and then pouring water on the head as a mark of cleansing and to mark the start of a new life in the church. For much of Christian history, baptism was performed as soon after the birth as possible, in case the baby died, in the belief that the act rids the baby of original sin and ensures entry into heaven. However, many Protestant traditions (Mennonites, Baptists, Adventists) practice adult or "believer's" baptism. In these traditions, an adult must decide to be baptized and baptism by full water immersion is more likely to be practiced. Undergoing adult baptism is considered part of the experience of being "born again" into the Christian faith. For infants, these churches are likely to offer prayers for the baby's safe arrival and future health; a service of dedication might be held in which the baby is brought to church a few weeks after birth to be welcomed into the community.

Some Hindu families welcome the baby into the world by writing OM/AUM on the baby's tongue with honey or ghee, or by placing some honey in the baby's mouth while whispering the name of God in the baby's ear. This may be performed immediately after birth or on the day of the naming ceremony, *namakarna*, traditionally held on the 11th day of the baby's life. In some communities, a celebration is held on the sixth day after the birth, when the women of the community gather to congratulate the mother, pray, give thanks, and bring presents for the baby.

Sikh parents might welcome their baby in a similar manner to Hindu parents by placing honey in the baby's mouth and whispering the *mool mantar* (the main chant or root verse) in the baby's ear. Some Sikh families also hold a ceremony on the 13th day after birth at which prayers are said and the baby is blessed. Another ceremony might be held when the baby is about 40 days old and is taken to the *gurdwara* for the first time. The baby's name is often chosen during this ceremony: the *granthi* opens the *Guru Granth Sahib* at random and recites a passage, the parents then choose a name beginning with the first letter of the passage, which is then announced to the congregation and *karah parshad*, a sweet dish, is distributed in celebration and thanksgiving.

Sarah Harvey

See also: Church of Scientology; Roman Catholic Church; Sikh Dharma; Yoga.

References

Gaskin, Ina May. *Spiritual Midwifery*. 4th ed. Summertown, TN: Book Publishing Company, 2002.

Klassen, Pamela. *Blessed Events: Religion and Homebirth in America*. Princeton, NJ: Princeton University Press, 2001.

Knodel, Natalie. *The Thanksgiving of Women after Childbirth, commonly called the Churching of Women*. 1995. http://users.ox.ac.uk/~mikef/church.html#intro.

Leboyer, Frederick. *Birth Without Violence*. Rev. ed. Rochester, VT: Inner Traditions/Bear and Company, 2002.

Schott, Judith, and Alix Henley. *Culture, Religion and Childbearing in a Multiracial Society: A Handbook for Health Professionals*. London: Butterworths Heinemann, 1997.

Ward, Gary L. ed. *Churches Speak on Abortion: Official Statements from Religious Bodies and Ecumenical Organizations*. Detroit, MI: Gale Research Company, 1989.

Birth of the Báb

Sayyid 'Alí-Muhammad, known by his spiritual title as the "Báb" (the "Gate"), was born on October 20, 1819, in Shíráz, Persia (now Iran). The Báb was the founder of a 19th-century new religious movement generally known as Bábism. The Báb declared himself to be the long-awaited Qá'im (Ariser/Resurrector), the expected eschatological deliverer (known in both Shia and Sunni Islam as the Mahdi), who, according to Islamic tradition, would come to revive Islam when it was at its lowest ebb. While proclaiming himself to be an independent "Manifestation of God," the Báb also spoke of the imminent advent of the Promised One, or "Him whom God shall make manifest." One of the Báb's followers, Bahá'u'lláh (1817–1892), would later receive revelations confirming that he was that Promised One heralded by the Báb.

Armin Eschraghi has argued that the new faith proclaimed by the Báb fulfilled all the criteria of an independent religion: a new founder, newly revealed scriptures, a new set of metaphysical and theological teachings distinct from those of Islam, new religious laws and principles. In revealing his new code of laws (called the Bayán), the Báb pursued three major goals: (1) paving the way for the advent of the Promised One; (2) provoking the clerical establishment and shattering the foundations of their often-abused institutionalized authority; and (3) proving the independence of his own religion as distinct from Islam.

Soon after the Báb publicly proclaimed his prophetic mission beginning on the evening of May 22, 1844, the Islamic government then in power in Persia began to suppress the movement and violence ensued. The Báb was arrested and executed by a firing squad of 750 musketeers on July 9, 1850, in Tabríz, Persia. Subsequent to an unauthorized and ill-fated attempt on the life of the shah of Persia in 1852, the shah ordered the most brutal tortures and deaths of a great number of Bábís, with estimates ranging from around 5,000 to 20,000 martyrs.

In the fall of 1852, in the wake of the Báb's execution, Bahá'u'lláh was imprisoned in the notorious Siyáh-Chál (Black Pit), during which time he experienced a series of visions that awakened him to his prophetic destiny. He was released, but banished—exiled successively to Baghdad (1853–1863), Constantinople/Istanbul (1863), Adrianople/Edirne (1863–1868), and finally to the prison-city of 'Akká, considered the vilest penal colony of the Ottoman Empire. In 1892, Bahá'u'lláh passed away in Bahjí, near 'Akká in Palestine (now Israel).

In his article on "Bábism" published that same year, Professor Browne wrote: "I say nothing of the mighty influence which, as I believe, the Bábí faith will exert in the future, nor of the new life it may perchance breathe into a dead people; for, whether it succeed or fail, the splendid heroism of the Bábí martyrs is a thing eternal and indestructible." The "Bábí faith" that Browne spoke of evolved into the Baha'i Faith, which has since spread worldwide to become the most widely diffused world religion next to Christianity, according to the 2001 *World Christian Encyclopedia*.

Today, Baha'is accept the Báb as a John the Baptist figure, whose words and actions heralded the arrival of Bahá'u'lláh. However, unlike John the Baptist, the Báb revealed much in substance, both in terms of doctrine and religious laws, that was subsequently revoiced and reenacted, with certain revisions, by Bahá'u'lláh.

The Báb did not instruct his followers to formally observe the day of his birth; however, for that occasion, Bahá'u'lláh had revealed the *Lawh-i Mawlúd*, which awaits an authorized translation. Today, Baha'is worldwide annually celebrate the birth of the Báb on October 20 as a holy day, with work and school suspended for the day. There being no required observances, Baha'is are free to creatively organize commemorative activities which, although attended mostly by Baha'is, are open to people of all faiths and persuasions.

J. Gordon Melton and Christopher Buck

See also: Baha'i Faith; Bahá'u'lláh; Birth/Ascension of Bahá'u'lláh; Temples—Baha'i Faith.

References

Bahá'u'lláh et al. *Twin Holy Days: Birthday of Bahá'u'lláh, Birthday of the Báb: A Compilation.* Los Angeles: Kalimát Press, 1995.

Browne, Edward G. "Bábism." In *Religious Systems of the World: A Contribution to the Study of Comparative Religion*, edited by William Sheowring and Conrad W. Thies, 333–353. London: Swann Sonnenschein, 1892.

Eschraghi, Armin. "'Undermining the Foundations of Orthodoxy': Some Notes on the Báb's Shar'ah (Sacred Law)." In *A Most Noble Pattern: Essays in the Study of the Writings of the Báb*, edited by Todd Lawson. Oxford: George Ronald, forthcoming.

Keil, Gerald. *Time and the Baha'i Era: A Study of the Badí' Calendar.* Oxford: George Ronald, 2008.

Saiedi, Nader. *Gate of the Heart: Understanding the Writings of the Báb.* Waterloo, ON: Wilfrid Laurier University Press, 2008.

Walbridge, John. "The Birthday of the Báb." In *Sacred Acts, Sacred Space, Sacred Time*, 217–218. Oxford: George Ronald, 1996.

Birth/Ascension of Bahá'u'lláh

The Baha'i Faith was founded by Mírzá Husayn-'Alí Núrí, known by his spiritual title, Bahá'u'lláh (1817–1892), and by Sayyid 'Alí-Muhammad of Shíráz (1819–1850), better known as the Báb (the "Gate"), who claimed to be the Qá'im (Ariser/Resurrector), the messianic figure expected in Shia Islam, the majority faith in Iran. Throughout his six-year ministry, the Báb heralded "Him Whom God Shall Make Manifest," whose advent was imminent. Most of the Bábís (followers of the Báb) came to accept Bahá'u'lláh as that messianic figure. Most current Baha'i laws, in fact, were originally instituted by the Báb and were subsequently selectively ratified and revised by Bahá'u'lláh and set forth in the preeminent Baha'i scripture, The Most Holy Book (Kitáb-i-Aqdas). The birth of Bahá'u'lláh and the birth of the Báb are therefore closely linked.

Bahá'u'lláh was born on November 12, 1817, in Tehran, Persia (now Iran). As a young nobleman, he became a prominent figure in the Bábí religion. In 1852, while in prison during the unrest that followed the Báb's execution in 1850, Bahá'u'lláh experienced a series of visions and accepted his role as the Promised One foretold by the Báb and in the messianic texts of all religions.

By imperial decree, Bahá'u'lláh was subsequently exiled to Baghdad (1853–1863), to Istanbul (1863), to Adrianople (1863–1868), then to 'Akká (Acre) in Palestine (1868–1892), where he would spend the rest of his life in custody, although the last years were in relative comfort under house arrest. Bahá'u'lláh died on May 29, 1892, in Bahji, Palestine. Today, members of the global Baha'i Faith commemorate both Bahá'u'lláh's birth and ascension.

As the co-founders of the Baha'i Faith, Bahá'u'lláh and his predecessor, the Báb, are often referred to as the "Twin Manifestations," and the occasions of their respective births are similarly called the "Twin Birthdays."

In the Most Holy Book (Kitáb-i-Aqdas), Bahá'u'lláh established four great festivals of the Baha'i year: "All Feasts have attained their consummation in the two Most Great Festivals, and in the two other Festivals that fall on the twin days." The "two Most Great Festivals" are the Declaration of Bahá'u'lláh (known as the Festival of Ridván [Paradise]) from April 21 to May 2 (commemorating Bahá'u'lláh's initial proclamation of his prophetic mission in Baghdad, April 21–May 2, 1863), and the Declaration of the Báb, which occurred

on the evening of May 22, 1844 (but is dated May 23 since, in the Baha'i calendar, the new day begins at sunset the previous day).

The birthdays of the Báb and Bahá'u'lláh fall on two consecutive days in the Islamic lunar calendar. "The Birth of the Abhá Beauty [Bahá'u'lláh]," Bahá'u'lláh wrote, "was at the hour of dawn on the second day of the month of Muharram, the first day of which marketh the Birth of His Herald [the Báb]. These two days are accounted as one in the sight of God." The explanation for this statement is that, in the Muslim lunar calendar, the birth of the Báb was on the first day of the month of Muharram 1235 AH (October 20, 1819), while the birth of Bahá'u'lláh took place on the second day of Muharram 1233 AH (November 12, 1817).

While the present Baha'i calendar (of 19 months of 19 days, plus intercalary days) is solar and roughly conforms to the Common Ear calendar), Baha'is in many countries of the Middle East observe these two Baha'i Holy Days according to the country's Islamic lunar calendar (which is incidentally how they were observed by Bahá'u'lláh himself), while Baha'is of the West and elsewhere (such as among the Baha'is in Syria and Lebanon) celebrate these occasions by their corresponding Common Era calendar dates. In the future, the Universal House of Justice (the institution that guides the Baha'i community internationally) will determine whether these "Twin Days" will be celebrated on a solar or lunar basis.

There is no prescribed ceremony or service for celebrating the anniversary of the birth of Bahá'u'lláh. But it is common for Baha'is to meet together for collective worship and fellowship, often through devotional meetings or musical programs. These programs are open to all to would like to attend.

The birth and ascension of Bahá'u'lláh are considered major holy days, during which work is suspended as well as school activities.

Bahá'u'lláh passed away at 3:00 a.m. on May 29, 1892, in Bahjí, near 'Akká, in Palestine (now Israel). A telegram bearing the news, "The Sun of Bahá' has set," was immediately dispatched to Ottoman Sultan Abdul-Hamíd II (r. 1876–1909), with a request for permission to bury Bahá'u'lláh at Bahjí, which was granted. After the ascension of Bahá'u'lláh, his eldest son, 'Abdu'l-Bahá (1844–1921), was appointed, pursuant to Bahá'u'lláh's will and testament and to provisions of the Most Holy Book, as the appointed "Centre of the Covenant" (successor to Bahá'u'lláh), as the perfect exemplar of Baha'i ethics and virtues, and as the infallible expounder of his father's teachings.

Local Baha'i communities worldwide will therefore gather at that time (3:00 a.m.) to commemorate their founder with Baha'i prayers and scriptures, usually culminating in the chanting in Arabic, or recitation in translation, of what is known as the "Tablet of Visitation," a special prayer reserved for the commemoration of the Báb as well as Bahá'u'lláh. Some Baha'is arrange, through the Office of Pilgrimage at the Baha'i World Centre in Haifa, Israel, to schedule their pilgrimages around the time of the birth or ascension of Bahá'u'lláh.

During their pilgrimage, Baha'is visit the shrine of the Báb in Haifa, and the shrine of Bahá'u'lláh in Bahjí, near Acre, where Bahá'u'lláh lived the last years of his life. (On July 8, 2008, the UN Educational, Scientific and Cultural Organization [UNESCO] World Heritage Committee designated the shrine of the Báb on Mount Carmel in Haifa, Israel, and the shrine of Bahá'u'lláh, located near Old Acre on Israel's northern coast as World Heritage sites—the first modern religious edifices to be added to the UNESCO List.) A large gathering was held there in 1992 on the centenary of Bahá'u'lláh's passing, following which the Universal House of Justice, the international governing body of the global Baha'i community, declared the period from April 1992 to April 1993 as the second "Baha'i Holy Year" to mark both the centenary itself and the inauguration of the Covenant of Bahá'u'lláh in November 1892.

J. Gordon Melton and Christopher Buck

See also: Baha'i Faith; Bahá'u'lláh; Birth of the Báb; Pilgrimage; Temples—Baha'i Faith.

References

Bahá'u'lláh et al. *Twin Holy Days: Birthday of Bahá'u'lláh, Birthday of the Báb: A Compilation.* Los Angeles: Kalimát Press, 1995.

Keil, Gerald. *Time and the Baha'i Era: A Study of the Badí' Calendar.* Oxford: George Ronald, 2008.

Momen, Moojan. *Bahá'u'lláh: A Short Biography.* Oxford: Oneworld Publications, 2007.

Walbridge, John. "The Ascension of Bahá'u'lláh." In *Sacred Acts, Sacred Space, Sacred Time,* 242–244. Oxford: George Ronald, 1996.

Walbridge, John. "The Birthday of Bahá'u'lláh." In *Sacred Acts, Sacred Space, Sacred Time,* 231–232. Oxford: George Ronald, 1996.

Blavatsky, Helena P.

1831–1891

Helena Petrovna Blavatsky, usually called simply Madam Blavatsky or her initials, H.P.B., was the primary theoretician of the Theosophical Society, cofounded by herself, Henry Steel Olcott (1832–1907), and William Quan Judge (1851–1896) in New York City in 1875. The Theosophical Society went on to become one of the most influential Western Esoteric organizations of the 20th century. It facilitated the movement of Eastern religions to the West and gave birth to numerous additional Esoteric groups.

Blavatsky was born Helena Hahn, July 30, 1832, in Ekaterinoslav (now Dnepropetrovsk), Ukraine. She grew up in an affluent Russian family and came of age as Spiritualism was spreading through segments of Russian society. As a teenager, she was involved in various spiritual experiences, including automatic writing. Her teen years were spent with her grandfather who provided a home following her mother's death in 1843. She was but 16 when she married a much older man, General N. V. Blavatsky. The marriage proved an unhappy experience for the young woman, and abandoning her husband, she moved to Constantinople. She stayed in Turkey only a relatively short time. She preferred travel and took the opportunity to roam through Asia and Europe. She traveled around the world twice during the 1850s, and in 1856, while in India, made a clandestine attempt to get into Tibet, then forbidden territory to outsiders. Whether she succeeded in her quest remains a debatable topic. In any case, investigating paranormal phenomena during her travels occupied much of her time. She became a medium and in 1871, in Cairo, she founded a Spiritualist society. The

Helena Petrovna Blavatsky was a Russian student of spiritualism and occultism. In 1875, Blavatsky cofounded the Theosophical Society in New York. (Ridpath, John Clark, *Ridpath's History of the World,* 1901)

organization allowed fraudulent phenomena to enter its activities and soon collapsed.

Blavatsky settled in New York City in 1873 and quickly integrated herself into the American Spiritualist community. At the time materialization séances were becoming prominent and she joined in the effort to produce a variety of what were termed "physical phenomena." At one point, she traveled to Vermont where she demonstrated her own ability at materialization in cooperation with the Eddy brothers, some famous American mediums. Here she met journalist Henry S. Olcott. Their friendship, later enlarged to include a lawyer, William Q. Judge, led to the formation of the Theosophical Society in 1875. The Society was devoted to exploring various esoteric philosophies, exploring paranormal phenomena, and promoting world brotherhood. She also began work on her first book, *Isis Unveiled* (1877), a compendium of Esoteric philosophy and knowledge. In 1879, she and Olcott launched the society's periodical, *The Theosophist*. In 1882, Blavatsky and Olcott moved to India. They reestablished the Society's international headquarters in Madras and left Judge in charge of the American work.

In transcending Spiritualism, Blavatsky drew heavily on the Esoteric traditions, especially speculative Freemasonry. She replaced the emphasis on contact with spirits of the dead, the bedrock of Spiritualist experience, with contact from a set of masters or mahatmas, teachers of Esoteric wisdom believed to inhabit some elevated planes of existence. She received messages written on paper from these mahatmas that would be discovered within a specially constructed cabinet at the Theosophical headquarters.

Blavatsky visited London in 1884, and, while there, she demonstrated her abilities to produce a range of phenomena before representatives of the Society for Psychical Research. They were duly impressed. Their initial favorable opinion, however, was soon refuted by a disgruntled former Blavatsky associate in India, Emma Cutting Coulomb, who charged that she was perpetuating fraudulent phenomena. In 1885, the Society for Psychical Research (SPR) sent Richard Hodgson (1855–1905) to India to investigate these charges. During his visit, he discovered a number of incidents of deception, was shown the various tricks used to produce seemingly paranormal phenomena, and reluctantly concluded Blavatsky was an accomplished fraud. The SPR published his findings.

The resulting scandal rocked the Theosophical world and drove Blavatsky from India to a relatively low-profile existence in Germany. She later settled in London. While there she completed what was to become her major work, *The Secret Doctrine* (1889). Above and beyond the charges of fraud, this book established her as an accomplished teacher of Esotericism and would become one of the most influential Esoteric texts of the 20th century. Its effect on the society was immediate in that it was instrumental in the conversion of the noted atheist orator Annie Besant (1847–1933) to Theosophy. Blavatsky recognized her leadership qualities and left the Society's Esoteric Section to Besant.

Following Blavatsky's death in London on May 8, 1891, Besant would successfully withstand a challenge from Judge for leadership of the Esoteric Section.

Then in 1907, following Olcott's death, Besant would become the international president of the Theosophical Society and would lead it for the rest of her life.

J. Gordon Melton

See also: Besant, Annie; Western Esoteric Tradition.

References

Blavatsky, Helena P. *H. P. Blavatsky: Collected Writings.* Comp. by Boris de Zirkoff. Wheaton, IL: Theosophical Publishing House, 1950–1995. 15 vols. http://www.katinkahesselink.net/blavatsky/. Assessed March 1, 2009.

Blavatsky, Helena P. *Isis Unveiled: A Master Key to the Mysteries of Ancient and Modern Science and Theology.* 1877; rpt.: Los Angeles: The Theosophy Company, 1982.

Blavatsky, Helena P. *The Sacred Doctrine.* 1888; rpt.: Los Angeles: The Theosophy Company, 1974.

Johnson, Paul K. *The Masters Revealed: Madame Blavatsky and the Myth of the Great White Brotherhood.* Albany: State University of New York Press, 1994.

Meade, Marion. *Madame Blavatsky.* New York: G. P. Putnam's Sons, 1980.

Ryan, Charles J. *H. P. Blavatsky and the Theosophical Movement.* Pasadena: Theosophical University Press, 1974.

Bodh-Gaya

The region of Gaya is a prominent Eastern Indian pilgrimage area located in the state of Bihar. Gaya is the name of a character in the Hindu scriptures who was a great devotee of the deity Vishnu. A temple at Brahma-Gaya honoring Vishnu, built in 1787 and housing the footprints of Vishnu, is the primary focus of Hindu pilgrims to the area. The majority of pilgrims in the area are not Hindus, however, but Buddhists. At Bodh-Gaya, some seven miles from Brahma-Gaya, Gautama Buddha, the founder of Buddhism, found enlightenment, the main event from which Buddhism originated.

Buddha had engaged in a variety of austerities for several years when he realized their futility. He then sat under a Gayan fig tree vowing not to rise until he attained his goal. He now battled with Mara, the Lord

Monks praying under the Bodhi Tree, Mahabodhi Temple, Bodh-Gaya, India. The ancient Indian custom of worshipping trees is still practiced today, and the Bodhi Tree in Bodh-Gaya maintains a special degree of sacredness as it is said to be the tree under which Prince Gautama Siddhartha gained enlightenment. (Luciano Mortula/Dreamstime.com)

of illusion, and subdued his mind. Having finally attained enlightenment, he continued at the tree for 21 additional days that included 7 days of sitting meditation, 7 days of walking meditation, and then 7 more days under the tree. At this point, usually dated to 623 BCE (others suggest 588 BCE), Gautama emerged as the Buddha, the Enlightened One, and began the mature phase of his life during which he taught his close disciples. The Bodhi Tree, a large fig tree located at Bodh-Gaya, is acknowledged by Buddhists as the originating point of their faith.

Several centuries later, the third-century BCE Indian Emperor Ahsoka, the first ruler in India to be a practicing Buddhist, marked the site of Buddha's enlightenment with one of his inscribed pillars, identified by its elephant capital. After his angry wife attacked the tree, he had a protective wall built around it. Ahsoka's daughter Sangamitta, a Buddhist nun, took a cutting from the tree to Sri Lanka where King Devanampiyatissa planted it at the monastery in the old capital of Anuradhapura. This present tree at Anuradhapura, which derives from the Bodhi Tree, is now the oldest continually documented tree in the world.

The oldest structure at Bodh-Gaya is the Mahabodhi (or Great Enlightenment) Temple, located adjacent to the Bodhi Tree site. Originally a stupa, in the second century, it was replaced by the present Mahabodhi Temple. Next to the temple is an area now designated as the Jewel Walk, reputedly the place where the Buddha practiced walking meditation for seven days following his enlightenment. In the first century CE, a stone rail was erected around the perimeter of the entire site. It included representations of the Vedic gods Indra and Surya. When he visited the area around 400 CE, the Chinese pilgrim Fa-hien noted that the temple contained several statues and monuments.

In the meantime, the tree at Bodh-Gaya became a focus of Hindu-Buddhist tensions and was cut down on several occasions. A century after Ahsoka, King Puspyamitra (second century BCE), had it cut down, and an offshoot of the original tree would have to be planted in its place. In 600 CE, King Sesanka again destroyed the tree and a new tree was again planted by King Purnavarma 20 years later. The temple was refurbished during the Pala-Sena period (750–1200).

Buddhism itself was largely destroyed in India in the 12th century as a result of the Muslim invasion of the area. For a time in the 14th and 15th centuries, Burmese Buddhists undertook the care of the Mahabodhi Temple, but in the 16th century, a Hindu ascetic, Mahant Gosain Giri, took control of the site and in 1590 established his *math* (monastery) there. His successors controlled the place until 1949. In the 19th century, British archaeologist Alexander Cunningham visited Bodh-Gaya. He found the Mahant followers practicing Hindu rites in the temple and the tree largely weakened by rot. He subsequently documented the destruction of the last remnant of the tree in a 1876 storm. In the wake of the storm, several people had

collected seeds, and in 1881 Cunningham planted the seeds. What emerged was the Bodhi Tree that is to be found at Bodh-Gaya today. Cunningham also gained the support of the British authorities for the restoration of Bodh-Gaya.

In the 1890s, Anagarika Dharmapala (1864–1933), a Sri Lankan Buddhist, founded the Maha Bodhi Society to raise the money to purchase Bodh-Gaya and return it to Buddhist control. He did not live to enjoy any success in his endeavor, but finally in 1949, the Bodhgaya Act recognized the site as a Buddhist holy place and a new temple management committee assumed control. While a majority of the committee, including its chairperson, are Hindus, Buddhists participate.

In the 1950s, the committee began to develop Bodh-Gaya as an international pilgrimage site. Subsequently, Buddhists from Sri Lanka, Thailand, Burma, Tibet, Bhutan, and Japan established monasteries, temples, and housing for pilgrims, all within easy walking distance of the Mahabodhi compound. In 1983, the Japanese opened the Shakado, topped with a reliquary that houses relics of the Buddha, the main building of the Daijokyo Buddhist Temple. Five years later, the Dalai Lama being present, they consecrated the Great Buddha Statue. Standing 80 feet, it is the first Buddhist mega-statue in India.

In 2002, the temple at Bodhgaya was named a world heritage site by the UN Educational, Scientific and Cultural Organization (UNESCO).

Edward A. Irons

See also: Ashoka; Buddha, Gautama; Enlightenment; Relics; Statues—Buddhist.

References

Ansari, Abdul Quddoos. *Archaeological Remains of Bodhgaya*. Delhi: Ramanand Vidya Bhavan, 1990.

Asher, Frederick M. *Bodh Gaya*. Oxford: Oxford University Press, 2008.

Barua, Dipak K. *Buddha Gaya Temple, Its History*. Buddha Gaya: Temple Buddha Gaya Management Committee, 1981.

Bauddh, Shanti Swaroop. *Badhgaya*. New Delhi: Samyak Prakashan, 2005.

Brockman, Norbert C., *Encyclopedia of Sacred Places*. Santa Barbara, CA: ABC-Clio, 1997.

Harshananda, Swami. *Hindu Pilgrimage Centres*. Bangalore: Ramakrishna Math, 2005.

Trevithick, Alan. *Revival of Buddhist Pilgrimage at Bodh Gaya, 1811–1949: Anagarika Dharmapala and the Mahabodhi Temple*. Delhi: Motilal, 2007.

Bodhidharma

ca. 470–ca. 534

Bodhidharma (aka Da Mo in Chinese or Daruma Daishi in Japanese) is the fabled First Patriarch of the lineage from which Chan (Zen) Buddhism has been passed to the contemporary world and the reputed originator of the modern disciplines of the martial arts. For a person of such importance, however, we know relatively little. He is said to have been born in southern India, the third son of a king, around the year 470 CE. Traditionalist practitioners of Zen see him as transmitting a lineage of meditative masters reaching back to the Buddha.

Bodhidharma seems to have spent most of his life in northern China as a wandering monk. A decade of these years (515–526) was spent at Yong Ming monastery in Loyang (soon to become the Chinese capital). At some point, Bodhidharma practiced meditation for a requisite time to attain enlightenment. He would then be able to pass along the seal of enlightenment (*inkashome*) to anyone who was recognized as having attained a like realization of truth. According to one story, he meditated for nine years, during which time his leg muscles atrophied. This unverified legend gave birth to the Japanese *daruma* dolls that always resume an erect sitting position when tipped over.

According to tradition, Bodhidharma passed his lineage to Hui Ke (or Hui-k'o) (ca. 487–ca. 593), cited in the lineage as the second Chan Patriarch. That lineage would subsequently be passed to successive masters until it reached Hui Neng (638–713), the Sixth Patriarch. It is following Hui Neng's death that Zen master Shen Hui (684–758) emerged as a teacher. He would in his mature years receive royal favor and used his position to promulgate a lineage of Indian Buddhist meditation masters leading to Bodhidharma and named the masters that served as the patriarchs of the Southern School of Bodhidharma, that branch of the movement that Shen Hui then headed. During his lifetime, Chan Buddhism was transformed from just another small Chinese Buddhist sect into one of its most vigorous branches. His promotion of Bodhidharma as the transmitter of the lineage from Indian to China provided the context in which many stories about Bodhidharma could be initially published and subsequently embellished.

The stories about Bodhidharma, any of which may carry a core of historical truth, begin with his arrival in China. Reportedly, the Emperor Wu Di, who was already a Buddhist, met with Bodhidharma at Nanjing. He was unable to convince the emperor that the many temples he was starting to build were valuable enough to receive the emperor's approbation.

The most famous stories tied to Bodhidharma relate to his wandering into the Song Mountains where he found the Shaolin Temple. He taught the monks Chan meditation, but equally important, upon observing their relatively poor physical condition, he developed a program of physical techniques designed to strengthen their bodies. The regimen allowed them not just to survive but to thrive in the rather isolated location where they had chosen to live. These techniques evolved into what is today called Kung Fu (*gongfu*), the fountainhead of all other martial arts.

Edward A. Irons

See also: Meditation; Zen Buddhism.

References

Broughton, Jeffrey. *The Bodhidharma Anthology*. Berkeley: University of California Press, 1999.

Dumoulin, Heinrich. *Zen Buddhism: A History*. Vol. 1: *India and China*. New York: Macmillan, 1988.

The Zen Teachings of Bodhidharma. Trans. by Red Pine. New York: North Point Press, 1987.

Bodhisattva

The bodhisattva, a key concept in Mahayana and Vajrayana Buddhism, is narrowly defined as an advanced individual who chooses not to attain nirvana, the enlightened state that is the ultimate goal of Buddhist attainment, and chooses instead to remain in the

Depiction of a bodhisattva surrounded by deities. In Buddhism, a bodhisattva is one who has achieved enlightenment but has chosen to remain in this world to help others. (Corel)

world of *samsara*, the present world dominated by the cycles of birth, death, and rebirth, in order to assist others in attaining enlightenment. The bodhisattva ideal is crucial for understanding the distinctiveness of Mahayana (and Vajrayana) thought relative to Theravada Buddhism, which has tended to focus its interest in the *arhats*, Buddhas (aka enlightened saints) who have through arduous persistent practice attained nirvana. Mahayanists while admiring the accomplishment of the arhat, has criticized them for their lack of *karuna* (compassion). The bodhisattva, while fully ready to attain the final release to nirvana, out of compassion has chosen to delay entrance until all sentient beings are free of sufferings and on their way to nirvana as well. As Mahayana developed in China, the bodhisat-

tva ideal also distinguished Buddhism from Confucian thought, which privileges the cultivated scholar, and Daoism, which valued the solitary recluse.

Mahayana recognized a number of bodhisattvas, but a relatively small number became ubiquitous to Mahayana practice and became known for a unique variation on the original vow. For example, Amitabha Buddha was known to have made 48 vows in which he outlined a plan to create a heavenly land, which came to be known as Sukhavati (Perfect Bliss) and is the Western paradise or Pure Land to which Pure Land believers aspire. He then vowed to bring all beings who called upon his name and thereby placed their hopes of salvation in him, to the Pure Land. Avalokitsvara (Guan Yin) has a special mission to save people who call on him or her from their sufferings. Guan Yiin has become the embodiment of the Buddhist ideal of compassion. Ksitigarbha (aka Jizo or Bodhisattva Earth Repository) has a special concern for the souls trapped in the hell realms and has vowed to delay his entrance into nirvana until hell is emptied. Medicine Buddha made 12 vows to cure all illness and lead all people to enlightenment.

In fact, in Mahayana thought, even Gautama Buddha himself has technically remained a bodhisattva until his final movement to nirvana.

The concept of the bodhisattva developed from a Theravada understanding of it as a being "destined for enlightenment." In Mahayana thought, the concept was considerably broadened, initially by identifying a number of individual deity figures as bodhisattvas ready to be admired and venerated. Then the term was applied to any individual who has made the first steps to embark on the bodhisattva path. In the last century, it was even further broadened in some Chinese groups to mean all Buddhist believers in general.

The future bodhisattva begins their path by making four basic vows: (1) to save innumerable living beings; (2) to eradicate unlimited earthly desires; (3) to master inexhaustible teachings; and (4) to attain unsurpassed enlightenment.

Edward A. Irons

See also: Amitabha's Birthday; Guan Yin's Birthday; Mahayana Buddhism; Pure Land Buddhism; Tantrism; Theravada Buddhism.

References

Gyatso, Geshe Kelsang. *The Bodhisattva Vow: A Practical Guide to Helping Others.* Conishead Priory, Cumbria, UK: Tharpa Publications, 1995.

Kariyawasam, A. G. S. *The Bodhisattva Concept.* Bodhi Leaves Publication No. 157 Kandy, Sri Lanka: Buddhist Publication Society, 2002. http://www.saigon.com/~anson/ebud/ebdha238.htm. Accessed May 15, 2009.

Ray, Reginald A. *Buddhist Saints in India: A Study in Buddhist Values and Orientations.* New York, Oxford: Oxford University Press, 1994.

Shantideva. *The Way of the Bodhisattva.* Boston: Shambhala, 2008.

Thomas, Edward J. *The Life of Buddha as Legend and History,* 1, 29, 147, 223–224. New Delhi: Munshiram Manoharlal, 1992.

Trungpa, Chogyam, et al. *The Bodhisattva Vow: A Sourcebook.* Halifax, Nova Scotia: Vajradhatu Publications, 2005.

Bohras

The Bohras continue a lineage of Ismaili Islam, who in the 11th century acknowledged the authority of al-Mustali (caliph in Egypt, 1094–1101), and later al-Tayyib, a subsequent heir to the throne. Following the death of his father, al-Mustali, the younger son of Caliph al-Afdal, became the focus of a struggle between his supporters and those of his elder brother, al-Nizar. He won, and his elder brother was executed. Al-Nizar's supporters relocated to Persia (Iran) and Mesopotamia (Iraq) and continued their movement from there. Today the Nizari Ismailis are the larger Ismaili group and now exist under the leadership of His Holiness Prince Aga Khan Shia Imani Ismaili Council.

However, at the end of the 11th century, the Ismailis in Egypt (where the Fatimid Caliphate ruled), Syria, and Yemen recognized al-Mustali. During the early 12th century, his successors in office were assassinated, and after the death of Caliph al-Azir in 1130, an infant son, al-Tayyib, remained as the heir. Given al-Tayyib's age, leadership of the Fatimid Empire fell to an older cousin, Abd-al Majid (d. 1131). Over the next years, al-Tayyib was never seen in public, and most to this day presume that he was killed. In 1132, al-Majid had himself named caliph, an event that sparked yet another division of the Ismaili community. The new party formed around those who looked for the rise of al-Tayyib.

The supporters of al-Tayyib, refusing to support the caliph and the authorities in Cairo, were suppressed in Egypt, but found a haven in Yemen, where the queen supported their cause. Over the next decades, leaders came to believe that al-Tayyib had survived, had been secretly taken out of Egypt, and had married and produced progeny. In Yemen, in the absence of any visible manifestation of al-Tayyib or his sons, the queen appointed a substitute who took the title of *al-mutlaq* (administrator). The al-mutlaq was granted full authority, almost as if he were an imam, to head the Ismaili community on behalf of the Hidden Imam (al-Tayyib) in his absence.

The Yemenite community preserved significant quantities of Ismaili literature, most of which was lost when the Egyptian libraries of the Fatimid dynasty were looted and burned by the Ottoman conquerors. In Yemen, moreover, the Ismailis had to contend with the Zaydites, a Shia group with its major strength in the region. Further trouble followed the rise of the Ottoman Empire, which overran Yemen in 1517. As a direct result of the intolerance of the Ottomans (followers of the Hanafite School of Islam), the al-mutlaq and the headquarters of the movement moved to Gujarat. Over the centuries, a sizable Ismaili community had developed in western India, and the al-Tayyib followers had built additional support in Gujarat. The Gujarati group had survived even after a Sunni Muslim ruler annexed the region in 1298.

The main body of al-Tayyib Ismailis, who came to be known as Bohras (traders), as many of the men engaged in trading businesses, suffered a major split over succession to the office of the al-mutlaq in 1589. The larger group acknowledged Da'ud (or Dawood) Burhan al-Din (d. 1612) as the new leader. A minority accepted the claims of Sulayman b. Hasan al-Hindi. Sulayman's strength was in Yemen, where his followers were in the majority. In subsequent years, additional problems with succession led to the formation of a number of Ismaili groups, though those that have survived are quite small.

The supporters of Dawood Burhan al-Din remained strong in Gujarat, though in 1785 the headquarters was moved to what were seen as more tolerant British-controlled territory in Surat. There a school for training of future leadership was founded. The community, some 700,000 strong, continues as the Shiah Fatimi Ismaili Tayyibi Dawoodi Bohra community (also popularly known as the Daud Bohras). Through the 20th century the Daud Ismaili community was affected by the emergence of a reformist community that asked for changes in light of modern life. The largest group of reformists organized themselves under the Central Board of the Dawoodi Bohra Community to challenge what they saw as the overly authoritarian role assumed by many Bohra priests.

The Sulaymani Ismailis eventually made their headquarters in northern Yemen at Najran, near the border with Saudi Arabia. In fact, in 1934 Najran was included in territory annexed to Saudi Arabia. From there, the Sulaymani Ismaili al-mutlaq leads a following of some 100,000 believers.

J. Gordon Melton

See also: Hanafite School of Islam; His Highness Prince Aga Khan Shia Imani Ismaili Council; Ismaili Islam; Shiah Fatimi Ismaili Tayyibi Dawoodi Bohra; Zaydites.

References

Amiji, H. M. "The Bohras of East Africa." *Journal of Religion in Africa* 7 (1975): 27–61.

Corbin, Henry. *Cyclical Time and Ismaili Gnosis*. London: Kegan Paul International, 1983.

Daftary, Farhad. *A Short History of the Ismailis*. Princeton, NJ: Marcus Wiener Publishers, 1998.

■ Bolivia

Located in the center of South America, Bolivia is surrounded by Chile, Peru, Brazil, Paraguay, and Argentina. About one-third of its territory is located in the high Andes Mountains, while about two-thirds is composed of tropical lowlands in the Amazon basin. The highest peak in Bolivia is Nevado Sajama at 21,463 feet, located in the Department of Oruro. Lake Titicaca, located at 12,500 feet above sea level, sits on the border between Bolivia and Peru. Bolivia is totally landlocked but that has not always been the case. In 1883, Chile annexed the Bolivian Department of Litoral during the War of the Pacific (1879–1884), thus taking away Bolivia's access to the Pacific Ocean. The remaining land (419,000 square miles) is now home to 9.2 million people (2008 estimate), with La Paz as its capital since 1898.

Bolivia is one of the least developed countries in South America, with almost two-thirds of its people, many of whom are subsistence farmers, living in poverty. The nation's major industries are mining, smelting, petroleum, food and beverages, tobacco, handicrafts, and clothing; its major exports are natural gas, soybeans and soy products, crude petroleum, zinc ore, and tin.

About 55 percent of the population are Native American Indians (Amerindian: mainly Quechua, Aymara, Chiquitano, and Guaraní who speak their ancestral languages), about 30 percent are *mestizo* (mixed heritage: Amerindian and European), and about 15 percent are white (mainly of Spanish ancestry but includes those of German, Italian, Basque, Croatian, Russian, Polish, and U.S. ancestry as well as other minorities). The small Afro-Bolivian population, numbering about 50,000, is descended from African slaves who worked in Brazil and then migrated westward into Bolivia. They are mostly concentrated in the Yungas region in the Department of La Paz. The nation's official languages are Spanish, Quechua, and Aymara.

Amerindians inhabited the Andean region for several thousand years during which time they produced several sophisticated civilizations. In the ninth century CE, a kingdom centered on Tiahuanaco spread along the Andes Mountains. By the 12th century it had been replaced by the Inca Empire from the Cuzco Valley of Peru, which absorbed many of features of the earlier kingdom. By the 16th century the Inca Empire reached from Ecuador to northern Chile and Argentina, and included the Aymara and Quechua peoples of Bolivia. Today, the Quechua (2,900,000) occupy southern Bolivia and the Andean highlands adjacent to Lake Titicaca in La Paz Department; the Aymara (1,800,000) occupy the upper valleys of the Andes in the central and western regions. There are dozens of small, no-

Bolivia

Religion	Followers in 1970	Followers in 2010	% of Population	Annual % growth 2000–2010	Followers in 2025	Followers in 2050
Christians	3,985,000	9,223,000	91.9	1.97	11,359,000	13,626,000
Roman Catholics	3,963,000	8,644,000	86.2	1.87	10,500,000	12,160,000
Protestants	185,000	1,140,000	11.4	5.10	1,500,000	1,900,000
Independents	42,200	330,000	3.3	4.53	470,000	690,000
Ethnoreligionists	69,900	359,000	3.6	1.99	320,000	300,000
Baha'is	94,000	225,000	2.2	2.00	285,000	360,000
Agnostics	40,000	180,000	1.8	3.98	330,000	500,000
Atheists	15,000	27,200	0.3	2.00	50,000	80,000
Buddhists	4,000	6,600	0.1	2.00	9,000	17,000
Jews	2,000	3,400	0.0	2.00	4,000	5,500
Muslims	500	2,400	0.0	2.00	4,000	8,000
Spiritists	1,000	2,000	0.0	2.01	3,000	3,600
New religionists	500	2,000	0.0	2.00	3,500	7,500
Chinese folk	100	460	0.0	2.00	600	900
Total population	**4,212,000**	**10,031,000**	**100.0**	**2.00**	**12,368,000**	**14,908,000**

madic Amerindian tribes in the Amazon lowlands of eastern Bolivia, in addition to the Chiquitano (47,000) in the eastern region of Santa Cruz Department and the Guaraní (40,000) in the southern departments of Chuquisaca and Tarija near the Paraguayan border.

The Spanish conquistadors moved into Inca territory early in the 1500s and in 1545 occupied the silver mines at Potosí, which went on to become one of the largest cities in the world in the 17th century. By the late 16th century, Bolivian silver was an important source of revenue for the Spanish Crown. A generation of struggle for independence from Spanish rule that began in 1809 finally led to success in 1825 under the leadership of the liberator Simon Bolívar (1783–1830), after whom the independent nation was named. The coming of Independence did not help the Amerindian peoples, because the Spanish families who had settled the land years earlier now took full control. Two wars in 1879–1884 (War of the Pacific) and in 1932–1935 (the Chaco War) cost Bolivia over half of its national territory.

Beginning with the assassination of President Gualberto Villarroel López (1908–1946) in 1946, Bolivia has been the scene of successive waves of new governments in failed attempts to establish democracy and to deal with the country's peculiar political, economic, and social problems. Bolivia had a total of 193 coups

d'état from Independence until 1981, averaging a change of government once every 10 months.

The National Revolutionary Movement (MNR) led a successful revolution in 1952, which ended the nearly continuous rule of the Conservatives since Independence; and this resulted in the first presidency of Víctor Paz Estenssoro (1952–1956). His administration, and the later government of President Hernán Siles (1956–1960), implemented many important structural reforms, including the extension of universal suffrage to all adult citizens (Amerindians and illiterates included), the nationalization of the country's largest tin mines, comprehensive land reforms, and promotion of rural education. The existing military apparatus, which had served the interests of the oligarchy prior to the Revolution, was dismantled and reorganized as an arm of the MNR.

What is especially significant about the 1952 Revolution is that the Bolivian state, for the first time in its Republican history, sought to incorporate into national life the Aymaras and Quechuas, which together constituted about 65 percent of the total population. Although the policies pursued by the MNR were largely corporatist and assimilationist, it marked a significant turning point in Bolivia's contested history of indigenous-state relations. The 1952 Bolivian Revolution has been called one of the most significant sociopolitical

BOLIVIA

events that occurred in Latin America during the 20th century, together with the Mexican Revolution of 1910–1920.

After 12 more tumultuous years of national reform, the country was bitterly divided between left, right, and moderate factions. For example, mining union-

labor leader Juan Lechín Oquendo founded the Partido Revolucionario de Izquierda Nacionalista in 1963, which supported the 1964 military coup against President Paz Estenssoro (1960–1964) at the beginning of his third term in office. This military intervention in national politics is an event that many assert brought an end to the National Revolution and marked the beginning of nearly 20 years of repressive military rule.

This unstable context provided an arena for the emergence of the insurrectionist activities of Ernesto "Che" Guevara (born in Argentina in 1928), a well-known leftist leader and participant in the 1956 Cuban Revolution, who was killed by the Bolivian military in 1967 while leading a small anti-government guerrilla force, called the Army of National Liberation (ELN).

The death of President René Barrientos (1919–1969), a former member of the military junta who was elected president in 1966, led to a succession of weak governments. Alarmed by growing public disorder, Colonel Hugo Banzer Suárez (1926–2002) was installed as president in 1971 with the support of the military, the MNR, and other political factions. Banzer, who ruled from 1971 to 1974, became impatient with discord within his political coalition, replaced civilians with members of the armed forces, and suspended all political activities. Although the economy grew significantly during Banzer's presidency, the people's demands for greater political freedom undermined his support base.

The national elections of 1978, 1979, and 1980 were inconclusive and marked by fraud, according to many observers. There was a sequence of military coups, counter-coups, and caretaker governments. In 1980, General Luis García Meza (b. 1932) came to power in a ruthless and violent coup; and his government was denounced for human rights abuses, narcotics trafficking, and financial mismanagement.

Although Bolivia returned to democratic civilian rule in 1982, its political leaders faced the difficult problems of deep-seated poverty, social unrest, and illegal drug production and trafficking. By the mid-1990s, Bolivia accounted for about one-third of the world's coca production that was being processed into cocaine. Bolivian law allows the cultivation of approximately 40,000 acres of coca to supply the traditional demand among the nation's indigenous people, where the chewing of coca leaves and coca tea are age-old customs used to mitigate the effects of high altitude in the central highlands. In recent decades the Amerindian peoples have significantly heightened their participation in the country's political structure as a means of slowing the encroachment upon their lands and cultures.

Many of the Amerindian peoples, especially the Quechua and Aymara in the western highlands and the Guaraní in the south, have retained their traditional animistic religions, although most would also declare themselves Roman Catholics. These indigenous religions are polytheistic and tend to see the Earth as populated with spirit entities (animism). Religious leaders, who function variously as shamans (*chamanes*), healers (*curanderos*), and divines (*brujería*), keep the largely oral traditions alive and have become increasingly important as symbols of cultural persistence.

Beginning in 2006 the populist government of President Evo Morales (an Ayamara) of Movement Toward Socialism (MAS) began to stress a revival of traditional Amerindian religious beliefs and rituals, which now occasionally precede official government events. Some government officials attend both Catholic Masses and indigenous religious rituals in the course of their official functions. Since taking office, Morales's controversial political and economic strategies have exacerbated racial and economic tensions between the Amerindian peoples in the Andean highlands and the non-indigenous communities (*mestizos* and whites) in the eastern lowlands.

The Spanish brought the Roman Catholic Church with them, and Bolivia was incorporated in a new Diocese of Cusco (Peru) in 1537. The first Amerindian groups to be Christianized were the Parias and Chacras. Over the next century and a half the Franciscans and Jesuits established a number of missions, with the Jesuits developing their well-known cooperative villages among the Moxos and Chiquitos. Through the 19th century, the Catholic Church had a virtual monopoly on organized religious life, but because of a shortage of trained priests many Amerindians are nominally Catholic while continuing their allegiance to traditional animistic beliefs and rituals in various admixtures (religious syncretism). Through the 20th century, the Catholic Church was slow to produce Bolivian priests and had to rely on foreign-born clergy and religious workers.

The Catholic Church of Bolivia is led by the Archbishop of La Paz (established as a diocese in 1605 and elevated to an archdiocese in 1943). In 1986 the

Chapel and cemetery in San Juan, Bolivia. (Pierre Jean Durieu/Dreamstime.com)

Catholic Church was reorganized into four archdioceses (La Paz, Santa Cruz, Cochabamba, and Sucre), six dioceses, two territorial prelatures, five apostolic vicariates that serve various Amerindian peoples, and one military ordinariate. There were approximately 750 priests, most of whom were foreigners, and the lack of priests significantly limited the effectiveness of church activities. For example, in 2004, the Archdiocese of Sucre only had 83 priests to minister to the needs of an estimated 474,000 Catholics (1:5,710) in 44 parishes, dispersed over 31,069 miles.

The Catholic Church retains its role as the official state religion, although other religions are now allowed some degree of toleration and freedom. The permeation of Catholicism into Bolivian society also means that both lay Catholics and priests are found across the political spectrum.

Several diverse tensions arose within the Roman Catholic Church in Bolivia during the 1960s and following years, resulting from challenges posed by the Latin American Bishops Conference in Medellín (Colombia) in 1968, Latin American Liberation Theology, and the Catholic Charismatic Renewal. These new movements polarized Catholic bishops, parish priests, religious workers, and the laity into various factions. *Traditionalists* wanted the church to remain as it was prior to the reforms approved by the Second Vatican Council (late 1960s). *Reformers* supported the church's modernizing stance. *Progressives* sought to implement the new vision for "a preferential option for the poor" through social and political action, aimed at transforming Bolivian society and establishing social justice through peaceful democratic means. *Radicals* adopted Liberation Theology, with its Marxist ideology, and advocated violent revolution by the people as a means of overthrowing the oligarchy and creating a Socialist state that would serve the poverty-stricken masses. *Charismatic agents* (priests, nuns, and lay members) sought to transform the spiritual and communal life of Catholics through the power and gifts of the Holy Spirit (including the "baptism of the Holy Spirit and speaking in tongues").

In 1970, Dominican priest Father Francis MacNutt (b. 1925) and Methodist pastors Joe Petree and Tommy Tyson (1922–2002) from the United States arrived in Bolivia to share their experiences in the Charismatic Renewal movement, among both Catholics and Protestants. MacNutt and his team led a retreat near Cochabamba with the participation of about 70 people.

MacNutt stated that the CCR in South America began with his visit to Bolivia and Peru in 1970; however, there is evidence that the Argentine Renewal movement that began among evangelicals in 1967 soon spread to Roman Catholics in Buenos Aires and other parts of the county during 1968–1969. As in Argentina, the CCR movement in Bolivia expanded mainly among middle- and upper-class Catholics and not among the lower classes as did the church's Base Communities (Comunidades Eclesiales de Base). In early 1971 MacNutt and several members of his team visited Bolivia, where they addressed groups of priests and nuns who could understand English, many of whom in turn became Charismatics and began to organize small groups of laypeople for prayer and Bible study. These charismatic groups began to multiply among Catholics spontaneously. MacNutt subsequently left the priesthood and married.

The remarkable ministry of a young Catholic layman, Julio César Ruibal Heredia, began in La Paz during 1972 after he returned to his homeland from the Los Angeles, California, area where he had been studying and came into contact with the famous Pentecostal faith-healer Kathryn Kuhlman (1907–1976), under whose ministry he experienced a personal conversion to Christ and was baptized in the Holy Spirit.

In Bolivia Ruibal began to share his newfound faith in the homes of his family and friends and in local Catholic parish churches, where he began to preach the gospel and heal the sick and the oppressed. His first public meetings took place in the parish of San Miguel Arcangel on the south side of La Paz, where numerous healings occurred. Between December 1972 and February 1973, Ruibal held a series of impromptu three-day crusades at soccer stadiums in La Paz, Santa Cruz, and Cochabamba with more than 200,000 people in attendance, according to news reports, and with remarkable results. In January 1972, Ruibal preached to a crowd of 25,000 in the Hernando Siles Stadium in La Paz, where many were touched by his message and allegedly experienced supernatural manifestations, such as glossolalia and physical healing, which were reported widely in Bolivian and international news media.

In May 1974, a group of about 300 persons organized an autonomous congregation under Ruibal's leadership in La Paz, which was incorporated in June 1975 under the name Ekklesia Misión Boliviana. Between 1976 and 1986, Ruibal and several of his leaders ministered in Colombia while others expanded the ministry to other Bolivian cities, such as Santa Cruz. However, in 1995, after Ruibal was murdered in Colombia, the leadership of the movement he founded was continued by his disciples under the administration of pastoral teams in many parts of Bolivia. Currently, this independent denomination has a strong presence in the nation, with affiliated churches in at least 10 countries, and is a member of the National Association of Evangelicals of Bolivia.

In January 2001 the Catholic Charismatic Renewal movement claimed an estimated 40,000 participants nationwide. Its lively worship services often resemble an evangelical tent revival and are controversial among traditional Catholics because of the similarities to evangelical practices.

The Catholic Church in Bolivia tries to resist encroaching alternative religions. Television priests are competing with Protestant televangelists, and Catholic bookstores sell decals to display on home windows that read: "We are Catholics and are not interested in changing our religion. Please don't insist."

Although the majority of the population still claims affiliation with the Roman Catholic Church, the percentage of Catholics has declined considerably since the 1950s. According to the 2001 national census, 78 percent of Bolivians claimed to be Roman Catholic, 16.2 percent were Protestant, 3.2 percent were affiliated with other Christian denominations, 2.4 percent claimed no religious affiliation, and less than 0.2 percent was affiliated with non-Christian religions. The non-Protestant marginal Christian groups include the God is Love Church, Growing in Grace Churches, Jehovah's Witnesses, Mormons (Church of Jesus Christ of Latter-day Saints and the Reorganized Church of Jesus Christ of Latter-day Saints, now called the Community of Christ), Israelite Mission of the New Universal Covenant, Light of the World Church, Unity School of Christianity, Universal Church of the Kingdom of God, and Voice of the Cornerstone. The Church of Jesus Christ of Latter-day Saints (Mormons), which claimed a national membership of 158,427 with 245 congregations for 2007, have established their presence throughout the country and have a particularly large following in Cochabamba, where their temple is one of the largest Mormon temples in the world. By contrast, the Jehovah's Witnesses only reported 17,843 "peak witnesses" and 208 congregations for 2005.

Occasional Protestant missionary activity in Bolivia was conducted by British and American Bible Society colporteurs after the establishment of the republic in 1825. However, the first permanent Protestant activity was initiated in 1895 by the Christian Brethren (the open Communion branch of the Plymouth Brethren movement); the Canadian Baptists arrived in 1898 and the American Methodists in 1901. Early mission work by the latter two missions centered on the building of schools and membership growth was relatively slow. However, these missions developed into the Evangelical Methodist Church in Bolivia and the Bolivian Baptist Union, two of the more prominent Protestant bodies.

Through the 20th century a wide spectrum of Protestant mission agencies and denominations arrived, primarily from the United States. The nondenominational Bolivian Indian Mission (now called the Andes Evangelical Mission) opened work among the Quechuas in 1907. It was joined in 1937 by the Evangelical Union of South America. Together they collaborated in producing a Quechua New Testament and finally merged their work in 1957 as the Evangelical Christian Union, the third largest Protestant denomination in the country.

The Seventh-day Adventist Church opened its now extensive work among the Aymara people in 1907. A people movement occurred among the Aymara around Lake Titicaca between 1915 and 1934 that greatly increased Adventist adherents. After World War II, the Adventists responded to a call from the Aymara to build schools (heavily subsidized by foreign funds)

among them, and that action led to a mass movement into the church as well.

The Peniel Missionary Society (an independent Holiness body that merged with World Gospel Mission in 1949) arrived in 1911; the Salvation Army and the Oregon Yearly Meeting of Friends in 1920; the South American Missionary Society (Anglican) in 1922; Lutherans from the independent World Mission and Prayer League established a mission among the Aymara people in 1939, which has grown into the Bolivian Evangelical Lutheran Church; the Church of God (Anderson, Indiana) arrived in 1944, and the Church of God (Holiness) and Church of the Nazarene in 1945. Several nondenominational mission agencies began work during the 1930s–1940s: New Tribes Mission in 1934, Gospel Missionary Union in 1937, and the World Gospel Mission in 1943.

Mennonite settlement in Bolivia began in 1954, when 12 families from Paraguay relocated near Santa Cruz. During the following years German- and Russian-heritage Mennonite settlers arrived from Canada, Mexico, Belize, and elsewhere. All Mennonite settlements in Bolivia are located in the Santa Cruz region of the eastern lowlands where the new settlers established self-sustained farming communities out of the thick forest, thereby helping to create a new agricultural frontier. Most Mennonites came to Bolivia with more experience in colonizing than in similar ventures elsewhere. Rainfall and temperature are especially favorable for soybean, corn, and wheat, and Mennonite farms produce a large percentage of Bolivia's cheese. Today multinational companies rely on their soybean and sunflower harvests to produce cooking oils and animal feed. These exports have transformed Bolivia's 40,000 Mennonites into a bloc of relatively prosperous landowners who mainly reside in 42 agricultural colonies.

Pentecostalism, though not as prominent in Bolivia as in some neighboring countries, is represented by mission agencies from most of the more notable U.S. denominations, including the International Church of the Foursquare Gospel that arrived in 1928, the Assemblies of God in 1946, the Church of God (Cleveland, Tennessee) in 1960, and the United Pentecostal Church International in 1974. Also, Pentecostals from Sweden, Norway, Trinidad, Argentina, Chile, Colom-

Estimated Membership for Largest Protestant Denominations in Bolivia, 1960–2000 (Sorted by estimated membership in 2000)

Denominational Name	1960 Members[1]	1967 Members[2]	1990 Members[3]	2000 Members[4]
Assemblies of God	800	1,431	15,000	43,100
Seventh-day Adventist Church	5,815	15,143	25,000	38,000
Evangelical Christian Union	2,166	7,000	10,000	32,100
Friends National Evangelical Church (Oregon Yearly Meeting of Friends)	2,062	4,700	5,500	16,800
Friends Holiness Bolivian Mission (Holiness Friends Mission)	400	800	1,750	14,200
Bolivian Baptist Union (Canadian)	1,200	2,475	8,500	13,000
Church of the Nazarene	856	1,398	4,000	12,100
Evangelical Methodist Church	1,400	3,680	5,000	11,500
Bolivian Evangelical Church of God (Anderson, IN)	250	1,500	3,750	9,350
Mennonite Church	150	1,700	3,500	7,970
Christian Brethren (Plymouth Brethren)	60	1,200	3,300	7,070
Evangelical Lutheran Church	250	1,500	3,000	6,560
Bolivian Holiness Church (Methodist)	100	950	2,000	5,670

Sources:

[1]Clyde W. Taylor and Wade T. Coggins. *Protestant Missions in Latin America: A Statistical Survey.* Washington, DC: Evangelical Foreign Missions Association, 1961; Keith Hamilton, *Church Growth in the High Andes.* Lucknow, UP, India: Lucknow Publishing House, 1962.

[2]William R. Read, Victor M. Monterroso and Harmon A. Johnson. *Latin American Church Growth.* Grand Rapids, MI: Eerdmans, 1969; plus estimates by PROLADES.

[3]Lausanne Bolivia Country Committee. *Bolivia: A People Prepared.* La Paz, Bolivia: Lausanne Bolivia Country Committee,1989; plus estimates by PROLADES.

[4]Brierly, Peter. *World Churches Handbook.* London: Christian Research, 1997.

bia, and Brazil have initiated work in Bolivia since the 1920s. In addition, non-Pentecostal evangelical groups from Switzerland and Latvia have also begun missionary work in Bolivia. In turn, these diverse denominations have become the seedbed for scores of Bolivian-based national church bodies.

In 1960, 27 Protestant missions and denominations reported 34,219 adherents in Bolivia. Along with church planting and leadership training they carried on various social programs, especially in health and education. Today, more than 130 Protestant denominations are reported to exist in Bolivia.

The National Association of Evangelicals of Bolivia (ANDEB) was founded in 1966 with 28 institutional members, but has since experienced a division between groups that were more ecumenically oriented and associated with the World Council of Churches (WCC) and the more conservative evangelical groups. Today, the latter dominate ANDEB (membership includes 83 evangelical denominations and service agencies), which is associated with the World Evangelical Alliance. Four small Protestant denominations are affiliated with the WCC-related Latin American Council

of Churches (known as CLAI): the Bolivian Evangelical Lutheran Church, the German-Speaking Lutheran Church, the Evangelical Methodist Church in Bolivia, and the Methodist Pentecostal Church of Bolivia.

The first Jewish residents settled in La Paz about 1905. The very small community grew measurably in the 1920s with the addition of Russian immigrants and, after 1935, German refugees. Today, there are some 640 Jewish residents, the majority of whom still reside in La Paz. Círculo Israelita is the national representative Jewish organization.

A wide variety of non-Christian religions have come to Bolivia since World War II, including Shinto, Mahikari, and Mahayana Buddhism brought by Japanese immigrants who found work in the rubber and mining industries. The Baha'i Faith, first incorporated in Bolivia in 1947, now has nine local spiritual assemblies nationwide. Afro-Brazilian Spiritism (Umbanda and Condomblé centers) also are present. Other small religions include Hinduism, Islam, Ancient Wisdom and Spiritualist-Psychic-New Age groups (50 Esoteric groups are listed in the official government registry, 1970–2000).

Bolivian devil dancers perform a traditional "Diablada" dance during carnival celebrations in the city of Oruro, south of the Bolivian capital of La Paz on February 5, 2005. (AP/Wide World Photos)

Because of the Catholic Church's weak presence in rural areas, the vast majority of Amerindians have developed their own brand of folk-Catholicism, which is far removed from orthodox Christianity. Indigenous rituals and fragments of Roman Catholic worship were interwoven in the elaborate seasonal fiestas that are the focus of village social life.

The contemporary cosmology of the Amerindians (approximately 35 ethnolinguistical groups) is a mixture of Catholic and preconquest animistic religion. A deity identified as the virginal daughter of the Inca sun god was incorporated into Catholic ritual as the Virgin Mary. Many of the supernatural forces are linked to a specific place, such as a lake, waterfall, river, or mountain. The earth mother, Pachamama, and fertility rituals play a prominent role as does Ekeko, a traditional indigenous god of luck, harvests, and general abundance, whose festival is celebrated widely on January 24. The Aymara New Year, the *machakmara*, is cele-

brated with music and offerings by crowds of people who ritually await the first rays of the sun on the morning of the winter solstice in the Southern Hemisphere. Some Amerindian leaders have sought to discard all forms of Christianity; however, this effort has not yet led to a significant increase in the number of "indigenous-belief only" adherents.

There are numerous holy places (shrines and sanctuaries) in Bolivia honoring Catholic saints and Amerindian deities (or a mixture of both): the Sanctuary of the Virgin of Candelaria in Copacabana, next to Lake Titicaca, contains a statue of the Virgin Mary (called the Black Madonna) allegedly carved by an Inca craftsman in 1576, which is believed to work miracles and is the most important pilgrimage destination in Bolivia between February 2 and 5 and during Holy Week; the festival of the Virgin Mary of Urkupiña in Quillacollo, also in the Department of Cochabamba, is celebrated from August 14 to 16, which draws together pilgrims from all over Bolivia and the neighboring countries. One of the most popular annual folk festivals in the country is the Carnaval de Oruro, celebrated in Oruro, the folklore capital of Bolivia. This carnival, which lasts for 10 days each year before Lent, marks the Ito festival for the Uru people, whose ceremonies stem from preconquest Andean customs. The ancient Amerindian invocations are centered on Pachamama (Mother Earth, transformed into the Virgin Mary via Christian syncretism) and Tio Supay (Uncle God of the Mountains, transformed into the Christian devil, hence the famous masked "devil-dances"). Christian icons are used to conceal portrayals of Andean gods, and the Christian saints represent other Andean minor divinities. The festival features music, dance, and crafts; it is highlighted by a ceremonial parade lasting 20 hours and covering 2.5 miles, and involving 20,000 dancers and 10,000 musicians.

J. Gordon Melton and Clifton L. Holland

See also: Assemblies of God; Baha'i Faith; Bolivian Evangelical Lutheran Church; Charismatic Movement; Christian Brethren; Church of God (Anderson, Indiana); Church of God (Cleveland, Tennessee); Church of Jesus Christ of Latter-day Saints; Church of the Nazarene; Evangelical Methodist Church of Bolivia; Franciscans; International Church of the Foursquare Gospel; Jehovah's Witnesses; Jesuits; Latin American Council of Churches; Mennonites; Pentecostalism; Roman Catholic Church; Seventh-day Adventist Church; Shinto; Spiritism; Umbanda; United Pentecostal Church International; World Council of Churches; World Evangelical Alliance.

References

Grimes, Barbara F., ed. *Ethnologue: Languages of the World.* 12th ed. Dallas, TX: Summer Institute of Linguistics, 1992.

Holland, Clifton L. *Toward a Classification System of Religious Groups in the Americas by Major Traditions and Family Types.* San José, Costa Rica: PROLADES, 2008. http://www.prolades.com/cra/clas-eng.pdf. Accessed March 1, 2009.

PROLADES Religion in the Americas database, "Religion in Bolivia." http://www.prolades.com/cra/regions/sam/bol/bol-rd.htm. Accessed March 1, 2009.

Rivière, Gilles. "Bolivia: el pentecostalismo en la sociedad aimara del Altiplano," in *Nuevo Mundo Mundos Nuevos*, BAC, 2007. http://nuevomundo.revues.org/index6661.html. Accessed March 1, 2009.

Thomas, Harold. "An Historical Profile of Religion in Bolivia in 1996." http://www.prolades.com/cra/regions/sam/bol/bolivia-eng.html. Accessed March 1, 2009.

U.S. Department of State. *International Religious Freedom Report 2007: Bolivia.* http://www.state.gov/g/drl/rls/irf/2007/90243.htm. Accessed March 1, 2009.

Wagner, C. Peter. *The Protestant Movement in Bolivia.* South Pasadena, CA: William Carey Library, 1970.

Weber, Linda J., and Dotsy Welliver, eds. *Mission Handbook of U.S. and Canadian Christian Ministries Overseas (2007–2009).* Wheaton, IL: Evangelism and Missions Information Service, 2007.

Bolivian Evangelical Lutheran Church

The Bolivian Evangelical Lutheran Church is the largest Lutheran body operating among the Native population of South America. It began in 1938 with the arrival of representatives of the World Mission and Prayer League (WMPL). The League had grown out of a student prayer movement in Minneapolis, Minnesota, earlier in the decade. WMPL is supported primarily by Midwestern Lutherans of Scandinavian descent.

After consultation with other Protestant groups working in the area, the League decided to direct its efforts to the Aymara people. Though nominally Roman Catholic, they were judged to be without significant spiritual care. The first two missionaries settled in Sorata in the Andean Mountains and opened a Bible school, a clinic, and a home for orphans. These facilities, located on a farm, became the center for evangelization. They learned the Aymaran language and found that laypeople developed an unusual level of participation in spreading the message of the church throughout the Aymara community.

The WMPL sent additional missionaries over the years, and their work was expanded by lay pastors trained in the school. A headquarters was established in La Paz and work was begun among the Spanish-speaking population. The headquarters complex included a school (now the Lutheran Center of Theological Education), a bookstore, offices, and a worship sanctuary.

The continued success of the League was expressed not only by the growth of Spanish-speaking congregations but through work initiated by the Aymara members among the Quechua Indians, whose traditional territory included parts of Peru. However, in 1969 the League faced a major crisis when the Spanish-speaking members withdrew and formed the Latin American Lutheran Church. Three years later the WMPL mission became autonomous as the Bolivian Evangelical Lutheran Church. It is organized congregationally, and national governance is through a synod and elected officers. Both churches hold to traditional Lutheran doctrinal statements such as the Augsburg Confession.

In recent years, although there have been attempts to heal wounds caused by the separation, the two bodies have moved in separate directions. The Latin American Lutheran Church, the smaller of the two bodies, has identified with the more conservative Protestant and Free church bodies and affiliated with the National Association of Evangelicals of Bolivia, which is in turn affiliated with the World Evangelical Alliance. At the same time the Bolivian Evangelical Lutheran Church has identified with the global ecumenical movement and joined the Lutheran World Fellowship and in 1991 the World Council of Churches. Pastors from both churches, as well as from the German-speaking Evangelical Lutheran Church in Bolivia, participate in the Conference of Lutheran Pastors of Bolivia.

In 2005, the church reported a membership of 20,000 in 95 congregations.

Bolivian Evangelical Lutheran Church
Calle Río Piraí (Zina El Tejar)
La Paz
Bolivia

J. Gordon Melton

See also: Free Churches; Lutheran World Federation; Lutheranism; World Council of Churches; World Evangelical Alliance.

Reference

Bachmann, E. Theodore, and Mercia Brenne Bachmann. *Lutheran Churches in the World: A Handbook.* Minneapolis, MN: Augsburg Press, 1989.

Bon Religion

The Bon religion is commonly regarded as the oldest of the Tibetan spiritual traditions. Although it is frequently described as "animist" or "shamanic," in practice Bon appears broadly similar to the Nyingma (rNying-ma) school of Tibetan Buddhism but with a number of unique features. Its adherents are found throughout the culturally Tibetan regions of the Himalayas, and it has also attracted a small number of Western converts.

The origins of Bon remain the subject of controversy and conjecture. The traditional texts of the Bonpos (followers of Bon) suggest that their religion was first promulgated by Tonpa Shenrab (sTon-pa gShenrab) some 20,000 years ago in an *axis mundi* called Olmo lun-rin ('Ol-mo lun-ring), the geographical location of which is identified in some texts as Ta-zig (sTag-gzig: Iran?). From there it is said to have spread into Shan-shung (Zhang-zhung: Western Tibet), and then throughout Tibet itself. Bon became the Tibetan national religion and remained so until its position was gradually usurped by the newly introduced Buddhism during the 8th to 11th centuries CE. Bon-pos typically now divide Bon into three phases, Nying ma'i Bon (rNying ma'i Bon: ancient Bon), Yung Drung Bon (gYung drung Bon: Bon of the Swastika), and Sar ma Bon (bon gsar ma: new Bon), but there is no general agreement on the exact meaning of the terms, and their usage without careful qualification remains problematic.

Early non-Tibetan studies of Bon (often following arguably tendentious Buddhist sources) suggest that the religion was the original, primitive, folk-religion of Tibet, but that it adopted many Buddhist texts and

A Bon lama in ceremonial regalia, Dolpo region, Nepal. (Craig Lovell/Corbis)

practices following their introduction into Tibet from India. More recent scholarship has suggested that the Bon religion might actually have its roots in an early Central Asian (as opposed to Indic) diffusion of Buddhism into Tibet, which was heavily flavored with both Indo-Iranian and autochthonous religious beliefs. In the millennium or more that has passed since Bon and Buddhism met in Tibet, the two religions have developed side by side and have clearly adopted much from each other.

Regardless of its historical origins, it is clear that Bon as it is now practiced is a genuine, if unconventional form of Buddhism, a point that has been acknowledged by the 14th Dalai Lama, Tenzin Gyatso (Bstan-dzin rgya-mtsho, b. 1935). Thus although the texts of the Bon-pos and Buddhists differ in detail, they enjoy a common vocabulary of belief. Both religions refer to the founder of their religion as Sangye (Sans-rgyas, used to translate Buddha; literally, "fully purified") and divide their canon into Kanjur and Ten-jur (bKa-'gyur and bsTan-'gyur, Bon orthography: brTen-'gyur), the former comprising the texts that contain the authoritative words and teachings, and the latter important commentaries. Zealous practitioners of both religions aim to achieve chang-chu (byang-chub: awakening) and to attain liberation from the cycle of suffering and rebirth for all creatures. In the case of practitioners of Dzogchen (rDzogs-chen: Great Perfection), a series of contemplative practices common to both Bon and the Nyingma School of Tibetan Buddhism, the aim is more specifically to achieve "oneness," an undifferentiated unity with the inner and outer cosmos. Also in common with Nyingma, Bon has a tradition of non-celibate "householder" (sngags-pa) lamas, who preserve particular teaching lineages within a family. In larger Bon monasteries monks are educated in a way similar to that of the Gelugpa (dGe-lugs-pa) sect of Buddhism: following the Vinaya (monastic code), practicing dialectical debate, and being trained in philosophy and logic.

Although Bon is mainly concentrated in the eastern provinces of Tibet, enclaves of Bon exist throughout the country, and in the ethnically Tibetan regions of Western Nepal, in Bhutan, and in a number of the northern states of India. Accurate population statistics do not exist, although a reasonable estimate might be that about 10 percent of the Tibetan population follow Bon. Some Bon teachers lecture internationally, but the religion does not actively proselytize beyond its own community and outside converts are few.

Both Bon-pos and Buddhists suffered persecution as a result of the Chinese occupation of Tibet, particularly in the years immediately following the invasion in the 1950s and during the period of the Cultural Revolution. Following the destruction of their principal monastery, Menri (sMan-ri), in 1959 many Bon-pos fled as refugees, mostly to India and Nepal. There they have established a number of monasteries, the largest of which is Palshenten Menri Ling (dPal gShen-bstan sMan-ri-gling), in Himachal Pradesh, which is home to the current head of the Bon religion, Abbot (mKhan-po) Sangye Tenzin Yong-dong (Sangs-rgyas bsTan-'dzin lJong-ldong). In recent decades the Bon religion has been able to reassert its presence in Tibet, and reconstruction work has taken place on a number of monasteries that were damaged or destroyed.

Palshenten Menri Ling
Bon Monastic Centre
Dolanji Village
PO Ochgat
Via Solan
Himachal Pradesh
India

Keith Richmond

See also: Nyingma Tibetan Buddhism; Tibetan Buddhism.

References

Bon Foundation: http://www.bonfoundation .org/

Karmay, S. G. *The Treasury of Good Sayings: A Tibetan History of Bon*. London Oriental Series, vol. 26. London: Oxford University Press, 1972.

Kvaerne, P. *The Bon Religion of Tibet. The Iconography of a Living Tradition*. London: Serindia, 1995.

Snellgrove, D. L., ed. and trans. *The Nine Ways of Bon* [Excerpts from the GzI-brjid]. London Oriental Series, vol. 18. London: Oxford University Press, 1967; rpt.: Boulder, CO: Westview Press, 1980.

Snellgrove, D. L., and H. E. Richardson. *A Cultural History of Tibet*. London; 1968; rev. ed.: Boston: Shambhala, 1986.

Borobudar

Borobudar, the largest Buddhist stupa in the world, was for many centuries lost, buried in the jungle in the center of Java, Indonesia. It is a primary artifact documenting the Buddhist kingdom that previously dominated Java. Buddhists erect stupas as shrines to the deceased.

Borobudar was built on a site formerly used as a Hindu temple. The local Hindu residents chose the original site because of its resemblance to Allahabad, India. Here, two rivers converge; their physical presence is then believed further to converge with a spiritual river, the whole generating a place where immortality can be experienced.

Under the Buddhists, Borobudar became a center of Vajrayana Tantric worship. Practitioners claim that the practice of Vajrayana accelerates the process of attaining enlightenment. It is most often associated with Tibetan Buddhism, though it originated in India and spread to most of the main Buddhist countries. It then spread through Southeast Asia and to Indonesia in the eighth century, when it became the religion of the powerful Sailendra dynasty. The several Sailendra who ruled in the late eighth and early ninth centuries developed the Borobudar complex into the center of Buddhism on the island. However, by the end of the ninth century, the Sailendra kingdom had been pushed out of central Java, and religious hegemony in the area was again assumed by Hinduism. Then in 1006, Java was shaken by a massive earthquake and an accompanying eruption of the Merapi Volcano. Ash from the volcano covered the site, and it was abandoned. Through the various political and religious changes in the governing powers in the region, many villages of central Java have continued to practice Buddhism to the present day, though they had lost knowledge of the massive monument to their faith buried in the jungle overgrowth.

Borobudar remained lost to the larger world until the 19th century. In 1814, Sir Thomas Stanford Raffles rediscovered the Borobudar site and subsequently led the effort to clear and survey it. Early in the 20th century, a massive restoration effort was pursued, to be followed by a more recent effort in the 1980s by the UN Educational, Scientific and Cultural Organization (UNESCO). The archaeological attention has finally led to its being reclaimed from the jungle, if not returned to Buddhist worship, and it has become an important tourist site.

The mound, which holds the temple above the jungle floor, has some 50,000 cubic feet of stone. The temple base is some 500 feet on each side. Above the base are eight terraces, each home to a number of relatively small stupas, memorials to enlightened individuals (or Buddhas), and many statues of the Buddha. A pilgrim ascends the temple along a spiral pathway that features pictures depicting scenes from those Buddhist scriptures depicting the path to nirvana. The pathway leads to a central terrace upon which rests a large stupa surrounded by 72 small stupas. The central stupa is 105 feet high.

Borobudar Temple in Java, Indonesia, the largest Buddhist stupa in the world. (Photos.com)

Viewed from above, Borobudar presents a picture of the cosmos not unlike that seen on some mandalas. Its overall shape derives from Mount Meru, the fabled home of the Buddhist deities. Its division into three basic levels, the base, the terraces, and the giant central stupa, represents the three divisions of the universe in Buddhist cosmology—the level of earthly entanglements, the terraces where one separates from the world and purifies desire, and the highest levels of emptiness and formlessness. The giant central stupa has two empty spaces into which a pilgrim may enter and experience the nothingness of nirvana.

Scholars have concluded that Borobudar was originally constructed to house a relic of Gautama Buddha, whose relics were distributed through the Buddhist world as significant centers emerged. Given its size and elaborate nature, however, Borobudar became a sacred site in and of itself. Today, located as it is in an overwhelmingly Muslim land, only a relatively few

Buddhists have discovered it and made their way to visit it.

In 1991, Borobudar was added to the list of World Heritage Sites designated by the United Nations.

J. Gordon Melton

See also: Devotion/Devotional Traditions; Relics; Statues—Buddhist; Tantrism.

References

Dumarçay, Jacques. *Borobudur*. Oxford: Oxford University Press, 1978.

Forman, Bedrich. *Borobudur, the Buddhist Legend in Stone*. New York: Dorset Press, 1992.

Miksic, John. *Borobudar: Golden Tales of the Buddha*. Hong Kong: Periplus Editions, 1991.

Wickert, Jurgen. *Borobudur*. Jakarta: Pt. Intermasa, 1993.

■ Bosnia and Herzegovina

Bosnia and Herzegovina, a former republic of the Federated Republics of Yugoslavia, asserted its independence as a new country in 1991. Largely land locked, its 18,772 square miles has a very small outlet on the Adriatic Sea. The 15 miles of coast line is immediately north and south of the city of Neum. In 2009, 4,613,000 people resided in the country.

The territory of Bosnia and Herzegovina was originally inhabited by the tribes of the Illyrian people who in the second century BCE were conquered by the Romans. In the seventh century CE, Serbs settled in the region. At the end of the 10th century, the land was overrun by an expansive Bulgarian ruler. During this time, the Gnostic religion of the Bogomils took hold in the region, and Bosnia became one of its strongest centers. Christian forces in neighboring lands fought Crusades to wipe out what they saw as heresy, but they were unable to defeat the Bosnian armies.

Bosnia and Herzegovina became a province of the Turkish Ottoman Empire in the 15th century. The Muslim Turks placed great pressure on the Bogomils to convert to Islam. The result was an unusual mixture of Muslim, Roman Catholic, and Eastern Orthodox believers in the country. Turkish rule continued until the 19th century, but the country became free in stages. In 1878, the Congress of Vienna assigned Bosnia and Herzegovina to Austrian control. However, many Bosnians had become committed to a united southern Slav kingdom, and it was the assassination of the Austrian Archduke Ferdinand in Sarajevo in 1914 that occasioned the beginning of World War I and the eventual collapse of the Austrian Empire. Bosnia became a part of Serbia.

Bosnia was occupied by the Germans during World War II and was then incorporated into the Federated

Pocitelj Mosque, Bosnia and Herzegovina. (Liane Matrisch/Dreamstime.com)

Bosnia & Herzegovina

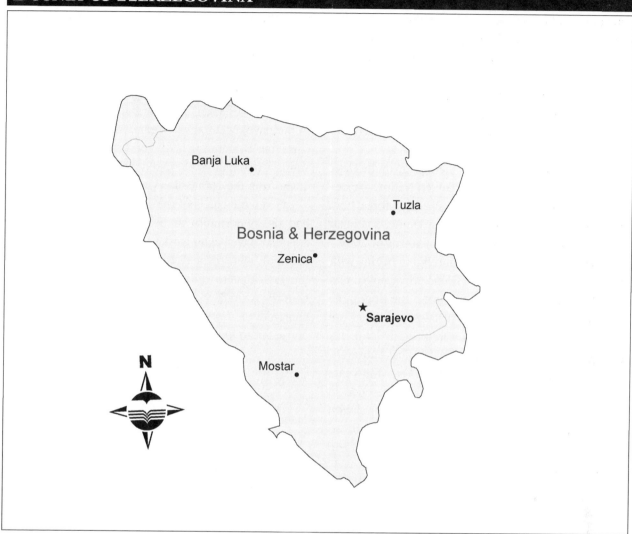

Bosnia & Herzegovina

Religion	Followers in 1970	Followers in 2010	% of Population	Annual % growth 2000–2010	Followers in 2025	Followers in 2050
Muslims	1,400,000	2,198,000	55.8	0.67	2,110,000	1,830,000
Christians	1,650,000	1,552,000	39.4	0.67	1,486,000	1,200,000
Orthodox	1,012,000	1,087,000	27.6	0.38	1,050,000	850,000
Roman Catholics	620,000	470,000	11.9	0.27	440,000	360,000
Protestants	1,800	4,800	0.1	1.53	6,000	8,000
Agnostics	350,000	140,000	3.6	0.67	120,000	100,000
Atheists	164,000	51,600	1.3	0.67	35,000	30,000
Jews	0	380	0.0	0.68	350	500
Total population	**3,564,000**	**3,942,000**	**100.0**	**0.67**	**3,751,000**	**3,160,000**

Republics of Yugoslavia after the war. In 1991 Bosnia and Herzegovina declared itself independent of Yugoslavia, the leaders opting for a multiethnic and multireligious country. Following a plebiscite that approved the establishment of an independent country in 1992, war broke out. Bosnian Serb troops opposed Bosnian Muslim and Croatian (Roman Catholic) troops. The war continued through the mid-1990s and exacted heavy losses of life, especially among the residents of Kosovo.

The war ended in 1995 with the signing of the Dayton accords and the entry of the United Nations peacekeeping forces of 60,000. The peacekeeping force, now under the authority of the European Union, has been steadily reduced and stood at some 2,500 as of 2009.

The story of modern Bosnian religion begins with the attempt of Orthodox forces from Serbia and Roman Catholic forces from Croatia to convert the Bogomils. The Orthodox efforts in the Crusades paralleled the rise of the Serbian Orthodox Church and its struggles to gain independence from the Ecumenical Patriarchate, headquartered in Constantinople. Over the years the Serbian church developed a strong presence in Bosnia and claimed some 30 percent of the population as members. In like measure, Roman Catholics based in Croatia developed a strong presence in the land and claimed some 17 percent.

The Muslims, of the Sunni Hanafite School, became the dominant religious force in the land. Following the Turkish conquest, Muslims had the necessary time to devote to the full conversion of the Bogomils to Islam. Eventually, Sarajevo became the seat of the Supreme Council of Islam. During the 20th century, the Supreme Council provided leadership for the more than 2,000 mosques of the Muslim community in Bosnia and the associated neighboring republics. More than 40 percent of the population is Muslim.

The war, which began in 1992, occurred as troops of the former Yugoslavia who happened to be Bosnian Serbs and members primarily of the Orthodox Church turned their armament on their fellow Bosnians. The Bosnian majority included Croats, Serbs, and Muslims, but the Serbian forces were particularly brutal against the Muslim element of the population, and as they gained control of part of the country in 1993, they killed the Muslims or drove them from the land.

Though they make up a very small percentage of the population, various Protestant and Free churches have come into Bosnia. The Church of the Nazarene came into the area in the 1870s. The Baptists had begun a decade earlier with the efforts of a former Nazarene, Franz Tabor, who moved to Sarajevo in 1865. Over the years the Baptist work was destroyed, and it started anew in the 1990s. The single Baptist church is located in Sarajevo. Methodists began work in the 1800s, the Christian Brethren in 1905, and the Seventh-day Adventist Church in 1909. An older Lutheran presence that dated from the 16th century appears to have died out.

Given the chaos of the 1990s, little new work has had the opportunity to be started. A few Christian agencies have begun work as the war ended. The International Society for Krishna Consciousness is one of the few Eastern religions that have moved into the country. A small community of Jews, now some 1,100, centered on Sarajevo, survived the Holocaust and chose not to move to Israel.

J. Gordon Melton

See also: Christian Brethren; Church of the Nazarene; Ecumenical Patriarchate; Free Churches; Hanafite School of Islam; International Society for Krishna Consciousness; Serbian Orthodox Church; Seventh-day Adventist Church.

References

Cuvalo, Ante. *Historical Dictionary of Bosnia and Herzegovina*. Lanham, MD: Scarecrow Press, 1997.

Malcolm, Noel. *Bosnia: A Short History*. New York: New York University Press, 1994.

The Muslims of Bosnia-Herzegovina: Their Historical Development from the Middle Ages to the Dissolution of Yugoslavia. Cambridge: Center for Middle Eastern Studies, Harvard University, 1996.

Velikonja, Mitja. *Religious Separation and Political Intolerance in Bosnia-Herzegovina*. College Station: Texas A&M University Press, 2003.

■ Botswana

The southern African nation of Botswana, formerly known as Bechuanaland, lies immediately north of

BOTSWANA

South Africa. It also shares borders with Namibia and Zimbabwe. It is separated from Angola by the Caprivi Strip, a long, narrow park and nature reserve that extends outward from Namibia's northeast corner. Some 1,991,000 people live in the 231,804 square miles of Botswana's landlocked territory. Most live in the eastern half of the country, as much of the western land is taken up by the Kalahari Desert.

Botswana, located in south-central Africa, was given its name by the 'Tswana people who settled there in the 17th century and were in residence when the Europeans arrived in the next century. The 'Tswana's homeland became a bone of contention between England and Portugal, and each tried to build a route across the continent to unite their coastal colonies. The first Europeans to settle the land, however, were Afrikaners (also called Boers) who had left Cape Town following the British takeover. About the same time, the Zulus began to expand into 'Tswana territory, and the conflict between the three groups continued through the rest of the century. In 1894, representatives of the three groups met in London to resolve their differences,

Botswana

Religion	Followers in 1970	Followers in 2010	% of Population	Annual % growth 2000–2010	Followers in 2025	Followers in 2050
Christians	254,000	1,283,000	65.7	2.15	1,644,000	2,073,000
Independents	44,700	730,000	37.4	2.91	970,000	1,265,000
Protestants	96,900	200,000	10.2	0.56	220,000	250,000
Roman Catholics	21,200	90,000	4.6	1.46	120,000	150,000
Ethnoreligionists	443,000	640,000	32.8	−0.37	580,000	558,000
Baha'is	3,400	16,400	0.8	1.21	22,000	45,000
Muslims	200	5,200	0.3	1.21	6,000	12,000
Hindus	0	3,400	0.2	1.21	6,000	1,500
Agnostics	0	3,000	0.2	1.21	5,000	10,000
Buddhists	0	1,100	0.1	1.19	1,200	2,000
Jews	100	370	0.0	1.25	400	500
Sikhs	0	270	0.0	1.23	400	600
Atheists	0	150	0.0	1.05	200	400
Chinese folk	0	110	0.0	1.22	200	400
Total population	**701,000**	**1,953,000**	**100.0**	**1.21**	**2,265,000**	**2,703,000**

the outcome of their meeting being the establishment of a British protectorate in what was then called Bechuanaland. Through the early 20th century, the Afrikaners were able to take control of the agricultural production.

Botswana gained independence in 1966. British-trained Seretse Khama (1921–1980)—whose marriage to Ruth Williams, a white European, was the subject of a scandal in England—became the country's first president and sought means to reconcile his people with the Afrikaners, who had come to own some 80 percent of the country's wealth. Although a relatively poor country, it was able to experience economic growth during the 1980s, and in the 1990s the wealth (in diamonds and beef) began to filter down to the larger part of the population.

Traditional religions survive in Botswana, and between a third and a half of the people continue to follow them. The San people (often called Bushmen), the original inhabitants of Botswana who had been pushed aside by the 'Tswana, have been particularly resistant to Christian missionary efforts. The San possess a sophisticated religion built around the belief that certain creatures (such as the praying mantis) and the celestial bodies (Sun, Moon, etc.) are particularly manifestations of the divine.

Protestantism came into the country early in the 19th century. The London Missionary Society (LMS) launched a mission in the region in 1816 and the resultant United Congregational Church became and has remained the largest church in the country. LMS missionaries were responsible for the translation of the Bible into Setswana, the first translation into one of the southern African languages. Eventually, the congregations in Botswana were united with the United Congregationalist Church of Southern Africa (formed in 1859).

Over the next years several other churches entered the country from South Africa, including the Methodist Church of South Africa (1822), the Dutch Reformed Church (1830), and the Evangelical Lutheran Church in Southern Africa (1857). The Methodist and Lutheran churches remain a part of their parent body, though the Dutch Reformed Church of Botswana has been autonomous since 1979.

The first Roman Catholic Church mission was opened in 1895; throughout the first half of the 20th century, however, work was conducted in the country from bases in three of the neighboring countries. Finally in 1959, an Apostolic Prefecture was established for the country, and a bishop for Gabonne was consecrated in 1970. The Church of England entered in 1899, and its work is now a part of the Church of the Province of Central Africa. The Diocese of Botswana was established in 1972.

The Seventh-day Adventist Church did not enter the country until 1921, but over the next decades emerged as the second largest of the churches produced directly by the missionary endeavor. The work is currently organized as two fields (North Botswana and South Botswana) attached to the church's Eastern Africa Division. More recently, the Lutherans have challenged the Seventh-day Adventists in membership.

Botswana has proved fertile ground for indigenous churches, especially in the last half of the 20th century. The most successful has been the Spiritual Healing Church, founded around 1950 by representatives of the Moshoeshoe Berean Bible Readers Church founded early in the century by Lesotho prophet Mattita. Other groups originating in neighboring countries include the Zion Christian Church of South Africa and St. John's Apostolic Faith Mission Church of South Africa. The latter church has had a Botswana schism known as St. Peter's Apostolic Faith Healing Church. Many of these independent churches are products of Pentecostalism, which appears to have entered the country through them. The Swedish Holiness Union Mission did not open work until 1960, the American-based Assemblies of God until 1963, and the Church of God (Cleveland, Tennessee) until 1968.

The Muslim community in Botswana is minuscule, as is the Jewish one. There is a small community of adherents of the Baha'i Faith. The Hindu temple in Gaborone and the Shiva-Vishnu temple at Selebe-Phikwe serve the Asian Indians in the country. There is also a center sponsored by the International Society for Krishna Consciousness. The Church of Jesus Christ of Latter-day Saints initiated a missionary effort in 1990. Although there is a growing diversity in Botswana, its relative isolation and small population has made it less attractive than some other African countries to the spread of the new religions from Asia, North America, and Europe.

J. Gordon Melton

See also: Assemblies of God; Baha'i Faith; Church of England; Church of God (Cleveland Tennessee); Church of Jesus Christ of Latter-day Saints; Church of the Province of Central Africa; Dutch Reformed Church; Evangelical Lutheran Church in Southern Africa; International Society for Krishna Consciousness; London Missionary Society; Methodist Church of Southern Africa; Pentecostalism; Roman Catholic Church; Seventh-day Adventist Church; Spiritual Healing Church; United Congregational Church of Southern Africa; Zion Christian Church.

References

Amanze, James N. *African Christianity in Botswana. The Case of African Independent Churches.* Oxford: Mambo Press, 1994.

Botswana Handbook of Churches: A Handbook of Churches, Ecumenical Organizations, Theological Institutions and Other World Religions in Botswana. Gaborone, Botswana: Pala Press, 1994.

Fako, T. T. *A Guide to the Registered Churches of Botswana.* Gaborone: University of Botswana, 1983.

Parratt, S. N. "Muslims in Botswana." *African Studies* 48, no. 1 (1998): 71–82.

Bradlaugh, Charles

1833–1891

Charles Bradlaugh, British orator, social activist, and freethinker, founded the National Secular Society, one of the early successful organizations supporting the emerging atheist tradition in the West. He also championed birth control, assisted by Annie Besant, like Bradlaugh an outstanding orator, and culminated his career with a stint in the House of Commons.

Bradlaugh was born September 26, 1833, in Hoxton, East London, England. He was raised an Anglican but doubts about faith led to his refusing confirmation. He left home as a young teen and began to associate with a group of freethinkers in London who gathered around the widow of Richard Carlisle (1790–1843), an early 19th-century freethinker. Bradlaugh delivered his first public lecture expressive of his developing ideas and authored his first pamphlet (criticizing Christian beliefs) in 1850. He became a clerk to a solicitor and though unable to overcome the obstacles to becoming a lawyer, he learned a lot about the law, knowledge that served him well in later life.

Bradlaugh's Freethought career really began in 1858 when he assumed editorship of the *Investigator*, a Freethought periodical notable for its more militant

Charles Bradlaugh (1833–1891), political activist, atheist, and founder of the National Secular Society. (Arnold Wright and Philip Smith. *Parliament Past and Present*, 1902)

stance, relative to more conservative secularism being advocated by Charles Jacob Holyoke, then the most prominent leader in British Freethought circles. The paper was discontinued six months later, but in 1860, Bradlaugh took over the *National Reformer*, the newspaper he would be identified with for the rest of his life. Meanwhile, to support his wife and two daughters, he also took a job as a clerk with a lawyer who shared many of his Freethought views.

Bradlaugh relinquished control of the *National Reformer* for several years in the mid-1860s, but in 1866 resumed the editorship and at the same time announced the formation of the National Secular Society. The Society would become the leading voice of Freethought concerns for the next quarter century. Several years later he took the lead in forming the National Republican League, which would focus his political program of Republicanism, a Freethought format that supported the uplift of the laboring classes

while opposing both the communalism then advocated by Holyoke and Robert Owens and the Paris Commune (1871) and the prerogatives of the British aristocracy.

Bradlaugh became deeply involved in the birth control issue in the 1870s, by which time Annie Besant, former wife of an Anglican minister and future Theosophist, had joined the cause. In 1877, the pair founded the Freethought Publishing Corporation to reissue *The Fruits of Philosophy*, a book on birth control that had landed its author, Charles Knowlton, in court. Only Bradlaugh's knowledge of the law kept the pair out of jail.

In 1880, after several unsuccessful attempts, Bradlaugh was elected to Parliament, but had to fight for six years before being allowed to take his oath of office and assume his seat in the House of Commons. In the meantime, he also had to defend himself in court for acting as an M.P. prior to his being seated. He won the case.

In Parliament he was active on a wide range of issues. Relative to Freethought directly he sponsored an Oaths Act that allowed freethinkers to make a simple affirmation rather than take a (sacred) oath. His ability to win elections was in large part attributed to his opposition to Socialism and promotion of individualism.

In 1889, his health began to fail. The following year he resigned as president of the National Secular Society. He died on January 30, 1891. His work was carried on by his surviving daughter, Hypathia Bradlaugh-Bonner, who republished his writings and authored a biography. By the time of his death, Annie Besant had left Freethought to begin her career as an international leader of the Theosophical Society. The *National Reformer* lasted only a few years after Bradlaugh's death, but the National Secular Society has continued to the present, while mutating with the times. Bradlaugh is remembered as standing at the fountainhead of the widely diverse 20th-century British secular atheist community.

J. Gordon Melton

See also: Atheism; Besant, Annie; Freethought.

References

Arnstein, W. L. *The Bradlaugh Case.* Oxford: Oxford University Press, 1965.

Bradlaugh, Charles. *The Autobiography of Mr. Bradlaugh: A Page of His Life.* London: Watts, 1873.

Bradlaugh, Charles. *A Selection of the Political Pamphlets of Charles Bradlaugh.* Ed. J. Saville. New York: Kelly, 1970.

Bradlaugh-Bonner, Hypathia, and John M. Robertson. *Charles Bradlaugh: A Record of His Life and Work.* London: Unwin, 1894.

Tribe, David. *President Charles Bradlaugh, M.P.* London: Elek, 1871.

Brahma Kumaris

The Brahma Kumaris World Spiritual University (BKWSU), headquartered in India, describes itself as an international nongovernmental organization rather than as a religion. It does nonetheless accord a central role to concepts such as reincarnation and karma, and teaches that each of us is an eternal spirit or soul, with the one God, the Supreme Soul, envisioned as a point of light. The organization offers students throughout the world a wide range of courses, foremost among which are their Raja Yoga meditation classes. A distinctive feature of the movement is the prominent role played by women (Brahma Kumaris means "daughters of Brahma"), although there is also a significant degree of participation by male members.

The movement was founded in the late 1930s in Karachi (now Pakistan), by Lekhraj Khubchand Kirpalani (1877–1969), a wealthy diamond merchant and devout Hindu, who later took the spiritual name Prajapita Brahma. In his mid-fifties, Dada Lekhraj (known to students as Brahma Baba) decided to sell his business and devote himself to spiritual pursuits. He was disturbed both by the materialism of commerce and by the treatment of women, and had received a number of visions, including an experience of Siva speaking through him in order to create a new world order. He began a movement, the Om Mandli, and many of the women (married and single) attending the religious gatherings took vows of celibacy. In 1938 some aggrieved husbands and relatives founded the Anti-Om-Mandli Committee, resulting in sensational newspaper articles, persecution, and lawsuits. After about a

Brahma Kumaris headquarters in suburban London. (J. Gordon Melton)

year the furor died down, and a new organization known as the Brahma Kumaris was created. After the partition of India into India and Pakistan in 1947, it moved to Mount Abu in Rajasthan, where the BKWSU headquarters is still located.

In 1971 branches were established beyond India, and in 1980 the BKWSU became affiliated with the United Nations, through which it runs several international projects. By the year 2008, with more than 8,500 centers in 100 countries, the movement claims to have more than 825,000 regular students.

The Brahma Kumaris' lifestyle is ascetic. A few live in centers and work full-time for the movement; most live outside and have normal jobs but will rise early to mediate at a local center. Fully committed members practice celibacy, are strict vegetarians, and wear white when teaching. Nearly all those in positions of spiritual authority are women. Although donations are accepted and members give regularly to the organization, meditation courses and retreats are offered free of charge and the activities are run by volunteers.

The Brahma Kumaris are not aggressive proselytizers, but they do have an extensive outreach through education, health care, prisons, and other areas. They produce a notable array of books, pamphlets, magazines, newsletters, cassettes, and videos; they also organize a large number of meetings, retreats, and conferences, and offer numerous classes in meditation and other spiritual and practical skills.

The Raj Yoga embraced by the Brahma Kumaris does not involve any mantras, special postures, or breathing techniques. It is usually practiced in a sitting position with the eyes open, facing a picture of red and orange rays emanating from a center of light. Meditators are encouraged to focus on a "third eye" behind their forehead, the objective being to practice "soul consciousness," recognizing the self not as a body but as a soul. The Raj Yogi is one who has a mental link with Siva, God the Supreme Soul, the source of all goodness. *Om shanti*, used as a greeting, is a reminder of the original state of peace of the soul.

Brahma Kumaris
Mount Abu
Rajasthan 307501
India
www.bkwsu.com

Eileen Barker

See also: Meditation; Reincarnation; Vegetarianism; Yoga.

References
Church, Anthea. *Inner Space: A Book of Hope for Busy People*. London: Brahma Kumaris Information Services, 1997.
Hodgkinson, Liz. *Peace and Purity: The Story of the Brahma Kumaris: A Spiritual Revolution*. London: Rider, 1999.
Howell, Julia Day, and Peter L. Nelson. "Demographic Change and Secularization in an Asian New Religious Movement: The Brahma Kumaris in the Western World, Parts I & II." *Research in the Social Scientific Study of Religion* 9 (1998): 1–34; 11 (2000): 225–239.
O'Donnell, Ken. *New Beginnings: Raja Yoga Meditation Course*. 6th ed. London: Brahma Kumaris Information Services, 1999.
Walliss, John. *The Brahma Kumaris as a 'Reflexive Tradition.'* Aldershot: Ashgate, 2001.

Brahmo Samaj

The Brahmo Samaj (The Society of Worshipers of One God) was founded in 1828 by Raja Rammohun Roy (1772–1833) in Calcutta, India. The Brahmo Samaj started as an attempt at religious and social reconstruction in the 19th century, in response to the challenges posed by Christian missionary work and Western ideas, both of which entered India in the wake of British colonialism. Part of the Bengal renaissance, it aimed to reform Hinduism, purging it of its idolatry, caste system, and other debasing features, and preserving its higher elements of truth, spirituality, and essential religion. It takes its stand distinctly on theism—the worship of one God, omniscient and omnipotent. Though distinctly Hindu in its origins, the Brahmo Samaj has adopted concepts from other religions, especially from Christian reform movements. It believes that all truth is of God and respects the prophets of all religions. Raja Rammohun Roy (1772–1833), Devendranath Tagore (1817–1905), and Keshub Chunder Sen (1838–1884) were especially important in shaping the Brahmo Samaj.

Rammohun Roy was born in the eastern state of Bengal. He acquired an intimate knowledge of Hinduism, Islam, and Buddhism, and learned Sanskrit, Arabic, Persian, and English. He developed a zeal for reform, in part from Hindu and Muslim thought and later from Unitarian doctrine. In the religious sphere his reforming zeal took the form of rejection of image worship as indicative of prejudice and superstition, and contrary to reason and common sense. He rejected also the violation of human rights perpetrated in the name of religion involving *sati*, or suttee, the burning of widows on the funeral pyres of their husbands. Roy and his followers formed the Brahmo Sabha (later Brahmo Samaj) to promote these ideals and reform society. The followers met regularly for religious services, during which passages were read from the *Upanishads*, sermons delivered, and hymns sung.

The Brahmo Samaj went into decline after Roy's death. In 1838, Devendranath Tagore, father of the famous Indian poet Rabindranath Tagore, revived and reorganized the Samaj. Tagore did not share the cosmopolitan vision of Rammohun and was definitely opposed to Christian missions. He believed firmly in the infallibility of the Hindu scriptures and developed the Samaj's identity in accordance with his beliefs. Under his guidance and leadership, the Samaj became an active Hindu missionary organization, drawing adherents from among educated Hindus, and it established branches in several towns in Bengal and other states.

Keshub Chunder Sen's work had a mixed impact on the Society, which ultimately fragmented into three factions. Sen rejected the caste system and child marriages, and promoted remarriage of widows and women's education. He gave the Samaj a universal character by drawing upon world scriptures. In 1865 the differences between him and other members of the Brahmo Samaj became sufficiently acute that he split off from the parent group and formed the Brahmo Samaj of India. A further schism occurred as a result of the marriage of his underage daughter to the maharaja of Kuch Bihar. Sen's claims that the marriage was in accordance with God's will disenchanted some of his associates, and they, in 1878, founded the Sadaran Brahmo Samaj. Sen continued as leader of the Brahmo Samaj of India, and in 1881 his group adopted the name the Navavidhan Samaj, or Church of the New Dispensation.

Sivanath Sastri was one of the prime movers of the Sadaran Brahmo Samaj, the largest group in existence today. While maintaining traditional Brahmo practices of faith in a personal God, congregational worship, and condemnation of idol worship, the Sadaran Samaj also emphasizes brotherhood, opposes caste distinctions, and promotes a well-ordered organization.

Today, the Brahmo Samaj is a very small minority with mostly hereditary membership. Though it was not able to reform Hinduism of what it saw as its idolatry and superstition, the Brahmo Samaj provided the basis for a rational critique of religious thought and practice that contributed to the establishment of a secular, democratic Indian society. There is a related Brahmo Samaj chapter in London, England, some members of which maintain an expansive website.

Sadaran Brahmo Samaj
211 Bidhan Sarani
Calcutta 700 006
India
www.chanda.freeserve.co.uk/brahmoframe.htm

Abhi P. Janamanchi

References

Banerjee, Dipankar. *Brahmo Samaj and North-East India*. New Delhi: Anamika Publishers & Distributers, 2006.

Kopf, David. *The Brahmo Samaj and the Shaping of the Modern Indian Mind*. Princeton, NJ: Princeton University Press, 1979.

Lavan, Spencer. "The Brahmo Samaj: India's First Modern Movement for Religious Reform." In *Religion in Modern India,* edited by J. L. Baird. New Delhi: South Asia Publications, 1981.

Lavan, Spencer. *Unitarians and India: A Study In Encounter and Response*. Chicago: Exploration Press, 1991.

Sastri, Sivanath. *History of the Brahmo Samaj.* 2nd ed. Calcutta: Sadharan Brahmo Samaj, 1974.

Branch Davidians

The Branch Davidians were a small and relatively unknown group until they were besieged by federal authorities in 1993. Their history begins with Victor Houteff (1885–1955), a 1907 Bulgarian immigrant who converted from Orthodoxy to Seventh-day Adventism, moved to Los Angeles, and in 1929 began to publish his views. Houteff affirmed the truth of leading Adventist teachings, including the imminent return of Christ, Saturday worship, pacifism, and observance of Old Testament dietary regulations. But Houteff believed that the denomination had grown lax in its observances, and that Christ would never return to an impure church to begin his millennial reign. Hence, Houteff stressed strict observance of church regulations and a simple style of life that allowed no compromise with the world.

Houteff believed that scripture held hitherto unknown truth that he could reveal. His message was that a remnant of 144,000 faithful and holy Adventists—the Davidians—would form the true church and would receive preferential treatment when Christ returned.

A Texas Department of Public Safety helicopter buzzes past the Mount Carmel Branch Davidian compound on March 27, 1993, near Waco, Texas. (AP/Wide World Photos)

His life mission was therefore to convert Seventh-day Adventists to his views. His followers accepted his message and viewed him as a prophet. However, the Seventh-day Adventist Church rejected Houteff's reform initiative. In 1935 he moved with a few followers to a site they named Mount Carmel, near Waco, Texas. There the Davidians created a viable community of about 65 people. They printed massive quantities of Houteff's teachings, which they sought to distribute to Seventh-day Adventists. They hoped that the prophet's truth would enlighten the Adventists, but their missionary effort produced meager results.

When Houteff died in 1955, Ben Roden formed another splinter group, which he called Branch Davidians. Houteff's wife, Florence, moved the group to a second site, New Mount Carmel, and retained power until 1959, when the Davidians split into many factions. Roden's group won control of Mount Carmel in 1962. Each new prophet legitimated leadership by

offering teachings based on new scripture. Roden stressed the importance of the founding of Israel as a prelude to Christ's return. His wife and successor, Lois, taught that the Holy Spirit is female, and that women should be ordained. Her son, George, succeeded her and taught that he was the Messiah.

In 1983 Lois befriended a new follower, Vernon Howell (1959–1993). George drove Howell away at gunpoint in 1985. But Howell and his followers returned and exchanged gunfire with Roden in 1987. Following appearances in court, Roden was jailed and the Howell faction occupied the Branch Davidian land. In 1990 Howell changed his first name to David, suggesting his messianic role, and his second name to Koresh (Hebrew for Cyrus), suggesting one who frees God's people from their enemies (as Cyrus the Great freed the Hebrews from their Babylonian captivity). The tradition of deferring to the new teachings of a prophet allowed Koresh to develop new lines of thought and practice that diverged radically from the older Branch Davidian tradition yet still retained a loyal following of Branch Davidians. Koresh stressed his prophetic role in opening the Seven Seals, which for him meant properly interpreting the symbolic language of the New Testament book of Revelation. He also taught that he was one of several Christs. Whereas the first one was sinless and pacifist, he said that he would destroy God's enemies. In place of pacifism Koresh stockpiled weapons. Whereas Houteff taught strict tradition morality, Koresh taught that he should father the children of his new kingdom. Thus he announced that he was the sinful messiah and that he alone would have sexual relations with the Branch Davidian women. The core Davidian idea of millennialism remained central for Koresh, but he changed much of traditional Branch Davidian thought and practice.

In February 1993, the Bureau of Alcohol, Tobacco, and Firearms (BATF) raided the Branch Davidians for possession of illegal firearms. The 2 groups exchanged gunfire and 10 people died. A 51-day standoff followed. It ended on April 19 when government tanks began knocking down the Davidian home. Fire broke out, and some 81 Branch Davidians died at Mount Carmel. The Branch Davidian standoff received worldwide coverage. The event raised many issues for reflection, such as the nature of religious authority, the limits of arms accumulation, the responsibility of the media, the staying power of millennial ideas, and government treatment of minority religions. The fallout from the event included a temporary rise in the militia movement and the bombing of the Oklahoma City Federal Building (which occurred in 1995 on the second anniversary of the Waco fire). The Branch Davidians are known around the world, not because of their religious ideas, but because of the deadly 1993 confrontation.

Following the fire at Waco, the few survivors of the Branch Davidian group reorganized and formed rival factions. Some faced trial on various charges growing out of their confrontation with the BATF and FBI and served prison sentences. The major remnant at Mount Carmel was led by Clive Doyle, who was loyal to Koresh. In 2006 he left the property. Charles Pace, the new leader at Mount Carmel, distances himself from Koresh.

Davidians do not reveal statistics, but the combined membership at the apex of the groups' strength appears to have been fewer than a thousand. They typically gather in small communities led by forceful personalities. There is no national organization. In addition to Mount Carmel near Elk, Texas, Davidian and Branch Davidian groups exist in Missouri, South Carolina, and New York, as well as in the United Kingdom and Australia.

William L. Pitts Jr.

See also: Seventh-day Adventist Church.

References

Note: Extensive sources on every aspect of the Branch Davidians are now available on various Internet sites and in several U.S. government reports. The Texas Collection at Baylor University contains an enormous amount of material on this group. The following items represent a selection of essential primary and secondary books for developing an overview of the group and the final conflagration.

Houteff, Victor. *The Shepherd's Rod Series*. Rpt.: Salem, SC: General Association of Davidian Seventh-day Adventists, 1990.

Houteff, Victor. *The Symbolic Code Series*. Rpt.: Tamasee, SC: General Association of Davidian Seventh-day Adventists, 1993.

Newport, Kenneth G. C. *The Branch Davidians of Waco: The History and Beliefs of an Apocalyptic Sect*. Oxford: Oxford University Press, 2006.

Tabor, James D., and Eugene V. Gallagher. *Why Waco? Cults and the Battle for Religious Freedom in America*. Berkeley: University of California Press, 1995.

Wright, Stuart A., ed. *Armageddon in Waco: Critical Perspectives on the Branch Davidian Conflict*. Chicago: University of Chicago Press, 1995.

Branham Tabernacle and Related Assemblies

The Branham Tabernacle was established in Jeffersonville, Indiana, by William Marrion Branham (1909–1965), a prominent Pentecostal healing evangelist in the decade following World War II. Branham, the son of a Baptist minister, began to hear a voice he identified as an angel of the Lord during his childhood. Then as a young man he was healed in a Pentecostal church and became a preacher. He was visited by an angel in 1946, and the event led to his becoming an evangelist who emphasized healing in the revival services he conducted.

In Oregon, he encountered Gordon Lindsey (d. 1973), pastor of an Assemblies of God congregation. Lindsey joined Branham's team and began editing the *Voice of Healing* magazine in 1948. Branham's work created the movement that in the 1950s led Oral Roberts (1918–2009) and others to fame as healing evangelists. Around 1960, a split developed between Branham and the majority of the healing evangelists, as Branham began to express divergent theological opinions in his sermons. He denounced denominationalism and the doctrine of the Trinity, and promoted the "Oneness" Pentecostal position of baptism in the name of the Lord Jesus Christ.

The split between the other evangelists and Branham widened in 1963, when he began to focus upon God's promise in Malachi 4:5 to send his prophet, Elijah. Although Branham never identified himself as that messenger, he hinted that it was acceptable to believe that he was the one spoken about by Malachi. In the midst of the controversy, he was killed in a car accident in 1965. Those who believed that Branham had been one with the spirit of Elijah immediately began to preserve and spread his message. To accomplish this task, tapes of sermons were reproduced and circulated by The Voice of God Recordings, Inc. (Box 950, Jeffersonville, IN 47130), while sermon transcripts were distributed by Spoken Word Publications. In 1986, Spoken Word merged into The Voice of God, which now houses the complete archive of Branham's tapes and written material. It is headed by Branham's son, Joseph M. Branham. Voice of God Recordings has an Internet site at www.branham.org.

The William Branham Evangelistic Association, led by another of Branham's sons, Billy Paul Branham, was formed to perpetuate Branham's missionary work. That work is centered upon the Branham Tabernacle and a large number of independent churches also follow the Branham teachings. Although the movement is concentrated in North America (with more than 300 congregations), there are many Branhamite congregations around the world. There is no organization, only an informal fellowship of congregations that support the Voice of God and receive and distribute the Branham tapes and sermon booklets. The literature is regularly translated into more than 30 languages. There are numerous Branhamite sites on the Internet.

Voice of God
Box 950
Jeffersonville, IN 47131
www.branham.org

James R. Lewis

See also: Angels; Assemblies of God; Pentecostalism.

References

Harrell, David Edwin, Jr. *All Things Are Possible.* Bloomington: University of Indiana Press, 1975.

Jorgonsen, Owen. *Supernatural: The Life of William Branham.* Tucson, AZ: Tucson Tabernacle, 1994.

Lindsey, Gordon. *William Branham, a Man Sent from God.* Jeffersonville, IN: William Branham, 1950.

Weaver, C. Douglas. *The Healer-Prophet, William Marrion Branham: A Study in the Prophetic in American Pentecostalism.* Macon, GA: Mercer University Press, 1987.

■ Brazil

Brazil, the largest country in South America, dominates the east-central portion of the continent and is home to the Amazon River Basin. Its 3,286,488 square miles makes it the fifth largest country in the world by size (and the largest in the Southern Hemisphere), while its 190,833,000 citizens make it the fifth largest by population. The Amazon River is the second longest river in the world and its basin is home to an all-important rain forest.

During the course of Portuguese colonization the Roman Catholic Church established itself as the single official religion and held this status for nearly four centuries. The ideological role of the Catholic Christianity brought by the Europeans and the intimate rela-

A nun shades her eyes as she gazes upward at the clouded-over Christ the Redeemer statue in Brazil. (Rodrigo Arena/Dreamstime.com)

tionship between the Portuguese Crown and the church was already evident in the first name the colonizers initially gave the newly discovered territory: Terra de Santa Cruz, or Land of the Sacred Cross. As if it were the most natural thing in the world, the early cities are named after saints (for example, Sao Vincente), or even after the sum total of all the saints (Santos). These and other newly founded villages were laid out in a manner that put the church at the geographic center of the community. Catholicism kept its monopoly until the proclamation of the republic in the year 1889 and the Constitution of 1891, which legally confirmed the religious neutrality of the Brazilian state. This political

development had already begun near the beginning of the century, when trade agreements with the British led to the toleration, within certain limits, of non-Catholic Christian communities in Brazil. The prohibition against religious persecution enacted in the first Constitution of 1824 was an important milestone in this process of religious liberalization.

On the other hand it is revealing that the first national census, taken in 1872, classified only 0.28 percent of the total population as non-Catholic. Everyone else was considered a member of the Catholic Church. Eighteen years later the census indicated that 98.92 percent of the population was Catholic and 1.08 percent non-Catholic. In 1940 more than 95 percent of the population was still Catholic and in 1960 it was slightly more than 93 percent. In 1980, this figure fell below the 90 percent mark for the first time. In the following decade, Catholicism witnessed a dramatic statistical decline of 5.6 percent. According to the Brazilian Institute of Geography and Statistics (IBGE), only 83.3 percent of the total Brazilian population associated itself with the Catholic Church in 1991. Later studies confirmed the basic trend. From 1990 to 1992 a regional count of newly founded local churches and parishes was undertaken in the Rio de Janeiro metropolitan area. It focused on newly founded facilities of both the Catholic Church and Pentecostal denominations. Of every 10 new parishes only one was Catholic and the rest were Pentecostal. From 1992 to 1995 a similar study was undertaken in the state of Rio Grande do Sul. It addressed a wider spectrum of recently founded religious institutions. Only one new local Catholic church was inaugurated annually. Meanwhile, Pentecostal Christians established 125 temples, Spiritists founded 79 new centers, and Afro-Brazilian circles opened 125 new *terrenos* during the same period.

In August and September 1994 the Datafolha-Institute provided data referring to the adult population entitled to vote. The survey indicated that 74.9 percent of this population was made up of Catholics. However, there were differences according to geographical regions. In percentage terms, the northeast (80.4 percent) is the most Catholic part of Brazil. The city of Salvador (65.3 percent), capital of the state of Bahia, is a notable exception. The percentage of Catholics is

Brazil

Religion	Followers in 1970	Followers in 2010	% of Population	Annual % growth 2000–2010	Followers in 2025	Followers in 2050
Christians	91,396,000	180,932,000	90.9	1.39	203,758,000	222,469,000
Roman Catholics	85,107,000	144,000,000	72.4	−0.42	153,000,000	154,000,000
Protestants	7,301,000	31,000,000	15.6	3.05	39,000,000	50,500,000
Independents	5,083,000	21,330,000	10.7	1.43	29,900,000	35,870,000
Spiritists	2,540,000	9,730,000	4.9	1.20	11,000,000	12,200,000
Agnostics	780,000	4,787,000	2.4	1.86	9,000,000	13,000,000
New religionists	165,000	1,543,000	0.8	2.87	2,500,000	3,000,000
Atheists	200,000	690,000	0.3	4.83	950,000	1,200,000
Buddhists	313,000	534,000	0.3	1.41	720,000	1,100,000
Ethnoreligionists	300,000	310,000	0.2	2.10	300,000	280,000
Muslims	90,000	204,000	0.1	1.41	300,000	450,000
Jews	155,000	140,000	0.1	0.07	140,000	140,000
Chinese folk	30,000	46,000	0.0	1.41	65,000	90,000
Baha'is	13,000	47,000	0.0	1.41	70,000	110,000
Hindus	5,000	11,000	0.0	1.42	20,000	30,000
Shintoists	2,000	8,000	0.0	1.42	10,000	16,000
Total population	**95,989,000**	**198,982,000**	**100.0**	**1.41**	**228,833,000**	**254,085,000**

also relatively high in the south (78.4 percent). On the other hand, the southeast, at 71.4 percent, is clearly below the national average. This figure is strongly influenced by the region's two major cities, São Paulo and Rio de Janeiro, where Catholics make up 65.2 percent and 59.3 percent, respectively, of adults entitled to vote. In the Rio de Janeiro metropolitan area, a representative study, conducted in 2000 by the Higher Institute of Religious Studies (ISER), counted only 55.7 percent Catholic.

More recent data indicate that Brazilian Catholicism continues to statistically decline. While according to the last national census 73.57 percent of the population had identified itself as Catholic in 2000, a study at the Federal Universities of Sao Paulo and Juiz de Fora (state of Minas Gerais) concluded that in 2006 the number had dropped to 68 percent.

However, a proper evaluation of these statistics requires a closer look. The project undertaken by the Datafolha-Institute in 1994, for example, found that of the 74.9 percent of adult Brazilians who called themselves Catholics at that time, 61 percent were "traditional" believers, characterized by a lack of commitment to the church as an institution. This majority attends religious services only sporadically, usually on the occasion of rites of passage. Only the other 14 per-

cent are considered engaged members of the church. These consciously identify themselves as Christians within an increasingly secularized society, and they actively take part in one of the church's subsidiary organizations and movements. Thus, from the 14 percent engaged Catholics, 1.8 percent are connected to a Base Community (CEB), and 3.8 percent represent the Charismatic Renewal movement (RCC). The remaining 7.9 percent belong to one of the minor, more specific Catholic groups that, for example, promote a certain devotional practice or attend to the needs of families, couples, or adolescents.

The CEBs emerged in the 1960s and 1970s. In principle these groups, which average 20 members, are orientated toward Liberation Theology, which means they side with the worries, needs, and rights of the poor. The leaders of the CEB movement plead for greater political participation among Catholics in the here and now in order to contribute to the construction of a more equitable, humane society. Datafolha results show that neither the previously estimated number of up to four million CEB members nor the other extreme assumption that there are only about 250,000 CEB members is adequate. Rather, based on the Datafolha results, it seems fair to assume that around two million Catholics are affiliated with a CEB. However, it appears that, compared to the past, many CEBs have become less political, while still offering a space where members can share their religious aspirations in an intimate setting.

The RCC spilled over from the United States in the 1970s. Since the second half of the 1980s it has witnessed a steady increase in members. Its impact on the general public has to do with the popular success of its most prominent representatives, first and foremost Father Marcelo Rossi (Padre Marcelo). Like a number of other, lesser known singing priests, Padre Marcelo attracts a growing number of fans with his show-like Masses, television presentations, and bestselling CDs. From two different perspectives the RCC can be seen as a religious antithesis. From within the Catholic Church it is in a certain sense at the opposite pole from the CEBs, since it propagates an individual apolitical spirituality and a conservative Catholic morality, with a focus on family life. At the same time it competes with Pentecostalism. Like the latter, the RCC emphasizes the Holy Spirit and spiritual gifts, such as healing and glossolalia. On the other hand, the RCC's members are devoted to Our Lady (the Virgin Mary) and stress their Catholic identity and loyalty to the pope.

If one leaves aside the relatively brief colonial-era invasions by the Dutch and French, as well as the rare cases of individual Protestant immigrants, the history of manifest Protestant religious activities in Brazil begins early in the 19th century.

The first Protestant place of worship was an Anglican chapel established in 1819 in São Paulo. In order to avoid provoking a Catholic backlash, the chapel, used only by Englishmen working in the city, was not recognizable as a religious building from the outside. Lutherans who had emigrated from Germany inaugurated the second (1823 in Nova Friburgo) and the third (1824 in Sao Leopoldo) Protestant churches on Brazilian territory, both in the state of Rio de Janeiro. Waves of immigration, ongoing until the 1930s, brought approximately 70,000 German and Swiss Lutheran Christians to Brazil. As a result of the regional concentration of Lutheran settlement and their efforts to preserve their cultural identity, there emerged relatively self-sufficient Lutheran enclaves. From a religious point of view, these communities have succeeded until today. Currently, the Lutheran Church in Brazil numbers about

one million members, or more than one-quarter of the total membership of all the denominations of the so-called historic branch of Protestantism combined. Regional variation in the density of Lutheran population is a result of historic immigration patterns. Because German immigrants preferred the south, about 80 percent of all Lutheran Christians in Brazil live in this region. Next is the southeast, with about 12 percent. Besides immigration Protestantism, predominantly of European origin, other denominations associated with a so-called conversion Protestantism, of North American origin, also left their mark on Brazil. Immigration from the United States occurred almost exclusively between 1865 and 1867 (following the American Civil War) and in very limited numbers. Only 2,000 North Americans came to Brazil, either individually or in single families. They dispersed throughout the country and assimilated quickly into the host society. Thus, the arrival of Presbyterian, Methodist, and Baptist ministers was not connected to immigration but possessed from the very beginning the character of missionary work.

The first three Presbyterian ministers arrived in Brazil between 1859 and 1860. The first Presbyterian meeting took place in 1865 in the English Reading Room in São Paulo, and led to the formation of the Presbyterian Church in Brazil. Their desire to emancipate themselves from North American patterns and financial dependency led some Presbyterian ministers to found a national branch of the church, the Independent Presbyterian Church of Brazil (Igreja Presbiteriana Independente) in 1903. Today it coexists with the Igreja Presbiteriana Conservadora, founded in 1940. Together, the three churches contain approximately 13.5 percent of all Brazilians who declare themselves members of what is usually termed a historic Protestant church (about 3,700,000 people).

In 1871 Baptist missionaries became active in the eastern part of the state of São Paulo. However, the first church was established only in 1892, in Salvador, Bahia. According to the national census of 1991, the Baptists (divided into some 14 denominations) make up the strongest group within the historic Protestant spectrum. It has about 1.5 million members, or approximately 41.5 percent of the combined membership of all the historic Protestant denominations in Brazil.

Statistically much less significant is the Methodist Church in Brazil, whose first chapel was established in 1876, in Rio de Janeiro. In 1991 they numbered only 140,000 members, or about 3.7 percent of the membership of all the historic Protestant churches. Although exact figures do not exist, it is evident that, in terms of membership, the Episcopal Anglican Church of Brazil and the Congregational Christians are even less important. In the 1991 census both denominations were included in the category "other traditional Protestants," which altogether represent only 2.9 percent of all historic Protestants.

The category "Protestants" appeared in a national census for the first time in 1872. The corresponding value was only one percent. Fifty years later 2.6 percent of the population declared themselves Protestants. The censuses of 1950, 1960, and 1970 indicated a steady growth of approximately one percentage point per decade. During the 1970s the increase was 1.5 percent and in the 1980s it was 2.4 percent. Thus, the census in 1991 revealed the existence of 13,189,282 Protestants in Brazil, which corresponds to 8.98 percent of the total population. The results of the 1994 Datafolha study revealed that 13.3 percent of voting-eligible respondents were Protestant. This figure was confirmed by Brasmarkt, a private research firm, in 2000. The survey of 200,000 voting-eligible adults in 449 Brazilian cities found that 13.6 percent were Protestants. The national census of the same year counted 15.41 percent Protestants nationwide.

The national census of 1980 was the first IBGE study that distinguished between historic and Pentecostal Protestants. Although at that time 51 percent of Protestants were of historic denominations, the situation had changed dramatically by 1991 in favor of the Pentecostals, who made up more than 60 percent of the total. According to Datafolha, in 1994 the Pentecostals were more than three times more numerous than historic Protestants among the approximately 21,000 voting-eligible adults sampled. Even in Rio Grande do Sul, characterized by a very high rate of membership in historic Protestant denominations, mainly the Lutheran Church, Pentecostals represent today about 70 percent of all Protestants. According to the IBGE figures referring to 2000 more than two-thirds of Brazil-

ian Protestants were Pentecostals (10.58 percent) while the rest were classified as "traditional," a category that embraces denominations such as the Lutherans (0.63 percent), the Baptists (1.89 percent), and the Presbyterians (0.58 percent).

The dynamics within the wider field of Brazilian Protestantism were already becoming visible during the 1980s, when Pentecostalism grew almost three times faster than the population, while historic Protestant denominations stagnated or even witnessed a decline relative to the growth of the total population. The study in the Rio de Janeiro metropolitan area conducted by ISER in the mid-1990s indicated that the Pentecostal denominations are especially successful among people who are underprivileged, in terms of both income and education.

The development of Pentecostalism in Brazil went through three different phases. It began with the arrival of European missionaries who, inspired by the first outbreak of Pentecostalism in the United States at the beginning of the century, had converted to this movement in Chicago. In 1910 the Christian Congregation of Brazil (Congregação Cristã do Brasil) was founded as the first Pentecostal church on Brazilian soil, followed only one year later by the Assemblies of God (Assembléia de Deus), established in Belém, the capital of the state of Pará. Since these two denominations generally reproduced North American patterns of Pentecostalism, Brazilian sociologists see them as paradigmatic for the first wave (1910–1950) of Pentecostalism, considered "classic." Emphasizing the gift of glossolalia and believing in the imminent return of Christ, both churches were initially characterized by a sectarian rejection of the outer world and a strong anti-Catholicism. Today, these groups have a less strained relationship with the rest of Brazilian society.

The case of the Assembléia de Deus, today split into two subdenominations, is particularly notable. This church is an integral part of Brazil's religiously tolerant society. However, what has remained is a conservative morality and relatively strict rules of social behavior, visible even in a particular type of hairstyle and apparel, which in common fashion catalogues sometimes appears under the category "gospel." The last national census of 2000 revealed that together

BRAZIL

the two denominations possessed almost 11 million adherents. A total of 2,489,113 Brazilians declared themselves members of the Congregação Cristã. The Assembléia de Deus, with about 8.5 million adherents, is not only the largest Pentecostal church by far but also the largest Protestant denomination.

The second wave of Pentecostalism (1950–1970) coincided with radical demographic and economic changes that transformed Brazil from a largely rural to an industrial and mass society. In this period Pentecostalism gained momentum, particularly in São Paulo. The churches began to use modern means of communication and started to organize mass events in

theaters, cinemas, and even soccer stadiums. As for spiritual practice, the emphasis shifted from the gift of glossolalia to the gift of healing. The Brazilian Branch of the International Church of The Foursquare Gospel, founded in 1953 under the name Igreja do Evangelho Quadrangular (1,318,805 members in 2000), represents a particularly notable example of Pentecostal churches imported from the United States. However, the majority of newly established denominations, such as Brazil for Christ (Brasil para Cristo) (1955), God Is Love (Deus é Amor) (1962), and Casa de Bênção (1964), are of Brazilian origin. Among these three churches founded during the second phase of Pentecostalism, the largest is Deus é Amor (774,830 in 2000), followed by Brasil para Cristo (175,610) and Casa de Bênção (128,676).

From the mid-1970s on, Brazil witnessed the third wave of Pentecostalism, frequently designated *neo-pentecostalismo*. In terms of doctrine, this wave has been characterized by an emphasis on the spiritual battle against the devil and the "health and wealth gospel" (the "birthright" of a "true" Christian to live her or his life here and now in happiness, material affluence, and perfect health). The geographical center of neo-Pentecostalism is Rio de Janeiro, and its most successful and polemical expression is undoubtedly the Universal Church of the Kingdom of God (Igreja Universal do Reino de Deus [IURD]). Founded in 1977 by Edir Macedo, the church expanded dramatically in the 1980s. At the beginning of the decade it had 21 temples in 5 states. The IURD has a considerable influence on politics and public opinion via TV-Record, Brazil's third largest national television network, which Edir Macedo acquired in 1889. The national census of 2000 counted slightly more than 2,100,000 IURD members.

Syrians and Lebanese who began to immigrate at the end of the 19th century brought Orthodox Christianity to Brazil. Later, especially after World War I, they were joined by other nationalities, such as Russians, Ukrainians, Armenians, Greeks, and Romanians. In 1897, the first official Orthodox service was held in a rented hall in São Paulo. In the same year, members of the São Paulo community realized the first Orthodox procession ever on Latin American soil. The first official Orthodox church was established in 1904, also in São Paulo. In 1915, the second church was founded in São Nicolao, state of Rio de Janeiro. Ten years later the third church was founded in São Jorge, state of São Paulo. Between 1933 and the mid-1980s, 16 more Orthodox churches were founded in different parts of the country, including the Orthodox cathedral in São Paulo, in 1958. The total number of Orthodox Christians in Brazil is rather low. In 1991 there were at most 35,396, almost the same number (32,507) that appeared in the national census of 2000. In terms of membership, the Orthodox Church has its strongholds in the states of São Paulo, Minas Gerais, Goiás, and Paraná.

As for other Christian minorities, at least three should be mentioned here because of their statistical relevance. The Church of Jesus Christ of Latter-day Saints, whose first missionary activities go back to the year 1928 and who established their first church in Brazil in 1935, experienced especially strong membership growth in the 1980s. However, the official figures and those released by the church itself are highly contradictory. Although the 1991 census counted 93,190 members, the church claimed to have 600,000 adherents.

The Seventh-day Adventist Church began its mission work in 1879 in Santa Catarina and established their first church in 1896 in the same state, in the city of Gaspar Alto. In 2000 the national census counted 1,142,377 adherents, that is 0.67 percent of the total population.

North American mariners who testified their faith in the harbor district of Rio de Janeiro in 1923 became the first known Jehovah's Witnesses in Brazil. Today the denomination is represented all over the country and has its headquarters in Cesário Lange, state of Sao Paulo. In 1991 the IBGE counted 725,576 Brazilian Jehovah's Witnesses. The 2000 census confirmed that the denomination is one of the fastest growing religious organizations.

Due to various common characteristics, particularly the significance of human mediators between the worldly and spiritual spheres, Brazilian scholars subsume Spiritism (in the tradition of Allan Kardecistic), Candomblé, and Umbanda in the category of mediumistic religions. In 1991, 1,644,354 Brazilians, or 1.12 percent of the population, declared themselves Kardecists. In 2000 the number had increased to 2,262,401 (1.33 percent). As for the other two religions, the 1991 census, which treated Candomblé and Umbanda as a statistical unit, counted 648,463 members (0.44 percent of the total population). The 2000 census provided separate figures. Accordingly, 397,431 Brazilians (0.23 percent) declared themselves practitioners of Umbanda, and 127,582 (0.08 percent) opted for the category Candomblé in the OIBGE questionnaire. However, the official counting is in striking contrast to the estimation of Federação Nacional de Tradição e Cultura Afro-Brasileira that takes for granted that 70 million Brazilians are participants of either Candomblé or Umbanda.

In 1812, an initial group of Spanish Jews settled in the Amazon region. From 1850 on, Jews of different origin immigrated, and at the beginning of the 20th century Jews from Eastern Europe arrived in considerable numbers. After 1933, the immigration of German Jews escaping from the Nazis increased. The first synagogue was established in 1910, in Rio de Janeiro. According to the last national census, in 1991 there were 86,421 Jews living in Brazil. The 2000 census counted almost the same number, that is, 86,825 corresponding to 0.05 percent of the population. Different from these official figures, the Federação Israelita do Estado de Sao Paulo estimates that in 2001 there were about 120,000 Jews in Brazil. The highest numbers are found in the states São Paulo, Rio de Janeiro, and Rio Grande do Sul.

During the 18th and 19th centuries an Islamic minority arrived along with other African slaves brought to Bahia. Their beliefs were interspersed with elements of African tribal religiosity, and after the slave trade came to an end, they did not survive as a religious group. In 1880 Arabic immigration began. Even today most Brazilian Muslims are of Syrian, Lebanese, or Palestinian origin. The first mosque was inaugurated in 1929 in Sao Paulo. Today there are about 50 mosques in Brazil. The figures produced by the IBGE are extremely unsatisfactory and do not even remotely correspond to the numbers estimated by Brazilian scholars. The national census from 1940 to 1991 subsumed Islam in the category "other Oriental religions," and in 1991 the IBGE identified 50,829 persons within this general rubric, without any further differentiation. The last census revealed an even less auspicious figure, suggesting that in 2000 only 27,239 Muslims (0.02 percent of the total population) lived in Brazil. Non-official sources disagree from the IBGE counting, asserting a total number of about 500,000 Brazilian Muslims, including approximately 200 non-Arabic descendants who, from the 1970s on have converted from Catholicism. Since the state of Paraná was once the preferred destination of Arabic immigrants, the border area next to Paraguay has today the highest concentration of Muslims in Brazil.

The first Baha'i group was founded in 1940 in Salvador, Bahia, by a North American adherent. In 1955, 20 Persian families came to Brazil in order to establish themselves in different cities and to work as missionaries among the local people. Their activities led to the establishment of various Baha'i centers, the first of which was inaugurated in 1957 in Curitiba. Four years later a national umbrella organization was founded. According to the Brazilian Baha'i headquarters, in 2008 the community counted some 50,000 members. However, there are considerable regional differences. For example, more than 13,000 members live in the state of Bahia, but only around 500 in the state of Rio de Janeiro.

About 1.26 million Brazilian inhabitants are of Japanese origin. According to data published by the Japanese embassy in 1985, 90 percent of them hold on to their traditional religions, mostly Shinto and Buddhism. However, empirical research disproves this statement. No data whatsoever are available regarding Shinto, except the information that there are about 150 Shinto shrines in Brazil. With regard to Buddhism, a detailed analysis by the IBGE in 2000 indicated a total of 214,873 Buddhists (0.14 percent of the Brazilian population). Only 81,345 were of Asian origin. Within this category, Japanese Buddhists were dominant. Although most Chinese temples and the one Korean Buddhist institution in existence appeared after 1980, several Japanese Buddhist temples were founded as early as the 1950s. The wave of Japanese temple foundations was stimulated by a fundamental change of mentality, stemming from Japan's defeat in World War II. Initially intending to stay only as long as necessary to acquire a considerable amount of wealth, the immigrants suffered a profound identity crisis, which in turn led to the decision to settle permanently in Brazil. Today, the Japanese Buddhist field contains temples and centers of almost every type, including various neo-Buddhist groups. All told, there are about 160 Buddhist institutions in Brazil. There are differences in terms of orientation, size, and level of organization, ranging from small circles, such as the Casa de Dharma in Sao Paulo (one of only three Theravada groups in Brazil), to highly frequented Amida temples, with dozens of affiliated centers all over the country, especially in those states in which the Japanese influence is strong.

Due to its frequent appearances in the media, Tibetan Buddhism is often considered the fastest growing

The main square of the Zulai Buddhist Temple in Cotia, Sao Paulo, Brazil. (Fagundes/Dreamstime.com)

branch of Buddhism. However, in terms of individuals affiliated with a local group, the total of 3,000 is not very significant. This is especially true when one compares this figure with that of the Brazilian branch of Soka Gakkai. When the movement was formally established in 1960, the association had less than 150 members, all of Japanese origin. In the last few decades, the Associação Brazil Sōka Gakkai International has evolved into a Buddhist group with centers in almost every region of Brazil. According to official information from SOKA Gakkai International, there are currently 130,000 adherents in Brazil; only 15 percent of them are descendants of Japanese immigrants.

A similar relation between Japanese and non-Japanese members can be found in some new religions of Japanese origin, particularly in the cases of Perfect Liberty Kyodan, Seicho-No-Ie, and Sekai Kyusei Kyo (Igreja Messiânica, or Messianic Church).

Perfect Liberty was introduced to Brazil by Japanese immigrants at the end of the 1950s. Just one decade later, more than half of its members were Brazilians of non-Japanese origin. In the 1990s only 5 percent of the estimated 360,000 members were born in a Japanese family. Seicho-No-Ie became active in Brazil in 1932, and at the time was exclusively supported by Japanese immigrants. In 1999, there were 2,000 Seicho-No-Ie centers nationwide with a total staff of 5,000, 70 percent of whom were Brazilians of non-Japanese origin. The national headquarters indicates that Seicho-No-Ie in Brazil currently has about one million practitioners. This figure is obviously an overestimate, but serious independently investigated numbers do not exist. Nonetheless, Brazilian scholars assume that only 20 percent of the Seicho-No-Ie adherents are of Japanese origin. Japanese immigrants established the Brazilian branch of the Messianic Church in 1955, in Rio de Janeiro. In 2000 there were 659 local centers. The Messianic Church is the only Japanese New Religion that appeared in the 1991 IBGE study, which counted 81,344 members. Ninety percent are Brazilians who are not descendants of Japanese immigrants. According to the last national census the number had increased to 102,961 in 2000.

The situation is different for Sukyo Mahikari and Tenrikyo. Mahikari was introduced to Brazil in 1974, Tenrikyo was brought by immigrants in 1929. In both cases, the great majority of the members come from a family of Japanese immigrants. However, precise numbers are still unavailable.

The various groups of Hindu origin have as yet not been sufficiently investigated. Hence, while the Brazilian branch of the International Society for Krishna Consciousness (ISKCON) has been studied in detail, not much is known, for example, about the Ramakrishna movement, Brahma Kumaris, or Elan Vital (formerly the Divine Light Mission). The 2000 census counted 1,560 Hindus in Brazil, a figure presumably predominantly referring to Indian immigrants.

The first Brazilian disciples of Bhaktivedanta Prabhupada belonged to the counterculture, and they came in contact with the ISKCON in Europe or the United States. Only in the second half of the 1980s did the movement increase rapidly, as temples were opened in every large city. In the 1990s, the ISKCON witnessed a decline, but the remaining devotees laid the groundwork for a more stable and future-oriented movement. This is due to a well-planned and suitably organized farm project called Nova Gokula. In the 1980s as many as 800 ISKCON members were engaged in the farm. Today, the community is composed of about 200 individuals who have decided to stay there permanently. One indicator of the durability of the project is the fact that the Nova Gokula community runs a primary school authorized by the government.

The religious search within the counterculture has led to the spread of the three Brazilian Ayahuasaca religions: Santo Daime, Barquinha, und União do Vegetal, which emerged in the decades after 1930 in the Amazon region. The core of these religions is an intoxicating tea extracted from two rain forest plants. The União do Vegetal, in particular, has various adherents among middle-class Brazilians, and it has about 7,000 groups, found in nearly every large city. It is currently the most significant Ayahuasaca line.

In a highly dynamic religious country such as Brazil, it is difficult to find reliable data on the socio-logically diffuse phenomenon often described using terms like "New Age" and discussed elsewhere in this encyclopedia as Western Esoteric tradition. As in other countries, in Brazil this complex is subject to constant changes, and in many cases it manifests itself only sporadically, for example when "Esoteric fairs" are held in São Paulo or Rio de Janeiro. Thus, often, only indirect indicators can verify the existence of a New Age boom. In this context, scholars refer to the dramatic increase in the production of Esoteric literature since the mid-1980s and the fact that a considerable proportion of calls to "0900" numbers are associated with New Age issues. However, the New Age movement's appeal to Brazilians has taken a concrete, institutional form for the first time in the area of Planaltina, about 37 miles away from the federal capital, Brasília. In this region, there exists a gigantic subterranean crystal, and local inhabitants believe that this rock transforms cosmic rays into life-supporting energy and makes the area the world of New Age culture. This explains why, since the mid-1970s, more than 500 religious groups have established their centers there.

Frank Usarski

See also: Assemblies of God; Baha'i Faith; Baptists; Brahma Kumaris; Christian Congregation of Brazil; Church of Jesus Christ of Latter-day Saints; Elan Vital/Divine Light Mission; Episcopal Anglican Church of Brazil; International Church of The Foursquare Gospel; International Society for Krishna Consciousness; Jehovah's Witnesses; Methodist Church in Brazil; Pentecostalism; Perfect Liberty Kyodan; Presbyterian Church of Brazil; Roman Catholic Church; Santo Daime; Seicho-No-Ie; Sekai Kyusei Kyo; Seventh-day Adventist Church; Shinto; Soka Gakkai International; Spiritism; Sukyo Mahikari; Tenrikyo; Tibetan Buddhism; Umbanda; Universal Church of The Kingdom of God; Western Esoteric Tradition.

References
Bastide, Roger, and Helen Sebba. *The African Religions of Brazil: Toward a Sociology of the Interpenetration of Civilizations.* Baltimore: Johns Hopkins University Press, 2007.

Dawson, Andrew. *New Era–New Religions: Religious Transformation in Contemporary Brazil.* Surrey: Ashgate, 2007.

Japanese Religions in Brazil, special issue (35, no. 1 [2008]) of the *Japanese Journal of Religious Studies*. http://www.nanzan-u.ac.jp/ SHUBUNKEN/publications/jjrs/jjrs_cumulative_list.htm#special2008.

Selka, Stephen. *Religion and the Politics of Ethnic Identity in Bahia, Brazil.* Gainesville: University Press of Florida, 2007.

Serbin, Kenneth P. *Needs of the Heart: A Social and Cultural History of Brazil's Clergy and Seminaries.* Notre Dame, IN: Notre Dame University Press, 2006.

Brazil, Japanese Religions in

Japanese religions propagated abroad in two different ways from the second half of the 19th century on. One was through the colonial enterprise: Shinto shrines were erected in Korea, Taiwan, and other places as a diacritical mark of Japanese hegemony; Buddhist chaplains followed the army and some did proselytize in the newly conquered territories; there were also cases of colonial farming projects for believers of specific religions. Religion also spread by means of emigration as Japanese laborers went to Hawaii, Guam, California, and various destinations to work on rice fields, coffee or cotton plantations, railway construction, and the like. These emigrants started making their way to Latin America by the end of the 19th century, arriving in Mexico in 1897, in Peru in 1899, and in Brazil in 1908. Throughout the 20th century they established major or, more frequently, tiny enclaves in many countries in this region of the world. Japanese religions pursued the trails of these emigrants and a few of them managed to conquer non-Japanese believers as illustrated below by the Brazilian case.

Prewar Diversity of Religious Practices At the beginning the religious life of Japanese immigrants in Brazil was at best improvised, discontinuous, and sporadic. They could not count on professional bonzes partially due to Japan's government policy of forbidding non-Christian missionaries to move to Brazil. This measure was intended to avoid hostility and xenophobia toward the immigrants due to the Catholic pre-dominance, which could in the end risk jeopardizing the whole immigration business. Responding to the social pressure of the host society, many Japanese had their children baptized in the Catholic Church. Evangelization of Japanese seems to have started with German priest Lourenço Fützbauer from 1919 on. Through his intercession, the first Japanese priest, Father Nakamura Chôhachi, was sent to Brazil in 1923. It is estimated that around 60 percent of the Japanese and their descendants became Catholics, of whom only 10 percent today are still practicing.

As for the Protestant side, in 1923 Kobayashi Midori founded the Church of São Paulo while Ito Yasoji established the Episcopal Church in São Paulo. Since then, other groups have also opened missions within the Japanese Brazilian community: the Evangelical Holiness Church (1925), the Free Methodist Church (1928), the Salvation Army (1936), and many others.

Despite the unfriendly environment for Japanese religions, some religions were present among prewar immigrants. The pioneer was Honmon Butsuryushu, a neo-Buddhist sect that had a member among the first immigrants of 1908. Other groups such as Oomoto, Tenrikyo, Seicho-No-Ie, traditional Buddhism, and Shinto also established local missions, meeting places, shrines, churches, and the like.

Traditional Buddhism tended to function in an informal manner until the 1950s. Without the support of fully ordained monks, prewar immigrants counted on anyone among them who could recall part of a sutra or could say a prayer to dispatch their deceased considering that many succumbed to accidents or fatal diseases such as malaria. Despite this lack of official activity, from the mid-1920s on some lay Buddhist meetings of Higashi and Nishi Honganji, Shingon and Nichirenshu were organized.

A few Shinto shrines were built in Japanese agricultural settlements in the 1920s. The first known Shinto shrine in Brazil is the Bugre Jinja, built in 1920, in the city of Promissão, after Native graves were found in the premises of the Uetsuka colony. In 1928, immigrants from Nagano Prefecture tried to build a shrine with the same name (Suwa Jinja) as one already existing in their native prefecture. More shrines were built in different parts of Brazil, such as Pará, Amazonas, Mato Grosso do Sul, and Brasília. In most cases,

Brazilian children of Japanese origin participate in a Buddhist ceremony in Sao Paulo, Brazil, June 18, 2003. The ceremony was part of the celebration of the 95th anniversary of the arrival of the first Japanese in Brazil, which is now home to the largest community outside Japan. (AFP/Getty Images)

these initiatives were done by postwar immigrants. But, as anthropologist Takashi Maeyama has pointed out, purely Shinto activities, organization, and architecture are uncommon in Brazil.

Between both wars, a few Japanese new religious movements were also active. Besides the already mentioned Honmon Butsuryushu, adepts of Tenrikyo arrived in Brazil around 1914 as regular immigrants with no missionary purposes. Then, in 1929, some families affiliated with the Nankai Main Church moved together to the Tietê colony and eventually propagated their faith among fellow Japanese.

Two other new movements also became active in the prewar period. In 1924 Oomoto adept Oyama Terukichi crossed to Brazil, but the turning point occurred two years later when Ishido Tsugio and Kondo Teiji emigrated with their families. Despite the lack of official support, the two of them combined their regular

jobs with an active missionary performance. Seicho-No-Ie was introduced into Brazil by means of publications in 1932, just two years after its creation in Japan. However, its landmark was when Daijiro Matsuda claimed to have been miraculously cured from amoebic dysentery by simply reading one of founder Taniguchi's works. Soon after, Matsuda and others spread this new movement among the immigrants in the interior of São Paulo.

The Situation after World War II The Higashi branch of the Jodo Shinshu sect established its official mission in 1952. The Nishi (Honpa) branch awaited the visit of its patriarch in 1954 to officially open its Brazilian mission. This Nishi branch incorporated most of the informal prewar lay movements in many parts of the country and became the largest traditional Buddhist organization. Soon after, other traditional and new religions were introduced into the country such as Jodoshu (1954), Soto Zen (1955), Sekai Kyuseikyo (1955), Perfect Liberty Kyodan (1957), Nichiren Shoshu/Soka Gakkai (1960), Rissho Koseikai (1971), Reiyukai (1975), and others.

Nowadays, almost all major Japanese religions have opened branches in Brazil. There are more than 60 different Japanese ethical-religious groups there, from traditional Shinto and Buddhism to new religious movements, from groups created in Japan to movements established in Brazil by Japanese immigrants, from formal religious organizations to groups aiming at fostering ethics and morals as a way to reach happiness and peace as is the case of the Institute of Moralogy.

Although the ethnic group has always been the focus of proselytism among almost all the Japanese religions, this community has certainly served as a springboard to further diffusion among non-Japanese from the 1960s on. The most successful groups were those that tried hard to find a way of Brazilianizing their practices. In terms of organizational structure most of them still retain a strong Japanese flavor with the top rank being composed of Japanese and descendants, the divisions by sex and age, and an evident focus on Japanese cultural values. Some adopted the Portuguese language and partially indigenized their rituals. Even more important was the formation of a large contingent of non-Japanese Brazilians to work on the frontline of proselytism. Perfect Liberty, for instance, started its movement in São Paulo in 1957. From there it propagated quickly to the states of Rio de Janeiro and Minas Gerais. Just 20 years later, it established a training academy for new instructors, with emphasis on Brazilians, both Nikkei and non-Nikkei. Its leaders also pushed hard to translate its teachings into Portuguese. The result was a sharp increase of Brazilian members of non-Japanese descent while Nikkei followers pulled out of the church. In the same line, Seicho-No-Ie, which had targeted Japanese immigrants prior to the war, changed its orientation in the 1960s to become the most successful Japanese religion in Brazil. This new orientation soon paid off with amazing results. In 1967, the movement claimed some 15,000 followers in Brazil, 900,000 in 1978, and 3 million in 1992, some 70 percent of whom had no Japanese ancestry.

Transnationalization of Japanese Religions in Latin America and Beyond Japanese religions seem to have been introduced in most Latin American countries. Currently, Soka Gakkai has a strong presence in most of Latin America. Zen is another tradition that has been introduced in many Latin American nations by means of different Zen masters. Other groups managed to open branches in Argentina, Bolivia, Colombia, Ecuador, Mexico, Paraguay, Peru, Uruguay, and some French Caribbean territories. In Peru, for instance, Jodoshu was introduced in 1903, followed by Soto Zen (1938), Seicho-No-Ie (1965), Soka Gakkai (1966), Tenrikyo (1967), Sekai Kyuseikyo (1974), Reiyukai (1979), Mahikari (1980s), and others.

Some religions have used their Brazilian branches as a propagating basis in the context of their internationalization strategy. For others, Brazil plays a crucial part in their messianic teachings. This means that Japanese religions have started to perform a more active role in the process of religious transnationalization in Latin America and elsewhere. To begin with, members of Perfect Liberty have been responsible for its spread in other countries. A case in point is Silvina Ferreira, who became a member of the Brazilian Perfect Liberty in 1971 and migrated to Ottawa, Canada, the following year. She spent a few years receiving guidance and print material from Perfect Liberty churches in Los Angeles and New York. This way Perfect Liberty was able to formally open its first church in Canada in 1979 with almost 150 practicing members. Brazilian members of Perfect Liberty have also contributed to the propagation of this group in Portugal, Italy, and elsewhere in Europe.

The most impressive case is that of Brazilian members of Sekai Kyuseikyo, who have been active in proselytizing activities in nearly 60 countries. Some of them are regular members who have moved to another country and started spreading their faith among friends. However, in most cases they had received proper training in Brazil and Japan before they were sent to those missionary assignments.

Other examples of propagation from Brazil come from Zen. The monk Ryotan Tokuda created more than 15 temples and meditation centers in Brazil. Over time he built an international network of disciples in Brazil, France, Belgium, and Argentina. Another Zen monk,

Daigyo Moriyama, lives in the southern city of Porto Alegre but constantly travels to Argentina and Uruguay to assist a group of devotees in these countries.

It is true that many Japanese religions were introduced in other Latin American countries by the same wave of Japanese immigrants. This is the case of Zen and Mahikari in Peru, Soka Gakkai in Mexico and Argentina, and Pure Land Buddhism in Bolivia. However, it must be noted that, since the 1960s, Brazilian headquarters of some of these religious groups have become their Latin or South American administrative headquarters, training and/or religious centers, as is the case of Soto Zenshu and Mahikari. A few groups such as Perfect Liberty and Sekai Kyuseikyo have also built "sacred lands" in Brazil, which attracts adepts and pilgrims from different parts of South America.

The *Dekasegi* Phenomenon's Impact on the Religious Field   Since the mid-1980s a flow of Japanese Brazilians to Japan (*dekasegi*), mainly as unskilled workers, came to constitute the second foreign minority in Japan, with approximately 300,000 people. This phenomenon caused an impact in many areas of Japanese Brazilians' lives, including religion. Especially those religions with their basis in the Nikkei community tended to shrink and lose key leaders when they moved to Japan. Interestingly, the loss of Nikkei members opened the way for non-Japanese Brazilians to ascend to higher ranks of leadership. For instance, in the 1990s, Reiyukai lost about 30 percent of its membership, including top-rank leaders. As a result, for the first time, non-Japanese members were elected to compose its board of directors.

Another aspect of this phenomenon was that other channels of exchange have been opened up between Brazil and Japan, and from there to other places. There is at least one religious group that was introduced in Brazil in connection with the dekasegi phenomenon: Shinji Shumeikai, a dissident branch of Sekai Kyusei Kyo, was brought to Brazil by Japanese Brazilians who converted while working in Japan. Also some religions like Seicho-No-Ie, Sekai Kyusei Kyo, and Soka Gakkai have organized groups of dekasegi throughout Japan. Additionally, the dekasegi have opened doors to the diffusion of Brazilian religions in Japan such as Pentecostal churches, Kardecist-Spiritism, Santo

Daime, and others. In the past decades, many dekasegi have resorted to Catholicism as a way to reconstruct their identities and preserve their Brazilianness within Japanese society. In doing so, they are helping to reinvigorate the small Catholic Church in Japan, although occasionally ending up establishing "parallel congregations" there.

Ronan Alves Pereira

See also: Free Methodist Church of North America; Nichiren Shoshu; Omoto; Pentecostalism; Perfect Liberty Kyodan; Pure Land Buddhism; Reiyukai; Rissho Kosei-kai; Salvation Army; Santo Daime; Seicho-No-Ie; Sekai Kyusei Kyo; Soka Gakkai International; Soto Zen Buddhism; Spiritism; Sukyo Mahikari; Tenrikyo; Zen Buddhism.

References

Clarke, Peter B., and Jeffrey Somers, eds. *Japanese New Religions in the West*. Folkestone: Japan Library, 1994.

Clarke, Peter B., ed. *New Religions in Global Perspective*. London: Routledge, 2006.

Maeyama, Takashi. "Japanese Religions in Southern Brazil: Change and Syncretism." *Latin American Studies* (University of Tsukuba) 6 (1983): 181–238.

Matsouka, Hideaki. *Japanese Prayer below the Equator: How Brazilians Believe in the Church of World Messianity*. Lanham, MD: Lexington Books, 2007.

Nakamaki, Hirochika. *Japanese Religions at Home and Abroad*. London and New York: Routledge Curzon, 2003.

Pereira, Ronan A., and Hideaki Matsouka, eds. *Japanese Religions in and Beyond Japanese Diaspora*. Berkeley: University of California/ Institute of East Asian Studies, 2007.

Rocha, Cristina, 2006. *Zen in Brazil: The Quest for Cosmopolitan Modernity*. Honolulu: University of Hawai'i Press, 2006.

Brethren

The term "Brethren" has been applied to several distinct Christian Free church groups that emerged in

Europe at various times, groups that protested against the state church system and were motivated by a desire to return to the organization and practice of the early church as they saw it portrayed in the Bible.

In the 1520s in Switzerland, some of those who participated in the Reformation of the Roman Catholic Church wished to break both with Rome and with the state and form a simple church of believers only. Conrad Grebel (1498–1526) initiated the movement that was later known as the Swiss Brethren by performing the first baptisms in 1525. The movement was persecuted in Switzerland, and it spread as believers scattered to escape the legal authorities. It finally found a place of relative safety in the Netherlands, and there it was eventually transformed into the Mennonite movement, after the Dutch leader, Menno Simons (1469–1561). Periodically, a new Mennonite group would take a name reminiscent of their Swiss Brethren origins, the most significant one being the Brethren in Christ.

At the beginning of the 18th century a similar Free church impulse grew up in the Palatinate (western Germany) when a group decided to separate from the state church. They found the church spiritually dry and wished to found a group that emphasized personal piety over doctrinal conformity. In 1708, under the leadership of Alexander Mack, eight people covenanted together and formed a "church of Christian believers." As part of their new beginning, they were rebaptized. They found their homeland unwilling to accept them and their new church as had the Swiss Brethren, and many moved to America, where they were informally known as the Brethren or the German Brethren and over the years organized as the Church of the Brethren. Through the 19th and 20th centuries, the church became the birthing ground of a spectrum of new denominational bodies, some of whom argued for further change, but most of whom rejected such change as had occurred.

In the 19th century, a group emerged in the British Isles who wished to separate from the state church and to return to what they saw as the simple life of the biblical church, including the rejection of the various denominational labels (Baptist, Anglican, Methodist, etc.). Rejecting any name, they were commonly referred to as the brethren. The first congregation was in Plymouth, England, and outsiders commonly called the group the Plymouth Brethren. As the group grew and splintered, a variety of designations were used to distinguish the different factions; among the more interesting was a numbering system adopted by the U.S. census early in the 20th century. During the late 20th century most of the factions yielded to society's need for labels and adopted (at least informally) a designation, the largest group now being known as the Christian Brethren.

Although the informal designation of any Christian group as the brethren is widespread, where it is used in a formal sense, the group almost always fits into one of the three traditions mentioned above.

J. Gordon Melton

See also: Brethren in Christ; Christian Brethren; Church of the Brethren.

References

Durnbaugh, Donald F., ed. *The Brethren Encyclopedia*. Philadelphia: Brethren Encyclopedia, 1983.

Wilson, Bryan R. *The Brethren: A Current Sociological Appraisal*. Oxford: All Souls College, 1981.

Brethren in Christ

The Brethren in Christ is a small American denomination in the Mennonite tradition. Many of the original members had been influenced by the Dunkers (now the Church of the Brethren) and had come to accept their practice of baptism by triune, or triple, immersion. Peter Witmer and Jacob Engel were among the first of the small group, which met in Engel's home in Lancaster County, Pennsylvania, to act upon their new insight. When the group organized formally in the 1770s, the members designated Engel as their first bishop.

The River Brethren, as they were originally known, drew most of their doctrine from the Anabaptist tradition, but a century later the members were dramatically influenced by the Methodist Holiness movement and came to believe in its teaching on sanctification. Holiness teachings emphasized the possibility that by an act of the Holy Spirit it was possible for a believer to become perfected in love in this life. Such an experience became the norm of Christian life within the Holiness churches. The adoption of Holiness teachings by the Brethren led to a number of members withdrawing and forming other new churches.

The church accepted its present name in 1865. It finally incorporated in 1904. Through the 20th century members began to move to different parts of the United States and Canada, and during the last half of the century its membership in North America tripled to its present level of 27,000 (2009). While having an evangelical thrust in North America, it also developed an extensive mission program, which now includes work in more than 15 countries in Africa, Asia, and Latin America. A majority of the members (65,000) now reside outside North America.

The Brethren in Christ church supports Messiah College in Grantham, Pennsylvania, and Niagara Christian College in Canada. It is a member of the Christian Holiness Partnership, the Mennonite Central Committee, and the National Association of Evangelicals, through which it relates to the World Evangelical Alliance.

Brethren in Christ
431 Grantham Road
PO Box A
Grantham, PA 17027-0901
www.bic-church.org

J. Gordon Melton

See also: Christian Holiness Partnership; Church of the Brethren; Holiness Movement; World Evangelical Alliance.

References

Sider, E. Morris. *Windows to the Church: Selections from Twenty-five Years of Brethren in Christ History and Life*. Grantham, PA: Brethren in Christ Historical Society, 2003.
Wittlinger, Carlton O. *Quest for Piety and Obedience*. Nappanee, IN: Evangel Press, 1978.

British Forest Sangha

The British Forest Sangha is a Theravada meditation-centered community that follows the meditation practices established in Thailand in the 19th century by monks dissenting from the secularization of the larger state-supported Buddhism of the country. The dissenting monks abandoned the cities for the remote forests of northern Thailand, where some Westerners discovered them in the 20th century.

The British Forest tradition came to England in 1977 when Ajahn Chah (1917–1992), founder of a famous hermitage monastery, Wat Pah Pong in northeast Thailand, visited the West. He arrived in Britain in company with a small group of Western disciples who had been ordained as monks in Thailand. The visit was arranged by the English Sangha Trust (EST), formed in 1956 with the express intention of establishing an indigenous Theravada Buddhist monastic order in Britain. In the intervening years lay members of EST sponsored a series of lone Western monks as incumbents of a *vihara* (monk's dwelling) at premises in Hampstead, London. Each encountered problems in maintaining monastic rules. Most were junior, in terms of the length of time that they had spent as monks in Asia. In Britain they had no teachers to guide them. In addition, individual monks could not perform the important corporate rituals, which require a quorum of four.

Ajahn Chah returned to Thailand, leaving his disciples at the Hampstead vihara. The most senior was the American monk, Ajahn Sumedho (b. 1934), who had acted as abbot of Wat Nanachat, a branch monastery that Ajahn Chah had established to accommodate his Western disciples. Ajahn Sumedho and his monks gained a reputation as effective meditation teachers, a reputation that, together with their strict interpretation of the monastic rules (Pali: *vinaya*) attracted a growing number of British lay supporters. British lay supporters are attracted to Buddhism by a strong desire for self-cultivation that leads them toward the practice of meditation. Many small meditation groups scattered across Britain became affiliated with the Forest Sangha monasteries.

In the summer of 1979, the EST exchanged the Hampstead premises for larger quarters in Chithurst, Sussex. Adjoining woodlands were donated to the trust, and the monks began referring to themselves as the British Forest Sangha. A key event took place at Chithurst in 1981 with the first ordination ceremony, held in front of a crowd of 100 laypeople. Since then ordination ceremonies have been conducted regularly. Branch monasteries were founded in Devon and Northumberland. In 1984 the EST purchased extensive premises in Hertfordshire to found Amaravati Buddhist Centre, a monastery designed to receive large numbers of lay visitors. Currently, about 40 affiliated meditation groups exist throughout Britain, and some 1,500 recipients receive the *Forest Sangha Newsletter*.

The success of the British Forest Sangha was facilitated by innovations, introduced in consultation with Theravada ecclesiastical authorities in Thailand. Among the most notable of these are the founding of a nuns' order and the institution of a new kind of postulancy in the form of the *anagarika* (homeless). A nun is known as a *siladhara* (upholder of virtue). The nuns follow rules elaborated from the Ten Precepts of the traditional *samanera* (novice) ordination. An anagarika is permitted to handle money and to cook food, activities forbidden to monks. The introduction of the anagarika meant that laypeople did not have to be consistently available to assist with the upholding of monastic rules, as they had during EST's earlier attempts to support monks. These adaptations have been important to the successful establishment of branch monasteries in Italy, Switzerland, North America (California), Australia, and New Zealand.

Great Gaddesden
Hemel Hempstead, Hertfordshire
HP1 3BZ
United Kingdom

Sandra Bell

See also: Meditation; Theravada Buddhism.

References

Ajahn Chah, Disciples of. *Seeing the Way: Buddhist Reflections on the Spiritual Life.* Hertfordshire, UK: Amaravati Publications, 1989.

Batchelor, Stephen. *The Awakening of the West: The Encounter of Buddhism and Western Culture.* Berkeley, CA: Parallax Press, 1994.

Bell, Sandra. "Being Creative with Tradition: Rooting Theravada Buddhism in Britain." *Journal of Global Buddhism* 1 (2000): 1–30. http://www.globalbuddhism.org/toc.html.

Bell, Sandra. "British Theravada Buddhism: Otherworldly Theories, and the Theory of Exchange." *Journal of Contemporary Religion* 13, no. 2 (1998): 149–170.

■ British Indian Ocean Territory

The British Indian Ocean Territory (BIOT) consists of a set of islands in the middle of the Indian Ocean that have been colonized by the United Kingdom for their strategic military value. The islands were uninhabited, and currently the only residents are the several thousand British and American navy personnel, including workers from India, who are temporarily stationed there. They all reside on the single island of Diego García, which includes 17 square miles of the 23 square miles of the territory's land.

Diego Garcia had been a French colony; it was turned over to the British following the defeat of Napoleon. Through the 19th century, a number of Madagascans and Africans came to the island, where they developed as a distinct group known as the Ilios. It was considered part of Mauritius (which was in a process of becoming independent that was completed in 1968) until 1965, when it was separated as part of the new BIOT. At this time, the Ilios were removed to Mauritius, where, much to the scandal of both governments, they were abandoned by the authorities and largely forgotten. Two years later, the British leased the island to the Americans for a 50-year period.

The religious among the British and Americans are primarily Christians, drawn from across the spectrum of Christian churches in their home countries. There are no clergy among those stationed on the island; however, Roman Catholic priests and Anglican ministers visit the island from Mauritius (where the Roman Catholic Church's Diocese of Port Louis is headquartered and the Diocese of Mauritius of the Church of the Province of the Indian Ocean is located).

It is also the case that military personnel are drawn from across the religious community in the United States and the United Kingdom, but there are no organized services for these other faiths. The religious among the Indian workers are primarily Hindu, Muslim, and Sikh, but none have developed any permanent

BRITISH INDIAN OCEAN TERRITORY

Peros Banhos

Salomon Islands

British Indian
Ocean Territory

Nelson's Island

INDIAN OCEAN

Three Brothers

Eagle Islands

Danger Island

CHAGOS ARCHIPELAGO

Egmont Islands

N

Diego Garcia

British Indian Ocean Territory

Religion	Followers in 1970	Followers in 2010	% of Population	Annual % growth 2000–2010	Followers in 2025	Followers in 2050
Christians	900	1,700	85.0	0.00	1,700	1,700
Roman Catholics	500	900	45.0	0.00	900	900
Anglicans	100	460	23.0	0.00	460	460
Agnostics	0	220	11.0	0.00	240	240
Hindus	900	50	2.5	0.00	50	50
Atheists	0	20	0.8	0.00	20	20
Muslims	200	20	0.8	0.00	20	20
Total population	**2,000**	**2,000**	**100.0**	**0.00**	**2,000**	**2,000**

religious facilities or organized regular events for worship.

J. Gordon Melton

See also: Church of the Province of the Indian Ocean; Roman Catholic Church.

References

Banjunas, Vytautas B. *Diego Garcia: Creation of the Indian Ocean Base.* N.p.: AuthorHouse, 2001.

Edis, Richard. *Peak of Limuria: The Story of Diego Garcia.* London: Bellew, 1993.

British Israelism

British Israelism, or Anglo-Israelism, refers to a strain of thought within millenarian Christian British that identifies the British people and the related peoples of the Commonwealth Nations and the United States as the true lineal descendants of the ancient Israelites. Israelism is associated with several small organizations rather than any single major organization. Although British Israel organizations never boasted many members, British Israel thinking had some influence upon William Miller (1782–1849), whose ideas gave rise to the Adventist tradition within Protestantism, and upon Charles F. Parham (1873–1929), founder of Pentecostalism. William Herbert Armstrong, founder of the Worldwide Church of God, accepted British Israelism and introduced his 100,000 followers to the doctrine, but since Armstrong's death, the Worldwide Church of God has repudiated British Israelism.

Although the notion that the English have been chosen by God for a special destiny dates back somewhat farther, the first individual to articulate the British Israel ideology in a formal way was the Canadian Richard Brothers (1757–1824). Brothers remained an isolated figure with few followers, and it was not until the publication of *Lectures on Our Israelitish Origin* by Scotsman John Wilson (d. 1871) in 1840 that British Israelism as a religious movement can really be said to have begun. In the years following the publication of Wilson's book, a number of organizations were formed to promote British Israel ideology and to foster communication among adherents. The movement never developed into a sect or denomination but remained a loose network of people with a common interest in but often-different interpretations of the British Israel idea. At the peak of its popularity in England in the 1920s, British Israelism may have had as many as 5,000 adherents in addition to smaller followings in the Commonwealth nations and the United States.

While not all versions of British Israelism are explicitly racist and anti-Semitic, British Israelism has been a major source of inspiration for the Christian Identity movement, which has developed it in a decidedly racist direction. Such small, but militantly rightist organizations as The Order, The Church, The Sword, and The Arm of the Lord, and The Church of Jesus Christ, Christian, Aryan Nations derive their religious and political stances from a radicalized version of British Israelism.

The core tenet of British Israelism is the belief that the Anglo Saxon people can trace their lineage back to the 10 lost tribes of Israel. Jews are the heirs of the

Kingdom of Judah rather than the Kingdom of Israel and are therefore not the group referred to in the biblical book of Revelation. To those who interpret Revelation as a blueprint for the millennium, this is significant because it means that prophecies concerning Israel refer to the British and related peoples. Christian Identity groups have taken the anti-Semitism implicit in this point of view to its extreme by positing that Jews are not only not really Israelites but are in fact the biological descendants of the devil.

British Israelism has also sometimes been associated with Pyramidology, the belief that the great Pyramid of Cheops was built for a divine purpose and that the proper interpretation of its measurements has much to reveal about the unfolding of sacred history.

British Israel World Federation
121 Low Etherley
Bishop Auckland DL 14 OHA
UK
www.britishisrael.co.uk

Arthur L. Greil

See also: Parham, Charles Fox; Pentecostalism.

References

Allen, J. H. *Judah's Sceptre and Joseph's Birthright.* A. A. Beauchamp, 1930.
Barkun, Michael. *Religion and the Radical Right: The Origins of the Christian Identity Movement.* Chapel Hill: University of North Carolina Press, 1997.

■ British Virgin Islands

The British Virgin Islands are a set of some 40 islands located in the Caribbean east of Puerto Rico and north and east of the Virgin Islands of the United States. Some 24,000 people (2008) reside on the islands 59 square miles of land. When Christopher Columbus visited the Virgin Islands in 1493, he found them inhabited by the Carib and Arawak peoples. Both were exterminated over the next two centuries. He also gave the islands their present name, a reference to the legendary Saint Ursula and the 11,000 virgins associated with her. The Spanish took control of the islands but created only one settlement for the purpose of mining copper. The Dutch took an interest in them, and in 1648 they established a settlement on Tortola Island.

Finally in 1672 the British began to push the Dutch out, a feat finally accomplished in 1680. The British introduced sugarcane and its seemingly necessary component, slavery. They began the introduction of African workers, who today constitute the largest segment of the population. Slavery was abolished in the 1830s.

British rule continues. In 1872 the islands were incorporated into the Leeward Islands colony but were again separated in 1956. Since 1960, the British government has appointed a governor, but legislative matters have been placed in the hands of a locally elected legislature. The United Kingdom bears responsibility for defense, foreign affairs, and internal security.

British Methodists came to the islands in 1789 as part of Methodism's initial missionary thrust into the Caribbean, prompted in part by the separation of the Methodists in the former American colonies. Openly allied to the African peoples, they grew to claim the great majority of the population (at one point more than 70 percent), though their percentage dropped as the island secularized in the later 20th century. Today the Methodist work has been incorporated into the larger Methodist Church in the Caribbean and the Americas.

The Church of England was established in 1700, many decades before the Methodists, but largely identified with the ruling white elite. Their membership was concentrated on Virgin Gorda Island. In 1916, administration of the Anglican work was turned over to the Episcopal Church based in the United States, which had developed work in the American Virgin Islands (purchased from the Dutch in 1917). In 1947 a diocese serving both the British and American territory was created. That diocese is today a part of Province II in the Episcopal Church, which includes New York, New Jersey, Haiti, and the congregations in Europe.

Only a few additional churches have entered the British Virgin Islands, its small population of 12,000 offering little prospect for growth. The Roman Catholic Church established a parish in 1960 that is currently

BRITISH VIRGIN ISLANDS

British Virgin Islands

Religion	Followers in 1970	Followers in 2010	% of Population	Annual % growth 2000–2010	Followers in 2025	Followers in 2050
Christians	8,900	19,700	84.4	1.42	21,900	22,800
Protestants	5,700	11,700	50.2	1.03	12,600	12,300
Anglicans	1,500	3,200	13.7	1.39	3,700	4,000
Independents	270	1,400	6.0	2.47	1,900	2,500
Spiritists	700	2,000	8.4	1.41	2,200	2,400
Agnostics	50	900	3.9	1.42	1,300	1,700
Hindus	40	280	1.2	1.43	400	500
Muslims	30	270	1.2	1.40	400	500
Baha'is	60	200	0.9	1.36	300	400
Atheists	0	30	0.1	0.79	40	70
Total population	**9,800**	**23,300**	**100.0**	**1.42**	**26,500**	**28,300**

attached to the Diocese of St. John's (Antigua). There are also a few members of the Jehovah's Witnesses, the Church of God International (Cleveland, Tennessee) the Church of the Nazarene, and the Seventh-day Adventist Church. A small group of Baptists is divided between the Southern Baptist Convention and the Baptist Missionary Association of America.

Immigrants from India and Pakistan have introduced Hinduism and Islam into the islands, and there is a small community of the Baha'i Faith.

J. Gordon Melton

See also: Baha'i Faith; Baptists; Church of England; Church of God International (Cleveland, Tennessee);

Church of the Nazarene; Episcopal Church; Jehovah's Witnesses; Methodist Church in the Caribbean and the Americas; Methodism; Roman Catholic Church; Seventh-day Adventist Church; Southern Baptist Convention.

References

Blackman, F. W. *Methodism: Two Hundred Years in the British Virgin Islands.* Bridgetown, Barbados: Methodist Church of the British Virgin Islands, 1989.

Dookan, Isaac. *History of the Virgin Islands.* Kingston, Jamaica: University Press of the West Indies, 2000.

Mason, D. G. *The Church in the Process of Development in the British Virgin Island.* S.T.M. thesis, Drew University, 1974.

Brotherhood of the Cross and Star

Apart from some outward similarities, such as members wearing white *soutanes* (robes), the Brotherhood of the Cross and Star (BCS) in southeastern Nigeria is not an Aladura church but a messianic and deliberately syncretistic movement that claims not to be a church, although it does claim to be Christian. The organization was founded in 1956 in Calabar by Olumba Olumba Obu (b. 1918), a healer and miracle worker known as O.O.O. (members paint these letters on homes and cars for protection) and as Leader Obu, "Sole Spiritual Head" of this movement.

Unlike most founders of African new religious movements, Obu did not belong to a church, did not receive a divine call, and did not undergo a period of seclusion and training. He is believed to have become aware of his divine mission and to have performed miracles at the age of five, and to know the Bible because he is its author. Nevertheless, Obu teaches that all of the Bible, except the book of Revelation, is a closed and useless book, and he teaches a pantheistic idea of God, the fallibility of Jesus, and reincarnation. He lives simply in Calabar, which he has not left since 1954; he preaches always in his native Efik; and he rejects Western clothing, watches, and footwear.

Although he appears to have handed over the movement to his son (who goes by the same name) the

Brotherhood of the Cross and Star Service, ca. 1990s, Great Britain. (Corbis)

aging Obu stands at the center of this movement. By 2009 he had not been seen publicly for several years and was said to be blind. His followers believe him to be the Messiah and the eighth and final incarnation of God—the seventh incarnation being Jesus. Although he at first denied his deity, Obu began to proclaim it publicly in 1977, and the BCS hymnbook abounds with references to him as divine. The movement's website refers to him as "the Sole Spiritual Head of the Universe." His son and successor is also now referred to as "the King of Kings and the Lord of Lords." Apart from its central emphasis on the person of Obu, the movement emphasizes spiritual and material prosperity, healing, and deliverance from witchcraft; it has aroused opposition from most other Nigerian churches. BCS practices baptism by immersion, foot washing before a Sunday congregational feast, the use of holy oil and holy water, and healing in the "powerful name" of Obu. It rejects some traditional beliefs, such as the existence and powers of witchcraft, and condemns cultural societies and traditional diviners, as well as polygyny.

The BCS may have had one million members worldwide in 2000 (BCS sources put this figure much higher), and it has expanded in West Africa, Europe, Asia, and North America. It has more recently developed links with other religious bodies, including several groups led by Hindu teachers, Rosicrucianism, and the Unification movement. Olumba O Obu and various leaders in the Brotherhood have published numerous small publications through Brotherhood Press over the years.

Brotherhood of the Cross and Star
34 Ambo Street
PO Box 49
Calabar
Nigeria
http://www.ooo-bcs.org/

Allen H. Anderson

See also: African Initiated (Independent)Churches; Aladura Churches; Reincarnation; Unification Movement.

References

Amadi, Gabriel I. S. "Power and Purity: A Comparative Study of Two Prophetic Churches in Southeastern Nigeria." Ph.D. diss., University of Manchester, 1982.

Hackett, Rosalind I. J. *Religion in Calabar*. Berlin: Mouton de Gruyter, 1989.

The Handbook of the Brotherhood of the Cross and Star. Calabar, Nigeria: Brotherhood Press, n.d.

Mbom, Friday M. *Brotherhood of the Cross and Star: A New Religious Movement in Nigeria*. Frankfurt am Main: Peter Lang, 1992.

Bruderhof

See Church Communities International.

■ Brunei

The Sultanate of Brunei Darussalam, located on the island of Borneo, is the smallest country in Southeast Asia, in terms of population. It is the remnant of a 15th-century sultanate, which lost control over Borneo during the colonial period that began in the 17th century. The British created a protectorate over Brunei in 1888 that lasted until 1984, when Brunei became an independent country.

Brunei's 2,228 square miles of territory is home to approximately 388,600 citizens (2008). Of this number 67.2 percent are ethnic Malays, the absolute majority of which are Muslims. Other ethnic Malay groups, which include the Kadayans, Dusuns, Muruts, Bisayas, Belaits, and Tutongs, account for 6 percent of the population. A majority of this group practice traditional premodern religions, although a marginal number among them have converted to Christianity and Islam. Among the immigrant population, ethnic Chinese (who have arrived in the area through the 20th century from China, Hong Kong, and Taiwan) now account for 15 percent of the population. Members of this group practice a spectrum of religions traditionally associated with China (Buddhism, Daoism, Confucianism). Some are also Christians, while a handful among them have converted to Islam. Freethinkers, Hindus, and others of unstated faiths account for the remaining 11.8 percent of the total population.

The most recent census of Brunei in 1991 indicated that 67 percent of the population identified themselves as Muslims, 13 percent as Buddhists, 10 percent as Christians, and the remaining 10 percent "other," which includes freethinkers, Hindus, Sikhs, members of the Baha'i Faith, undeclared, and so on.

Although Islam is the official religion of the country, and the state funds many Muslim religious organizations through the Ministry of Religious Affairs, religious minorities have the right to observe their religious values and traditions. According to the Constitution of the state of Brunei (1959), "the religion of the State shall be the Muslim religion, provided that all other religions may be practiced in peace and harmony by the persons professing them in any part of the State."

Brunei

Religion	Followers in 1970	Followers in 2010	% of Population	Annual % growth 2000–2010	Followers in 2025	Followers in 2050
Muslims	76,100	228,000	55.1	2.31	306,000	422,000
Christians	7,300	63,300	15.3	2.31	87,200	116,000
Roman Catholics	0	30,000	7.2	1.83	38,000	49,000
Independents	1,500	21,000	5.1	3.84	32,500	45,000
Protestants	1,600	7,000	1.7	2.66	10,000	15,000
Ethnoreligionists	18,900	44,000	10.6	2.31	50,000	55,000
Buddhists	16,000	40,000	9.7	2.31	38,000	43,000
Chinese folk	10,000	21,000	5.1	2.31	21,500	12,500
Confucianists	0	7,800	1.9	2.31	10,000	13,000
Agnostics	0	4,700	1.1	2.31	7,000	10,000
Hindus	1,300	3,500	0.8	2.32	4,500	6,000
Baha'is	530	1,300	0.3	2.31	1,500	2,500
Atheists	0	150	0.0	2.36	200	300
New religionists	0	100	0.0	2.29	200	300
Total population	**130,000**	**414,000**	**100.0**	**2.31**	**526,000**	**681,000**

BRUNEI

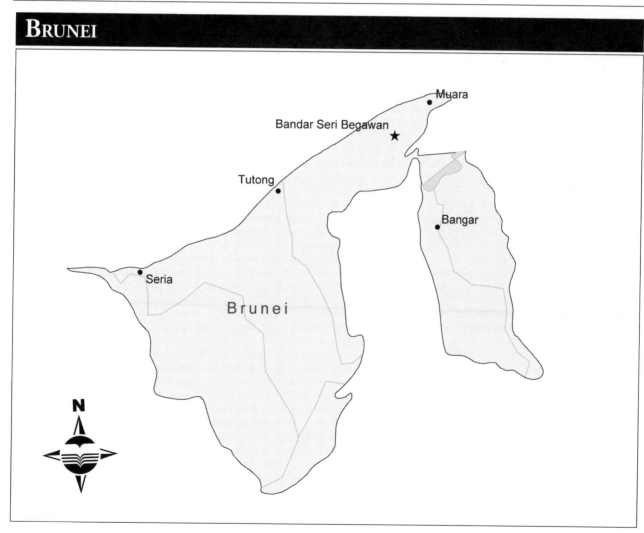

Religious and educational institutions for both Muslims and non-Muslims are scattered around the country. There are 102 mosques and Muslim prayer halls. There are also seven Christian churches (two in Bandar Seri Begawan [BSB], three in Seria, and two in Kuala Belait), the majority being congregations of the Roman Catholic Church. In addition to the above, there are three Chinese temples (the Kuan Yin or the Goddess of Mercy temple in BSB, the Ching Nam in Muara, and the Fook Tong Keng temple in Tutong) and two small Indian temples located in BSB and Seria. Although the small Sikh community in Brunei (approximately 500 people) has no official religious institutions, weekly services are held in members' homes. Of the religious educational institutions, 115 are Islamic religious schools, which operate in conjunction with the government schools. In addition, a number of Christian-based schools established during the colonial period are still in operation today. Such schools include St. George's and St. Andrew's in BSB, and St. Michel's and St. Angela's in Seria. There are eight Chinese schools in Brunei managed by the Chinese community in the country, including the well-known Chung Hwa Middle School in the capital.

Dr. Niew Shong Tong, a former senior lecturer at Universiti Brunei Darussalam (UBD), has discovered more than 40 socio-religious and cultural Chinese associations established in Brunei. These include dialect-locality groups, trade-occupational, cultural-recreational, mutual help-benevolent, religious, and community-wide associations.

The primary Christian association operating in Brunei is the Borneo Evangelical Society, which is essentially an umbrella organization operating on behalf of Christians on the Island of Borneo (including the East Malaysian states of Sabah and Sarawak).

There are two Indian-related organizations/associations in Brunei. The oldest is the 58-year-old Hindu Welfare Board in Brunei, which functions as a Hindu religious organization and has approximately 3,000 members, both foreigners and locals. The second major Indian organization is the 51-year-old Indian Association, which is considered a social organization for the Indian community and has 300 registered members.

Brunei annually celebrates a number of religious holidays, including Eid al-Fitri (the festival marking the end of Ramadan), Eid al-Adha (the festival of sacrifice), the Prophet's birthday, the First of Muharram, Nuzul al Qur'an (descension of the Koran), the Fast of Ramadan, and Isra (the night journey) and Miraj (ascension) for Muslims. The Christian New Year and Christmas are also officially recognized holidays, as is the Chinese New Year. Although they are not recognized as national holidays, the Hindu community in Brunei celebrates both Thaipusam (a celebration of exotic rituals) and Diwali (the festival of lights). On regional and local levels, Hari Gawai, an annual festival commemorating the rice harvest, is celebrated by the Iban tribe.

Ahmad F. Yousif

See also: Baha'i Faith; Brunei, Islam in; Diwali; Eid al-Adha; Ramadan; Roman Catholic Church.

References

Awang Mohd. *Jamil al-Sufri, Haji. Brunei Darussalam: The Road to Independence.* Bandar Seri Begawan: Brunei History Centre, Ministry of Culture, Youth and Sports, 1998.

Brunei Darussalam Statistical Yearbook. Brunei: Statistic Division, Ministry of Finance, issued annually.

Brown, Carrie C. "Notes on the First Chinese Temple of Brunei Town." In *From Buckfast to Borneo: Essays Presented to Father Robert Nicholl on the Eighty-Fifth Anniversary of His Birth*, edited by Victor T. King and A. V. M. Horton. Hull, UK: University of Hull Press, 1995.

Niew Shong Tong. "Brunei." In *The Encyclopedia of the Chinese Overseas*, edited by Lynn Pan, 138–139. Singapore: Archipelago Press, 2006.

Niew Shong Tong. "Chinese Society in Brunei: A Survey." In *Southeast Asian Chinese: The Socio-Cultural Dimension*, edited by Leo Suryadinata. Singapore: Times Academic Press, 1995.

Tan Pek Leng. "A History of Chinese Settlement in Brunei." In *Essays on Modern Brunei History*, edited by Tan Pek Leng et al. Brunei Darussalam: University Brunei Darussalam, Department of History, 1992.

Brunei, Islam in

Historical documents dating back to 414 CE show that Brunei, an independent sultanate in Borneo, was originally a Hindu-Buddhist city-state. Historians have suggested different theories regarding the coming of Islam to Brunei. Some say that Islam came to Brunei from China during the 10th century, while others trace it to Arab traders who came to Southeast Asia during the 14th century from Yemen and possibly Hujurat, India. Still others argue that Islam first came to Brunei during the 14th century, with the conversion of Awang Alak Betatar and his brother, Bateh Berbai. Awang Alak Betatar, who changed his name to Muhammad Shah, subsequently became the first Muslim sultan of Brunei.

Whatever the origins of Islam in the region, it is certain that from the 15th to the mid-16th centuries, the Sultanate of Brunei became a dominant regional power, with sovereignty over the whole island of Borneo and the Philippines. During this period, there were a number of sultans who were particularly active in the promotion of Islam. For example, Sultan Sharif Ali (1425–1432), the third leader of Brunei (said to be a descendant of the Prophet's grandson, Hussein), established religious institutions such as mosques and schools, and implemented the Shariah (Islamic law code based on the Koran) in Brunei.

With the coming of the Spanish and the British to the region in the latter half of the 16th century, Brunei's power became gradually eroded, until it became little more than a British protectorate in 1888. During

Sir Omar Ali Saifuddien Mosque in Brunei. (J. Gordon Melton)

the initial period of British penetration, two sultans, Saiful Rijal (1533–1581) and Hassan (1582–1598), played a significant role in promoting Islam, as well as protecting the people from Christianization.

As in the past, Islamic values and ethics continue in the modern period to be incorporated and manifested within Brunei culture, society, and politics. No greater proof of the continuous link between religion and state, past and present, exists than the continuation of the MIB (Melayu Islam Beraja, or Malay Muslim Monarchy) concept, which has been in existence since Brunei first declared itself a Muslim Malay Sultanate six centuries ago. MIB is the cornerstone of the religio-political philosophy of Brunei, which stresses the importance of maintaining the Malay race, language, and culture, and the Muslim religion of the nation. The significance of this concept was reaffirmed during the reign of Sultan Haji Omar Ali Saifuddien (1950–1967) when it became officially recognized in the 1959 Brunei Constitution.

Today Islam, primarily of the Shafiite School of jurisprudence, is alive and thriving in Brunei. Birth, marriage, divorce, burial, and other social ceremonies in Brunei are generally done according to the Islamic law. According to the Department of Mosque Affairs, the number of mosques and prayer halls reached 102 in 1999. This number includes two major state mosques, Masjid Omar Ali Saifuddien (Kampong Sultan Lama, Bandar Seri Begawan, Brunei Darussalam) and Jame'Asr Hassanal Bolkiah (Kampong Kiarong, Bandar Seri Begawan, Brunei Darussalam), both of which are considered major tourist attractions for visitors to Brunei.

The majority of Islamic organizations or departments in Brunei are established and funded by the government. For example, the Ministry of Religious Affairs (Kementrian Hal Ehwal Ugama, Jalan Mentri Besar, Barakas, BB3910, Bandar Seri Begawan, Brunei Darussalam; website address: religious-affairs.gov.bn/?tpl =th003_english_org), established in 1986, is comprised of five different departments, namely, Mosque Affairs, Hajj, Islamic Studies, Shariah Affairs, and Administration, in addition to the Islamic Da'wah Center (propagation center). As far as nongovernmental Islamic religious organizations are concerned, they are few in number. These include the National Association of Qur'anic Reciters and Memorizers (IQRA'), which trains and assists members to properly read and memorize the Koran, the New (Muslim) Converts Association, and the Ikhwan al-Muslimeen, which is based in the district of Kuala Belait. Of these groups, only the first two can be genuinely classified as active.

A number of Islamic institutions of an economic nature have also been established in Brunei. These include Tabung Amanah Islam Brunei (TAIB), an Islamic trust fund founded in 1991, and Insurance Islam Taib and the Islamic Bank of Brunei (IBB), both of which were established in 1993.

Islam in Brunei is well represented in the local print and electronic media. For example, Radio-Television Brunei (RTB) devotes more than 20 hours a week to religious or religion-related television programming. Such programs include coverage of the weekly Friday khutbahs, or religious sermons, the annual Koran competition, Muslim festivals and celebrations, and the like. In addition to the above, the government also funds the religiously oriented Nurul-Islam (Light of Islam) radio station.

In addition to the above organizations and groups, Sufi orders, or *tariqahs* (mystical paths), such as al-Ahmadiyya and al-Naqshabandiyya, have also established themselves in the country. Some of these tariqahs trace their roots directly to the Middle East, while others entered Brunei via neighboring countries such as Indonesia and Malaysia. Many of these groups engage in Mawlud Dhikir, a socio-religious ceremony in which religious poems are read and chanted. In this century, the Ahmadiyya Muslim movement has also established itself.

The 20th century witnessed the growth and development of Islamic religious education in Brunei. In 1956, 7 full-time Islamic schools were officially opened. By 1999, the number of religious schools had increased to 115. Islamic education is also promoted under schools and colleges affiliated with the Ministry of Religious Affairs, where traditional Islamic subjects are taught in both Malay and Arabic languages. Some of the more renowned religious institutes in the country are the Sultan Haji Hassanal Bolkiah Tahfiz al-Quran Institute in Bandar Seri Begawan (BSB), the Brunei College of Islamic Studies (Ma'had) in Tutong, and the University College Religious Teachers

Training College (Maktab Perguruan Ugama) in BSB. Religious (*ugama*) classes are also taught in the public schools. The majority of students study under the "old system" and accordingly have four hours a week of Islamic studies at the elementary level and three hours in the secondary level. Under the "new system," which is presently in operation in 15 schools in the country, the amount of Islamic instruction has been increased to 8 hours per week for elementary students and 6 hours at the secondary level. In addition to the above, a Kefahaman Islam (Islamic understanding) course has recently been introduced for non-Muslim students on a trial basis in three schools, St. George, St. Andrew, and Chung Hwa, all of which are located in the Bruneian capital.

At the tertiary level, the newly (2007) established Sultan Sharif Ali Islamic University (UNISSA) has four faculties and three centers, and offers undergraduate and postgraduate programs on Islamic Studies and others.

Ahmad F. Yousif

See also: Ahmadiyya Movement in Islam; Naqshabandiyya Sufi Order; Sufism.

References

Ahmad, Mohamed Deli, ed. *Brunei Darussalam in Brief.* 7th ed. Brunei: Information Department, 1997.

Brown, Donald E. *Brunei: The Structure and History of Bornean Malay Sultanate.* Brunei: Brunei Museum, 1970.

Hughes-Hallett, H. R. "A Sketch of the History of Brunei." In *Papers Related to Brunei.* Malaysia: Malaysia Branch of the Royal Asiatic Society, 1998.

Ibrahim, Yahya. "Islam in the History of Brunei: A Study of the History of the Administration of Islamic Law up to the Promulgation of the Constitution of 1959." In *Constructing the Past: National History and Historiography in Brunei, Indonesia, Thailand, Singapore, the Philippines, and Vietnam,* edited by Putu Davies, 158–174. Brunei: University Brunei Press, 1996.

Mansurnoor, Iik Arifin. "Islamic Education, State and Society in Brunei." Paper presented at the International Seminar of Islamic Studies in the ASEAN: History, Approaches and Future Trends, Pattani, Thailand, 1998.

Osman, Mohd Taib. "The Malay Sultanate: Past and Present Functions, with Particular Reference to Negara Brunei Darussalam." In *Proceedings for the International Seminar on Brunei Malay Sultanate,* vol. 2. Brunei: University Brunei Press, 1994.

Tuah, Duraman. "The Development of Melayu Islam Beraja (MIB) in Upholding Negara Brunei Darussalam as an Independent and Sovereign Nation." *Jurnal Institut Perkhidmatan Awam* (Brunei) (February 1999): 27–47.

Yousif, Ahmad F. "Islamic Science: Controversies, Possibilities and Implications for Scientific Education in Brunei Darussalam." *Journal of Religious Studies and Theology* (Canada) 20, no. 1 (2000): 81–107.

Buddha Purnima

See Wesak.

Buddha, Gautama

566–486 BCE

Buddha, a title meaning the Enlightened One, was initially ascribed to an individual born to the royal family of a tiny northern Himalayan kingdom of the Sakyas (in what is now Nepal). Sakyamuni, or sage of the Sakyas, as he is sometimes called, was given the name Siddhartha and called Gautama (descendent of the sage Gotama). As is true of many ancient figures, the facts about Siddhartha have been called into question by modern scholars given the several centuries that passed before the documents recording the Buddha's life began to be written down.

The Sakya regime was centered at the city of Kapilavastu. Some have identified ruins along the Nepal-Indian border as those of Kapilavastu, but none have been positively identified. Ancient Kapilavastu was most likely absorbed into the empire of the Magadhas, which flourished during and after the Buddha's period.

Statue of Gautama Buddha, Taos, New Mexico. (J. Gordon Melton)

It is also the case that the Sakya lineage is known only through Buddhist sources, and much elaboration was added over the centuries. It seems likely that the leader of the Sakya state was simply a regional ruler in a larger state. The Sakya rulers were from the *kshatriya* (warrior) class (caste) of the Gotama clan. The original ancestor was a *rishi* (seer) named Gotama who was of the *brahmin* (priestly) class. It remains an unresolved quandary as to why the descendents of a person of the higher brahmin class would later claim the status of kshatriya, a lower class. Possibly, Vedic regulations concerning strict membership in particular castes were not fully functional within the Sakya tribe.

Today, few doubt the existence of the Buddha, and all traditions agree that he lived for eighty years and taught in India. That being said, a variety of dates have been suggested for his birth—cases being made for 566, 563, and as early as 623 BCE. Some traditions

date him even earlier to the sixth century BCE. Most scholars have used the 566–486 dating (thus making him a contemporary of Mahavira (c. 599–527 BCE), the founder of the Jain tradition in India. This question of his dating is complicated because all records were oral and the sutras, the discourses he gave, were not committed to writing for several hundred years. Accounts of his life were created by a process of compiling data from all the sutras into a narrative.

Siddhartha was the son of Suddhodana, the king of the Sakyas, and Maya, the queen. Maya gave birth in the forest of Lumbini. One popular account describes the queen being showered with perfumed blossoms as her son was born. Immediately after his arrival, the infant stood up, took seven steps, and announced "I alone am the World-Honored One!" Siddhartha was raised by Maya's sister, Mahaprajapati, whom his father had also married. We are unaware of any other children of Suddhodana, but Siddhartha had a number of cousins, among them being Ananda, a major disciple, and Devadatta, who betrayed him. Siddhartha grew up as a prince in line for the throne. He married a woman named Yasodhara who bore him a son. The birth of his son became the occasion of a personal crisis in his spiritual quest and soon afterward he left his family and princely life. He was 29 years old.

From the large body of material assembled once the sutras were written down, what is known as the Pali Canon (Pali being the language in which they were written), material for the first biography, the Asvaghosa's Buddhacarita (or Acts of the Buddha) was composed in the second century CE and is an important early biography. It appears to mix legendary materials with a core of historical truth. Later generations added additional details and embellishments.

According to the widely accepted biography, King Suddhodana took pains to keep his son from the more unpleasant realities of life. The young prince lived in luxury and was given a quality education but was confined within the royal compound. As he matured, Siddhartha desired to know about the larger world outside the walls. He secretly conspired with his charioteer, Channa, to escort him through the countryside. What he saw shocked him to his core. He saw misery and pain in the realities of old age, illness, suffering, and even death. His experience outside the walls contradicted much of the picture of the world communicated in his education. By the time his son was born, he decided to leave his home and seek truth by himself.

Thus, Siddhartha bid his wife, Yashodhara, and baby son, Rahula, farewell and left the compound for the last time. He rode with his horse and charioteer some distance before abandoning both, and, ordering them to return, he cut himself off from his previous enclosed life. He soon met five wandering ascetics, men who had given up all physical and social attachments as part of a process hopefully leading to spiritual insight and wisdom. Siddhartha decided to join the ascetics on their quest for spiritual understanding, and during the next four years he engaged in a variety of extreme physical deprivations in hope of overcoming the influence of the physical body. He eventually concluded that asceticism was simply another extreme and would not lead to true wisdom. He left his companions and contemplated his alternatives. Finally settling in a forest grove, beneath a fig tree (now called the Bodhi Tree) at a place now called Bodh Gaya, he began to contemplate his life experiences. After forty days he achieved what is invariably described as enlightenment, a complete and pervasive shift in understanding of the nature of reality. Siddhartha, the former prince and wondering ascetic, had become the Buddha, that is, the enlightened one.

The Buddha's subsequent story involved his forty-five-year career as a teacher. Shortly after gaining enlightenment, he traveled to the Deer Park at Sarnath, near Benares, where he gave his first discourse (or sermon), laying out the basics of his new insights. He also reconnected with the five ascetics he formerly lived with and organized the community of monks, the Sangha. His growing following of mendicant monks wandered the countryside with him as he taught, settling down for a lengthy annual retreat during the rainy season. He also later facilitated the organization of an order of nuns.

After more than four decades of teaching, the Buddha sensed his health was deteriorating and chose a forest setting (at present-day Kushinagar, India) to die, which is generally termed entering Parinirvana. Though most often pictured in the sitting position, the Buddha is also shown reclining on his side, his head resting on the palm of his hand, delivering his last teaching prior to his passing. The Buddha's body was subsequently cremated and the relics were divided and placed in structures called stupas. Some of these relics are believed to have survived to the present and are quite valued items within the larger Buddhist community.

At a later date, many Buddhists came to believe that he was born, reached enlightenment, and passed away on the same day of the year, namely the evening of the full moon in the Indian month of Vaisakha (April or May on the Common Era calendar). This day, called Wesak, is now celebrated each year. Others, however, such as the Buddhists of Japan, celebrate the three events on different days. The places associated with the major events of the Buddha's life—Lumbini, Bodh Gaya, Sarnath, and Kushinagar—have become pilgrimage sites. The site of Buddha's enlightenment fell into non-Buddhist hands when Buddhism was largely wiped out in India in the twelfth century, and an effort was begun in the late nineteenth century to recover the site. Led by the Maha Bodhi Society, the effort has met with moderate success.

J. Gordon Melton

See also: Bodh-Gaya; Enlightenment; Kushinagar; Lumbini; Maha Bodhi Society; Mahavira; Monasticism; Pilgrimage; Relics; Sarnath; Statues—Buddhist; Wesak.

References

Bagchee, Moni. *Our Buddha*. Kuala Lumpur, Malaysia: Buddhist Missionary Society, 1999.

Johnston, E. H., trans. *The Buddhacarita, Or, Acts of the Buddha*. 3d ed. Delhi: Motilal Banarsidass, 1984.

Ling, Trevor. *The Buddha*. Harmondsworth, UK: Penguin, 1973.

Robinson, Richard H., and Willard L. Johnson. *The Buddhist Religion: A Historical Introduction*. Belmont, CA: Wadsworth Publishing Company, 1997.

Saddhatissa, Hammalava. *The Life of the Buddha*. London: Unwin, 1976.

Thomas, Edward J. *The Life of Buddha as Legend and History*. New Delhi: Munshiram Manoharlal, 1992.

Buddhasasananuggaha Association

The Venerable U Sobhana Mahathera, more widely known as Mahasi Sayadaw (1904–1982), was born on July 29, 1904, in Seikkhun village, near Shwebo, in northern Burma. After demonstrating extraordinary precociousness in the mastery of Pali Buddhist texts as a novice monk (*samanera*), he became an ordained *bhikkhu* (monk) in 1923. Although U Sobhana continued to excel in his scholastic achievement and the intellectual mastery of the texts of Theravada Buddhism and remained steadfastly committed to this pursuit throughout his entire life, he was also determined to apply the practical aspects of those texts to the practice of meditation. He therefore set out to find an appropriate meditation teacher, a most difficult task due to the unfortunate fact that methodical meditation training had become nearly extinct in Theravada Buddhist countries

by the early 20th century. However, eight years after his ordination the opportunity arose for U Sobhana to enter what he later described as "a most intensive practical course of *satipatthana* (Foundations of Mindfulness) meditation under the personal guidance of the Most Venerable Mingun Jetavan Sayadaw of Thaton." In 1938 he began his own career as a teacher of the intensive practice of satipatthana, directing his efforts largely toward laypeople, who had essentially no means of learning rigorous meditation technique.

He began teaching meditation at a monastery in Seikkhun village known as Maha-Si Kyaung, due to a large (*maha*) drum (Burmese: *si*) located there. The many practitioners who learned meditation under him at this location thus came to call him Mahasi Sayadaw ("Sayadaw" being Burmese for Great Teacher). In 1944, in response to requests from students, Mahasi Sayadaw completed his great treatise, *The Method of Vipassana Meditation*. Some brief quotes from this work may suffice to demonstrate the essence of the meditation technique he taught:

"Try to keep your mind (but not your eyes) on the abdomen. You will thereby come to know the movements of rising and falling of this organ . . . Then make a mental note, *rising* for the upward movement, *falling* for the downward movement . . . What you actually perceive is the bodily sensation of pressure caused by the heaving movement of the abdomen . . . and do not think of *rising* and *falling* as words. Be *aware only of the actual process of the rising and falling movement of the abdomen.*"

This method, adapted from Mingun Jetavan, was further developed by Mahasi Sayadaw to include making mental notes for all activities throughout the day. Thus, for example, while eating:

"When you bring the food to the mouth, *bringing* When you bend the neck forward, *bending* When the food touches the mouth, *touching.*

In this way insight (*vipassana*) into the impermanent (*anicca*), unsatisfactory (*dukkha*), and unsubstantial (*anatta*) nature of all conditioned (i.e., non-*nibbana*) phenomena is developed."

Venerable Mahasi Sayadaw succumbed to a sudden heart attack on August 14, 1982. His life exemplified a rare combination of profound erudition in Pali

Buddhist texts, deep meditation experience, and practical teaching ability.

In 1947, Sir U Thwin and others founded the Buddhasasananuggaha Association in Rangoon. Sir U Thwin served as its first president and donated a plot of land for the erection of a meditation center. He also proposed that Mahasi Sayadaw be invited to teach at the center. Subsequently, the Buddhasasananuggaha Association became the vehicle for the dissemination of the Mahasi Sayadaw Vipassana technique around the world.

The Buddhasasananuggaha Association is located in Yangon (Rangoon). A related Internet site can be found at http://web.ukonline.co.uk/buddhism//mahasi.htm#biography. Affiliated centers are found in 41 countries in Asia and Europe as well as the United States. Approximately one million people have received formal training in the Mahasi Sayadaw Vipassana technique at meditation centers around the world devoted to teaching this approach to meditative practice. Over the two decades since his death, as the Mahasi Sayadaw meditation technique has become increasingly influential in the West, there has been a concomitant propagation of some of the hermeneutical disputes that arose during his life within the Burmese Sangha concerning the precise textual/scriptural basis of his approach to Vipassana practice.

Buddhasasananuggaha Association
No 16, Sasana Yeiktha Road
Bahan, Yangon (Rangoon) 11201
Myanmar

Jeffrey M. Schwartz

See also: Meditation; Theravada Buddhism; Vipassana International Academy.

References

Mahasi Sayadaw. *Practical Insight Meditation.* Kandy, Sri Lanka: Buddhist Publication Society (BPS), 1971. (Excerpt from *The Method of Vipassanā Meditation*, 1944).

Mahasi Sayadaw. *Satipatthana Vipassana: Insight through Mindfulness.* Kandy, Sri Lanka: Buddhist Publication Society, 1990. www.accesstoinsight.org/lib/bps/wheels/wheel370.html. Accessed June 15, 2009.

Nyanaponika Thera, *The Heart of Buddhist Meditation.* York Beach, ME: Samuel Weiser, 1973.

U Sulananda Sayadaw. *The Four Foundations of Mindfulness.* Boston: Wisdom Publications, 1990.

◆ Buddhism

Today's approximately 400 million Buddhists can look back on 2,500 years of history with diverse developments and a wide spectrum of cultural expressions. Although the different traditions emphasize specific concepts, practices, and lifestyles, all Buddhists relate back to these three fundamental principles: the Buddha, the Teachings, and the Order. They call these principles the three Jewels or "Gems of Buddhism."

It is generally assumed that Buddha Shakyamuni lived from 560 to 480 BCE. However, in the later 20th century, Indological research questioned those dates and placed the lifetime of the Buddha at the turn of the fifth to the fourth centuries BCE. And though the debate has not yet come to an end, scholars provide good evidence to adopt as the lifetime of the historical Buddha the span between 448 and 368 BCE, with a margin of 10 years. As a consequence of this recalculation, the Buddha's life, the order's development, and Buddhist history in general move much closer to the reign of King Ashoka (ca. 268–239 BCE), and thus to the earliest reliably datable accounts in Indian history.

The name Buddha is an honorific title meaning "the Awakened One." Born as Siddhartha Gautama in a royal family in a region of northern India (in Lumbini, now southern Nepal), Siddhartha spent his childhood and youth in luxury. He was married at 16 and became the father of his son Rahula 12 years later. Upon leaving—and while away from—the protected world of the palaces, the "four sights" provoked a major change in the course of his life. The 29-year-old saw an aged man bent by the years, a sick man scorched by fever, a corpse followed by mourners weeping, and a mendicant ascetic. Becoming aware of the transitoriness of life, Siddhartha left the palace and became a wandering monk. In those days monks and ascetic orders commonly sought to find and teach final solutions to the human sufferings of old age, sickness, and

Painting inside a Buddhist temple in Luang Prabang, Laos. (Luciano Mortula/Dreamstime.com)

death, and their perpetual recurrence. For six years Siddhartha engaged in strict practices of asceticism designed to deny the pleasures of the senses. When that severe self-denial failed to bring the solution desired, he withdrew to a balanced form of asceticism, called the Middle Path. This approach avoids the extremes of self-denial and self-indulgence. At the age of 35, while meditating in a resolved manner under a tree known as the Bodhi Tree (*Ficus religiosa*), Siddhartha attained enlightenment (Sanskrit/Pali: *bodhi*). In Buddhist accounts, here at Bodh Gaya he became "awakened" from the sleep of delusion—that is, from the ignorance that binds living beings to the suffering of this world.

From now on, the homeless ascetic was called the Buddha, the Enlightened or Awakened one. Buddha spread his insight and the teaching of the Middle Path through conversation, parable, and speech. He preached for 45 years in northern India, where he founded an order of monks and nuns. Laymen and laywomen supported the newly founded order by donating food and clothes and offering accommodations. For centuries the Teachings were transmitted orally, and it was no earlier than about 300 years after the Buddha's death that they were written down in Pali, and later in Sanskrit. Buddha did not nominate a successor. It was

rather his Teachings that succeeded him, after the "extinction" of his physical death.

Buddha adapted the Vedic and Brahmanic concepts of rebirth and dependent origination—that is, the principle of cause and effect. According to those theories, the next life is dependent on the meritorious and bad deeds (Sanskrit: *karma*) of the present life. In order to leave the endless cycle of rebirths (*samsara*), a practitioner would have to fully understand and follow the Buddhist teachings. Thus the aim of the teachings is to overcome the suffering or dissatisfaction (*duhkha*) that is caused by being imprisoned in the cycle of rebirths. The Four Noble Truths describe and analyze the existence of suffering and provide a way to extinguish it. According to Buddhist tradition, in his very first sermon at Deer Park in Sarnath (near Benares), the Buddha had preached these Truths, a sermon later known as the "first turning of the Wheel of *Dharma*." The truth of Suffering points to the fundamental reality that nobody is able to escape birth, old age, illness, and death. The truth of the Origin of Suffering states that desire (*tanha*) and thirst after life are the causes of suffering. The truth of the Cessation of Suffering says that it is possible to put an end to suffering by overcoming desire and thirst. The fourth truth, the truth of the Path to the Cessation of Suffering, consists of eight parts. Called the Noble Eightfold Path, it is pictured as an eight-spoked wheel, an important Buddhist symbol. This Path consists of: (1) right view, (2) right intention, (3) right speech, (4) right conduct, (5) right livelihood, (6) right effort, (7) right mindfulness, and (8) right concentration. For convenience and clarity, the Path's eight components are regrouped into three categories: wisdom (1–2), ethics (3–5), and meditation (6–8).

Basic to the Four Noble Truths and Buddhist teaching is that every existence is unsatisfactory (duhkha). This is because nothing has an enduring substance or self (*anatman*), due to the fact that everything is subject to change and is transitory in the final end (*anicca*). These three "characteristics of existence" are to be found in everything that is born and comes into existence. Clinging to the idea of a lasting satisfaction or something that is enduring in perpetuity is both desire and a false view—that is, ignorance (*avidya*). The Noble Eightfold Path provides practical advice and exercises both to acquire an understanding of these principles and to embark on the liberating path to extinguish the "thirst" (*trishna*). This path is directed to reach the ultimate goal, *nirvana* (Sanskrit) or *nibbana* (Pali), the "blowing out" of the fire of desire and ignorance.

Strictly speaking, only the monks (*bhiksu*) and nuns (*bhiksuni*) constitute the members of the *sangha*, the Buddhist monastic order. They have undergone a formalized ordination and taken vows to live in celibacy and simplicity. Monks and nuns are responsible for preserving and passing on the teaching and providing the social context for its practice. The ordained are intended to serve as inspiring ideals to the laity and to teach them the dharma. The sangha is an autonomous body that is, ideally, self-regulating. There is no individual or collective body that can make decisions for the sangha as a whole. As a consequence, divisions according to different monastic rules (*vinaya*) and ordination lineages occurred, resulting in a variety of monastic traditions and schools (*nikaya*).

According to Mahayana Buddhist interpretation, however, not only the ordained but also male and female lay supporters are a part of the sangha. All Buddhists, the ordained as well as the laypeople, take refuge in the "threefold refuge": the Buddha, the Teachings

(dharma), and the community (sangha). Tibetan Buddhists additionally take refuge in the teacher (Tibetan: *bla ma*, pronounced *lama*). All Buddhists promise to refrain from killing, stealing, undue sexual contacts, lying, and taking intoxicants. The ordained pledge themselves to numerous further self-disciplines, the number of precepts varying according to the monastic tradition they belong to. In the southern tradition (Theravada), the monks have to observe 227 rules and the nuns 311.

The Primary Buddhist Traditions During the tradition's first two centuries of existence, a fair number of distinct branches or schools (nikaya) evolved. The various schools of so-called "early Buddhism"—Buddhist tradition speaks of 18 and the texts state names for about 30 different schools—differed according to their interpretation of monastic rules and later of specific doctrines. All these schools may be summed up under the designation of *Shravakayana*, "the Vehicle of the listeners (of Buddha's word)." Of these, the "school of the Elders," the Sthaviravadin (Sanskrit) or Theravada (Pali), is the only one to have continued until today.

Around the beginning of the Common Era, the reformist movement of Mahayana Buddhism, the "Great Vehicle," emerged within the Buddhist community in India. The followers of the Mahayana criticized the established schools to the effect that the ultimate goal of liberation was granted only to monks and nuns—that is, that the ordained ascetic, the self-sufficient or "worthy" (Sanskrit: *arhat*) was exclusively held to have attained nirvana. Pejoratively they designated these schools as "Hinayana," the Lesser Vehicle. In contrast, Mahayana Buddhists emphasized the ideal of the unselfish "living being committed to awakening" (Sanskrit: *bodhisattva*). The bodhisattva, though capable of reaching enlightenment, has delayed entering nirvana. Motivated by compassion for the suffering beings, the bodhisattva remains in the world in order to help these beings attain enlightenment. Mahayana Buddhism also enhanced the status of laypeople, as it declared that not only an ordained but also a layperson is able to become a bodhisattva. The new emphasis and interpretation praised itself as the "second turning of the Wheel."

Responding to the new ideal and soteriological path, Shravakayana Buddhists laid emphasis on the view that it is only they who painstakingly had passed on the teaching of the Buddha. Advocates of the Shravakayana, and the surviving Theravada tradition, placed its legitimacy on the Pali canon that was (and is) held to have preserved the "original" word of the Buddha. This canon was written down on palm-leaves and collected in three thematic "baskets" (Sanskrit: *tripitaka*). First is the basket of the monastic rules (vinaya); the second basket contains discourses attributed to the Buddha and his immediate disciples (*sutra*); the third basket consists of treatises expounding Buddhist doctrine in abstract and theoretical terms (*abhidharma*). Within early Buddhism, there had existed other collections with different text groups. The Pali Tipitaka of the Theravada school is the only surviving closed canon, first committed to writing in the first century BCE in Sri Lanka. The Mahayana Buddhism refers not only to the Pali scriptures but also to the sutras (teachings) written in Sanskrit and later translated into Chinese and Tibetan. This new genre of scriptures, among them the *Prajnaparamita* sutras, the *Saddharmapundarika* sutra, and the *Lalitavistara* were composed between the first and fifth centuries CE. They hold that the sutras present the teachings of the Buddha in a more appropriate way than the former texts.

Tibetan Buddhism looks upon the transplantation of Tantric Mahayana Buddhism from northern India beginning in the seventh century on as a "third turning of the Wheel." The use of Tantric practices that make use of bodily experiences, instrument of thought, sequence of sounds (Sanskrit: *mantras*), and circle (Sanskrit: *mandalas*) are based on late Indian Mahayana teachings. They are held to provide a quick path to final liberation. The *lama* plays a central role in guiding the disciple and giving initiations. Like Mahayana Buddhism in China and East Asia, the self-designated Thunderbolt or Diamond Vehicle (Sanskrit: *Vajrayana*) lays emphasis on the selfless actions of the bodhisattva. Its primary reliance is upon texts called *tantras* rather than upon the sutras. Emphasis is laid on meditation practices as visualizations and a characteristic type of liturgical meditation (Sanskrit: *sadhana*). While becoming established over a period of 500 years, a variety of syncretic forms evolved in absorbing native

Bon concepts and rituals then current in Tibet. These forms remained basic, on a popular, lay-oriented level, with rites to accumulate merit, honoring local and personal tutelary deities, wearing protective amulets, conducting pilgrimages, and much more.

Finally, at the turn of the 21st century, Western Buddhists in North America and Europe began to outline the contours of a new, fourth vehicle (Sanskrit: *yana*). According to them, the encounter of Western culture and Buddhist ideas, ethics, and practices is currently molded into a new Buddhism, self-consciously named the "fourth turning of the Wheel." This new Vehicle (Sanskrit: *Navayana*) or World or Global Vehicle (Sanskrit: *Lokayana*) takes impulses from socially and politically engaged Buddhists, feminist interpretations of Buddhist concepts and practices, psychological and scientific approaches, and, last but not least, the meeting and encounter of Buddhist schools and traditions in Western localities.

Spread and Local Development Buddha and the members of his order preached the dharma in northern India on the plain of the River Ganges, in Magadha and Kosala. Compared with competing ascetic orders in the fifth and subsequent centuries BCE, the Buddhist community grew fairly rapidly. It gained support from the economically better-off strata of society. This enabled the building of residences (*vihara*) and later monasteries. Parallel to the settled monks and nuns, dwelling in monasteries, a tradition of forest-dwelling monks practicing intense austerities and meditational practices persisted throughout Buddhist history.

During the time of Ashoka in the third century BCE, the model of rulers who assumed the role of "righteous king" (*dharmaraja*) came into being. These rulers supported the sangha and protected the monasteries. In return, the king received a sense of moral and religious legitimacy. This relationship, beneficial for both sides, was confirmed and celebrated in festivities and processions. The spread of Buddhism in China, Korea, Japan, and Tibet was greatly assisted by the patronage of Buddhist rulers. In Southeast Asia a close association between the practice of Buddhism and the institution of monarchy existed throughout its history.

With the encouragement of King Ashoka, Buddhist monks and nuns started to spread the dharma be-

A row of Thai Buddhist Monks in prayer at the Dhammakaya Temple north of Bangkok, Thailand. (Ilgitano/Dreamstime.com)

yond the borders of the vast empire, covering the whole of northern and central India. The ordained reached the northwestern parts of the subcontinent, and from the first century on, order members and Buddhist traders traveled from the Kusana Empire's center, Bactria (today's northern Afghanistan), to Chinese Turkestan.

In India itself, Buddhism blossomed with the development of the philosophical Mahayana schools of Madhyamika and Yogacara. Also, for the whole of the second half of the first millennium, the monastic University of Nalanda (in the north of India) became the center of learning. There and in other huge monasteries of the time, monks and nuns adhering either to schools of the Mahayana or Shravakayana lived side by side, following the same vinaya rules. The seventh century gave rise to Tantric ideas and practices within Buddhism. This new emphasis, with its focus on mantras, body-based experiences, and ritual, brought Buddhism nearer to concepts and devotional forms current

in Hindu traditions. The gradual absorption of Buddhism into Hinduism and the destruction of the Buddhist centers of learning by Muslim invaders in the 12th century brought about the end of Buddhism in India as a lived religious tradition. In Nepal, Tibet, and Bhutan, however, the forms of Indian Buddhism survived and continued in culturally translated versions. It was no earlier than the late 19th and mid-20th centuries that Buddhism gained a new footing in its land of origin. In 1891 the Sinhalese Anagarika Dharmapala (1864–1933) founded the Maha Bodhi Society with the purpose of regaining control of the Maha Bodhi temple at Bodh Gaya and resuscitating Buddhism in India. In 1956, Bhimrao Ramji Ambedkar's (1891–1956) conversion to Buddhism set in motion a mass conversion movement among the West Indian Mahars, a caste of unskilled laborers designated as untouchables. Mainly because of that development, in 1991 the census counted some six and a half million Buddhists in India.

According to Buddhist tradition, the monk Mahinda, declared to be a son of Ashoka, brought Buddhism in its Theravada form in the mid-third century to the island of Ceyon. Mahinda built a monastery in the capital, Anuradhapura, and propagated Buddhist teachings and practices at the court and among the elite. Of utmost symbolic importance, during this time a cut from of the Bodhi Tree at Bodhi Gaya was planted in the ancient capital. Later, the relic of a tooth of Buddha, venerated to this day, was brought in an annual grand procession to Kandy. The sacred status of the tooth is symbolic of the close relationship between the sangha and the king. It represented the royal protection of the sangha and the king's legitimation on religious grounds. During succeeding centuries, the interweaving of kingdom and monastic order resulted in the establishment of prosperous monasteries, the monks of which becoming landlords with endowed villages and lands. With European colonialism from the 16th century on, a process of disestablishment and loss of privileges of the sangha began. In the late 19th century, as Western technologies (such as the press), scientific concepts, and Christian missionaries arrived, a Buddhist revival gained momentum. Responding to these challenges, Buddhist monks and laypersons like Anagarika Dharmapala (1864–1933) emphasized rationalist elements in Buddhist teachings, accompanied by a tacit elimination of traditional cosmology, a heightened recognition and use of texts, a renewed emphasis on meditational practice, and a stress on social reform and universalism. The two broad strands of Buddhism —that is, modernist and traditionalist, or village-based Buddhism—existed side by side, at times in tension. The involvement of the monastic order in the politics of the country has lasted, especially so as certain parts highlight the status of Sri Lanka as a "Buddhist nation" and the custodian of Buddhist tradition. This claim is to the detriment of ethnic and religious minorities in present-day Sri Lanka, observable also in the current Sinhalese–Tamil civil war.

Burma/Myanmar Buddhism spread in the form of Theravada to Burma. As in Sri Lanka, a close relationship with the kings and dynasties evolved. Although Theravada seems to have been introduced to the region around the start of the Common Era, it was in the 11th century that Buddhist teachings and practices began successfully to penetrate the nations and devotional forms. The Burmese King Anuruddha (1044–1077) was converted by a Buddhist monk from the Mon people, resulting in a lasting patronage of the sangha. Succeeding kings were also influential in sangha reforms and the introduction of an important ordination lineage from Sri Lanka (1476). Burma, like Sri Lanka, has been widely recognized among South Asian Buddhists as a guardian of Theravada Buddhism and of the Pali texts. The fifth and sixth Buddhist councils, with the recitation of the authoritative texts, were held in Mandalay in 1868–1871 and in Rangoon in 1954–1956. Unlike Thailand, Burma became a colony of the British Empire in the second half of the 19th century. The disestablishment of the sangha led to a revival of Buddhism and a renewed emphasis on meditation practices. Buddhism and Buddhist monks became an influential factor in the political independence movement. On a global scale, Burmese meditation masters such as Sayagyi U Ba Khin (1899–1971) and Mahasi Sayadaw (1904–1982) instigated the spread of Theravada meditation practices through their Western disciples to North America and Europe.

Thailand, Cambodia, and Laos Traveling Buddhist monks and traders had introduced Buddhism in its Mahayana form from India in the first millennium CE in Southeast Asia. In a parallel way, Hindu traditions and their ritual forms had become established. Both enjoyed privileged status at the royal courts and strengthened the political legitimation of the rulers.

In Thailand (then Siam), Theravada Buddhism became powerful from the mid-13th century on, also holding a paramount influence in Cambodia and Laos. Several times, the Siamese kings reformed the sangha with the import of Sri Lankan monks and their ordination lineage. In the mid-19th century, King Mongkut (1804–1868, r. 1851–1868), having been a monk for 27 years before ascending to the throne, established the Dhammayuttika (Thai: Thammayut) as the most influential school. This school follows a strict compliance with the monastic rules (vinaya), whereas a majority of monks and schools, summarized under the designation Mahanikaya (Thai: Mahanikai), opposed the imposed reforms. Monkut's son, King Chulalongkorn

(1868–1910), continued the reform for a more standardized and Bangkok-centralized Theravada Buddhism in Thailand. The Sangha Act of 1902 created a sangha bureaucracy with a "Supreme Patriarch," bringing the hitherto decentralized sangha with its diverse lineages into line with the civilian government hierarchy. In contrast to this monastery-based Buddhism, the austere life of monks, living as wandering ascetics in the forest and dedicated to the practice of meditation, continued, and it even witnessed an efflorescence. In the early 1970s, new Buddhist foundations or movements, such as the Dhammakaya and the Santi Asoka, were formed, and Thai meditational practices and approaches of engaged Buddhism became globally known through the work of Ajahn Chah (1924–1993) and Buddhadasa (1906–1993). Parallel to these forms of "official" Buddhism, a multitude of "popular" Buddhist practices, such as healing, warding off malevolent spirits, and bespeaking protective amulets, persist and take importance for the laity.

Cambodia   In Cambodia, most widely known are the monuments of Angkor Wat (12th century), providing evidence in stone of the syncretism of Hindu and Indian Mahayana traditions, the cult of the divine king (Sanskrit: *devaraja*) forming the most important ritual. From the 13th century on, Theravada Buddhism was introduced and adopted by the royal Khmer court. Political and cultural influences from neighboring Siam (Thailand) increased and pushed back the ruling Khmer. Also via Thailand, the ordination lineages from Sri Lanka were adopted, and in 1855 King Norodom imported the reformed Dhammayuttika-Nikaya (Cambodian: Thommayut) from Thailand. The Sangha-state relationship and its administrative structure was formed along the Thai model, although not without opposition from the Mohanikay School. The reign of terror of the Khmer Rouge from 1975 to 1979 aimed to annihilate all religious expression, resulting in the murder of most monks and the destruction of the temple-monastery (Thai: *wats*) and traditional Khmer Buddhism. During the 1980s, Buddhist practices remained constrained by the Communist government installed by Vietnam in 1979. The restrictions were lifted in 1988, enabling the rebuilding of wats and ordaining of Buddhist novices and monks.

Laos   Although the earliest traces of Buddhism in Laos date back to the 10th century, it was around 1350 that, with the creation of the kingdom of Laos, Theravada became the dominant religious tradition. The sangha enjoyed political patronage and high social prestige. Thailand had a strong political and religious influence until the late 19th century, when in 1893 Laos became a French colony. In 1953, Laos gained independence and Buddhism became the state religion. With the Communist takeover in 1975, the sangha and Buddhist traditional lifestyle lost much of its former dominance. However, some of the monasteries were allowed to continue their work, albeit under restrictions. Since the mid-1980s, less restrictive policies have enabled a moderate resurgence of Buddhism.

Whereas Theravada Buddhism dominates in these countries of South and Southeast Asia, and therefore at times is also designated as southern Buddhism; so-called northern Buddhism, or Mahayana Buddhism, is prevalent in Central and East Asia.

China   Monks and pious laypersons from central Asia had brought Buddhist teachings and practices along the trade route to China in the first century CE. The Indian concepts of rebirth and personal awakening, as well as the monastic lifestyle of a person who is not manually productive and does not fulfill filial duties, aroused at best curiosity among the Chinese. With the end of the Han Empire (220 CE), Buddhism having existed in China for at least 150 years, Buddhism still remained a marginal, foreign, and exotic phenomenon. During the period of political disunity (311–589) Buddhism gained a footing among the educated elite and higher aristocracy. Monks no longer were exclusively "foreigners," but also sons and daughters of Chinese origin. Sanskrit texts were translated into Chinese, and wealthy monasteries came into existence as centers of learning, sponsored by local courts and the cultural elite. The number of monastics and local temples rose considerably, so that with the reunification of China in 589, Buddhism had become an established religious community, on par with other Chinese religions such as Confucianism and Daoism. Imperial patronage, coupled with bureaucratic control of the sangha and Buddhism's alignment to Chinese indigenous concepts, developed into a Sinicized Buddhism. During the T'ang dynasty (618–906), Buddhist masters elaborated proper Chinese Buddhist traditions, mainly on the basis of Mahayana concepts. Zhiyi (538–597) advocated the centrality of the Lotus Sutra and formed the Tiantai School. In the seventh century, Pure Land Buddhism (*Ching-tu*) developed, focusing on devotion and faith in Buddha Amitabha. Although the actual school reached the end of its life in the ninth century, it remained indirectly influential in the way that virtually all Chinese schools had accommodated aspects of it. In Japan, ideas of Pure Land Buddhism developed into proper schools from the 12th century on. During the seventh century, Chan Buddhism arose as a blending of Chinese (notably Daoist) and Mahayana concepts and practices. The school emphasized meditational practice and developed a genealogical lineage of "patriarchs," placing the sixth-century semilegendary Indian monk Bodhidharma in the position of its first patriarch. A variety of schools and branches developed in due course. In 13th-century Japan, Chan Buddhism was elaborated into different schools of Zen Buddhism—Soto and Rinzai.

Following the flourishing of Buddhism during the T'ang period, Confucianism regained strength during the succeeding dynasties. Buddhist and Taoist schools faced repeated oppressions during the Ming (1368–1644) and Qing (1644–1912) dynasties. Monasteries were deprived of their privileges, and Buddhism steadily declined. In the early 20th century a revival of Buddhism began, with the reformist monk Tai Hsu (or Taixu, 1890–1947) playing a leading role. The Sino-Japanese War (1937–1945) and the establishment of the Communist Chinese People's Republic in 1949 brought an end to those activities. The Cultural Revolution (1965–1969), had a devastating effect on Buddhist clergy and institutions. Since the late 1970s, however, restrictions on religious activities have become less stringent, and Buddhism has started to recover. In line with the Chinese aims of political stability and control, Buddhist clergy and laypersons are organized in a paragovernmental association.

Republic of China (Taiwan) Following the Communist victory on mainland China, Buddhist monks and nuns moved to Taiwan in 1947 along with the Kuomintang. The Buddhist Association of the Republic of China was designed to represent all Buddhists in the Republic. It mainly served to communicate the official politics to the sangha and laypeople and to report concerns to the party. The Association had the right to ordain only monks and nuns. In 1989 the Law on Civic Organizations removed restrictions on all forms of Buddhist institutionalization and ordination. As a result, during the 1990s a dynamic emergence of hitherto marginalized Buddhist organizations and movements has come to the fore. Organizations such as the Buddhist Compassion Relief Tzu Chi Association, Dharma Drum Mountain, and the Foguangshan have been able to gather a substantial membership in the republic, as well as to establish branches and monasteries globally.

Vietnam Buddhism reached the region of today's Vietnam via the north, from China, and via the sea, from India, during the first millennium. The north of Vietnam formed the southernmost part of the Han Empire, resulting in a Sinization of the elite and the adoption of Confucian, Daoist, and Chan Buddhist concepts. Sea-traveling monks and traders had brought Buddhism in its Theravada tradition. The flourishing of Buddhism started with Vietnam's independence in the mid-10th century. The Dinh dynasty (968–980) introduced royal sponsorship of Buddhism, which reached its apogee under the Ly dynasty (1009–1224). The Ly court lavishly patronized the Sangha, supported the building of monasteries, and elevated Buddhism to the rank of official state religion. In due course, Buddhism spread among the population. The evolved Vietnamese synthesis of Chan and Pure Land Buddhism mixed with local creeds and customs, notably the cult of spirits and divine village patrons. The later Le dynasty adopted neo-Confucianism as its central ideology, causing a steady decline of Buddhism. Under French colonialism (1860–1940), Catholicism was introduced, which provoked a Buddhist revival movement in the 1930s. In 1951, Buddhist leaders formed the National United Sangha (Vietnamese: Tong Hoi Phat Giao Viet Nam), which included all Chan, Pure Land, and Theravada groups. The division of Vietnam at the 17th parallel in 1954 split the newly formed association into a renamed northern part, controlled by the Communists, and a southern part, under

Interior of a Buddhist temple, South Vietnam. (Natalia Pavlova/Dreamstime.com)

strong pressure by the regime of the Catholic Ngo Dinh Diem. Anti-governmental demonstrations by monks and nuns protested imposed restrictions, culminating in the public self-immolation of Buddhist monks in 1963. The formation of the Unified Buddhist Church of Vietnam (UBC) in 1963 in Saigon sought to provide peaceful answers to the military government, increasing U.S. involvement in Vietnam and the Second Indo-Chinese War (1964–1975). One of the early leaders was Thich Nhat Hanh. With the fall of Saigon in 1975 and the establishment of the Socialist Republic of Vietnam, Buddhist activities faced restrictions; numerous monks and nuns were imprisoned, and the UBC had to continue underground. A large-scale exodus of South Vietnamese people via unseaworthy boats across the Chinese Sea began in 1978, bringing refugees to Europe, Australia, and North America. In 1986 the Vietnamese Communist Party launched a national economic renovation (Vietnamese: *doi moi*) policy that since the 1990s has lifted some of the restrictions on religious activities.

Korea Buddhism was introduced from China at the three Korean courts in the late fourth century. The cultural elites regarded the new religious teachings and practices as part of advanced Chinese civilization, including in particular the use of Chinese script. The seventh century saw the unification of Korea under the royal house of Silla (688–917) and the sending of Korean monks for study in T'ang China. Some monks even traveled to India. All Chinese Buddhist traditions,

including Chan, Tientai, Pure Land, and Tantric Chenyen, gained a footing in Korea. Patronized by the royal court, many Chinese-style temples and monasteries were built. This period and the following Koryo dynasty (918–1392) formed the classical age of Korean Buddhism. As evidence of this, in the 11th and again in the 13th century, official sponsorship made possible the production of complete printed editions of the Buddhist canon. The more than 80,000 printing blocks are still preserved in the Haein Monastery near Taegu. The popularity of Chan Buddhism led to the gradual absorption of most other schools. Under the Yi or Choson dynasty (1392–1910), much as in China, neo-Confucianism gained status as the official ideology, leading to a steady decline and marginalization of Korean Buddhism. Since the late 19th century and during Japan's annexation of the peninsula (1910–1945), Japanese Buddhist traditions such as the Nichiren Shoshu and the Jodo Shinshu sent their missionaries, the Tokyo government using religion as a tool of colonization. Following the Japanese capitulation, the Communists took power in the northern part of the Korean Peninsula. Under the Stalinist leadership of Kim Il Sung (r. 1945–1993), all religious institutions were subjected to governmental control and later closed or destroyed. Religious believers were prosecuted and killed, and Buddhism has come to an end as a lived and practiced tradition. In the south, the reign of Park Chunghee (r. 1962–1979) strongly supported Buddhism for nationalist and anti-Communist reasons. Under the next president, the staunch anti-Buddhist Chun Doohwan (r. 1980–1987), Buddhism and the Chogye Order in particular came under the strict surveillance of government agents. As a consequence, order members became politicized and led antigovernmental rallies. Since the late 1980s, however, the succeeding governments aimed less to use Buddhism and Buddhist orders for their political purposes. Despite the strong rivalry by Christian churches, Buddhist traditions such as the dominating Chogye Order; the Won School, established 1910; the Pomun Order, founded 1971; and the globally spread Kwan Um School, founded 1983 have been able to arouse a growing interest.

Japan Korea served as the transmission belt of Buddhism to Japan. Following a Korean embassy to the

Japanese emperor in the mid-sixth century, carrying with it Buddhist texts and items, Buddhism began to be spread as a foreign faith among the imperial court and nobility during the reign of Prince Shotoku-Taishi (574–622). The newly ruling family was looking for a philosophy that would serve as an ideological basis for a centralized state and a legitimation of its power. Under Shotoku's regency, grand temples were built, a first embassy was dispatched to the court of Sui China in 607, and Chinese script, art, and science were adopted. The seventh and eighth centuries saw the introduction of the six Chinese schools, all Mahayana-based, existent in those days. The cultural translation of these and other Buddhist traditions imported to Japan went along with an adoption of native religious concepts, and it led to numerous varieties of Shinto-Buddhist amalgamation. This trend intensified during the Heian period (794–1185), especially after the transmission of the Lotus Sutra–based Tiantai School by Saicho in 805 and the Chinese tantric tradition of Chen-yen by Kukai in 806. These two traditions incorporated numerous aspects of Shintoist devotional faith and of the formerly imported Buddhist schools. With this, decisive steps had been taken to spread Buddhist teachings and practices to all social strata. A close interweaving between the imperial court and Buddhist temples, some of which maintained monastic armies, was also characteristic. The Tendai or Tiantai School or sect (Japanese: *shu*) developed into the dominant religious tradition in Japan. Tendai perspectives were superseded in the mid-11th century by the apocalyptic notion of living in the final period of the dharma (*mappo*). Only the invocation of the devotional formula *namu-amida-butsu* (surrender to the Buddha Amida) would make possible entrance to the Western Paradise of the Buddha Amida—that is, the "Pure Land." Based on this picture, Honen (1133–1212) systematized the idea of relying only on the "Other Power" (*tariki*)—that is, on the compassionate Buddha Amida—and established the Jodo-shu, or Sect of the Pure Land in 1175. His disciple Shinran Shonin (1173–1262), with a different emphasis, founded the Jodo Shinshu, or True Sect of the Pure Land in 1207.

As Japanese culture had started to emancipate itself from Chinese tutelage during the Heinan period, it was during the early Kamakura period (1185–1333)

that other Japanese Buddhist schools were set up. Following studies in China, the Tendai monks Eisai (1141–1215) and Dogen (1200–1253) brought to Japan the teachings and practices of Chan Buddhism, forming the meditational schools of Rinzai Zen and Soto Zen. In contrast to the Jodo schools, Zen placed its emphasis on "Own Power" (*jiriki*)—that is, the ability to reach enlightenment through one's own efforts. Later devotional forms of worship to local deities (*kami*) and rites for deceased family members were incorporated, placing emphasis on temple rituals rather than on austere meditational practice. Finally, in 1253 the Tendai-trained Nichiren (1222–1282) proclaimed that the title of the Lotus Sutra (Japanese: *Myoho-renge-kyo, Hokekyo* for short) embraced the essence of the whole sutra. The invocation of the title (*daimoku*) by way of uttering *namo-myoho-renge-kyo* (Homage be paid to the Lotus sutra of the Wonderful Dharma) would be sufficient to find oneself in the state of the highest enlightenment of the Buddha Shakyamuni.

During the Muromachi period (1336–1573) the various Buddhist schools became firmly established, the Rinzai School being lavishly supported by the military government. The Tokugawa or Edo period (1573–1867) saw the closing of Japan to foreigners, the strengthening of neo-Confucianism, and a bureaucratic control of Buddhist temples and monasteries. The enforced opening of Japan to foreign trade (1853) sounded the end of the rigid feudal system. During the Meiji period (1868–1912) the new imperial regime modernized Japan's political, economic, and social system. Ideologically, a restoration was carried out in establishing Shinto as the state cult, to the detriment of Buddhism. The picturing of Buddhism as a foreign, non-Japanese element forced Buddhist leaders into reforms. Most brought Buddhism in close relationship to nationalistic tendencies, reaching a disastrous climax in the fatal support of fascism during World War II. During the Taisho (1912–1926) and Showa (1926–1945) periods, individual Nichiren priests and lay leaders founded various new societies, among them the Nipponzan Myohoji, Reiyukai, Soka Gakkai, and Rissho Kosei-Kai. Within the tradition of Shinto, the Shinnyoen and Gedatsu Kai were founded in the 1930s. Earlier on, reforms of Zen had set on, similar in terms to the modernization of South Asian Theravada in the late 19th century. Zen modernists emphasized rational, scientific, demythologized, and lay-based elements, paving the way for the global spread of Zen meditational practices since the 1950s. Since 1945, Japan has witnessed a continuous proliferation of other Buddhist subsects. This contrasts with the steady decline of long-established Buddhist schools, which are seen to have become commercial, worldly, and unspiritual in the eyes of their critics. Finally, worldwide migration, already begun in the late 19th century, and the travel of Japanese masters to teach Westerners, have spread many of the Buddhist traditions and schools globally.

Tibet Buddhism in its Indian, Tantric Mahayana form reached the vast, mountainous regions north of the Himalayas from the seventh century on. King Songtsen Gampo (ca. 618–650) established Tibet as a powerful empire and, according to tradition, his two wives, one from Nepal, the other from China, introduced Buddhism to the royal court. The court adopted the Indian script, and the Jo-khang was built as the first Buddhist temple in 653 in Lhasa. Patronage of Buddhism continued during the eighth century, though rivaled by families and priests of the native Bon faith. King Trisong Detsen (ca. 740–798) invited Santaraksita and Padmasambhava, an Indian scholar-monk and a Tantric master, to spread Buddhist teachings and practices. Following the foundation of the first Buddhist monastery at Samye in 775, monks took residence and established the order of the Nyingma (adherents of the Old [Tantras]). Tantric Buddhism absorbed many of the native Bon ideas and ritual practices, thus paving the way for a culturally translated form of the Buddhist teachings and practices. Up until the mid-ninth century, Buddhist monks were able to gain a strong influence in the political sphere. The assassination of King Relbachen (r. 815–836) was followed by a temporary persecution of Buddhism. This brought to an end the "first dissemination" of Buddhism.

It took two centuries until, with the arrival of the Indian monk Atisa (982–1054) in 1042, the restraining of strengthened Bon began and a renewal of monastic discipline was initiated. During this "second dissemination," outstanding teachers, supported by local ruling families, formed the new orders of the Kadampa (later absorbed by the Gelukpa), the Sakyapa, and the Kagyupa with its various suborders (such as the Karmapa). A close contact with the Buddhist centers of learning in India existed during this time, and a steady flow of Tibetan pilgrims crossed the Himalayas. A multitude of Buddhist Sanskrit texts were translated into Tibetan, collected in the Tibetan Canon of the *Kanjur* (108 volumes, vinaya texts, sutras, and tantras) and the *Tanjur* (225 volumes, treatises and commentaries). The Nyingmapa compiled their voluminous "Compendium of Old Tantras" and thus codified their own doctrines. Although the schools differed in their emphasis on specific teachings and methods of practice, they all followed the same monastic rule (the vinaya of the Mulasarvastivadin). In the early 15th century, Tsong Khapa (1357–1419) founded Ganden monastery and established the reformist order of the Gelukpa. The school placed a strong emphasis on scholarship and monastic life.

In 1577, the Gelukpa abbot Sonam Gyatso (1543–1588) converted the Mongolian ruler Altan Khan to Tibetan Buddhism. The ruler bestowed the honorary title of Third Dalai Lama (ocean of wisdom) on the abbot, thus establishing the lineage of reborn Dalai Lamas. With the support of the Mongolian ruler Gusri Khan, in the mid-17th century the dominant Red Hat Karmapa was deprived of power and the Gelukpa gained supremacy in Tibet. The Fifth Dalai Lama, Ngawang Losang Gyatso (1617–1682), became the undisputed master of Tibet. During this time, Mongolian-backed Tibet established a far-reaching empire, acknowledged by the Chinese Manchu dynasty as a politically independent territory in 1653. Nevertheless, during the 18th and 19th centuries, Tibet came under temporary foreign control, and the Manchus were able to establish a "patron-and-priest" relationship.

Until the late 18th century, the system of government (with the Dalai Lama as ruler) and religious and social life remained virtually unchanged, reinforced by the sealing off of Tibet to foreigners from 1792 on. Under the 13th Dalai Lama, Tupden Gyatso (1876–1933), Tibet gained political independence as the Manchu dynasty collapsed in 1911. The incipient steps of the 13th Dalai Lama to reform political and social life came to an abrupt end as, in the autumn of 1950, the Communist regime of China sent its army into Tibet. Following the Chinese annexation, a systematic looting of monasteries; the execution, imprisoning, or forceful disrobing of monks and nuns; and a suppression of religious life took place. The years of the so-called Cultural Revolution had been disastrous to Buddhism in Tibet, though antireligious campaigns during the 1950s had already been intense and destructive.

In 1959, the 14th Dalai Lama, Tenzin Gyatso (b. 1935), fled to India and established a government-in-exile in Dharamsala. Tens of thousands of Tibetans have since fled from Tibet. They were resettled in various camps and villages in the Himalayan foothills, in Nepal and in South India (Karnataka). Some of the head monasteries have been rebuilt, and monks and nuns work to preserve Tibetan culture and its specific religious tradition. Small exile communities also came into being in Switzerland, Canada, and the United States. Since the late 1960s, numerous Tibetan lamas have come to the West to teach Westerners. The lamas and their Western disciples have founded a multitude of teaching centers, monasteries, and groups globally.

Buddhism in the West Currently, Buddhism in the West is experiencing an enthusiastic growth of interest and a dynamic proliferation of groups and centers. During the 1990s the news media repeatedly declared Buddhism as "in" and as the "trend religion" of the 21st century. In this wave of positive adoption, it is worthwhile to remember that Europeans and North Americans had no coherent conception of Buddhism until 150 years ago.

Europe First information about Buddhist concepts can be traced to the records of the Greek philosopher Plutarch (first century CE). Plutarch writes about the Indo-Greek king Menander (second century BCE) and his commitment to Buddhist ideas. The Pali text *Milindapanha* (*Menander's Questions*) gives a detailed account of this conversation between the Buddhist monk Nagasena and the king. The rise of Christianity and later of Islam blocked any further exchange until the travels of Franciscan friars to Mongolia in the 13th century. Reports by Jesuit missionaries to Tibet, China, and Japan from the 16th century on provided further

data, although fragmentary and distorted in nature. In the course of European colonial expansion, information was gathered about the customs and history of the peoples and regions that had been subjected to British, Portuguese, and Dutch domination. Around 1800, texts and descriptions about Indian religions had become known in literate and academic circles in Europe, and a glorifying enthusiasm for the East took hold. In particular, the Romantic movement and the Eastern Renaissance discovered the Asian world and its religious and philosophical traditions. In the 1850s, Europe witnessed a boom of studies and translations, paving the way for an enhanced knowledge of and interest in Buddhist teachings.

The sudden discovery of "Buddhism"—a concept systematized and coined by the French philologist Eugène Burnouf (1801–1852) in 1844—was essentially treated as a textual object, being located in books and Eastern libraries. During the 1880s, Europeans, self-converted by reading Buddhist treatises of the Pali canon, took up Buddhism as their guiding life-principle. Around the turn of the century initial Buddhist institutions were founded, the first being the Society for the Buddhist Mission in Germany, established in 1903 in Leipzig. The close contact of early Western Buddhists with the revival of Theravada Buddhism in South Asia was of much importance. European men traveled to South Asia to be ordained as Buddhist monks. On their return to Europe, they were active in propagating Buddhist ideas. The Ceylonese Anagarika Dharmapala traveled to Europe and the United States numerous times, founding sister branches of his Maha Bodhi Society, first established in 1891. During this time a philosophical interest in Buddhist ideas and ethics dominated. The texts of the Pali canon rather than the actually lived and practiced Theravada tradition formed the focus of interest. The few Buddhists came mainly from the educated middle strata, some from the upper strata of society.

After World War I (1914–1917) Buddhists in Germany and Great Britain started to take up religious practices such as spiritual exercises and devotional acts. Outstanding Buddhists during the 1920s and 1930s were Paul Dahlke (1865–1928) and Georg Grimm (1868–1945) in Germany and Christmas Humphreys

(1901–1983) in Great Britain. In other European countries, Buddhist activities remained low-key (if present at all) until the 1960s.

The postwar years saw the influx of Mahayana traditions from Japan and a growing interest in meditational practice. Zen in particular caught the interest of many spiritual seekers. The Zen boom of the 1960s was followed by an upsurge of interest in Tibetan Buddhism since the mid-1970s. Within only two decades, converts to Tibetan Buddhism were able to found a multitude of centers and groups, at times outnumbering all other traditions in a given country. This rapid increase, accompanied by an expansion of the already existing institutions of Theravada Buddhism and nonsectarian societies, led to a considerable rise in the number of Buddhist groups and centers on the side of convert Buddhists. In Britain, for example, within only two decades the number of organizations quintupled from 74 to 400 groups and centers (1979–2000). In Germany, interest in Buddhism resulted in an increase from some 40 to more than 500 groups, meditation circles, centers, and societies (1975–2001). Often ignored and hardly noticed in public, considerable numbers of Buddhists from Asian countries have come to Western Europe since the 1960s. In France, as a former colonial power in Indo-China, strong communities of refugees from Vietnam, Laos, and Cambodia have emerged; Paris has become the central place for Southeast Asian Buddhist migrants. Informed estimates speak of a million Buddhists currently living in Europe, two-thirds of whom are made up of Buddhists from Asia and their offspring. Among the convert strand, Tibetan Buddhism and Zen are favored most. Buddhism in the country is heterogeneous and plural, with Buddhist schools from the Theravada, Mahayana, and Tibetan Buddhist traditions, as well as newly founded Western Buddhist groups. Buddhism is very well organized in many European countries, often with a national umbrella organization that works for mutual cooperation between the different Buddhist traditions.

North America The intellectual approach toward Buddhism, dominant in Europe during the 19th century, also characterized the adoption of Buddhist ideas by American sympathizers and early convert Buddhists.

Writers such as the Transcendentalists Ralph W. Emerson (1803–1882) and Henry D. Thoreau (1817–1862) spread Buddhist ideas in their essays to members of the middle and upper classes. The Theosophist Society, founded in 1875, additionally aroused an interest in Buddhist concepts. The Chicago World's Parliament of Religion in 1893 became important for the history of convert Buddhism in North America, as Buddhist speakers such as Dharmapala and the Japanese Zen master Soyen Shaku (1859–1919) presented Buddhism as a rational and scientific religion. It was in Chicago, as well, that the German-American Carl Theodor Strauss (1852–1937) became the first American to take refuge formally in the Buddha, dharma, and sangha, in 1893. Although Dharmapala succeeded in founding an American branch of the Maha Bodhi Society in 1897, and three Rinzai Zen masters resided in the United States as of 1905, interest in Buddhist teachings and practices was minimal. It wasn't until the lecture tours of Daisetz T. Suzuki (1870–1966) during the 1950s, which spread a modernist understanding of Zen Buddhism, that a broader interest in Zen came about among artists, poets, and members of the counterculture. Zen as a meditational practice started with the influence of the Beat Generation and increased in the 1960s with the arrival of Japanese teachers (Japanese: *roshis*) and American disciples returning from Japan to teach and establish meditation centers. The Zen masters were followed by Tibetan lamas and Theravada bhiksus from the 1970s on, further enriching the increasingly plural spectrum of Buddhist options in North America.

Parallel to these processes, since the mid-19th century Buddhism had spread along a very different line to North America. Chinese and later Japanese migrants had come to the West Coast to find work and gold. By the 1880s, the number of Chinese in Gold Mountain (California), Montana, and Idaho had grown to more than 100,000, with an additional 10,000 in Canada. Upon their arrival, Chinese temples were built, the first two in San Francisco in 1853. During the next 50 years, hundreds of so-called joss-houses, where Buddhist, Daoist, and Chinese folk traditions mingled, spread throughout California and Canadian British Columbia. In striking contrast to the high esteem that Buddhist texts and ideas had gained among East Coast

The Great Stupa of Dharmakaya at the Shambhala Mountain Center at Red Feather Lakes, Colorado. (Julie Crea)

intellectuals, in the American West, residents devalued East Asian culture as strange and incomprehensible. In 1882 the Chinese Exclusion Act restricted further immigration of Chinese nationals to the United States. Japanese immigrants during this time were treated no better. For their religious guidance, two Jodo Shinshu priests were sent to the United States in 1899, and the Buddhist Mission to North America was formally established in 1914. Renamed the Buddhist Churches of America in 1944 during the internment of 111,000 people of Japanese ancestry, the Jodo Shinshu Buddhists have become a part of the broader middle class in U.S. society since the 1960s.

Following the change of U.S. immigration laws in 1965, further Buddhist traditions arrived from Asia with Sri Lankan, Thai, Chinese, Taiwanese, Korean, and Japanese teachers and adherents. Among these traditions and schools, one of the most vigorous turned out to be the Soka Gakkai International, gaining a stronghold with a claimed membership of 500,000

people in the mid-1970s. As in Europe, Buddhism is a heterogeneous and very diversified phenomenon. Although well established in a multitude of groups, centers, and monasteries, intra-Buddhist cooperation and exchanges are on a much lower level than in the "Old World." Estimates of the number of Buddhists in the United States and Canada run from around one million to about four and a half million convert and immigrant Buddhists.

Australia   The history of Buddhism in Australia begins with the arrival of Chinese immigrants in 1848. As in North America, the Chinese came to work in the gold fields. Numerous joss-houses were set up, followed by more established temples such as the one in Melbourne in 1856. During the 1870s other workers came from Sri Lanka and Japan, and a Sinhalese Buddhist community came into being in 1876 on Thursday Island. Two Bodhi Tree saplings were planted on the island, and Buddhist festivals were strictly observed. With the Immigration Restriction Act of 1901, the community slowly began to disperse. The same applied to the Chinese and Japanese communities, paying tribute to the racist "White Only" policy. Around the turn of the century, Theosophist ideas caught an increasing interest among the better educated citizens of the upper-middle class. Henry Steel Olcott (1832–1907), cofounder of the Theosophical Society, visited Australia in 1891 and spent several months lecturing. A strong influence of Theosophy remained until the 1950s, the Sydney Theosophical Lodge having been the largest and wealthiest in the world in the 1920s. Melbourne has the credit for having staged the first two convert Buddhist organizations, the Little Circle of Dharma in 1925 and the Buddhist Study Group in 1938. In the early 1950s, Buddhist societies were set up in the states of Victoria, New South Wales, Queensland, and Tasmania, assisted by the visits of the American-born Theravada "nun" Sister Dhammadina (1881–1967) and prominent Theravada monks from Burma and Sri Lanka. At the end of the decade, in 1958, the Buddhist Federation of Australia was formed as a national body; it is still existent today. The first Buddhist organizations were made up with a membership of mainly well-educated citizens, emphasizing philosophical and ethical aspects of Southern Buddhism. In particular,

Charles F. Knight (1890–1975) and Natasha Jackson (1902–1990) saw Buddhism as a triumph of rationalism, banishing all ritual and religious devotion as accretions of traditional Buddhism, an approach that dominated the small Buddhist scene until the early 1970s.

The 1960s and 1970s saw the introduction of Japanese Mahayana traditions to Australia. Zen meditational groups came into being, the Diamond Sangha being one of its pioneers. Jodo Shinshu and the Soka Gakkai formed their first institutions in Australia. With the 1970s, an increased influence of monastics on the hitherto lay-dependent presence of Buddhism in Australia began. Theravada monasteries were built to house residential monks, and Tibetan lamas began to visit incipient groups. The influx of more than 100,000 Vietnamese, Laotian, and Cambodian refugees during the 1980s proved to be decisive for Buddhism in Australia, however. The overall number of Buddhists grew from 35,000 to 200,000 between 1981 and 1996. Subsequently, the number of Buddhist groups and centers rose from 167 to 315 between 1991 and 2000. The largest Buddhist complex in the Southern Hemisphere came into being in the 1990s, the Taiwanese Fokuangshan order setting up the Nan Tien Temple at Wollongong, south of Sydney. Buddhism in Australia is well established with a wide spectrum of Buddhist traditions and schools, forming a multifarious part of Australia's plural society.

South Africa Although the history of Buddhism in southern Africa can be traced back to 1686, when three Thai bhiksus were shipwrecked on the west coast and compelled to stay four months, Buddhist activities in organized form did not start until the 20th century. In 1917, the Indian Rajaram Dass established the Overport Buddhist Sakya Society and called low-caste Hindus working in Natal to embrace Buddhism in order to escape the degrading social and religious position imposed on them by Hindu custom. The movement did not really gain momentum, however, and after reaching its peak with some 400 families during the 1930s (one percent of the total Indian population), in the course of time it gradually declined. Buddhist activities started to take off from the 1970s on as small, local meditational groups were founded in the main

metropolitan areas. The important Buddhist Retreat Center near Ixopo (Natal) started operating in 1979, offering established Theravada meditation courses but also meditative practice combined with artistic expression and nature awareness. The 1980s saw an influx of visiting U.S. and Asian teachers, establishing a variety of Zen and Tibetan centers. Groups formerly rather open to a variety of Buddhist practices changed to sharpening their doctrinal identity and lineage adherence. Other traditions, such as the Soka Gakkai and the Foguangshan Order, have established themselves, the latter working on building a huge monastery and the Nan Hua temple near Bronkhorstspruit since 1992. During the 1990s, Tibetan Buddhism was able to gain a comparatively strong following, as teachers began to stay on a permanent basis. Likewise, Zen teachers and Theravada monks settled and firmly established their traditions. Estimates on the number of Buddhists in 2001 range from 6,000 to some 30,000, although the lower informed guess seems more reliable, especially in view of the 1994 census, giving a total of only 2,400 Buddhists.

Buddhism has gained a footing in numerous other countries outside Asia, among them Brazil, Mexico, Ghana, Israel, Eastern Europe, and New Zealand. A rapid growth in terms of founding groups and centers took place in the 1980s and 1990s in particular. Buddhism in the West is deeply marked by its plurality and heterogeneity. A multitude of schools and traditions have successfully settled in urbanized, industrialized settings. The presence of the main traditions of Theravada, Mahayana, and Tibetan Buddhism is heavily subdivided according to country of origin (for example, Laos, Burma, Sri Lanka, or Thailand), lineage (Gelukpa, Karma-Kagyu, Sakyapa, or Nyingma; Rinzai, or Soto), teacher (Asian and Western, manifold), and emphasis on specific Buddhist concepts and practices. In addition to the publicly, more visible convert groups, monasteries and societies established by Asian migrant Buddhists and their offspring have increasingly come to the fore and claimed recognition in the presentation of Buddhism. The marked plurality of Buddhism outside Asia has been intensified by the globalization of once local organizations. The British-based Friends of the Western Buddhist Order or the France-based International Zen Association have spread worldwide.

This applies also to various Zen and Vipassana organizations with teachers from the United States and prominent Vietnamese and Korean meditation masters. In a similar way, Tibetan Buddhist organizations have created global networks with lamas untiringly touring the globe. Apart from institutional aspects, Buddhists in the West work to adapt and change Buddhism as they place emphasis on lay practice and participation, critically evaluate women's roles, apply democratic and egalitarian principles, favor a close linkage to Western psychological concepts, conceptualize a socially engaged Buddhism, and create an ecumenical, non-sectarian tradition. The study of Buddhism in the West has grown into a subdiscipline of Buddhist Studies, and the 21st century will prove to be most fascinating in following up in what ways and directions a "Western Buddhism" and possibly a "fourth turning of the Wheel" will emerge.

Martin Baumann

See also: Ambedkar Buddhism; Angkor Wat; Ashoka; Benares; Bodh-Gaya; Bodhisattva; Bon Religion; Buddha, Gautama; Buddhist Compassion Relief Tzu Chi Association, The; Dalai Lama III, Sonam Gyatso; Death; Dharma Drum Mountain Association, The; Diamond Sangha; Dogen; Enlightenment; Foguang-shan; Gedatsu Kai; Gelugpa; International Zen Association; Jodo-shinshu; Kagyupa Tibetan Buddhism; Karma-Kagyupa Tibetan Buddhism; Kukai (Kobo Daishi); Lumbini; Maha Bodhi Society; Mahayana Buddhism; Monasticism; Nichiren; Nichiren Shoshu; Nipponzan Myohoji; Nyingma Tibetan Buddhism; Pomun Order of Korean Buddhism; Pure Land Buddhism; Reincarnation; Reiyukai; Relics; Rissho Kosei-kai; Sacred Texts; Saicho; Sarnath; Shingon Buddhism; Shinnyoen; Shinto; Soka Gakkai International; Soto Zen Buddhism; Thai Forest Monks; Theosophical Society (Adyar); Theravada Buddhism; Tian Tai/Tendai Buddhism; Tibetan Buddhism; Unified Buddhist Church; Western Buddhist Order, Friends of the; Won Buddhism; Zen Buddhism.

References

The Three Jewels and Main Traditions
Bechert, Heinz, and Richard Gombrich, eds. *The World of Buddhism*. London: Thames and Hudson, 1984.

Gombrich, Richard F. *How Buddhism Began: The Conditioned Genesis of the Early Teachings*. London: Athlone, 1996.

Harvey, Peter. *An Introduction to Buddhism: Teachings, History, and Practices*. Cambridge: Cambridge University Press, 1990.

Harvey, Peter. *An Introduction to Buddhist Ethics: Foundations, Values and Issues*. New York: Cambridge University Press, 2000.

Prebish, Charles S. *Historical Dictionary of Buddhism*. Delhi: Indian Books Centre, 1995.

Reynolds, Frank E., and Jason A. Carbine, eds. *The Life of Buddhism*. Berkeley: University of California Press, 2000.

Strong, John. *The Experience of Buddhism: Sources and Interpretations*. Belmont, CA: Thomson, 1995.

Williams, Paul. *Mahayana Buddhism: The Doctrinal Foundations*. London: Routledge, 1989.

Spread and Regional Development
Harris, Ian, ed. *Buddhism and Politics in Twentieth-Century Asia*. London: Pinter, 1999.

Lamotte, Ètienne. *History of Indian Buddhism: From the Origins to the Saka Era*. Louvain-la-Neuve: Université Catholique de Louvain, 1988.

Lopez, Donald S., Jr., ed. *Curators of the Buddha: The Study of Buddhism under Colonialism*. Chicago: University of Chicago Press, 1995.

Queen, Christopher S., and Sallie B. King, eds. *Engaged Buddhism: Buddhist Liberation Movements in Asia*. Albany: State University of New York, 1996.

Sharf, Robert H. "Buddhist Modernism and the Rhetoric of Meditative Experience." *Numen* 42 (1995): 228–283.

Takeuchi, Yoshinori, ed. *Buddhist Spirituality: Later China, Korea, Japan and the Modern World*. New York: Crossroad, 1999.

South and Southeast Asia
Gombrich, Richard. *Theravada Buddhism: A Social History from Ancient Benares to Modern Colombo*. London: Routledge, 1988.

Gombrich, Richard, and Gananath Obeyesekere. *Buddhism Transformed: Religious Change in Sri*

Lanka. Princeton, NJ: Princeton University Press, 1988.

Harris, Ian. *Cambodian Buddhism: History and Practice.* Honolulu: University of Hawaii Press, 2005.

Houtman, Gustaaf. *Mental Culture in Burmese Crisis Politics.* Tokyo: Institute for the Study of Languages and Cultures of Asia and Africa, Tokyo University of Foreign Studies, 1999.

Kamala, Tiyavanich. *Forest Recollections: Wandering Monks in Twentieth-Century Thailand.* Honolulu: University of Hawai'i Press, 1997.

Ray, Reginal. *Buddhist Saints in India: A Study in Buddhist Values and Orientations.* New York: Oxford University Press, 1994.

Seneviratne, H. L. *The Work of Kings: The New Buddhism in Sri Lanka.* Chicago: University of Chicago Press, 1999.

Tambiah, Stanley J. *The Buddhist Saints of the Forest and the Cult of Amulets.* Cambridge: Cambridge University Press, 1984.

Taylor, James. *Buddhism and Postmodern Imaginings in Thailand: The Religiosity of Urban Space.* Surrey: Ashgate, 2008.

Trainor, Kevin. *Relics, Ritual and Representation in Buddhism: Rematerializing the Sri Lankan Theravada Tradition.* Cambridge: Cambridge University Press, 1997.

China and East Asia
Arai, Paula Kane Robinson. *Women Living Zen: Japanese Soto Buddhist Nuns.* Oxford: Oxford University Press, 1999.

Ch'en, Kenneth K. S. *Buddhism in China: A Historical Survey.* Princeton, NJ: Princeton University Press, 1964, 1972.

Dumoulin, Heinrich. *Zen Buddhism: A History.* 2 vols. 2nd rev. ed. New York: Macmillan, 1988.

Gernet, Jacques. *Buddhism in Chinese Society: An Economic History from the Fifth to the Tenth Centuries.* New York: Columbia University Press, 1995.

Jones, Charles Brewer. *Buddhism in Taiwan: Religion and the State, 1660–1990.* Honolulu: University of Hawai'i Press, 1999.

Lancaster, Lewis R., and C. S. Yu, eds. *Assimilation of Buddhism in Korea.* Lancaster, CA: Asian Humanities Press, 1991.

Payne, Richard, ed. *Re-Visioning "Kamakura" Buddhism.* Honolulu: University of Hawai'i Press, 1998.

Porcu, Elisabetta. *Pure Land Buddhism in Modern Japanese Culture.* Leiden and Boston: Brill, 2008.

Victoria, Brian. *Zen War Stories.* Richmond, UK: Curzon Press, 2002.

Watanabe, S. *Japanese Buddhism.* Tokyo: Kokusai Bunka Shinkokai, 1968.

Welch, Holmes. *Buddhism under Mao.* Cambridge: Harvard University Press, 1972.

Welch, Holmes. *The Buddhist Revival in China.* Cambridge: Harvard University Press, 1967.

Williams, Duncan Ryūken. *The Other Side of Zen: A Social History of Sōtō Zen Buddhism in Tokugawa Japan.* Princeton, NJ: Princeton University Press, 2005.

Tibet
Bishop, Peter. *Dreams of Power: Tibetan Buddhism and the Western Imagination.* London: Athlone, 1993.

Godstein, Melvyn, and Matthew Kapstein, eds. *Buddhism in Contemporary Tibet: Religious Revival and Cultural Identity.* Berkeley: University of California Press, 1998.

Lopez, Donald S., Jr. *Prisoners of Shangri-La: Tibetan Buddhism and the West.* Chicago: University of Chicago Press, 1998.

Powers, John. *Introduction to Tibetan Buddhism.* Ithaca: Snow Lion, 1995.

Samuels, Geoffrey. *Civilized Shamans: Buddhism in Tibetan Societies.* Washington, DC: Smithsonian, 1993.

Snellgrove, David. *Indo-Tibetan Buddhism: Indian Buddhists and Their Tibetan Successors.* London: Serindia, 1987.

The West
Adam, Enid, and Philip J. Hughes. *The Buddhists in Australia.* Canberra: Australian Government Publishing Service, 1996.

Batchelor, Stephen. *The Awakening of the West: The Encounter of Buddhism and Western Culture.* Berkeley, CA: Parallax, 1994.

Baumann, Martin. *Deutsche Buddhisten: Geschichte und Gemeinschaften.* Marburg: Diagonal, 1995.

Baumann, Martin. "Global Buddhism: Developmental Periods, Regional Histories and a New Analytical Perspective." *Journal of Global Buddhism* 2 (2001): 1–43.

Baumann, Martin, and Charles S. Prebish, eds. *Westward Dharma: Buddhism Beyond Asia.* Berkeley: University of California Press, 2002.

Cadge, Wendy. *Heartwood: The First Generation of Theravada Buddhism in America.* Chicago: University of Chicago Press, 2004.

Clasquin, Michel, and Kobus Krüger, eds. *Buddhism and Africa.* Pretoria: University of South Africa, 1999.

Croucher, Paul. *Buddhism in Australia: 1848–1988.* Kensington, Australia: New South Wales University Press, 1989.

Kraft, Kenneth. *The Wheel of Engaged Buddhism: A New Map of the Path.* New York: Weatherhill, 1999.

McMahan, David. *The Making of Buddhist Modernism.* Oxford: Oxford University Press, 2008.

Numrich, Paul David. *Old Wisdom in the New World: Americanization in Two Immigrant Theravada Buddhist Temples.* Knoxville: University of Tennessee Press, 1996.

Numrich, Paul David., ed. *North American Buddhists in Social Context.* Leiden and Boston: Brill, 2008.

Obadia, Lionel. *Bouddhisme et Occident: La diffusion du bouddhisme tibétain en France.* Paris: L'Harmattan, 1999.

Queen, Christopher S., ed. *Engaged Buddhism in the West.* Boston: Wisdom Publications, 2000.

Prebish, Charles S. *Luminous Passage: The Practice and Study of Buddhism in America.* Berkeley: University of California Press, 1999.

Rocha, Cristina. *Zen in Brasil. The Quest for Cosmopolitan Modernity.* Honolulu: University of Hawai'i Press, 2006.

Seager, Richard Hugh. *Buddhism in America.* New York: Columbia University Press, 1999.

Snelling, John. *Buddhism in Russia: The Story of Agvan Dorzhiev—Lhasa's Emissary to the Tsar.* Shaftesbury, Dorset: Element Books, 1993.

Spuler, Michelle. *Facets of the Diamond: Developments in Australian Buddhism.* Richmond, UK: Curzon, 2002.

Tweed, Thomas A. *The American Encounter with Buddhism 1844–1912: Victorian Culture and the Limits of Dissent.* Bloomington: Indiana University Press, 1992, 2000.

Williams, Duncan Ryuuken, and Christopher S. Queen, eds. *American Buddhism: Methods and Findings in Recent Scholarship.* Richmond, UK: Curzon, 1999.

Buddhist Association of Thailand

The Buddhist Association of Thailand is the major normative and nongovernmental Buddhist association in Thailand. It was founded by a group of 33 devout Thai Buddhists, led by Phra Rajadharma-nidesa, a well-known nobleman of the time, on February 28, 1933. The founders were scholars, noblemen, and people of high social status who, during their meeting at the Samagayacarya Club in Bangkok vowed to adhere to the Buddha's teachings and to propagate Buddhism throughout the country. Its significance rests in its leading in the Buddhist propagation and development at the national level. Being led and administered by a group of respectable people of the country and supported by the king of Thailand, the Association is unanimously trusted by all Thai Buddhists to run all religious activities in the name of the people. Originally, the Association was named Buddha-Dharma Society, but it was later changed to the Buddhist Association in order to embrace the Triple Gem, the name given to the three pillars of Buddhism: the Buddha himself, the basic principles of human life as he taught them (the dharma), and the fellowship of Buddhists who have chosen the perfected life of the monk (the sangha).

The Buddhist Association of Thailand is supported by the Royal Institution and the Thai Sangha (monks' order). Its work is in accordance with national policies and the Thai Buddhist tradition. Its creative activities

Buddha statues at the temple ruins of Ayutthaya, Thailand. (Luciano Mortula/Dreamstime.com)

are the annual Visakha (Vesakh festival) Celebration at Phra Meru Ground, Bangkok, where people have joined the Thai government in offering food to Buddhist monks. In 1935 this festival also included the establishment of the yellow Buddhist flag with the symbolic emblem of the Wheel of the Law at its center, which originally decorated the Phra Meru Ground during the Visakha Celebration, and, since then, has been used in all major Buddhist ceremonies and celebrations. In addition, in 1935 the Buddhist Association published palmleaf books of the Buddhist doctrine for distribution to all Thai provinces to be used as teaching manuals in Buddhist monasteries.

In 1950, the Buddhist Association of Thailand joined with Buddhist associations of other countries to found the World Fellowship of Buddhists (WFB) in Colombo, Sri Lanka. As a WFB regional center, its work and activities are increasingly international.

Within Thailand, the Buddhist Association of Thailand works primarily for the benefits of Thai Buddhists, that is, monks and novices, students, and all the needy. Its primary objectives are (1) to support all Buddhist activities within the country and abroad; (2) to study, spread, and uphold Buddhist doctrine; (3) to provide unity; and (4) to render public services and serve social welfare. Regularly, it propagates the Buddhist doctrine at its office and outside, for example, at schools, in prisons, and around the country. Dharmic lectures and discussion are held at its office from 2:00 p.m. to 4:30 p.m. every Saturday and at some radio stations occasionally. Since 1934, it has organized a writing contest on Visakha Day and rewarded the winners. It opened a free clinic in its office building in 1975 to render services to monks, novices, and members from 2:00 p.m. to 5:00 p.m. on Sunday.

As to its international role beginning in 1950, the Buddhist Association of Thailand has published many Buddhist books in English, for distribution within Thailand and abroad, especially the Visakha Puja, the annual Buddhist text for the Visakha Celebration. The text is widely popular for its contents, which include Buddhist teaching, art, and literature. Apart from this, the Buddhist Association of Thailand also joins the World Fellowship of Buddhists Headquarters in hosting the WFB General Conference whenever the conference is held in Thailand.

There are now approximately 7,500 members (2009) registered at the main office of the Buddhist Association of Thailand, though the number of members in all of its 70 branches throughout the country is unknown.

Buddhist Association of Thailand
41 Phra Arthit Road
Bangkok 10200
Thailand

Pataraporn Sirikanchana

See also: World Fellowship of Buddhists.

Reference

Buddhist Association of Thailand under Royal Patronage. *The Buddhadharma Journal.* The Office of National Buddhism Printing, 2008.

Buddhist Association of the Republic of China

The Buddhist Association of the Republic of China (BAROC) is not a religious denomination but an association that claims to represent all Chinese Buddhists. The BAROC had sought after 1947 to rebuild in Taiwan the association that had been previously set up in China by the reformist monk Tai Hsu in 1927, even though only a fraction of the original clergy could move to Taipei along with the KMT government in 1949. Although a few reformers subscribing to the ideas of Tai Hsu initially controlled the BAROC, more traditionalist figures opposed to his innovations led the Association after 1957. This clergy upheld a theologically conservative view in the Chinese Mahayana Buddhism orthodoxy that was in tune with the Confucian tradition of deference to the secular leader. As a result of this, the BAROC's leaders have designed their Association in such a way that it has long served as a transmission belt for the government. That is, the Association was expected to communicate to members of the sangha and lay devotees instructions from

the KMT, and was in return expected to aggregate, articulate, and express the concerns of the whole Buddhist community to the ruling party. Until 1989, the KMT had granted the Association the exclusive right to represent Buddhists in Taiwan, but this privilege was lost with the passing of the Law on Civic Organizations that year. As a result of this evolution, very few Buddhists in Taiwan now take seriously the assertion that the BAROC represents them.

Taiwanese Buddhists initially accepted the claims of the BAROC because of the circumstances that prevailed in Taiwan when the KMT took control of the island: the monks who came from the continent in 1947 were then the only individuals with some measure of prestige among Buddhists. After 1989, however, other organizations could ordain monks and nuns, thus depriving the Association of its monopoly on ordination, the only effective instrument with which it could control the sangha. The BAROC suffers from the fact that its leadership does not reflect the current dynamic of Taiwanese Buddhism, which embraces the reforms proposed by Tai Hsu. In particular, the leadership of the BAROC is under the control of ecclesiastics, even though the dynamism and the influence of the religion on the island are increasingly a function of laypeople's activism. Two other characteristics of the BAROC leadership are also at odds with current trends in Taiwanese Buddhism. First, men continue to govern the BAROC despite the fact that women significantly outnumber men among Taiwanese Buddhists. Second, the leadership of the Association remains the preserve of people from the Chinese mainland, even though a majority of Buddhists in Taiwan, like most other inhabitants of the island, do not identify with China. As a response to its diminution of standing, the BAROC has tried in vain during the mid-1990s to pressure the government into passing legislation that would help it reassert its authority over Taiwanese Buddhists, despite almost unanimous opposition from most other Buddhist organizations.

Buddhist Association of the Republic of China
6, North Shao-hsing Street
Taipei
Taiwan

André Laliberté

References

Jones, Charles Brewer. *Buddhism in Taiwan: Religion and the State, 1660–1990.* Honolulu: University of Hawai'i Press, 1999.

Laliberté, André. *The Politics of Buddhist Organizations in Taiwan, 1989–2003.* London: Routledge-Curzon, 2004.

The Buddhist Compassion Relief Tzu Chi Association

The Buddhist Compassion Relief Tzu Chi Association is one of the two largest Taiwanese Buddhist organizations in the ROC, and its leader Cheng Yen (b. 1937) is one of the most prominent public figures on the island. Tzu Chi is officially registered as a charitable foundation and a lay organization, but it is in fact a religious organization under the authority of a charismatic leader. Its activities in the provision of relief and free health care to poor people, vocational education for nurses, campaign for a bone marrow registry, the establishment of a publishing house, and the operating of a television broadcast station have made it the largest of its kind in Taiwan. Cheng Yen originally established Tzu Chi to perform a mission of "helping the poor and educating the rich," and the members of the organization enthusiastically perform their charitable activities because they believe it brings them spiritual merit. The enthusiasm of Tzu Chi members for charity work is not limited to the ROC. The provision of international relief started in 1991, when the American branch of Tzu Chi in Los Angeles helped victims of a cyclone in Bangladesh, and in 2000, many

Displaced residents receive blankets, cash, and food supplies from the Chinese Buddhist Tzu Chi Foundation during relief distribution in Marikina, east of Manila, Philippines, on November 19, 2009, following massive flooding in the capital and surrounding provinces. (AP/Wide World Photos)

people outside of the overseas Chinese communities of North America, Europe, and Asia have joined the Association. In 1999, during the deadly September 21 earthquake that struck Taiwan, the Association was among the first to organize relief in the disaster area. In 2008, after the devastating Sichuan earthquake, Tzu Chi was finally authorized to register in China.

Tzu Chi was founded in 1966. Its functioning rests entirely on the authority of its charismatic leader, whose decisions are not questioned. Although people both inside and outside Tzu Chi are reluctant to call Cheng Yen "leader," there is no question as to the source of authority within the foundation. Her awe-inspiring authority is sustained by devotion to her within the organization and admiration from the Taiwanese media, which has dubbed her as the "Mother Teresa of Taiwan." The leadership of Cheng Yen needs to be situated in the context of the ascendancy of humanistic Buddhism in Taiwan. This approach, developed by Taixu and his Taiwanese Yinshun, emphasizes the importance of the laity and charitable activities in the propagation of the dharma.

In 1966, Cheng Yen established her foundation with only 5 disciples and 30 followers. Today, Tzu Chi has an estimated membership of about four million people in Taiwan and abroad. Its core monastic community comprises only 110 nuns and is vastly outnumbered by the few thousand active lay members of the organization. Another important distinguishing feature of Tzu Chi is the importance of women in the organization. Because of a Buddhist practice that allows nuns only to initiate women, Cheng Yen's following within the small monastic community she leads is exclusively female. Indeed, the prevalence of women in Tzu Chi is not limited to the monastic community but extends to the whole of the lay organization.

Buddhist Compassion Relief Tzu Association
21, Kang Leh Village
Shin Cherng Shiang
Hualien County, Taiwan

André Laliberté

See also: Devotion/Devotional Traditions.

References

Huang, Julia. *Charisma and Compassion: Cheng-yan and A Global Buddhist Movement from Taiwan.* Cambridge: Harvard University Press, 2008.

Laliberté, André. *The Politics of Buddhist Organizations in Taiwan, 1989–2003.* London: RoutledgeCurzon, 2004.

Buddhist Institute

The Buddhist Institute was founded in 1930 as part of a reorganization of the Royal Library established in 1921. Coordinated by librarian Suzanne Karpelès, the Institute was the first research and publication center in Cambodia, with branches established in Laos and Cochin-China (in southern Vietnam, locus of a large ethnic Khmer community). Together with the School of Higher Pali Studies established in 1922, it was initiated by the French in part to sever an educational, cultural, and political dependence, by monks in particular, on Siam (Thailand) and as a means to promote an Indochinese identity. The Institute incorporated the Tripitika Commission, established in 1929 to translate the Pali canon into Khmer, a vast oeuvre (110 volumes) completed in 1969. Its general editor, the Venerable Chuon Nath, the reformer of Buddhism in Cambodia, also produced the first Khmer dictionary, published by the Institute, in 1934.

The Institute took over Cambodia's first literary periodical, *Kambuja Suriya* (*Sun of Cambodia*), a monthly published since 1926 at the Royal Library. In 1934, a Mores and Customs Commission was established with the help of Eveline Porée Maspéro to collect ethnographic and literary materials, and by 1938 it published a seven-volume *Collection of Cambodian Tales and Legends*. On a political level, intellectuals associated with the Institute (Pach Chhoen, Sim Var, Son Ngoc Thanh) created a moderate nationalist movement in the mid-1930s with the publication of *Nagaravatta*, the first Khmer-language newspaper. After the July 1942 monks' "umbrella" demonstration calling for the release of an incarcerated monk, Hem Chieu, the French authorities banned the paper.

By the 1970s, the Institute's library, with its 40,000 titles and collection of ethnographic materials, was the largest of its kind in the country. The 1975 Communist revolution ended work at the Institute until its formal reappearance in 1992, together with its parent Ministry of Cults and Religious Affairs. Although plagued by the loss of qualified personnel, the semi-autonomous Institute has received Japanese and German assistance to reprint books, rebuild the library, and gradually re-establish its previous structure, if not stature. *Kambuja Suriya* resumed publication as a quarterly in 1994, and a more spacious Japan-financed building was opened in 1998.

Buddhist Institute
PO Box 1047
Phnom Penh
Kingdom of Cambodia

Peter Gyallay-Pap

See also: Theravada Buddhism.

References

Centers of Buddhist Studies in Cambodia. Phnom Penh: Buddhist Institute, 1963.

Harris, Ian. "Buddhism in Extremis: The Case of Cambodia." In *Buddhism and Politics in Twentieth-Century Asia,* edited by Ian Harris, 54–78. London and New York: Pinter, 1999.

Karpelès, Suzanne. "The Revival of Buddhism in Cambodia and Laos." *Jayanti* 1, no. 7 (1955).

Buddhist Missionary Society

The Buddhist Missionary Society (BMS), with head-quarters at the Buddhist Maha Vihara, a Sinhalese Buddhist Temple, in Brickfields, Kuala Lumpur, Malaysia, was registered on April 3, 1962. In 1996, following an amendment to its constitution to allow it to establish branches, its name was changed to Buddhist Missionary Society Malaysia (BMSM). It now has two branches in Malaysia. The founder of BMSM is the Venerable Dr. K. Sri Dhammananda Maha Nayaka Thera (1919–2006), a Sri Lankan monk who came to Malaysia in 1952 as a Buddhist missionary. Dhammananda was a prolific writer with more than 50 books on Buddhism to his credit.

The objectives of BMSM are as follows: (1) to study and promote Buddhism and Buddhist culture; (2) to encourage, foster, and develop the qualities of Truth and Compassion, and to cultivate religious harmony and understanding in the practice of Buddhism; (3) to print Buddhist literature; (4) to provide proper guidance in practicing the Buddhist way of life; and (5) to render spiritual solace, guidance, and advice to Buddhists in case of sickness or death.

The official organ of the society is its biannual journal, *Voice of Buddhism*, which first appeared in 1963. However, BMSM is well known for the millions of Buddhist pamphlets written by Dhammananda that it has distributed free to different parts of the world. Many of the titles are now translated into various foreign languages.

With regard to temple activities and projects, BMSM organizes on an annual basis the Wesak Celebrations, All-Night Chanting, the Buddhist Novitiate Program, and the Kathina ceremony. This is done jointly with the Sasana Abhiwurdhi Wardhana Society (SAWS), which manages the Buddhist Maha Vihara. Other activities held at the temple include the New Full and Full Moon Services, Dharma talks on Friday evenings, and Sunday morning service and talks.

The Society established the Endowment Fund in 1996 to assist needy students, the physically handicapped, and victims of natural disaster. In 1997, a similar Scholarship and Loans Fund was set up. The BMSM, together with SAWS and the Malaysian Buddhist Association, is represented in the Malaysian Consultative Council of Buddhism, Christianity, Hinduism, and Sikhism (MCCBCHS). This forum was formed in 1983 to promote interreligious harmony in Malaysia.

The BMSM began with 27 members in 1962. By 2009, its membership had grown to more than 10,000 members all over the world.

Buddhist Missionary Society Malaysia
c/o Buddhist Maha Vihara
123 Jalan Berhala
Brickfields, Off Jalan Tun Sambanthan
50470 Kuala Lumpur
Malaysia
http://www.bmsm.org.my/

Benny Liow Woon Khin

See also: Theravada Buddhism; Wesak.

References

Liow, Benny. *K. Sri Dhammananda Felicitation: Essays In Honour of His Eightieth Birthday.* Petaling Jaya: Buddhist Gem Fellowship, 1999.

Liow, Benny, ed. *Pictorial Retrospect of K. Sri Dhammananda.* Petaling Jaya: Buddhist Gem Fellowship, 1997.

Voice of Buddhism. Kuala Lumpur, Buddhist Missionary Society, biannually. 1963–present.

Buddhist Society, The

The Buddhist Society is the oldest existing Buddhist institution in the United Kingdom, having been founded in 1924 by Christmas Humphreys (1901–1983). His interest in Buddhism drew him to the Theosophical Society and the work of Helena P. Blavatsky (1831–1891). His conviction that Buddhism was "the noblest and least defiled of the many branches of an Ancient Wisdom Religion" led him to set up a Buddhist Lodge within the Theosophical Society. An earlier Buddhist Society of Great Britain and Ireland (1907–1926) had consisted primarily of scholars. However, with the growth of the Buddhist Lodge the emphasis shifted, and the beginnings of a community of practicing Buddhists in Britain emerged. The Lodge's "threefold object" stated that it was founded "to form a nucleus of such persons as wished to study, disseminate and attempt to live the fundamental principles of Buddhism." In 1925 the Society opened a public shrine room at Lancaster Gate. However in 1926, due to certain philosophical differences, the Buddhist Lodge parted company with the Theosophical Society, and in 1943 the Buddhist Society of today came into being. Over the following years the Society was housed in various London locations, finally settling at 58 Eccleston Square in London in 1956. Organizationally it is structured around a council of 12 members, a general secretary, and two vice presidents.

The Buddhist Society is a lay organization, and being nonsectarian in nature, it aims to "publish and make known the principles of Buddhism and to encourage the practice of those principles." In its early years it did have a stronger connection with the Theravada School and with the monk, Anagarika Dharmapala (1864–1933). However, with a rise in interest in the Mahayana, the Society became increasingly inclusive. Consequently, today classes and courses are offered in Rinzai Zen, Theravada, Tibetan Gelugpa, and

The Buddhist Society, London, England. (J. Gordon Melton)

Pure Land Buddhism, as well as a general introduction to Buddhism. Various teachers from these traditions, both ordained and lay, are invited to give classes. Other activities include special study and practice days, retreats, an annual summer course, and occasional major study courses on topics such as Indian Mahayana and Chinese Buddhism. A correspondence course covering the fundamental principles of Buddhism, including characteristics of the major schools and an outline of its history, is also available.

Current membership stands today at around 2,000, though many of these people may also be members of other Buddhist groups. Its publishing activities, however, including a magazine called *The Middle Way* (issued thrice annually) and the *Buddhist Directory*, have meant that many people worldwide have come into contact with the Society. The recent growth of Buddhism in the United Kingdom has meant that the Society is no longer in a position to represent all schools and traditions. Its position of nonalignment with any one tradition or school means that the Society does not have its own distinctive religious practices or texts. Rather it draws in and makes available teachers from various traditions and groups to teach both practice and doctrine as part of an eclectic program. Members do usually however align themselves with one or another of these traditions. For further details regarding the practices and sacred literature of the traditions presented within the Buddhist Society, please refer directly to the entries on the various traditions elsewhere in this encyclopedia.

Buddhist Society
58 Eccleston Sq.
London SW1V 1PH
United Kingdom
www.buddsoc.org.uk/

Jamie Cresswell

See also: Blavatsky, Helena P.; Pure Land Buddhism; Theosophical Society (Adyar); Theravada Buddhism; Zen Buddhism.

References

Biddulph, D., ed. *The Middle Way.* London: Buddhist Society, 1943–2000.
Buddhism in Britain. Vols. 1–17. London: The Buddhist Lodge, 1926–1943.
Humphreys, Christmas. *Sixty Years of Buddhism, 1907–1967: A History and Survey.* London: Buddhist Society London, 1968.
Oliver, Ian P. *Buddhism in Britain.* London: Rider, 1979.

Builders of the Adytum

The Builders of the Adytum (BOTA) is a mystery school in the Western Esoteric tradition and the major representative of the initiatory magical current originated by the Hermetic Order of the Golden Dawn (HOGD), a new magical group founded in England in the 1880s. The HOGD developed a membership throughout the English-speaking world before it fell apart early in the 20th century. Paul Foster Case (1884–1954) was an American initiate of the HOGD. Several years after the disintegration of the HOGD, in 1922, Case founded BOTA as a school of practical occultism.

Like the HOGD, BOTA emphasizes the Christian Kabbalah (or Qabalah) as it had been appropriated from Jewish mysticism in the 16th century. The Kabbalah presents a system for understanding the universe grasped through numbers and letters. According to this system, the cosmos emanated from God as 10 realms (called *sephirots*) that are connected to each other by 22 paths. These are pictured in a diagram called the Tree of Life, which is seen as a representation of both the outer visible world and the inner psychological world of each person. During the magical revival in France in the 19th century, the 22 paths of the Kabbalah were identified with the 22 trump cards of the Tarot. The basic work of the BOTA consists of introducing its members to the mystical workings of the Kabbalah and Tarot. The symbols of the Tarot are believed to speak directly to the universal structure of the human soul.

The practical occultism of BOTA leads to an affirmation of the oneness of God, the brotherhood of man, and the kinship of all life. The order has posed as its objective the promotion of the welfare of humanity, as exemplified in its seven-part program of working for (1) Universal Peace, (2) Universal Political Freedom, (3) Universal Religious Freedom, (4) Universal Education, (5) Universal Health, (6) Universal Prosperity, and (7) Universal Spiritual Unfoldment. It is believed that work with the Tarot and Kabbalah will bring with it individual spiritual enlightenment and that the transformed person will be better able to influence the larger social environment.

BOTA is an outer school, behind which stands an inner mystery school that offers instructions for those members who wish to participate. Members may relate to BOTA either as individuals or through joining a group (*pronaos*). After initiation in a pronaos, the member may participate in BOTA group rituals.

BOTA is headed by a board of stewards and the proculator general, the primary link between the outer order and the inner school (which exists only in the invisible magical realms). BOTA was largely confined to Southern California until the mid-1970s, but in the last quarter of the 20th century, groups were founded in most of the states of the United States and also in Canada, Great Britain, the Netherlands, New Zealand, Colombia, and Aruba.

Builders of the Adytum
5105 N. Figueroa
Los Angeles, CA 90042
www.bota.org

J. Gordon Melton

See also: Hermetic Order of the Golden Dawn.

References

Case, Paul Foster. *The Tarot*. Richmond, VA: Macoy Publishing Company, 1947.

Case, Paul Foster. *The True and Invisible Rosicrucian Order*. The author, 1928.

Frazer, Feliz J. *Parallel Paths to the Unseen World*. Los Angeles: Builders of the Adytum, 1967.

Bukhara

Bukhara, a city in what is now Uzbekistan, became a Muslim city in the eighth century and grew in impor-tance over the next millennium. In the 14th century it emerged as a prominent educational center and the origin point of the Naqshbandiyya Sufi Order. It was a key stop for traders traveling the Silk Road, and later was established as a center for the Uzbek people.

Settlement at Bukhara dates to the third millen-nium BCE, but around 500 BCE the several communi-ties that had formed at what was a desert oasis built a protective wall and emerged as a urban center. Its aus-picious placement between Persia to the east and China to the west made it a attractive target for king-doms seeking to expand.

In 708, Arab Muslims of the Umayyad Caliphate established themselves in Damascus. Located on the eastern edge of the empire, Bukhara would frequently switch hands as one-by-one Persians, Turks, and Mongols emerged. In the 14th century, a native of the area who came to be known as Tamerlane (1336–1405) emerged as a leader and took control from the weak-ened Mongol leadership that had been imposed by Genghis Khan (1167–1227). Under Tamerlane, Bukhara

View of the Islamic monuments of Bukhara, Uzbekistan. Under the Abbasid dynasty, especially from the eighth to ninth centuries CE, the city of Bukhara became one of the most important cities for Islamic art, culture, and education. (Shutterstock)

emerged as a prominent center of Islamic learning. Also, Baha al-Din Naqshband, founder of the Naqshbandiyya Sufi Order, was a resident of the city at this time. Bukhara shared its role in the region with Samak, where Tamerlane and his successors had established their capital.

Early in the 16th century the Uzbek people invaded and took control of Bukhara, and in 1557 the Uzbek leader Abd Allah ibn Iskander Khan (d. 1598) designated it his new capital, and the city gave his name to his new state. Under the Bukhara Khanate, the city prospered and became a center of Islamic architecture. As seem to be the course of dynasties, however, the Khanate was weakened by internal feuding and in 1740 the Persians took control of the city. It took 13 years for it to regain its independence in 1753, but by then the Uzbek state had lost both size and power.

When the Russians moved into the region, they made the Bukhara Khanate a protectorate (1868), and maintained the ruling dynasty in power. The protectorate provided the environment for the emergence of a Muslim intellectual reform movement. The Young Bukharans found stiff resistance from both the Islamic community leadership (the *ulama*) and the ruling emir. Russian control disappeared briefly as the Russian Revolution took attention away from the edges of the empire, but the Young Bukharans became allies of the Soviet Union, taking back control of the country in 1920, at which time the emir fled into exile.

The Soviet Union established the Bukhara People's Soviet Republic, which in 1924 was divided into the Uzbek, Tajik, and Turkmen Soviet Socialist Republics (the precursors of the present states of Uzbekistan, Tajikstan, and Turmenistan). Through the 20th century, the Sik Road having long since lost it function, the city of Bukhara steadily declined in importance.

Today, Bukhara continues as an important regional seat of Islamic learning. Among its notable surviving architectural sites are the 16th-century Kalyan Mosque (Masjid-i kalyan), (often compared to the Bibi-Khanym Mosque in Samarkand), and the Ismail Samani mausoleum, which dates from the 10th century, when the Persians ruled the city.

J. Gordon Melton

See also: Naqshbandiyya Sufi Order; Sufism.

References

Burton, Audrey. *The Bukharans: A Dynastic, Diplomatic and Commercial History 1550–1702*. New York: St. Martin's Press, 1997.

Frye, Richard N. *The History of Bukhara*. Princeton, NJ: Markus Wiener Publishers, 2007.

Gangler, Annette. *Bukhara—The Eastern Dome of Islam*. Fellbach, Germany: Edition Axel Menges, 2004.

Khalid, Adeeb. *The Politics of Muslim Cultural Reform*. Berkeley: University of California Press, 1998.

Petrocciolli, Attilo, ed. *Bukhara: The Myth and the Architecture*. Cambridge: The Aga Khan Program for Islamic Architecture, 1999.

Bukkyo Dendo Kyokai

The Bukkyo Dendo Kyokai (BDK), or Society for the Promotion of Buddhism, is a Japanese-based organization devoted to the propagation of Buddhism worldwide. It was founded in 1965 by Reverend Dr. Yehan Numata (1897–1994), a businessman and Shin Buddhist priest. Numato founded Mitutoyo Manufacturing Company in 1934. The founding of BDK resulted from his reflections upon his company's 30th anniversary and the success it had enjoyed globally.

For years, Numata had dreamed of ways to familiarize the world's population with Buddhist teachings. As his thoughts matured, he mobilized a group of people from a spectrum of Japanese Buddhist groups to back a non-sectarian mission to transmit Buddhism globally. The Society initiated its work with the publication of a basic text on Mahayana Buddhism, *The Teachings of the Buddha*, a book that was originally published in 1925. It was an anthology of essential Buddhist teachings that a group of Japanese scholars had compiled. They distributed it during the closing years of the Meiji regime (which officially supported Shinto).

The Teachings of the Buddha had been translated into English and published in 1934, and even before founding BDK, Numata had reprinted the English edition (1962). BDK subsequently assembled a group of scholars who were assigned the task of preparing a new English-Japanese edition. As the group of scholars expanded, it was translated into more than 30 additional languages.

The BDK leadership studied the program of the Gideons, the American group that specializes in placing Bibles in hotel rooms. From them they learned various techniques for distributing *The Teaching of Buddha*. Through the first decade of the 21st century, they placed more than 6 million copies in hotel/motel rooms in more than 50 countries. While developing this distribution program, BDK affiliates emerged in Japanese diaspora communities around the world.

BDK's interface with the academic world led to its founding of a number of Numata Chairs in Buddhism at different universities. It also began publishing the Tripitaka Translation Series, a program to issue copies of the Buddhist scriptures. In addition, Numata has established several Shin temples called Ekoji (Temple of the Gift of Light). Several are located in Japan and one each has been opened in the Washington, D.C., metropolitan area; in Dusseldorf, Germany; and in Mexico City. BDK is headquartered in Tokyo. The temples are affiliated with the Jodo Shinshu Buddhists internationally, and the single American temple with the Buddhist Churches of America.

Bukkyo Dendo Kyokai
Ekoji Buddhist Temple
6500 Lake Haven Lane
Fairfax Station, VA 22039-1879

Edward A. Irons

See also: Jodo-shinshu; Mahayana Buddhism.

References

Buddhist Denominations and Schools in Japan. Tokyo: Bukkyo Dendo Kyokai (Society for the Promotion of Buddhism), 1984.

The Teaching of the Buddha. Tokyo: Bukkyo Dendo Kyokai (Society for the Promotion of Buddhism), 2001.

■ Bulgaria

Bulgaria, a southeast European country, is located on the Black Sea between Turkey and Romania. It also

Icon of God the Father with saints around Him, at the Rila Monastery, Bulgaria. The monastery, built in the 14th century, is a major landmark in Bulgaria and has hosted monks, two schools, and countless visitors. (Petar Neychev/Dreamstime.com)

shares a border with Greece, Macedonia, and Serbia. The great majority of the 7,260,000 people (2008) who inhabit the 42,857 square miles of land that makes up what is now Bulgaria share the heritage of the Bulgars.

Bulgaria was settled by Slavic peoples as early as the seventh century BCE. They found the area occupied by Traco-Illyrian people, some of whom were displaced and others absorbed into the new dominant Slavic community. In the wake of the coming of Attila and his Huns into the region, the Bulgars, a Central Asian people known for their warlike character, settled in north of the Black Sea (fifth century CE). Several centuries later they were forced into present-day Bulgaria by the Kazars. The Byzantine emperor recognized their existence as an autonomous state in 681. Once established in the area between the Byzantines

Bulgaria

Religion	Followers in 1970	Followers in 2010	% of Population	Annual % growth 2000–2010	Followers in 2025	Followers in 2050
Christians	5,668,000	6,269,000	83.9	−0.59	5,524,000	4,195,000
Orthodox	5,534,000	6,055,000	81.0	−0.77	5,400,000	4,090,000
Protestants	68,500	145,000	1.9	1.63	100,000	100,000
Roman Catholics	57,000	78,000	1.0	−0.76	80,000	75,000
Muslims	934,000	904,000	12.1	−0.65	792,000	600,000
Agnostics	1,180,000	220,000	2.9	−1.65	180,000	120,000
Atheists	700,000	73,300	1.0	−2.31	50,000	30,000
Jews	7,000	3,700	0.0	−0.65	3,600	3,000
Baha'is	100	650	0.0	−0.67	900	1,100
Total population	**8,490,000**	**7,471,000**	**100.0**	**−0.65**	**6,551,000**	**4,949,000**

to the south and the Magyars (Hungarians) to the north, they adopted the Slavic language and eventually Christianity. The Bulgarian king was baptized in 870.

The borders of Bulgaria changed frequently. It expanded greatly in the 10th century during King Simeon's rule (893–927), reaching across the Balkans to the Adriatic. In 1014 the kingdom was incorporated into the Byzantine Empire. During the 10th-century expansion, Simeon's armies captured the Macedonian territory, which had become the home of a new Gnostic religious movement, the Bogomils, followers of a peasant named Bogomil. He taught a dualism similar to Manicheanism, which viewed the world as a battleground for the struggle between a good deity, who had created the heavens, and an evil one, who had created the Earth. Leadership of the Bogomils was vested in an ascetic celibate priesthood. The movement spread through Bulgaria and on to Constantinople. Though frequently the target of persecution, the movement survived as a popular form of religious life until the Muslim invasion and capture of Bulgaria by the Ottoman Turks in 1393. Bulgaria remained a part of the Ottoman lands through the empire's decline in the 17th and 18th centuries. Then in 1810 and again in 1823, Russian invaded, but did not stay.

A spirit of independence emerged strongly in the 19th century, and Bulgarians aligned with the Russians in their ongoing battles with the Turks. In 1878, the Berlin Congress carved out a semi-independent Bulgarian state. A constitutional monarchy was installed, with a grandson of the czar as the ruler. The state continued to change boundaries in the series of Balkan wars that occurred over the next generation. Bulgaria aligned with Germany in both World Wars. It was invaded by the Soviet Union in 1944. After the war the country aligned with the Soviet Union. As the Soviet Union was falling apart, in 1989–1990, the Marxist hold on Bulgaria also gave way to a new democratic government, which began a new relationship with the rest of Europe.

Christianity had entered what is now Bulgaria by the second century. As Christianity emerged to dominance in the Mediterranean Basin, both Roman and Greek missionaries established churches. Their almost equal strength was demonstrated in the ninth century when King Boris (828–907) (a Bulgar) first accepted baptism from the Greeks, then became a Roman Catholic, and still later returned to the Greek church, which in 870 named a Bulgar priest the archbishop of Bulgaria. Subsequently, priests were sent to Constantinople (Istanbul) for training. In 889, Boris abdicated in favor of his son Vladimir, who tried to reestablish Paganism and was deposed in 893 in favor of his brother, Simeon (r. 893–927). As part of building his empire, Simeon supported the establishment of a Bulgarian patriarchy independent of Constantinople. Thus the Bulgarian Orthodox Church came into existence.

When Bulgaria fell to Byzantium in 1186, the Patriarchate was suppressed. It reappeared briefly in 1235, but was again suppressed during the days of the Ottoman Empire, when it was again made subordinate to the patriarch in Constantinople. It only reappeared in 1870, and it was not reconciled to the Ecumenical Patriarchate until 1945. During the early 20th century,

BULGARIA

the church claimed the allegiance of 85 percent of the Bulgarian people. It suffered greatly during and after World War II and only began to recover after the fall of Marxism in 1990.

Non-Chalcedonian Orthodoxy is represented in Bulgaria by the Armenian Apostolic Church, which originated with the movement of Armenians into Bulgaria as early as the fifth century, though the first church does not appear to have been built until the middle of the 11th century. Through the centuries the Armenians have been able not only to remain, but to resist assimilation.

The Roman Catholic Church continued its presence in Bulgaria even after the country's alignment with Greek Orthodoxy. Missionaries came with the Crusaders, and priests of various orders arrived at different times. In the 17th century Franciscans arrived in numbers and had the greatest success, most present Catholics being descendants of people converted during this period. In 1758 a vicariate was established in Sofia. The Diocese of Nicopoli was erected in 1789.

In the 1870s, Rome accepted a group of Orthodox believers who were allowed to keep their Bulgarian Orthodox rite. The Eastern-rite Bulgarians, now numbering around 7,000, constitute one of the small Eastern-rite enclaves in the Roman church.

The Roman church suffered the most damage under the post–World War II Marxist government. It lost all of its institutions and most of its buildings. All foreign religious leadership was expelled in 1948. The bishop of Nicopoli was executed in 1952, and for several decades the church existed without episcopal leadership. Only in the 1970s was a new bishop consecrated.

Islam entered the country in force in 1393. Although there was no attempt to force conversion on the people, it is believed than many of the Bogomils and some Roman Catholics were among the converts. There are also many Gypsies who profess Islam. Through the years of Ottoman control, many Turks settled in Bulgaria. They created a large Muslim community, primarily in the eastern part of the country. This community numbered more than 500,000 in the mid-1960s. The Turks lived in somewhat segregated communities, and in 1989 there was a marked attempt to assimilate them into the larger society. They resisted, and the Bulgarian government moved to suppress their demonstrations with force. In June 1989 they began deporting the Turkish Bulgarians to Turkey. Over the summer some 300,000 were forced out, at which point Turkey closed its borders. The situation led to a demand by the Muslims for religious freedom, a demand now seen as one of the first steps in the downfall of the Marxist government. The Bulgarian Muslims are primarily of the Hanafite School of Islam. The community is headed by its grand mufti.

Meanwhile, in the 1850s, missionaries from the American Board of Commissioners for Foreign Missions established a small mission in Bulgaria. Colleagues from the Methodist Episcopal Church (now a constituent part of the United Methodist Church) followed the next year. However, the larger Protestant enterprise originated from Russia. Russian Baptists came in 1865, Seventh-day Adventists in 1891, and Pentecostals in 1921. The Pentecostals, though dividing into the Pentecostal Evangelical Church and the Free Pentecostal Church, became the largest element in the Protestant/Free church community.

The Jewish community in Bulgaria appeared in the second century CE. As World War II began, there were some 50,000 members of the community, but in the decade after the war the great majority migrated to Israel. Today only about 6,500 remain. They are organized through the Central Jewish Religious Council and Synagogue in Sofia. The associated Organization of the Jews in Bulgaria operates a Jewish museum, publishing house, and resource center, also in Sofia. The Sofia Synagogue, which resembles the famous Sephardic house of prayer in Vienna, was opened in 1909.

In the wake of changes at the beginning of the 1990s, a number of both Eastern and Western religious groups have appeared in Bulgaria, beginning with an indigenous Bulgarian esoteric group, the White Brotherhood, which was able to revive. There is a spectrum of Hindu groups and several of the new religions, including The Family/Children of God and the Unification Church. The Church of Jesus Christ of Latter-day Saints established work that led to the creation of the Bulgaria Sofia Mission in 1990. The Reorganized Church of Jesus Christ of Latter-day Saints also has a following.

A host of Christian evangelical groups have begun missionary activity, among the most important being the Campus Crusade for Christ, the Greater Europe Mission, and SEND International. The very conservative Wisconsin Evangelical Lutheran Synod began a mission in 1992. The sudden emergence of so many unfamiliar groups in Bulgaria in the 1990s has presented a new challenge to a country with little experience with the radical religious pluralism that became the common way of life of most of the world's countries in the 20th century.

There is no council of churches in Bulgaria, and no church headquartered in the country is a member of the World Council of Churches. However, evangelical groups have formed the Bulgarian Evangelical Alliance, which cooperates with the World Evangelical Alliance. The Evangelical Congregational Churches in Bulgaria, the outgrowth of the American Board mission, is a member of the World Alliance of Reformed Churches.

J. Gordon Melton

See also: American Board of Commissioners for Foreign Missions; Armenian Apostolic Church (Holy See of Etchmiadzin); Bulgarian Orthodox Church; Church of Jesus Christ of Latter-day Saints; Ecumenical Patriarchate/Patriarchate of Constantinople; Franciscans; Free Churches; Hanafite School of Islam; Roman Catholic Church; Unification Movement; United Methodist Church; White Brotherhood; Wisconsin Evangelical Lutheran Synod; World Alliance of Reformed Churches; World Council of Churches, World Evangelical Alliance.

References

Fox, Frank. *Bulgaria*. Charleston, SC: Bibliobazaar, 2007.

Hopkins, James L. *The Bulgarian Orthodox Church: A Socio-Historical Analysis of the Evolving Relationship between Church, Nation, and State in Bulgaria*. New York: East European Monographs, 2008.

Mojzes, P. B. "A History of the Congregational and Methodist Churches in Bulgaria and Yugoslavia." Ph.D. diss., Boston University, 1965.

Oschlies, W. *Kirchen und religöses Leben in Bulgarien*. Cologne: Bundesinstitut für Ostwissenschaftliche und Internationale Studien, 1983.

Riis, Carsten. *Religion, Politics and Historiography in Bulgaria*. New York: East European Monographs, 2002.

Neuberger, Mary. *The Orient Within: Muslim Minorities and the Negotiation of Nationhood in Modern Bulgaria*. Ithaca, NY: Cornell University Press, 2004.

Stoyanov, P. *Churches and Religions in the People's Republic of Bulgaria*. Sofia: Synodical Publishing House, 1975.

Bulgarian Alternative Orthodox Church

In Bulgaria, in the wake of the fall of the Berlin Wall and the end of the Communist-led governments in Eastern Europe, a controversy broke out in Bulgaria. In 1992, the Board of Religious Affairs of the Bulgarians' post-Communist government challenged the status of the head of the Bulgarian Orthodox Church by suggesting that he held office illegally. He had been appointed by the former atheist government. Soon afterward, three of the Bulgarian bishops called for Patriarch Maxim (b. 1914) to resign. Metropolitan Pimem of Nevrokop emerged as the leader of the dissidents. He found some initial support from government officials and in 1996 was installed as the new patriarch for the dissenting group. In 1998, the church's bishops consecrated the new metropolitan archbishop of the dissenting Montenegrin Orthodox Church, with whom they have remained aligned.

In 1997, the group suffered a major setback when the country's supreme court ruled against it and rejected its registration as a religious body. At that point, the country's president, Petar Stoyanov (b. 1952, r. 1997–2002) stepped in with an unpopular suggestion that both patriarchs resign and that a new candidate be chosen that would satisfy all. From that point events turned against what had become known as the Bulgarian Alternative Orthodox Church. First, in 1999 Patriarch Pimen died and no successor was elected. In 2002, a new religion law was passed in Bulgaria that marginalized the church. By this time the church had possession of some 250 church facilities. Then, during the evening hours of July 20–21, 2004, the priests and bishops of the Alternative Church were forcibly ejected from those facilities by government authorities, now decidedly behind Patriarch Maxim.

The loss of their property was devastating for the Alternative Church, but it has continued. In 2008, it held a synod at which a new patriarch was elected.

The Bulgarian Alternative Orthodox Church is in full communion with several autonomous Orthodox bodies: the Ukrainian Orthodox Church–Kiev Patriarchy, the Chiesa Ortodossa in Italia, and the Montenegrin Orthodox Church. None of these churches are in communion with the Ecumenical Patriarchate.

J. Gordon Melton

See also: Bulgarian Orthodox Church; Chiesa Ortodossa in Italia; Montenegrin Orthodox Church; Ukrainian Catholic Church.

References

"The Orthodox Church of Bulgaria." CNEWA (Catholic Near East Welfare Association). http://www.cnewa.org/ecc-bodypg-us.aspx?eccpageID=20&IndexView=toc. Accessed May 15, 2009.

"Strasbourg to solve Bulgarian Church conflict." http://www.hrwf.net/religiousfreedom/news/2004PDF/Bulgaria_2004.pdf. Accessed May 15, 2009.

Bulgarian Catholic Church

The Bulgarian Catholic Church is an Eastern-rite church, originally composed of members of the Bulgarian Orthodox Church who converted to Roman Catholicism in the 1850s. As had occurred elsewhere, the Roman Catholic Church (which had had a Latin-rite presence in the country for many centuries) allowed this group to keep a revised version of their Orthodox liturgy in Old Slavonic when the church was established in 1859.

As part of the process of founding the new church, Joseph Sokolsky was consecrated the first Bulgarian Catholic prelate in 1859. Unfortunately, soon afterward, he was abducted by the Russians and interned for the next 18 years. Throughout the 19th century, the Bulgarian Orthodox had sought various means of freeing themselves from the control of the Ecumenical Patriarchate in Istanbul. Then in 1870, the Turkish sultan finally allowed the Bulgarians to establish themselves independently of the Patriarchate. This break occurred as the Bulgarian Catholic Church reached its peak at the beginning of the 1870s, when it counted some 80,000 faithful. Following the reestablishment of an independent Bulgarian Orthodox Church, 60,000 members of the Bulgarian Catholic Church left the fold and returned to Orthodoxy.

The number of members of the Bulgarian Catholic Church dwindled to around 7,000 in the 1970s. It revived in the 1990s and now reports approximately 15,000 members. The church is headed by its Bishop Christo Proykov (b. 1946), the Apostolic Exarch for Catholics of the Byzantine-Slav Rite in Bulgaria, who resides in Sofia.

Bulgarian Catholic Church
c/o Assumption Cathedral
5, Ljulin planina Str.
1606 Sofia
Bulgaria
http://www.catholic-bg.org/eng/

J. Gordon Melton

See also: Bulgarian Orthodox Church; Ecumenical Patriarchate/Patriarchate of Constantinople; Roman Catholic Church.

Reference

Roberson, Ronald G. *The Eastern Christian Churches—A Brief Survey.* 5th ed. Rome: Edizioni Orientalia Christiana, Pontificio Istituto Orientale, 1995.

Bulgarian Orthodox Church

The Bulgarian Orthodox Church is the largest Christian body in Bulgaria. Over the centuries, the idea of church membership merged with the national identification of most of the country's citizens. Christianity came to Bulgaria as early as the second century CE. Through the next centuries the area became a battleground in which Roman Catholicism and Eastern Orthodoxy vied for control, with the latter, due in large part to the proximity of Constantinople, the eventual victor. In 870, the orientation of Bulgaria toward the East was solidified when King Boris convinced Constantinople to appoint a Bulgar as archbishop of Bulgaria. Boris retired in 889 to become a monk. His son Simeon (r. 893–927) actively pursued the substitution of Slavonic for Greek in the church's liturgy (utilizing the translation by the Greek missionaries Methodius and Constantine). He also pushed the Bulgarian bishops to declare their autonomy, in spite of the opposition of the Ecumenical Patriarchate in Constantinople.

In 1018, the Bulgarian kingdom fell to Byzantine forces, and the new authorities suppressed the Bulgarian Patriarchate. It was reestablished in 1235. But then in 1396 Bulgaria fell under the domination of the Ottoman Empire. After the fall of Constantinople, the Bulgarian Church once again came under the control of the Ecumenical Patriarchate in Constantinople. Only

Interior of the Dormition of the Theotokos Cathedral in Varna, Bulgaria. (Tass/Dreamstime.com)

in 1870 did the Turkish authorities allow the Bulgarians again to set up independently. Then two years later, the Greek Orthodox authorities excommunicated the Bulgarians. Only in 1945 did the Bulgarian Orthodox Church reconcile with the Ecumenical Patriarchate. A new patriarch was elected and enthroned in 1953.

Unfortunately, by the time that it had the Ecumenical Patriarchate's approval, the country had fallen under the control of a Marxist government, with its antireligious perspective. All the monasteries were appropriated by the new government, though they were returned in 1953 after the church made a formal statement of allegiance to the new government. It is estimated that the church went from counting the adherence of 85 percent of the population to around 25 percent by the mid-1960s. Through the years to the overthrow of the Marxist government at the beginning

of the 1990s, the church received financial support from the government, but only at a survival level. The two theological seminaries, Tcherepich Seminary and the Sofia Theological Seminary, were allowed to remain open.

Through the 20th century, Orthodox church members became part of the diaspora that brought many Eastern Europeans to Western Europe and North America. Congregations began to appear soon after the beginning of the 20th century. A diocese was created in America in 1937. In 1974, the American diocese incorporated separately as the Bulgarian Eastern Orthodox Diocese of the U.S.A., Canada, and Australia, and announced that it could no longer accept direction from the Patriarchate in Sofia. The split was partially healed in 1962, when the patriarch recognized the independent jurisdiction. That reconciliation led to a schism within the American church and the formation of an anti-Communist Bulgarian Orthodox Church (Diocese of North and South America), which has not yet reconciled to the parent church. There is also a diocese for Western and Central Europe, now headquartered in Germany.

In 1998, the Bulgarian Orthodox Church claimed that its 12 dioceses held the loyalty of more than 85 percent of the people, though other estimates are considerably lower. The church is led by its patriarch, currently His Holiness Patriarch Maxim, enthroned in 1971. The church supports the Theological Seminary St. John of Rila in Sofia.

Amid complaints of a lack of ecumenical openness, in 1998 the church withdrew from the World Council of Churches in protest of its dominance by Protestants and its concentration on a set of liberal theological issues such as the status and role of women, liturgical reform, and sexuality.

Bulgarian Orthodox Church
Oboriste 4
BG-1090 Sofia
Bulgaria
www.bulch.tripod.com/boc/contentsen.htm
  (in English)

J. Gordon Melton

See also: Ecumenical Patriarchate/Patriarchate of Constantinople; World Council of Churches.

References

Raikin, S. T. "Nationalism and the Bulgarian Ortho-dox Church." In *Religion and Nationalism in Soviet and East European Politics,* edited by P. Ramet. Durham, NC: Duke University Press, 1989.

Slijepcevic, D. *Die bulgarische orthodoxe Kirche, 1944–1956.* Munich: R. Oldenburg, 1957.

■ Burkina Faso

Burkina Faso is a country of more than 15 million people in central Africa. A landlocked country, its 105,792 square miles of land is surrounded by the Ivory Coast, Ghana, Togo, Benin, Niger, and Mali.

More than 60 distinct African peoples reside in the country, though the Mossi people established themselves as dominant in the 11th century. Through its leadership and organization of the various peoples, this group was able to fend off attempts by different African neighboring kingdoms to expand into its territory. It was not as successful in stopping invasion by the French in the years between 1895 through 1904. French forces burned villages, slaughtered livestock, and killed thousands of individuals. Their harsh rule was challenged in 1916, but the insurrection looking to throw off French control was violently repressed.

In 1919, Upper Volta, as it was called at the time, was incorporated into the colony of Upper Senegal-Niger. Its colonial status went through several changes prior to the area being granted freedom in 1960. A series of government coups followed. Thomas Sankara was brought to power by such a coup in 1983. The next year he changed the name from Upper Volta to Burkina Faso. In 1991, a new democratic constitution was adopted, and some stability appears to have been brought to the country.

Burkina Faso has been one of the more resistant areas of the world to both Muslim and Christian

The Grand Mosque in Bobo Dioulasso, the second largest city in Burkina Faso. (Torsius/Dreamstime.com)

BURKINA FASO

proselytization, understandable given the violent nature of its interactions with both its Muslim neighbors to the north and with Europeans in the 20th century. Each of the different peoples has its own language and its own religion, though the different indigenous faiths have some similarities with each other. Among the more famous of the groups are the Dogon people, whose traditional land reaches into neighboring Mali.

Islam entered the area in the 18th century, and toward the end of the century a mosque was built and an imam installed in Ouagadougou, the country's present capital. Islam spread successfully among some peoples, such as the Fulani, Masina, Sia, Songhai, Udalan, Wala, and Zerma. In 1962, the Muslim Community, a national organization, was founded. Most Muslims follow the Sunni Malekite School of Islam, but there is a significant presence by the Tijaniyya and Qadariyya Sufi brotherhoods. The Ahamdiyya Muslim movement is also active in the capital.

Christianity appears to have been established in Upper Volta only in 1901, when the White Fathers opened a mission at Ouagadougou. From the center

Burkina Faso

Religion	Followers in 1970	Followers in 2010	% of Population	Annual % growth 2000–2010	Followers in 2025	Followers in 2050
Muslims	1,880,000	7,876,000	48.9	3.24	11,946,000	19,058,000
Ethnoreligionists	3,045,000	4,710,000	29.3	1.41	5,900,000	7,801,000
Christians	523,000	3,401,000	21.1	6.46	5,696,000	10,234,000
Roman Catholics	416,000	1,850,000	11.5	3.64	3,100,000	5,500,000
Protestants	97,000	1,600,000	9.9	10.07	2,650,000	4,800,000
Independents	7,100	92,000	0.6	2.55	180,000	400,000
Agnostics	500	106,000	0.7	3.24	180,000	400,000
Baha'is	340	3,500	0.0	3.24	5,000	8,000
New religionists	100	700	0.0	3.25	1,000	1,700
Atheists	0	600	0.0	3.22	800	1,000
Total population	**5,449,000**	**16,097,000**	**100.0**	**3.24**	**23,729,000**	**37,503,000**

of the country the work reached out to various peoples, and in spite of the nature of the French domination of the country, steadily expanded. The vicariate of Ouagadougou was erected in 1921. The next year, an indigenous religious order, the Black Sisters of the Immaculate Conception, was formed. Ouagadougou became an archdiocese in 1955.

The Assemblies of God (AOG) pioneered Protestant/Free church presence in Upper Volta. AOG missionaries settled in the capital in 1921. In 1933 they opened a Bible school and began turning out numerous educated lay workers. The Christian and Missionary Alliance began work in Dioulasso in 1923 and joined their strength to the AOG in translating the Bible into the indigenous languages.

The first indigenous church was an independent congregation in the capital city, Temple Apostolic. Over the last half of the 20th century several other independent groups emerged, and a number came in from neighboring countries. Very conservative evangelical churches have dominated the Christian community in Upper Volta, and they created the country's primary Christian cooperative association, the Federation of Evangelical Churches and Missions in the Upper Volta, in 1961. The federation is associated with the Association of Evangelicals of Africa and Madagascar and the World Evangelical Alliance. Until 2005, Burkina Faso did not have a church in the World Council of Churches, but that year the Association des Églises évangéliques réformées du Burkina Faso, an indigenous church formed in 1977, joined.

In the relatively free religious environment created by the country's constitution, Burkina Faso has become home to different global religious groups such as the Baha'i Faith, the Jehovah's Witnesses, and the Ancient and Mystical Order Rosae Crucis.

J. Gordon Melton

See also: Ahamdiyya Movement in Islam; Ancient and Mystical Order Rosae Crucis; Assemblies of God; Baha'i Faith; Christian and Missionary Alliance; Dogon Religion; Free Churches; Jehovah's Witnesses; Malekite School of Islam; Qadiriyya Sufi Order; Tijaniyya Sufi Order; White Fathers; World Council of Churches; World Evangelical Alliance.

References

Barrett, David, ed. *The Encyclopedia of World Christianity.* 2nd ed. New York: Oxford University Press, 2001.

Bissio, Roberto Remo, et al. *Third World Guide 93/94.* Montevideo, Uruguay: Instituto del Tercer Mundo, 1992.

Flavien, T. I. *Églises et mouvements évangéliques au Burkina Faso.* Burkina Faso: Ouagadougou, 1990.

Kouanda, A. "'L'état de la recherche sur l'Islam au Burkina." *Islam et Sociétés du Sud du Sahara* 2 (1988): 94–105.

Burma

See Myanmar.

■ Burundi

Burundi, one of the poorer countries of the world, is located in central Africa between the northeast shore of Lake Tanganyika and Rwanda. It also shares borders with Tanzania and the Democratic Republic of the Congo. In 2008, 8,691,000 people resided in its 9,900 square miles of territory. Ethnically, the people are divided among three very different ethnic communities: the Hutu (85 percent), Tutsi (14 percent), and Twa (one percent),

Like Rwanda, its neighbor to the north, it was originally settled by the Hutu and Twa peoples and then overrun by the Tutsi (or Watusi) people in the 15th century. Much of the history of Burundi has been written in the continuing ethnic struggle between the conqueror and the conquered, the same struggle that has had such disastrous results in Rwanda. The Tutsi held sway until the late 19th century, when Germany moved into the area and established the colony of Rwanda-Urundi. Following World War I, Belgium took over from Germany, divided Burundi from Rwanda, and merged it into the Congo. Under the Belgian system, Tutsi, though a minority, were placed in all the local governing positions.

Burundi gained its independence in 1963. Following four years of instability, a Tutsi prime minister staged a coup, and as president purged the government of Hutu officials. In 1971, still during the rule of the Tutsi Michael Micombero (r. 1966–1976), more than 350,000 Hutu were killed and an additional 70,000 fled the country. Jean-Baptiste Bagaza (r. 1976–1987), supported by the Hutu majority, succeeded Micombero. More recent decades have been marked by attempts to hold democratic elections and several coups; Burundi's president was assassinated in 1993. His death led to widespread ethnic violence between the Hutus and the Tutsis. Though attracting less attention than the fighting in Rwanda, Burundi saw 200,000 of its citizens die over the next dozen years, and the level of violence forced additional hundreds of thousands from their homes, many fleeing into neighboring countries. Finally, in 2003, a power-sharing agreement between the two factions led to a transition process for peace. Initially, an integrated defense force was established. Two years later a new constitution was adopted and elections brought a majority Hutu government led by President Pierre Nkurunzizi to power. With South African assistance, the last rebel group still holding out was pacified in 2006.

The original religions of the several groups that constitute Burundian society have survived, to some extent among the Hutu, but especially among the Twa. Prior to 1966, the country was ruled by a king who was assisted by a set of priests (called *ganwa*), and the overthrow of the king did not help the survival of traditional religion. Among the Twa, the Creator is known as Imana. A popular form of the traditional religion that originated in Rwanda is focused on a hero figure known as Kiranga. The Kiranga religion is a semi-secret group with a hierarchical organization. Followers are known as Abana b'Imana (children of Imana).

Burundi

Religion	Followers in 1970	Followers in 2010	% of Population	Annual % growth 2000–2010	Followers in 2025	Followers in 2050
Christians	2,579,000	8,879,000	92.9	3.43	14,102,000	27,087,000
Roman Catholics	2,108,000	5,850,000	61.2	3.57	9,300,000	17,500,000
Protestants	147,000	1,350,000	14.1	3.54	2,300,000	4,500,000
Anglicans	45,000	750,000	7.9	3.71	1,300,000	2,500,000
Ethnoreligionists	903,000	525,000	5.5	2.21	700,000	784,000
Muslims	30,000	130,000	1.4	3.34	208,000	390,000
Hindus	300	6,800	0.1	3.34	10,000	17,500
Baha'is	1,600	6,700	0.1	3.34	12,000	22,000
Agnostics	100	5,000	0.1	3.54	8,000	14,000
Atheists	0	180	0.0	5.37	300	500
Total population	**3,514,000**	**9,553,000**	**100.0**	**3.34**	**15,040,000**	**28,315,000**

BURUNDI

Kiranga, who is seen as an intermediary, is assigned the ability to facilitate or stop a person's access to Imana.

The original attempt to establish a Christian mission in Burundi was launched in 1879 by the White Fathers. Two years later, two priests were killed, and no further efforts were made to evangelize the land until 1899. By this time Burundi had come under German control. When the Belgians took over, they forced the closure of the German missions, and French priests began to flow into the area. In 1922 the Roman Catho-

lic Church in the area was formed into a vicariate apostolic. Suddenly, in 1930, the number of adherents began to grow rapidly, and by 1937 almost a half million new members had been added. The present University of Bujumbura was originally founded as a Catholic institution by priests from the Society of Jesus (Jesuits).

The first African bishop (a Tutsi) was appointed in 1959. The church has been deeply affected by the intertribal warfare that erupted into violence in 1972–1973. Eighteen priests were killed in massacres that took 100,000 lives. Most of the Hutu intelligentsia were killed, including a number of Catholic medical workers. The church has tended to favor the Tutsi elite, and during the early 1980s it opposed a number of reforms instituted by then president Bagaza that attempted to end discrimination against the Hutu. Bagaza forced a number of missionaries from the country and confiscated church property. The government and church were not reconciled until 1989, at which time the church's former property was returned.

Protestantism entered the country in 1907 when German Lutherans opened a mission, but they were soon forced out by the Belgians. Since Belgian Protestants were unable to take over from their German colleagues, Danish Baptists established work in 1928. In the meantime, Seventh-day Adventist missionaries had found their way into the country (then a part of the Congo). During the 1930s, a variety of Protestant and Free church bodies established missions, including the Kansas Yearly Meeting of Friends (now the Evangelical Friends) (1932), the Free Methodist Church (1935), the Swedish Free Mission (1935), and the Christian Brethren (1938). The Swedish Free Mission, a Pentecostal body now known as the Églises de Pentecoste, has become the second largest church in the country. Three American churches with a Wesleyan Holiness background, the Churches of Christ in Christian Union, the Congregational Methodist Church, and the Evangelical Methodist Church, supply support to the Église Evangélique Mondiale.

The Church of England also entered the country in 1934 with the arrival of Church Missionary Society missionaries and were greatly assisted by a religious revival that swept through East Africa right at the time they were setting up work. The mission founded a variety of medical facilities and a teacher training school, Warner Theological College. The first African bishop was named in 1965, and the following year Burundi became a diocese in the Church of the Province of Uganda, Rwanda, and Burundi. As the work grew, Uganda was separated and the Congo (Zaire) added. More recently, Burundi was established as a separate province. The Church of the Province of Burundi, now the third largest religious group in the country, is a member of the World Council of Churches.

The Kimbanguist Church/Église de Jésus Christ sur la terre par le prophète Simon Kimbangu, which entered in 1965 from the Congo (then Zaire), was the first of the African Initiated Churches to gain a significant following. Three years earlier, there had been a schism from the Anglican Church in southern Burundi, but the Église de Dieu au Burundi, as the new church was called, lost most of its members when it was officially suppressed in 1965. Even earlier there was a schism from the Friends church, but it soon died out.

Approximately two-thirds of Burundi's 5,500,000 citizens are Christian, the majority being Roman Catholics. Many of the Protestant churches are united in the National Council of Churches of Burundi, which in turn is affiliated with the World Council of Churches. The majority of the remaining population follow traditional African faiths. There are about 50,000 Muslims. Most of the African Muslims are Sunnis who follow the Malekite School of Islam. There is a minority of Asians who follow Ismaili and Shia Islam and a few Bohras (members of the Shiah Fatimi Tayyibi Dawoodi Bohra). Most Muslims live in western Burundi near Lake Tanganyika.

J. Gordon Melton

See also: Bohras; Christian Brethren; Church Missionary Society; Church of the Province of Burundi; Evangelical Friends International; Free Methodist Church of North America; Jesuits; Kimbanguist Church; Malikite School of Islam; Roman Catholic Church; Seventh-day Adventist Church; Shiah Fatimi Ismaili Tayyibi Dawoodi Bohra; White Fathers; World Council of Churches.

References

Barrett, David, ed. *The Encyclopedia of World Christianity.* 2nd ed. New York: Oxford University Press, 2001.

Bikangaga, J. *The Church of Uganda, Rwanda, and Burundi: Survey on Administration and Finance of the Church in Uganda.* Kampala, Uganda: Uganda Bookshop, 1969.

Eggers, Ellen J. *Historical Dictionary of Burundi.* Metuchen, NJ: Scarecrow Press, 2006.

Hohensee, D. *Church Growth in Burundi.* South Pasadena, CA: William Carey Library, 1978.

Kastfelt, Neil. *The Role of Religion in African Civil Wars.* London: Hurst & Co Ltd., 2001.

Perraudin, J. *Naissance d'une église: histoire du Burundi Chrétien*. Usumbura, Burundi: Presses Lavigerie, 1963.

Watt, Nigel. *Burundi: The Biography of a Small African Country*. New York: Columbia University Press, 2008.

Bwiti

One of the largest new religious movements in Gabon, in western equatorial Africa, is the syncretistic and ethnically based Bwiti movement, also known as Église de Bwiti (Church of the Initiates) and the Eboga religion, after the bitter hallucinogenic root iboga (*Tabernanthe iboga*), which is used ritually in all-night vigils. Found among the southern Fang people, Bwiti is a group of several religious movements named after a traditional initiation society. It is essentially a revitalization of ancient Fang ancestor rites, a movement originating at the end of the 19th century and persecuted by colonial and Catholic authorities alike. By 1945 it had incorporated some Christian (especially Catholic) elements, and the religion is constantly changing. The Gabon government legalized it in 1970 on an equal footing with Christianity and Islam.

Bwiti members meet all night with traditional music and dance, have an elaborate mythology, and use the traditional narcotic drugs to acquire religious power and encourage communication with the ancestors. The Bwiti savior, identified with Christ, is called Nzambia-Pongo, and is at the heart of initiation and other rituals, as is the iboga drug. In these vigils, traditional music on a sacred harp and dancing led by the *Nganga*, who represents Christ, together with the consumption of iboga, prepare initiates, known as *banzie*

European women rest in a temple, after taking iboga during an initiation to the Bwiti rite, September 2005, in Libreville, the capital and largest city of Gabon. (AFP/Getty Images)

(angels), to fly away to another world, where they achieve a state of "one-heartedness" and are reunited with the ancestors and the Mother of God.

In 1983 a *Catechism of the Bwiti Religion* was publicly displayed. The movement spawned a united organization called the Association of Eboga Members, founded by Ovono Dibenga Louis-Marie in 1984. By 2000, the movement was thought to have some 60,000 members in Gabon and Equatorial Guinea, perhaps 20 percent of the Fang people. There is a related initiation movement known as Mbiri (named after spirit beings known collectively as *imbwiri*), which also is found among the southern Fang, uses iboga in rituals, and is primarily a healing and anti-sorcery cult seeking direct communication with the ancestors.

The headquarters of the Bwiti movement is in Libreville, Gabon.

Allan H. Anderson

See also: African Initiated (Independent) Churches.

References

Fernandez, James W. *Bwiti*. Princeton, NJ: Princeton University Press, 1982.
Swiderski, Stanislaw. " L'Ombwiri société d'initiation et de guérison au Gabon." *Studi e Materiali di Storia della Religione* (Rome) 1, nos. 40–41 (1971): 125–204.
Swiderski, Stanislaw. *La Religion Bwiti*, Tome 1: Histoire. Ottawa: Éditions de l'Université d'Ottawa, 1990.

Byakko Shinko Kai

Byakko Shinko Kai is a Japanese new religion founded by Goi Masahisa (1916–1980) in 1951. As a teacher of Seicho-no-Ie, Goi devoted himself to others who were suffering, but he gradually doubted the practice and teachings of the religion, and then he broke away from it. After various spiritual experiences he received a special message from God, May Peace Prevail on Earth, and founded his own religious movement. According to Goi's teachings, words and thoughts are waves vibrating at different frequencies, and peace prayer vibrating at the highest possible level has a purifying effect on people and the world. Byakko Shinko Kai emphasizes prayer for world peace and teaches that human beings derive from the universal *Kami* (Deity) and that everyone has *shugorei* (guardian spirits) and *shugoshin* (guardian deities). The prayer for world peace is as follows:

> May peace prevail on earth
> May peace be in our homes and countries
> May our missions be accomplished
> We thank thee, Guardian Deities and Guardian Spirits.

Following Goi's death in 1980, his adopted daughter Saionji Masami became the spiritual leader. It is believed that Goi sends spiritual messages to the Earth using Saionji as a medium. Byakko Shinko Kai distributes stickers and erects Peace Poles, and has conducted world peace prayer ceremonies in such cities as Los Angeles and Assisi.

As the new century began, Byakko Shinko Kai claimed some 500,000 members. Although the great majority of members reside in Japan, some have joined the Japanese diaspora and may now be found in the United States, South America, and Europe.

Byakko Shinko Kai
5–26–27 Kokubunn
Ichikawa-shi, Chiba prefecture
Japan 272
www.byakko.or.jp (in Japanese)

Keishin Inaba

See also: Seicho-No-Ie.

References

Numata, Kenya. "Shinshûkyô ni okeru Charisma to Shamanism: Byakko Shinko Kai wo chûshin tosite." *Bunkajinruigaku* 6 (1989).
Reader, Ian. "The Rise of a Japanese 'New New Religion.'" *Japanese Journal of Religious Studies* 15, no. 4 (1988): 253–261.

Index